47 ⁹⁵
Dev Chen

MICROPROGRAMMING AND FIRMWARE ENGINEERING METHODS

edited by

STANLEY HABIB

 Van Nostrand Reinhold
New York

Copyright © 1988 by Van Nostrand Reinhold

Library of Congress Catalog Card Number 88-261

ISBN 0-442-23554-2

All rights reserved. No part of this work covered by the copyright hereon may be reproduced or used in any form or by any means—graphic, electronic, or mechanical, including photocopying, recording, taping, or information storage and retrieval systems—without written permission of the publisher.

Printed in The United States of America

Designed by Karin Kincheloe

Van Nostrand Reinhold
115 Fifth Avenue
New York, New York 10003

Van Nostrand Reinhold Company Limited
Molly Millars Lane
Wokingham, Berkshire RG11 2PY, England

Van Nostrand Reinhold
480 La Trobe Street
Melbourne, Victoria 3000, Australia

Macmillan of Canada
Division of Canada Publishing Corporation
164 Commander Boulevard
Agincourt, Ontario M1S 3C7, Canada

16 15 14 13 12 11 10 9 8 7 6 5 4 3 2 1

Library of Congress Cataloging-in-Publication Data

Microprogramming and firmware engineering methods.
    Bibliography: p.
    Includes index.
    1. Microprogramming.   2. Computer firmware.
I. Habib, Stanley.
QA76.6.M495 1988   005.6   88-261
ISBN 0-442-23554-2

To Mim

contents

preface   vii

contributors   ix

one
A BRIEF CHRONOLOGY OF MICROPROGRAMMING ACTIVITY
STANLEY HABIB   1

two
FUNDAMENTAL CONCEPTS OF MICROPROGRAMMING
ROBERT A. MUELLER AND JOSEPH VARGHESE   33

three
AN ASYNCHRONOUS APPROACH TO MICROPROGRAMMING
HAROLD W. LAWSON   95

four
HIGH-LEVEL MICROPROGRAMMING LANGUAGES
SCOTT DAVIDSON   145

five
VERTICAL MIGRATION
TOM WEIDNER AND JOHN STANKOVIC — 191

six
DYNAMIC MICROPROGRAMMING
ROBERT I. WINNER — 223

seven
AN EMULATION ENVIRONMENT AND ITS APPLICATION
CHARLES J. NEUHAUSER AND MICHAEL J. FLYNN — 275

eight
TRADITIONAL MICROPROGRAM DEVELOPMENT TOOLS
WILL TRACZ — 337

nine
HORIZONTAL MICROCODE COMPACTION
JOSEPH L. LINN — 381

ten
PRINCIPLES OF FIRMWARE VERIFICATION
SUBRATA DASGUPTA — 433

INDEX — 483

preface

This book is a collective effort involving thirteen members of the microprogramming community who are committed to the notion that twenty years of microprogramming methodology should be documented for future reference. Many others contributed a great deal of theory and applications to this methodology, and it would be difficult to list all of them here. Many of the names appear in the references cited in the various chapters.

We offer a special recognition to Professor Maurice Wilkes, first because he has written seminal papers that you will see mentioned in more than one chapter in this book. But Wilkes has also been very special to those of us writing here because he has participated in so many of the annual microprogramming workshops that each of us has attended as well, providing stimulating keynote presentations and overall leadership.

The book contains ten chapters. The first is a brief summary of microprogramming activity. It is presented in chronological form; however, certain topical areas, such as emulation, compaction, high-level language enhancements, migration, tools, dynamic microprogramming, asynchronous machines, and verification, seem to thread throughout the history of this methodology.

The second chapter is intended to acquaint the reader with a tutorial (yet up-to-date in notation) introduction to microprogramming concepts. Chapter 3 describes research performed in the area of asynchronous behavior in microprogramming and architectures designed around the methodology discussed. Over the years there have been many suggestions for possible high-level languages for microprogramming, and chapter 4 is a summary of much of this effort. Although we have not achieved a universally accepted language, it is important to record past efforts so that we do not repeat them.

Chapter 5, on vertical migration, is a culmination of many years of study on the kinds of software that lend themselves to incorporation into firmware. The notions presented form an integral part of firmware engineering. The concept of vertical migration serves as a natural antecedent to dynamic microprogramming discussed in chapter 6: the first provides motivation for the second, which then provides additional methodology.

Emulation has been an essential topic in microprogramming since the early 1960s, and chapter 7 provides tutorial as well as real application experience in emulation studies. Microcoding tools bear a familiar relationship to high-level languages for microprogramming in that there is no universally accepted set of such tools; however, the history of previous attempts to provide them should be useful to anyone working in this area. Chapter 8 provides us with some of this history. Chapter 9, on microcode optimization and compaction, also presents tutorial material and insights into the particular problems of microcode as contrasted with coding at the higher machine-language level.

Finally, there has been a great deal of interest lately in software verification theory, and chapter 10 studies the special problem of microcode verification.

This book is intended for reference and professional development. It may also be used as a text, although no problems appear at the ends of chapters (one can surely devise projects and questions based on the material contained in each of the chapters). The authors represent academia, research laboratories, and industrial organizations involved in both applied and research aspects of microprogramming methodology. Indeed, this mix of professional activity has been characteristic of the field.

The contributors believe that the almost twenty years of microprogramming methodology documented in this book will prove to be a valuable tool for practicing professionals, future microprogramming theorists, and future microprogrammers.

A few individuals offered some helpful comments to this book: thanks are due to Edward Armbruster, Bruce Shriver, and Steve Vegdahl for their comments.

contributors

STANLEY HABIB (editor) is Professor of Computer Science at City College of New York of the City University of New York and is a member of the board of the ACM SIGMICRO.

SCOTT DAVIDSON is a member of the technical staff at the AT&T Engineering Research Center in Princeton, N.J.

SUBRATA DASGUPTA is USL Foundation Professor of Computer Science at the University of Southwest Louisiana in Lafayette, La.

MICHAEL J. FLYNN is Professor of Electrical Engineering at Stanford University in Stanford, Ca.

HAROLD W. LAWSON is Professor of Computer Science at Linköping University in Linköping, Sweden.

JOSEPH L. LINN is a research staff member at the Institute for Defense Analysis in Alexandria, Va.

ROBERT A. MUELLER is Professor of Computer Science at Colorado State University in Fort Collins, Colo.

CHARLES J. NEUHAUSER is a vice president at Palyn Associates, Inc., in San Jose, Calif.

JOHN STANKOVIC is Professor of Computer Science at the University of Massachusetts in Amherst, Mass.

WILL TRACZ is Advisory Programmer in the Systems Integration Division at IBM in Owego, N.Y., and is Chairman of the ACM SIGMICRO.

JOSEPH VARGHESE is a member of the technical staff at the Microelectronics and Computer Technology Corporation in Austin, Tex.

TOM WEIDNER is a member of the technical staff at the Burroughs Corporation in Mission Viejo, Calif.

ROBERT I. WINNER is Deputy Director of the Computer and Software Engineering Division at the Institute for Defense Analysis in Alexandria, Va.

one
A BRIEF CHRONOLOGY OF MICROPROGRAMMING ACTIVITY

STANLEY HABIB

Microprogramming was introduced as an innovative approach to the design of the control unit in the central processing unit of a computing system. The microprogram consists of a set of microinstructions. A sequence of microinstructions typically corresponds to a macroinstruction execution sequence. The control unit executes the sequence through a step-by-step accessing and decoding of the microinstructions in the microroutine. The collection of all the microroutines in the microprogram provides a complete set of commands that then determines the instruction set of the computing system's central processor. Most people who have been following the field of microprogramming agree that microprogramming began with the seminal paper delivered by M. V. Wilkes entitled "The Best Way to Design an Automatic Calculating Machine" (1951). Wilkes's paper introduced the notion of register transfer and its association with microorders, the matrix concept of control store, and the logical structure of a stored microprogram. While he included no specific reference to microinstruction, microroutine, or microprogrammable control stores, the illustration he presents in his article provides the groundwork for these concepts. In his example, he refers to a microprogram for add, subtract, multiply, shift, and other operations. We see an implied microprogrammed architecture in which each macroinstruction is executed during its execution cycle through a branch to a microroutine stored in the control portion of the microprogrammed machine. Wilkes also suggested the possibilities of personally tailored opcodes and even dynamically changeable control stores, stores that contain both read and write capabilities and can be altered during program execution. Wilkes may not have anticipated much exploitation of this "fascinating possibility," but many individuals later tried to take advantage of the flexible, practical, yet logical advantage of this architectural construct.

As people became more and more interested in investigating the microprogrammed approach to the design of the control store, many new areas of research evolved. The notion of instruction sets that can be tailored to particular orientations led to various applications in emulation. Some of the obvious and useful advantages of being able to change instruction sets easily suggested migration of software into the microcode. These ideas led to explorations into vertical migration and firmware engineering. Efforts were also made to develop high-level languages and compiler-simulation tools for microprogramming. Moreover, because of the high degree of parallelism in microcode, studies in optimization and verification developed.

Much of the history of microprogramming is relayed through annual microprogramming workshops. Such workshops started in 1967, initiated by a small group at a meeting in California. The formation of the workshops accompanied the development of a Special Interest Group in Microprogramming (SIGMICRO) within the Association for Computing Machinery (ACM). SIGMICRO and the Institute of Electrical and Electronic Engineers Technical Committee on Microprogramming groups continue to sponsor the annual workshops, which usually take place in the fall of each year.

In addition to these workshops, Euromicro Workshops that encompass microprogramming and microprocessor concepts also formed. Several special workshops have also been held over the years to address the state of the art of microprogramming. Issues of the *IEEE Transactions on Computers* and *Computer* have also been completely devoted to microprogramming concepts. The relevant literature has certainly not been limited to these journals. Various trade journals have published tutorial articles, and on several occasions special issues of the ACM journals have contained sections devoted to the various methodologies associated with microprogramming.

Much of the history of microprogramming comes from the reporting of the highlights of the annual microprogramming workshops; this is what will be featured here. In addition to reporting on the workshops, other allied meetings of significance will also be discussed.

THE EARLY YEARS, 1967 TO THE EARLY 1970s: LANGUAGE ENHANCEMENT, DIAGNOSTICS, EMULATION

The first and second annual microprogramming workshops, held in 1967 and 1968, provided the foundation for the following annual workshops, as well as the inspiration for the Special Interest Group in Microprogramming (ACM SIGMICRO). This was followed soon after by the formation of the IEEE Tech-Micro (Technical Committee on Microprogramming).

The third annual microprogramming workshop (MICRO-3) was held in October 1970 in Buffalo, New York. This workshop's format became the model for future workshops. It consisted of several keynote papers of general interest followed by two days of nonparallel sessions. One of the keynote papers (Gardner 1970) defined functional memory and its applications in control store. The latter parts of the paper discussed the field and branching delay problems associated with use of functional memories in microprogrammed control store. (While the full text of the paper was not presented in the proceedings of the workshop, it was later published in the *IEEE Transactions on Computers*.) MICRO-3 also included two papers that discussed emulation using microprogramming, not included in the final proceedings, and early papers on language enhancements through microprogramming. These concepts were the forerunners of vertical migration.

From the very beginning microcoded aids to diagnostics have been of interest as an important application of microprogramming, and in fact many individuals saw this as the only useful application of microprogramming.

Diagnosis of hardware faults can be made either through self-diagnosis or macrodiagnosis. Self-diagnosis involves the use of microcode to diagnose the control store itself, while macrodiagnosis uses microcode to diagnose the noncontrol portion of the architecture (the functioning of units other than the control unit). One paper (Beuscher, Sisson, and Toy 1970) describes an original scheme for self-diagnosing the microprogrammed control portion of the machine through single parity-error checking. Although the application of microprogramming to the generation of microdiagnostic routines was and is widely used, the topic received less attention at future workshops in microprogramming.

It is worth noting that a paper on optimization did appear at the third annual microprogramming workshop (Ramamoorthy 1970), although interest in microcode optimization techniques did not flourish until later.

One area that received a great deal of attention at this workshop was that of high-level languages and their relationship to microprogramming. In fact, this topic consists of two distinct parts: high-level languages developed specifically for microprogramming and enhancements to familiar high-level languages to make them useful for microprogramming. The first area was addressed in several papers at the workshop. One (Eckhouse 1970) examined the syntax of PL/I to determine which constructs of the language could be used as a microprogramming language. At that time Eckhouse concluded, "Interestingly enough, although it is possible to conceive of a dialect of PL/I, no such need has occurred since careful scrutiny of the language has discovered syntax for all of the problem cases." The second area was addressed in several papers, which emphasized translation and compilation improvements that can be made through microprogramming. One (Habib 1970) demonstrated technique in which interpretively driven operations (IDOs) were used to perform the translation of high-level language statements into target code. These IDOs were then coded into microcode, thereby removing the constraint of the manufacturer's macroinstructions. Use of IDOs was not new, but the idea of encoding them directly into microcode and using them as the firmware primitives was introduced here.

There had previously appeared in the literature other illustrations of high-level language enhancement through microprogramming (Weber 1967). This paper, published in the Communications of the ACM, described a microprogrammed implementation of EULER and provided a new exposure to the process of interpretive code.

Emulation was becoming popular at the time of the MICRO-3 workshop, but no distinction was made between emulation applied to migration of macroinstruction opcodes into microcode as opposed to complete replacement of one machine by another through emulation. Earlier work on emulation (Tucker 1965, 1967) demonstrated how emulation was used to provide compatibility among several models of the IBM 7000 series. At this time emulation was viewed as a migration technique in which certain software features were incorporated into firmware. The emphasis at the workshop was on making portions of operating systems into firmware or on replacing one operating system by another but without replacing entire architectures—that is, without changing entire instruction sets. We will refer later to a paper (Reigel 1970) in which an interpreter is introduced; this notion suggested conversion of one high-level language machine to another.

Following the third microprogramming workshop, the concepts of microprogramming flexibility in architecture design, language enhancement through microprogramming, emulation, and formalism became leading topics. One paper, presented at MICRO-4 (Nichols 1971), stressed the flexibility available through microprogramming and also discussed the advantages of simulation as opposed to expensive hardware construction. As stated in the paper, proper experimentation with different machine designs is best achieved through actual construction of the hardware but can alternatively be tested through modeling with a software simulator. The simulator described here was used in the early stages of microprogramming research and employed horizontal microprogramming only. As indicated in the conclusions of the paper, shortcomings include:

no provision for input/output operations; the requirement that the control and memory cycles be identical (no asynchronous operations); and the lack of a high-level language for microassembling.

The fourth annual workshop on microprogramming (MICRO-4), held in 1971 at the Santa Cruz Campus of the University of California, saw a continued interest in microprogramming education. It contained a good deal of working sessions without formal papers, offering the opportunity to exchange recent ideas. Among the subjects raised was whether a microprogramming text should emphasize theoretical aspects of optimization, formal description of microprogramming languages, and verification. At the time it was felt that a full course in microprogramming was necessary for graduate computer-science students only. In future years microprogramming was included in most architecture textbooks at all levels of electrical-engineering and computer-science education.

MICRO-4 also contained several papers on microprogramming research in design and emulation underway at SUNY Buffalo. The work was done in conjunction with Nanodata Corporation and utilized QM-1 hardware. The chief characteristic of this particular hardware was its multilevel emulation capabilities; it was also one of the first truly user-microprogrammable machines. The user-programmable capabilities at the microprogramming level led to a number of research studies in emulation and operating-systems development, spearheaded by R. Rosin and others.

Firmware implementation of high-level language components is a perennial topic at all micro workshops. The idea is to recode primitives that are particularly suited to the language being implemented at the microcode level. One of the implementations often discussed at MICRO-4 were the attempts to design microcoded primitives for APL machines. At this workshop several such implementations were presented (Zaks 1971).

User microprogrammability on manufacturers' hardware remained scarce (except for the QM-1). Even if the manufacturers supplied user programming, users had to dig out the documentation and decipher it as best they could themselves. In addition, documentation was not only surreptitious but often incorrect. Since that time, writable control stores, user-microprogrammable machines, and firmware engineering have become more readily available.

It is interesting to note that at MICRO-4 there was some discussion of microcoded controllers. Microcoded processors were initially used to perform bit sampling and character assembly, with no hardware assist. The use of remote displays in place of keyboard printers had added to the need for more sophisticated microcoded controllers. Microcoded controllers did not play a large part in the workshop presentations, though they were of great interest to the manufacturers. They are more practical than microcoded control units for central processing units (CPUs), because they have a smaller instruction set and are much less confusing and tedious to use compared to the extensive set of microroutines used in complete systems.

Although much of the microprogramming activity has been reported in the annual microprogramming workshops, there have been many publications that have simultaneously reported developments. In the early 1970s a paper (Reigel 1970), described the Burroughs Interpreter. This interpreter is composed of three logic packages: the logic unit, the control unit, and the memory control unit. In addition, two memory levels are provided: the microprogram memory and the nanoprogram memory. This report gave evidence of successful applications of the interpreter to peripheral controllers, emulators, high-level language executors, and special function operators. The wide applicability of the interpreter is due to the versatility of its design.

By the time of the fifth annual microprogramming workshop (MICRO-5), the concept of enhancements to a high-level language was well established. In fact, the possibility of complete machine design based on the direct execution of high-level languages was fairly well reported. In a panel on higher-level language machines, the discussion centered around the question of how to justify choosing a particular set of machine instructions for implementation. At that time the discussion of suitable primitives was focused on the PL/I variety; little attempt was made to address I/O primitives in firmware. There was also a tendency to lock the design of primitives into established architectures such as the QM-1, Microdata, or Nova.

During this period a further conceptualization of emulation took place. Emulation was now conceived of as the realization of one machine architecture on another machine. (The "emulation" should be credited to Michael Flynn, who actually defined it in the context of microprogramming.) Papers on emulation concepts (Tucker and Flynn 1971) began to appear. One of the strongest distinctions to be made involved the differences between emulation and simulation. One paper (Freider 1977) pointed out that if emulation is instantiated by other than a hardwired realization done with hardware and software, then it forces us to include that software as a part of the emulator.

In May 1973 the SIGPLAN/SIGMICRO Interface meeting took place in Harriman, New York (Wexelblat 1973). It provided an opportunity for the members of both the Special Interest Group in Programming Languages (SIGPLAN) and the SIGMICRO group to discuss common interests of these two disciplines. The meeting not only refined the concepts of emulation and high-level language enhancement but also started us on the way toward formalism in microprogramming specification.

In the keynote paper (Reigel and Lawson 1973), the programming language–microprogramming interface was defined. The paper presented architecture as a structured organization consisting of: level i, microprogramming architecture; level $i+1$, microprogramming; and level $i+2$, microprogrammed implementation of programming languages. The paper emphasized the direct execution of programming languages, which was further defined with respect to interpretation. The term "interpretation" generally involves two functions: analysis and execution. The analysis portion involves translation into an intermediate form, which is then executed through branches to microcoded microroutines, each of which corresponds to the intermediate pseudocodes.

Another paper at the SIGPLAN/SIGMICRO Interface meeting (Lawson and Blomberg 1973) provided the first look at asynchronous microprogram control and the strong use of vertical microprogramming. It described the Flexible Central Processing Unit (FCPU) developed at Datasaab.

An early attempt at formalizing the representation of microprogramming languages for horizontally microprogrammed machines was also presented (Rauscher 1973). The argument was made that earlier attempts at such formalism contained unnatural symbolism and inflexible formats as well as a lack of certain constructs needed for microprogramming languages. While the syntax described was geared toward a particular language, it still opened the discussion of the need for formalism in the description of microprogramming languages.

Just after the SIGPLAN/SIGMICRO Interface meeting, the sixth annual microprogramming workshop (MICRO-6) was held. This workshop featured continuing experience with the design of microprogramming languages, microprogramming enhancements to high-level languages, the emergence of formalism, applications to graphics, and increasing appreciation of controller design using microprogramming.

The keynote paper (Ramamoorthy and Shanker 1973) discussed correctness and equivalence of straight-line microprograms. Automatic methods for the testing of correctness and equivalence of straight-line segments of microcode were reviewed, and the paper also provided a formal means for describing a microprogrammed architecture, which was then used to define correctness. Quite a bit of research done in this area in succeeding years was influenced by this paper.

MICRO-6 also featured a description of the very interesting Burroughs B-1726 computer (Dewitt, Schlansker, and Atkins 1973). The B-1726 has an interesting architecture from two points of view. First, it is a high-level-language machine that attempts to execute the language directly by using a stack-oriented architecture. Second, in its direct execution of intermediate code (reverse Polish) it branches to microcoded subroutines, each of which is microcoded to execute the Polish operator directly. Earlier descriptions of Burroughs high-level-language machines using microprogrammed architecture had been given (Wilner 1973; Burroughs 1972).

Although we were introduced to the specific architecture of the B-1700 series, geared towards direct execution of high-level languages using microcoded subroutines, there was a great deal of interest in new architecture designs— at least on paper. Three papers (Chu 1983; Habib 1973; Kimmel 1973) were concerned with designing architectures for language interpretation. In some cases attempts were made to design an entire architecture, and in others

(Chu, 1973; Habib, 1973) the familiar problem of enhancements to portions of language translation or execution through microcoding was covered.

THE MID 1970s: HIGH-LEVEL LANGUAGE MACHINES; HIGH-LEVEL LANGUAGES FOR MICROCODING

The seventh microprogramming workshop (MICRO-7) was held in 1974. It featured a continued discussion of microprogrammed control-unit architectures, language enhancements, and emulation. Attendees at the MICRO-7 workshop displayed interest in theoretical modeling of microprogramming and in what was to become a field of great interest, microcode optimization.

Microprograms can be optimized through detection of concurrently executable microoperations: "Since it (horizontal microprogramming) is highly machine dependent and requires knowledge of highly intricate features of a machine," only limited effort had been made so far to derive an algorithm for detection of microprogram parallelism (Tsuchiya and Gonzales 1974). There had been well-developed techniques for optimizing concurrency, but the horizontal-microprogramming optimization problem is constrained by resource contention. Consequently, one must not only develop an effective algorithm for horizontal microprograms with respect to parallelism, but one must also develop an effective resource-allocation scheme. At this time, the formal description of the microprogramming model was carried further. Formal descriptions of microoperations and resource allocations were better identified, and these descriptions were used to derive and illustrate an optimization algorithm.

MICRO-7 saw the evaluation of the areas of language enhancement and emulation. In one paper (Fuller 1973) a survey of past development and future trends in microprogramming was presented. The authors began by pointing out that the state of semiconductor technology is a major factor in the architecture of microprogrammed processors. Two views of microprogramming were stated: on the one hand, microprogramming can be seen as an economical way to implement a complex instruction set on a single processor; on the other, microprogramming provides software designers with an extra degree of representational freedom—that is, the ability to develop multiple instruction sets with different sets for different tasks.

Throughout the latter part of 1974 there was an ongoing parallel interest in microprogramming, emulation, and interpretation. The interpreter was characterized as a system "that carries out the execution of a program in one representational framework by dynamically mapping each statement or instruction...into a sequence of statements in another environment which realize the semantics of the mapped statement." Features needed to simplify microprogramming emulators, such as more high-speed registers, larger control stores, memory management, and microinterrupts, were some of the central concerns.

Another unique feature of MICRO-7 was the indication by manufacturers of a willingness to provide user-writable control stores. Unfortunately, the availability of the writable control store was not accompanied by sufficient supporting documentation. A paper on the Hewlett-Packard 21MX (Matheson 1974) stated that it offered a versatile microprogrammable minicomputer as well as a viable philosophy of design for user microprogrammability in the minicomputer. The writable control store is a separate board that is inserted into a standard I/O slot and cabled to the rest of the control store. It is loaded using the I/O system but assumes the function of ROM in the control portion.

MICRO-7 exposed the microprogramming community to multimicroprocessor structures (Siewiorek 1974). Many attendees had given thought to such structures, but prior to this workshop there had been very little discussion of the applications of microprogramming to them. Siewiorek showed how microprogrammed special-purpose instructions could be helpful in dealing with problems of deadlock prevention. One of the main points was that a synchronizing primitive encoded in microcode could provide sufficient speed improvement to avoid deadlock problems encountered in multiprocessor systems.

In late 1974 we continued to see papers on high-level language enhancement through microprogramming (Hoevel 1974) and on proof of program correctness and the application of structured programming techniques to microprogramming (Jones 1974). But there was an even stronger interest in hardware organization, not only from the point of view of teaching microprogramming but also that of the use of microprogrammed control as a framework for teaching computer architecture. In one paper (McKeeman 1974), a simple computer used as a teaching tool at the University of California, Santa Cruz, was described. The goal was to present a computer architecture that left the student with a good understanding of computer organization. The intent of the paper was to provide a unified approach to machine instruction sets without any bias toward a particular manufacturer. The discussion also described a simulator for this simple computer, a precursor of the many microprogrammed architectures later simulated through software.

The interest in structured design and its relationship to microprogramming was presented in another paper (Boulaye 1974). Boulaye reiterates that synthesis is movement from the global to the detailed. The paper discusses the global nature of design by viewing the layers of the machine, the different intermediate machines, and the domains of the hardware and software.

In the same year another paper, entitled "The Significance of Microprogramming" (Rosin 1974), reexamined the subject. The author argued that microprogramming had previously been used to bridge the gap between hardware and software but that in fact it had actually disguised the gap. Since "microprogramming is the implementation of hopefully reasonable systems through interpretation on unreasonable machines," it hides the nature of unreasonable machines by constructing reasonable systems on top of them. Unreasonable machines are neither a good idea nor are they necessary: microprogramming should be avoided whenever possible on them; and if one is faced with an unreasonable machine, then microprogramming is a necessary tool.

The SIGMICRO Newsletter contained a paper (Lloyd 1974) suggesting design considerations for microprogramaming languages. The distinction was made between providing a hospitable target machine vs. a hospitable high-level programming language. To be sure, target-machine development and high-level microprogramming-language development can occur simultaneously, but this assumes complete freedom in both arenas. One of the interesting features here was the categorization of microcode-generation difficulties, including the combinatorial complexity that derives from the number of microorders within each microinstruction, the microinstruction dependency deriving from the number of shared resources which must be managed, and the timing dependency, or the scheduling of operations that require more than one cycle to complete. One of the interesting discussions concerned the design of a higher-level language that can be built on a given host machine. In discussing this topic the authors provided an interesting set of levels associated with high-level language design.

During the mid 1970s computer scientists began to design their own microprogrammable hardware. In one paper (Kornerup and Shriver 1975) a dynamically microprogrammable processor was described. The processor was designed to be used as a tool in emulator and processor research. The system—MATHILDA, as it was called—also proved to be a successful educational tool for graduate courses in microprogramming.

While much thought was given to the migration of operating systems into microcode, research and applications in this area were spotty. One paper (Brown, Eckhouse, and Goldberg 1976) discussed what we mean by microgramming in operating systems. As stated by the authors, the hardware/software interface in an operating system is represented by the extensions made to the base-level machine. File systems and access-control mechanisms are higher-level extensions, while synchronizing primitives and queue management are low-level facilities. Extensions that are candidates for firmware implementation are those that would be too specific for hardware, would be unlikely to change with time, and would suffer from the slower execution rate of software. In the late 1970s research areas in the migration of operating systems into microcode included the need to compare the implementation of executive functions at the micro- and macrolevels and techniques for constructing an entire system by utilizing firmware (or a split between kernel functions and special-purpose functions).

Discussion of language enhancements through microprogramming had focused on the interpretive execution of intermediate instruction streams such as the execution of Polish-string opcodes. Chu (Chu 1976) was a proponent of direct-execution computer architecture in which the high-level language is taken directly as the machine language; there is no Polish-string language, no assembly language, and no relocatable or absolute language. As stated in the article, the high-level language is the machine language and the architecture is direct-execution architecture. A direct-execution computer need not have only one high-level language, nor need it be either a single-processor or multiprocessor machine; the design of the high-level language is a separate issue. "Direct execution" means direct execution of a high-level language program. There is neither a compiler or an intermediate language nor an assembler or assembly language. Again, the high-level language is the machine language. Emulation and firmware make multiple languages implementable but do not necessarily become locked into the primitives for a particular language.

During this period a new technology that provided an important research-and-development arena in the microprogramming field, microprogrammable microprocessors, started to flourish. One paper (Mick 1976) introduced the concept of microprogramming for the hardware engineer. The microprogrammable microprocessor became more than a development fantasy due to the introduction and design of the Advanced Micro Devices Am2901 four-bit-slice microprocessor and the Am2909 microprogram sequencer. These devices are low-power Schottky integrated circuits utilizing microprogramming. In addition to the architecture of the Am2900 series, the paper described the engineering design of microprogramming architectures. The difficulty of designing with microprogrammed microprocessors arises from the flexibility of the microinstruction format. The approach used with design engineers suggested using only one format for the microprogram word. Engineers were spared the tradeoff decision required when using various formats. After the initial architecture is laid out, the design proceeds in such a way that small groups of microinstructions are written for machine instructions. As the small portions of firmware are written, economy of space and timing is incorporated. The distinguishing feature of the Am2900 series is its suitability for high-performance computer control units using overlap fetch of the next instruction.

Another paper (Ehlers and Harmon 1976) discussed an always interesting topic, emulation of one architecture on another. It defined simulation as an operating system using mathematical or physical models that attack specifically devised problems in a time-sequential method similar to itself. Emulation via microprogrammed modifications allows the host to project an image of the target machine's architecture. The point made in this paper is that the emulator allows an exchange of packages between two architectures: the HP 2100 and Varian 72. In the years that followed several papers and projects demonstrated the emulation of one hardware on another.

In 1976 one of the first books on microprogramming since *Microprogramming Principles and Practices* (Husson 1970), *Foundations of Microprogramming* (Agrawal 1976), was published. The field was still at a stage where it was not clear whether it was an art or a technical discipline. The shortcomings of any book on microprogramming stem from the lack of a suitable universal high-level language, the fact that one must have access to a suitable microprogrammable device in order to really understand the subject, and the fact that many architectures are so specialized that they do not lend themselves to a universal approach to formalization.

During this period, microprogrammable microprocessors were especially interesting to researchers, since hardware existed on which to try them out. At the ninth microprogramming workshop (MICRO-9) a paper was presented on bit-slice architectures (Andrews 1976). It focused on the Intel 3000 architecture (which has since been minimally, if at all, supported by Intel, which served as another interesting prototype of an architecture on which microprogrammed concepts could be understood and implemented. The application discussed was a concrete example of bit-slice implementation, along with the modifications needed to use this particular architecture as a model for educational purposes. The application demonstrated was a hardwired floating point processor. The CPE functions are more latchlike than accumulator-like, and further modifications are needed to relate the Intel 3000 to a horizontal microprogrammable computer. A simulator made the microprogramming architecture easier to understand.

In keeping with the interest in a high-level language for microprogramming, another paper (DeWitt 1977) discussed extensibility in microprogramming languages. The author reviewed some of the essential features of microprogramming languages, such as readability, machine independence, efficient microcode generation, and structured design. The novel feature of the paper is its introduction of extensibility into microprogramming languages. Microprogramming languages are somewhat unique in terms of extensibility, since transportability of microcode is particularly sensitive to architecture design. The paper introduced a language (EMPL), the first extensible microprogramming language, and illustrated its use. At that time a compiler did not exist.

THE LATE 1970s: MICROPROGRAMMABLE MICROPROCESSORS, MICROPROGRAMMING TOOLS

In late 1976 and early 1977 there was a growing interest in microprogramming tools. Manufacturers of microprogrammed architectures created a good many tools for their own purposes, but they tended to be locked into a particular hardware. Researchers quickly realized the need for a high-level language assembler to avoid the bit-by-bit microcoding approach. This led to a variety of manufacturer-generated microprogramming assembly languages of the symbolic variety. Intel devised one for the Intel 3000 series, and AMD did the same for the Am2900 series. A second need was for a simulator; many of the same microassemblers devised for the specific architectures also provided a simulator, but again they were tailored to the manufacturers' specific architectures and microassembly languages.

Concurrent with manufacturer-developed microassemblers and simulators were general-purpose microassemblers that were not tied to any particular architecture and thus provided some original designs. These general-purpose assembler/simulators also enabled the user to build a particular architecture as well. A typical example of a general-purpose microassembler and simulator was given in one paper (Adamowicz and Mirza 1977). As stated in the introduction, one reason for developing high-level assemblers and simulators is to provide a tool for teaching computer architecture. High-level simulators not only remove the tedium of low-level coding but also provide a well-defined notation for describing architectures. A simulator provides feedback by allowing the user to check a proposed design.

The basic components of a design language include the control line; outputs that control the flow of data between registers and that decode and execute instructions; next-address branching, which either sequences control to the next microinstruction or causes branching to a microinstruction computed from the next address and branch condition(s); and the constant, or "emit," field of the microinstruction. These components also describe the format of the microinstruction of a general-purpose architecture. In building a microprogramming assembler and simulator, one needs to build the register definitions, the data paths, the microroutines for the macroinstructions, and in the case of some architectures, particularly microprogrammable microprocessors, the microfunctions.

Very little activity has taken place in the area of operating-system enhancement through firmware. Several descriptive papers on this topic appeared in the tenth annual microprogramming workshop, MICRO-10 (Flink 1977; Frieder 1977; Dalrymple 1977). The particular model considered involved a closed queuing network model with routing probabilities. One of the interesting points made by the authors is that microprogramming is of little practical value if we are not able to measure the improvement using the new primitives. The long-range hope of the research presented was to develop a hardware-based operating-system nucleus. While the study did not succeed in implementing the entire nucleus, it did provide some insight into which primitives could advantageously be migrated into microcode.

One exciting initiation at MICRO-10 was the award for the outstanding contribution to microprogramming. On the tenth anniversary of the meeting, the community of attendees presented the first award to Dr. Maurice Wilkes. In his "Ten Years and More of Microprogramming" (Wilkes 1977), Wilkes restated his view of microprogramming as a systematic method of control design.

Emulation, he stated, is an additional bonus but not the essential feature of microprogramming. At this time Wilkes viewed high-level language support through microprogramming as a disappointment and in fact maintained that hardware improvement through memory such as cache would provide the larger part of speedup. The paper also foresaw the impact of microcomputer accessibility in the form of personal computers. The combination of shared multiprogrammed computer systems and writable control stores offered the ability to provide individuals with microprograms especially adapted to their needs. Microprogramming can be used to personalize a computer to an individual's needs—for example, LISP vs. large numerical computation programs.

Late 1977 witnessed continuing interest in firmware engineering and migration across the software-hardware boundaries. One paper (Davidson 1977) is an example of the state of the art at the time. The process described in the paper represents the use of microcode to implement an algorithm. It was implemented on a microprogrammable machine that also offered the capability of extended microinstructions to provide new macroinstructions. The study made some observations regarding the advantages available from microprogramming of primitives for a particular algorithm. Some of the observations may appear to be obvious: for example, a program that spends a great deal of time in loops is a candidate for an extended instruction set. Programs that are extremely processor-intensive are candidates; this means that I/O is kept to a minimum.

It seems that migration and emulation are inextricably connected. Research in both areas overlaps a great deal. In one paper (Flynn 1977), the author discusses classes of emulators. The paper defines different types of emulation. On the one hand, emulation transforms all images into the true machine, which duplicates all failure modes. In contrast, there are transformations of image programs that appear to be correct but may fail certain tests. The third class involves transformation of subsets of the image programs. The author makes an interesting comparison of easy and difficult problems solvable through emulation. On the one hand, the addition of extra instructions on some image machine is relatively easy to handle in emulation except for the problem of lack of space. On the other hand, memory protect is viewed as a difficult problem to solve, since in emulation this feature affects alteration of the instruction cycle time.

As was mentioned earlier, hardware manufacturers were actively involved at this time in developing microprogrammable microprocessors. Adams (Adams 1978a) surveyed microprogrammable microprocessors, including Intel, Monolithic Memories, Fairchild, Texas Instruments, Motorola, Advanced Micro Devices, and Signetics. In a follow-up article (Adams 1978b) Adams lists the criteria for microprogrammable comparisons. These include basic clock cycle time, dual-port features, nonfixed register size, register width per chip, microinstruction power, and sequencer addressability. As may not be surprising, certain conclusions drawn include the ease of design with larger data-path microchips, large addressability sequencers, and dual-port architectures.

In the late 1970s many special-purpose designs (a form of turnkey systems) appeared at the microprogramming workshops. The eleventh annual microprogramming workshop, MICRO-11, included several such examples. A paper by Johannsen (1978) describes the advantage of LSI technology. The subject is a microcoded LSI processor. The original design included five LSI chips plus standard memory parts. There is a division between the data chip, which contains the register file, and the multibit shifter, arithmetic logic unit, and bit-modification unit. Instructions for the chip come from the microcode unit, which of course is ROM. The success of this project stems from the fact that the data chip and the controller chip were actually fabricated. The actual masks are shown in the paper. The paper demonstrated various possibilities obtainable through different topologies as a result of nMOS and LSI technology.

A second illustration of special design systems is given in another paper (Stritter and Tredennick 1978). In this work a design for a single-chip microprocessor using LSI is presented. While many of the advantages of microprogrammed architecture had been cited earlier, this contribution and the preceding paper demonstrated how the advent of LSI technology made it possible to implement some of these notions. Some of the reasons for microprogrammed design may well be repeated here: design time constraints seem to be eased by microcoding; the regular structure of the microprogrammed architecture decreases the complexity of the control unit and simplifies the layout of the chip; and designers can delay some binding decisions. Once the basic structure is determined, the circuit designers can go to work and fill in the microcode later.

LSI implementation of microprogrammed architecture offers important features. An array of read-only memory cells should take less chip area than the equivalent combinational logic. It also eases simulation and testing. As has been noted earlier, microcode offers the ability to add new instructions or modify existing ones; in the case of chip design, such modifications may be possible without major redesign of the chip. Moreover, clocking functions in microprogrammed control are much cleaner than in combinational approaches.

It is probably worthwhile to review some of the aspects of horizontal vs. vertical microcode. Vertical microcode is highly encoded and requires a significant amount of combinational logic to decode the microinstructions. Horizontal microcode, on the other hand, drives the execution unit with less levels of intervening logic. Vertical microcode also requires more cycles to emulate a given macroinstruction. It does have the advantage of a reduced control store, since horizontal code tends to be wide and often repetitious.

Stritter and Tredennick (1978) put forth the interesting suggestion of two-level control store consisting of a mix of vertical and horizontal structures. They analyzed two-level control and cited some of the problems. One problem is that access to memory is not instantaneous and requires sequential access. A second problem is that conditional branching leads to an excessive delay. Needless to say, branching operations occur frequently in micro control stores.

In conclusion, the authors stressed the novelty of two-level hybrid vertical and horizontal controls, which foreshadowed a new generation of microprocessor control.

The eleventh annual microprogramming workshop (MICRO-11) featured a number of presentations describing how microprogramming can be used in architectures for signal-processing applications. The advantages include speed and the ability to tune to the specific application.

The first paper of interest (Mulrooney 1978) discussed a microprogrammed FFT machine. One of the useful aspects of the paper is that the author reviewed the FFT algorithm and demonstrated which parts are best improved with microcode. The author stated in the summary remarks that microprogramming enhances performance by eliminating the unnecessary decoding of the instruction register and by being able to take advantage of simultaneous memory and arithmetic operations. The speed advantages were two to three times greater than conventional assembly-language routines.

Also at MICRO-11 Dasgupta proposed a microprogramming-language schema (1978). The schema is a Pascal-influenced language. Characteristics of a microprogramming schema were given, including the ability to construct the control structures for sequential and parallel flow of control, the ability to declare microprogramming data objects, and the ability to test the correctness of microprograms. In addition to the sequential constructs introduced in the paper, the author introduced microparallelism constructs such as the cocyle. This paper was an attempt to provide a universal microprogramming schema, in contrast to earlier presentations that tended to favor special architectures and special-purpose applications. The introduction of this high-level language approach to microcode program writing carried existing high-level languages one step further in their development.

The twelfth annual microprogramming workshop (MICRO-12) continued to exhibit a strong interest in microprogramming languages, microprogramming tools, and emulation. In the second area one paper took the total approach, including assemblers, loaders, and simulators (Tamura and Tokoro 1979). The authors described a general-purpose microprogramming generating system that provides a general-purpose development support system for LSI processor modules. The generator has a three-level hierarchical structure: the lowest level is the microassembler; the second level is an optimizer of the microinstructions; and the highest level is for a high-level language for microprogramming.

Another paper presented at the MICRO-12 proceedings described a medium-level compiler (Marti and Kessler 1979). It pointed out some of the problems in working directly with existing microcode. The first difficulty mentioned was that, since the registers were not general-purpose, the coder is restricted to using the registers for the special purpose that they were designed to serve. Performing input/output from microcode is extremely difficult, and it proved easier to handle at the operating-system/service-routine level. In order to overcome the shortcomings of the built-in microcode ability, the authors devised a medium-level compiler generation system. Microprogramming tools were also discussed in terms of real-world experience in several other papers presented at the proceedings.

One of the most successful emulation tools is the EMMY, which is still in operation at the Computer Systems Laboratory at Stanford University. The results of research were given in another paper presented at MICRO-12 (Huck and Neuhauser 1979). The research topic was emulator construction for a variety of machines including conventional architectures as well as original designs. In the paper the authors stated various design objectives of emulation, such as speed in transfer rate, so that the emulation is not slower than the actual device, and flexibility in terms of device representation. In the emulation of a device the authors argued that it is better to use redirection of I/O.

Another paper presented at MICRO-12 described research in a machine-independent microprogramming language (Patterson, Lew, and Tuck 1979), YALLL (yet another low-level language). Features of the research are that the authors compiled the language on a couple of architectures, compared the efficiency of microarchitectures, and extolled the advantages of microprogramming versus macroprogramming.

Low-level microprogramming languages refer to transfers between registers, transfers between registers and memory, data manipulations between registers, and both conditional and unconditional branches. The results of the study pointed to some of the difficulties in porting microcode, such as the transparency of addressing at the macroinstruction level. At the microprogramming level it is not easy to disguise addressing to the microcoder. Another area causing efficiency problems is the width of the path to memory. Various masking techniques apparently need to be employed to compensate for different bit-width paths. The authors also pointed to the difficulty mentioned in the Marti paper (Marti and Kessler 1979) in that the special-purpose nature of registers could pose a problem for the microcoder. In spite of the lack of universality in microprogram portability, the authors argued for a less powerful but useful language. In any event, the language is transportable within a family of computers.

THE EARLY 1980s: FIRMWARE ENGINEERING, VERTICAL MIGRATION, OPTIMIZATION

A meeting was held in the early months of 1980 in Linz, Austria, entitled "Firmware, Microprogramming, and Restructurable Hardware." The topic receiving the most attention (according to the report of the meeting) was firmware engineering. One paper (Davidson and Shriver 1980) surveyed the field and pointed out the parallel between it and software engineering. It further predicted that new advances made in software methodology will be matched in firmware methodology. Still to be developed at that time were a high-level language, improved simulators and assemblers, and the availability of hypothetical and real machines for hands-on experience. These tools would in turn allow the construction of larger microprograms, improved verification techniques, and effective tradeoffs between software and firmware.

A second topic of interest at the meeting was migration. It was covered primarily through panel discussions. It was agreed that support for operating systems, high-level languages, and application programs should be supplied by microprograms. Synchronization, virtual memory management, and scheduling also lend themselves to microprogramming.

Additional topics discussed at the meeting included restructurability, verification, and issues in microprogramming language design (Davidson and Shriver 1980; Crocker 1980; Dasgupta 1980a).

The strong interest in microprogramming tools and microcode optimization continued into the early 1980s, as evidenced by the papers presented at the thirteenth annual microprogramming workshop, MICRO-13. One of the papers (Poe 1980) indicated the new emphasis on global as opposed to straight-line code optimization. Global optimization has parallels in data-flow analysis. Both start with interior loops, which constitute the basic blocks. Taking into account data and control dependencies, microoperations are migrated above and below basic blocks. The paper is tutorial in nature and provides a useful complement to other works on global optimization.

Another significant discussion of optimization combined with binding was presented at MICRO-13 (Fisher 1980). It discussed logically independent tests that can be used to determine microprogram jumps. As the author argued, such testing becomes more and more a necessity if horizontally microcodable machines are to become wider. The author pointed to a problem well known to microprogrammers, the complexity of horizontal microcode. One of the interesting clarifications that the author made in the paper is that more accurate terms for microcode optimization are "compaction" and "parallelization." The paper provided an overview of parallelization within basic blocks and went on to discuss the more complex and important problem, that of parallelization beyond blocks. A serious defect of very wide microengines is that only one test instruction may be scheduled per wide instruction. The optimization algorithm proposed in the paper introduced a multiway independent jump that allows independent tests to be specified and states many possible true and false paths.

The MICRO-13 workshop also summarized the state of high-level microprogramming languages. In one paper (Sint 1980) the author reviewed some of the high-level language proposals made to date and recapitulated the special considerations of microprogramming language design. The point was made that horizontal microcode is much more complicated because it exercises direct control over the hardware and provides for inherent parallelism. There are more complicated timing considerations in the parallelism that must be taken into consideration. Another factor in microcode is the necessity for efficiency. This is especially true in emulation, where speed is important. Finally, the author pointed out that whatever microcodable machines do exist are so tied into specific hardware that it is impossible to make full use of flexibility for efficiency.

The paper provided a good summary of the languages proposed to date and also pointed to the fact that difficulty of implementation, not language design, is the major problem. Of the ten languages reviewed in the paper, only two leave the composition of the microinstructions to the programmer, and only two allow the programmer to work with symbolic variables instead of registers. These conclusions could be interpreted as useful requirements for further development in microprogramming languages.

The fourteenth annual microprogramming workshop (MICRO-14) took place in 1981. The meeting reflected the continuing interest in firmware engineering, compaction (optimization), and tools. One of the papers presented at this workshop (Mueller and Johnson 1981), though tutorial in nature, compared the terms "translation," "verification," and "synthesis." Translation systems, the authors pointed out, have been successful for software development but have had little impact in the domain of firmware development. In addition to some of the problems mentioned above (Sint 1980), there is not as much motivation for developing powerful and efficient languages for microprogrammable machines. Verification techniques have not been widely used in the macro software arena, but there is some evidence that they may have practical value when applied to microcode, primarily due to the lack of complex data structures and control constructs and the smallness of microprograms. Synthesis is the attempt to derive a program for some target machine given only a functional specification of the program. As is the case of verification, automated synthesis of microcode seems to have greater potential than synthesis applied to macroprogramming.

About the time of the MICRO-14 workshop, Wirth introduced a great deal of material concerning his MODULA language and LILITH machine (Wirth 1981). One of the papers presented at MICRO-14 (Habib and Yang 1981) described the use of a meta-assembler to build a subset of MODULA interpreter. The MODULA machine is emulated on a set of AMD2900 chips using AMD2901/3 microfunctions. The paper typifies the dependency on existing microprogramming hardware for microcoding.

Another tools paper (Roskos and Winner 1981) made use of writable control store. The discussion was once again related to a specific hardware. Still another paper presented at MICRO-14 (Geyer and Lake 1981) was similar in that it also addressed software tools from the assembler level to the target-machine level. It described a set of software tools used to develop microcode for the Bolt, Beranek, and Newman machine, which contains vertically oriented microinstruction format, RAM-based microcode, and a multitask operating system that provides various utilities to the microprogrammer. Both of the sets of tools described above had been used successfully and so were well beyond the development stage.

In the early 1980s the notion of reduced instruction sets was introduced (Patterson 1981). As the name suggests, reduced-instruction-set machines have a select group of instructions that are often used in combination with an architecture that provides for fast execution. The architecture is also based on register-to-register macroinstructions, thereby eliminating high overhead memory accesses. The combination of VLSI and microprogrammed control makes the design of a faster architecture much easier.

This interesting idea for machine design became a major topic at the Fifteenth Annual Microprogramming workshop (MICRO-15). It generated controversy because it represented a serious rethinking of many years of instruction-set design. Wilkes (1982) pointed out that using reduced instruction sets generates much less dense code than we are accustomed to. One of the arguments put forth is that memory bandwidth is customarily the limiting factor in improved performance and the use of reduced instruction sets imposes severe demands on memory access and memory management.

Wilkes went on to distinguish the purposes of the microprogramming unit. On the one hand, it expands the information coded in the instruction; on the other, it commands the execution of the instruction. He suggested that code be stored in a compacted form and expanded to the reduced format. This process was compared to macroexpansion, with the microprogram unit playing the role of the macroexpander. Wilkes proposed this as a mechanism for wider acceptance of reduced instruction sets.

The availability of VLSI offered new challenges to the field of microprogramming. Its implications for development of microprogrammed architectures were explored in two papers at MICRO-15 (Burke 1982; Li 1982). Both papers suggested that microprogrammed implementation techniques coupled with VLSI enable designers to create rather sophisticated functions. Illustrations were given of operating-system primitives and controller primitives implemented in the microprogrammed control store. One of the drawbacks mentioned in the latter paper is that, while microprogrammed architecture offers advantages, a different type of tool than what is currently available is needed for development. In fact, what is most needed is a high-level microprogramming language.

Microcode optimization, which had become important during the late 1970s (Fisher 1979, 1981), continued to command attention in the 1980s. One paper (Vegdahl 1982) presented algorithms for optimization. The author suggested a method of constant unfolding as an optimization method the employs heuristic search. The author also illustrated code-generation techniques using the method.

THE MID 1980s: DYNAMIC MICROPROGRAMMING, VERIFICATION, SPECIFICATION

The sixteenth microprogramming workshop (MICRO-16) started off with a continued interest in instruction-set design. A keynote address (Flynn 1983) concerned instruction-set evaluation. It distinguished between primary and secondary factors. Primary factors include static measures, such as the fact that smaller static code is better, and compilation time, with the obvious considerations of optimization. Some of the secondary factors mentioned include compatibility, by which the author meant that the "primary level of transportability and compatibility of programs is the instruction set." Even when source code for the high-level language is available, the variety of dialects creates many compatibility problems. Another point made in this discussion is the fact that as the hardware becomes less costly, it makes more sense to design hardware for specific applications to the extent that the environment is known.

In this discussion of instruction-set choice microprogramming plays a role, and the implications for implemetation through microcode were discussed. For example, the definitions of universal host machine and universal executing host machine are given. The role of the microstore vis-à-vis each of these environments is described. This address also described the DEL (directly executed language) project at Stanford and the general aspects of language-oriented architectures that provide "the understanding of customizing an architecture to an environment. . ."

As we have indicated earlier, a substantial theoretical foundation for microcode compaction emerged during the late 1970s. The continuing interest in and importance of compaction is demonstrated in several papers presented at MICRO-16 (Linn 1983; Lah and Atkins 1983). The papers presented different approaches to code compaction and raised unresolved issues. For example, Linn pointed out the problem of delayed branches. He also suggested that not enough use of global compaction is made in local compaction issues. The third paper asserted that further efforts can be made to apply compaction technique to microprograms with longer critical paths and higher probability of resource conflicts.

The appeal of microprogramming workshops to both theoreticians and practitioners has been apparent throughout their history. Eager (1983) described a comprehensive set of microprogramming tools that were used in advanced micro devices development. The tools provide a high-level yet usable set for the assemble/link/load process.

For many years research-and-development efforts were based on static microcode. The 1970s saw increased interest in dynamic microprogramming, "the ability of a system user to place microcode dynamically into a writable control store, thus effectively extending the programming architecture of the machine" (Winner and Carter 1983). In this same paper the authors described a research project in which the interactions of dynamic microprogramming, vertical migration, and data abstraction were explored. The project investigated the feasibility of migration of abstract data types using dynamic microprogramming. While the project leaves unexplored areas, it offers a view of redefinable computer architecture. It appears that more research will be forthcoming in this area. There had been earlier work on dynamic microprogramming (Tucker and Flynn 1971), but it was highly architecture-dependent.

At about the same time, parallels between software and microcode verification were being investigated. Microcode verification is analogous to software verification based upon Floyd and Hoare's (Floyd 1967; Hoare 1969) assertion methods. Formal verification is also identified with high-level language programming and hence suggests the existence of a high-level language for microcode. The practical advantage of high-level verification is the avoidance of serious errors caused by incorrect low-level microcode. Wagner and Dasgupta (1983) illustrate the use of formal verification techniques in the environment of the S*(QM-1) microprogramming language. This is a machine-specific microprogramming language based on Dasgupta's scheme S*(Dasgupta 1980b). The paper represents one of a very few that address the issue of formal verification of microcode, and it raises the kinds of issues that arise in microcode verification. It takes the position that microcode is subject to verification just as is familiar software.

The continuing use of microprogramming for the design of new architectures was particularly evident at the seventeenth annual workshop (MICRO-17) at which several papers were presented on the VLSI VAX microcomputer (Brown and Sites 1984; Gries and Woodward 1984; Samudrala 1984; Sherwood 1984). This set of papers describes this microarchitecture and the microcode strategies that achieve VAX 11/780 performance. An accompanying set of software tools was used to develop the microcode. In addition, a global view of some VLSI design tools used for design verification, hardware debugging, and microcode testing was given. While VLSI design tools had been available for some time, their specific application to microcode testing was of great interest to the microprogramming community.

Concomitant with the strong interest in high-level languages for expert system design and research was a concern with PROLOG machines. (Ponder and Patt 1984; Doby, Patt, and Despain 1984). The thrust of these papers was chiefly to propose architectures for improved language performance. A microengine is at the heart of the control, and the control unit is entirely microprogram-based. The results seemed encouraging, although at the time they were arrived at through simulation.

Verification, specification, and firmware engineering were also of continuing interest at the seventeenth annual workshop (Dasgupta 1984b; Damm 1984). Dasgupta discussed micromachine models of the past and put forth a generalized micromachine model in both a notational and a formal sense. The description relies on interacting stores, functional (and operational) modules, clocks, and a "system-wide" timekeeper. The major focus was to capture machine description in a somewhat abstract though not obscure manner. The Damm paper offered a set of axioms intended for use in verification of timing behavior and conflict avoidance of microprograms expressed in high-level languages. The framework for the language is S*, previously proposed by Dasgupta (Dasgupta 1980b).

Retargetability received a great deal of attention during the early and mid 1980s. Two presentations at MICRO-17 expanded local retargetable microcode to global retargetability (Mueller, Varghese, and Allan 1984a; Mueller, Duda, and O'Haire 1984b). They dealt with the ability to translate a machine-independent intermediate language (compiler- or parser-generated) into a machine-specific target. The methodology employs flow analysis and optimization.

The eighteenth annual workshop on microprogramming (MICRO-18) contained papers that reported additional activity in the area of microcode verification (Damm 1985a, 1985b). The approach taken is to adapt the hierarchical design method to firmware-design methods (Levitt and Robinson 1979). Microarchitecture, architecture at the microorder level, imposes resource-allocation constraints that are unique to design at this level. The approach here is to modify the HDM methodology for microarchitecture design.

Microcoding tools still had not reached a universal state—and still have not. They remain locked into specific architectures. One paper (Tracz 1985) demonstrated the advanced nature of the tools used at IBM, though they were still somewhat architecture-dependent.

CONCLUSION

The chronological history presented in this section seems like an annotated bibliography of microprogramming workshops. That is because such a large portion of the research and development has been reported at these workshops. Other important contributions have been made at other conferences and in journals and newsletters. The *IEEE Transactions on Computers* over the years has contained original research-project reporting as well as summary papers on the state of microprogramming. The annual conferences on computer architecture and design automation have also included microprogramming-research-project reports. Discussions of microprogramming are often embedded in broader subjects, such as VLSI architectures, RISC machines, I/O controllers, and specific-purpose architectures. Microprogramming has played a crucial role in education and usually comprises a complete chapter in textbooks on computer architecture.

The microprogramming workshops continue to be held every year as of this writing, and they provide a forum for the presentation of projects from both the academic and the industrial communities. We are encouraged by the steady attendance at these workshops and look forward to the further resolution of unanswered issues and the introduction of new issues that arise as the technology and the application of computer architectures changes.

In recognition of over seventeen years of microprogramming activity, a special repository has been formed. Known as the Microprogramming Repository, it has been established at the University of Southwest Louisiana. It was formed under the inspiration and leadership of Dr. Bruce Shriver and contains archival documents collected over many years.

We hope that the twenty years or so of microprogramming methodology that we have witnessed to date will provide a continuing foundation in the architecture pyramid. If one were to list the areas of continuing interest for research and application in microprogramming methodology, they would include: microcode development, language enhancement, architecture design employing microprogramming, compaction, specification, emulation, verification, migration, and high-level language design for microcoding. It will be curious to observe how new architecture approaches refocus these areas.

REFERENCES

Adamowicz, M., and Mirza, J. 1970. "MDSL: A Microcomputer Design and Simulation Language." *SIGMICRO Newsletter*, 8 (2).

Adams, P. M. 1978. "Microprogrammable Microprocessor Survey." *SIGMICRO Newsletter*, 9 (1) and 9 (2).

Adams, P. M. 1979. "A Microprogrammable Microprocessor Survey Part II." *SIGMICRO Newsletter*, 9 (2).

Agrawala, A. K., and Rauscher, T. G. 1976. "Foundations of Microprogramming; Architecture, Software, and Applications." *ACM Monograph*. New York: ACM Press.

Andrews, M. 1976. "A Bit Slice Architecture for Microprogrammable Machines." *The Ninth Annual Workshop on Microprogramming*. New Orleans, LA: IEEE Computer Society Press.

Andrews, M. 1980. Principles of Firmware Engineering in Microprogram Control Computer Science, 1980

Banerji, J. K., and Raymond, J. 1982. *Elements of Microprogramming*. Englewood Cliffs, NJ: Prentice-Hall.

Beuscher, H. J.; Sisson, W. H.; and Toy, W. H. 1970. "A Self-checking Microprogram Control." *The Third Annual Workshop on Microprogramming*, Buffalo, NY: IEEE Computer Society Press.

Boulaye, G.; Mermet, J.; and Anceau, F. 1971. International Advanced Summer Institute on Microprogramming, Paris, France.

Boulaye, G. 1974. "Microprogramming and Structured Design." *SIGMICRO Newsletter*, 5 (2).

Boulaye, G. G. 1975. *Microprogramming.* New York: Halsted Press.

Brown, G. E., Eckhouse, R. H., Jr.; and Goldberg, R. P. 1976. "Operating" System Enhancement Through Microprogramming." *SIGMICRO Newsletter*, 7 (1).

Brown, J. F. III, and Sites, R. L. 1984. "A Chip Set Microarchitecture for a High-Performance VAX Implementation." *Proceedings of the Seventeenth Annual Microprogramming Workshop.* New Orleans, LA: IEEE Computer Society Press.

Burke, G. R. 1982. "Control Schemes for VLSI Microprocessors." *The Eleventh Annual Microprogramming Workshop.* Palo Alto, CA: IEEE Computer Society Press.

Burroughs Corporation. 1972. *Burroughs B1700 Reference Manual.* Philadelphia, PA: Burroughs Corporation.

Chattergy, R., and Pooch, U. W. 1977. *Microprocessors, Microprogramming, and Minicomputers.* North Hollywood, CA: Western Periodicals.

Chroust, G., and Muhlbacher, J. R. 1980. "Firmware, Microprogramming and Restructurable Hardware." *Proceedings IFIP Working Conference on Firmware, Microprogramming and Restructurable Hardware.* New York: Elsevier.

Chu, Y. 1972. *Computer Organization and Microprogramming.* Englewood Cliffs, NJ: Prentice-Hall.

Chu, Y. 1973. "Recursive Microprogramming in Syntax Recognizer." *Proceedings of the Sixth Annual Workshop on Microprogramming.* Palo Alto, CA: IEEE Computer Society Press.

Chu, Y. 1976. "Direct-Execution Computer Architecture." *SIGMICRO Newsletter*, 7 (1).

Cline, B. E. 1981. *Microprogramming Concepts and Techniques.* New York: Petrocelli.

Crocker, S. D.; Marcus, L.; and van-Mierop, D. 1980. "The ISI Microcode Verification System." *Proceedings of the IFIP Working Conference on Firmware, Microprogramming and Restructurable Hardware.* Linz, Austria: North-Holland.

Dalrymple, S. H. 1977. "The QM-1 Computer Emulation Facility." *TIE (Technical Idea Exchange).* August.

Damm, W. 1984. "An Axiomatization of Low-Level Parallelism in Microarchitectures." *Proceedings of the Seventeenth Annual Microprogramming Workshop.* New Orleans, LA: IEEE Computer Society Press.

Damm, W. 1985a. "Design and Specification of Microprogrammed Computer Architectures." *Proceedings of the Eighteenth Annual Workshop on Microprogramming.* Pacific Grove, CA: IEEE Computer Society Press.

Damm, W. 1985b. "Verification of Microprogrammed Computer Architectures in the S*-System: A Case Study." *Proceedings of the Eighteenth Annual Workshop on Microprogramming.* Pacific Grove, CA: IEEE Computer Society Press.

Dasgupta, S. 1978. "Towards a Microprogramming Language Schema." *Proceedings of the Eleventh Annual Microprogramming Workshop.* Pacific Grove, CA: IEEE Computer Society Press.

---. 1980a. "Some Implications of Programming Methodology for Microprogramming Language Design." *Proceedings of the IFIP Working Conference on Firmware, Microprogramming and Restructurable Hardware.* Linz, Austria: North-Holland.

---. 1980b. "Some Aspects of High-Level Microprogramming." *Computing Surveys*, 12 (3).

---. 1984a. *The Design and Description of Computer Architectures.*" New York: John Wiley and Sons.

---. 1984b. "A Model of Clocked Micro-architectures for Firmware Engineering and Design Automation Applications." *Proceedings of the Seventeenth Annual Microprogramming Workshop.* New Orleans, LA: IEEE Computer Society Press.

Davidson, S. 1977. "A Case Study of the Migration of an Algorithm Across Software—Firmware Boundaries." *SIGMICRO Newsletter,* 8 (4).

Davidson, S., and Shriver, B. D. 1980. "MARBLE: A High-Level Machine Independent Language for Microprogramming." *Proceedings of the IFIP Working Conference on Firmware, Microprogramming and Restructurable Hardware.* Linz, Austria: North-Holland.

DeWitt, D. J. 1976. "Extensibility—a New Approach for Designing Machine Independent Microprogramming Language." *Proceedings of the Ninth Annual Workshop on Microprogramming.* New Orleans, LA: IEEE Computer Society Press.

DeWitt, D. J.; Schlansker, M. S.; and Atkins, D. E. 1973. "A Microprogramming Language for the B-1726." *The Sixth Annual Workshop on Microprogramming.* Palo Alto, CA: IEEE Computer Society Press.

Dobry, T. P.; Patt, Y. N.; and Despain, A. M. 1984. "Design Decisions Influencing the Microarchitecture for a PROLOG Machine." *Proceedings of the Seventeenth Annual Microprogramming Workshop.* New Orleans, LA: IEEE Computer Society Press.

Eager, M. J. 1983. "M29—An Advanced Retargetable Microcode Assembler." *Proceedings of the Sixteenth Annual Microprogramming Workshop.*" Downingtown, PA: IEEE Computer Society Press.

Eckhouse, R. H., Jr. 1970. "An Investigation into the Use of a Higher-level, Machine-Independent Language for Writing Microprograms." *Proceedings of the Third Annual Workshop on Microprogramming.* Buffalo, NY: IEEE Computer Society Press.

Ehlers, B. L., and Harmon, G. L. 1976. "Reflective Emulations of the HP 2100A and VARIAN 72" *SIGMICRO Newsletter,* 7 (2).

Fisher, J. A. 1979. The Optimization of Horizontal Microcode Within and Beyond Basic Blocks: An Application of Processor Scheduling. Ph.D. diss., Courant Institute of Mathematics, New York University.

---. 1980. "2-Way Jump Microinstruction Hardware and an Effective Instruction Binding Method." *Proceedings of the Thirteenth Annual Microprogramming Workshop.* Colorado Springs, CO: IEEE Computer Society Press.

---. 1981. "Trace Scheduling: A Technique for Global Microcode Compaction." *IEEE Transactions on Computers*, C-30(7).

Flink, C. W. II. 1977. "EASY—An Operating System for the QM-1." *Proceedings of the Tenth Annual Microprogramming Workshop.* Niagara Falls, NY: IEEE Computer Society Press.

Floyd, R. W. 1967. "Assigning Meanings to Programs." *Mathematical Aspects of Computer Science,* 19.

Flynn, M. J. 1977. "Classes of Emulators." *SIGMICRO Newsletter,* 8 (4).

Frieder, G., and Miller, J. 1977. "An Analysis of Code Density for the Two Level Programmable Control of the Nanodata QM-1." *Proceedings of the Tenth Annual Workshop on Microprogramming.* Niagara Falls, NY: IEEE Computer Society Press.

Fuller. 1973. "Past and Future Trends in Microprogramming." *Proceedings of the Seventh Annual Microprogramming Workshop.* Palo Alto, CA: IEEE Computer Society Press.

Gardner, P. L. 1970. "Functional Memory—Microprogramming Implications." *Proceedings of the Third Annual Workshop on Microprogramming.* Buffalo, NY: IEEE Computer Society Press.

Geyer, S., and Lake, A. 1981. "Development Tools for User Microprogramming." *Proceedings of the Fourteenth Annual Microprogramming Workshop.* Chatham, MA: IEEE Computer Society Press.

Gries, R., and Woodward, J. A. 1984. "Software Tools Used in the Development of a VLSI VAX Microcomputer." *Proceedings of the Seventeenth Annual Microprogramming Workshop.* New Orleans, LA: IEEE Computer Society Press.

Habib, S. 1970. "Microprogrammed Higher Level Computers." *Proceedings of the Third Annual Workshop on Microprogramming.* Buffalo, NY: IEEE Computer Society Press.

———. 1973. "Name Resolutions Using a Microprogrammed Interpretive Technique." *Proceedings of the Sixth Annual Microprogramming Workshop.* Palo Alto, CA: IEEE Computer Society Press.

Habib, S., and Yang, Xue-Liang. 1981. "The Use of a Meta-Assembler to Design an M Code Interpreter on AMD2900 Chips." *Proceedings of the Fourteenth Microprogramming Workshop.* Chatham, MA: IEEE Computer Society Press. Oct., 1981.

Hartenstein, R., and Zaks, R. 1975. "Microarchitecture of Computer Systems." The First EUROMICRO Symposium on Microprocessing and Microprogramming. Paris, France, June.

Hoare, C. A. R. 1969. "An Axiomatic Basis for Computer Programming." *Communications of the ACM,* 12 (10).

Hoevel, L. W. 1974. "Ideal, Directly Executed Languages an Analytical Argument for Emulation." *IEEE Transactions on Computers,* C-23.

Huck, J., and Neuhauser, C. 1979. "I/O Device Emulation in the Stanford Emulation Lab." *Proceedings of the Twelfth Annual Microprogramming Workshop.* Hershey, PA: IEEE Computer Society Press.

Husson, S. S. 1970. *Microprogramming Principles and Practices.* Englewood Cliffs, NJ: Prentice-Hall.

Johannsen, D. 1978. "Our Machine, A Microcoded LSI Processor." *Proceedings of the Eleventh Annual Microprogramming Workshop.* Pacific Grove, CA: IEEE Computer Society Press.

Jones, L. H. 1974. "Microinstruction Sequencing for Structured Microprogramming." *Proceedings of the Seventh Annual Microprogramming Workshop.* Palo Alto, CA: IEEE Computer Society Press.

Kimmel, M. J. 1973. "PRIME—A Processor Design for Character Recognition." *Proceedings of the Sixth Annual Microprogramming Workshop.* Palo Alto, CA: IEEE Computer Society Press.

Kornerup, P., and Shriver, B. D. 1975. "An Overview of the MATHILDA System." *SIGMICRO Newsletter*, 5 (4).

Kraft, G. D., and Toy, W. N. 1981. *Microprogrammed Control and Reliable Design of Small Computers.* Englewood Cliffs, NJ: Prentice-Hall.

Lah, J., and Atkins, D. E. 1983. "Tree Compaction of Microprograms." *Proceedings of the Sixteenth Annual Microprogramming Workshop.* Downingtown, PA: IEEE Computer Society Press. Oct., 1983.

Lawson, H. W., and Blomberg, L. 1973. "The DataSaab FCPU Microprogramming Language." *Proceedings of SIGPLAN-SIGMICRO Interface Meeting Programming Languages—Microprogramming.* Harriman, NY: ACM Press.

Lawson, H. W.; Berndt, H.; and Hermanson, G. 1978. "Large Scale Integration: Technology, Application, and Impacts." The Fourth EUROMICRO Symposium on Microprocessing and Microprogramming. Paris, France, June.

Levitt, K., and Robinson, L. 1979. "Proof Techniques for Hierarchically Structured Programs." In *Current Trends in Programming Methodology II*, edited by R. Yeh. Englewood Cliffs, NJ: Prentice-Hall.

Li., T. 1982. "A VLSI View of Microprogramming System Design." *The Fifteenth Annual Microprogramming Workshop.* Pacific Grove, CA: IEEE Computer Society Press.

Linn, J. 1983. "SRDAG Compaction—A Generalization of Trace Scheduling to Increase the Use of Global Context Information." *Proceedings of the Sixteenth Annual Microprogramming Workshop.* Downingtown, PA: IEEE Computer Society Press.

Lloyd, G. R. 1974. "Design Considerations for Microprogramming Languages." *SIGMICRO Newsletter*, 5 (1).

Mallach, E., and Sondak, N. 1983. *Advances in Microprogramming*, 2nd ed. New York: Artech House.

Marti, J. B., and Kessler, R. R. 1979. "A Medium Level Compiler Generating Microcode." *Proceedings of the Twelfth Annual Microprogramming Workshop.* Hershey, PA: IEEE Computer Society Press.

Matheson, W. G. 1974. "User Microprogrammability in the HP-21MX Minicomputer." *Proceedings of the Seventh Annual Microprogramming Workshop.* Palo Alto, CA: IEEE Computer Society Press. Sept. 1974.

McKeeman, W. 1974. "Language Aspects of Microprogramming." *Proceedings of the Seventh Annual Microprogramming Workshop*. Palo Alto, CA: IEEE Computer Society Press.

Mick, J. R. "Microprogramming for The Hardware Engineer." *SIGMICRO Newsletter*, 7 (2).

Mueller, R. A., and Johnson, G. R. 1981. "Contrasting Translation, Verification and Synthesis in Software and Firmware Engineering." *Proceedings of the Fourteenth Annual Microprogramming Workshop*. Chatham, MA: IEEE Computer Society Press.

Mueller, R. A.; Varghese, J.; and Allan, V. H. 1984a. "Global Methods in the Flow Graph Approach to Retargetable Microcode Generation." *Proceedings of the Seventeenth Annual Microprogramming Workshop*. New Orleans, LA: IEEE Computer Society Press.

Mueller, R. A.; Duda, M. R.; and O'Haire, S. M. 1984b. "A Survey of Resource Allocation Methods in Optimizing Microcode Compilers." *Proceedings of the Seventeenth Annual Microprogramming Workshop*. New Orleans, LA: IEEE Computer Society Press.

Mulrooney, T. J. 1978. "Microprogrammed Spectrum Analysis." *Proceedings of the Eleventh Annual Microprogramming Workshop*. Pacific Grove, CA: IEEE Computer Society Press.

Nichols, A. J., III. 1971. "A Microprogramming Framework for Experimental Machine Design." *SIGMICRO Newsletter*, 2 (2).

Nicoud, J. D.; Wilmink, J.; and Zaks, R. 1977. "Microprocessing and Microprogramming Microcomputer Architectures." The Third EUROMICRO Symposium on Microprocessing and Microprogramming. Paris, France, June.

Patterson, D. A.; Lew, K.; and Tuck, R. 1979. "Towards an Efficient, Machine-Independent Language for Microprogramming." *Proceedings of the Twelfth Annual Microprogramming Workshop*. Hershey, PA: IEEE Computer Society Press. Nov., 1979.

Patterson, D. A., and Sequin, C. H. 1981. "RISC 1: A Reduced Instruction Set VLSI Computer." Proceedings of the Eighth Symposium on Computer Architecture. Minneapolis, MN: 443.

Poe, M. D. 1980. "Heuristics for the Global Optimization of Microprograms." *Proceedings of the Thirteenth Annual Microprogramming Workshop*. Colorado Springs, CO: IEEE Computer Society Press.

Ponder, C., and Patt, Y. N. 1984. "Alternative Proposals for Implementing PROLOG Concurrently and Implications Regarding their Respective Microarchitectures." *Proceedings of The Seventeenth Annual Microprogramming Workshop*. New Orleans, LA: IEEE Computer Society Press.

Ramamoorthy, C. V., and Kleir, R. L. 1970. "A Survey of Techniques for Optimizing Microprograms." *Proceedings of the Third Annual Microprogramming Workshop*. Buffalo, NY: IEEE Computer Society Press.

Ramamoorthy, C. V., and Shanker, R. 1973. "Correctness of Straight Line Microprograms." *Proceedings of the Sixth Annual Microprogramming Workshop*. Palo Alto, CA: IEEE Computer Society Press.

Rauscher, T. G. "Towards a Specification of Syntax and Semantics for Languages for Horizontally Microprogrammed Machines." *Proceedings of SIGPLAN-SIGMICRO Interface Meeting Programming Languages—Microprogramming.* Harriman, NY: ACM Press. May, 1973.

Reigel, E. W. 1970. "The Interpreter, a Microprogrammable Building Block System." *Proceedings of the SJCC.* New York: ACM Press.

Reiger, E. W., and Lawson, H. W. 1973. "At The Programming Language— Microprogramming Interface." *Proceedings of SIGPLAN-SIGMICRO Interface Meeting Programming Languages—Microprogramming.* Harriman, NY: ACM Press.

Richter, L. 1981. "Implementing Functions: Microprocessing and Firmware." Proceedings of the Seventh EUROMICRO Symposium on Microprocessing and Microprogramming. Paris, France, June.

Rosin, R. F. 1974. "The Significance of Microprogramming." *SIGMICRO Newsletter*, 4 (4).

Roskos, J., and Winner, R. 1981. "Toward User Sharing of the Microprogramming Level Under Unix on the Perkin-Elmer 3220." *Proceedings of the Fourteenth Annual Microprogramming Workshop.* Chatham, MA: IEEE Computer Society Press.

Salisbury, A. B. 1976. *Microprogrammable Computer Architecture.* New York: Elsevier.

Sami, M. G. 1980. "Microprocessor Systems: Software, Firmware and Hardware." The Sixth EUROMICRO Symposium on Microprocessing and Microprogramming. Paris, France, June.

Samudrala, S. 1984. "Design Verification of a VLSI VAX Microcomputer." *Proceedings of the Seventeenth Annual Microprogramming Workshop.* New Orleans, LA: IEEE Computer Society Press.

Sherwood, W. 1984. "A Prototype Engineering Tester for Microcode and Hardware Debugging." *Proceedings of the Seventh Annual Microprogramming Workshop.* New Orleans, LA: IEEE Computer Society Press.

Siewiorek, D. P. 1974. "Modularity and Multi-Microprocessor Structures." *Proceedings of the Seventh Annual Workshop on Microprogramming.* New Orleans, LA: IEEE Computer Society Press.

Sint, M. 1980. "A Survey of High Level Microprogramming Languages." *Proceedings of the Thirteenth Annual Microprogramming Workshop.* Colorado Springs, CO: IEEE Computer Society Press.

Sondak, N., and Mallach, E. 1977. *Microprogramming.* New York: Artech House.

Stritter, S., and Tredennick, N. "Microprogrammed Implementation of a Single Chip Microprocessor." *Proceedings of the Eleventh Annual Microprogramming Workshop.* Pacific Grove, CA: IEEE Computer Society Press.

Tamura, E., and Tokoro, M. 1979. "Hierarchical Microprogram Generating System." *Proceedings of the Twelfth Annual Microprogramming Workshop.* Hershey, PA: IEEE Computer Society Press.

Tiberghien, J.; Carlstedt, G.; and Lewi, J. 1979. "Microprocessors; Microprogramming." The Fifth EUROMICRO Symposium on Microprocessing and Microprogramming. Paris, France, June.

Tracz, W. 1985. "Advances in Microprogramming Support Software." *Proceedings of the Eighteenth Annual Microprogramming Workshop.* Pacific Grove, CA: IEEE Computer Society Press.

Tsuchiya, M., and Gonzalez, M. J., Jr. 1974. "An Approach to Optimization of Horizontal Microprograms" *Proceedings of the Seventh Annual Microprogramming Workshop.* Palo Alto, CA: IEEE Computer Society Press.

Tucker, A. B., and Flynn, M. J. 1971. "Dynamic Microprogramming: Processor Organization and Programming." *Communications of the ACM*, 14 (4).

Tucker, S. G. 1965. "Emulation of Large Systems." *Communications of the ACM*, 8 (12).

———. 1967. "Microprogram Control for System/360." *IBM Systems Journal*, 6 (4).

Van Spronson, J. W., and Richter, L. 1982. "Microsystems: Architecture, Integration and Use." The Eighth EUROMICRO Symposium on Microprocessing and Microprogramming. Paris, France, June.

Vegdahl, S. R. 1982. "Phase Coupling and Constant Generation in an Optimizing Microcode Compiler." *Proceedings of the Fifteenth Annual Microprogramming Workshop.* Palo Alto, CA: IEEE Computer Society Press.

Wagner, R., and Dasgupta, S. 1983. "The Use of Hoane Logic in Verification." *Proceedings of the Sixteenth Microprogramming Workshop.* Downington, PA: IEEE Computer Society Press.

Ward, B. 1975. *Microprocessor/Microprogramming Handbook.* Blue Ridge Summit, PA: TAB Books.

Wexelblat, R. L. 1974. "Programming Language/Microprogramming Proceedings." *SIGPLAN Notices*, 9 (6).

Wilkes, M. V. 1951. "The Best Way to Design an Automatic Calculating Machine." Report of the Manchester University Computer Inaugural Conference. Manchester University, Manchester, England, July.

Wilkes, M. V. 1977. "Ten Years and More of Microprogramming." *SIGMICRO Newsletter*, 8 (4).

———. 1982. "The Processor Instruction Set," *Proceedings of the Fifteenth Annual Microprogramming Workshop.* Palo Alto, CA: IEEE Computer Society Press.

Wilmink, J.; Sami, M. G.; and Zaks, R. 1976. "Microprocessing and Microprogramming." The Second EUROMICRO Symposium on Microprocessing and Microprogramming. Paris, France. June.

Wilner, W. T. 1972. "Design of the Burroughs B1700." *Proceedings of the FJCC.* Washington, DC: AFIPS Press.

Winner, R., and Carter, E. 1983. "Toward Type-Oriented Dynamic Vertical Migration." *Proceedings of the Sixteenth Annual Microprogramming Workshop.* Downingtown, PA: IEEE Computer Society Press.

Wirth, N. 1981. "The Personal Computer LILITH." Institut für Informatik, ETH, Zurich. Report #40.

Zaks, R. 1971. "Microcoded APL Machines." *Proceedings of the Fourth Microprogramming Workshop.* Chicago, IL: IEEE Computer Society Press.

Zaks, R. 1978. *Microprogrammed APL Implementation.* Berkeley, CA: Sybex.

two
FUNDAMENTAL CONCEPTS OF MICROPROGRAMMING

ROBERT A. MUELLER
JOSEPH VARGHESE

Even though microprogramming was initially formulated as a technique for simplifying the control units of digital computers, it has evolved into a mature discipline in its own right. In this chapter, some of the basic concepts of microprogramming are reviewed prior to the introduction of more advanced concepts in subsequent chapters of this book.

INTRODUCTION TO CONTROL IN VON NEUMANN MACHINES

Essential to the understanding of microprogramming is the concept of control within traditional von Neumann machines. The next section is devoted to this issue; the historical evolution of the discipline of microprogramming in this context is the subject of the following section. After the introductory sections, the organization of control units is discussed, including control-store memories and their structure and microinstruction sequencing and execution. Since microprogrammed control forms the lowest level in the architectural hierarchy, efficiency is an important issue in firmware engineering. Microprogramming has evolved in directions other than machine-architecture emulation, and some of these applications are discussed in the section on alternate roles of microprogramming.

Organization

Although several people are credited with the ideas that led to the construction of the first digital computers, the name that is most often associated with these early machines is that of the mathematician John von Neumann. In particular, he is acknowledged as being among the first to formulate and refine stored program methods in computer architectures. Since these ideas have survived in some form in machine architectures up to the present, these architectures are now known as *von Neumann architectures*.

The organization of von Neumann machines is fairly simple and well understood. They can be partitioned into four components:

1. Storage unit
2. Input/output unit
3. Arithmetic and logic unit
4. Control unit

A block diagram of a simple von Neumann machine is shown in figure 2-1. The storage unit can transfer data to and from the input/output unit and the arithmetic and logic unit. The control unit does not participate directly in these transfers of data but merely oversees them and the internal operations of the other units.

In the earliest machines, such as the ENIAC (Stone 1975), storage was used only to hold data being worked on or generated during intermediate stages of computation. When larger storage devices became available, it appeared feasible to store the programs that manipulated data along with the data itself. This uniformity in the methods for storage of programs and data enabled programs to be treated as data and vice versa; manipulations of data are also applicable to manipulations of programs. In present-day systems, the storage component usually consists of a hierarchy of memories, with the portions of data and programs that are used more often being stored on faster memory devices. For the purposes of this exposition, however, storage is treated as one monolithic unit.

The input/output unit is the machine's interface with its environment. There may be several types of input/output devices that are connected to the machine, but all of them together can be considered as a single unit that provides the machine with input and that consumes the output of the machine's endeavors. The input/output unit communicates with the rest of the system through the storage unit. Input is stored in and output read from the storage unit under the supervision of the control unit.

The arithmetic and logic unit (*ALU*) is the portion of the machine in

Figure 2-1. Basic organization of von Neumann machines.

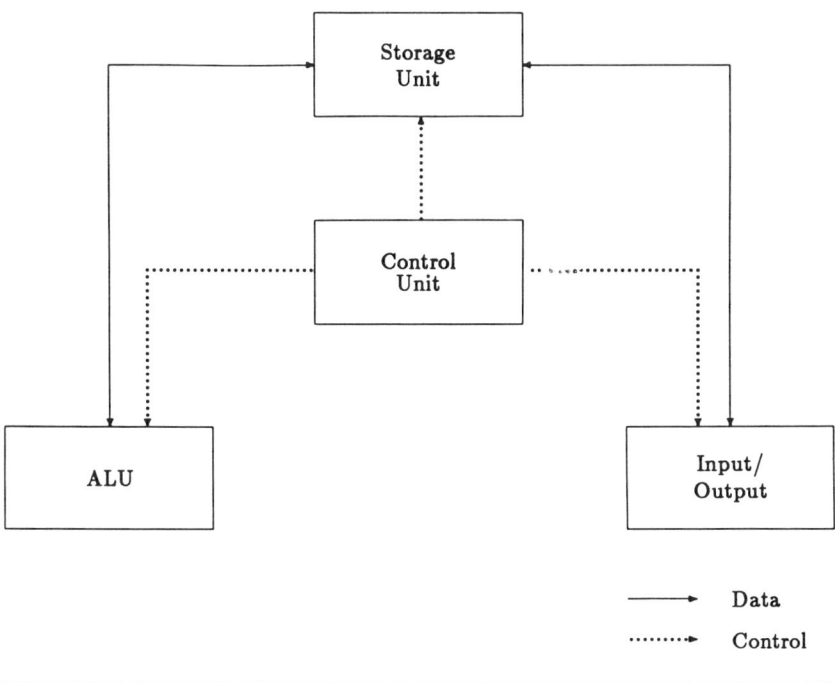

which data can be manipulated and transformed. Data from the storage unit is imported to ALU, where it can be subjected to a variety of arithmetic and logical operations. The results of these operations can then be stored in local storage within ALU or in the storage unit (or both). Movements of data between ALU and the storage unit and within ALU itself are performed under the direction of the control unit.

The control unit supervises the other components of the machine and the movements of data among them. It, in turn, is supervised by the programs in the storage unit. Individual instructions from these programs are retrieved from memory, decoded, and then executed in an order that can be determined by the results of the execution. This unit is probably the most complex part of the machine; the next section is devoted to a discussion of its operation.

Operation of the Control Unit

As explained in the previous section, the control unit oversees the execution of the programs in the storage unit. In this section, the role of the control unit will be elaborated. For explanatory purposes, the machine depicted in figure 2-2a will be used. Even though it is less skeletal than the machine in figure 2-1, it is still a very simple machine.

In this machine the storage unit consists of a memory block together with its interface. This interface consists of the memory address register (MAR) and the memory data register (MDR). Data can be read from a location in memory by placing the address of the desired location in MAR and then sending a READ control signal from the control unit to the memory unit. This control signal forces the contents of the specified location to be placed in MDR. Similarly, data can be written into the memory unit by placing the data in MDR and the address of the location where this data is to be

Figure 2-2. *a.* Simple von Neumann machine organization; *b.* instruction format.

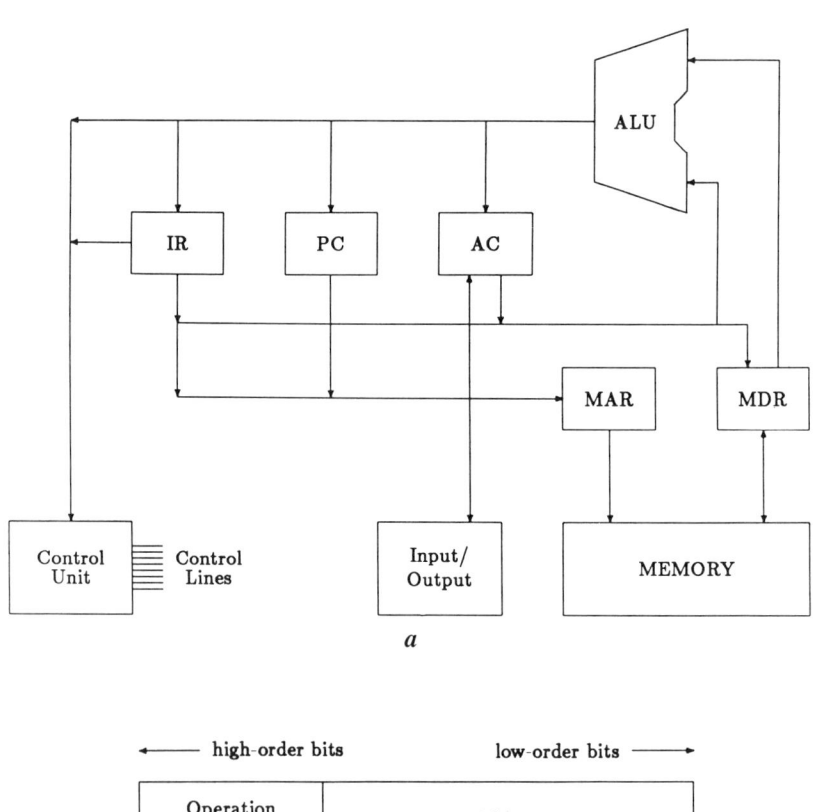

placed in MAR and then sending a WRITE control signal from the control unit to the memory unit. In this hypothetical machine, the memory contains 4,096 16-bit words. Therefore, 12 bits are required to address a location in memory, and for this reason the MAR register is only 12 bits wide.

As before, the input/output unit is the machine's interface with its environment. In this case, however, it communicates with the memory through the accumulator register (AC). ALU gets one of its inputs from the memory through MDR and the other input from either the instruction register (IR) or AC. ALU can perform various arithmetic operations on its inputs, or it can pass them through unchanged. The output of ALU can be stored in AC, IR, or the program counter (PC).

AC is a register that is used as an implicit operand in many instructions. Its main function is to store intermediate computation results. The program counter (PC) contains the address of the program instruction being executed. It has the ability to increment its value by one in order to enable the sequential execution of programs in the memory. The output of PC can in turn be fed into MAR. Since it only keeps track of memory addresses, it, like MAR, is 12 bits wide. When accepting input from ALU, it only accepts the lowest 12 bits. The instruction register (IR) holds the instruction currently being executed. It can place the lowest 12 bits of its value in MAR or can feed its value to ALU.

The control unit accepts data as input but can only send control signals as output. The input data to the control unit merely determines its future actions. In its basic mode of operation, it fetches the instruction referred to by PC into the instruction register (IR), decodes it in IR, and then performs the actions specified by it. Once it has completed this instruction, the control unit starts the cycle all over again. This method of operation is sometimes referred to as the fetch/decode/execute method. A program can also specify a deviation from this sequential mode of execution by giving the address of an instruction that it wishes to have executed next. In this case the control unit gets the address for the next instruction directly from IR instead of PC.

Programs for this machine consist of sequences of instructions. An instruction resides in one word of memory. To specify an operation, an instruction simply specifies both the operation and a memory location. For most operations the memory location is one of two operands. The other (implicit) operand is the accumulator register (AC), which may also serve as the (implicit) output location. Thus, when an addition operation and memory location X are specified, the result of adding the contents of memory location X to the contents of AC is stored in AC. Since a reference to a memory location takes up 12 bits and since the locations in memory are 16 bits wide, only 4 bits remain for the specification of the operation. This enables up to 16 different operations to be specified. The format for instructions is depicted in figure 2-2b. The meanings of the various operation codes (opcodes) in the instruction are given in Table 2-1.

Table 2-1 Opcode Table.

Opcode	Operation	Meaning
0	NOP	Does nothing
1	LOAD X	AC ← MEMORY[X]
2	STO X	MEMORY[X] ← AC
3	ADD X	AC ← AC + MEMORY[X]
4	MPY X	AC ← AC × MEMORY[X]
5	SUB X	AC ← AC − MEMORY[X]
6	DIV X	AC ← AC ÷ MEMORY[X]
7	OR X	AC ← AC ∨ MEMORY[X]
8	AND X	AC ← AC ∧ MEMORY[X]
9	EXOR X	AC ← AC ⊕ MEMORY[X]
10	NEG X	AC ← − (MEMORY[X])
11	IO	for input/output
12	STOP	halts execution
13	JUMP A	branch to or start execution of instruction in MEMORY[A]
14	JZ A	if result of previous ALU operation is zero then branch to MEMORY[A]
15	JN A	if result of previous ALU operation is negative then branch to MEMORY[A]

In the fetch/decode/execute mode of operation, the machine performs the following steps in the given order for every instruction.

1. Fetch the instruction referred to by the address in *PC* and place this instruction in *IR*.
2. Increment *PC* by one so that it now addresses the next instruction in memory.
3. Decode the highest 4 bits of *IR* to determine the actions to be performed.
4. If the address component specifies an input operand required by this operation, then transfer the lowest 12 bits of *IR* to *MAR* and initiate a READ operation. Once all the operands are available, perform the operation specified by the instruction. This execution may require more data transfers among the registers and memory.

After the execution of the fourth step, control passes once again to the first step. The control unit performs this cycle until an external interrupt causes it to temporarily suspend execution or until a STOP instruction is executed. Once a STOP instruction is executed, the machine has to be manually started using console switches. External interrupts may cause a suspension of program execution in order to process the interrupt, after which execution resumes where it left off.

To illustrate, take the sequence of instructions in Table 2-2 where W, X, Y, Z, and A are integers between 0 and 4,095. Assume that PC initially contains the value W where MEMORY[W] contains the instruction LOAD X. In the first step of the first instruction, the instruction LOAD X is fetched into IR. In the next step, PC is incremented by one so that it now has the value W + 1 and hence points to the ADD instruction. The third step sees the decoding of the LOAD instruction, and in the next step the control unit causes the contents of location X to be placed in AC.

At the end of the fourth step, the control unit starts the first step for the second instruction by fetching the contents of MEMORY[W + 1] into IR. During the second step PC is incremented so that it now contains the value W + 2. In the third step, the control unit looks at the highest four bits of IR to see what kind of instruction has been fetched. Since it is an ADD instruction, the contents of MEMORY[Y] have to be fetched into MDR so that ALU can work on it. The control unit then schedules the fourth step, in which an addition operation takes place in ALU, taking the contents of MDR and AC as operands. The result of the operation is placed in AC. This signals the end of the second instruction, and the control unit now fetches the instruction stored in MEMORY[W + 2] and starts the cycle all over again. In a similar manner, during the execution of the STO instruction the control unit causes the contents of AC to be placed into MEMORY[Z].

The kind of sequencing described above, where instructions are executed in the order in which they are stored, is not sufficient for most programs. It is sometimes necessary to take actions that depend on the value of intermediate results or to transfer control to a portion of the program that does not immediately follow the instruction being executed. These requirements are met by branch instructions, which can cause transfers of control. For example, the instruction JUMP A causes the control unit to initiate and execute the instruction stored in location A.

At this point in the execution of the above program, PC contains the value W + 3 as a result of performing the STO instruction. In the first cycle the control unit places the contents of location W + 3 in IR. In the second step, the control unit increments PC by one so that it indicates that the next instruction to be executed is in location W + 4, and in the third step, the control unit decodes the operation code of the current instruction.

The highest four bits of IR indicate that a transfer of control is to take place, and during the fourth step, this causes the control unit to place the lower 12

Table 2-2 Sample instruction sequence.

W:	LOAD	X
	ADD	Y
	STO	Z
	JUMP	A

bits of *IR* (the branch address) in *MAR* before fetching the next instruction. The control unit also places these lower 12 bits in *PC* (overwriting the previous contents of *PC*) so that the address of the next instruction is updated. Once it has performed these steps, the control unit then begins execution of the instruction stored at location A, thus completing the execution of the program sequence in the example.

EVOLUTION OF MICROPROGRAMMING

As demonstrated in the previous section, machine instructions are usually abstractions for sets of individual operations of the underlying machine. The control unit enables and sequences these individual operations so that their net effect is the required machine instruction. In the earliest machines the control unit was entirely hardwired and, as a consequence, very complex and unwieldy.

Wilkes's Concept

M.V. Wilkes of the Cambridge Mathematical Laboratory introduced the notion of microprogramming as a way to simplify the design of control units (1951, 1969). He used the term "microprogramming" to emphasize the similarity between the decomposition of programs into machine instructions and the decomposition of machine instructions into individual operations. Since then, microprogramming has undergone significant growth and change.

Figure 2-3 is a depiction of microprogramming as expounded by Wilkes. The contents of the microinstruction register (*MIR*) determine the operations to be performed in the next cycle in a manner similar to the effect of *IR* on the operations of the von Neumann machine described in the previous section. The decoding-tree component of the control unit is an n-line to 2^n-line decoder that transforms the contents of *MIR* into control signals. At any point in time only one of the horizontal control lines emanating from the decoding tree is active. These horizontal control lines may in turn intersect one or more of the vertical control lines.

The vertical lines of matrix A control the arithmetic unit and the other registers of the machine. Each possible register, arithmetic unit, or other individual operation has a vertical control line associated with it. An operation is enabled if the currently active horizontal line intersects its vertical line at a diode junction (denoted by dark circles).

Operations that depend on the values of flip-flops in the machine are referred to as *conditional operations*. The branching in the horizontal control lines where they intersect input lines from flip-flops in the machine indicates this dependence. These branch points can be considered as extensions of the decoding tree. The vertical lines of matrix B determine the contents of *MIR* during

Figure 2-3. Wilkes's concept of microprogramming.

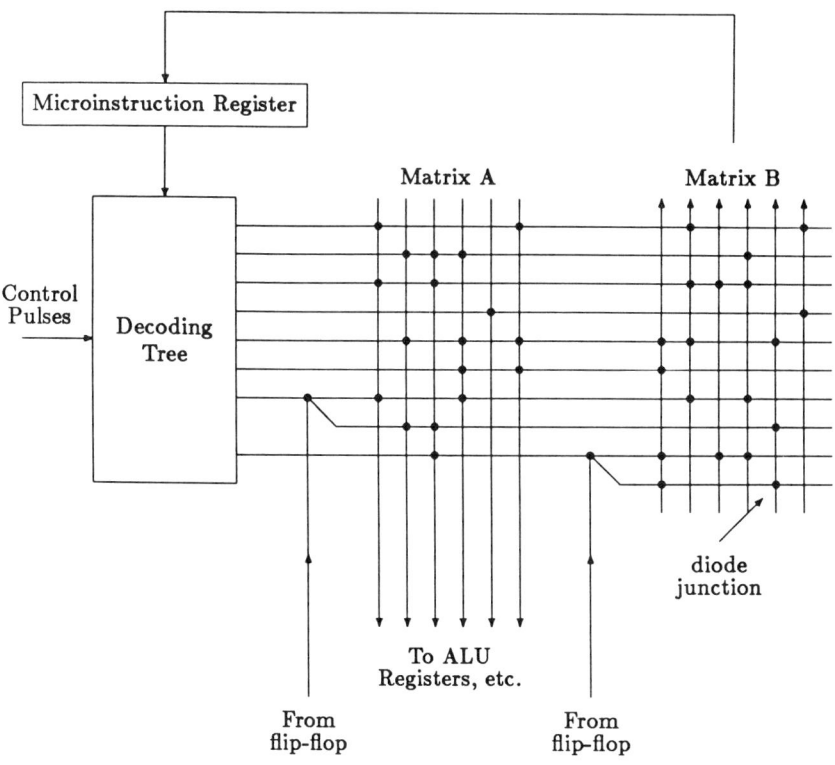

the next cycle and are analogous to mechanisms for determination of the next address in branch instructions.

The decoding tree, along with the diode matrices and *MIR*, form what is called the *control store* for this machine, because these units hold programs that implement the control unit. Since the diode matrices are fixed and cannot be changed without rewiring, this is a form of read-only control store. This method of control store was efficient at the time because it was very fast compared with conventional memory. This meant that memory access dominated the time required to execute an instruction.

Microprogramming for Machine Emulation

With the emergence of fast storage technologies, microprogramming underwent a period of change. When memory access times were relatively slow, there could be many microsteps in the interpretation of a single instruction, and consequently, the number of operations performed per step could be small. As memory technology developed, the number of operations per step had to increase in order to keep pace. The gap between access times for read-only control stores and main memories had narrowed to the point where a new rationale was necessary for microprogramming as an implementation method.

In 1964, IBM introduced its System/360 series, in which several microprogrammable machines implemented a common instruction set (Tucker 1967). In addition, as a marketing gesture, some of these systems could also execute the instruction sets for earlier machines such as the IBM 1401 and 7096. These applications come under the domain of *machine emulation*. Emulation can be distinguished from simulation by the presence of hardware support for the machine being emulated; simulation is done entirely by software.

The method proposed by Wilkes is somewhat inefficient in some respects. For example, all the different ALU operations require one control line to activate them, but at any one time only one of these operations can be enabled. Therefore, there is a significant amount of wasted control store. If there were 2^n such mutually exclusive operations, they could be controlled by n lines in the A matrix. These n lines could then be decoded afterwards using an n-line to 2^n-line decoder in order to enable the individual operations. This method is sometimes referred to as *bit-packing*, and the corresponding control store is referred to as a *packed* control store. In contrast, the original method is also known as the *unpacked method*.

As storage techniques progressed, it became possible to use some of these methods in the implementation of the control store. Control stores began to resemble main memory-storage units in their construction, and since they did not need to be writable stores, they could still be made much faster than writable storage units. With the use of these storage units and the use of bit packing in control stores, words in control store began to resemble instructions in appearance. Because of this, each word of control store was referred to as a *microinstruction*, and the individual operations that were controlled by these microinstructions were referred to as *microoperations*. Similarly, a set of microinstructions that performs a well defined task is a *microprogram*.

To illustrate the principles of machine emulation, consider the emulation of the (hypothetical) machine with the instruction set of Table 2-1 by the machine in figure 2-2. In order to avoid confusion, we will refer to the two machines as the *image machine* and the *host machine*, respectively (Flynn 1975). The microinstruction format for the host machine is given in figure 2-4.

There are two types of microinstructions, type 0 and type 1. In type-0 microinstructions, the highest bit is a zero; they are mostly register-transfer-type operations. Correspondingly, in type-1 microinstructions the highest bit is equal to one, and they deal with control transfers within the control store. Corresponding to *IR*, there is a microinstruction register (*MIR*) within the control unit that holds the microinstruction being executed. Type-0 microinstruc-

Figure 2-4. Microinstruction formats.

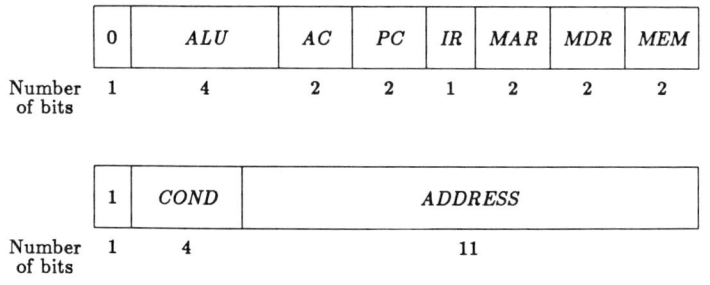

tions, on completion of execution, pass control to the next microinstruction in control store. The meanings of the various microinstruction fields are given in Table 2-3. Not all the possible actions are listed in this table for the sake of brevity.

Within a microinstruction, the various operations are not executed simultaneously but in four steps. To distinguish the time for these steps from the cycle time for a microinstruction, they are referred to as *minor cycles*. The schedule for the various operations is given in figure 2-5. The first minor cycle is for the execution of the ALU operations. Once ALU has finished, it can set the values of the PC, IR, and AC registers in the second minor cycle. During the third minor cycle, MAR and MDR can change their values by reading in the contents of IR, PC, or AC, depending on the allowable operations. The next and last cycle is for the performance of memory reads and writes. If a memory read is performed, the data that is read is available in MDR at the start of the next microinstruction cycle.

In the case of a type-1 microinstruction, there are two fields. The COND field selects the condition under which the branch is to be made. If the value of COND is 0, the branch is an unconditional branch. There are other possible conditions for branching, as given in Table 2-3, and the address for these branches is given in the ADDRESS field of the microinstruction. Although the ADDRESS field has 11 bits, only the lowest 8 are used in determining the next address. If the COND field value is 1, then the branch is made to an address in control store such that the lower four bits of the address are 0 and the next higher four bits are equal to the contents of the highest four bits of IR. This enables the control unit to branch to different locations in control store, depending on the opcode in IR. This facility is exploited in decoding image machine instructions.

Some sample microprograms for image machine instructions are given in Table 2-4. The IFETCH routine is the routine that fetches the next instruction

Table 2-3 Microinstruction interpretation

Field	Value	Action
ALU	0	No action
	1	ALU ← MDR
	2	ALU ← AC
	3	ALU ← IR
	4	ALU ← MDR + AC
	5	ALU ← MDR + IR
	6	ALU ← MDR × AC
	7	ALU ← MDR × IR
AC	0	No action
	1	AC ← ALU
PC	0	No action
	1	PC ← ALU[12:1]
	2	PC ← PC + 1
IR	0	No action
	1	IR ← ALU
MAR	0	No action
	1	MAR ← PC
	2	MAR ← IR[12:1]
MDR	0	No action
	1	MDR ← AC
	2	MDR ← IR
MEM	0	No action
	1	Read (MDR ← MEMORY[MAR])
	2	Write (MEMORY[MAR] ← MDR)
COND		branch to control store address specified by address in ADDRESS field under the following conditions:
	0	unconditional branch
	1	unconditional branch to control store address specified by highest four bits of IR multiplied by 16
	2	ALU = 0
	3	ALU < 0
	4	CARRY = 1

Figure 2-5. Microoperation schedule.

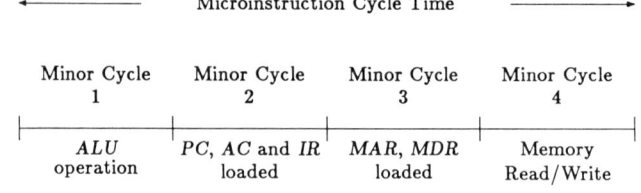

from memory and branches to the appropriate microprogram, depending on the opcode of the instruction. This microprogram interprets the instruction and then branches back to IFETCH in order to start the processing for the next instruction. It is in this manner that the host machine emulates the image machine.

Historically, the earliest commercial applications of machine emulation appeared in the IBM System/360 series of machines (Tucker 1967; Husson 1970). Using microprogramming, the manufacturer could market machines with differing characteristics, all of which would execute the same programs with the same results. The advantage to the customer was obvious. The customer could purchase low-performance machines to start with and expand into the higher-performance machines later without having to reprogram all the applications. The fact that the machines were microprogrammed also meant that the manufacturer could expand the instruction set to handle special-purpose tasks such as file handling with little or no hardware modifications. As Tucker (1967) has pointed out, once the cost of the control storage and supporting hardware has been met, additional features require only the cost of developing and changing microprograms, which is marginal.

The smaller machines in the series, such as the Model 30, were built with general-purpose data paths, whereas larger systems were built specifically to emulate the System/360 series machine-instruction set. Some machines, such as the Model 75, required such high performance standards that they were designed using conventional methods without microprogramming. The models that were microprogrammed differed widely in performance and design, with the Model 20 having 3.6 microsecond main-memory and .625 microsecond control-store access times compared with the Model 85, with .96 microsecond main-memory and .08 microsecond control-store access times. The technologies for the control stores varied from card-capacitor read-only store (CCROS) to transformer read-only store (TROS) to capacitor read-only store (CROS). There was also a large variation in CPU cycle times (.08 microseconds for the Model 85, 1 microsecond for the Model 30), memory size, and other important criteria that are closely linked with performance.

As another facet of upward compatibility, the Model 30 could also emulate the IBM 1401 (Tucker 1967). Some additions to the microoperation repertoire were required, and data had to be treated differently in order to do so. The read-only storage also had to be expanded in order to handle the extra emulator. The emulation of some IBM series 7000 instruction sets on other System/360 machines required changes in hardware, and some instructions were even executed by software. Thus, users could execute programs for these older machines in a more cost-effective manner on the newer machines. Several other series of machines, such as the RCA Spectra/70, DEC PDP-11, and the DEC VAX-11 series, were also built with the same idea of a single instruction set being emulated by microprogrammable machines with differing performance characteristics.

Table 2-4 Sample microinstructions with encoding.

Function	MI	Minor Cycle			
		1	2	3	4
LOAD	1		PC ← PC + 1	MAR ← IR[12:1]	read
	2	ALU ← MDR	AC ← ALU		
	3	Branch IFETCH			
ADD	1		PC ← PC + 1	MAR ← IR[12:1]	read
	2	ALU ← MDR + AC	AC ← ALU		
	3	Branch IFETCH			
STO	1		PC ← PC + 1	MAR ← IR[12:1]	write
				MDR ← AC	
	2	Branch IFETCH			
JUMP	1		PC ← IR[12:1]		
	2	Branch IFETCH			
IFETCH	1			MAR ← PC	read
	2	ALU ← MDR	IR ← ALU		
	3	Branch to address IR[16:13] × 16			

a. Microinstructions for sample functions

Function	MI	Mode	ALU	AC	PC	IR	MAR	MDR	MEM
LOAD	1	0	0	0	2	0	2	0	1
	2	0	1	1	0	0	0	0	0
	3	1	COND = 0, ADDRESS = address of IFETCH						
ADD	1	0	0	0	2	0	2	0	1
	2	0	4	1	0	0	0	0	0
	3	1	COND = 0, ADDRESS = address of IFETCH						
STO	1	0	0	0	2	0	2	1	2
	2	1	COND = 0, ADDRESS = address of IFETCH						
JUMP	1	0	0	0	1	0	0	0	0
	2	1	COND = 0, ADDRESS = address of IFETCH						
IFETCH	1	0	0	0	0	0	1	0	1
	2	0	1	0	0	1	0	0	0
	3	1	COND = 1, ADDRESS = IR[16:13] × 16						

b. Encoding for microinstructions

Writable Control Stores

From the point of view of some programmers, the machine-emulation principle as described in the previous paragraphs had a basic flaw. The fact that the control stores in some of these machines were read-only stores meant that only the manufacturer could expand the instruction set. A case could be made for writable control stores by citing the potential gain in efficiency if programmers could define their own image machine-level instructions. But this kind of programmer freedom raises several issues about security and data protection.

According to Flynn (1975), the move towards writable control stores will have important effects on computer architectures. Since the programmer will have more control over machine resources, the image machine instruction set can be made much simpler. Correspondingly, with the transfer of responsibility for the best utilization of resources from the designer of the instruction set to the programmer or the compiler, more intelligent use of resources is possible, leading to significant improvements in performance. Flynn predicted an order of magnitude improvement in performance.

It could be argued that such advances have been made. The move towards *dynamic microprogramming*, in which the contents of the control store could be changed under program direction, was not as much of a success as was hoped for due to the fact that the cost of manually producing large amounts of microcode proved to be too high. But with the advent of *reduced instruction set computer* (RISC) architectures (Patterson and Sequin 1981; Hennessy et al. 1982) some of these predictions have been fulfilled. RISC architectures tend to have very simple instruction sets, and much of the responsibility for features such as branch delays has been transferred to the compiler. These architectures have been demonstrated to offer large improvements in performance as compared to architectures with more complex instruction sets. The instruction sets for RISC machines resemble the microinstruction sets for simple microprogrammable machines. Presumably, if compiler technology improved to the point that efficient compilers for the production of more complex microinstructions were possible, even more improvements in performance could be expected.

Several machines were built with dynamic microprogramming in mind. These include the Nanodata QM-1 (Nanodata 1974) and the Burroughs B1700 (Wilner 1972a). The Burroughs machine was constructed with the explicit purpose of providing an environment for *directly executable languages*. The memory is bit-addressable, and variable-size operands and operations are possible. Several emulators for high-level languages such as FORTRAN and COBOL were available for this machine. The Nanodata machine was built for the emulation of more traditional machine instructions. It has a two-level writable control store. The instructions at the higher of the two levels are interpreted by the lower-level instructions, and the bus structure of the machine is dynamic.

CONTROL-UNIT ORGANIZATION

Microprogrammed Control Units

A microprogrammed control unit can be distinguished from other control schemes, such as *hardwired implementations*, in that the generally complex operations it controls reside in a memory unit as a sequence of primitive operations. Each primitive operation, called a *microoperation* (MO), typically controls a single hardware resource of the machine. The memory unit that holds the MOs is called the *control store*. The control store is generally distinct from the stored program memory of the machine.

Collections of MOs can be grouped into logical units, called *microinstructions* (MIs), to obtain more sophisticated functions. The operation of a microprogrammed control unit is thus an analog of the classical fetch/decode/execute sequence characteristic of von Neumann machines. That is, a basic step in the operation of a microprogrammed control unit entails fetching an MI from the control store, decoding it into a collection of MOs, and then executing the MOs according to some partially ordered timing sequence.

This is achieved by the use of two control unit registers: the *control-store address register* (CSAR) and the *microinstruction register* (MIR). The CSAR contains the control-store address of the next MI to be fetched and executed and is therefore an analog of the "program counter" that contains the main memory address of the next machine instruction to be executed. The execution of an MI begins with the transfer of the control store word(s) addressed by the CSAR to the MIR, which is an analog of the "instruction register" to which machine instructions are fetched. The MIR holds the MI while it is decoded and executed. To achieve greater performance, the execution of the current MI can be overlapped with the fetch phase of the subsequent MI. This is usually achieved by using another register, the *microinstruction buffer register* (MIBR), to hold the next MI to be executed while the MIR holds the currently executing MI. An architectural view of the microprogrammed control-unit concept is shown in figure 2-6.

Microprogramming was originally conceived as an alternative approach to the control-unit implementation of machine instructions. While it has since been effectively applied to other applications (e.g., "universal host machines" for the emulation of widely differing architectures), its use in the interpretation of machine instructions continues to predominant. We will illustrate some of the fundamental concepts of microprogramming by introducing a simple, hypothetical microprogrammed machine and then presenting the microprogrammed implementation of several hypothetical machine instructions. Figure 2-7 depicts the architecture of the hypothetical microprogrammed machine (HMM), and figure 2-8 contains its microinstruction set repertoire.

Each MI on the HMM is executed in four minor cycles. In the first cycle, the contents of any one of the MAR, MDR, IR, or file registers is placed on the SBUS. Next, both an ALU operation and an (optional) main-memory operation take place. The operands of the ALU are the ACC, the SBUS, or the constants 0 or 1. It can perform various arithmetic/logic functions on the operands or simply pass operand values straight through. Main-memory reads transfer the contents of the word addressed by MAR to MDR, and memory writes transfer the contents of MDR to the word addressed by MAR.

Figure 2-6. Architectural view of microprogrammed control.

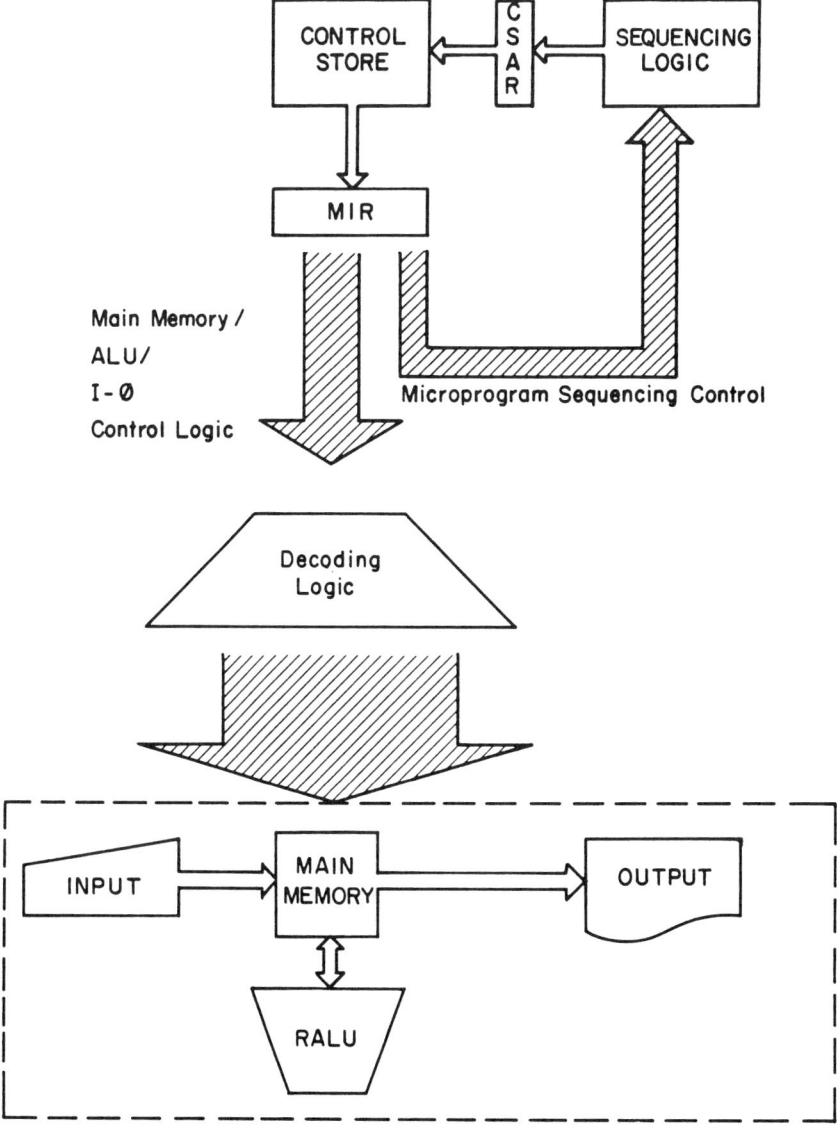

In the third cycle the *ALU* contents are transmitted through the shifter either directly or with an arithmetic/logical shift or a rotate, and the address of the next MI to be executed is determined. In the final cycle, the output of the shifter can be gated into any one of the MAR, MDR, IR, or file registers, concurrently with optional gating into the ACC.

The use of multiple minor cycles in the execution of an MI relies on a technique called *polyphase execution*. We will simply assume that any MO completes its execution during the cycle in which it is initiated. This cannot

Figure 2-7. Hypothetical-microprogrammed-machine (HMM) organization.

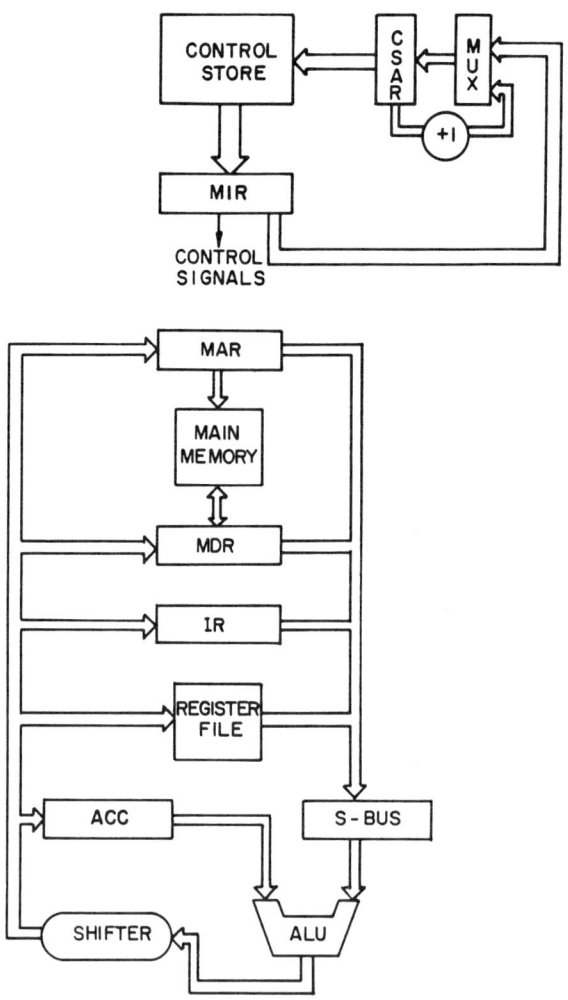

Figure 2-8. HMM microinstruction set repertoire.

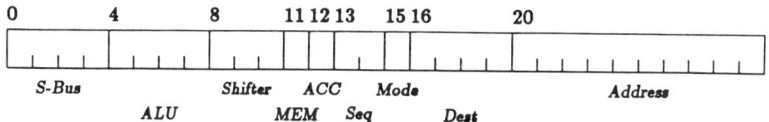

MEM	MO
2	MDR ← MEM[MAR]
3	MEM[MAR] ← MDR

ACC	MO
1	ACC ← Shifter

Dest	MO
$0 \leq i \leq 7$	R_i ← Shifter
8	IR ← Shifter
9	MAR ← Shifter

SBUS	MO
$0 \leq i \leq 7$	SBUS ← R_i
8	SBUS ← IR
9	SBUS ← MAR
10	SBUS ← MDR

Seq	MO
0	next sequential MI
1	CSAR ← Address
2*	if CARRY = 1 then CSAR ← Address
3*	if ZERO = 1 then CSAR ← Address

*Conditions inverted when Mode=1.

ALU	MO
1	ALU ← ACC
2	ALU ← SBUS
3	ALU ← ACC + SBUS
4	ALU ← ACC − SBUS
5	ALU ← SBUS − ACC
6	ALU ← ACC ∧ SBUS
7	ALU ← ACC ∨ SBUS
8	ALU ← ¬SBUS
9	ALU ← SBUS + 1
10	ALU ← ACC + 1
11	ALU ← 0
12	ALU ← 1

Shifter	MO
0	Shifter ← ALU
1	Shifter ← shift_left_logical(ALU)
2	Shifter ← shift_right_logical(ALU)
3	Shifter ← rotate_left(ALU)
4	Shifter ← rotate_right(ALU)
5	Shifter ← shift_left_arithmetic(ALU)
6	Shifter ← shift_right_arithmetic(ALU)

generally be assumed, since, for example, a slow main-memory access time would cause the second cycle of HMM to be very long. We will also assume that ALU, SBUS, and shifter are all *transient storage elements*, as opposed to *permanent storage elements* such as conventional flip-flops. Transient storage elements don't latch their contents and therefore typically hold assigned values for only short periods of time. In the HMM, we'll assume that all transient storage elements hold any value assigned to them in minor clock cycle i long enough for it to be read in minor clock cycle $i + 1$ and no longer.

The first example of an HMM microprogram is a machine-instruction fetch

Figure 2-9. HMM microprogram for machine-instruction fetch. Note: unspecified fields are implicitly no-ops.

Specification: IR ← MEM[R0] ; R0 ← R0 + 1

HMM Microprogram:

MI	HMM Encoding
(1) SBUS ← R0, ALU ← SBUS, Shifter ← ALU, MAR ← Shifter, next microinstruction	SBUS = 0, ALU = 2, Shifter = 0, Dest = 9, Seq = 0
(2) SBUS ← R0, ALU ← SBUS + 1, Shifter ← ALU, R0 ← Shifter, MDR ← MEM[MAR], next microinstruction	SBUS = 0, ALU = 9, Shifter = 0, Dest = 0, MEM = 2, Seq = 0
(3) SBUS ← MDR, ALU ← SBUS, Shifter ← ALU, IR ← Shifter, next microinstruction	SBUS = 10, ALU = 2, Shifter = 0, Dest = 8, Seq = 0

Note: Unspecified fields are implicitly no-ops.

---

interpreter that moves the main memory word addressed by file register R0 to IR and then increments file register R0. Its specification and an HMM microprogram are shown in figure 2-9. Each MI is given by the MOs that effect it and their field encodings. To illustrate how the microprogram accomplishes its designated function, suppose R0 initially has contents addr, and MEM[addr] initially has contents inst. Figure 2-10 shows snapshots of the HMM execution of the microprogram, highlighting the polyphase form of its execution.

A second, more sophisticated example is a memory-block-move microprogram. We assume that file register R1 initially contains the negated number of words to be moved, file register R2 contains the address of the first word of the block to be moved, and file register R3 contains the address of the initial location where the block is to be written. The specification and microprogram are given in figure 2-11.

While both the HMM and the machine instructions shown were particularly

Figure 2-10. Polyphase execution of HMM microprogram in figure 2-9.

MI	Minor Clock Cycle	HMM State
0	(initially)	$R0 = addr$, $MEM[addr] = inst$
1	1	$R0 = addr$, $MEM[addr] = inst$, $SBUS = addr$
	2	$R0 = addr$, $MEM[addr] = inst$, $ALU = addr$
	3	$R0 = addr$, $MEM[addr] = inst$, $Shifter = addr$
	4	$R0 = addr$, $MEM[addr] = inst$, $MAR = addr$
2	1	$R0 = addr$, $MEM[addr] = inst$, $MAR = addr$ $SBUS = addr$
	2	$R0 = addr$, $MEM[addr] = inst$, $MAR = addr$ $ALU = addr + 1$, $MDR = inst$
	3	$R0 = addr$, $MEM[addr] = inst$, $MAR = addr$ $Shifter = addr + 1$, $MDR = inst$
	4	$R0 = addr + 1$, $MEM[addr] = inst$, $MAR = addr$ $MDR = inst$
3	1	$R0 = addr + 1$, $MEM[addr] = inst$, $MAR = addr$ $MDR = inst$, $SBUS = inst$
	2	$R0 = addr + 1$, $MEM[addr] = inst$, $MAR = addr$ $MDR = inst$, $ALU = inst$
	3	$R0 = addr + 1$, $MEM[addr] = inst$, $MAR = addr$ $MDR = inst$, $Shifter = inst$
	4	$R0 = addr + 1$, $MEM[addr] = inst$, $MAR = addr$ $MDR = inst$, $IR = inst$

simple for the sake of illustration, we can still draw on the examples for several important points of contrast between machine operations and MOs, machine instructions and MIs, main memory and control-store memory, and the interpretation of machine programs and microprograms.

First, a machine instruction typically embodies a single operation, which may be complex and involve the use of sophisticated addressing modes in accessing its operands. Alternatively, an MI may comprise a very large collection of MOs. The Nanodata QM-1 (Nanodata 1974) and several recent military signal-processing machines have control words with over 300 bits that may represent over 50 MOs! Further, each MO is usually a very simple operation that moves data between storage and operational unit resources. As many of the MOs in an MI are mutually "independent" in terms of the resources they utilize, groups of independent MOs in MIs often execute concurrently.

Figure 2-11. HMM microprogram for block memory move: *a.* microprogram specification; *b.* HMM microprogram. Note: unspecified fields are implicitly no-ops.

```
Specification :  while R1 < 0 do begin   R1 ← R1 + 1 ;
                                         MAR ← R2 ;
                                         R2 ← R2 + 1 ;
                                         MDR ← MEM[MAR] ;
                                         MAR ← R3 ;
                                         R3 ← R3 + 1 ;
                                         MEM[MAR] ← MDR
                 end while
```

a

HMM Microprogram:

MI	HMM Encoding
(1) SBUS ← R1, ALU ← SBUS, if ZERO = 1 then CSAR ← "end_address"	SBUS = 1, ALU = 2, Seq = 3, Address = "end_address"
(2) SBUS ← R1, ALU ← SBUS + 1, Shifter ← ALU, R1 ← Shifter, nextmicroinstruction	SBUS = 1, ALU = 9, Shifter = 0, Dest = 1, Seq = 0
(3) SBUS ← R2, ALU ← SBUS, Shifter ← ALU, MAR ← Shifter, nextmicroinstruction	SBUS = 2, ALU = 2, Shifter = 0, Dest = 9, Seq = 0
(4) SBUS ← R2, ALU ← SBUS + 1, Shifter ← ALU, R2 ← Shifter, MDR ← MEM[MAR], nextmicroinstruction	SBUS = 2, ALU = 9, Shifter = 0, Dest = 2, MEM = 2, Seq = 0
(5) SBUS ← R3, ALU ← SBUS, Shifter ← ALU, MAR ← Shifter, nextmicroinstruction	SBUS = 3, ALU = 2, Shifter = 0, Dest = 9, Seq = 0
(6) SBUS ← R3, ALU ← SBUS + 1, Shifter ← ALU, R3 ← Shifter, MEM[MAR] ← MDR, goto "begin_address"	SBUS = 3, ALU = 9, Shifter = 0, Dest = 3, MEM = 3, Seq = 1, Address = "begin_address"

b

Some distinctions between main memories and control-store memories are visible when one considers the differing factors that influence their word size. Main-memory size is determined in part by the need to encode data, the number of operations in the instruction set, the availability of addressing modes, and the availability of program-control sequencing modes. For example, machines using the ASCII character set are likely to have main memory words whose width is a multiple of eight. Likewise, numerically oriented machines will most likely have very wide word widths that permit representation of real numbers with many significant digits. The data-representation issues must be weighed against the machine-instruction representation issues, which include, for example, the number of machine operations, the encoding of addressing modes, and the choice between one, two, or three address instructions.

The determinants that influence control-store word size are quite different. They include the degree of MO concurrency desired, the extent of decoding logic required in the presence of encoded fields, control word addressing, and the architecture of the machine. The issues of MI sequencing, MI organization, and MI execution will be discussed in detail in the following subsections.

The *length* of the memories are also determined by different factors. Since the performance of a microprogrammed machine depends heavily on the efficiency of the control-unit operation, control-store memories are often implemented with very high-speed technologies. The complementary high cost associated with such technologies can be compensated for by keeping the length of the control memory small (e.g., 4K words). On the other hand, address space is paramount in most machines. Large main-memory banks are tolerated through the use of somewhat cheaper technologies, with the associated degradation in access time.

Types of Control-Store Memories

The main memories of general-purpose, stored-program computers allow the programmer to both write to and read from constituent words. This is not generally the case with control-store memories. We can distinguish two major types of control-store memories: *read-only memories* (ROMs) and *writable control stores* (WCSs). In some ways, the different control memories can be treated uniformly. For example, the choice of control memory has little influence on MI organization or the accompanying decoding logic. There are, however, some important points of distinction.

Let's begin with memory technology. ROM implementations are characterized by a matrixlike structure in which columns correspond to individual bits and rows correspond to words, as shown in figure 2-12. An element of the ROM is accessed by activating, first, a word row, which subsequently enables a subset of the bits in that row. A bit is *active* if there exists a *coupling* between the bit and the activated word in which it resides. Generally, such a coupling represents the logical value 1, and its absence represents the logical value 0.

Figure 2-12. Basic ROM structure.

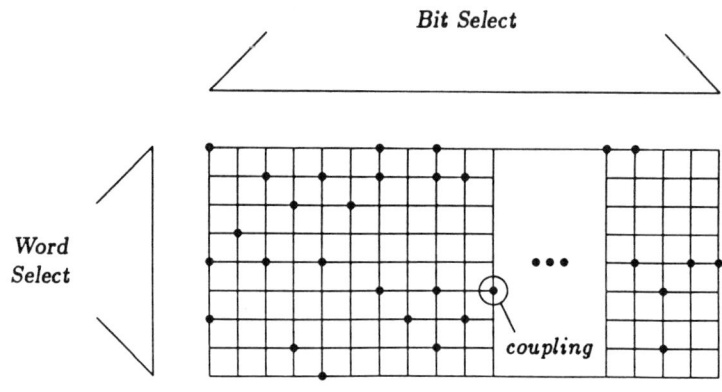

Alternate technologies are distinguished by the implementation of the matrix couplings. An early ROM implementation used resistors for coupling elements. A *card-resistor read-only memory* (CRROM) containing 500 words of at most 60 bits, with a cycle time of about 10 microseconds, was developed by IBM (Husson 1970). The IBM System/360 machines used an improved version of CRROMs in which resistors were replaced by capacitors. The operation of the *card-capacitor read-only memory* (CCROM) required transmission of a drive current along a word line. Those capacitively coupled matrix elements would then be charged and emit the logical value 1 (and likewise, uncoupled elements would remain uncharged and transmit the logical value 0). This technology enabled the development of a 2,816-word memory, with each word having a width of 100 bits and a cycle time of about 200 nanoseconds.

Another approach uses inductive elements, such as magnetic cores, for the coupling elements. The result is a read-only analog of the once-popular read-write core memories. The simplicity of the read-only structure permitted higher speeds than those attainable with comparable read-write core memory. Finally, the coupling elements can be implemented with either diodes or transistors. In the transistor-coupled ROM, the emitter of the coupler is connected to a bit line, while the collector is connected to a supply voltage. Semiconductor implementations of diode/transistor coupled devices are popular modern-day choices, since they are compatible with other semiconductor processing elements and offer the conventional advantages of semiconductor devices, such as reliability, density, speed, and small power demands.

Read-write memories are implemented with *random-access memory* (RAM), a misnomer that has been perpetuated. The RAM technologies available for control-store implementation are the same as those used for implementing main memories, and are generally classified as either *metal-oxide semiconductor* (MOS) or *bipolar*. Semiconductor implementations offer the advantages stated above. Bipolar technologies, such as *transistor-transistor logic* (TTL) are faster at the expense of higher cost and greater power dissipation. Another bipolar technology is the *integrated injector logic* (I^2L). I^2L memories are also high-speed, but have much lower power requirements and permit higher chip density.

While the ROM offers a much better speed/cost ratio than an equivalent-sized RAM, there are several other issues to consider. ROM implementations are commonly programmed by the machine's manufacturer and remain fixed for the life of the machine. This approach is the traditional and still predominant one. In contrast, a WCS affords the flexibility of user microprogrammability. Thus, the machine can be assigned custom instruction sets for higher performance or be used for the experimental emulation of alternative machine designs and implementations.

It is evident that the control-unit design issues are different for ROM and WCS implementations. The designer of a WCS-based control unit must heavily weigh the user "microprogrammability" of the machine, a much less significant issue in ROM-based design. On the other hand, the architecture of the ROM-based machine can be "optimized" with respect to fixed criteria, including the microprograms. That is, one can first define a collection of microprograms that serve as a specification of a *virtual machine*. The control unit, data paths, ALU, main-memory unit, and other architectural components can then be designed around the microcode to efficiently implement the virtual machine. This option is not available for WCS-based microprogrammable control units.

It should also be mentioned that there is another alternative, which can be construed as a "compromise" between the ROM and WCS schemes: the *programmable read-only memory* (PROM). PROMs differ from ROMs in that they are *field-programmable*. That is, PROMs are manufactured so that couplings exist at all points of the bit matrix (i.e., all bits in the matrix initially have logical value 1). Programming a PROM involves *fusing* (i.e., destroying) those couplings for which a bit value of 0 is desired. In effect, the PROM offers the flexibility of user programmability available in the WCS scheme along with the higher densities and lower costs characteristic of ROMs. Note, however, that once a coupling has been fused it cannot be reestablished.

If reprogrammability of PROMs is desirable, one has the option of using an *erasable programmable read-only memory* (EPROM). EPROMs are implemented using MOS technology, with the additional property that their programming is erased whenever a sufficient dose of ultraviolet light is transmitted through a window on the chip. Thus, the EPROM can be inexpensively programmed and erased. This makes it ideal for prototyping applications. However, the relatively slow access time and higher price of the EPROM vis à vis the ROM make the former undesirable for production use.

Control-Store Structure

The overwhelming choice of past and existing machines is likewise the simplest: each control-store word contains a single MI. This approach is popular since it makes microprogramming conceptually simple and has a straightforward hardware implementation. A simple deviation from this approach is to store two or more MIs in a single control word. This has the advantage of reducing control-store accesses but requires more complex control hardware.

A more substantial variation is to organize the control store into *pages* of memory. The result is the ability to partition control-store addresses into those within the current page and those that fall outside the current page. Since a much shorter offset is required in the former case, considerable savings in space will result when locality of reference tends to be the rule. For example, the 4K-word control store of the Microdata 3200 (Microdata 1974) is hierarchically organized into 16 pages of size 256, and each page is partitioned into 16 blocks of size 16. Each control-store word contains two MIs, designated the +MI and the −MI. Further, each next MI address descriptor contains four fields: a four-bit page address, a four-bit block address, a four-bit location address, and a single +/−MI selector bit. A sophisticated scheme is then employed in which condition codes can be used to mask or modify any of these fields. The result is a powerful collection of next-address selection modes.

Another twist is to use a *split* structure, in which two distinct memory units with different word sizes comprise the control store. This scheme is used in the Burroughs Interpreter (Reigel, Faber, and Fisher 1972), which has a microprogram memory and a nanoprogram memory. MIs in the microprogram memory are 16 bits long and perform two functions: the transfer of a literal to a general register and the determination of an MI in the nanoprogram memory to be executed. In contrast, words in the nanoprogram memory are 54 bits wide and represent a collection of concurrently executed MOs. The advantage of the split-structured control store is space economy, as fewer bits are needed for microprogram storage when the short MIs that perform data transfers are frequently executed and a single long MI is referenced by many short MIs. The major drawback is the additional time needed to access two levels of storage.

A related control-store structure is the *two-level* control store, in which MIs in the lower level interpret MIs in the higher level. Note the facsimile of this approach to the use of MIs to interpret machine instructions. The Nanodata QM-1 (Nanodata 1974) uses a two-level control structure. The lower level, called the *nanostore*, is comprised of a maximum of 1,024 words, each containing 360 bits. The upper level, called the *microstore*, contains up to 16K words, with the word width being 18 bits. The two levels of control store offer flexibility, which is particularly useful in emulation. However, the QM-1 is an extremely complex machine and is very difficult to program, particularly at the nanostore level. Those interested in studying the QM-1 further are encouraged to read Chapter 11 of *The Design and Description of Computer Architectures* (Dasgupta

1984). A two-level control store is also used in the microprogrammed implementation of the Motorola MC68000 single-chip microprocessor. Those interested in reading about the microprogrammed implementation of the MC68000 are referred to "Microprogrammed implementation of a single-chip microprocessor" (Stritter and Treddenick 1978).

It was stated earlier that one of the distinguishing characteristics of microprogrammed control is the separation of main memory from control store. This is not always the case, however, as exemplified by the Burroughs B1712 and B1714 machines (Wilner 1972b). Finally, it may be useful to augment the control store with a high-speed cache memory in order to compensate for a slower, less expensive control-store memory. The cache has no bearing on user microprogrammability, as its operation is transparent to the microprogrammer.

Microinstruction Sequencing

Control-store sequencing is the process of determining the next MI in the control store to be executed. There are two major approaches to control-store sequencing. The *implicit-addressing* approach is analogous to the sequencing scheme used to determine the next machine instruction to be fetched for execution from the main memory. Specifically, the next MI to be fetched to the *MIR* is the MI that resides in the next sequential location in the control store following the MI last executed, unless an explicit directive to the contrary is contained in that MI. This is usually implemented architecturally by augmenting the *CSAR* with an incrementing unit.

To direct the control unit to an MI other than that residing in the next sequential control-store location, we can use any of a number of addressing modes that parallel those commonly available in machine instructions. In general, we can deviate from sequential execution through either conditional or unconditional branch MOs. The address of the next MI to be processed can be found in a variety of different sources. One possibility is to allocate an MI field to hold the effective address, an offset for the relative address computation of the effective address, or some other variation on this theme.

Another approach is the *index-register* scheme, in which either a special register or one of a bank of general registers is designated in a field of the MI to hold the effective address. A third possibility is to retrieve the address from a hardware stack. This is particularly useful as a mechanism for facilitating subroutine linkage and/or interrupt processing. Another simple variation on implicit sequencing is the conditional (unconditional) skip, which can be used to implement if-then-else control constructs.

The philosophy behind implicit sequencing is that sequence in control flow is the rule rather than the exception. This is the case when the straight-line sequences of MIs with single entry points and single exit points in the microcode tend to be long. We would expect this to be the case for machines with short

Figure 2-13. Branching instructions for the Standard Logic CASH-8.

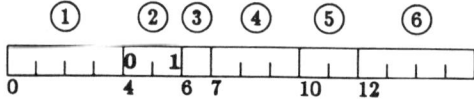

1. Register Select

2. Branch Select Encoding

3. Condition test mode (branch on condition *true/false*)

4. Auxiliary Operation

Encoding			Interpretation
1	0	0	move contents of selected register to lower 8 bits of *CSAR*
1	1	0	move the address of the next *MI* to selected register and its successor. load *CSAR* with the contents of the next two registers
1	0	1	load *CSAR* with the contents of selected register and its successor
1	1	1	load *CSAR* with the contents of the vector register
0	X	X	test condition is contained in register select field; contents of condition select field are moved to lower 8 bits of *CSAR*

5. Not used

6. Condition Select

Encoding				Interpretation
0	0	0	0	$ACC \leq 0$
0	0	0	1	$ACC \neq 0$
0	0	1	0	$CARRY = 1$
0	0	1	1	
	...			External lines 0-3 set
0	1	1	0	
0	1	1	1	Unconditional
0	b_0	b_1	b_2	ACC bit $b_0 b_1 b_2$ set

word-length MIs that contain few MOs (the so-called *vertical* MIs), since many MIs are then required to effect complex tasks. As such, the information needed to specify sequencing in each MI is reduced.

A simple example of a machine that uses implicit sequencing is the Standard Logic CASH-8 (Standard Logic 1973). The CASH-8 has a 16-bit MI. When the value of the bits in positions 4 to 5 is anything other than 01, an ALU operation, data transfer, or I/O operation is specified, and implicit sequencing is used. The assignment of value 01 to this field designates an explicit branch operation, as shown in figure 2-13. In this case, the value of the bits in positions 0 to 3 specifies which one of 16 general-purpose registers holds the effective address; bit position 6 specifies either conditional or unconditional branching; the value of the bits in positions 12 to 15 determines which condition is to be tested (only meaningful when conditional branching is enabled); and the bits in positions 7 to 9 specify an ancillary data-transfer operation between the CSAR and some other storage resource.

In the explicit-sequencing scheme, the control-store address of the next MI to be executed is stored in the MI currently being executed. In effect, the microcode in the control store becomes a *linked list*. To accomplish conditional branching, several approaches may be feasible. The first is to simply include n addresses in the MI when an n-*way* conditional branch is required. This simple-minded approach can, however, be very control-store-space-inefficient. The amount of space required for large address-space control stores can be moderated by adding a base register to hold the current address and place *relative addresses* in the MI. A simple variation to handle conditional branching would be to store alternate addresses in other storage resources (e.g., index register or hardware stack).

Another possibility is to modify the next MI control-store address field contingent on the outcome of conditional evaluation. For example, to implement such an n-*way* conditional branching scheme, we provide the capability to modify the low-order n bits of the next address field. This approach trades off added control-unit complexity and possibly slower speed for more efficient control-store utilization.

The philosophy behind explicit sequencing is that short sequences in control flow tend to characterize microprogram flow. We would expect this to be the case for machines with very wide word MIs that contain many MOs (the so-called *horizontal* MIs), since complex tasks can be effected using large numbers of MOs in a single MI, keeping MI sequences relatively short. As such, the machine can avoid wasting both space and time on the repeated use of branch instructions by permitting the specification of both functional operations and arbitrary control sequencing in a single MI. Another advantage of explicit sequencing lies in the simplicity of editing linked sequences of MIs during microprogram development with EPROMs or WCSs. An example of a machine that uses a complex explicit-sequencing scheme is the Varian 73 (Varian 1973).

Microinstruction Organization

There are two important facets of microinstruction execution: the number of MOs executable in a single MI (or, equivalently, MI word width) and the degree of encoding in the representation of MOs in the MI. MIs are usually classified into three groups as regards the first criterion.

In a *vertical* MI, there is generally only a single MO. The organization of a vertical MI closely resembles a traditional machine instruction, with the exception that the vertical MI lacks the complex operand-addressing modes often present in machine instructions. As such, the word width of a vertical MI is typically less than 25 bits.

Examples of several commercial machines with vertical MIs are the Burroughs B1700 Series machines (Wilner 1972a) and the Standard Logic CASH-8 (Standard Logic 1973). The organization of the CASH-8 is shown in figure 2-14. Its salient feature is simplicity of microprogramming. The CASH-8 MI repertoire has four groups of instructions: arithmetic/logic MIs, branch MIs, register-file and I/O transfer MIs, and shift/rotate MIs. The control-word template for the branching MIs, shown in figure 2-13, illustrates the simplicity characteristic of the vertical MI.

Simplicity of user microprogramming is clearly one of the virtues of vertical MIs. Another is the ability to fully utilize each MI without the need to apply complex microcode-compaction methods. Disadvantages include the failure to exploit potential concurrent execution of independent MOs in a microprogram and the need to write long sequences of MIs to implement even modestly complex operations.

Machines with MIs that have multiple but limited numbers of MOs are (facetiously) called *diagonal* MIs. Diagonal MIs offer the compromise of greater machine resource control and efficient resource utilization without undue complexity in user microprogrammability. Commercial examples of machines with diagonal MIs include the HP 21-MX family (Matheson 1974), which has 24-bit MIs, and the Interdata Model 85 (Interdata 1973) and the Microdata 3200 (Microdata 1974) machines, each of which has 32-bit MIs. The simple hypothetical microprogrammed machine exhibited in the section "Microprogrammed Control Units" (fig. 2-6) is another example of the diagonal MI approach.

At the other end of the spectrum is the *horizontal* MI. A horizontal MI generally offers the microprogrammer a large number of parallel MOs in the MIs of a microprogrammed machine. This allows the talented individual (or powerful automated translator) the potential to fully exploit the underlying architecture and thus perform high-speed machine operations. As such, the horizontal MI structure is a popular choice for microprogrammed signal-processing machines that operate under demanding real-time constraints. Some commercial examples of horizontally structured machines include the Varian 73 (Varian 1973), which has a 64-bit MI partitioned into 25 fields; the Digital VAX 11-780 (Digital 1979), which has a 96-bit MI formed by 30 distinct fields; and the Nanodata

Figure 2-14. Standard Logic CASH-8 organization.

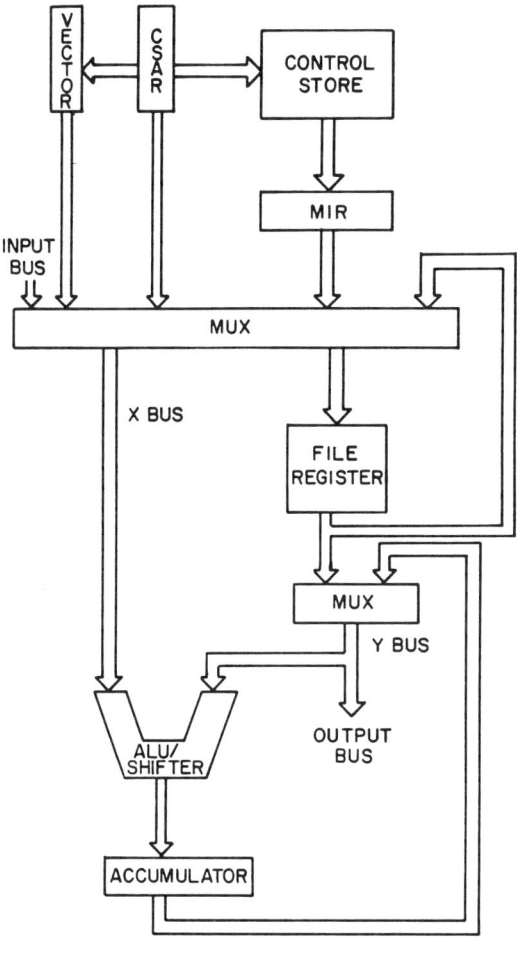

(MAIN MEMORY USES INPUT AND OUTPUT BUS)

QM-1 (Nanodata 1974), which has a 360-bit nanoword comprised of a 72-bit "K" vector containing 21 fields and four 72-bit "T" vectors, each containing 41 fields (for a total of 185 fields!).

There are several disadvantages to using horizontal MIs. While they offer great resource control, data-dependency constraints often limit the number of MOs that can be placed in an MI. The result is poor control-store space utilization. There is also the complexity of user microprogrammability that results from compositely trying to exploit machine resources to the fullest extent while preserving the intended function of the microcode and not illegally placing resource-dependent MOs in a common MI. As a result, automated tools are essential for the development of horizontal microcode.

The second important MI organizational issue is the degree of encoding used in representing MOs in an MI. The simplest form of MO representation in an MI is to use a single bit to enable/disable each distinct MO, as illustrated in figure 2-15a. This approach was one of the first MI encoding schemes proposed (Wilkes 1951), and is still used to a limited extent in machines with highly horizontal MIs. Its obvious disadvantage is the unnecessarily wide MIs used to accommodate the absence of encoding.

A more popular generalization is to use an n-bit MI field to represent up to 2^n different operations that control a single resource. This method is called *single-level*, or *direct, encoding*. Single-level encoding has the important advantage of space efficiency over the fully decoded method, since the single-level field for n operations requires at most $[\log_2 n]$ bits, as opposed to n bits for the fully decoded approach. Since one can conserve control-store space and still enable large numbers of parallel MOs in a single MI, most horizontal machines employ single-level encoding. The single-level encoding scheme is shown in figure 2-15b.

When the meaning of a single field depends in part on the encoding of other fields, we have *two-level*, or *indirect, encoding*. This approach is commonly used with vertical MIs, with the (single) operation code used to interpret the remaining fields. When the other fields are also contained in the MI, we have the *bit-steering* scheme. The bit-steering approach is shown in figure 2-15c. Bit steering is used in the RCA Spectra 70, the Honeywell H1700, and the IBM System/360 machines (Andrews 1980). The other field can also be a component of some machine register, which produces a *format-shifting* scheme. Format shifting can be used to conditionally direct MI execution based on machine states in applications such as I/O processing.

Microinstruction Execution

The execution of an MI has several parameters. One is the way in which the execution of the MI controls the resources of the machine. Typically, the MOs in an MI directly control machine resources. We call this *immediate control*. A variation used in the Nanodata QM-1 (Nanodata 1974) is to have the execution of the MI (conditionally) assign values to control registers (called *setup registers*) and use the setup registers to exercise direct control over machine resources. This approach is called *residual control*.

The advantage of residual control arises when, say, an arithmetic/logic operation must be repeatedly executed many times. The operation need only be placed in an MI in the control store once, yielding savings in control-store space. Thus, a machine with a vertical MI may still obtain some of the parallel

Figure 2-15. Microinstruction encoding alternatives: *a.* fully decoded MI; *b.* single-level encoded MI; *c.* MI with bit-steering control.

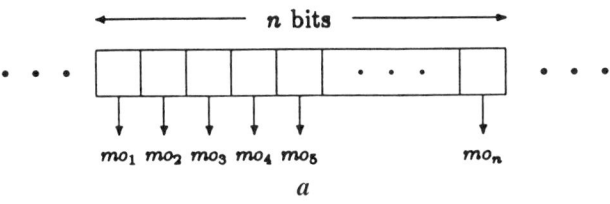
a

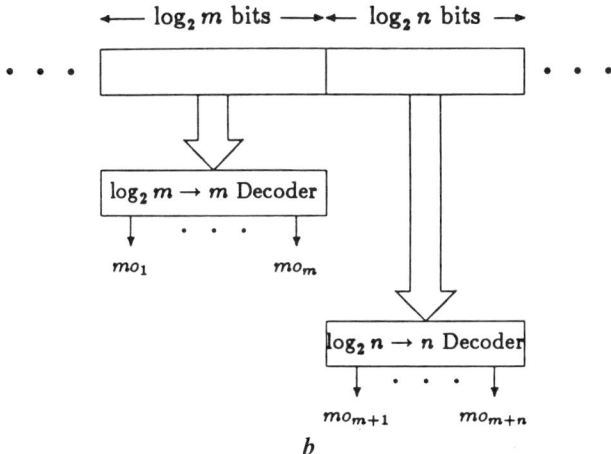
b

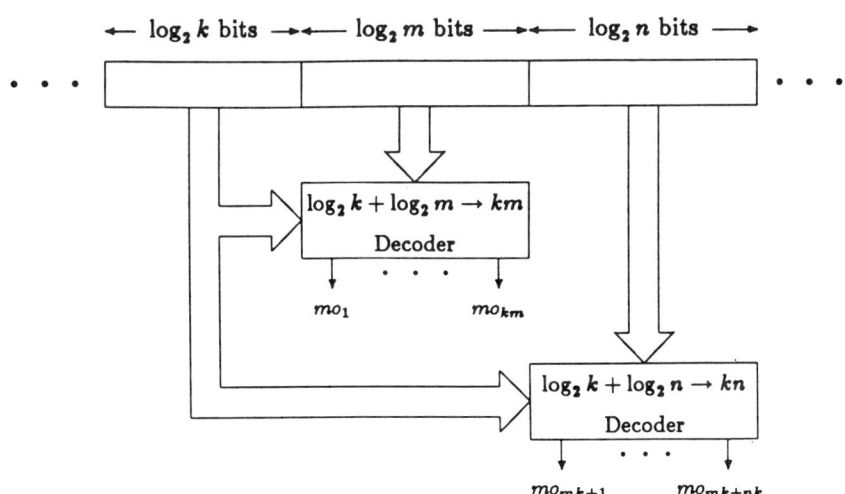
c

resource control afforded by horizontal structures without the wide control-word width.

A second parameter of MI execution is the timing patterns used to sequence the MOs within the execution of a single MI. The simple approach is to execute all MOs concurrently in a single clock cycle, called the *major clock cycle*. This is called *monophase timing*. Monophase timing is useful when the MOs tend to be very simple (e.g., simple data transfers), and it has the advantage of requiring a simple hardware implementation.

When the execution of the MOs in an MI requires sequencing, the major clock cycle can be broken up into several *minor cycles*. With *polyphase timing*, collections of resource-independent MOs can execute in a common minor cycle, and the need to complete the execution of some MO m_i prior to executing another m_j can be realized by simply placing m_i in a minor clock cycle preceding that in which m_j is placed. A timing diagram illustrating monophase and polyphase timing is shown in figure 2-16.

Polyphase timing can be either *synchronous* or *asynchronous*. In synchronous polyphase timing, the major clock cycle is decomposed into a fixed number of minor cycles. As with monophase timing, synchronous polyphase timing has a simple hardware realization (e.g., a simple counter scheme).

A more general approach is to make the number of minor cycles variable, depending on the complexity of constituent MOs. This yields asynchronous polyphase timing. The advantage of asynchronous polyphase timing is the ability to fully utilize the time within a major clock cycle, when, for example, synchronous timing yields potentially large idle time if a microprogram is characterized by MIs containing very simple MOs. Its disadvantage is the sometimes complex hardware required for realization.

The third parameter of MI execution is the timing of the fetch/decode/execute sequence. *Serial implementations* are those in which the execution of the current MI always completes before the initiation of the fetch phase for the subsequent MI begins, as illustrated by the Gantt chart in figure 2-17a. A serial implementation preserves functional determinacy with no special hardware checks but fails to exploit the potential overlap of independent operations and the resulting efficiency gains.

In a *parallel implementation*, the execution of the current MI is overlapped with the fetch phase for the next MI to be executed, as shown in figure 2-17b. The problem with parallel implementations is, in general, the need to guess the control-store address of the next MI to be executed. This specifically occurs in cases of conditional branching.

To compensate for this, the control unit may be designed to "guess" the address of the next MI to be executed (e.g., the next sequential address). In this case, hardware for both checking for incorrect guesses and correcting the address must be a part of the control unit. Another possibility is to use hardware to detect conditional branch instructions and inhibit prefetch until the next

Figure 2-16. Monophase (*a*) and polyphase (*b*) MI implementations.

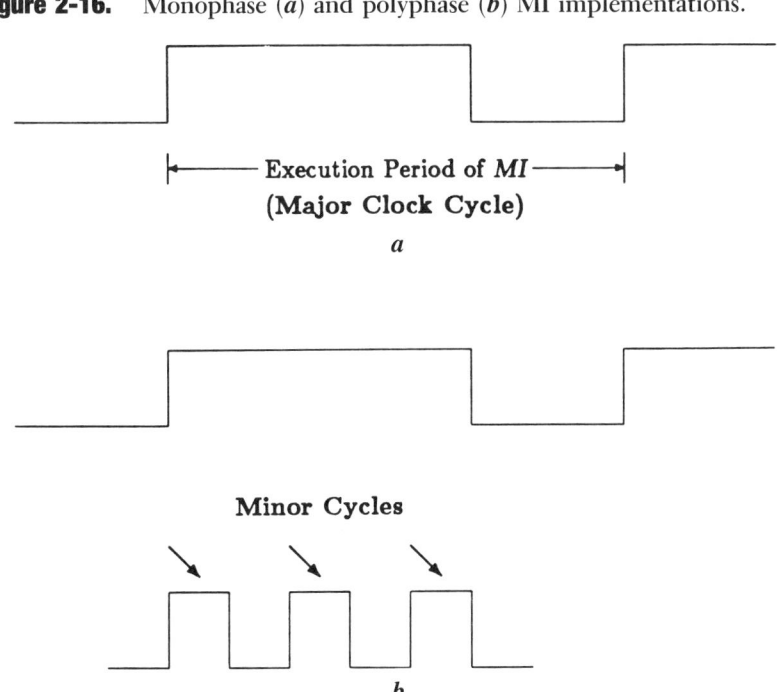

control-store address has been determined. Finally, the control unit may rely on the microprogrammer/automated translator to ensure determinacy in the presence of conditional branches. The associated software optimization of the "delayed branch problem" for the latter alternative will be discussed in more detail in the next section, "Efficiency Considerations."

It has been noted that polyphase timing is an auspicious alternative when a parallel implementation is used and the control-store access time is slow relative to the processor time (Dasgupta 1979). The poor performance that accompanies slow access times is moderated by the composite effect of fewer accesses and efficient overlapped operation.

EFFICIENCY CONSIDERATIONS

The microprogrammed control unit is embedded deep in the hierarchical-structured computing system. As such, its performance heavily influences that of the entire system. There are several important factors to consider in designing efficient microprogrammed control units and efficient microprograms.

Figure 2-17. Serial (*a*) and parallel (*b*) MI implementations.

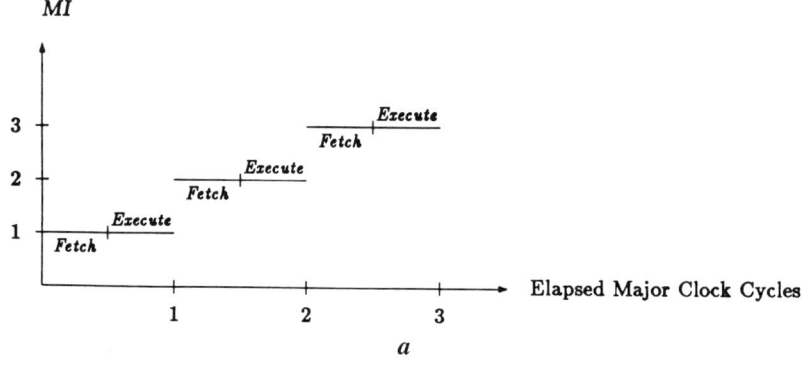

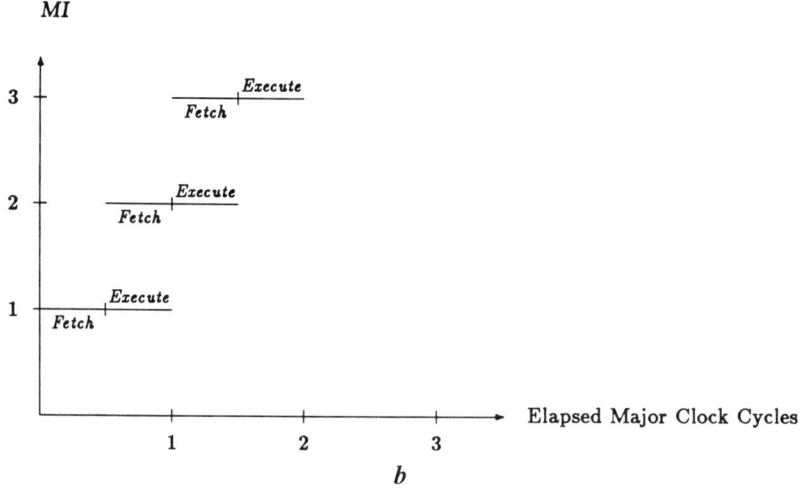

First, we would like to employ a high-speed memory technology for the control store. This, however, means higher costs. While advances in memory technology make high-speed memory available at much lower prices, it may still be important to be frugal with control-store space. We can improve the space requirements by carefully designing both the organization of the MI control word and the organization of the MOs in the microcode. Finally, architectural considerations can also influence the speed of the control unit through the integration and effective use of resources.

In this section we will review the fundamental concepts of and problems associated with efficient microprogrammed control-unit design and present some simple (and sometimes naive) approaches to their solution. Detailed treatment of this subject is given in other chapters of this book, especially Chapter 9, ("Horizontal Microcode Compaction").

A general theme to keep in mind throughout the reading of this section is the computational intractability of most problems associated with *optimal* microprogrammed control-unit design. Formally, we refer to these problems as being NP-hard; informally, this characterization can be interpreted to convey the uncertainty that there exists a practical, efficient algorithm for solving the problem. Examples of NP-hard microprogrammed control-unit optimization problems are those associated with minimizing the dimensions of the control store: the microcode-bit optimization problem (Robertson 1979) and the microcode-word optimization problem (DeWitt 1976).

We will look at four different efficiency factors: determination of control-word format given the microcode for a ROM-based design, minimization of the word size of a directly encoded control word given potentially parallel sets of MOs, minimization of the length of a microprogram for a diagonal/horizontal-control-word machine given MO conflict classes and a data-dependency graph representation of the microcode, and minimization of branch delays in a machine that employs MI prefetch.

Control-Word Format Determination

Suppose we are designing the MI control word and control-store space must be limited. A logical optimization criterion to establish would be the minimization of the ratio of control-word bits per executable MO in the MI. A simple analytical model that might help in weighing the tradeoffs inherent in vertical vs. horizontal word structures that is based on this criterion was first proposed by Ramamoorthy and Tsuchiya (1970).

Let M be the microprogram to be stored in the control store. The parameters of the problem are:

1. The number of *vertical* MIs required to represent M, W_v, when the MI word width is N_v
2. The number of *diagonal* or *horizontal* MIs required to represent M, W_{nv}, when the MI word width is N_{nv}
3. The average number of parallel MOs executable using the format of (2), Q

The total space requirement of M for the vertical format would be $N_v * W_v$, and for the nonvertical format $N_{nv} * W_{nv}$. Assuming that the number of MOs required to execute M is independent of the format of the MI, we can state the relation $W_{nv} = W_v/Q$ and express the space requirements for the nonvertical format as $W_v * N_{nv}/Q$.

We can now solve a simple linear inequality to determine the relative merits of the vertical and nonvertical formats. Specifically, when the slope of the curve for the ratio $Q/(N_{nv}/N_v)$ is less than one, format (1) is preferable. Likewise, a slope of greater than one makes format (2) the better choice. This is graphically depicted in figure 2-18.

This simple model can be extended to allow a similar decision to be made between formats that both permit concurrent MO execution in an MI. We leave this as an exercise to the reader.

Bit Minimization of Directly Encoded Control Words

Recall from the section "Control-Unit Organization" that the idea behind *directly encoded* control words is to group MOs that cannot be concurrently executed into fields. When there are n MOs in a group, a field of $[\log_2 n]$ bits in the MI is sufficient for its representation. When using such an MI structure, it is useful to determine an assignment of MOs to groups (and likewise MI fields) in such a way that: (1) no two concurrently executable MOs belong to the same group, and (2) the width of the MI is minimized. We will call this the *microcode-bit optimization problem*.

Figure 2-18. Tradeoff between vertical/nonvertical format. In region v, a vertical format is more efficient; in region nv, a nonvertical format is more efficient.

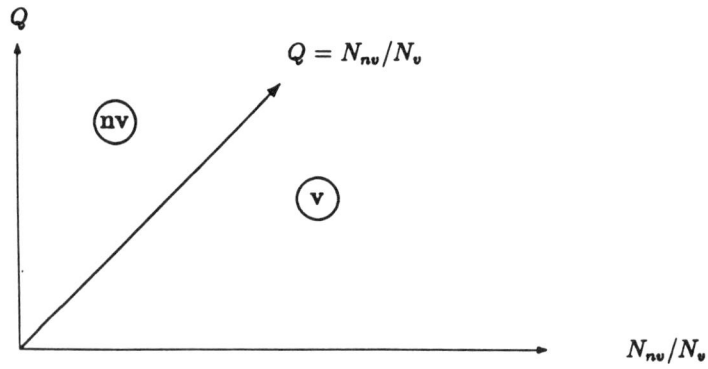

Region v: Vertical format is more efficient

Region nv: Non-vertical format is more efficient

FUNDAMENTAL CONCEPTS OF MICROPROGRAMMING 71

To begin with, the binary relation on MOs called *potentially parallel* (PP) must be computed. It is generally found in different ways, depending on whether we have a ROM- or WCS-based control unit. In the case of a ROM-based control unit, the relation PP is taken from the microcode given, e.g., a data-dependency graph representation.[1] For WCS-based control units, the criterion is essentially machine resource dependencies (Dasgupta and Tartar 1975).

Compatible MOs are those pairs that do not belong to PP. A *compatibility class* (CC) is any set of MOs that are pairwise compatible. As such, any CC constitutes a valid group of MOs to be represented by a single MI field. Figure 2-19 shows the PP relation for a set of MOs and several corresponding CCs.

In terms of the microcode-bit optimization problem, a *feasible* solution is then any collection of CCs $\{C_1, \ldots, C_k\}$ that *partition* the set of MOs.[2] If we let $|C_i|$ denote the number of MOs in set C_i and allow for each field to have an additional "no-op" encoding, an *optimal* solution to the microcode-bit optimization problem is any feasible solution $\{C_1, \ldots, C_k\}$ that minimizes the sum

$$L = \sum_{i=1}^{k} \lceil \log_2(|C_i| + 1) \rceil$$

Several general approaches to solving the problem have been proposed. One is to view the problem as a *minimal graph covering* problem (Das, Banerji, and Chattopadhyay 1973; Schwartz 1968; Grasselli and Montanari 1970; Dasgupta and Tartar 1975), and the other is to view it as a *linear programming* problem (Jayasri and Basu 1976). We will overview a straightforward method based on the first approach, with the intention of illustrating the more important elements of the covering technique.

There are two major steps in the covering procedure for microcode-bit optimization: computing maximal compatible sets of MOs and finding a minimal cover for the set of maximal compatibles. A *maximal compatibility class* (or *maximal compatible* for short) is a CC that is maximally closed under the compatibility relation—that is, a CC that is a proper subset of no other CC. We will refer to maximal compatibles simply as MCs.

In computing MCs, we will assume that the compatibility relation on a set of MOs is supplied as input. The compatibility relation can be represented as a set of n *adjacency lists* for any set of n MOs, $\{m_1, \ldots, m_n\}$. The initial adjacency

---

1. Data-dependency graphs are discussed in the next subsection, "Microcode Compaction."

2. Formally, a *partition* on a set S is any set of nonempty subsets of S with the property that each element of S is contained in exactly one of the subsets.

Figure 2-19. Parallel MO sets (*a*) and corresponding compatible classes (*b*).

1. {1,3,6}
2. {2,4}
3. {2,5}
4. {2,7}
5. {1,6,7}
6. {5,6}
7. {5,7}
8. {7,8}

a

1. {1,4}, {3,5,8}, {2,6}, {7}
2. {1,2}, {4,6}, {3,7}, {5,8}
3. {1,2,8}, {3,4,5}, {6}, {7}

b

list for m_i is a list of all CCs of the form (m_i, m_j) such that $i < j$ and (m_i, m_j) is a compatibility pair. The adjacency-list representation of the compatibility relation corresponding to the example in figure 2-19 is shown in figure 2-20.

To get MCs from the adjacency lists, we begin with list n {$CC_n 1,\ldots,CC_n k$} and then attempt to *merge* each $CC_n i$ with each of the CCs in the $(n - 1)$ list. When merging is possible, the new CC is entered into list n. Otherwise, the pair is simply added to list n.[3] A CC merge is simply the union of two CCs that results in a CC (note that the union of two CCs does not always produce a CC). The resulting list of CCs must then be processed against each of the remaining $n - 2$ lists, $n > 2$. The algorithm terminates when $n = 2$, with the list of CCs produced in the last iteration being the desired set of MCs. The skeleton of the algorithm, described in detail by Unger (1969), is given in figure 2-21, and the iterative computation of the algorithm for the adjacency lists in figure 2-20 is shown in figure 2-22.

---

3. Actually, there is no need to work from the end of the adjacency lists toward the front. Any ordering that processes each list against all other lists is valid.

Figure 2-20. Adjacency-list representation of binary parallel relation.

[1] {2, 4, 5, 8}

[2] {3, 6, 8}

[3] {4, 5, 7, 8}

[4] {5, 6, 7, 8}

[5] {8}

[6] {8}

[7] ∅

The second phase of the procedure is to find a subset of the MCs with the property that each MO is contained in at least one of the MCs. We call such a set a *cover*. Tabular methods for computing covers from sets of MCs have been used in the computation of *prime implicants* in switching functions (Kohavi 1970) and were subsequently applied to the microcode-bit optimization problem (Schwartz 1968; Grasselli and Montanari 1970; Das, Banerji, and Chattopadhyay 1973). We will overview the approach described in the last of these.

Let M = $\{MC_1, \ldots, MC_k\}$ be the set of maximal compatibles for a compatibility relation on a set of MOs $\{m_1, \ldots, m_n\}$. We can then construct a *cover table* with n columns, such that MC_i is listed under column j if and only if m_j is contained in MC_i. For example, the cover table for the MCs computed in figure 2-22 is shown in figure 2-23.

The cover table is useful for exhibiting several important properties of MC sets. In particular, whenever a column representing m_j contains exactly one entry, MC_i, we call m_j a *distinguished* MO and MC_i an *essential* MC. Note

Figure 2-21. Unger's algorithm for computing maximal compatibles.

comment: *let $L[1] \ldots L[n]$ be the n adjacency lists*;

begin

    $MC := L[n]$;

    for $i := n - 1$ downto 1 do $MC := \text{cc\_merge}(MC, L[i])$;

end

Figure 2-22. Iterative computation of maximal compatibles using Unger's method on the parallel sets in figure 2-17.

Iteration	MCC
0	$\emptyset$
1	$\{\{6,8\}\}$
2	$\{\{5,8\},\{6,8\}\}$
3	$\{\{4,5,8\},\{4,6,8\},\{4,7\}\}$
4	$\{\{3,4,5,8\},\{4,6,8\},\{3,4,7\}\}$
5	$\{\{2,3\},\{2,6\},\{2,8\},\{3,4,5,8\},\{4,6,8\},\{3,4,7\}\}$
6	$\{\{1,2,8\},\{1,4\},\{1,5\},\{3,4,5,8\},\{4,6,8\},\{3,4,7\}\}$

that in the cover table shown in figure 2-23, m_2, m_6, and m_7 are distinguished and MC_1, MC_5, and MC_6 are essential. Clearly, any cover must contain each of the essential MCs.

There are, in general, many covers, and we must be careful to compute them so that an optimal solution can always be found. Problems such as this, with potentially large search spaces, are usually attacked by first applying heuristic rules that eliminate candidates that can easily be shown to be nonoptimal (or less desirable than other candidates). An example of such a heuristic is based on the *principle of column dominance*.

Figure 2-23. MCs and cover table.

1.$\{1,2,8\}$ 2.$\{1,4\}$ 3.$\{1,5\}$ 4.$\{3,4,5,8\}$ 5.$\{4,6,8\}$ 6.$\{3,4,7\}$

1	2	3	4	5	6	7	8
1	1	4	2	3	6	5	1
2		5	4	4			4
3			5				6
			6				

FUNDAMENTAL CONCEPTS OF MICROPROGRAMMING 75

An MO m_i dominates m_j when the MCs in column j of the cover table are a subset of the MCs in column i. When m_i dominates m_j, we can eliminate column i from the search. The validity of and motivation behind this principle are clear, since we are simply observing that the MCs in column j cover both m_i and m_j more "economically" than those in column i. For the cover table in figure 2-23, note that m_2 is dominated by m_1 and m_8, m_6 is dominated by m_4 and m_8, m_7 is dominated by m_3 and m_4, and m_3 is dominated by m_4.

After eliminating the dominating columns, we examine the remaining nondistinguished MOs. In our example, only column 5 remains. MO m_5 is covered by both MC_3 and MC_4. Thus, combining all possible ways to cover the remaining nondistinguished MOs with the essential MCs that cover the distinguished MOs, we get a set of feasible solutions that contains an optimal solution. There are two solutions for our example:

$$S_1 = \{MC_1, MC_3, MC_5, MC_6\}$$

or

$$S_2 = \{MC_1, MC_4, MC_5, MC_6\}$$

The final step is the elimination of *redundant* MOs, and determination of the optimal solution from the set of *nonredundant* solutions. In S_1, m_1 is redundant in that it is contained in both MC_1 and MC_3. Allowing redundant MOs in the cover simply means that there would be multiple ways of executing the MO in a single MI format. This can be rectified by eliminating the redundant MO from all but one of the MCs of which it is a member.[4] The set of all nonredundant solutions computed from S_1 and S_2 is shown in figure 2-24. From the set for S_1, the minimal optimization criterion sum (6 bits) is associated with S_{11},

$$S_{11} = \{\{m_1, m_2, m_8\}, \{m_5\}, \{m_6\}, \{m_3, m_4, m_7\}\}$$

In general, minimal covers are not unique. For our example, another 6-bit solution can be derived from the set associated with S_2:

$$S_{21} = \{\{m_1, m_2, m_8\}, \{m_3, m_4, m_5\}, \{m_6\}, \{m_7\}\}$$

As a final note it should be mentioned that, in practice, optimal algorithms for microcode bit minimization are much too slow, owing to the NP-hard property of the problem. Accordingly, the more effective solutions are efficient algorithms that tend to produce near-optimal solutions. Examples of such algorithms can be found in two readings (Baer and Koyama 1979; Rao and Biswas 1983).

---

4. Eliminating all redundant MOs may not always lead to the most desirable MI organization. Dasgupta (1979) discusses some important tradeoff issues.

Microcode Compaction

Microcode designated for vertical machines is essentially a linear sequence of MOs. While alternate sequences of the MOs may achieve the same function, the vertical MI structure inhibits any potential parallelism between MOs, and thus only limited performance improvement from sequence perturbations is possible. In contrast, horizontal machines can offer considerable flexibility in exploiting the functional independence of MOs in a microprogram.

Informally, the *microcode compaction problem* is to determine a minimal-length microprogram for a partially ordered sequence of MOs on a selected horizontal machine. The result of compaction can be both a reduction in control-store space and microcode execution time. The nature of the compaction problem differs depending on the scope of the microprogram under scrutiny.

The *local compaction problem* deals strictly with straight-line sequences of MOs that have a single entry point and a single exit point, called *basic blocks*. Every program can be decomposed into a *flow graph*, the nodes of which are basic blocks and the edges of which indicate potential control flow between basic blocks. Efficient algorithms for the task can be found in a number of readings (Aho and Ullman 1977; Hecht 1977; Kou 1977). Basic blocks are often simpler to analyze due to the absence of internal control loops, and thus much literature has been published on the flow analysis of basic blocks (Aho and Ullman 1977; Hecht 1977; Muchnick and Jones 1981), code generation for basic blocks in both conventional compilers (Aho and Ullman 1977; Aho and Johnson 1976; Sethi and Ullman 1970), and microcode compilers (Baba and Hagiwara 1981; DeWitt 1976; Ma and Lewis 1981; Marwedel 1984; Mueller 1984; Sheraga and Geiser 1981; Vegdahl 1982), and, of course, compaction of basic blocks of microcode (Landskov et al. 1980 and Chapter 9 of this book, "Horizontal Microcode Compaction").

The *global compaction problem* is more general in that MOs can be moved beyond basic-block boundaries. It has been reported that the length of basic blocks on highly horizontal machines tends to be short; thus, local compaction is of limited value and global compaction is essential to producing quality code (Fisher 1979). Algorithms for performing global compaction have appeared more recently and tend to be more sophisticated than most local-compaction algorithms. Some notable examples of global techniques can be found in a number of readings (Dasgupta 1977; Tokoro et al. 1978; Wood 1979b; Fisher 1979; Poe 1980; Fisher 1981; Tokoro, Tamura, and Takizuka 1981).

For simplicity, we will examine the fundamentals of the local compaction problem; detailed treatment is given in Chapter 9 ("Horizontal Microcode Compaction"). Before we can discuss algorithms for solving the local compaction problem, the representation of the microcode and the constraints that inhibit sequencing must be considered.

A simple way to represent a basic block of MOs would be to list them in a strict linear sequence, as is done with assignment statements in programming

Figure 2-24. MC cover table.

$C_1=\{1,2,8\}$	$C_1=\{1,2,8\}$	$C_1'=\{1,2\}$	$C_1'=\{1,2\}$
$C_3'=\{5\}$	$C_3'=\{5\}$	$C_2'=\{5\}$	$C_2'=\{5\}$
$C_5'=\{6\}$	$C_5'=\{4,6\}$	$C_5'=\{6,8\}$	$C_5'=\{4,6,8\}$
$C_6=\{3,4,7\}$	$C_6'=\{3,7\}$	$C_6=\{3,4,7\}$	$C_6'=\{3,7\}$
S_{11} (6 bits)	S_{12} (7 bits)	S_{13} (7 bits)	S_{14} (7 bits)
$C_1'=\{2,8\}$	$C_1'=\{2,8\}$	$C_1'=\{2\}$	$C_1'=\{2\}$
$C_3'=\{1,5\}$	$C_3'=\{1,5\}$	$C_3'=\{1,5\}$	$C_3'=\{1,5\}$
$C_5'=\{6\}$	$C_5'=\{4,6\}$	$C_5'=\{6,8\}$	$C_5'=\{4,6,8\}$
$C_6=\{3,4,7\}$	$C_6'=\{3,7\}$	$C_6=\{3,4,7\}$	$C_6'=\{3,7\}$
S_{15} (7 bits)	S_{16} (7 bits)	S_{17} (7 bits)	S_{18} (7 bits)

Solution 1.

$C_1=\{1,2,8\}$	$C_1=\{1,2,8\}$	$C_1=\{1,2,8\}$	$C_1=\{1,2,8\}$
$C_4'=\{3,4,5\}$	$C_4'=\{4,5\}$	$C_4'=\{3,5\}$	$C_4'=\{3,5\}$
$C_5^r=\{6\}$	$C_5'=\{6\}$	$C_5'=\{6\}$	$C_5'=\{4,6\}$
$C_6'=\{7\}$	$C_6'=\{3,7\}$	$C_6'=\{4,7\}$	$C_6'=\{7\}$
S_{21} (6 bits)	S_{22} (7 bits)	S_{23} (7 bits)	S_{24} (7 bits)
$C_1'=\{1,2\}$	$C_1'=\{1,2\}$	$C_1'=\{1,2\}$	$C_1'=\{1,2\}$
$C_4=\{3,4,5,8\}$	$C_4'=\{4,5,8\}$	$C_4'=\{3,5,8\}$	$C_4'=\{3,5,8\}$
$C_5'=\{6\}$	$C_5'=\{6\}$	$C_5'=\{6\}$	$C_5'=\{4,6\}$
$C_6'=\{7\}$	$C_6'=\{3,7\}$	$C_6'=\{4,7\}$	$C_6'=\{7\}$
S_{25} (7 bits)	S_{26} (7 bits)	S_{27} (7 bits)	S_{28} (7 bits)

Solution 2.

languages such as FORTRAN and PASCAL. This scheme is not suitable, however, since it fails to highlight potentially parallel MOs. Accordingly, we wish to explicitly indicate sequencing only when it is necessary. Sequencing between MOs is necessitated when any one of three relations below hold between the MOs:

1. An MO m_j is *data-dependent* on MO m_i if m_i produces data required by m_j.
2. An MO m_i is *data-antidependent* on MO m_j if m_i destroys data required by m_j.
3. Finally, an MO m_i *conflicts* with MO m_j if m_i and m_j cannot execute in the same MI.

Traditionally, a *data-dependency graph* for a basic block of MOs is defined to be a directed graph whose nodes are the set of MOs; in addition, an edge is directed from m_i to m_j if m_j is data-dependent on m_i, an edge is directed from m_j to m_i if m_i is data-antidependent on m_j, and there are no edges otherwise. Note that the conflict relation is determined by the microprogrammable machine rather than the microcode and is not represented in a data-dependency graph.

Consider, for example, the basic block of MOs in figure 2-25. A data-dependency graph for this basic block is given in figure 2-26a. Note that an edge in the illustration depicts a data dependency unless the edge is labeled with an asterisk (*), in which case it represents a data antidependency. Data-dependency representations are not, in general, unique. This is due in part to the presence of antidependent edges. In our example, we can also construct the data-dependency graph shown in figure 2-26b from the basic block in figure 2-25, assuming the value of C assigned to F in figure 2-25 is not read by a subsequent MO.

Figure 2-25. Sample program.

1. $A \leftarrow B$

2. $C \leftarrow A$

3. $E \leftarrow A$

4. $F \leftarrow C$

5. $C \leftarrow G$

6. $H \leftarrow C$

7. $I \leftarrow H$

Figure 2-26. Data-dependency graphs for the program in figure 2-25.

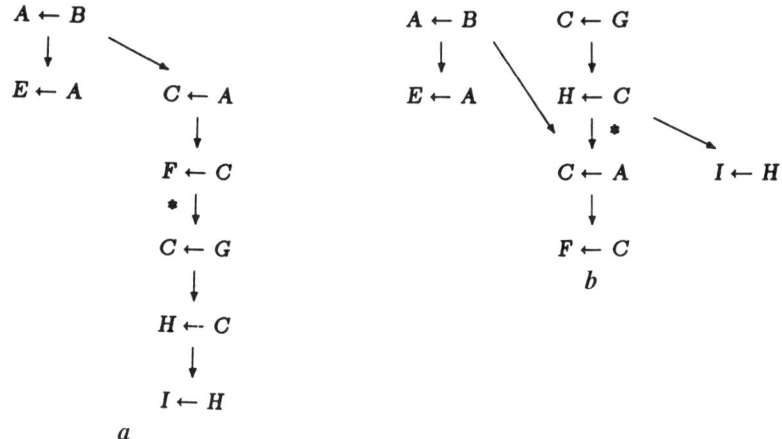

In the world of compaction, this nonuniqueness property is important, since most compaction algorithms do not consider alternate representations of a data-dependency graph supplied as input, and the choice of data-dependency graph can profoundly influence the effect of compaction (Vegdahl 1982). If we simply look at the graph D_1 in figure 2-26a and D_2 in figure 2-26b, we note that the longest path in D_1 is five edges long, whereas the longest path in D_2 is only three edges long. Any maximal-length path in a data-dependency graph is called a *critical path*, and the length of the critical path plus one is a lower bound on the number of MIs in any compacted microprogram for that graph.[5] Thus, the best we could hope for from D_1 would be a six MI microprogram, whereas D_2 might yield a four MI microprogram. This is ultimately determined by the conflict relation.

Given the definition of the three sequencing relations, we can formally define the *local microcode compaction problem* to be that of finding any minimal-length sequence of MIs for a basic block of MOs (M) over all data-dependency-graph representations of the block $\{D_1,\ldots,D_k\}$ such that for some D_m, $1 \leq m \leq k$,

1. No conflicting MOs are members of a common MI in M
2. MO m_j is placed in a later MI of M than MO m_i whenever there is a path in D_m directed from m_i to m_j

---

5. Strictly speaking, this is true of monophase implementations but is not generally true for polyphase implementations. However, this point is peripheral to the immediate discussion, so we will assume, for convenience, a monophase implementation.

Vegdahl suggests the related problem obtained by restricting the search to a single data-dependency graph be called the *classical microcode compaction problem*, since this assumption was made in many of the early algorithms (Vegdahl 1982).

Many algorithms for solving the local compaction problem have appeared in the literature. Some are exhaustive and guarantee the computation of an optimal solution but are generally too slow to use in practice, owing, again, to the NP-hard property of the local microcode compaction problem (DeWitt 1976). Examples can be found in two readings (Astopas and Plukas 1971; Yau, Schowe, and Tsuchiya 1974). Approximation algorithms that are efficient and tend to produce optimal solutions (rather than guarantee them) are the choices of practice. Examples of these include the algorithms found in other readings (Dasgupta and Tartar 1976; Tsuchiya and Gonzalez 1974; Wood 1979a; Gosling 1981).

For the sake of example, we will overview the method given in the second approximation solution, called the *critical-path partitioning algorithm*. The motivation behind critical-path methods is that the ith MO on any critical path must be placed in the ith MI if a minimal-length solution is to be obtained under ideal conflict-relation conditions. Thus, we place the *critical* MOs first in their critical positions, moving MOs when needed to comply with resource conflicts, and repeat the process for the remaining noncritical MOs.

We illustrate this method with an example. Assume the resource-conflict relation given in figure 2-27, and consider the compaction of D_1 in figure 2-26a. There is only one critical path in D_1; viz. $<m_1, m_2, m_4, m_5, m_6, m_7>$. Thus, the first iteration of the algorithm produces the MI placement shown in figure 2-28a. There is only one remaining noncritical MO, m_3.

The noncritical MOs are placed in their *earliest possible partition*; that is, the earliest MI placement that does not violate any of the three relations. For m_3, the earliest possible partition corresponds to MI (3). Thus, the compacted microcode for D_1 is given in figure 2-28b.

To demonstrate the importance of compacting from the "right" data-dependency graph, consider the compaction of D_2 in figure 2-26b using the same conflict relation given in figure 2-27. Again, there is only one critical path; viz. $<m_5, m_6, m_2, m_4>$. The placement of these critical MOs yields the MI placement shown in figure 2-29a. The remaining noncritical MOs are m_1, m_3, and m_7.

Figure 2-27. Sample conflict relation for MOs of the program given in figure 2-25.

$\{conflict(A \leftarrow B, H \leftarrow C), conflict(E \leftarrow A, H \leftarrow C), conflict(C \leftarrow A, I \leftarrow H)\}$

Figure 2-28. Compaction of microprogram represented in DDG of figure 2-26a: *a.* placement of critical path MOs; *b.* placement of all MOs.

MI	MO's
1	$A \leftarrow B$
2	$C \leftarrow A$
3	$F \leftarrow C$
4	$C \leftarrow G$
5	$H \leftarrow C$
6	$I \leftarrow H$

a

MI	MO's
1	$A \leftarrow B$
2	$C \leftarrow A, E \leftarrow A$
3	$F \leftarrow C$
4	$C \leftarrow G$
5	$H \leftarrow C$
6	$I \leftarrow H$

b

The earliest possible partition for m_1 is 1, since there are niether data-dependency, data antidependency, nor conflict relations with m_5. Based on the data-dependency graph, we would first attempt to place m_3 in MI(2); however, since it conflicts with m_6, which already resides in MI(2), it is placed in MI(3). Similarly, we would first attempt to place m_7 in MI(3) based on the data-dependency graph, but it conflicts with m_2, which already resides in MI(3). Thus, it is placed in MI(4). The resulting microcode is shown in figure 2-29b. Note that this solution has two fewer MIs than that computed from D_1.

Minimizing Branch Delays

In the section "Control Unit Organization" we discussed the merits of using MI prefetch to obtain overlapping phases and thus performance improvements. The

Figure 2-29. Compaction of microprogram represented in DDG of Figure 2-26b: *a.* placement of critical path MOs; *b.* placement of all MOs.

MI	MO's
1	$C \leftarrow G$
2	$H \leftarrow C$
3	$C \leftarrow A$
4	$F \leftarrow C$

a

MI	MO's
1	$C \leftarrow G, A \leftarrow B$
2	$H \leftarrow C$
3	$C \leftarrow A, E \leftarrow A$
4	$F \leftarrow C, I \leftarrow H$

b

major problem with such a scheme is the management of conditional branch MIs when the address of the next MI is not determined until the current MI has executed. While this may not seem to be a major problem, it should be noted that a survey of machine instructions executed on some architectures revealed that 25%-30% of the instructions were branches (Shustek 1977). Investigations into the nature of MIs executed on horizontal machines also reveals that a substantial percentage tend to be branches (Fisher 1979).

There are several approaches to the problem. The first is to employ additional control-unit hardware to detect the presence of a branch instruction and delay the prefetch until the address of the successor instruction is determined. While this is a fairly simple fix, it is plagued by at least two problems. One is the resulting degradation in processor performance. Experiments reported by Riseman and Foster (1972) indicate that such a scheme virtually nullifies the potential performance improvements that motivated the integration of prefetching. Another problem is the desire to simplify control units for VLSI implementations consistent with the *reduced instruction set computer* (RISC) theme. For example, neither the Berkeley RISC machine (Patterson and Sequin 1981) nor the Stanford MIPS machine (Hennessy et al. 1982) possesses hardware detection and delay hardware.

The second approach is to organize the instructions in such a way as to preserve functional integrity and minimize the branch delays. Algorithms for performing such optimizations can be performed automatically on handwritten microcode or integrated as the final phase of a compiler. We will describe some of the optimization methods proposed by Gross and Hennessy (1982). As the techniques apply to both MI prefetch and the more general problem of pipelined instruction-stream execution, we will talk in more general terms of the problem and its solution.

First, the problem centers around the execution of branch instructions. For our purposes, a *branch instruction* can be interpreted as any instruction that alters the flow of program control. Examples include conventional conditional and unconditional branches, as well as the more exotic TRAP (supervisor-call) instructions. Associated with each branch in a pipelined machine is the number of instructions sequentially following the branch that are executed regardless of whether the branch is taken.

More precisely, a branch instruction at location b to location L is a *delayed branch* with delay n if the instructions at locations $b, b + 1, \ldots, b + n, L$ are executed whenever the branch is taken. For example, consider the instruction sequence shown in figure 2-30. If instruction (3) is a delayed branch with delay 1, then each time the branch is taken the machine executes instruction sequence 1,2,3,4,7. Thus, if the value of variable B is equal to that of Q on entrance to instruction (1), the execution of the sequence assigns X the value $q + 1$, where q is the initial value of variable Q.

The simple solution to masking the undesirable effects of prefetch is to place n no-op instructions after each branch of delay n. This is unacceptable for two reasons. The first is the performance degradation analogous to that resulting from the use of detection and delay hardware. The second is the increased memory requirements for the storage of the no-op instructions.

There are several effective *code motion* optimization techniques that are conditionally applicable. Suppose we have a branch of delay n. The first technique is to move the branch instruction to immediately precede the n instructions that precede the branch. This can be very effective, but it is only applicable when none of the preceding n instructions affect the determination of the branch condition. In general, we can move the branch instruction to immediately precede the k instructions that precede the branch, where k is the maximal number of preceding instructions that have no effect on the branch condition, $1 \leq k \leq n$.

When the first optimization can be used to move only $k < n$ instructions, there are two other possible techniques to consider. The second optimization is the duplication of the first n instructions beginning at the given target address of the branch, additionally placed immediately after the branch instruction, and the modification of the target address of the branch to that which immediately follows the original n instructions. This optimization can be performed only when the target address is known (e.g., the target address for a trap call is generally not known), and none of the n instructions are data-antidependent on any of the instructions that are executed when the branch is not executed. This second optimization requires additional space for the duplication of the instructions but saves time when the branch is taken.

Similarly, we can simply place the n instructions that are executed when the branch is not taken immediately after the branch. Again, this optimization can be performed only when the address of the instructions executed when the branch is not taken is known, which is typically the case, and none of the n instructions are data-antidependent on any of the instructions that are executed when the branch is taken. This third optimization requires no additional space and saves time only when the branch is not taken.

To illustrate these optimizations, we return to the code sequence given in figure 2-30. If instruction (3) had a branch delay of one, we could perform the first optimization and move the branch to the place between instructions (1) and (2), as shown in figure 2-31. This is ideal, since it requires no additional space and completely masks the branch delay.

Suppose instead that the branch delay was two. Then the first optimization could be used as above, but there would still remain a delay of one. In this case, the second optimization is applicable, allowing for the duplication of instruction (7), its placement between instructions (2) and (4), and the modification of the target branch address to that which immediately follows

Figure 2-30. Sample program.

1. $A \leftarrow B$
2. $B \leftarrow B - 1$
3. if $A = Q$ then goto $L1$
4. $Q \leftarrow Q + 1$
5. $D \leftarrow E$
6. $E \leftarrow F$
7. $L1: X \leftarrow Q$

---

the original instruction (7). The result is shown in figure 2-32. Note that we were able to completely mask out the delay but incurred the cost of the space for one additional instruction.

ALTERNATIVE ROLES OF MICROPROGRAMMING

Microprogramming is applied in many ways other than the interpretation of machine-language instructions. In this section we will discuss four important roles of microprogramming: machine emulation, directly executable languages, dynamic microprogramming, and vertical migration of system functions. As each of these is covered in detail in subsequent chapters, the discussions will be brief.

Figure 2-31. Transformation of sample program of figure 2-30 assuming branch delay of 1.

1. $A \leftarrow B$
3. if $A = Q$ then goto $L1$
2. $B \leftarrow B - 1$
4. $Q \leftarrow Q + 1$
5. $D \leftarrow E$
6. $E \leftarrow F$
7. $L1: X \leftarrow Q$

Figure 2-32. Transformation of sample program in figure 2-30 assuming branch delay of 2.

1. $A \leftarrow B$
3. if $A = Q$ then goto $L2$
2. $B \leftarrow B - 1$
7. $X \leftarrow Q$
4. $Q \leftarrow Q + 1$
5. $D \leftarrow E$
6. $E \leftarrow F$
7. $L1: X \leftarrow Q$
8. $L2:$

Machine Emulation

The concept of machine emulation (hereafter, simply *emulation*) has changed over the last twenty years. In the early years of microprogramming, emulation was associated with the microcode in a control store. As Rosin stated in his article entitled "Contemporary Concepts in Microprogramming and Emulation": "Throughout this paper we use the term 'emulator' to describe a complete set of microprograms which, when embedded in a control store, define a machine" (Rosin 1969, 197). An even earlier use of the term "emulator" that reflects the use of microprogramming in the realization of the IBM System/360 series machines described an emulator as "a package that includes both special hardware and a complementary set of software" (Tucker 1965, 753).

The concepts of *emulation* and *interpretation* were distinguished by Rosin (1969), with the latter connoting the execution of machine instructions. This distinction has seemed to prevail and causes some confusion. Flynn correctly points out that the notions of emulation and interpretation are equivalent and the distinction based on the execution of microinstructions vs. machine instructions is arbitrary (Flynn 1975).

More recently, the emulator has come to be associated with general-purpose architectures that are user-microprogrammable. This is reflected in Tredennick's categorization of "microprogramming cultures" (Tredennick 1982). Specifically, he distinguishes the concept of a *microprogrammed machine* endemic to the *commercial machine culture*, in which the machine is designed to support one architecture, from the *microprogrammable machine* of the *microprogrammable machine culture*, which is designed to support many architectures. The machine that executes the microprograms (i.e., the microprogrammable machine) is usually called the *host machine*, and the machine defined by the emulator is usually called the *image machine* or *target machine*.

Contemporary emulation is usually considered to involve the use of microprogramming to realize a machine's architecture on a (distinct) microprogrammable machine (Banerji and Raymond 1982). However, there is still no precise, universally accepted definition of the term.

Directly Executable Languages

In general, there is considerable difference between the statements of a high-level algorithmic language and the instructions of a computing machine. This is due to the distinct goals of simplifying the programming process and improving the performance of program execution. The result of trying to simultaneously satisfy both goals is a system with an effective programming environment and high-speed machine instructions. However, the problem of *translating* source programs into efficient image-machine representations is most likely complex and computationally costly.

The advantage of reducing the *semantic gap* between source language and image-machine language is therefore the simplification of the compilation process. The *directly executable language* (DEL) strategy is to make the image-machine representation as similar as possible to a selected source language. Ideally, there will be a one-to-one correspondence between the source-program objects and their image-machine counterparts.

The representation of a source program is influenced by its property of transparency. Flynn (1980) defines "transparency" to be a property of the host-machine/image-machine correspondence in which the state transitions of both the image and host machines occur in the same order, and the image machine states are always preserved at the end of an image instruction execution (implying that the result of an image-machine action must be reflected in the image-machine memory vis à vis a component of the host-machine memory that is not part of the image-machine memory). Thus, transparency provides the advantages of synchronization and debugging.

The design of a DEL and the underlying machine poses a formidable problem that involves issues of language design, architectural design, and microprogramming (should the image instructions be emulated by microprograms). From the engineering-economy standpoint, the DEL design problem weighs tradeoffs between compilation and direct execution.

A contemporary and controversial issue centers around the benefits and shortfalls of RISC machines, which contain a small and rather simple repertoire of image instructions. The contention of RISC proponents is that optimizing compilers cannot effectively exploit large, elaborate instruction sets, and thus the image-machine instruction set should be simplified to improve the efficiency of image-instruction execution. To achieve this efficiency, the image and host instruction sets are "unified" by making the host MIs appear as normal image-level instructions (Hennessy et al. 1982). This is possible due to the simplicity of the instructions. Thus, we have the DEL concept applied one level lower in the machine hierarchy.

Dynamic Microprogramming

With the advent of fast storage technologies, it became possible to design systems with writable control stores. Since techniques for the production of microcode have not kept pace, it is not possible to evaluate this development in a fair manner. But the concept of dynamic microprogramming, in which the microprograms in the control store can be modified dynamically, has several potential benefits and pitfalls.

Among the advantages cited for dynamic microprogramming, one of the earliest was the ability to customize the instruction set of the image machine in a dynamic manner (Tucker 1967). Taking this concept one step further, one could easily visualize systems in which a high-level language such as FORTRAN or COBOL could be interpreted using microprograms. Programs in these languages would be compiled into high-level machine instructions that reflect the semantics of these languages more closely than traditional instruction sets. Such systems could offer tremendous improvements in performance when compared with traditional compilation methods. Compilers for these languages could themselves be microprogrammed in order to provide better performance during compilation. Weber demonstrated such a compiler for the language EULER (Weber 1967). Other system functions would also then become targets for such improvement. A discussion of this issue appears in the next section on vertical migration.

Flynn (1975) predicted that dynamic microprogramming would cause radical changes in computer architectures, resulting in the simplifications of machine instruction sets and the transfer of responsibility for dealing with complexity to the programmer or to the compiler. Recent developments in RISC architectures (Patterson and Sequin 1981; Hennessy et al. 1982) seem to support this view.

From the perspective of the IBM System/360 architects, microprogramming was only a way of implementing a common instruction set on different machines. The microprogrammability of these machines was transparent to its users. Allowing users access to the control store would result in considerable overhead in monitoring the use of this resource (Husson 1970; Rosin 1969). Above all, security and data integrity would become primary concerns if such access were permitted to occur. Presumably, similar constructs for operating systems could be adapted to the microprogramming environment for the sake of protection, but the overhead cost might be too high to justify such an approach.

Vertical Migration

Computer systems can be thought of as layered multilevel systems, with hardware the lowest level and application programs the highest level. There may be several intervening levels, such as the firmware level and the various levels in a hierarchically structured operating system. Each level provides primitives that can be used at the same level or at higher levels. Such a decomposition into levels facilitates the design and maintenance of complex systems.

One of the problems with implementing systems in such a hierarchical fashion is that there is a certain amount of overhead associated with each level in order to provide sufficient generality for higher levels. A program written at a lower level in the hierarchy usually performs better than the same program written at a higher level. Some paths in programs at a certain level may be used with sufficient frequency that it may be cost-effective to implement that path at a lower level in the hierarchy. This kind of movement of programs from higher to lower levels in the hierarchy is known as *vertical migration* (Heller and van Dam 1981; Stockenburg and van Dam 1978).

The performance improvement in primitives that migrate to lower levels could sometimes be measured in orders of magnitude, and this may be reflected in improvements of a factor of two in application programs (Stockenburg and van Dam 1978; Stankovic 1981; Stankovic 1982). Selecting the candidates for migration is not an easy task. Frequency of execution is not the only criterion for selection. Other factors such as locality of data reference also have to be considered, and algorithms and data structures frequently have to be modified in order to increase potential gains.

Since firmware constitutes the lowest level of programmability, migrations to microcode usually give the best performance improvement. This migration to firmware of primitives from higher levels constitutes a form of architecture synthesis. In *manual architecture synthesis* (Stockenburg and van Dam 1978), the programmer manually recodes the primitives in microcode, whereas in *heuristic architecture synthesis* (Winner and Carter 1983; Abd-Alla and Karlgaard 1974) the transformation to microcode is done by the system. However, with the use of writable control stores, problems of security and data integrity are again introduced, as they are in dynamic microprogramming.

SUMMARY

Since its inception, the discipline of microprogramming has undergone several changes, both drastic and evolutionary. Architecture emulation was the application that launched the discipline in the commercial sphere. Although new applications, such as vertical migration and directly executable languages, have come to the forefront, machine-architecture emulation remains the primary one.

Since microprograms are stored in and are executed out of a control store, evolution of the discipline has depended heavily on the technology of high-speed memories. Even though significant advancements have been made in this area, efficiency considerations require the use of techniques for minimizing the dimensions of the control store.

Issues similar to those in software engineering have crept into firmware engineering as well. Since reliability and efficiency are even more critical in this context, several tools have been proposed and implemented for the development of firmware. High-level languages for microprogramming (Davidson 1983; Dasgupta 1980) and other firmware tools (Davidson and Shriver 1980) have alleviated some of the problems of developing reliable microcode, but the accomplishments have still lagged behind those of software engineering.

REFERENCES

Abd-Alla, A.M., and Karlgaard, D.C. 1974. "Heuristic Synthesis of Microprogrammed Computer Architecture." *IEEE Transactions on Computers*, C-23(8):802–7.

Aho, A.V., and Johnson, S.C. 1976. "Optimal Code Generation for Expression Trees." *Journal of the ACM*, 23(3):488–501.

Aho, A.V., and Ullman, J.D. 1977. *Principles of Compiler Design.* Reading, MA: Addison-Wesley.

Andrews, M. 1980. *Principles of Firmware Engineering in Microprogram Control.* Potomac, MD: Computer Science Press.

Astopas, F., and Plukas, K.I. 1971. "Method for Minimizing Computer Microprograms." *Automatic Control*, 5(4):10–16.

Baba, T, and Hagiwara, H. 1981. "The MPG System: a Machine-independent Efficient Microprogram Generator." *IEEE Transactions on Computers*, C-30(6):373–95.

Baer, J.-L., and Koyama, B. 1979. "On the Minimization of the Width of the Control Memory of Microprogrammed Processors." *IEEE Transactions on Computers*, C-28(4):310–16.

Banerji, D.K., and Raymond, J. 1982. *Elements of Microprogramming.* Englewood Cliffs, NJ: Prentice-Hall.

Das, S.R.; Banerji, D.K.; and Chattopadhyay, A. 1973. "On Control Memory Minimization in Microprogrammed Digital Computers." *IEEE Transactions on Computers*, C-22(9):845–48.

Dasgupta, S. 1977. "Parallelism in Loop-free Microprograms." In *Information Processing 77*, edited by B. Gilchrist. Amsterdam: North-Holland.

———. 1979. "The Organization of Microprogram Stores." *Computing Surveys*, 11(1):39–65.

———. 1980. "Some Aspects of High-level Microprogramming." *ACM Computing Surveys*, 12(3):295–324.

———. 1984. *The Design and Description of Computer Architectures*. New York: Wiley-Interscience.

Dasgupta, S., and Tartar, J. 1975. "On the Minimization of Control Memories." *Information Processing Letters*, 3(3):71–74.

———. 1976. "The Identification of Maximal Parallelism in Straight-line Microprograms." *IEEE Transactions on Computers*, C-25(10)986–92.

Davidson, S. 1983. "High-level Microprogramming—Current Usage, Future Prospects." *Proceedings of the 16th Microprogramming Workshop*: 193–200. Downingtown, PA: IEEE Computer Society Press.

Davidson, S., and Shriver, B.D. 1980. "Firmware Engineering: An extensive update." *Proceedings of the IFIP, TC-10 Conference on Microprogramming, Firmware, and Restructurable Hardware*: 1–36. Amsterdam: North-Holland.

DeWitt, D.J. 1976. "A Machine-Independent Approach to the Production of Optimal Horizontal Microcode." Ph.D. diss., Department of Computer and Communication Sciences, University of Michigan.

Digital Equipment. 1979. *KA-780 Central Processor Technical Description Manual*. Maynard, MA: Digital Equipment Corporation.

Fisher, J.A. 1979. "The Optimization of Horizontal Microcode Within and Beyond Basic Blocks: An Application of Processor Scheduling." Ph.D. diss., Courant Institute of Mathematical Sciences, New York University.

———. 1981. "Trace Scheduling: a Technique for Global Microcode Compaction." *IEEE Transactions on Computers*, C-30(7):478–90.

Flynn, M. J. 1975. "Interpretation, microprogramming, and control." In *Introduction to Computer Architecture*, edited by H.S. Stone, 432–472. Palo Alto, CA: Scientific Research Associates.

———. 1980. "Directions and Issues in Architecture and Language." *IEEE Computer*, 13(10):5–26.

Gosling, J. 1981. "Some Issues and Techniques for Microcode Compilers." Unpublished report. See Vegdahl (1982) for a discussion of this report.

Grasselli, A., and Montanari, U. 1970. "On the Minimization of Read-only Memories in Microprogrammed Digital Computers." *IEEE Transactions on Computers*, C-19(11):1111–14.

Gross, T.R., and Hennessy, J.L. 1982. "Optimizing branch delays." *Proceedings of the 15th Microprogramming Workshop*: 114–20. Palo Alto, CA: IEEE Computer Society Press.

Hecht, M.S. 1977. *Flow Analysis of Computer Programs*. New York: North-Holland.

Heller, A., and van Dam, A. 1981. "Vertical and Outboard Migration—a Progress Report." *AFIPS National Computer Conference*: 69–74. Arlington, VA: AFIPS Press.

Hennessy, J.; Jouppi, N.; Przybylski, S.; Rowen, C.; Gross, T.; Baskett, F.; and Gill, J. 1982. "MIPS: a Microprocessor Architecture." *Proceedings of the 15th Microprogramming Workshop*: 17–22. Palo Alto, CA: IEEE Computer Society Press.

Husson, S.S. 1970. *Microprogramming: Principles and Practices*. Englewood Cliffs, NJ: Prentice-Hall.

Interdata. 1973. *Dynamic Control Store Manual* (#29-308R02). Oceanport, NJ: Interdata Corporation.

Jayasri, T., and Basu, D. 1976. "An Approach to Organizing Micro-instructions which Minimizes the Width of Control Store Words." *IEEE Transactions on Computers*, C-25(5):514–21.

Kohavi, Z. 1970. *Switching and Finite Automata Theory*. New York: McGraw-Hill.

Kou, L. 1977. "On Live-dead Analysis for Global Data Flow Problems." *Journal of the ACM*, 24(3):473–83.

Landskov, D.; Davidson, S.; Shriver, B.D.; and Mallett, P.W. 1980. "Local Microcode Compaction Techniques." *ACM Computing Surveys* 12(3): 261–94.

Ma, P-Y.R., and Lewis, T. 1981. "On the Design of a Microcode Compiler for a Machine-independent High-level Language." *IEEE Transactions on Software Engineering*, SE-7(3):261–73.

Marwedel, P. 1984. "A Retargetable Compiler for a High-level Microprogramming Language." *Proceedings of the 17th Microprogramming Workshop*: 267–74. New Orleans, LA: IEEE Computer Society Press.

Matheson, W.G. 1974. "User Microprogrammability in the HP-21MX Minicomputer." *Proceedings of the 7th Microprogramming Workshop*: 168–77. Palo Alto, CA: IEEE Computer Society Press.

Microdata. 1974. *Micro 32/S Computer Reference Manual*. Irvine, CA: Microdata Corporation.

Muchnick, S.S., and Jones, N.D., eds. 1981. *Program Flow Analysis: Theory and Practice*. Englewood Cliffs, NJ: Prentice-Hall.

Mueller, R.A. 1984. *Automated Microcode Synthesis*. Ann Arbor, MI: UMI Research Press.

Nanodata. 1974. *QM-1 Hardware Level User's Manual*. 2d ed. Williamsville, NY: Nanodata Corporation.

Patterson, D.A., and Sequin, C.H. 1981. "RISC-1: a Reduced Instruction Set VLSI Computer." *Proceedings of the 8th Annual Symposium on Computer Architecture*: 443–58, Minneapolis, MN: IEEE Computer Society Press.

Poe, M.D. 1980. "Heuristics for the Global Optimization of Microprograms." *Proceedings of the 13th Microprogramming Workshop*: 13–22. Colorado Springs, CO: IEEE Computer Society Press.

Ramamoorthy, C.V., and Tsuchiya, M. 1970. "A Study of User Microprogrammable Computers." *Proceedings of the Spring Joint Computer Conference*: 165–81. Montvale, NJ: AFIPS Press.

Rao, C.D.V.P., and Biswas, N.N. 1983. "On the Minimization of Wordwidth in the Control Memory of a Microprogrammed Digital Computer." *IEEE Transactions on Computers*, C-32(9):863–68.

Reigel, E.W.; Faber, U.; and Fisher, D.A. 1972. "The Interpreter—a Microprogrammable Building Block System." *Proceedings of the Spring Joint Computer Conference*: 705–23, Montvale, NJ: AFIPS Press.

Riseman, E.M., and Foster, C.C. 1972. "The Inhibition of Potential Parallelism by Conditional Jumps." *IEEE Transactions on Computers*, C-21(12):1405–11.

Robertson, E.L. 1979. "Microcode Bit Optimization is NP-complete." *IEEE Transactions on Computers*, C-28(4):316–19.

Rosin, R.F. 1969. "Contemporary Concepts of Microprogramming and Emulation." *Computing Surveys*, 1(4):197–212.

Schwartz, S.J. 1969. "An Algorithm for Minimizing Read-only Memories for Machine Control." *Proceedings of the 10th IEEE Symposium on Switching and Automata Theory*: 28–33, New York: IEEE Press.

Sethi, R., and Ullman, J.D. 1970. "The Generation of Optimal Code for Arithmetic Expressions." *Journal of the ACM*, 17(4):715-28.

Sheraga, R.J., and Geiser, J.L. 1981. "Automatic Microcode Generation for Horizontally Microprogrammed Processors." *Proceedings of the 14th Microprogramming Workshop*: 154–70. Chatham, MA: IEEE Computer Society Press.

Shustek, L.J. 1977. "Analysis and Performance of Computer Instruction Sets." Ph.D. diss., Stanford University.

Standard Logic. 1973. *CASH-8 Reference Manual*. Santa Ana, CA: Standard Logic, Inc.

Stankovic, J.A. 1981. "The Types and Interactions of Vertical Migrations of Functions in Multi-level Interpretive Systems." *IEEE Transactions on Computers*, C-30(7):505–13.

―――. 1982. *Structured Systems and their Performance Improvement through Vertical Migration*. Ann Arbor, MI: UMI Research Press.

Stockenburg, J., and van Dam, A. 1978. "Vertical Migration for Performance in Layered Hardware/Firmware/Software Systems." *Computer*, 11(5):35–50.

Stone, H.S., ed. 1975. *Introduction to Computer Architecture*. Palo Alto, CA: Scientific Research Associates.

Stritter, S., and Tredennick, N. 1978. "Microprogrammed Implementation of a Single-chip Microprocessor." *Proceedings of the 11th Microprogramming Workshop*: 8–16. Pacific Grove, CA: IEEE Computer Society Press.

Tokoro, M.; Takizuka, T.; Tamura, E.; and Yamaura, I. 1978. "A Technique of Global Optimization of Microprograms." *Proceedings of the 11th Microprogramming Workshop*: 41–50. Pacific Grove, CA: IEEE Computer Society Press.

Tokoro, M.; Tamura, E.; and Takizuka, T. 1981. "Optimization of Microprograms." *IEEE Transactions on Computers*, C-30(7):491–504.

Tredennick, N. 1982. "Cultures of Microprogramming." *Proceedings of the 15th Microprogramming Workshop*: 79–83. Palo Alto, CA: IEEE Computer Society Press.

Tsuchiya, M., and Gonzalez, M.J. 1974. "An Approach to Optimization of Horizontal Microprograms." *Proceedings of the 7th Microprogramming Workshop*: 85–90. Palo Alto, CA: IEEE Computer Society Press.

Tucker, S.G. 1965. "Emulation of Large Systems." *Communications of the ACM*, 8(12):753–61.

———. 1967. "Microprogram Control for IBM System/360." *IBM Systems Journal*, 6(4):222–41.

Unger, S.H. 1969. *Asynchronous Sequential Switching Circuits*. New York: John Wiley and Sons.

Varian Data Machines. 1973. *Varian Microprogramming Guide*. Irvine, CA: Varian Data Machines Corporation.

Vegdahl, S.R. 1982. "Local Code Generation and Compaction in Optimizing Microcode Compilers." Ph.D. diss., Department of Computer Science, Carnegie-Mellon University.

Weber, H. 1967. "A Microprogrammed Implementation of EULER on IBM 360/30." *Communications of the ACM*, 10:549–58.

Wilkes, M.V. 1951. "The Best Way to Design an Automatic Calculating Machine." *Report of the Manchester University Computer Inaugural Conference*: 16–18. Manchester: Electrical Engineering Department, Manchester University.

———. 1969. "The Growth of Interest in Microprogramming: a Literature Survey." *Computing Surveys*, 1(3):139–45.

Wilner, W.T. 1972a. "Microprogramming Environment on the Burroughs B1700." *COMPCON 72 Digest of Papers*: 103–6. IEEE Press.

———. 1972b. "Burroughs B1700 Memory Utilization." *Proceedings of the Fall Joint Computer Conference*: 579–86. Montvale, NJ: AFIPS Press.

Winner, R.I., and Carter, E.M. 1983. "Toward Type-Oriented Dynamic Vertical Migration." *Proceedings of the 16th Microprogramming Workshop*: 128–39. Downingtown, PA: IEEE Computer Society Press.

Wood, W.G. 1979a. "The Computer-aided Design of Microprograms." Ph.D. diss., University of Edinburgh, Scotland.

———. 1979b. "Global Optimization of Microprograms through Modular Control Constructs." *Proceedings of the 12th Microprogramming Workshop*: 1–6. Hershey, PA: IEEE Computer Society Press.

Yau, S.S.; Schowe, A.C.; and Tsuchiya, M. 1974. "On Storage Optimization of Horizontal Microprograms." *Proceedings of the 7th Microprogramming Workshop*: 98–106. Palo Alto, CA: IEEE Computer Society Press.

three
AN ASYNCHRONOUS APPROACH TO MICROPROGRAMMING

HAROLD W. LAWSON

The development of microprogrammable computer systems has centered around the utilization of synchronous logic, that is, the functional hardware is controlled in fixed-length time increments via a central clock. For simple microprogrammable computers this approach is manageable; however, as complexity of the microarchitecture increases, especially with increased attempts to achieve parallelism, the synchronous approach leads to several undesirable properties. Performance becomes tied to worst-case logic sequences, the structure becomes rigid (not easy to extend), and complexity of utilization is passed on to the microprogrammer.

During the first few years of the 1970s, a commercial product was developed in which an asynchronous approach for the microarchitecture was utilized. This microarchitecture, called the FCPU (F for flexible), was used as the CPU for the Swedish manufacturer DataSaab's D23 Computer System. Several advantages were obtained over conventional synchronous solutions to microprogrammable architectures. These ideas, while appropriate at that time, are even more appropriate in relationship to the use of the highly integrated circuits of today and tomorrow. The purpose of this chapter is to present the motivations for and the realization of the DataSaab FCPU as an asynchronous approach to microarchitecture, as well as to indicate the significance of asynchronous control for future integrated-circuit design.

INTRODUCTION

The original reason Wilkes (1951) considered the use of microprogramming was to provide an orderly means of designing the control section of a digital computer. After relatively little use in the 1950s, microprogramming became an important method for realizing compatible instruction sets among several different central processing units and providing for the emulation of past instruction repertoires on new central-processing-unit hardware (Tucker 1967).

The role of microprogramming then expanded to include, along with the above motivations, the use of microprogrammed processors as *adaptable architecture components*. That is, the processor can be used to accelerate the performance of key system and application software. Thus, it can be used to implement new instruction repertoires that contain features such as flexible addressing mechanisms, protection mechanisms, tailored instructions for programming-language translation and execution, and special data-structure processing instructions for vectors, queues, stacks, and the like. Several of these potential uses of future microprogrammed processors were pointed out at an early stage by various authors (Opler 1967; Wilkes 1969; Rakosi 1969; Husson 1970), and in particular several papers appeared describing the use of microprogrammed processors for the implementation of programming languages (Weber 1967; Melbourne and Pugmire 1965; Lawson 1968; McKeeman 1967).

These additional roles of microprogramming placed new demands on the design of central processing units. While some work had been done on these new directions of programming, it proceeded primarily with processors that were not designed with these future goals in mind. Both the hardware and the microprogramming-language tools were not adequate for convenient implementation of these new uses of microprogramming. The pioneering work in satisfying these new demands culminated in the design and implementation of the Standard Computer MLP-900 (Lawson and Smith 1971). These new directions were pursued also in the design of the QM-1 processor (QM-1). Several manufacturers, realizing the importance of these new directions as well as their link to the past (emulation), designed and developed more general microprocessors (*Computer Decisions* 1973; Wilner 1972). It was hoped that the design, implementation, and use of digital computers was finally moving in the direction of solving computation problems by addressing them with appropriate levels of implementation techniques rather than with expensive, complex hardware and software.

The FCPU described in this chapter represented another step forward in the design and utilization of processors for meeting past as well as future demands. Much of this presentation may seem like a defense of the thesis that the FCPU contained the appropriate architectural properties for satisfying the goals. It is intended to be such a discussion so that the reader can understand the *why*, not just the *what* and *how*, of the processor architecture. This presentation first considers the global architecture, microinstruction-processing strategy, and the rationale of the global design decisions. Next, each of the functional units is described, and the physical realization is considered. The properties of the high-level microprogramming language are discussed, and examples are presented that illustrate important applications of the microprogrammed processor. Finally, the project-design, development, testing, production, and maintenance aspects are reviewed. After the FCPU presentation, some implications of the architecture for future architectures, particularly in the context of VLSI structures, are considered.

In this chapter, reference is made to FCPU1, which was the first and only version of the FCPU to be implemented. In this version, some original FCPU facilities were excluded or included but in a subset form. The FCPU1 was used primarily as the CPU of the Swedish DataSaab D23 System. In this role, the full features of the FCPU were not required. However, since upward compatibility of design and high-level microprogram language were maintained, all facilities were planned for future versions.

GLOBAL ARCHITECTURE

A block diagram of the FCPU appears in figure 3-1. The processor is organized into three separate asynchronous parts, namely, the field access unit (FU), arithmetic unit (AU), and control unit (CU). The control unit contains the control storage and some *variable* hardware for accelerating performance of particular target systems. Communication between the units is handled primarily by passing register-width (64-bit) values from a sending unit to the TFR (to-and-from register) of another unit. This technique is very similar to that discussed by Dijkstra (1968) for process synchronization. Each unit contains eight TFR registers for inputs. Four of the registers are supplied by outputs from one of the units and the other four from the other unit. For example, FUTFR 0-3 are supplied from the AU and FUTFR 4-7 are supplied from the CU. These particular register assignments are indicated in figure 3-2.

The microinstructions for the three units contain fields that address the TFR registers as inputs and outputs. These registers are therefore in the register address space of each respective unit. Associated with each register is a *valid/invalid* switch. This switch is set to valid when a value is written into the register and invalid when a value is read from the register. Therefore, one level of communication exists for cooperation between the units. That is, after the register is set to valid, the next read of the register sets it to invalid. A read of a register that is invalid stalls the reading unit until the register becomes valid

Figure 3-1. Block diagram of the FCPU.

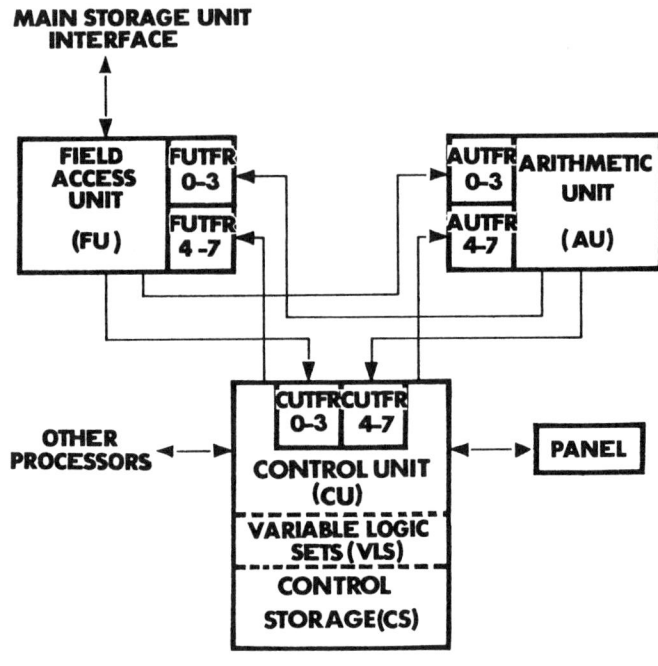

(that is, produced). A write of a register that is valid stalls the writing unit until the register becomes invalid (that is, consumed). The CU contains a time-monitoring function to avoid deadlocks resulting from machine errors or faulty microprograms.

The functions performed by the various units shown in figure 3-1 are summarized below.

Field Access Unit

The field access unit is designed to interface with a main storage or main storage processor (such as an associative register-address translation). The unit is equipped to handle *logical storage operations*. That is, a storage operation involves a word address, bit address, and bit length. The FU normally performs the operations, leaving read results in a TFR register of the AU or CU and processing write values that have been delivered from the AU or CU from a TFR register. The maximum length of a logical storage operation is 64 bits,

Figure 3-2. TFR register assignment.

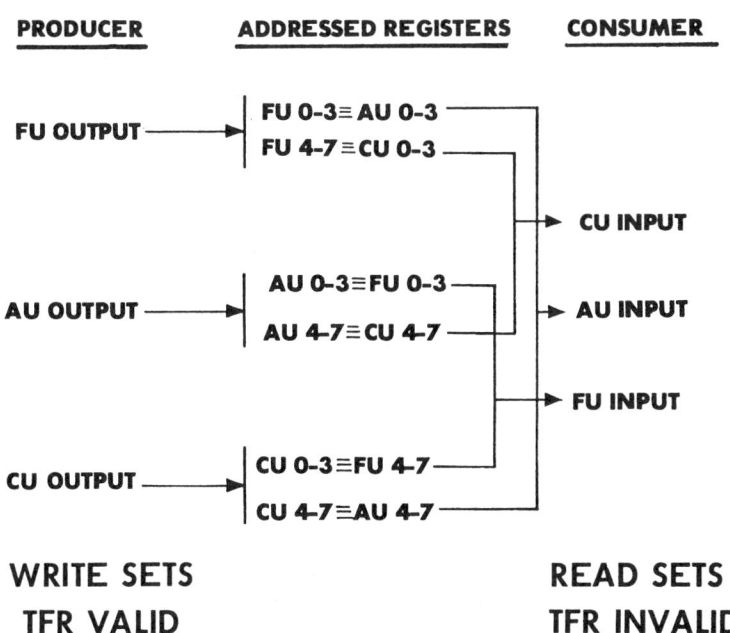

with the FU handling all the field extraction, insertion, and skewing between accessed physical cells.

Arithmetic Unit

The arithmetic unit contains a set of 16 (64-bit) general-purpose registers that, along with the AU TFR registers, can be used as the inputs for operations performed in the AU. Outputs produced can be routed to a general register or the TFR registers of the FU or CU. A maximum of eight processing modules can be accommodated in the AU. Each module contains its own logic for terminating its processing activities. That is, the execution time for each module is variable. The AU contains three standard modules. These modules are the MOM (move module) for fast register transfers, the SAM (shift and mask module) for high-speed shifting and bit field manipulation, and the ADM (adder module), which provides logical and arithmetic operations on binary and decimal values. The ability to incorporate new processing functions in the AU is an important property of the FCPU architecture.

Control Unit

The control unit accesses microinstructions from the read/write control storage (CS). It determines the class of microinstruction, prepares operations, and routes the microinstructions to the appropriate units (including the control unit itself). Since the units are run asynchronously (that is, all units can be active at the same time), the CU can prepare microinstructions on a streaming basis, as discussed in the next section.

The CU contains counting registers for controlling iterative operations and status flip-flops for maintaining the state of the FCPU and target systems. Real-time and interval clocks are provided in the CU. Facilities are provided for the stacking of return locations for microprogrammed subroutines and for the processing of interrupts.

Up to four variable logic sets (VLS) can be accommodated in the CU to provide special-purpose functions for critical operations of the implemented target languages. It is through the VLS structure that hardware adaptability is accomplished. The VLS for a particular language is normally designed to accelerate target-instruction decomposition. The VLS can also be used to modify parts of a microinstruction prior to its execution. That is, register or flip-flop addresses, immediate values, and the like can be supplied from other sources prior to the execution of a microinstruction. The current VLS is selected by two bits in an MPS (microprogram-status register).

The FCPU contains a local maintenance and debugging panel. Communication with this alphanumeric display panel can be microprogrammed to provide for target-language-oriented and special-purpose displays as well as for manual control. The CPU can also be connected to other processors for both sending and receiving short messages.

Note that in FCPU1, the FU processes logical byte operations (one to eight bytes). That is, FCPU1 has variable byte addressing rather than variable bit addressing.

MICROINSTRUCTION PROCESSING STRATEGY

The read/write control storage is composed of 64-bit cells with two 32-bit microinstructions per cell. The maximum control storage contains 32K microinstructions. There are four classes of microinstructions; the first two bits indicate the class membership as follows:

    00   Field access unit (FU)
    01   Arithmetic unit (AU)
    10   Control unit processing (CUP)
    11   Control unit branch (CUB)

Within each class of microinstruction, there are various functions and register operands. Note that there are two types of CU microinstructions, one for the processing of CU registers, flip-flops, and the like and one for conditional branching. The CU, therefore, is further subdivided into two asynchronous units. That is, the CU parts that process each class of microinstruction can be activated simultaneously.

We shall now discuss one of the most important points of the FCPU architecture, namely, the mechanisms for microinstruction stream preparation and control. This process is illustrated in figure 3-3. Microinstructions are fetched two at a time from the control storage (CS) to the microinstruction register (MR). The CS address is indicated in a microinstruction location counter (MLC). The *next* microinstruction to be executed is selected from the MR or from the current VLS. That is, the VLS can at particular moments introduce the next microinstruction to be executed. The microinstructions introduced by the VLS can be modifications of previously entered microinstructions or newly generated microinstructions. When the next microinstruction is selected, it is examined to see whether VLS definition is specified. If VLS definitions are specified, the microinstruction is sent forward to the MIP (microinstruction preparation unit)

Figure 3-3. Microinstruction-stream preparation and control.

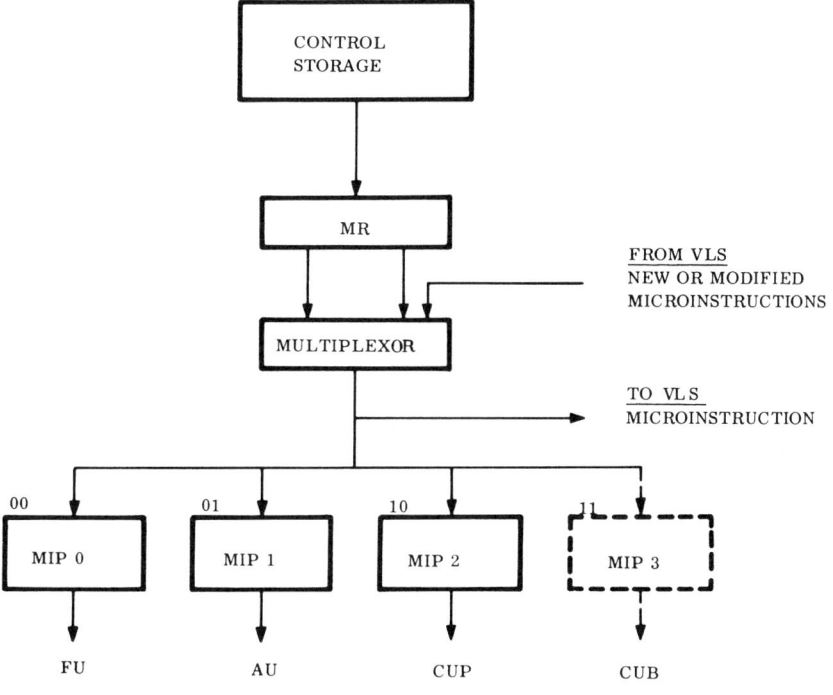

and VLS to be modified by the VLS and then reentered into the microinstruction stream. The microinstruction is held in the MIP until VLS definition is completed. It is during this time that the VLS can introduce new microinstructions.

Microinstructions are routed to one of four microinstruction preparation units based upon the two high-order bits as indicated above. If the MIP is unoccupied, the microinstruction is registered in the MIP as available for execution. If the unit is ready for its next microinstruction, it is accepted and the MIP is emptied so another microinstruction from the stream can be prepared. If the MIP is occupied and another microinstruction is routed to that MIP, the streaming stalls until the microinstruction is consumed from the MIP.

Consequently, for MIP 0, 1, and 2, the unit can be executing a microinstruction and have another ready to be executed. In the case of the FU (00) and CUP (10), there can be more than one microinstruction in execution in the unit, thus providing additional simultaneous capability for processing logical storage operations and processing control information. Whenever a CUB microinstruction is encountered, the stream is stalled; the microinstruction is set up directly for execution from MIP 3. The microinstruction for the false path is either in MR or on its way at the time of encountering the CUB microinstruction. In order to minimize delay, CS is referenced with the effective branch address (true path) but not gated into MR unless the branch condition is true.

The asynchronous nature of the FCPU and the microinstruction streaming provide for a high degree of time overlapping. Of course, the results of operations, registers, status, and the like must be coordinated. We have discussed how the TFRs are used in this connection. Status and other values are coordinated by providing status paths to flip-flops in the CU and by providing means of addressing several generations of status values.

DESIGN ALTERNATIVES

There are many tradeoff decisions made in designing a central processing unit. Of primary importance is making these decisions in a manner consistent with the goals of the product, tempered by the available component technology and the environment in which the product is developed. The purpose of this section is to discuss the more important global design decisions of the FCPU. The reader should bear in mind that these decisions were made in 1971–1972.

High-level Facilities

There was at that time a growing understanding of digital computation. The component producers and the computer user were less far apart than they had previously been. Component technologies of MSI and LSI provided more sophisticated functions at the chip level. System programmers were becoming more interested in understanding and using hardware facilities for the solution of difficult problems such as data protection, addressing mechanisms, and so on. Microprogramming offers an important level of understanding between hardware and software engineers. For these reasons, the FCPU used up-to-date component technology to provide higher-level basic functions such as logical storage operations, bit manipulations, high-speed decimal arithmetic, and so on. Also, the FCPU was modularly designed to incorporate new high-level functions in modules of the AU. Microprogramming in the FCPU is perhaps less micro than previous microprogrammed processors. For the FCPU, microprogramming can be viewed as a means of controlling well-understood, higher-level hardware functions.

To satisfy the goals specified in the introduction, it was clear that significant amounts of microcode would have to be written, debugged, documented, and maintained. It was also clear that a less complicated processor with appropriate software tools was required. By providing higher-level facilities, the microprogramming became less complex, and, in general, less microcode was required to achieve required functions. We can get some sense of this relationship in figure 3-4.

Here we see that the simplest microprogrammed device is the Universal Turing Machine (Turing 1936), which certainly lacks sophisticated functions but can accomplish higher-level functions by performing many microsteps organized in a sophisticated manner. The FCPU, on the other hand, relies less on sophisticated microcode and more upon higher-level processor functions. The

Figure 3-4. Processor-microcode relationship.

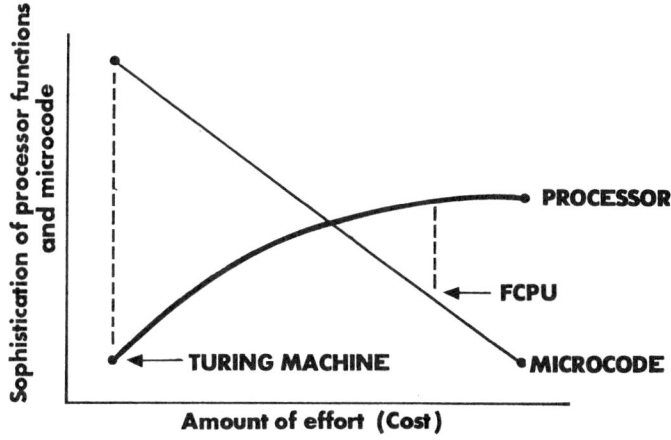

cost of structuring a processor is shown as a decaying function since we were provided with higher-level component functions, making it easier to develop a sophisticated processor. From a historical perspective, the development of large-scale integrated circuit technology in the 1970s and 1980s provides evidence that this direction was correct.

It is interesting to contrast the FCPU strategy of providing higher-level functions with the strategy used in the QM-1 (Salisbury 1976). In the QM-1, the higher-level functions at the microprogramming level were provided by introducing a lower-level (nano) language, environment, and control. Though this accomplishes the same goal, it does it with another level of programming rather than by incorporating high-level component technology. The nanoprogramming approach required another level of specialist in implementing the digital-computation hierarchy, thus moving hardware and software further apart. New languages and associated tools must be developed for this approach. The approach followed in the FCPU design is based on narrowing the gap between hardware and software. We speculated that *today's microprograms will be tomorrow's components*. This early speculation, again, is proving to be correct.

Minimally or Highly Encoded Microinstructions

Most of the microprogrammed medium-scale central processing units developed in the 1960s used rather large (50 to 300 bits) microinstruction words. The microinstruction words were divided into fields that controlled specific hardware gatings of registers and functions. Since the specific activities were directly specified, the microinstructions are considered *minimally encoded (horizontal)*; that is, requiring minimal hardware decoding. In some processors, a few encoded bits in the microinstruction word specified a redefinition of the fields, thus extending the number of operations. Another property of many of these processors was that the microinstruction remained active for several machine cycles or subcycles, while particular fields were selected in each cycle or subcycle. During specific cycles, several fields could be activated, thus providing for parallelism of activities in nonconflicting data paths.

In a *highly encoded (vertical)* strategy, a smaller microinstruction control word is utilized and more hardware decoding is required to determine the specific gatings and functions to be performed. Of course, this decoding does have a cost in time and hardware, but it must be put in the context of a number of issues. The first issue is the cost of control storage (particularly read/write storage). Obviously, the highly encoded strategy saves space. The second issue is the complexity of the microinstruction. Generally, highly encoded instructions are more similar to conventional target-language instructions and are more understandable at least to the programming community. Conventional assembly-language techniques can be applied to highly encoded formats. The codings specified in the minimally encoded format are generally difficult to understand and require special means of symbolically constructing microprograms.

The strategy for the FCPU was to utilize the highly encoded microinstruction format, primarily for the two reasons stated above. The highly encoded strategy, with its higher-level facilities, permitted easier production, debugging, and maintenance of FCPU microprograms. As an alternative to the single cycle or subcycle parallelism attainable in the minimally encoded format, the FCPU uses its asynchronous units to overlap the times of processor activities. This property will be discussed in the next part of this section. Minimally encoded and highly encoded microinstruction formats are discussed further elsewhere (Lawson and Smith 1971; Redfield 1971).

Synchronous or Asynchronous Processing

In general, it is much simpler and less expensive to design a synchronous processor with a single clock-pulse generator. This argument is certainly valid for small processors. For medium-scale processors, too, the synchronous strategy can be used, with varying amounts of data-path parallelism as discussed previously. The decision to use an asynchronous approach for the FCPU, with units and modules generating processing-terminating signals, was based upon a number of factors:

1. *Segmentation of design and implementation.* The various units and modules of the processor were assigned to different personnel for detailed design and implementation. The individual parts have their own timing logic so that stringent requirements of a single clock rate did not have to be accommodated.
2. *Performance.* By using the asynchronous approach, microinstruction streaming, and appropriate microprograms, the overall throughput of the processor could be increased.
3. *Tuning and accommodating new hardware.* The segmented asynchronous approach permits the fine-tuning of units that are found to be time-critical. New hardware technologies with very fast circuit times could be introduced. Also, as stated before, new high-level hardware facilities could be readily accommodated without a major redesign.

Writable Control Storage

In order to have an environment in which changes can be made easily, we elected to use a writable control storage. Semiconductor stores were available at sufficient speeds and at acceptable prices for a medium-scale processor. The advantages of using a writable control storage are as follows:

1. It provides a convenient environment for debugging and maintaining the processor. The ability to reassemble microprograms and load them into control store rather than having to physically change the control-storage medium is important. Field maintenance is more easily accomplished in installing changes by distributing new microprograms on an external-input medium.
2. It provides for convenient reloading with new emulators of known or experimental target languages. There is the possibility of swapping some segments of the CS on a dynamic basis. However, this is a complex matter that the FCPU design addressed. This point will be discussed in a later section describing the control unit.
3. New versions of microprograms could be loaded that include modifications to gather statistics about target programs being executed by the FCPU. This is valuable information for improving performance of hardware and microcode as well as providing information for improving systems and application software.

Of course, with a writable control storage, the danger always exists that an unauthorized change of CS contents can cause a system crash. To prevent this, a CWL (control-store write limit) register is used, which, when set upon program loading, can be locked by removing a physical key from the maintenance panel area. Each write into CS must then occur at an address above this limit. The storage below the limit is protected (effectively, read-only).

Processor Data Path Width

An early decision was to use 64-bit-wide data paths and processing functions within the FCPU. This data-path width must be considered as a maximum from the processor function standpoint, since appropriate facilities have been provided to deal with arbitrary precisions from 1 to 64 bits. This decision was made for the following reasons:

1. Most computing systems do not have a basic word size greater than 64 bits, thus permitting convenient implementation of emulators for a wide variety of processors.
2. Using 64 bits provides for extended precision arithmetic for special-purpose operations.
3. This width is useful in simplifying microprogramming and improving efficiency for multiple precision operations in emulating systems in which the multiple precision fits into 64 bits; for example, double precision is 48 bits in the DataSaab D23.
4. Logical storage operations for operands that do not conform to storage word size can be accommodated in single logical storage

requests to the FU. For example, the exact number of bytes of a decimal operand can be extracted and positioned up to a maximum of 8 bytes. This property improves storage-referencing performance.

There were many more decisions made in the FCPU design. We have attempted here to consider the more important global issues. Motivations for other more local FCPU features are considered in the following sections of this paper.

FIELD ACCESS UNIT

The field unit (FU) is designed for handling logical storage requests. The format of a logical storage-address request is shown at the top of figure 3-5. The address is composed of an L (length) part indicating 1 to 64 bits, a virtual or real MSU (main storage unit) address selecting a starting physical cell, and a starting bit address (B) within a cell. In terms of 64-bit cells, this means that an arbitrary selection of 64 bits is accomplished between bit B and bit $B+L-1$ of two consecutive cells, as indicated at the bottom of figure 3-5.

Note that in FCPU1, the MSU was composed of 32-bit cells. However, the FU still provided 64-bit logical cells for processing logical storage request, as indicated in the FU READ or WRITE microinstruction. There are three

Figure 3-5. Logical MSU addressing and field selection.

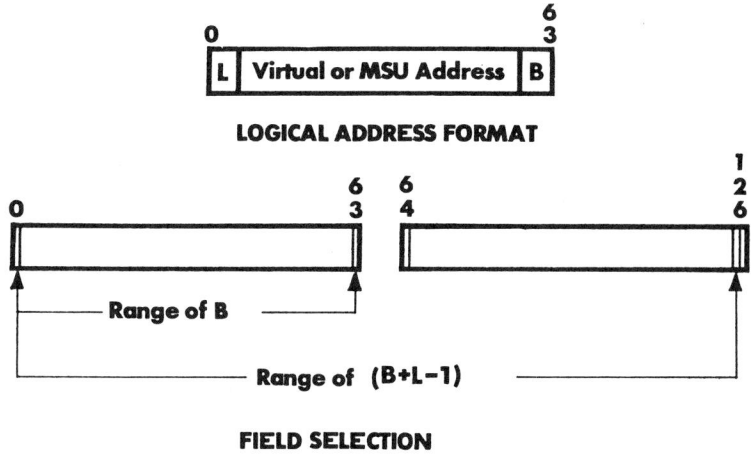

possible sources, as shown in figure 3-6: first, from the VLS, where an address could have been formed as a result of decoding and preparing a new target instruction; second, from an FU TFR; third, from one of four address-control registers (ACRs). Further, the address used may be incremented or decremented by L (length) values upon the execution of an FU microinstruction and stored in an ACR register. This provides a very powerful mechanism for sequencing through instruction streams and, more importantly, for efficient handling of regular information structures such as arrays and vectors.

The data and instruction values delivered from the MSU are placed in buffer data registers (DRs) before being field-extracted, as indicated in figure 3-7. The extracted values may be aligned left or right (with zero fill) in AU or CU TFR registers and are also sent to the VLS. This latter transmission is primarily for transmitting target instructions. Values to be written into storage are sent from FU TFR registers through a field-positioning mechanism. A mask pattern and the value to be written are supplied to the MSU so that only desired portions of physical storage cells are updated.

In FCPU1, the FU had the capability of executing two microinstructions simultaneously. This was provided by overlapping the time for performing physical storage operations with the time for the logical field extraction and positioning mechanisms. The FCPU control unit could also have prepared another FU microinstruction in MIP 0 that would be ready for FU execution as soon as it could be accepted.

The FU design is considered to be an important feature of the FCPU, since logical addressing removes many microprogramming and software burdens. The provision of ACR registers for handling regular information structures can enhance performance significantly for many important applications.

Figure 3-6. Physical MSU address generation and step control.

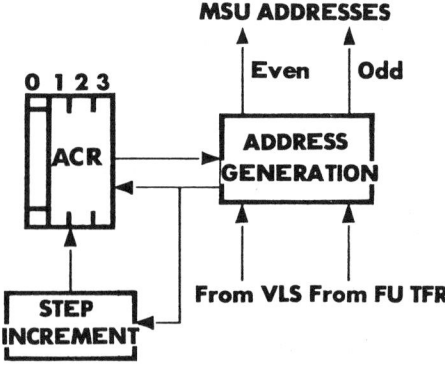

Figure 3-7. Logical READ and WRITE MSU transmission.

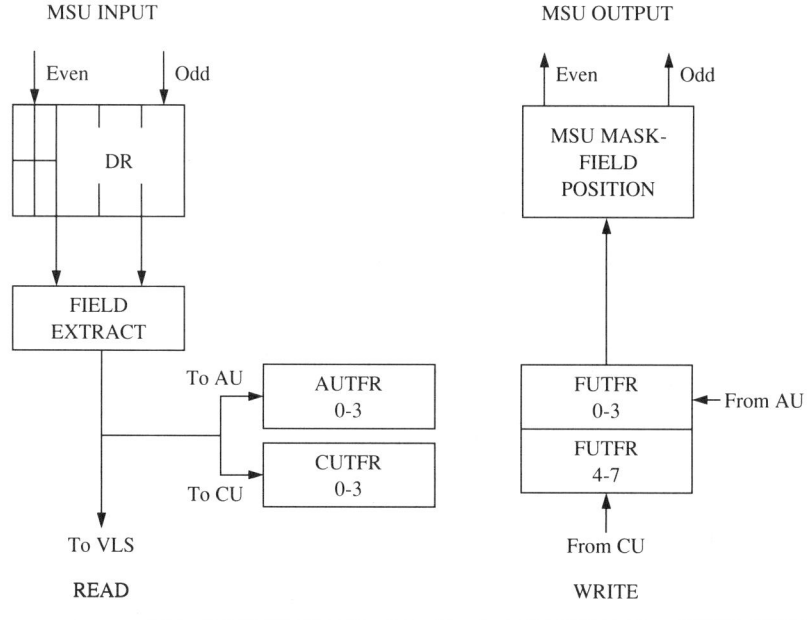

ARITHMETIC UNIT

The arithmetic unit (AU) is designed to provide standard arithmetic and logical functions and powerful data-manipulation, shifting, and status-generating facilities. Additional optional higher-level hardware functions can be incorporated. The AU contains 16 general registers (GRs), which can be used as inputs and outputs.

Inputs can also come from AU TFRs supplied from the FU or CU, and outputs may be delivered to FU or CU TFRs. These registers and the three standard AU modules are displayed in figure 3-8. The A and B buses are inputs; the C bus is the output that is available also to the VLS for special target-level-oriented inspections. Status outputs go to the CU and are available also to the VLS. The AU microinstruction indicates the module to be activated. We shall now consider a short description of each of the three standard modules.

The MOM (move module) provides for high-speed register-to-register transmission, constant-to-register transmission, and rapid status development.

The SAM (shift-and-mask module) provides for high-speed shifting of 0 to 63 bits (truncated or rotated) in one local cycle. Shifted results may be inserted into arbitrarily selected bit field positions of the target register. For arithmetic

Figure 3-8. Arithmetic-unit structure.

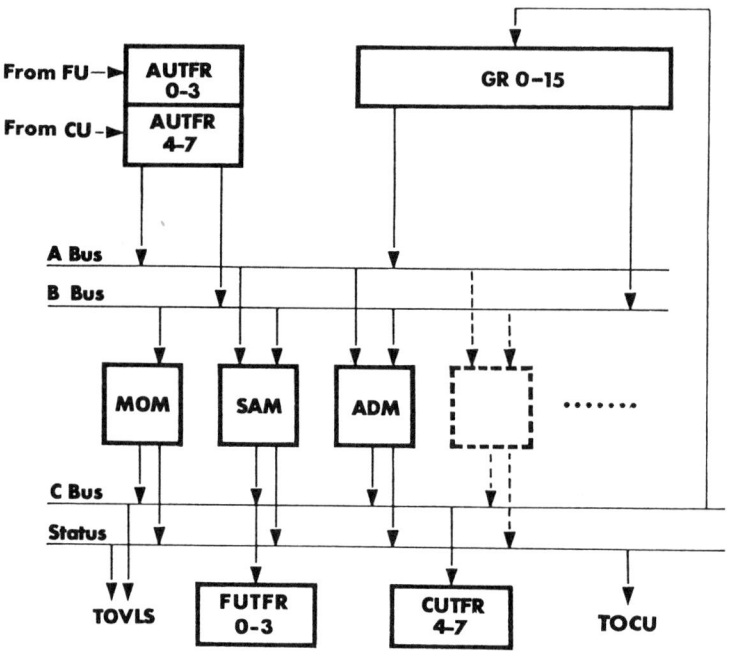

shifting, the high-order bit position may be sign-filled to the left. Unselected positions of the target register may be left undisturbed or zero-filled.

These first two standard modules provide operations of the form:

$$C \leftarrow f(B)$$

where f is a unary function. In each case, however, the following *standard status values* are developed:

Sign sense	(Copy of bit position 0 of the output data)
All zero	(Output data = 00 ... 000)
One sense	(Output data = 00 ... 001)
All one sense	(Output data = 11 ... 111)
NSA	(Normalization shift amount: 6 bits)

The latter status output (NSA) provides a shift value necessary to normalize the value. This value can be used in an SAM operation to accomplish the normalization in a single step. It is determined according to the first bit-value inversion in the 64-bit value (0 to 1 or 1 to 0). Two generations of AU status are saved in the status registers of the CU.

The ADM (adder module) provides 16 binary arithmetic functions, 16 logical functions, and 2 decimal (BCD) functions. The latter facility provides for performing 16-decimal-digit addition in a single ADM cycle. Result shifting of 1, 2, or 4 bits may be selected. Operations performed in the ADM are of the form:

$$C \leftarrow f(A, B)$$

where f is a selected binary function.

The standard status values indicated above are also developed after ADM execution. However, the following additional status outputs are provided:

    Carry out   (Carry from position 0 in arithmetic)
    Overflow   (Base 2 or 10 arithmetic)
    Shift out   (1, 2, or 4 bits shifted out)

Two generations of AU status outputs are saved in status bits in the control unit. The ability to add hardware modules to the AU was an important design criterion. This provides hardware as well as microprogram adaptability. The standard status values will always be developed; however, the new module can also develop unique status outputs. Since each module generates its own terminating signal, the modules can have different operation times. This permits easy adaptation of complex processing functions. Some module candidates included a high-speed multiply module and a data-editing module as well as floating-point and complete decimal-arithmetic modules. These latter two modules were made available in the D23 product as options.

CONTROL UNIT

The control storage accessing and microprogramming-preparation properties of the control unit (CU) were considered in the section on microinstruction processing strategy. The CU contains a variety of registers and status flip-flops used in accomplishing control functions in the FCPU host system. Several registers and functions are also provided to facilitate the microprogramming of control functions for the target system. These registers, their connection to the control-unit bus, and the primary control-unit functions are displayed in figure 3-9.

There are two classes of microinstructions that can be executed by the CU; namely, CUP (control-unit processing) and CUB (control-unit branch) microinstructions. We shall first consider the three types of CUP microinstructions.

MOVE provides for register-to-register movement along the control-unit bus. The registers indicated in figure 3-9, including the control storage, are possible sources or destinations of the MOVE operation. Movement can involve full

Figure 3-9. Control-unit registers and functions.

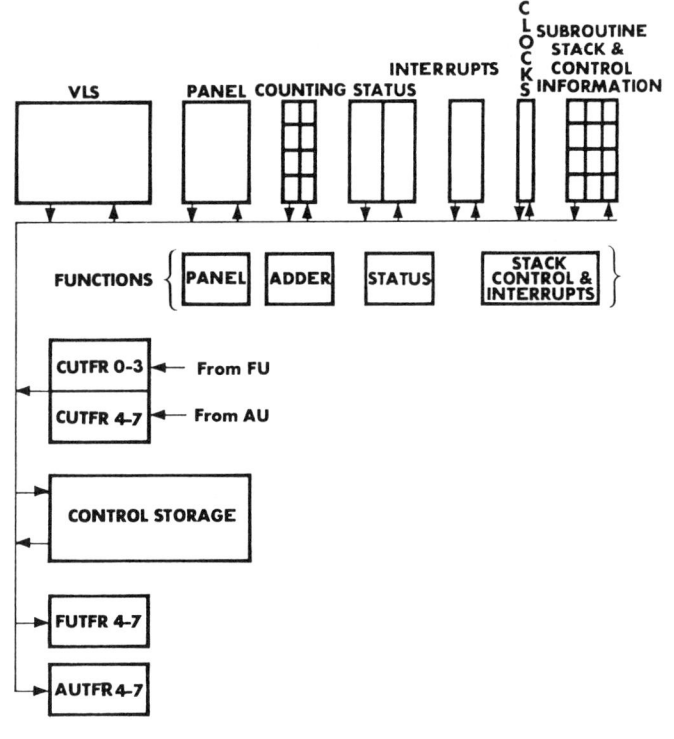

register width (64 bits) or partial register widths (<64 bits). This is provided by defining partial registers as having addresses in the address space of the MOVE microinstruction. The partial register values are transmitted right-aligned (zero filled to the left) on the bus. A good example of a partial register definition is the NSA (normalization shift amount) status from the AU, which is stored in six bits of the CU status registers. This six-bit field has a partial register address.

STATUS MANIPULATION provides for setting a status bit, interrupt bit, interrupt mask bit, or external signal as a function (AND, OR, EXCLUSIVE OR) of two input bit operands. The status and interrupt registers indicated in figure 3-9 are further subdivided into 64 bits of *soft status* (programmable status temporaries), 32 *interrupt* bits matched by 32 *interrupt mask* positions, 32 external *output* signals, and 96 bits of *working status* developed during execution of FU, AU, or CU microinstructions. The working-status bits may be inputs in a STATUS microinstruction, but they may not be indicated as outputs.

COUNTING REGISTER primarily provides for the incrementing and decrementing of counting values. There are eight counting registers of 16 bits each in the CU. The functions provided are of the form:

$$B \leftarrow f(A, B)$$

where f is a binary function.

The selected function can be one of 16 arithmetic or 16 logical functions. Thus, counting registers can be used for other control-type manipulations in addition to simply incrementing or decrementing. Status outputs developed from a CUP COUNTING microinstruction include sign sense, all one sense, and carry out. This status set is saved for the last three COUNTING microinstructions executed. These registers are important for controlling iterative microprograms (for example, vector operations); however, they may be used also for monitoring and statistics-gathering facilities in measuring CPU performance.

Control Mechanisms

Before we consider the CUB type of microinstruction, we shall first discuss some of the FCPU control mechanisms. The gross state of the FCPU at any instant of time is recorded in the MPS (microprogram status register). This important 16-bit partial register is pictured in figure 3-10. We shall consider the functions of each of the utilized fields of this register in the following paragraphs.

The ILI (interrupt level indicator) indicates whether normal state or interrupt state is currently active and, if the latter, which one of the interrupt levels (0, 1, or 2) is active. Level 0 specifies serious error interrupts. Level 1 is a trace interrupt, that is, an interrupt generated after executing each microinstruction. This facility is extremely useful for writing microcode to assist in debugging microprograms. Normal interrupts occur at level 2. If any of the 32 interrupts occurs, the CU generates a transfer of control to the control storage addresses 0, 2, 4, 6, ... , 62. The first two microinstructions of interrupt handling are placed at this point.

Figure 3-10. Microprogram status register.

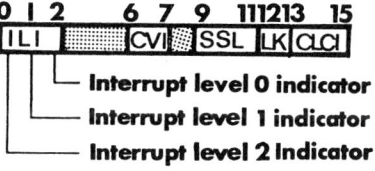

The CVI (current VLS indicator) field selects which of four possible VLS (variable logic set) structures is active at the current moment.

The CLCI (current location counter indicator) field indicates the level of the microprogram subroutine stack. These eight registers function as a push-down stack for recording return locations for microprogram subroutine returns and interrupt service returns. In order to provide a finer level of control over the microprogram structure, the SSL (subroutine stack limit) field may be set to a level number, and an interrupt will be generated if this limit is met on a subroutine call.

The LK (locking key) field indicates whether the locking key at the maintenance panel is on or off. If it is off and the WRITE CS key on the maintenance panel is lit, writing into all parts of the control storage is permitted. If it is on, writing is permitted only at control storage addresses greater than the address contained in a control-storage write-limit (CWL) register. The lower addresses effectively become read-only. In designing the control mechanisms, much attention was given to the protection of the FCPU. It is possible to construct a microprogram monitor to control global transitions in the FCPU. In addition to the mechanisms described for the MPS, it should be noted that when operating at a location counter level 0 (that is, CLCI = 0), writing is permitted into certain key registers including MPS, whereas at all other CLCI levels these key registers become read-only.

The alphanumeric maintenance and debugging panel is controlled by storing information in the panel registers. Functions from the panel cause an interrupt, and storing of information in the panel registers. Since much of the communications is microprogrammed, the display and input can be target-system-level-oriented as well as FCPU-oriented. A real time and an interval clock, both having partial register addresses, are incorporated in the CU for handling data functions and timing interrupts, respectively.

We shall now consider the five types of CUB (control-unit branch) microinstructions.

CONDITIONAL BRANCH provides for testing a status bit or its complement and branching if true to a control-storage address. The same instruction format can indicate that a subroutine is to be entered at the control-storage address, that a return from a subroutine is to be performed, or that the single microinstruction at the control-storage address is to be executed.

START TARGET indicates that processing a new target-level instruction is to begin. Execution of this microinstruction causes the activation of the VLS functions and specifies the base address of a branch vector in control storage to be used for the initial breakout from target-instruction-operation-code decoding. In both of these CUB microinstructions, the effective control-storage address can be optionally calculated by adding the MIX (microprogram index register).

START PROCESSOR brings the processor to a well-defined starting point or restarting point and branches to the indicated control-storage address.

WAIT stalls the processor until all indicated events are completed. Control then resumes at the next microinstruction. The events are related primarily to the completion of microinstructions in the various units. WAIT provides programmed rather than automatic synchronization. This microinstruction can be utilized to establish well-defined "clean points" in the microprogram where one or more units are quiescent.

MICROINSTRUCTION RECOVERY requests copies of microinstructions under execution in the various FCPU Units. It is used primarily in error-recovery procedures.

VARIABLE LOGIC SETS

In order to provide for accelerating performance of particular target-instruction sets, the FCPU design includes the capability of having from one to four variable logic sets (one per target language). Switching to a new active VLS is accomplished by changing the CVI (current VLS indicator) field in the microprogram status register.

There are no predefined functions for a VLS; however, several standard input/output signals and paths are provided for possible use. A VLS, when operating, has 64 addresses in the CUP MOVE instruction address space so that values may be communicated to and from the VLS. The VLS can contain registers and flip-flops used for keeping track of the target-instruction stream. In the case of the D23, the VLS23 contains the three target-system index registers and provides for effective address calculations for operand addresses.

One of the major signals that the VLS requires is the transmission of a START TARGET microinstruction. VLS23 inserts FU READ microinstructions into the microinstruction stream to access the D23 target-instruction stream. After isolating a target instruction, it calculates the effective operand addresses and, if a storage read is required, initiates this FU READ. VLS23 also decodes the operation code and causes a transfer of control to be executed in interpreting the target instruction.

All microinstructions contain a bit specifying whether VLS definition of parts of the microinstruction is to be performed. If this is the case, the CU routes the microinstruction to the VLS, where parts or all of the microinstruction may be modified. The VLS then returns the microinstruction to the microinstruction stream for execution. Modification is primarily for address and immediate value fields of the microinstructions. A good example would be the utilization of a push-down stack level counter in the VLS to modify the operand addresses in an AU microinstruction, thereby using some of the AU's general registers as a push-down stack.

The complexity of the VLS is basically a function of the performance requirements for the target language and the complexity of the target-language instruction formats. It is important to note that, where target-language instructions have high semantic content (that is, perform many steps), the power of the FCPU becomes readily apparent without the need for a sophisticated VLS structure. When the target language instructions have low semantic content, more sophistication is required to accelerate performance. That is, target-instruction processing rates must be accelerated.

THE PHYSICAL STRUCTURE

Figure 3-11 shows the disposition of the cabinets for the CPU portion of the D23 system. As you can see, the physical structure resembles the logical. The modularization and adaptability include the facility of moving the boxes around in the cabinets and/or adding cheaper or more powerful ones, due to the independence of interconnection interface cable lengths and standardized interface.

The FCPU1 is a separate processor that mainly communicates with the environment via the main storage unit (MSU), but has positions in an external input/output part for bit communication. The MSU interface consists of two identical interfaces, each with 32 bits of data width, due to the 32-bit MSU

Figure 3-11. Physical View of the FPCU in the D23 system.

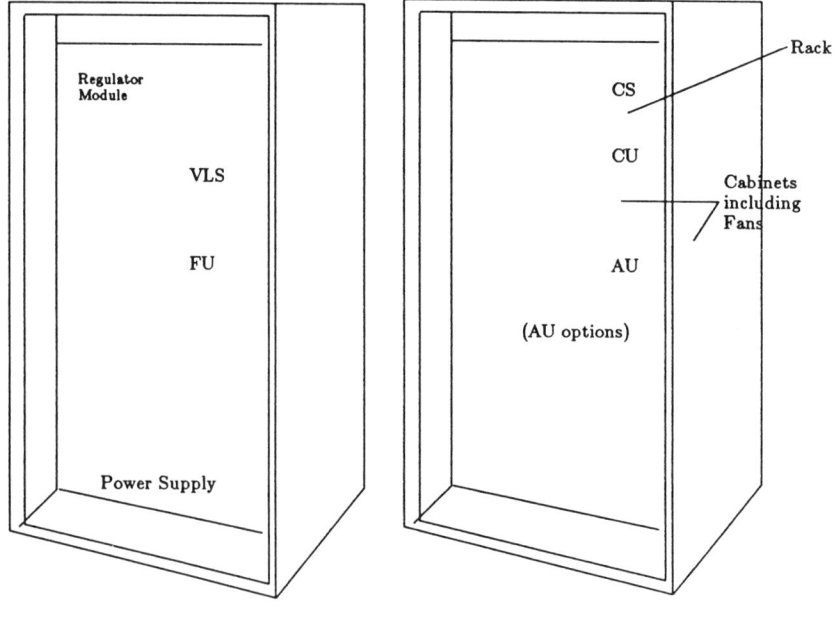

banks. The field manipulation facility, as discussed earlier, is used in implementing logical storage addressing and works with the D23 target system, which utilizes a basic word length of 24 bits.

The asynchronism means that each unit has its own control part, but most status manipulations are handled by the main control unit (CU). Because of the high internal speed and physical size there is no clock-pulse distribution, not even inside the separate units. Timing is constituted by delay lines. "Handshaking" is used in the asynchronous interfaces throughout the system, which results in high-speed performance and greater control of activity and is helpful for troubleshooting.

Microprogrammability in a read/write control storage (CS) makes it possible to give the FCPU1 different identities, that is, programming of hardware. For instance, during hardware test the identity is a processor "TEST," not a D23 target-system test. A specific facility is the microprogrammed maintenance panel. On the panel it is possible, through microprogram control, to display every register or whatever test is desired. The panel is designed to permit manual control on both the microprogram and the target-program level. In addition, the panel has two standard IO-interfaces so that the maintenance personnel can connect ordinary peripheral units or telecommunication equipment to initiate and analyze test program runs (locally or remote).

The control storage is $\leq$ 16 K, 32 bits, and can be divided in two parts, one high-speed (and expensive) and one low-speed (and less expensive). The low-speed part uses the same storage boards as the main storage unit, and of course it is possible to use only low-speed or high-speed control storage.

THE MICROPROGRAMMING LANGUAGE

Several languages had been developed for the programming of computer systems by utilizing a higher-level language-oriented syntax but with very machine-dependent semantics. PL/360 (Wirth 1968) and BSL (IBM) are two of these machine-dependent languages. Generally, the high-level-language expression of a program is easier to understand, debug, and maintain than the corresponding conventional assembly-language version of the program. In utilizing all these languages, the structure of the computer is always apparent. Each executable statement constructs maps, in a direct manner, into a single or very few machine-language instructions. Basically, the *translation function* involves minimal code generation. With conventional high-level languages such as FORTRAN, COBOL, PL/I, and ALGOL, the underlying computer structure is frequently less apparent (exclusive of individual implementation conventions), and the translation function involves significant amounts of code generation.

In considering the microprogramming of devices during the 1960s, the microinstruction format affected the manner of expressing microprogrammed algorithms. For minimally encoded (horizontal) microinstructions with several subfields, the language simply reflects the selection of field alternatives, as in the CAS system for the System/360 (Husson 1970). Where more highly encoded (vertical) microinstructions were utilized, conventional assembly languages had been applied, as in ICAP for the Standard Computer MLP-900 (Standard Computer 1970; Lawson 1971). The understandability of algorithms written for a minimally encoded microinstruction device is generally a direct function of the complexity of the device (e. g., number of fields, amount of parallel activity, interaction of facilities and functions). The use of conventional assembly languages for highly encoded microinstruction devices makes the program more readable to those who are accustomed to using assembly languages; but, again, understandability is basically a function of the complexity of the device.

The microprogramming languages developed in the past had been machine-dependent, and the translation function had been in most cases nongenerative. Generative aspects were normally accommodated via assembly-language macros. Due to the diversity of microprogrammed-device architectures it was and still is difficult to find a single microprogramming language from which efficient programs could be generated for all devices. Consequently, we were faced with machine-dependent, basically "one-for-one" microprogramming for some time into the future. However, this did not prohibit making a transition at the microlevel similar to the transition from conventional assembly language to the PL/360- or BSL-type languages. This was the approach taken in developing the microprogramming language (ML) for the FCPU. This approach was also utilized for the Burroughs B1700 (Wilner 1972). As before, one needed to learn the structure of this device to do effective microprogramming. However, in a departure from previous microprogrammed devices, the FCPU was designed as a "higher-level microprogramming device. " Consequently, the device was less complex than most previous medium-scale microprogrammed devices, making the algorithms written in the ML more understandable and easier to debug and maintain.

Significant attention was given to the organization of the FCPU and its microprogramming language, since we believed that there would be a significant increase in the use of microprogramming for the device in comparison with previous medium-scale microprogrammed central processing units.

Microinstruction Organization

To illustrate a 32-bit microinstruction format, let us consider the format for arithmetic-unit (AU) microinstructions displayed in figure 3-12. Basically, an AU microinstruction is a three-address format with three operand registers and the semantics

$$C \leftarrow f(A, B)$$

where f is a binary AU-function.

Figure 3-12. Arithmetic-unit microinstruction format.

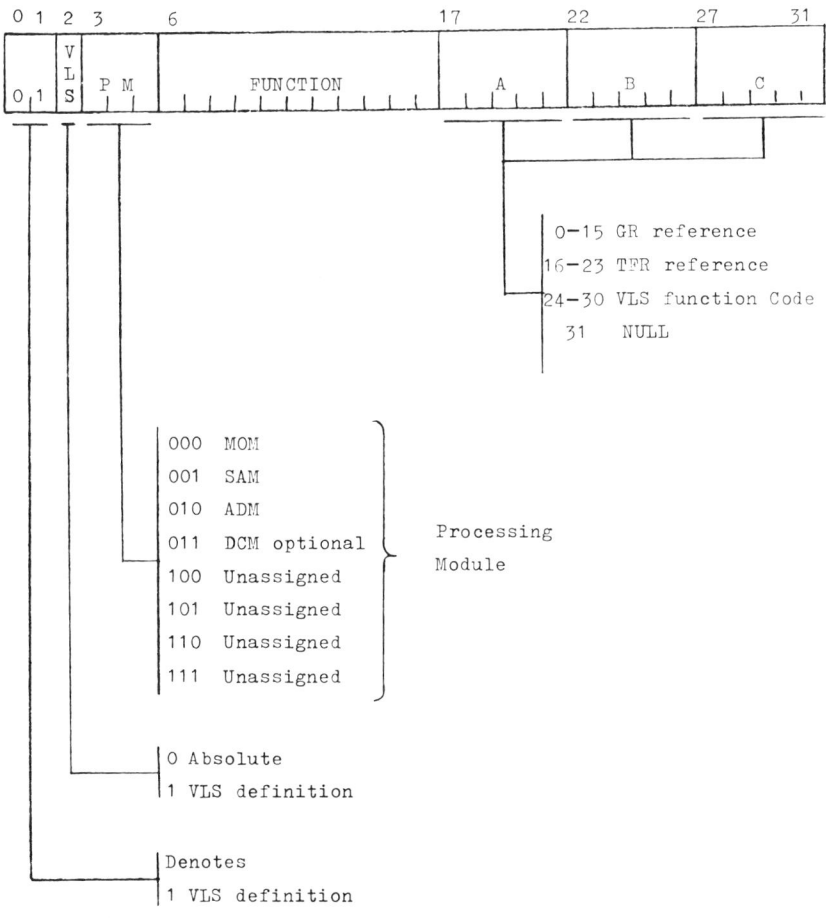

In some AU microinstructions only two addresses, B and C, are utilized with the semantics

$$C \leftarrow f(B)$$

where f is a unary AU-function, and various data manipulations are performed on B.

A brief description of the fields follows:

- Bits (0, 1): indicate an AU-class microinstruction.
- Bit (2): indicates whether the microinstruction is to be sent directly to the AU by the control unit as it is or premodified

by the currently active variable logic set (VLS). Note: Target-language adaptability is provided in this manner.
- Bits (3–5): select one of eight AU processing modules. Three of these modules, MOM (move module), SAM (shift-and-mask module), and ADM (adder module), are standard; others, such as DCM (decimal-conversion module), are optional or available for new AU processing functions (e. g., high-speed multiply/divide).
- Bits (6–16): select a function to be executed within the selected processing module. Subfields in this portion frequently specify modifiers for the operation or operands.
- Bits (17–31): indicate three operand fields each five bits in length. The address of each is decoded to (1) a direct reference to any one of 16 local general registers (GRs) contained in the AU, (2) any of the 8 input TFRs for A and B or any of the 8 output TFRs for C, (3) a VLS modification of the address, or (4) a NULL address where zeros are to be supplied for A or B or the storing is to be inhibited for C.

The detailed formats of the microinstructions for the other units will not be presented here. However, we can observe that a microinstruction from any of the units contains the following three types of information:

1. *Function:* the activity to be performed within the unit
2. *Operands:* the address of registers, flip-flops, and so on to be manipulated; or a control storage address for some of the CUP and for CUB microinstructions
3. *Modifiers:* encoded fields that indicate modifications to the basic function or to one or more of the operands

Microprogram and Language Structure

Basic Language Elements

The language has the *delimiters* = –, ( ) : / * and end-of-card. Blanks are significant so that, for example, identifiers must be separated by one or more of them.

Identifiers begin with a letter and contain a maximum of 12 letters and digits.

Constants are decimal or hexadecimal. Decimal constants are positive or negative and at most 7 digits. HEXR and HEXL are used to indicate right or left justified hexadecimal constants followed by 1 to 16 hexadecimal digits.

One statement is generally placed on each card and is ended by the end-of-card. However, a statement may be extended to a new card if the present card is ended with a /.

Comments begin with * and end with end-of-card; no continuation is possible.

Microprogram Structure
A microprogram has the following structure:

DECLARE
<global declarations>
BEGIN
  <statements>
    DECLARE
    <local declarations>
    BEGIN   } Inner block, may occur zero, one, or
    <statements>   several times
    END
END

In a program there is an outer block with global declarations and potentially several inner blocks with local declarations. The global declarations are valid throughout the program but the local declarations only in the block where they appear.

Control Storage Layout
The outer block with its constants and variables, followed by the inner blocks with their unique constants, are loaded from the beginning of control storage (fig. 3-13). The variables of the inner blocks share the memory at the highest addresses in control storage. The reason for this is as follows. The outer block may contain a monitor that handles the switching of different language emulators. The control write limit (CWL), the limit above which writing in CS is allowed, is set to CWL1 when the monitor is active and to CWL2 when any of the emulators are active. There was no initial need for a relocating loader, and consequently all the microprograms were translated together.

Declarations
In the declarations, users may define their own names for particular registers and functions in the FCPU, name constant values, and reserve control storage for variables and constants.

All registers and functions have *built-in* names either individually or as a group. When using a group name, a number must be supplied to indicate which member of the group is referred to. For example, the real-time clock has the built-in name RTC and the general registers in AU have the name GR.

A declaration involving these two facilities is:

    DECLARE CLOCK = RTC
             ACCUMULATOR = GR.4

It is not necessary to declare names for the registers; the built-in names can be used in the microinstructions. Examples of constant and variable declarations are:

```
DECLARE TEN = CONST, 10
        TENHEX = CONST, HEXR, A
        X = VAR, 1, 2, 3, 5, 8
        Y = VAR
        Z = VAR (10)
        FOUR = IMM, 4
```

Figure 3-13. Organization of microprograms in control storage.

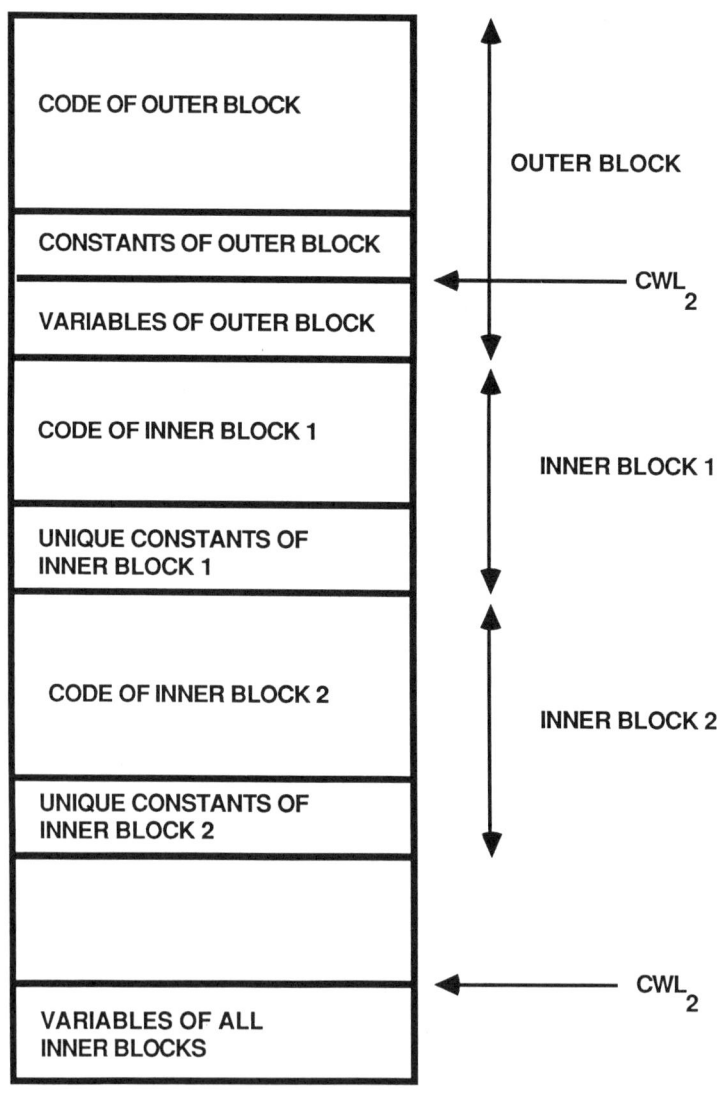

TEN and TENHEX are both constants with the decimal value 10. X is the declaration of five consecutive variables with initial values, the first of which is referred to by X. Y is a variable with the value 0. Z is the reference to the first of 10 variables all with initial value 0. FOUR is an immediate constant with value 4 that is not located in control storage but can appear as an immediate field in a microinstruction.

Label declarations are identifiers followed by a colon. Normally, programs are loaded from cell 0 in control storage. With an absolute label declaration, <identifier>(<constant>), the program will be loaded starting at CS address <constant>.

Grouping of Microinstructions

The language has facilities to aid the programmer in structuring groups of microinstructions. The simple DO statement and corresponding END statement cause several statements to be treated as one.

Branch Vectors

The DO CASE (n) statement is used to build a branch vector. Each statement, either a simple statement or a DO statement, constitutes one case. If less than n simple statements are specified for a case, additional no-operation (NOP) statements are inserted by the translator. Apart from these NOPs, no instructions are created by the translator in a DO CASE statement.

By means of the microinstruction index register (MIX), which must be loaded with n^* (actual case 1) and a branch statement using MIX, control is transferred to the actual case of the DO CASE statement.
Example:

```
L: DO CASE (4)
       GOTO L1      * CASE 1
       DO
           A = B    * CASE 2
           GOTO L2
       END
   END
```

A total of five extra NOPs are emitted by the translator. If case 2 is wanted, MIX is loaded with 4, and a GOTO, MIX L microinstruction is executed.

Loop Control

To facilitate the creation of iterative loops, a DO statement with loop control is provided. Three things may be specified:

1. A CU counting register in which the counting takes place that must be preloaded by the user; this must always be specified

2. A by factor that is either a CU counting register or an immediate value; this is the value by which the loop-controlling counting register is to be incremented
3. A to factor that indicates the condition of the loop-controlling counting register that finishes the loop

The to factor can be ONE, ZERO, POSITIVE, or NEGATIVE. Either the by or the to factor but not both may be left out. Either may separately be placed at the beginning or end of the loop; when appearing together the order is significant so that the user has full freedom in the order of incrementing and testing the loop-controlling register.

The translator generates appropriate conditional and unconditional branch statements and a counting register assignment for the to and by factors. Examples:

1. DO LOOP BY −1
   ...
   END LOOP TO ZERO

   The counting register LOOP is decreased by 1 until zero.

2. DO COUNT TO POSITIVE BY ELEMENTSIZE
   ...
   END

Subroutines

Any portion of the microcode may be treated as a subroutine since the return address is kept in a hardware stack within the FCPU. By executing an ENTER L instruction, the stack is pushed down, the address of L is placed on top of the stack, and the top element of the stack now acts as microprogram location counter (MLC).

By executing a RETURN instruction the element on top of the stack is removed from the stack (popped up), and the element that now becomes top element is the current MLC.

Microinstructions

The microinstructions for the various FCPU units contain several subfields to indicate functions (operations), operands, and modifiers to operands and operators. In general, the operands of a statement are placed inside parentheses and separated by commas. Exceptions are branch statements where no parentheses occur. Modifications to an operand or an operation in general follow them, separated by commas. The following examples illustrate the microinstruction structure.

FCPU Unit	Statement	Operation	Operands	Modifiers
FU	READ, NOACCESS (A,B)	READ	A,B	NOACCESS
AU	C = ADD, RIGHT, 4(A,B)	ADD	A,B,C	RIGHT, 4
CUP	C = X, HALF	assignment	C,X	HALF
CUB	IF A THEN GOTO, MIX L	GOTO*	A,L	MIX

*Note: all transfers of control are conditional.

This introduction to ML should provide the reader with a basic idea of the strategy used in designing the microprogramming language for the FCPU. Application examples in the following section show how ML can be applied. The chapter appendix contains a list of all of the FCPU built-in names as well as a summary of the ML syntax.

APPLICATIONS

We shall consider two application examples of FCPU microprogramming. One example is the coding of a low-semantic-content D23 target instruction from the D23 emulation, and the other is the encoding of some simple vector operations, illustrating the implementation of high-semantic-content instructions.

A D23 Instruction Implementation

The D23 target-system architecture includes an AR (accumulator register), MR (multiplier register), and three index registers. The basic word size of the D23 is 24 bits (3 bytes). We shall consider the encoding of the D23 target instruction += (add-to-AR and write). The instruction contains an operation code part, indexing indicator part, and an address part. At the execution of a START TARGET microinstruction, the VLS calculates the effective address and inserts the following microinstruction into the microinstruction stream:

READ (VLS, AUTFR.0, LEFT) SAVE (ACR.1)

The 24-bit logical cell will be delivered left-aligned in AUTFR.0, and the address of the operand will be saved in ACR.1. By issuing this FU microinstruction from the VLS, the memory reference starts much faster than if we were to wait to issue the FU microinstruction from control storage. While the operand fetch is being performed, the VLS is decoding the operation code part and causing the branch-vector breakout into control storage. This basic branch-vector structure is illustrated in figure 3-14. Note the use of START microinstructions.

An abstraction from the listings of the D23 emulator appears in figure 3-15. The declaration part shows some programmer names for referenced FCPU built-in facility names and immediate constants. The branch vector for initial D23 operation-code breakout is contained in a DO CASE in which each case can have eight microinstructions. Note that the assembler supplies NOPs (indicated as dummy CUP operations) when less than eight microinstructions appear for a case.

For operation $+=$, we enter the branch vector at the label OP07. We shall consider what is occurring at the execution of each microinstruction by referring to the hexadecimal control storage address of each microinstruction:

> 0009: waits if necessary until the 24-bit operand is read from storage and placed in the AUTFR.0, then adds this value to the AR
> 000A: stores the overflow status developed in the previous step into a soft status bit
> 000B: transmits the AR to the FUTFR.0 in the FU to prepare for writing to storage
> 000C: writes the FUTFR.0 contents into the MSU at the same address from which the input operand was fetched; note the READ issued by the VLS, indicating that the address was to be saved in ACR.1 in the FU

Figure 3-14. Target-language branch vector.

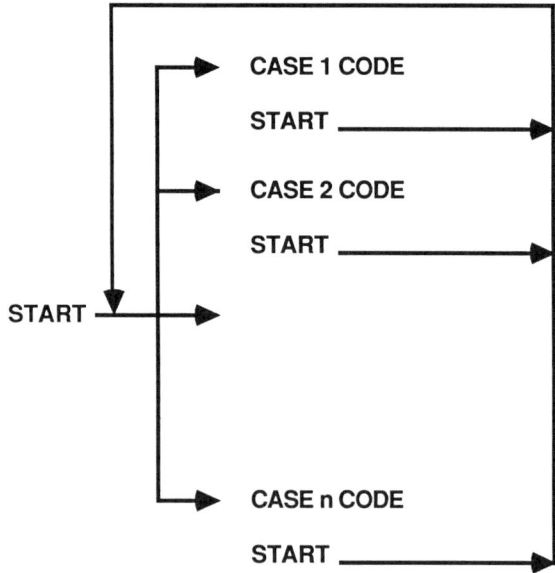

Figure 3-15. Part of the D23 emulator listing.

```
* SOME FACILITY DECLARATIONS FROM A D23 EMULATION
DECLARE    AR = GR.0
           MR = GR.1
           AU-OVERFLOW = WSBIT,37
           AU-SIGN = WSBIT.32
           SS-S-IND = SSBIT.0
           VLS-I-IND = CU-RIT-VLS.0
           TARGET = IMM, 0
           INITIAL = IMM,1
BEGIN
*
*FIRST D23 INSTRUCTION EXECUTION
START (INITIAL,D230P)
*
* OPCODE BRANCH VECTOR 128 CASES
D230P: DO CASE (8)
OP00:  DO
       NOP
       END
         .
         .
         .
OP07:  DO
       AR = ADD(AR,AUTFR.0)
       SS-S-IND = AU-OVERFLOW
       FUTFR,0 = AR
       WRITE (ACR.1, FUTFR,0, LEFT) LENGTH (24)
       VLS-I-IND = AU-SIGN
       START (TARGET, D230P)
       END
         .
         .
         .
       END
END
```

000D: stores the sign status of the AR into a VLS indicator bit
000E: starts the execution of the next target instruction

Since the processor is preparing the microinstructions on a streaming basis, the above microinstructions are not necessarily completed in the order specified. Remember, synchronization based upon value passing occurs when necessary. This aspect of time overlapping will be graphically demonstrated in the next example.

Vector Operations

The power of the FCPU becomes more evident when we consider the execution of instructions with higher semantic content. To illustrate this capability, we shall consider the inner-loop microcode and timing for the following simple vector operations:

$$\text{ASUM}$$
$$C_i = A_i + B_i, \; i = 1, 2, \ldots, n$$
$$\text{CASUM}$$
$$C_i = C_i + A_i + B_i, \; i = 1, 2, \ldots, n$$

The power of the FU stepping capability and ACR registers is apparent since we can increment addresses and save them in the FU in time overlapped with operand fetching or storing and element processing. The inner-loop microcode for the two operators is displayed in figure 3-16. Note that the FU READ and WRITE instructions specify stepping (STEPR) and saving of the incremented addresses in ACR registers named ASTREAM, BSTREAM, and CSTREAM. Counting of the number of elements processed is done in the counting register CR0. 1 and testing for completion is accomplished through the name DONE, which is equated to the zero sense of a counting register operation. The MIX (microprogram index register) is used to hold the operation code specifying which operator is to be executed. ASUM and CASUM could be one of several vector operations sharing the same address-control code. Note that the operator is entered and exited as a subroutine. Overflow checking is performed for each element processed.

The execution timing for ASUM and CASUM is displayed in figure 3-17. The microinstructions are numbered with their corresponding numbers from figure 3-16. Note that a microinstruction is readied for execution every 100 nanoseconds (unless a branch occurs).

The notation ⊨ indicates a timing delay. That is, the microinstruction cannot proceed until some other event has been completed. The overlapping of time is interesting, particularly in the case of instructions 4, 1.3, and 2.4, which are transfers of control with no time penalty or very little time penalty for branching. In these cases, subroutine exit occurs even before the subroutine is completed and execution resumes in the main line code. This is an interesting property provided by asynchronous control. The overlapping here provides an average microinstruction rate of approximately 170 nanoseconds. These timing properties vary quite widely, depending upon the semantic content of the target operations involved. Remember that microinstructions for the FCPU perform higher-level functions, and fewer microinstructions are normally required to execute a target instruction than on general-purpose microprocessors such as the MLP-900 (Lawson and Smith 1971). The incorporation of

Figure 3-16. Sample vector operations.

1	LOOP :	READ (ASTREAM, AVALUE) STEPR, SAVE (ASTREAM)
2		MIX = TOPCODE
3		READ (BSTREAM, BVALUE) STEPR, SAVE (BSTREAM)
4		ENTER, MIX ADDOP
5	RETUR:	CRO. 1 = DECR (CRO. 1)
6		WRITE (CSTREAM, CVALUE) STEPR, SAVE (CSTEAM)
7		IF OVERFLOW THEN GOTO OVERCODE
8		IF NOT DONE THEN GOTO LOOP
9		START ... * INSTRUCTION FINISHED
	ADDOP :	DO CASE (4)
		DO
1.1	ASUM:	CVALUE = ADD (AVALUE, BVALUE)
1.2	ISTORE:	OVERFLOW = AU-OVERFLOW
1.3		RETURN
		END
		DO
2.1	CASUM:	READ (CSTREAM, TVALUE)
2.2		AVALUE = ADD (AVALUE, BVALUE)
2,3		CVALUE = ADD (AVALUE, TVALUE)
2.4		GOTO ISTORE
		END
		END * END OF CASES

these vector operations into the FCPU microprograms provides a performance factor of about 3.5 to 1 over D23 target-language programs executing the same operations and could have made the FCPU competitive with many much more expensive scientific processors in performing operations on these regular information structures. A microprogram-supported vector-arithmetic package for integration into the D23 FORTRAN was indeed specified and an experimental microcode developed.

Figure 3-17. ASUM and CASUM execution timing.

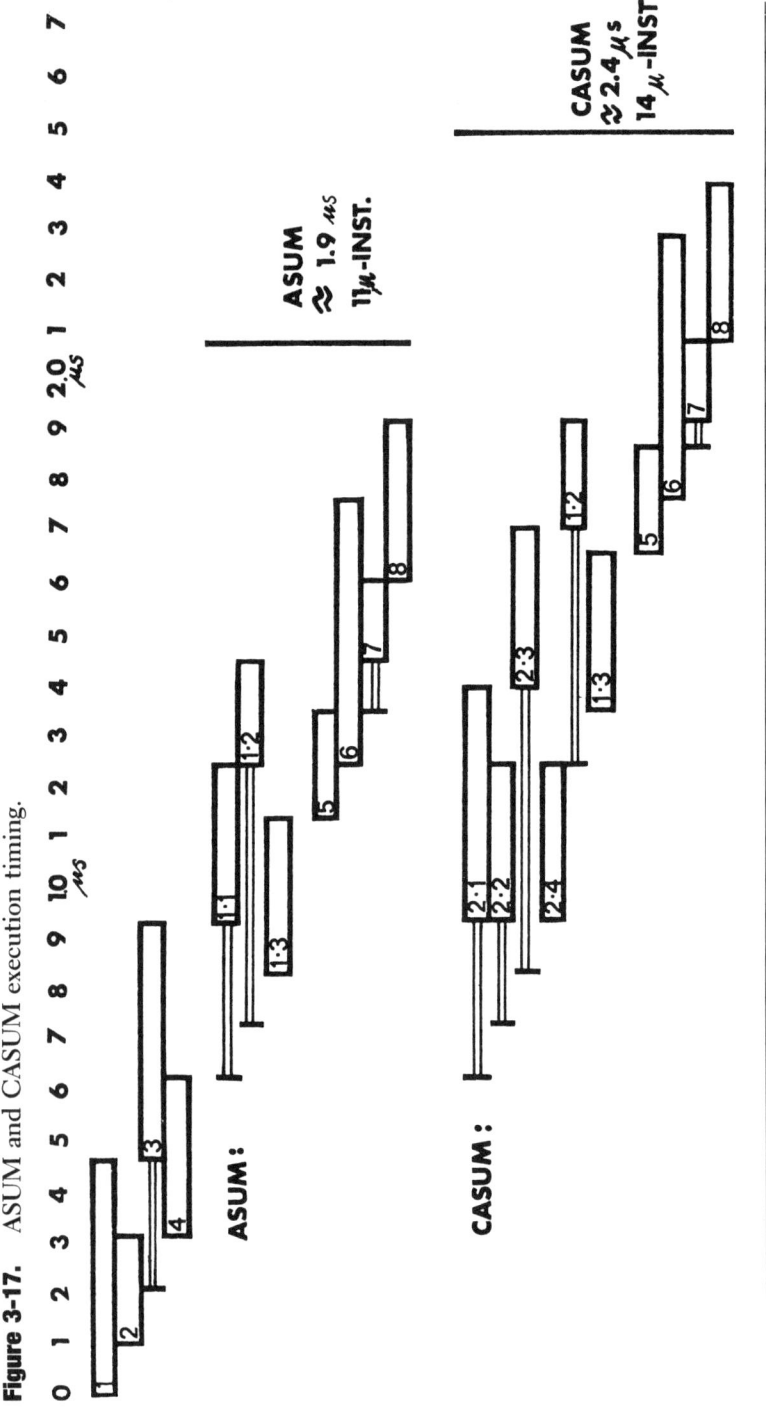

DESIGN, DEVELOPMENT, TESTING, PRODUCTION, AND MAINTENANCE

During all phases of the work with the FCPU, we exploited the structuring aspects of the product design. The logical design was made by a small group of highly experienced people, representing both hardware and software engineering.

This combination of personnel helped to soften the hardware facilities and vocabulary. During the design phase, the ML (microprogramming language) translator (MITRAN) and the FCPU simulator (MISIM) were developed, and because of this close cooperation between hardware and software project members, the hardware specification was thoroughly penetrated from a microprogram-consistency point of view. MITRAN and MISIM were implemented in the programming languages COBOL and ALGOL-GENIUS (a DataSaab-developed language), respectively, and were first made operational upon the previous-generation D22 systems.

The structural designers stated very early that due to short development time, easy and inexpensive production, high reliability, and low maintenance requirements, the design should include: 19-inch boxes, one standard board size with mixed wire-wrapped and -plated interconnections, TTL and S-TTL, common power parts, plus one separate regulating module per box and extrahigh common mode for interconnections. Due to the asynchronism between the units, it was possible to develop and test the different units independently of each other. One specific person was responsible for the important intra- and interconnections (including the to-and-from registers).

During the testing phase, the engineers utilized debugged test programs since they already had run successfully in the simulator (MISIM). To shorten the testing time, logical and time "hazard" errors were simulated before the hardware was available for testing. The testing of the FCPU consisted of three phases:

1. Parallel test of the separate units (AU, CU, CS, FU, VLS)
2. Test of joined units (CS, CU), (CS, CU, AU), (CS, CU, AU, FU), (CS, CU, AU, FU, VLS23)
3. Test of microprogram for system identity and performance

Phases 1 and 2 utilized the asynchronism to run test sequences on separate "test controllers," delivering sequences of microinstructions to test the units off-line.

Phase 2 started with the joining of CS and CU with extralong interconnection cables and proceeded in the order indicated above. The FU had been tested against the MSU and I/O system separately before integration with the FCPU. The input/output media used during testing were a card reader (microprogram loading) and a line printer connected directly to the maintenance panel. A specific debugging facility of interest is the TRACE function microsubroutine that stores variables of interest after an execution of a microinstruction. This interrupt facility was described in the section on the control unit.

For phase 3, the panel was prepared to step microinstructions and/or to step target instructions. In addition, microprograms could be loaded via the MSU from disk, tape, and so on.

In the production line, we exploited the asynchronism to produce and test units separately and then used the substitution method to verify system function, that is, to exchange modules on an already working reference FCPU.

The documentation was well coordinated between the development and production departments because of the well-structured hardware. From a database for the developed products' documentation files, control information was directly fed to the production machines.

For maintenance, there are several utility functions, which include the following:

- Input-output interfaces on the FCPU panel prepared for local or remote control and analysis
- A panel display for 256 characters, which can display the content of all the FCPU registers and its CS
- TRACE function
- STEP function on microprogram and target-program levels
- Asynchronous units with well-defined interconnection interfaces and highly encoded (vertical) microinstructions
- Test programs, for separate units or joined units, in ML and target language with well-prepared test points

In retrospect, we can state that all phases of the FCPU product life cycle were assisted by the asynchronous design philosophy.

FUTURE ARCHITECTURE IMPLICATIONS

The forecasting of what will happen in the future, particularly in a dynamically changing field, can be dangerous. However, experiences with microprogrammable computers and possible directions as a result of ongoing VLSI technology can lead to an indication of some possible new directions in the area of microarchitectures and, more importantly, system architectures.

Let us first clarify some of the important terminology and concepts used in the following discussion. When we refer to architecture, we mean the activities of design related to specifying the eventual assembly of available or new "building blocks," thus constructing a system or subsystem. In the computer environment, we can observe many levels of systems and subsystems. Traditionally, we divide the computer-system architecture into software and hardware parts. The architecture of a total computer system is a composite of many subarchitectural activities. We can also refer to architectural-design activities as the organizing and/or structuring of systems and their parts.

In order to improve our view of global computer-architectural activities, we shall abstract a common denominator of the activities. We shall view the building blocks used at all levels as *processes* and the architecture that is evolved at each level of the system as a whole as a *system of cooperating processes*. For example, gates are processes that, when combined into combinational and sequential circuits, form a system of cooperating processes. Likewise, collections of microsubroutines and subroutines (procedures, functions, and so on) of higher levels are processes that are organized into systems of cooperating processes.

We can make the observation that the cooperating processes of higher levels are dependent upon the cooperating processes of lower levels. This relationship has been referred to as an *interpretive hierarchy* (Lawson 1976). Going a bit deeper into this subject, we can state that *one level's system of cooperating processes forms a processor for the next higher level*.

Consequently, we can say that architects design processors. This point of view is valuable in forming a fundamental understanding of computer systems (Lawson 1981a) as well as in considering the new concepts presented in this discussion. The question as to what is micro to what in a system architecture is not always clear, and in order to achieve a uniformity in structure between various architectural levels, we should perhaps use the denotation *programmed logic* as a general concept that can be applied at all levels. Further, we can use the term *base logic* to refer to the lowest level of processes (nonreducible hardware actions in this case). This point of view is quite useful, since the realization of programmed logic can indeed vary among architectural levels (e. g. , programmable logic arrays, microprograms, or conventional programs written in lower- or higher-level languages).

Returning to the realm of microprogrammed architectures, let us consider the form in which parallelism is accomplished. The use of commonly known synchronous architecture strategies leads to what this author refers to as *unnatural parallelism*, that is, *man-made parallelism*. The possibilities for parallelism are designed into the architecture and must be thoroughly understood by the micro-/ or nanoprogrammer to be exploited, often with significant difficulties due to the magnitude and/or complexity of their structure.

It is possible, as demonstrated by the FCPU, to introduce *natural parallelism* at the microarchitecture level, parallelism that is achieved automatically by the nature of the implemented instruction-interpretation mechanism in relationship to base logic processes that have not been designed with the type of design-timing constants typical of the classical synchronous approach. The microprogrammer, while possibly being aware of potential parallelism, is not faced with the complexities of understanding and exploiting man-made parallelism that has been determined by stringent clock time-requirements and possible "glitches."

Natural Parallelism in the VLSI Environment

The availability of VLSI and especially CAD tools for VLSI will lead to the possibility of realizing new approaches to the programming of base logic. Synchronization mechanisms, for example, implemented by newly defined logic cells, will relieve the problem of costly implementation via standard MSI and SSI components.

A major research area for the future will investigate methods for evaluating alternative "processor" architectures to support the processes to be implemented. In many situations, particularly when the process is not complicated, it may be useful to construct a processor per process. In other cases, where the process is more complicated and/or a family of related processes is to be supported, more sophisticated programmed logic processors may be justified. This programmed logic can then be shared (multiplexed) among the higher-level processes to be executed by the processor. One trend that may evolve from these advances is that complicated general-purpose processors of the type we have built earlier may well be replaced by a "network" of special-purpose processors. Note that this trend is already underway with the expansion of computer network technology. What is being pointed to here is that this trend can well be extended into chip architectures. The PLA as one keystone of VLSI programmed logic is already well established due to the regularity of physical structure. It is clear that the use of this programming form for base logic will continue to be an important factor for low-level processor realization and in many cases will provide an alternative to more conventional microarchitecture-control strategies.

Consider the organization of several base-logic processes, particularly when the processing of less regular "data" (including instructions) is required. Shall we resort to the use of unnatural parallelism with all its possibilities for creating complicated structures that are difficult to microprogram, test, and maintain? In this author's opinion, that approach is asking for trouble. With VLSI, one will attempt more comprehensive architectures and be able to design, implement, and test them; one needs to reduce at all costs the complexity of process structures and their programmed base-logic processors.

While we have discussed in this chapter the use of asynchronous control for microarchitectures, which could be implemented using the VLSI strategy, the reader will observe that the structure proposed here can well apply to process realization in general. It is quite possible that with appropriate CAD tools and appropriate descriptive languages for expressing base logic (or convenient synthesis to base logic), newer forms of systems architectures may well, in many situations, avoid a microarchitectural level of the form we have discussed, be it horizontal or vertical (synchronous or asynchronous). Programmed logic for processor realization will only be introduced when deemed necessary for supporting families of similar processes and/or when advantages for design, testing, and maintenance can be obtained.

Diverging for a moment from the subject of microarchitectures for emulation and HLL instruction interpretation, we can observe that interesting applications of VLSI technology involving systolic algorithms have been proposed in which there is inherent natural parallelism that permits the design of regular arrays of logic, normally with homogeneous "data"-pipelined synchronous control of processing (Kung and Leiserson 1978). Unfortunately, emulation and HLL instruction interpretation do not fit into this class of "application" parallelism. Process execution in this environment is extremely heterogeneous. However, with the appropriate organization of asynchronous approaches we can hope to put some order into these complex processes.

To give a better idea of the new concepts introduced in this section, let us consider some processes of varying complexity with an idea of the type of processors required:

Process	*Processor*
Real-time clock	Sequential circuit with registers and random logic
Bus arbitration	Programmable logic array
Input/output control	Programmable logic via a static "control memory"
High-level language machine interpretation	Programmable logic via a dynamic "control memory"

The key point to be made here is that the processor-architecture complexity need only be as complex as required for the processes that it supports (executes). We can observe that the VLSI architecture concepts presented here provide for a form of distributed control. Remember that asynchronous control is the natural mechanism for permitting process execution at its own rate of speed, regardless of its physical location.

Implications of Improved Architectures

The possibilities of redistribution of functions between previous levels of hardware, firmware, and software architectures can be expanded with the introduction of a clearer notion of programmed logic and resulting process and processor organization. The view that all system architectural levels are composed of subsystems of cooperating processes, with clean intra- as well as interlevel interfaces, allows us to begin to understand redistribution possibilities (perhaps, in some cases, as mentioned above, eliminating what we know as microarchitecture today).

Global-design rules can hopefully be evolved that will allow a uniform view of activities at all levels and thus permit us to encapsulate redistribution possibilities into the CAD (in a broad sense) systems of tomorrow. In this environment, assuming the availability of powerful simulation engines, the necessary evaluation and insight can be gained. The synthesis of the programmed logic of processors at all levels (hopefully fewer levels than today) can be accomplished in a natural symbiosis between human and machine.

We can conclude that the 1980s will probably be an era of change for system architectures (including microarchitectures), due to the possibilities made available by VLSI and CAD systems. Hopefully, we shall move in the direction of producing highly structured systems that will be easier to design, implement, test, maintain, and utilize. Further, the systems of tomorrow will be easier to understand and provide for widespread education for new categories of "users" and layoperators. The generalization of the process-oriented approach advocated in this discussion has been used successfully in presenting a well-structured overview of computer system concepts and terminology for people (lay as well as professionals-to-be) from a variety of walks of life (Lawson 1981a). Hopefully, our architecture and educational activities will become closer in the future.

The discussion on future architectural implications in this section is based upon a paper presented at the 1981 National Computer Conference (Lawson 1981b). Since then, there has evidently been an increased interest in the use of asynchronous control, as indicated in the December 1985 issue of *Electronics* (Barney 1985). In the article entitled "Logic Designers Toss Out the Clock," the reader can observe many of the arguments, especially those related to complexity issues, that have been addressed in this chapter.

The use of asynchronous control has continued to be an active area of research for this author and his colleagues at Linköping University. As a concrete research area a project entitled ASAP (Architectural Strategy for Asynchronous Processing), sponsored by the Swedish National Board for Technical Development, is being pursued (Lawson and Lyles 1985). Note the convenient double meaning of "as soon as possible," which indicates the essence of asynchronous control.

SUMMARY

The experiences gained in the FCPU project certainly proved the feasibility and advantage of an asynchronous approach to the design of microarchitectures. The rationale applied in the development of the FCPU can be applied to future computer-system architectures. DataSaab constructed nine FCPUs for the D23 computer-system project. Thus, the FCPU was a working architecture. In fact, the last D23 was decommissioned in 1984. Unfortunately, for many reasons (nontechnical), DataSaab decided to abandon its medium-scale line of computer products in 1975. Thus, the FCPU was not further developed along the lines of its utilization as described in this chapter. Good technical ideas do not automatically lead to commercial success.

The computer club at Linköping University, LYSATOR, has been a repository for previous DataSaab computer products, including the FCPU-based D23. In fact, this group of enthusiastic students continually develops experiments with the FCPU, especially via microprograms. Projects including a FORTH language interpreter and UNIX operating-system support have been developed. Thus, the FCPU is still alive and some students have learned from experimenting with this "microprogrammable" device. The reader who wishes to investigate the FCPU further is referred to several publications (Lawson and Malm 1973a, 1974; Lawson and Blomberg 1973b; Lawson and Magnhagen 1975; Lawson 1983).

ACKNOWLEDGMENTS

The author is pleased to acknowledge the contribution of all those persons who participated in the design and development of the FCPU. Special appreciation is given to Bengt Malm, Håkan Niska, Torbjörn Granberg, Kerstin Berger, Lars Blomberg, Bengt Magnhagen, and Rolf Flisberg for their enthusiastic support and valuable contributions.

APPENDIX

This appendix is a summary of the syntax of simple statements in which there is a one-to-one correspondence between ML statements and microinstruction words. A list of the built-in names and a short statement of their use is also presented.

Built-in Names

Common to All Units
AUTFR　　　　　　　　The 8 to-and-from registers in AU.
CUTFR　　　　　　　　The 8 to-and-from registers in CU.
FUTFR　　　　　　　　The 8 to-and-from registers in FU.

Arithmetic Unit
ALF　　　　　　　　　Arithmetic-logic function of adder module (including carry in). Common names such as ADD, AND exist for the most frequently used ALF functions.

	GR	The 16 general registers.
	INSERT	Part of the target register in a SAM (shift-and-mask) instruction is replaced.
	INVERT	The mask of a SAM instruction is inverted.
	LEFT	Left shift logically 1, 2, or 4 binary steps of the result of an ADM (adder module) instruction.
	LOGICAL	The shift of a SAM instruction is performed as a logical shift.
	NULL	When appearing as a source register, the input is zero; when appearing as a result register, the result is not stored.
	RIGHT	Right shift logically 1, 2, or 4 binary steps of the result of an ADM instruction.
	RIGHT-A	Right shift arithmetically 1 binary step of the result of an ADM instruction.
	ROTATE	The bits shifted out at one end of the register are entered at the opposite end.
	SIGNPROP	Sign propagate in the mask function of a SAM instruction.
	SHIFT	Denotes a SAM dynamic shift instruction; i.e., the shift-and-mask amounts are supplied from an input register.
	SHL	Shift left static; i.e., the shift-and-mask amounts are stored in the instruction itself.
	SHR	Shift right static.
	ZEROFILL	Zerofill in the mask function of a SAM instruction.

Field Access Unit

	ACR	Denotes the four address control registers used to contain MSU addresses.
	LEFT	The data read or written is left-aligned.
	LENGTH	The length part of the MSU addresses replaced.
	NO ACCESS	No MSU access is made, used for setting and accessing values in the ACRs.
	STEPR, STEPL	Used together with SAVE to increment or decrement the MSU address by the length value prior to storing it in the ACR.
	WRITE	Transfer of data from FCPU to main storage unit.

Control-Unit Processing

AND	Logical and between two status flip-flops.
CARRY	The carry-out of the previous counting-register operation is used as carry-in to the current one.
CR	Counting registers addressable as two 64-bit registers or eight 16-bit registers.
CWL	Control write limit containing an address below which writing is prohibited.
EO	External output, a 32-bit register for communication with devices outside the FCPU, also addressable by bits.
FULL	All 64 bits are read from or written into control storage.
HALF	Half the length, 32 bits, are read from or written into control storage.
INDEX	When accessing control storage the content of one of the counting registers is added to the label reference to form the effective address.
INT	Interval timer, a 32-bit register counting microseconds.
IR	Interrupt register, indicating causes of interrupts, also addressable by bits.
MLC	Micro location counter stack; containing eight elements, the top element is the current location counter.
MRR	Microprogram recover register, a 64-bit register to which the current instruction of each unit can be read in case of an error in the FCPU.
NOT	The specified status flip-flop is completed.
OR	Logical or between two status flip-flops.
RTC	Real-time clock, a 40-bit register counting microseconds.
SS	Two 64-bit soft-status registers, also addressable by bits.
VLS-R	Eight 64-bit registers for communication with the VLS.
WSBIT	The 96 bits indicating the current status of the FCPU (contains status from FU, AU, and CU counting-register operations). Groups of WSBITs containing information

	of the same kind or from the same unit are addressable separately.
XOR	Exclusive or between two status flip-flops.

Control-unit Branch

ENTER	A subroutine is entered.
EXECUTE	An instruction is executed.
GOTO	Transfer of control.
MIX	The content of microprogram index register is added to the label reference to form the effective address.
RETURN	Return from subroutine.

Syntax

Notation

$$\begin{Bmatrix} - - - \\ - - - \\ - - - \end{Bmatrix}$$ One of the lines within the brackets must be chosen.

$[- - -]$ The expression inside the brackets may be left out.

Built-in names for groups of registers must be followed by an integer; its range is indicated inside ( ), e.g., GR(0, 15).

Arithmetic Unit

Move module:

$$C = B\,[,\,NSA]$$

Adder module:

$$C = \begin{Bmatrix} <\text{named function}> \\ ALF.\,(0, 509) \end{Bmatrix} \left[\begin{Bmatrix} ,RIGHT \\ ,RIGHT \\ ,RIGHT\text{-}A \end{Bmatrix} \begin{Bmatrix} ,1 \\ ,2 \\ ,4 \end{Bmatrix} \right] (A, B)$$

The first decimal digit in the ALF code indicates the function mode (logical, binary, BCD) and whether forced carry-in is to be applied. The last two digits indicate the function (15 logical and binary and 2 BCD).

$<$named function$>$ ::= built-in names for commonly used functions, e.g., ADD, AND, etc.

Shift and mask module:

$$C = \begin{Bmatrix} SHL \\ SHR \end{Bmatrix}, <\text{shift amount}>, \begin{Bmatrix} ZEROFILL \\ SIGNPROP \\ INSERT \end{Bmatrix},$$

$$<\text{mask position}> [, INVERT](B)$$

or

$$C = \text{SHIFT} \left[\left\{\begin{array}{l},\text{LOGICAL}\\,\text{ROTATE}\end{array}\right\}\right]\left[\left\{\begin{array}{l},\text{ZEROFILL}\\,\text{SIGNPROP}\\,\text{INSERT}\end{array}\right\}\right][,\text{INVERT}](A, B)$$

C is the target register for storing (i.e., the GRs, four FUTFRs, four CUTFRs, or NULL). A and B are input registers to be read from (i.e., the GRs, the eight AUTFRs, or NULL).

Field Unit

$$\left\{\begin{array}{l}\text{READ}\\\text{WRITE}\end{array}\right\} [, \text{NOACCESS}] \left(<\text{address source}>, <\text{FU register}> \left[\left\{\begin{array}{l},\text{RIGHT}\\,\text{LEFT}\end{array}\right\}\right]\right)$$

$$[\text{LENGTH}(<\text{constant}(1, 64)>)] \left[\left[\left\{\begin{array}{l}\text{STEPL,}\\\text{STEPR,}\end{array}\right\}\right]\text{SAVE } (<\text{acr}>)\right]$$

<address source> is the register from which the MSU address is taken (FUTFR, ACR, or VLS)
<FU register> is a CUTFR or AUTFR in a READ and a FUTFR in a WRITE.
<acr> is one of four address control registers in the FU.

Control-unit Processing

Status Manipulation, A, B, and C are status flip-flops.

$$C = \left\{\begin{array}{l}\text{AND}\\\text{OR}\\\text{XOR}\end{array}\right\} ([\text{NOT}]A, B)$$

Counting-register manipulation, B and C are 16-bit counting.

$$C = \left\{\begin{array}{l}<\text{named function}>\\\text{ALF.}(0, 315)\end{array}\right\} \left(\left\{\begin{array}{l}B\\<\text{constant } (-32768, 32767)>\end{array}\right\}\right)$$

See "Arithmetic Unit" for an explanation of the ALF Code. BCD function mode is not permitted. The operation is performed on C and B, and the result is stored in C.

CUP Move, B and C are the registers in CU in addition to TFRs.

$$\left\{\begin{array}{l}<\text{label reference}>\\C\end{array}\right\}\left\{\begin{array}{l},\text{FULL}\\,\text{HALF}\end{array}\right\} [, \text{INDEX}]\}$$

$$= \left\{\begin{array}{l}<\text{label reference}>\\B\end{array}\right\}\left\{\begin{array}{l},\text{FULL}\\,\text{HALF}\end{array}\right\} [, \text{INDEX}]\right\}$$

<label reference> is the name of a label in the microprogram or a declared constant or variable. Only one label reference is allowed; i.e., control-storage write or read is possible.

Control-unit Branch
A is a status flip-flop.

$$\left\{ \begin{array}{l} \left\{ \begin{array}{l} \text{GOTO} \\ \text{EXECUTE} \\ \text{ENTER} \end{array} \right\} [, \text{MIX}] <\text{label reference}> \\ \text{RETURN} \\ \text{IF [NOT] A} \quad \text{THEN} \left\{ \begin{array}{l} \text{GOTO} \\ \text{EXECUTE} \\ \text{ENTER} \end{array} \right\} [, \text{MIX}] <\text{label reference}> \\ \text{IF [NOT] A} \quad \text{THEN GOTO [,MIX]} <\text{label reference}> \\ \hspace{6cm} \text{ELSE RETURN} \\ \text{START} (<\text{VLS function code}>, <\text{label reference}>) \end{array} \right.$$

REFERENCES

Barney, C. 1985. "Logic Designers Toss Out the Clock." *Electronics*, December.

Bell, C. G., and Newell, A. 1971. *Computer Structures: Readings and Examples*. New York: McGraw-Hill.

Computer Decisions. 1971. "The Many Faces of Microprogramming." *Computer Decisions*, September.

Dijkstra, E. W. 1968. "Cooperating Sequential Processes." In *Programming Languages*, ed. F. Genuys. New York: Academic Press.

Husson, S. S. 1970. *Microprogramming Principles and Practices*. Englewood Cliffs, NJ: Prentice-Hall.

IBM. 1960. *IBM Corporation Basic Systems Language*.

Kung, H. T., and Leiserson, C. E. 1978. "Systolic Arrays (for VLSI)." *Proceedings of the Society of Industrial and Applied Mathematics on Sparse Matrices*, Philadelphia, PA: SIAM.

Lawson, H. W. 1968. "Programming-language-oriented Instruction Streams," *IEEE Trans. Comput.* C-17: 733–47.

——. 1976. "Function Distribution in Computer System Architectures." *Proceedings of the Third Annual Symposium on Computer Architecture*.Rockville, MD: IEEE Computer Science Press.

——. 1981a. *Understanding Computer Systems*. Rockville, MD: Computer Science Press.

——. 1981b. "New Directions for Micro- and System Architectures in the 1980s." *Proceedings of the National Computer Conference*, Chicago, Illinois.

——. 1983. "Flexibility and Asynchronism in Microprogrammable Computer Architectures," Ph.D. dissertation , Royal Institute of Technology, Stockholm.

Lawson, H. W., and Smith, B. K. 1971. "Functional Characteristics of a Multilingual Processor." *IEEE Trans. Comput.* C-20: 732–42.

Lawson, H. W., and Malm, B. 1973. "A Flexible Asynchronous Microprocessor." *BIT* 13(2).

Lawson, H. W., and Blomberg, L. 1973. "The DataSaab FCPU Microprogramming Language." *Proceedings of the SIGPLAN/SIGMICRO Interface Meeting*, Harriman, N.Y., May 1973.

———. 1974. "The DataSaab Flexible Central Processing Unit (FCPU)." *Infotek State of the Art Series, Report 17 on Computer Design*.

Lawson, H. W., and Magnhagen, B. 1975. "Advantages of Structured Hardware." *Proceedings of the Second Annual Symposium on Computer Architecture*, Houston, TX: IEEE Computer Science Press.

Lawson, H. W., and Lyles, J. B. 1985. "An Architectural Strategy for Asynchronous Processing." In *Concurrent Languages in Distributed Systems: Hardware Supported Implementation*, eds. G. L. Reijns and E. L. Dagless. Amsterdam: North-Holland.

McKeeman, W. 1967. "Language Directed Computer Design." *Proceedings of AFIPS SJCC* 31: 413–18.

Melbourne, A. J., and Pugmire, J. M. 1965. "A Small Computer for the Direct Processing of FORTRAN Statements." *Computer Journal* 8: 24–27.

Opler, A. 1967. "Fourth Generation Software." *Datamation* 13: 22–24.

QM-1. 1970. Nanodata Corporation. Williamsville, New York.

Rakozi, L. L. 1969. "The Computer-within-a-Computer, a Fourth Generation Concept." *Computer Group News* 2: 14.

Redfield, S. R. 1971. "A Study in Microprogramming Processors: a Medium-Sized Microprogrammed Processor." *IEEE Trans. Comput.* C-20.

Rosin, R. F. 1969. "Contemporary Concepts in Microprogramming and Emulation." *Computing Surveys* 1 (4):197.

Rosin, R. F.; Freider, G.; and Eckhouse, R. Jr. 1972. "An Environment for Research in Microprogramming and Emulation." *Communications of the ACM* 15 (8).

Salisbury, A. B. 1976. *Microprogrammable Computer Architectures*. New York: American Elsevier.

Standard Computer. 1970. *ICAP II Language Programmers Manual*. Santa Ana, CA: Standard Computer Corporation.

Tucker, S. G. 1967. "Microprogram Control for System/360." *IBM System Journal* 6 (4): 222–41.

Turing, A. M. 1936–7. "On Computable Numbers with an Application to the Entscheidungsproblem." *Proceedings of the London Mathematics Society* 2 (42): 230–65.

Weber, H. 1967. "A Microprogrammed Implementation of Euler on IBM 360/30." *Communications of the ACM* 10: 549–58.

Wilkes, M. V. 1951. "The Best Way to Design an Automatic Calculating Machine." *Proceedings of Manchester University Inaugural Conference*. Manchester, England: University of Manchester.

_____. 1969. "The Growth of Interest in Microprogramming." *Computing Surveys* 1(3):14.

Wilner, W. T. 1972. "Design of the B1700." *Proceedings of the FJCC*. Anaheim, CA.

Wirth, N. 1968. "PL/360, A Programming Language for the 360 Computers." *Journal of the Association for Computing Machinery*, 15-1: 37–74.

four
HIGH-LEVEL MICROPROGRAMMING LANGUAGES

SCOTT DAVIDSON

The great majority of software written today is written using higher-level languages (HLLs). It is therefore natural that a great deal of research has been done in higher-level microprogramming languages (HLMLs). Nonetheless, most microcode is written with either microassemblers or low-level languages. This chapter will investigate why this is the case.

First, why would we want to use an HLML? The reason is basically the same as for using an HLL, to increase programmer (microprogrammer) productivity. This occurs in several ways. The first is that the HLL is closer to the domain of the problem than an assembler language, and the programmer can thus state the solution to the problem in fewer steps, i.e., in terms of the algorithm, not details of the target implementation. This means that the complexity of the actual solution is reduced. Second, the HLL constrains the solution through the use of mechanisms such as type checking and syntax analysis. A program that has been successfully compiled is more likely to be correct than one that has been successfully assembled. Third, a variety of tools exist to assist the HLL programmer in constructing and debugging a program. The number of such tools has increased with the number of HLL users, while the fact that an assembly language is limited to one machine has tended to limit the number of tools. Widely used machine families, such as System/360, of course, have a better selection of tools available, but none so numerous as a language such as COBOL.

The wide use of an HLML would tend to bring such benefits to the microprogrammer. With a larger number of users, tools could be developed for that language. Fewer mistakes would be made in microcode, speeding the production process. Greater productivity would lower microcode cost, allowing more functions to be written in microcode. Larger microprogramming projects would also become more feasible with a reduced staff.

In the late 1960s the perception of a "software crisis" led to the development of the field of software engineering. The area of firmware engineering already exists, by analogy to software engineering, but its relevance is reduced by the lack of an HLML. We do not expect a "firmware crisis" because microcode can always be migrated up to software where necessary, but we do not know what the lack of an HLML is costing today.

First, let us define high-level microprogramming languages. A microprogramming language is simply a language designed to be compiled into microcode. An HLML is somewhat harder to define. It has the property that one statement of the language is compiled into several target-machine statements. The language must also contain constructs not directly implemented by the target machine. These are typically control constructs, such as **for** loops. This is necessary but not sufficient as a definition. We also require that an HLML have some of the data- and control-structuring features of an HLL.

The possibility that a language can also be interpreted or compiled into machine language is not excluded by this definition. Some HLMLs can be compiled into machine language; microTAL is one example (Bartlett 1981). Many HLMLs are adaptations of HLLs. microAPL (Hobson, Hannon, and Thornburg 1981) is an example of this, as are several microcode versions of C (Gurd 1983; Hopkins, Horton, and Arnold 1985; Duda and Mueller 1985).

If there is no theoretical difference between HLLs and HLMLs, what are the practical differences and similarities? Let us look at the similarities first. The class of language that HLMLs most resemble is the systems-implementation language (SIL). Languages of this type are meant for operating-system or utility design. They give direct or indirect access to target-machine resources and tend to be lean in that there is a good match between language constructs and the target. (By *target* we mean the machine for which microcode is to be generated. This usage is different from what is meant when discussing emulation.) SILs frequently do not contain I/O constructs but depend on operating-system calls. C is a popular SIL (Kernighan and Richie 1978).

HLMLs and SILs share the ability to support the writing of structured programs. They allow the use of subroutines, free-form program structure, the use of indentation for readability, the use of comments, and control structures such as **case** statements and **for** and **while** loops. They usually have **goto** statements for efficiency, as well as loop-exit statements. They also contain some methods of structuring data to allow several fields to be referenced together. Both classes of language support Boolean operations on bit vectors.

The differences between SILs and HLMLs arise in areas that HLMLs are not expected to support. HLMLs will usually not have a multiply operator, since many microprogrammable machines do not have a hardware multiply. SILs do, since even if a machine does not have either a firmware or hardware multiply, a call to a software multiply routine will not critically degrade performance in most SIL applications. SILs support pointers so that complex structures in memory can be easily built. HLMLs do not, since memory access is more expensive, and the use of memory in microcode is usually more limited. Floating-point operations are almost never found in an HLML.

HLMLs contain some features that many SILs do not. One is the ability to define fields of a bit string and to extract or insert values from or to these fields. Finally, many HLMLs, especially machine-dependent HLMLs, allow direct access to more of the target-machine resources than do SILs. HLMLs usually do not offer any protection to the programmer not found in the hardware.

We have described indirectly what can be expected to be found in an HLML. The features of some HLMLs will be given in more detail later in this chapter.

What are the advantages of HLMLs over microassembly languages? To some extent they are the same as the advantages of HLLs. A true HLML would require less of the programmer's effort to be expended in keeping track of the physical location of the variables in the program. In lower-level languages the microprogrammer must explicitly cause data to be transferred to and from memory. An HLML should be able to handle this. An HLML compiler should also include an optimizer to increase the efficiency of the produced code. All these factors should increase the microprogrammer's productivity. Interim work supports this hypothesis (Sheraga and Gieser 1981), but a complete study has yet to be done.

At the present state of the art in microcode compilers a person writing microcode can still do better than the compiler for small amounts of microcode. Even if this remains true in the future, the use of an HLML allows the possibility of higher-level improvements, to the algorithm, perhaps. A worker at the microassembly level tends to get lost in the details of the code; a worker at the HLML level can see its purpose more clearly. Patterson (1981a) reports that an emulator written in a high-level machine-dependent language took less space than the same program written in a microassembly language because of the identification of improvements that were visible at the higher level. Moving to still higher levels should increase this, perhaps to the point that the common advice to HLL programmers, "Optimize the algorithm, not the program," would also be applicable to HLML programmers.

Another advantage of HLMLs is the decrease in the distance between the algorithm being implemented and the language of the implementation machine. (Here, "algorithm" is being used loosely in the sense of a high-level implementation-independent description of the job to be done.) The writer of an HLL program does not have to keep two different problem domains in mind but only the one that the programmer is most interested in. The low-level-language programmer, on the other hand, must be an expert in the structure of the host machine as well as in the target problem domain. Certainly, the constraints of the language must be dealt with in both cases, but the higher the language level, the fewer the irrelevant constraints.

With all these advantages, why have HLMLs not been more widely accepted? One reason is that code written with an HLML compiler has been perceived as not as efficient as code written with a microassembler. An efficient HLML compiler is possible but difficult. Why is no such compiler available?

Let us consider where HLML compilers are written. In the academic environment the support does not exist for a production-quality compiler. Much work has been done on developing different techniques for the efficient production of microcode, but as yet they have not been put together into one widely available, well-supported compiler. The compiler and microprogramming support system reported by Young (1988) is a first step in this direction, however.

Work on compilers has also been done in the industrial environment, but here there are other reasons for their unavailability. The first is the proprietary nature of much industrial research. More efficient production of microcode represents a competitive advantage for a processor vendor, so such a vendor is unlikely to make the details available. Second, assuming an efficient compiler does exist, there is a limited outside market for it. A compiler in an industrial environment is developed for a specific target machine; and since most vendors discourage user microprogramming, the compiler would not be made available outside the microprogramming shop of that company. Third, since microprogramming usually produces a fairly limited amount of code for a particular target, there is less incentive to produce a compiler, because low-level techniques do work well for small amounts of code. Also, as mentioned above, assemblers and low-level languages are particularly fitted to the production of emulators, a large part of the microprogramming task.

In the industrial environment there are usually strict time constraints on a microprogramming project. A compiler would have to save more time than it would take to write it to be practical. There are two ways around this problem. The first would be to use a machine-independent language. Here, only the code generator needs to be written for a particular target, and much of the microprogramming could be done in parallel to compiler development. The problem is that we do not know how to write an efficient compiler for a machine-independent language intended for applications that require specific target-machine resources. The second possibility is to use a machine-dependent language, but since the structure of the target machine is bound to the structure of the language compiler, development could not begin until the design of the target hardware is complete, which is too late.

Another problem is the lack of a market for an HLML. There are enough users of any particular model of computer to make the production of compilers for that computer economic and, for vendors, necessary. The use of compatible instruction sets for several models increases the market for a compiler. Not only vendors but independent software suppliers provide compilers. This is not the case for microprogramming. In general, the market for an HLML for a particular target would be small. One exception would be the AMD 2900 series of bit-slice microprogrammable machines. These, however, have special problems in that they can be used in a great variety of configurations. Nonetheless, someone attempting to write a marketable HLML might want to start here. Certainly, microassemblers are commercially available for these machines. An easily retargetable compiler would also help, but this has proven to be quite difficult to implement.

Another exception is the case of a family of machines with somewhat similar microarchitectures. This situation extends the payback period for language development and makes the project more feasible. The language Ohne (Wagnon and Maine 1983) seems to have been developed in this environment.

The market for an HLML is small in another sense. Within a company only a limited number of people will be involved in microprogramming: the writers of an emulator for a new processor, applications microprogrammers, and a few people doing research. This is a more homogeneous group than the users of an HLL, and fewer aids to microprogramming are considered essential. Those in control of allocating research dollars must consider whether developing an HLML would significantly increase the productivity of these few people and whether many of these people would be willing users. Thus, there are social reasons for the lack of an HLML. We will not discuss these social issues any further, for they must be met in each microprogramming environment. The existence of a proven HLML would do a great deal to promote HLML acceptance in industry. Therefore, we will spend the rest of the chapter discussing technical issues.

Most of the rest of this chapter is composed of an extensive survey of microprogramming languages. (A good but less extensive survey can be found in Sint 1980.) We begin with a discussion of early microprogramming tools, bit-stuffers, and microassemblers. We will then discuss low-level and high-level microprogramming languages in more detail and give some examples of a microprogram written in several proposed HLMLs. Unfortunately, we can only compare the syntaxes of the languages and obtain some idea of the advantages and disadvantages of using each language. Since none of these languages is generally available, we cannot compare the efficiency of code produced for the example or make much of a quantitative analysis. We also include some examples of lower-level languages as a basis of comparison.

The next section also covers the technical reasons for the lack of HLMLs in more detail, building on the given examples. The final section of the chapter gives a summary and some suggestions as to the utility of HLMLs for different microprogramming applications. Much good work has been done on microprogramming languages, and successful languages are beginning to appear for certain limited applications. Still better HLMLs are possible, especially with an understanding of previous efforts.

The references give suggestions for further reading, with an extensive list of the papers on HLMLs that have appeared. Such a list is primarily of historical importance, for new and better HLMLs are reported each year. The only way of keeping up to date is to keep abreast of the literature.

EARLY MICROPROGRAMMING TOOLS

One might expect that the development of microprogramming languages would parallel the development of HLLs. This is not the case. The greater emphasis on lower-level microprogramming languages has caused these and assembly languages to be developed far beyond machine-language assemblers and low-level machine languages. Many of the same factors that have delayed the development of HLMLs have been successfully solved at this lower level. Microprogrammers have some of the best assemblers in the world!

Microcode, like machine code, was written before there were assemblers. The most primitive tool for writing microcode is called a bit-stuffer. This is a tool that allows the fields of a microinstruction to be filled in off-line. The bit-stuffer would then produce a guide to making the read-only memory (ROM) to implement the microcode. The first bit-stuffers accepted binary; later ones would allow fields to be specified in hexadecimal or octal.

The disadvantages of the bit-stuffer are clear. The microcode is very hard to read and write, and it is very easy to make errors in writing it. Illegal operations, wrong operations, and conflicting fields would be accepted without complaint. So, following the example of machine-language programmers, microassemblers began to be constructed.

Here we must make a distinction between vertical and horizontal microprogrammable targets. The structure of tools for vertical machines has closely followed the structure of tools for machine-language programming, because the use of only one or two microoperations per microinstruction closely parallels the case of machine language. There are other issues not faced by the machine-language programmer, such as expensive memory access and next-address fetching techniques driven by target-machine peculiarities, but these have not significantly affected language design. Most work has been in the area of tools for the generation of code for horizontal machines, and this is where we will place our emphasis.

The first microassemblers contained some simple but very useful improvements on bit-stuffers. First, the microprogrammer was given the ability to define labels and to reference them in branch microoperations, as is the case with machine-language assemblers. The second is the definition of mnemonics for legal values of the fields of the microinstruction. This prevents the microprogrammer from specifying an illegal value, and if the mnemonics are chosen properly, makes it less likely that an incorrect value will be specified. Reading mnemonics in place of binary or octal numbers gives the maintainer (and writer) of the microcode a much better idea of what is being done by the microinstruction. Comments could also be included, which are more valuable the lower the level of the program. Finally, the microinstructions could be formatted in such a way as to give a better indication of which value went into which field. An example of code written with a primitive microassembler appears in figure 4-1.

This technique hardly solves all the problems of low-level microprogramming. The semantics of the microinstruction sometimes constrain the value of one field, depending on the value of another field. There is no way of showing this with a primitive microassembler, and usually no way of checking for this type of error. Defaults are not allowed: each field must be assigned a value, even if that field is not participating in this microinstruction. There is still a great deal of hexadecimal notation being used instead of symbols. For instance, to specify an arithmetic-and-logic-unit (ALU) operation, one must give the number to be input to the ALU select lines for that operation, not a symbol for the operation. The operands are given in other fields, three other fields if a literal is used. Finally, in order to get a 16-bit literal into 8 bits, an encoding is used. The microassembler does not help with this encoding; the encoded value must be given. Still, this is a great improvement over the bit-stuffer.

Further improvements in microassemblers were made in three areas: the simplification of input, by using more of a free-form approach; the improvement of reliability by including syntactic and semantic checking within the microassembler; and the facilitation of the creation of these more complex microassemblers through the use of meta-assemblers. We will consider these areas in turn.

The main difficulty in allowing free-form input is that there are more fields

Figure 4-1. Example of microcode written with a simple microassembler.

DC Data to Accumulator Instruction Class

DS Data Set-up, Decode Operation

ADR	ROM 987654321	LB	FIELDS STACDXFYM21ZW	COMMENTS
03C	9BA93B570	DC	4AB22903B5700	<-IR&0X0700-1; IF E11S=0 GOTO LOC 57
03D	AB297E4F2		5LB02913E3F02	T<-IR&0X000F; IF E07S=1 GOTO DS(LOC3F); F=1
03E	AF27 9922		5LF027 99202	T=XR;IF E03S=1 GOTO LOC 92
03F	0 0 3 588	DS	00 00 0 5810	LOOKUP TABLE 5,8 FOR GEN OP 1
040	4A88E0FF4		2LA20B 20FF04	FB=T; C,V=0; GOTO (TABLE)
041	6 0 B F20		30 00 2 F200	F=2; BUS CYCLE

in a microinstruction of a horizontally microprogrammable machine than can fit on a single line. Two solutions to this have been implemented. The first was used by IBM for System/360 microcode (Husson 1970). The microoperations for a microinstruction word are placed in a flow-chart box (fig. 4-2). In this approach the microoperation to be specified is determined by its placement in the box. Each box (microinstruction) is partially identified by its placement on a page. This allows the value of a particular microoperation to be easily found by its position. Default values of microoperations can be specified by leaving a position blank, which quickly shows the reader which microoperations have been defaulted and tends to reduce the amount of information in a box.

The other approach, more widely used, is to attach a tag identifying the microoperation being specified to each value. Depending on the target architecture, this might be an identifier for each microinstruction field or one giving the microoperation type. In the latter case values may be assigned by the microassembler to several fields. In other instances the mnemonic for a value might also implicitly specify the field to which the value is to be assigned. The proper choice of mnemonics can give the microassembly language some of the appearance of an HLML. For instance, writing

$$R1 = R1 + A;$$

might cause values to be assigned to the two ALU source fields (for registers R1 and A), to the ALU destination field (to use the input general register), and to the ALU operation field (ADD). This is certainly easier to read and write than

$$\text{Add, R1, A, R1}$$

but it is less general than it looks, for saying

$$R2 = R1 + A;$$

should lead to a syntax error if it is not possible to specify three different

Figure 4-2. Example of microcode written in flow-chart notation.

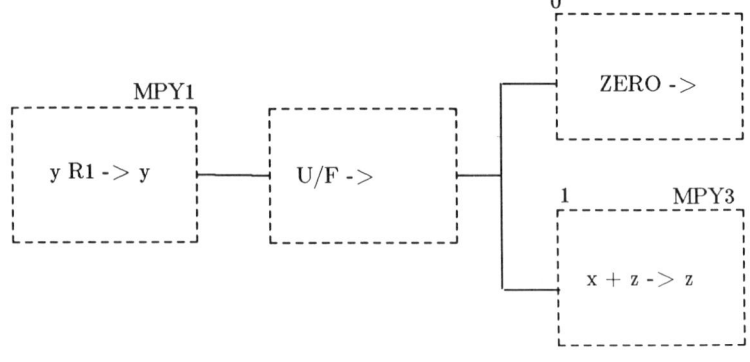

registers in a microinstruction. Microassemblers take little of the burden off the microprogrammer.

This second variety of microassembler has been more widely used because it fits the commonly available line-oriented text editor and paper terminal better than the flow-chart method. With today's more powerful terminals and editors, however, perhaps the two-dimensional approach should be more widely used outside IBM.

The discussion of errors in the specification of an arithmetic operation leads us to the second area of improvement in microassemblers: better checking of syntax and semantics. Constraints enforced by the architecture of the target machine should be checked by the assembler. These include constraints in register usage, as in the example above; limitations on which microoperations can be placed in the same microinstruction; constraints in the content of certain fields depending on what has been specified for other fields; and enforcement of sometimes nonobvious rules. Giving a set of mnemonics for the microoperations helps in this, for it limits the user's freedom. Exactly how much can be checked depends on the nature of the target machine and the sophistication of the microassembler.

The third advance in microassemblers has been to reduce the cost of creating an assembler for a new architecture. The use of table-driven or meta-assemblers allows the construction of a new assembler by simply defining the mnemonics for the microoperations and the format of the target microinstruction. Most of the work of creating an assembler has already been done. Another advantage is that all the assemblers created with the meta-assembler will have the same general structure; all the pseudo-ops will be the same; and in general the syntax of all the microassembly languages will be similar; therefore it will be easier for a user to learn second and subsequent languages for different machines. A good survey appears in "Meta-assemblers" (Skordalakis 1983).

There have been other advances in microassemblers, such as a self-commenting assembler, which reports in easy-to-read terms what each microinstruction does (Laws 1977). Far more research has been put into microassemblers than machine-language assemblers in the last ten years. An example of state-of-the-art microassembler design can be found in the M29 (Eager 1983).

With free-form input, relatively meaningful mnemonics, and assembler-development systems, microassembly languages have moved closer to lower-level-language quality. In the next section we discuss the development of low-level languages.

LOWER-LEVEL MICROPROGRAMMING LANGUAGES

In the past, lower-level microprogramming languages have had the most success. Being close to the semantics of the target machine in most cases, it was not difficult to write efficient code generators for these languages. Compiler technology is at a state where many people have the ability to write compilers and compiler-writing tools are common, making the job of writing a compiler for a low-level language neither difficult nor time-consuming. More difficult is the job of making the language easy for microprogrammers to use, but the advantages over microassemblers are so great as to make even a less than perfect language desirable.

The major difference between the low-level language and the microassembler language is not format but semantic sophistication. The microassembler language would accept only those constructs directly supported by the target machine. The low-level language accepts constructs that make sense at the algorithmic level. It is the job of the compiler to determine a sequence of microoperations to perform the given task. This is, of course, also true of high-level languages. The syntax and semantics of the low-level language enforce the use of low-level constructs that the relatively unsophisticated compiler can handle.

Efficient compilation of machine-independent microprogramming languages requires more sophistication in the structure of the compiler, especially in the code generator. For this reason low-level languages have been primarily machine-dependent. Another reason is that the effort of writing a low-level-language compiler for a target lies primarily in code generation, an effort not reduced by a machine-independent language and compiler.

Perhaps the best way to get a feel for a low-level microprogramming language is by an example. Figure 4-3 gives a multiply routine in the language GMPL (Guffin 1982). GMPL is targeted for a proprietary HP processor, but this exam-

Figure 4-3. Sample microprogram in GMPL.

```
INSTRUCTION Mult;
    Begin
        READ (B);                       Read From Memory
        INPUT WORD MREG ==> x;
        y AND M1 ==> ACC;               Mask
        READ (A);                       Multiplicand from memory
        INPUT WORD MREG ==> x;
        ACC + x ==> ACC;                Determine result sign
        x AND M2 ==> x;                 Magnitude of mcand in x
        ACC AND M1 ==> z;               Sign to result register
        y AND M2 ==> y;                 Magnitude of multiplier in y
* Beginning of loop. It is not a repeat because there is no variable
* to increment or decrement
    MPY1:   SHIFT y RIGHT 1 ==> y;
            IF U/F THEN MPY3;           A bit dropped?
            IF ZERO THEN MPY4;          All done?
    MPY2:   SHIFT x LEFT 1 ==> x;
            GOTO MPY1;
    MPY3:   x + z ==> z;                Accumulate result
            GOTO MPY2;
    MPY4:   OUTPUT WORD z;
            WRITE (C);
            EXIT;
```

ple is written as if it were targeted for another machine (Tucker and Flynn 1971).

This program does multiplication by the shift-and-add algorithm. The multiplier is in memory at location B; the multiplicand is at location A; and the result is to be placed in location C. The numbers are in sign and magnitude representation. This sign of the multiplier is stripped off and placed in the accumulator (ACC). The multiplicand is added to this to give the sign of the result, which is placed in the result register z. Then a standard shift and add is done, with the multiplicand added to the result whenever the low bit of the multiplier is 1. The multiplicand is shifted left and the multiplier is shifted right at every step. When the multiplier becomes 0, all significant bits have been considered, and the result is written into memory.

Even with the given comments, it is unlikely that the casual reader could have determined the details of the algorithm from the given program. That a knowledge of the target machine is necessary to understand a program is typical of low-level machine-dependent microprogramming languages. Examining this program statement by statement will give us some insight into the nature of this type of language.

The first two statements clearly fetch B from memory and place it in register y. From the second statement we see that another register, MREG, is also involved. Someone unfamiliar with the microprogrammable architectures might wonder what the difference is between READ and INPUT. A knowledge of the target would give the answer: READ (B) sets up the memory address register and initiates the READ command, while INPUT completes it. The data from memory is now in the memory data register (MREG), and is then moved to the y register. In a microassembler language this code would require at least four microoperations:

$$\text{MAR} \leftarrow \text{B; Start Read; Finish Read; } x \leftarrow \text{MREG;}$$

which might require as few as two microinstructions, depending on the parallel data paths available in the target.

The protocol for a memory read is somewhat hidden by the low-level language. The MAR is accessed implicitly, and we would expect that the location of the multiplier would be assigned by the compiler. However, the two-step nature of the process is still evident, and the data must be explicitly moved to a register before it can be used.

The third statement is a typical assignment statement. It is quite clear except for the use of M1. A sophisticated language might accept a constant here and automatically assign it to a mask register (for that is what M1 is), but if users of the language were assumed to be familiar with the target architecture, the name of the mask register would be used. Another solution would be to have an initialization section that would assign values to mask registers. Clearly, the first solution is the most machine-independent, showing that low-level languages can be more or less dependent on a target architecture.

The fourth and fifth statements read the multiplicand from A and place it in register x. We see that these statements could be considered a primitive of the language, perhaps defined by a macro. The target architecture, however, will determine whether this is a good idea. If the memory cycle time is long compared to the microinstruction execution time, it would be advantageous to place instructions not depending on the data being retrieved from memory between the initiation and the completion of the memory transfer. This can be done by the expert microprogrammer in the language as given, but it could not be done if the structure of the memory-transfer protocol were hidden by the language. This difficulty could only be rectified if the compiler were sophisticated enough to do this scheduling. This is an example of how the need for efficiency requires either sophisticated compilers or low-level languages.

The next four statements are three masks and an addition. Here, M2 contains 011...11. The next statement shifts register y right one bit. As is standard, this target fills the high bit of y with a 0. In this target, the bit lost by the shift sets a condition code called underflow (U/F), which can be tested at the next microinstruction. Allowing the condition to be tested is an example of the machine dependence of the language, since this is not a predicate that can be expected in a machine-independent language. As we will see, this section of code must be rewritten in some of the other languages we will consider.

The next statement again tests the result of the shift. A more readable version of this statement would be

$$\text{IF } y = 0 \text{ THEN MPY4};$$

but this would likely cause another ALU operation to be performed, and, depending on the sophistication of the compiler, require additional microinstructions and time. This is another example of how access to target-machine resources from the language can improve efficiency.

The THEN clause of the IF statement looks like BASIC. The next two statements are a shift left (putting a 0 in the least significant bit) and a GOTO. **Gotos** appear in all low-level languages, since they are easy to implement when complex procedure environments are not allowed.

The final three statements of the program, beginning at the label MPY4, write the register to memory location C and exit (the subroutine). Again we have a two-part memory operation, first putting the data in the MREG and then giving the write address. These statements are somewhat deceptive in that the MREG and the memory address register are not explicitly mentioned. Someone wishing to use these registers for data storage could easily introduce a subtle bug by inserting a write. This is an example of an often stated advantage of high-level languages: protecting a programmer from self-destruction.

We have seen some common features of low-level machine-dependent languages in this example: the use of register names for most data manipulation, semantics that may be either cryptic or deceptively simple for one not well versed in the details of the target machine, and the use of constructs mapping directly to target resources for efficiency. That this is a successful combination of features can be seen from the fact that low-level languages rank just behind assembly languages in popularity. The audience for these languages is comprised of those who are expert in a target but who wish to be freed from the tedium of repeatedly writing certain constructs in the assembler. For this audience low-level languages have proven quite successful, as will be seen in the next section.

A Survey of Low-Level Machine-Dependent Languages

We will describe in some detail four LLMDLs. There are far more reported in the literature and even more existing as proprietary languages, for the reasons mentioned above. These four, however, should give a feel for the state of this class of languages both when most research was being done on them in the mid-1970s and today.

The first language we will describe is ML (microprogramming language) for the DATASAAB FPCU (Lawson and Blomberg 1973). Much of any report on an LLMDL is a description of the target architecture, which is not relevant here. For our purposes it is sufficient to note that the FPCU had a vertical architecture and a 32-bit control word. Data could be stored in control store, unlike many microarchitectures, giving the machine more of the look of a standard architecture. Sequencing is done by a microprogram counter.

ML is a free-format language, with statements terminated by the end of line (though continuation characters were allowed). ML is somewhat block-structured, with one outer block and several inner blocks, all at one level below the outer block. Variables of the outer block are separated from the collected variables of all inner blocks, and constants are local to each inner block.

The first section of each block is for declarations. Machine resources are predeclared but can be given synonyms. Local variables can be declared, and it appears that constants used within each block have to be declared. Constants that can be specified as immediate operands have to be declared, though they are not allocated control-storage locations.

Most statements in the language correspond directly to target microinstructions and are built into the language. A number of control statements are available. **Case** statements are implemented by a DO CASE statement, which generates code using an indexed branch. Destinations not specified are automatically filled with a NO-OP. DO Loops are available. Examining this statement more closely will show why statements in low-level languages that look high-level may not be. The DO Loop allows the specification of an index variable, an increment, and a terminating condition, much as in HLLs. The index variable, however, must be one of the counting registers of the FPCU. This is a common restriction of microprogrammed architectures. The increment can be anything. The terminating condition, however, must be one of ZERO, ONE, ONES (all ones), POSITIVE, or NEGATIVE. More general terminating conditions, which I am sure could be supported, were not used because they were not directly supported by the target architecture.

As this example shows, how high a level the microprogramming language reaches is often directly dependent on the support of the target architecture for high-level constructs. The need for efficiency often precluded the use of high-level constructs that could be supported, though not directly.

The second example is ANIMIL (another interesting microprogramming language), developed for the signal-processing arithmetic unit (SPAU) of the AN/UYK-17 computer (Rauscher 1973). SPAU was a horizontal architecture, with 160-bit words divided into 68 fields.

The only sequencing command in ANIMIL is an IF statement. Its major claim to being high-level is a free-format syntax and the selection of data paths used for data transfers by the compiler. The complexity of the architecture made it unreasonable for the microprogrammer to completely specify the path for each transfer. Having the compiler do it must have been helpful.

One interesting aspect of ANIMIL was its solution to the problem of checking microoperation semantics, mentioned in the section on microassemblers above. As is often the case, many syntactically correct constructs in the language were semantically incorrect. An abstract interpreter was proposed to interpret the parse tree to check for invalid operands, and so on. ANIMIL demonstrated that sophisticated language issues are presented even by low-level microprogramming languages and that advanced compiler theory could be useful in addressing these issues.

The third example is GPM, a general-purpose microprogramming language for the MLP-900 processor project at USC Information Science Institute (Oestreicher 1973). The MLP-900 was a vertical machine, designed as a slave processor for a DEC-10.

GPM uses simple statements and allows a free format. The language has a syntactic block structure, which is a compile time artifact, with no local variables. All registers have reserved names but can be renamed on a block basis. This is useful in giving the microprogrammer the ability to give registers names meaningful in a local context, but it could introduce unexpected aliasing. Expressions of any complexity are allowed as long as no temporary registers are required. As in ANIMIL, specifying some data transfers caused the compiler to generate several microinstructions moving the data through several intermediate locations.

Three types of control statements are supported. The first is the standard IF. The DO statement heads a block representing the body of an infinite loop, exited by using a BREAK statement. The SWITCHON statement causes an indexed jump to a location specified by a CASE statement, with the jump table automatically generated.

The primitiveness of the semantics of GPM was a result of the primitiveness of the target microinstruction set. As we have seen, the language designer striving for efficiency has little choice but to design a language that does not make great demands on the target.

The three languages described above show the influence of 1973-style architectures. GMPL, a microprogramming language for a Hewlett-Packard proprietary 32-bit microprocessor (Guffin 1982), shows the effects of modern architectures on LLMDLs. Actually, we might say GMPL shows the effects of microprogramming languages on microarchitectures. The target of GMPL has many features that make microprogramming and the construction of a microprogramming language simpler. The target architecture is vertical, with a 32-bit microinstruction word. The microarchitecture is designed for emulation with an automatic macroinstruction prefetch. Returnable microinterrupts also make this aspect of the microprogrammer's job easier. In fact, the architecture is described as "microprogramming-language-directed."

GMPL is a free-format register-transfer-level language. As such, all data-resource names are predefined, and there is no declaration section. It is not clear whether expressions not directly implementable by a microinstruction are supported, but the ability of the microengine to extract, insert, and perform operations on fields of any size makes GMPL powerful in its ability to process operands of any size.

Four control constructs are supported. The IF statement can branch on any of 64 "indicator" states or on the Boolean combination of two such states. An ELSE clause is limited to subroutine exit. A DO loop, with the index variable being in a counting register, is supported, as well as REPEAT UNTIL and CASE statements. We have seen an example of a GMPL microprogram in figure 4-3.

The power of GMPL is attributable to the increased power of the microengine, due to cheaper hardware costs.

Summary

LLMDLs have the advantage of being efficient and the disadvantage of requiring a detailed knowledge of the target machine to use. The semantics of an LLMDL depends directly on the microinstruction set of the target machine, with language power depending more on the target than on the skill of the language designer. LLMDLs can do some things for the microprogrammer: fill in data paths, compile expressions, and protect from errors in syntax and semantics. Making the best use of the machine and bridging the gap between the problem and the implementation are the responsibility of the microprogrammer. Therefore, these languages are primarily useful for emulation applications and, while better for applications microprogramming than microassembly languages, are not as good as some of the higher-level languages to be discussed below.

LOW-LEVEL MACHINE-INDEPENDENT LANGUAGES

We see many common features in the low-level machine-dependent languages described in the previous section, so a natural next step is to design a low-level machine-independent language that contains features in the intersection of the machine-dependent languages. The basic assumption is that microcode can be generated that uses only those functional and control resources that can be found with a wide variety of targets. A microprogram written in such a language could be ported to many targets with few changes (perhaps only as many as required by a program written in an HLL being ported), and only the code generator of such a compiler need be changed to put the language on another machine.

Before discussing these issues in more detail, let us examine the multiply microprogram as it would appear in one such LLMIL. YALLL (yet another low-level language) is designed as a machine-independent intermediate microprogramming language also suitable for handwritten microprograms (Patterson, Lew, and Tuck 1979).

This is a particularly suitable application for an LLMIL, since code from a high-level machine-independent microprogramming language would not at this stage make use of machine dependencies, and the low-level nature of the language makes the intermediate language code easier to generate. Being human-readable, YALLL allows humans to modify or improve the code generated by the compiler, especially important given the then current state of HLMILs and the need for efficiency. YALLL also illustrates many LLMIL issues well.

A sample microprogram written in YALLL appears in figure 4-4. YALLL uses three address instructions, appropriate in an intermediate language for microprogramming. (Stack machine languages do not suit microprogrammed targets well, and many of the advantages of stack machines, such as expression evaluation and the saving of environments, are not useful in the generation of microcode.) YALLL is machine-dependent in the area of data resources in that target-machine registers are used, though they may be renamed, as was the case for many LLMDLs. Memory operations are done with target-machine-independent load and store operations.

The sample program (see figure 4-4) should be clear, if not especially easy to read. The machine-independent nature of YALLL means that there are no surprises hidden in the semantics of the language, and no knowledge of a particular target is required to understand the example. A major difference between this implementation and the GMPL implementation is that the U/F

Figure 4-4. Sample microprogram in YALLL.

```
reg mcand = x
reg mier = y                        ; illustrates renaming feature
reg product = z                     ; x, y, and z are machine dependent

MPY:
        load mier, B                ; YALL cannot handle memory to memory
;                                   operations, so consider x,y,z as registers
                and ACC,#100...00,mier
;                                   Clear ACC, set sign of B. First operand is the
;                                   destination
                load mcand, A
                add ACC, ACC, mcand
                and mcand,#011..1, mcand    ; Get mcand value
                and product,#100...0,ACC    ; Set result sign, clear value
                and mier,#011...1,mier      ; Get mier value
MPY1:   jump MPY3 if mier<0>=1      ; Test low bit
        jump MPY4 if mier=0         ; Done
MPY2:   srl mier,mier,1
        sll mcand,mcand,1
        jump MPY1
MPY3:   add product,product,mcand   ; Accumulate product
        jump MPY2
MPY4:   store product,C             ; Result to memory
        rtn
```

flag on the target machine cannot be accessed through YALLL. Therefore, the example must be rewritten to test the low bit of the multiplier before the shift is performed. In this case this has no major effect, but it is possible that some required target operations would take several YALLL statements but only one target microoperation. This is a major source of the inefficiency of machine-independent microprogramming languages. The semantic gap between YALLL and the target is greater than the gap between GMPL and the target.

This example illustrates some common features of LLMILs. Data resources consist of registers and variables to be found in memory. General registers, found in almost every target, can be easily bound to registers in the source microprogram. Having the microprogrammer do register allocation improves the efficiency of the microprogram without the expense of a complex compiler. Similarly, the use of memory operations to fetch data from memory to a register is common and easily mapped from the LLMIL to the target.

The functional resources supported by LLMILs are those found on a variety of machines: addition, subtraction, logical operations, and shifts. Common flags such as carry and overflow are also usually represented. A disadvantage of LLMILs is that less common but still useful microoperations (such as a microoperation implementing one step of a multiply operation) cannot be accessed from the LLMIL.

The control resources implemented by LLMILs include branches, **if** statements, multiway branches, and usually subroutine call and return statements. Older languages, designed when microstacks were not so common, may not have this last feature. **While** loops, easily implemented with an **If** and a branch, are sometimes found. **For** loops usually are not, since without a special counter register too much overhead is required to implement the loop.

The attractiveness of a machine-independent language and the relative simplicity of implementation resulted in proposals and design of several LLMILs. Five are surveyed in the next section.

A Survey of Low-Level Machine-Independent Languages

A microprogramming language described by Tirrell illustrates one code-generation method for LLMILs: using a table of target-machine features to drive the compiler (Tirrell 1973). A program in this language consists of two types of statements: declaration statements and command statements. The declaration statements describe the target to the compiler; the command statements are those usually found in microprogramming languages.

Seven tables are used by the compiler. The hardware-contents table gives the contents of a target register as set by a declaration or other statement. It appears that the contents of this table are only valid for registers not modified within a loop, though this issue is not discussed. The cross-reference table contains all target data-resource names and the data names stored in the register. Other information about the register, such as size and location of first reference, is stored in this table. The address-trace table gives the control flow for the microprogram, useful in the optimization phase of the compiler. The EO-substitution table (an EO, or elementary operation, is a microoperation) gives the assembly-language microcode that implements language statements. Code generation in this compiler is done by textual substitution. The prerequisite table gives microoperations that must be performed before other microoperations. An example is that data must be placed in the instruction register before a test of that register can be done. The alternative table gives microoperations that can be used in place of others under certain conditions. The last table, the combine-test table, gives conditions that can be combined into another condition, possibly allowing two microoperations to be merged.

Parts of these tables are prebuilt and parts are generated by the declaration statements. One element of the declaration statement, for instance, is a prerequisite field that is used to set the prerequisite table.

Declaration statements must precede any command statements that make use of the resource declared. The command statements are low-level and include the usual operations, **if** statements, **read** and **write** operations, branches, and **moves**. An example of the source language appears in figure 4-5.

Machine independence in this language comes from the tables, not from the syntax and semantics of the language. It might be possible to port a microprogram to another machine by changing the tables, but it is not likely. Programs

Figure 4-5. Example of microcode written in Tirrell's language.

```
*START
DCLG                        (PS=1).
DCL                         HLDA=F1%0-%1.
DCL                         HLDB=F2; L=2.
DCL                         CLWM=(OR#5=0).
DCL                         A=FFR1; PC=(R=X'02');STOR=HLDA.
DCL                         B=FFR1+1; PC=(R=X'02'); STOR=HLDB.

*                           NOTE :- OR REG SET TO X'0C' (CLWM)
*                                   OR X'2B' (SETWM) PRIOR TO
*                                   ENTERING ALGORITHM

WM01                    :   RD A TO HLDA%1; IF CLWM; BR WM11.
WM02                    :   AND X'BF' TO HLDA%1.
WM03                    :   WR A FROM HLDA%1.
WM04                    :   LET A = A-1.
WM05                    :   RD B TO HLDB%1.
&WM06    OR5EQ0WM13
WM07                    :   RESET HLDB%1#6.
WM08                    :   WR B FROM HLDB%1.
WM09                    :   SUB 1 FROM B.
WM10                    :   ENDA.
WM11                    :   OR X'40' TO HLDA%1.
WM12                    :   BR WM03.
WM13                    :   SET HLDB%1#6.
WM14                    :   BR WM08.
*END
```

written in the language are not machine-independent, though the language and the compiler are. This is typical of table-driven microprogramming languages.

An early example of a language with machine-independent syntax is SIMPL (Ramamoorthy, Tabandeh, and Tsuchiya 1973). SIMPL was modeled after ALGOL-60 and was designed to facilitate the compaction of code produced by the SIMPL compiler. SIMPL is a modified single-assignment language. In single-assignment languages, each variable can be assigned a value only once. This makes the construction of the data-dependency graph of the program (necessary for some compaction algorithms) easier. The cost is a very large number of variables. In SIMPL the single-assignment condition is relaxed to allow assignment to a variable only after all previous statements using that variable as input have been executed. Thus, the single-assignment principle is applied to the contents of a variable, not to the variable itself. In SIMPL variables represent target-data resources.

As mentioned above, SIMPL was designed to resemble ALGOL-60. Procedures, **while**, **for**, and **repeat** loops are allowed, as well as **if-then-else** statements. Variables, however, correspond to target registers, which could be renamed. Arrays are not allowed, since they are difficult to handle in a single-assignment language. Memory reads and writes are done explicitly, using an index register. Areas of memory can be allocated and named, thus creating what are effectively arrays.

The example in figure 4-6 shows a SIMPL program. Note that expressions are allowed only two operands and one operator. The binding of variables to target resources thus did not allow the allocation of temporaries for expression evaluation.

We consider SIMPL to be a low-level language because of its lack of storage allocation and because of its simple expressions. It also was meant to serve as an intermediate language, though its relatively advanced control structures would not be necessary here. SIMPL was used for research in the critical-path-compaction algorithm (Ramamoorthy 1974) but does not appear to have been used for production microprogramming.

An example of a microprogram written in YALLL has already been given. YALLL is not a free-format language. Data resources are limited to target resources but can be renamed. Operators defined in the language include **add**, **add1** (increment), **sub**, **sub1**, **and**, **or**, **xor**, and six types of shifts. **Jumps** and **ifs** are defined (but not **else**), as are **call**, **return**, **exit**, and a table jump, implementing a multiway branch.

Figure 4-6. Example of microcode written in SIMPL.

```
BEGIN    EQUIVALENCE   A≡X1,B≡X2,C≡X3,D≡X4,E≡X5,
                       F≡X6,G≡X7,I≡B1,J≡B2,K≡B3,
         READ A1.A,B1.B,C1.C,D1.D,E1.E,F1.F,G1.G,
              I1.I,J1.J,K1.K

         FOR I→ I STEP J UNTIL K DO
                 BEGIN

                         C/D→ G    ;
                         C/B→ C    ;
                         A+B→ D    ;
                         D*G→ B    ;
                         C*F→ D    ;
                         E*F→ E    ;
                         A+E→ A    ;
                         C+E→ G    ;
                         B/A→ E    ;
                         C*D→ F    ;
                         E/G→ A    ;

                 END

         END

         DATA

                 A1    :   DEC 1.0   ;
                 B1    :   DEC 2.0   ;
                 C1    :   DEC 1.5   ;
                 D1    :   DEC 1.1   ;
                 E1    :   DEC 1.0   ;
                 F1    :   DEC 4.0   ;
                 I1    :   DEC 1     ;
                 J1    :   DEC 1     ;
                 K1    :   DEC 20    ;
```

This machine-independent syntax allows, in some cases, microcode to be ported from one machine to another by changing only the register declarations. This was done for a string-translation microprogram, compiled for a VAX 11/780 and an HP 300. YALLL produced good code for the HP 300, but poor code for the VAX. This was attributed to the lack of an optimizing compiler. Rewriting the YALLL code could also have improved the result. This illustrates that even with a machine-independent language, better results can be obtained with some knowledge of the target. (This is also true for HLLs.) Finally, Patterson et al. speculate that for larger examples hand optimization becomes impractical, and optimization of the algorithm, easier to do using a higher-level language, would improve the YALLL code (Patterson, Lew, and Tuck 1979). This was found to be the case in the experiments done with the STRUM language (see below).

Another example of a table based-LLMIL is the microprogram-generator language MPGL (Baba and Hagiwara 1981). MPGL is part of the MPG microprogramming environment. An MPGL program consists of two parts, the machine-description section (MDS) and the algorithm-description section (ADS). This is similar to the Declare and Command statements of Tirrell's language.

The MDS is translated into tables for a MD table library (MDTL). This drives not only code generation but also the microassembler and simulator that are part of MPG. The MDTL describes the functionality of the microoperations of a particular target, which fields of the microinstruction word are occupied by the microoperations, and the bit patterns for the microoperations. The tables can handle simple and conditional microoperations.

Data resources in the ADS are machine-dependent, as defined in the MDS. **Goto**, **if** and **case** statements are allowed, as are general expressions. Machine-dependent address generation schemes and the use of residual control are also allowed if defined in the MDS.

An example of an MPGL program is given in figure 4-7. This is the ADS part of the program; the MDS is rather longer and more difficult to read. Of course, only one MDS need be written per target.

The same microprogram was written for two different machines. The code produced was close to that produced by hand assembly—within 10% of the space and 20% of the execution time of the assembly-language microprograms. As was the case with Tirrell's language but not with YALLL, a program in MPGL is not machine-independent but the language and compiler are.

The last language we will examine is ISPMET (Goessling and McDonald 1972), a language for emulation derived from ISP (Bell and Newell 1971). The goal of ISPMET is to convert an ISP description of an instruction-set processor into microcode, for the Meta-4 in this case. ISPMET is the most machine-independent of the languages we have examined so far in that no target dependencies at all appear in the language. The only major addition to ISP is a GOTO statement.

Figure 4-7. Example of microcode written in MPGL. From Baba 1981, © 1981 IEEE.

```
ADS MULT
AVAIL SPM0(X"39");
EXTERN ALG END (X"A20");
ALG MULT (X"A50");
*** SPM0(X"18") : ADDRESS OF MULTIPLIER
*** SPM0(X"19") : ADDRESS OF MULTIPLICAND
        SPM0(X"10") := MM(SPM0(X"18")'8:29');   /* read main memory and transfer to
        SPM0(X"11") := MM(SPM0(X"19")'8:29');      scratchpad memory */
        G := XL8"20";                           /* set counter G with "20" Hex */
        U := XL32"0";                           /* reset U and L */
        L := XL32"0";
L0:     SPM0(X"10") := <SRLA> SPM0(X"10");      /* shift scratchpad memory */
        IF SC'0' = BL1"0" THEN GOTO L1;         /* test the value of spilled bit */
        U := U <+> SPM0(X"11");                 /* Add U and scratchpad memory */
L1:     U := <SRL> U;                           /* Shift U and L. Spilled bit from U
        L := <SRC> L;                              becomes left input to L */
        > G;                                    /* Decrement G */
        IF G ~= XL8"0" THEN GOTO L0;            /* Test for end */
        MM(SPM0(X"18")'8:29') := L;             /*Product is stored in consecutive words
        SPM0("18") := SPM0("18") <+> XL32"4";      of main memory */
        MM(SPM0(X"18")'8:29') := L;
        GOTO END;                               /* return */
GLA;
SLA;
```

An ISPMET program is composed of five sections. In the first, registers are declared. Subfields of registers can be given names, and the compiler will properly assign those names to a section of the target register bound to the virtual register of the emulated machine. The Meta-4 has 32 registers, so it appears that the problem of more emulated registers than host registers was not considered. The ISPMET compiler does register allocation, but a BIND statement to force the allocation of target registers to host registers was suggested.

The second section of an ISPMET program allocates section of main memory and gives them names. The third section specifies instruction formats of the machine to be emulated. This is a characteristic of ISP descriptions and shows how ISPMET is a special-purpose language for emulation. The fourth section of an ISPMET program, a description of effective address calculation for the target, is also emulator-specific. The final section, instruction fetch and execution, is a feature more typical of a general-purpose microprogramming language.

Unfortunately, we are unaware of reports on ISPMET in the literature after the one cited. Many microprogramming languages are patterned after other languages, but ISPMET was the first patterned after a high-level architecture-description language. Such a language is a particularly good choice for microprogramming. The Meta-4 seems a good host for emulation, and though ISPMET was machine-independent, it is not clear how easy it would be to implement on a less friendly microprogrammable machine.

Summary

In our survey of LLMILs we have seen two approaches to machine-independent microprogramming languages. The first is to define a language that can generate code for any target by including only those features found on most targets. The second is to provide facilities for defining the target machine. In this case the language is machine-independent, but any program written in the language is likely to be machine-dependent.

The second approach seems better for low-level languages. In the first approach inefficient code may be generated without an increase in the productivity of the microprogrammer through the use of a high-level language (though an increase over the use of a microassembler is certainly possible). Though the tables for a particular machine may be difficult to generate, it is a one-time job, and the gain in efficiency seems worthwhile. Of course, to achieve this efficiency, the microprogrammer must again be an expert in the target, just as for LLMDLs. The use of the tables to generate a simulator and assembler, as in MPG, is very attractive.

In general, however, a LLMDL is easier to design and implement. This, together with the fact that there is little call for machine independence at this level, have meant that LLMDLs have been more successful. The field as a whole, however, influenced by work on HLLs, has moved towards higher-level microprogramming languages. We discuss these in the next section.

HIGH-LEVEL MACHINE-DEPENDENT LANGUAGES

The next step in microprogramming-language development was to incorporate the features of high-level programming languages. By doing this, the language designers wished to gain for microprogramming the advantages of HLLs, discussed above, especially faster microprogram development and reliability. These languages could be either machine-dependent, to simplify the compilation process and allow user-directed allocation of data and functional resources, or machine-independent, to allow use of the language for a number of target machines. ("Target" is used here in the sense of the machine for which code is generated.) In this section we discuss high-level machine-dependent languages.

HLMDLs seem machine-dependent in the semantics of the language rather than in the syntax. This is because they usually take their syntax from a previously existing HLL, such as Pascal. The data resources of the language are usually at least partially machine-dependent in that variables are assigned to registers, but the transfer of data from memory (usually defined by an array declaration) to a register is done by the compiler. The user must only write a simple assignment statement and therefore only has to worry about the allocation of storage when writing variable declarations. This significantly reduces the level of detail that needs to be considered when microprogramming.

Machine-dependent functional resources can easily be introduced into the language without affecting the syntax. This is done by the introduction of special operators (such as **shift**) or machine-dependent code sections. This is not difficult if the machine-dependent statements do not affect the control flow of the program.

Control statements in HLMDLs are almost always machine-independent and are identical to those found in HLLs. This makes HLMDL programs look like HLL programs. Restricting machine-dependent data-resource references to variable declarations also helps make the languages look high-level. Some machine-dependent HLMLs also allow the specification of low-level parallelism.

The major difference between HLMDLs and the higher-level machine-independent languages we will examine later lies in the structure of the compilers, not in the structure of the languages themselves. Compilers for HLMDLs are simpler to construct, because much of the binding of source-level resources to target-level machine resources is done by the user at variable declaration time or by the language designer when the language was developed. The language designer will only introduce those operators that can be implemented efficiently on the target, and the semantics of the language can be made to match the semantics of the target. Also contributing to the ease of compiler design is the fact that code for the target can be generated immediately and that target-dependent optimizations can be performed throughout the code-generation process. If an intermediate language is used, it can be designed to reduce the semantic gap between source language and target language. Machine-independent intermediate languages, used for HLMILs do not reduce the semantic gap nearly so well, and often machine-dependent intermediate languages are also used, increasing the number of compilation stages required. These stages are often omitted if only one target is envisioned, but this makes porting the compiler more difficult.

Another, less obvious advantage of the HLMDL is that the compiler can be made to do tedious but necessary operations for the programmer. An example in the HLMDL microTAL is that the compiler will insert checks for microinterrupts at appropriate places. In a machine-independent compiler this would have to be done late in the translation, and devising a general way of representing this would be difficult.

Let us now examine a sample microprogram in an HLMDL, in this case microTAL (fig. 4-8). This microTAL program has been written as if for the Tucker and Flynn machine. The program looks much like an HLL MULTIPLY program, except that the machine-dependent register ACC has been introduced and the machine-dependent flag U/F has been used. Except for these two cases, the machine dependency of the language is hidden from the user. We can say that HLMDLs are less machine-dependent (from the user's point

Figure 4-8. Sample microprogram in microTAL.

```
proc MULT (A, B, C)

int A, B, C, mier, mcand, result

begin
    ACC := (B and 100..0) + A
    mcand := A and 011...1
    mier := B and 011...1
    result := ACC and 100...0
    while mier <> 0 do
    begin
        mier := mier rshift 1
        if U/F   ! Machine dependent condition flag
        then result := result + mcand
        mcand := mcand lshift 1
    end
    C := result
end
```

of view) than LLMDLs. It seems that HLMDLs are designed by introducing machine dependency into an HLL (the SIL TAL in the case of microTAL), while LLMDLs are designed by simplifying the syntax of the target microinstructions.

A Survey of High-Level Machine-Dependent Languages

Because of the greater effort required to design an HLMDL as compared to an LLMDL, they are not as common. The two of which I am aware are microTAL (Bartlett 1981) and STRUM (Patterson 1975).

MicroTAL is a language targeted for a Tandem computer. It is a subset of an already existing systems-implementation language known as TAL, which is a member of the Algol-60 class of languages and resembles C. There are a number of advantages to adapting an already existing language for microprogramming use. The first is that a trained user base already exists. Second, the language design has had a chance to be refined and stabilized. Third, a compiler for the language already exists, which can be modified for use as the compiler for the microprogramming language. Fourth, it is possible to either use already existing programs as microprograms, which saves development costs, or to write new microprograms as HLL programs first, to use HLL software development tools to test them. This cannot completely test microprograms, since many timing problems cannot be detected, but it will allow the algorithm to be debugged with already existing debugging and testing tools. A microprogramming language designed in this manner need not be machine-dependent; microC (Gurd 1983) is one example of an HLMIL designed this way. MicroC will be described below.

MicroTAL is designed to allow the replacement of TAL procedures with microcode. Therefore, it is procedure-oriented. Procedures can have parameters in the HLL sense, not renamed global variables as is often the case in HLMLs. These are passed on a register stack. It is assumed that no register values are saved, making the register-allocation problem easier. Variables can be declared as being in registers or memory, and arrays can be declared to reserve a block of memory. No explicit **read** or **write** statements are required; data is transferred from arrays to variables by using assignment statements.

Three data types are supported: *integer* (16-bit values), *byte* (8-bit values), and *array*. A variable can be declared to be of type **string**. This might be an alias for **array** of **byte**.

Expressions of unlimited complexity are allowed, and temporary registers are allocated where necessary. The requirement for compatibility with an existing language has prevented many of the compromises we have seen in the previous sections. Control statements supported include **if then else, do until, while do**, and **goto**. Code statements, consisting of target microcode, are allowed for cases in which the language cannot adequately reference target resources. Macros are also supported.

As mentioned above, the compiler automatically inserts interrupt checks inside loops and at user-defined labels. This allows this essential task to be done without programmer intervention. Page faults in the target machine cause a branch to a hardwired microstore location two cycles after the memory operation was started. This means that a restart point must be placed before statements that may cause a page fault. The compiler inserts restart points before each statement and expression.

The microprogrammer can, by compiler option, manually insert interrupt checks and restart points into the microcode. For the most part, however, use of a high-level language hides many unpleasant implementation details from the microprogrammer and makes the job much easier.

STRUM (Patterson 1975) is a microprogramming language designed to assist in the verification of microprograms. (See Chapter 10 of this book for a discussion of this subject.) We will concentrate on STRUM (which stands for structured microprogramming language) as a language. STRUM is a Pascal-based language, designed to generate code for the Burroughs D machine. It was designed for a research project, not as a production language, but it was very successful in the applications presented. STRUM was made machine-dependent because of the easier compilation task and because no other target than the D machine was foreseen. Except for declarations, however, STRUM was effectively machine-independent. Optimization of generated microprograms had to be done by hand because of lack of time to develop an optimizer. In doing hand optimization Patterson differentiated between those improvements that could be automated and those dependent on target-machine tricks and the functionality of the source program.

Variable declarations in STRUM consist of giving the association between the variable and the target resource in which the contents of the variable are to be stored. This is the only typing done. Expressions in STRUM are limited to what can be done in one pass through the ALU and barrel shifter of the D machine. No temporary registers are allocated. Control statements in STRUM resemble those of Pascal—**while, repeat, for, if then else,** and **case**. Besides **call** (subroutine) there is also a subroutine exit statement. There is no **goto**, surely because one of the goals of the language was to support microcode verification. Macros were allowed, and parallelism could be explicitly specified in the source program. A sample STRUM program can be found in figure 4-9.

The most interesting result of the STRUM experiment related to language design is the comparison between the microcode generated by STRUM and that generated by assembly-language microprogramming. A Search routine written in STRUM generated 17 microoperations before hand optimization, as good as in assembly language. Optimization reduced this number to 9, about half the improvement coming from optimization that could be automated. A more interesting result is that STRUM produced better code for an emulator than did an assembly-language programmer (Patterson 1981a). Patterson attributes this result to the high-level improvements to the algorithm possible by using a high-level language. Small amounts of microcode can be written more efficiently by hand, but the level of detail in low-level microcode makes an analogous improvement impossible for large microprograms.

Summary

The advantages of high-level languages in all areas of programming have also been accepted in microprogramming. HLMDLs are an attempt to gain the advantages of high-level microprogramming by using relatively simple compilers that could generate efficient code by binding source resources to target resources at language-definition time. We have seen, however, that except for variable definitions the HLMDLs described in this chapter are machine-independent. Most of the machine dependence comes from the structure of the compilers. Allocating user-declared variables to registers is not difficult if the target supports an adequate amount of local storage. The use of compiler writing systems makes the construction of HLMDLs easier, as does the use of an already existing HLL. Therefore I expect more HLMDLs to be reported, possibly some already existing as proprietary products.

Since machine dependence is embedded in all phases of HLMDL compilers, the effort to create an HLML with a wide user base rests on research in machine-independent languages, with compilers designed to make the porting of the language to another target relatively easy. The next section describes these languages.

Figure 4-9. Sample STRUM program. From Patterson, 1976, © 1976 IEEE.

```
proc MULTIPLY
    (PARTIAL_PRODUCT = B, MULTIPLICAND = A1, MULTIPLIER = A2;)

        / WE WANT THE RESULT TO BE LESS THAN 2**15 /
    assume
        0 <= MULTIPLICAND.0 <= 181,
        0 <= MULTIPLIER.0 <= 181;
            /     181 * 181 < 2**15 /

    conclude
        PARTIAL_PRODUCT = MULTIPLICAND.0 mul MULTIPLIER.0,
        0 <= PARTIAL_PRODUCT <= 2 exp 15,
        MULTIPLICAND = MULTIPLICAND.0,
        MULTIPLIER = 0;

    PARTIAL_PRODUCT = 0;
    begin   MAC 'LSB OF MULTIPLIER = 1' = 1ST(MULTIPLER) CAM;

        declare I = DUMMY;

        for I := 0 to 7
            assert MULTIPLICAND.0 mul MULTIPLIER.0
                = PARTIAL_PRODUCT + MULTIPLICAND mul MULTIPLIER,
                MULTIPLIER = MULTIPLIER.0 shr I,
                MULTIPLICAND = MULTIPLICAND.0 shl I,
                0 <= MULTIPLICAND.0 <= 181,
                0 <= MULTIPLIER.0 <= 181

            do
                if 'LSB OF MULTIPLIER = 1'
                then PARTIAL_PRODUCT := MULTIPLICAND + PARTIAL_PRODUCT
                fi;

                MULTIPLICAND := MULTIPLICAND shl 1;
                MULTIPLIER := MULTIPLIER shr 1
        rof

        end;

        MULTIPLICAND := MULTIPLICAND shr 8

    corp;
```

HIGH-LEVEL MACHINE-INDEPENDENT LANGUAGES

Most microprogrammers and all microprogramming language designers have used HLLs. It is therefore natural to want to use an HLL, or a language that closely resembles one, for microprogramming. Current HLLs are machine-independent, so there is an incentive to design machine-independent languages. These have the obvious advantage of being useful for many targets, but they also hide target-machine details from the microprogrammer, allowing the use of parts of HLL compilers without modification and allowing the compiler to have full control over the use of target resources. All these factors make for a simpler source microprogram and for a compiler in which more effort can be devoted to optimization.

When a microprogramming language looks like an HLL, one would suspect that it is most useful for the same tasks as an HLL. This in fact appears to be the case. Two of the HLMILs described below, "HLL" and Microcode C, were designed for applications microprogramming, not for emulation. Nonstandard features of target machines are often designed to make emulation of the host instruction set easier and may be useful for other emulators. These target features are the ones for which code generation from HLMILs is difficult. Applications microprograms are more likely to make use of the microinstructions and target resources that are analogous to those found at the machine-language level: registers, standard operators, condition codes, and features supporting control structures. These features are the ones to be found in most microarchitectures; therefore, the assumption behind the HLMIL, that there exists a subset of target features to be found on all machines that will support the languages' functionality, is valid for applications microprograms. As we will see, data strongly supports the contention that an HLMIL can generate code as good as an assembly-language microprogrammer for applications microprograms. There is no such data for emulations, though there is for HLMDLs, as we have seen in Patterson's work.

Figure 4-10 shows a sample microprogram coded in an HLMIL, Microcode C in this case (Gurd 1983). This example is uninteresting in that the code is almost exactly what a C programmer would produce. It is very interesting for the same reason. It is clear that a C programmer could be easily trained to write microprograms simply by being told which features of C are not supported by

Figure 4-10. Sample microprogram in Microcode C.

```
int A,B,C;      /* These are globals */

multiply ();

{
  register mier, mcand, result;

  mier = B;
  result = ((mier & 0x80...0) + A) & 0x80...0;
  mier &= 0x7f..f;
  mcand = A & 0x7f...f;
  while (mier != 0)
  {
    if ((mier & 1) == 1)     /* Or if odd, if available */
       result += mcand;
    mier >>= 1;
    mcand <<= 1;
  }
  C = result;
}
```

Microcode C. How good the resulting microcode would be is a different story. Certain ways of writing in an HLMIL produce much better code than others. This is also the case for HLLs, but for the latter better optimizers may reduce some of the inefficiency, and cheap machine cycles mean that few applications need to be tuned. The need for tuning in microcode is much greater, since resources are relatively expensive, and increased speed is usually a major reason for migrating an application into microcode. (Other reasons are discussed in Chapter 5 of this book.)

HLMILs are a very popular research area in microprogramming languages. We will describe four in the next section: MPL, SUILVEN, HLL, and Microcode C. Other HLMILs include CHAMIL (Weidner 1980), VMPL (Ma and Lewis 1981), the DEC V Compiler (Patterson et al. 1981), and MIMOLA (Marwedel 1981). An example of an HLMIL without a compiler is Ada for the Intel 432, described at the 14th Microprogramming Workshop in 1981. Here, Ada, with a few additions for microprogramming, was hand-translated into microcode because of the lack of an Ada compiler. This approach had the disadvantage of hand translation but the advantage of having the microcode written initially in an easy-to-read form. Hand translation of an appropriate HLL to microcode, as has been suggested (Davidson 1983), is an approach for those who cannot afford a compiler or who require more efficient code than a compiler can produce.

HLMILs are valuable tools in the writing of large amounts of application microcode. In the next section we describe four HLMILs and see how their capabilities have grown over the last 12 years.

A Survey of High-Level Machine-Independent Languages

MPL is the first HLMIL described in the literature (Eckhouse 1971). MPL (for microprogramming language) is a small dialect of PL/I. Procedures are allowed, and scope rules apply to variables declared within these procedures. All data items are declared. Variables are declared as in PL/I, and the types of variables include registers (including virtual registers), central and microcode memory, and local and auxiliary storage. For the most part, though, declarations resemble those of PL/I. Events can also be declared; they are not like PL/I events but instead are basically Boolean variables that correspond to condition codes. IF statements are the means of testing events. Control statements include GOTOs, CALLs, and IF THEN ELSE. The WHILE statement does not appear to be in the language.

General expressions are allowed. One interesting feature of MPL assignment statements is that register concatenation is allowed on the left side of the assignment statement. A PL/I–like syntax is used to declare the substructure of variables. These subfields can be directly assigned, eliminating much of the need for subfield assignments.

As an early language, MPL is primitive compared to the HLMILs described below. However, it has all of their features: syntax resembling that of an HLL, no machine-dependent features in the source language, and implicit rather than explicit data-transfer operations between registers and memory. MPL seems to be targeted for emulation, which was the main application of microprogramming in 1971. No comparison with handwritten code was made.

SUILVEN is an HLMIL that is Pascal–like but not a dialect of Pascal (Sommerville 1979). The implementation reported generated code for a Burroughs B1700.

SUILVEN supports a number of data types. The most basic is the BITS type, which is used to declare a variable as being of a certain size. Arrays can be declared of a base type of BITS. Templates, a recordlike structure, can be used to give a variable an internal structure. Templates can be associated with a variable local to a procedure, so a variable can take on a number of structures depending on how it is used within a particular context. WITH statements, like those of Pascal, can be used to access the fields of a structure as defined by a template. Use of this statement is not only for programmer convenience; it also helps in register assignment by telling the compiler that the base address of the structure should be stored in a register.

The other type of data element is the flag. Flags are Booleans, representing condition codes. They are accessed by using the built-in functions TRUE and FALSE, which take a variable of type flag as a parameter, returning the truth value of the flag. These are used within IF statements. Flags are set or cleared by the built-in functions SET and UNSET.

Procedures are allowed in SUILVEN, but they cannot be nested (as in C). Variables local to procedures can be declared, and procedures can take parameters. Parameters can be passed by value or by reference. Macros are supported in SUILVEN.

Control statements supported in SUILVEN include IF THEN ELSE, CASE, and REPEAT UNTIL DO. This last statement allows a test in the middle of a loop without the use of a loop-exit statement. If the DO clause is empty, the statement becomes a standard REPEAT, as in Pascal.

Figure 4-11 shows a SUILVEN program. The DEFINE statement associates the variable INSTRUCT_REG with the template PINST. Fields of the variable are accessed as in Pascal.

Code from SUILVEN was compared against machine-language code for a Pascal interpreter, not against microassembly code. Though SUILVEN was used in emulation tasks, Sommerville believes that the language would be most useful for applications microprogramming.

The microprogramming language HLL (Sheraga and Gieser 1981) is part of a complete compiler, optimization, and machine specification system designed

Figure 4-11. A binary-search program in SUILVEN. From Sommerville, 1978, © 1978 North Holland Publishing Company. Reprinted by permission.

```
FUNCTION BINARY_SEARCH(BITS(WS) VALUE KEY, TABSIZE;
        BITS(WS) ARRAY TABLE);
    BITS(WS) INDEX, UPPER, LOWER;
    LOWER := 0; UPPER := TABSIZE;
    WHILE LOWER LEQ UPPER DO
        $(
            "In SUILVEN, all operators have the same precedence and
            expressions are evaluated from left to right. A right
            shift implements integer division by 2"
            INDEX := LOWER + UPPER SHR 1;
            IF TABLE[INDEX] = KEY THEN
                EXIT = INDEX
            ELSE
                IF TABLE[INDEX] < KEY THEN
                    UPPER := INDEX -1
                ELSE
                    LOWER := INDEX + 1;
        $)
    END = KEYNOTFOUNDVALUE;
```

---

for machine-independent applications microprogramming. The target problem is speeding up algorithms with a great deal of algebraic manipulation, not the usual emulation problem at all. The design of HLL reflects this type of problem.

Data types in HLL include integer, real, single and double precision and one- and two-dimensional arrays. HLL is the only microprogramming language of which I am aware that supports real variables, which are needed for its target application. Five common condition codes, Carry, Overflow, Zero, Minus, and Link, are defined in the language.

HLL has a richer set of functional resources than is common for HLMLs. Not only are all the standard ALU operators available, but so are built-in math functions (such as sin, log, etc.). The target-machine stack, if available, can be accessed using the pseudovariable STACK. Input and output, in the high-level-language sense, can be done using the pseudovariables INPUT and OUTPUT. This is also not usually included in HLMLs. For this application, however, I/O is necessary.

HLL supports the standard control structures—IF THEN ELSE, GOTO, FOR, and WHILE. Concurrency, the ability to execute tasks concurrently within the main program, is supported with synchronizing primitives.

The compiler performed almost as well as hand microcoding. In one case, where the assembly-level microcode was written by an inexperienced programmer, HLL did twice as well. As we have seen, these are not unique results. However, the productivity of the microprogrammers was also measured by coding time. Here, the handwritten code took about 350 hours to produce in each case, as against 5 hours for the microcode produced using HLL. For this situation, with large amounts of applications microcode to produce, the worth of an HLML is very clear.

An example of the direct adaptation of an already existing language is Microcode C (Gurd 1983), which has already been briefly described. Based on the language C (Kernighan and Richie 1978), Microcode C is lacking some features not considered necessary for microprogramming. For instance, only the integer and structure types are supported. Recursion is not allowed, as there is no run-time stack. There are no **goto** or **switch** statements. Additions to the language include built-in functions that can access target resources and the ability to include assembly-level code (also available in C). The compiler can be directed to put variables in registers, as in C. In general, any Microcode C program can be compiled by the C compiler, but the reverse is not true.

C, as a popular HLL with a readily available compiler, has become a popular basis for HLMILs. Others include a Microcode C from Burroughs (Hopkins, Horton, and Arnold 1985) and one from Colorado State University (Duda and Mueller 1985).

Summary

HLMILs appear to have been successful as applications microprogramming languages. The part of the target microinstruction set used in these applications can be efficiently bound to HLMIL source constructs. The knowledge gained from research in HLL compilers has shown how an HLMIL compiler can produce efficient code and be written by one person in a reasonable amount of time.

An especially important advantage of HLMILs is their ability to allow an algorithm to be written in an HLL, debugged and optimized, and then moved to the microprogram level. This is an important reason to base an HLMIL closely on an existing HLL, as was done for Microcode C.

So HLMILs, if not universally accepted, can be said to be a success for one type of microprogramming. But what of those who wish to do both emulation and applications microprogramming, or emulation on a wide variety of host machines? Can HLMLs that do emulation efficiently also be machine-independent? Recent research has suggested microprogramming languages with both machine-dependent and machine-independent components. These high-level mixed languages (HLMXLs) will be introduced in the next section.

HIGH-LEVEL MIXED LANGUAGES

The aim of research into high-level mixed languages is to meet the apparently contradictory goals of machine independence and efficiency through access to target resources from the HLMXL. Two approaches have been identified. The first is the schema approach, first proposed by Dasgupta (1978, 1980). In the second approach, first presented by DeWitt (1976), machine-dependent features are defined in the language in a machine-independent way, then used within the language.

A language schema is basically an outline for a language, with some elements of the language not yet defined. Defining these elements is called *instantiating* the schema into a particular language. We have noticed in the discussion of HLMDLs that only a small portion of the syntax of the language was machine-dependent. This is what is not defined in the language schema. This portion is typically language data resources, which will be bound to target resources, and some language functional resources.

We mentioned that most of the language dependence in HLMDLs lay in the compiler. A compiler can be designed to reduce the effort of generating a specific translator for a language instantiated from the schema. This can be done by making various parts of the language table-driven and by carefully distinguishing those parts of the compiler responsible for translating the machine-dependent parts of the language from those translating machine-independent parts.

The second approach to HLMXL design recognizes that an appropriate HLMIL can be used to simulate target-machine resources. A target-machine register can be simulated as an integer variable; a target-machine functional resource, such as a multiplier, can be simulated by a procedure that does a multiply. If a mechanism exists to identify these source-language constructs with target-machine resources, programs calling on the source constructs can make use of the target constructs directly if code is being generated for that target. If not, the source constructs can still be used, because they are valid machine-independent code segments. Thus, any program in this language can be ported to a different machine without change. Efficiency will of course suffer, because a procedure that is translated into one microinstruction on the intended target may require many microinstructions on another target. The identification of source constructs with target resources is called *resource binding*, and we will call this type of language a resource-binding language.

Each of these techniques has advantages and disadvantages. Languages instantiated from a schema are machine-dependent and are not compatible. It is somewhat similar to using an HLL, say, Pascal, as a model for many HLMDLs. The major difference is that the schema is designed to be well suited for microprogramming, making the many modifications that would be required to make Pascal a microprogramming language not necessary. The advantage of the schema approach is that programs written in each of the instantiated languages can be expected to be efficient and that the amount of machine dependence in the instantiated languages would be reduced to the minimum necessary.

The disadvantage of the resource-binding approach is that though programs may be ported without change, if the original program had a good deal of machine dependence, the ported program might be very inefficient. The advantages are that applications microprograms might be written using only the machine-independent portions of the language and that only the machine-dependent portions of a target required by a particular microprogram need to be described. We will describe two examples of each of these techniques below.

A Survey of High-Level Mixed Languages

S* is an example of a microprogamming language schema, and as mentioned above, is not a language but a language schema (Dasgupta 1980). We will not describe a particular language instantiated from S* but rather the schema itself. There is one primitive data type in S*, the bit, and three data structures. The sequence type allows a number of bits to be considered as a unit. A 16-bit variable would be declared

$$\text{var a: } seq\,[15..0]\ bit\,;$$

The array type has the characteristics of a standard array. The tuple corresponds to the Pascal record type.

Data objects are declared by an S* program and are defined by the semantics of the target machine. (By S* program we mean a program in a language instantiated from S*; strictly speaking, it is impossible to program in S*.)

Data-transfer operations are defined in S*, as are assignment statements, but expressions are not a part of the schema. Legal expressions in an instantiated language are determined by the semantics of the target. Therefore, most of what is defined in S* are control constructs. These consist of the selection statement, the **goto** statement, procedure calls, **repeat until**, and **while do**. The selection statement is a generalized **if then else** and is of the form

$$\textit{if}\ B1 \rightarrow S1\,||\,B2 \rightarrow S2\,||\,...\,||\ \textit{else} \rightarrow Sn\ \text{fi};$$

where at most one of the Bi can be true at a time. The Bi are predicates determined by the semantics of the target.

Several other less common control structures can be found in S*. The first is a method of synchronizing asynchronous regions of a program through the use of synchronization variables and the synchronizing actions **await** and **sig**. Another feature of S* is that parallel constructs can be specified to assist in the compaction of the microprogram. Parts of the program that have been optimized by the programmer can be specified by the region construct. No optimizing transformations will be applied to the statements within a region.

An example of a piece of a program written in S* instantiated for the QM-1 is given in figure 4-12. S* has been instantiated into languages for several machines, including the QM-1 (Klassen and Dasgupta 1981). There has also been work in instantiating S* for a machine described in the architectural description language AADL (Damm 1984).

Figure 4-12 Example of microcode written in S*(QM-1). From Klassen, 1981, © 1981 IEEE.

```
prog (test)

declaration

    /* included files expanded by preprocessor */
    #include "qm1_dec.h"

    syn immediate = control_store_output
    syn index_adr = index_alu_output
    syn base_register = a_par
    syn data_register = b_par

    macro INCR_MPC_2
        index[fmpc] := index[fmpc] + 2
    endmacro
endec

init
    /*
        local store register 24 set
        as the microprogram counter
    */
    fmpc := 24
endinit

proc add_relative (instruction, op=arel, fmt=r.r.c)

    fcod := data_register;

    region

        index_alu_output := local_store[base_register]
                            + immediate;

        local_store[fcod] := control_store[index_adr];
    endreg

    INCR_MPC_2;

    act fetch;

endproc

...
...
endproc
```

Another example of a family of languages based on the schema principle is Ohne (Wagnon and Maine 1983), a language developed at Burroughs. Ohne is part of the E-Machine workbench, a collection of tools for a family of Burroughs processors with stack-machine architectures. This architecture is called E-Mode, thus the name E-Machine.

The workbench consists of the language, a simulator, an editor coupled to the simulator, and a releaser. (Details are in the reference cited above.) The advanced nature of the tools is made possible because microcode must be written for a number of similar but not identical machines. This fact made the schema approach effective.

Ohne is actually the generic name for a number of variant languages. The languages are similar because the targets are similar. In Ohne data resources are determined by the semantics of the target in that variables are renamed target registers. Nonetheless, type checking is done by the compiler, and scope rules are enforced.

There are two basic units in the language. The first is the parameterless subroutine. The second is the operation. Operations are subroutines that are bound to E-Machine operators. This is somewhat similar to the bound functional resource of MARBLE (see below), except that the operation cannot be unbound.

A unique feature of Ohne is the **definition** concept. This is an English statement, placed in angle brackets within the code, which represents a piece of code to be defined later. In this way Ohne naturally supports stepwise refinement. When the definition is defined later in the program, it is given a number representing its level in the refinement. The sample Ohne program in figure 4-13 has the definition

<<read code word to be executed>>

within level 1. When this is defined, it is given the level 1.1. This code includes the definition

<<finish processing correct branch>>

which is given the level 1.2 when it is defined, and so forth.

There are three forms of control structure in Ohne, all using forms of the guarded command. In the alternative statement the guarded-statement list preceded by the true guard is executed. This statement is delimited by IFs. The repetitive statement continues to execute until all guards are false. A statement associated with a particular false guard within the repetitive statement is not executed. This statement is delimited by DOs. The CASE statement allows a guard to take on more than one value, and has semantics similar to the usual CASE statement. Guards are selected from target hardware conditions.

Hardware-dependent functions can be introduced into Ohne programs through the COMMAND statement. We see that, as in the case of S*, each instance of an Ohne variant is a machine-dependent language, but the language is machine-independent in the sense that the schema is suitable for many targets.

Ohne is being used as a part of the workbench. Using the workbench, 54,000 lines of microcode were written and tested in one year. This is an example of how an HLML could serve as the centerpiece of a firmware engineering tool, increasing microprogrammer productivity significantly.

Figure 4-13. Example of microcode written in Ohne.

```
/ OPERATION BRUN [PRIMARY 4'A2']

#1 << branch to pwi:psi >>:
    temp := ZERO EXCEPT (bits_15_to_0: NEXT_2_PARAMETERS),
      COMMAND_PROCESSOR (step_code_ptr_2_bytes);
    static_branch

\OPERATION BRUN;
```

Sample Operation

```
/SUBROUTINE static_branch

#1 << static branch definition >>:
    /IF psi_value_ok (temp) =>
        <<read new code word to be executed >>
    ! NOT (psi_value_ok) ->
        temp := isolate_psi_field(temp);
        invalid_index_in_temp_interrupt
    \IF

#1.1 << read new code word to be executed >>:
    COMMAND_MEMORY (read_code, PBR + isolate_pwi_field (temp));
    TEST isolate_pwi_field (temp) - PLI;
    /IF less =>
        << finish processing correct branch >>
    ! geq ->
        temp := isolate_pwi_field (temp);
        invalid_index_in_temp_interrupt
    \IF

#1.2 << finish processing correct branch >>:
    PWA := PBR;
%........note use of two concurrent operations below
    COMMAND_PROCESSOR (load_code_ptr, isolate_psi_field (temp)),
    PWA := PWA + isolate_pwi_field (temp)

\SUBROUTINE static_branch
```

The second approach is that of a machine-independent language that can describe machine-dependent target resources. An example of this type of language is MARBLE (Davidson 1980; Davidson and Shriver 1981). A MARBLE program uses the high-level constructs of the language to describe target-machine data and functional resources. Thus, MARBLE is totally machine-independent. When a target construct is to be used directly by a program, the description of that construct is bound to the target resource, then code using the resource directly is generated. If the program is to be ported to a machine without the target resource, the construct describing the resource is unbound, and the machine-independent MARBLE code describing the resource is used instead. An example of this will be given after the language is described.

MARBLE is Pascal-based. The *boolean* and *char* base types are supported, as are subranges, sets, enumerated types, and records. The bit type represents a 1-bit entity. The integer type for a 16-bit machine can be defined as

type int = *bit* 16;

This makes the machine dependency of the integer type explicit. It also assists in the definition of subfields. Another data type not found in Pascal is the *view*. This allows a particular area of storage to be accessed in different ways. For instance, several subfields of a register can be given different names as one view of the register. Other views can be defined on the same register; for instance, an instruction register can be considered as being composed of different combinations of subfields depending on the particular instruction being decoded. Views are a structured way of accessing subfields of a word.

Expressions in MARBLE are like those of Pascal, except that multiply and divide and pointer operations are not implemented. Neither are variant records and procedure parameters. The control constructs of MARBLE are identical to those of Pascal.

Figure 4-14 gives a sample MARBLE program. The elements that can be bound are data resources, such as registers, and functional resources, such as a multiplier. Data resources are represented by types. When a type is bound, variables declared to be of that type are assigned to the specific target-data resource. If the type is unbound, the variable is assigned to a region of memory of a size specified by the type definition. Functional resources are represented by procedures or functions. The body of the procedure should implement the semantics of the target functional resource to which the procedure is to be bound. It is possible to omit the body of a bound procedure, but the body must be included if the program is to be ported.

A MARBLE compiler was implemented but never used in a production environment. The principle of the resource-binding language is being used in the Ada-based language MARBLE/A (Linn, Shriver, and Dasgupta, 1983).

A variant of the idea of describing resources in the source language can be found in the microprogramming language LUKKO (Heinanen 1983). LUKKO is the inverse of MARBLE. It is the skeleton of an abstraction language, in which the types to be used are built out of the built-in type word. The only machine-independent feature of LUKKO is the procedure invocation. All other parts of the language are built up of machine-dependent code. This machine-language code can only refer to machine-dependent constructs. The interface between the higher-level parts of a program and the machine-dependent parts is by initialization of machine-dependent constructs.

LUKKO is built around the concept of abstract data types, whose semantics are defined by target-machine microcode. Thus, all operators are defined within an abstract data type and in terms of target microoperations. Control structures are also defined in this way, so the IF statement is actually a function call.

Figure 4-14. Sample microprogram in MARBLE.

```
/* Global declarations of bound resources */
type bound x,y,z = bit 64;
    /* Assumption: registers named x,y,z */

function bound UF returns boolean;
    bound;
        /* Representing the flag. Could also be
           declared as a bound
           data resource if more appropriate */

procedure multiply (in A, B: bit 64; out C: bit 64):

var  mier: bound y;
     mcand: bound x;
     result: bound z;
begin
    mier := B;
    mcand := A;
    result := ((mier and <b>100...0) + mcand)
              and <b>100...0;
    mier := mier and<b>011...1;
    mcand := mcand and <b>011...1;
    while mier <> 0
    begin
        mier := mier rshift 1;
        if UF
        then result := result + mcand;
        mcand := mcand lshift 1;
    end;
    C := result
end; /* of procedure multiply */
```

LUKKO is a way of structuring a microprogram using a particular programming methodology. It does not hide the target machine from the microprogrammer. It is machine-independent in the sense that the method of building source constructs is independent of the semantics of a particular target machine.

Summary

We have seen two approaches to language design in this section: the creation of a family of languages, differing only in those constructs determined by the target machine, and a type of language in which target structures to be used directly are defined in terms of the machine-independent parts of the language. Of great advantage to the schema approach would be a method of automatically instantiating a schema for a new machine by generating a compiler for the machine. This requires some means of describing the semantics of the target. Work has been done in this area (Sint 1981; Damm 1984). A microinstruction-description language would also be useful for the resource-binding approach in generating the part of the compiler that generates code for the portions of the microprogram using bound resources. The two approaches are thus somewhat compatible.

CONCLUSION

To make this chapter's content relevant to the microprogrammer, we will conclude it with advice on choosing a microprogramming language, as if it were possible to buy one. It is not, unfortunately, but the exercise is still rewarding, for those with an option of choosing a microprogramming language will either be designing it or influencing a designer. We recognize, of course, that many microprogrammers will have no such option, either because no language is available or because the choice of language is dictated to them.

The appropriate language depends on the programs that are to be written for a particular application. This is obvious for HLLs but has never been given as a reason for microprogramming language design. As mentioned above, machine-dependent languages seem to work best for emulation, and machine-independent languages are successful in supporting applications microprogramming. Why this is so can be seen by considering the concept of semantic gap. Using a language to reduce the semantic gap between problem and target machine is often given as a reason for the design and use of HLMLs. Implicit in this argument is that the semantics of the HLML lie somewhere between the semantics of the problem definition and the semantics of the target. The semantics of the problem would be expressed in mathematical terms for number-crunching problems, in a description of an instruction set for emulation, and in an HLL for a vertical-migration application.

The assumption that the level of an HLML is always between the problem and target domains is not valid. A microengine designed to support the instruction set of a particular machine might be much closer in semantics to the problem than a machine-independent microprogramming language that can only represent a certain application with a tortuous series of general operations instead of one or a few target operators specifically designed for the task. Thus, those rejecting HLMILs for emulation are right, for it would require a sophisticated compiler indeed to determine the target operation that would most efficiently implement a sequence of source operations. On the other hand, if the problem statement is essentially machine-independent, the use of an HLMIL does greatly reduce the semantic gap.

With this in mind, let us begin our survey with the problem of emulation. In the most common case, writing microcode for a target designed to support a particular instruction set, a machine-dependent language is most appropriate. The level of the language depends on the complexity of the instruction set to be emulated. Simple instruction sets, like those for early microprocessors, do not require complex control but only a few simple loops. A low-level language or an assembly language is adequate for this. For more sophisticated instruction sets and for applications such as control of a user interface to a console more complex control structures are used, and a higher-level machine-dependent language is appropriate. This might allow optimization of the algorithm, which for some complex applications may be of more advantage than the lower-level improvement available from writing at the assembly-language level.

Another class of emulation problem is emulating an instruction set on a machine designed to support some other instruction set. If the target is unreasonable enough, an HLMIL will do as well as a machine-dependent language, but usually a lower-level machine-dependent language will be necessary to make the emulator as efficient as possible by using whatever target resources support the emulation. If the target supports general emulation, it should not be difficult for an HLMDL to generate good code. Here, again, the possibility of high-level optimization warrants the use of a higher-level language.

This assumes that work will be done for a single target machine. If a number of targets are to be used, the situation is different. If they are similar, as is the case of the E-Machine, a schema approach could be taken to define a number of similar HLMDLs. If the targets are very different, this approach would require the generation of many different code generators and would also create a training problem, as many different targets would have to be learned. In this case a machine-independent language or a resource-binding approach would be appropriate.

In an applications-microprogramming environment it is likely that the target will not be designed to support the application. Therefore, only a subset of target resources would normally be used even if programming were done at the assembly level. In this case, using the HLMIL that is patterned after the HLL best suited to the application is the best approach. This will often be a SIL, but not always. A SIL would be an inappropriate language for an application with a large amount of numeric computation.

In any case, because of the high cost of designing and implementing a microprogramming language, it is a good idea to do an experiment to determine the suitability of an HLML for a particular application. This can be done by deciding on a language design and then hand-compiling a real application into microcode. A familiar HLL can also be used as the source language for this experiment; modifications necessary to make the HLML an effective microprogramming language will soon become apparent.

For users writing too little microcode to make the investment in a compiler worthwhile, this approach may be adequate. The language can be considered as high-level pseudocode, and improvements to the program carried out before translation to microcode is done. If an HLL is used as the pseudocode, many errors could be detected early. Intel used this approach for writing Intel 432 microcode, but the lack of an Ada compiler made it impossible to run their code even at the assembly-language level.

For those intending to write an HLML compiler, the benefit of this approach is that one can test the language before the compiler is written and build up a user community before the language is fully implemented.

From this survey it should be clear that no one microprogramming language will ever become universally accepted. Different applications will require different languages. The microprogramming community is too diverse for one language to become dominant. Within a particular segment of the community, such as one corporation, a language with a large enough user base for effective support can become established.

What is the next step? I believe that it is the creation of a microprogramming environment or microprogramming workbench that would support the entire range of microprogram development: specification, microcoding, debugging, prove-in on the target system, and maintenance. Such an environment has been proposed (Davidson 1983), and a workbench in production use has been described (Wagnon and Maine 1983). It is interesting to note that this E-Machine workbench was created in an environment in which one language was used for microprogramming several different targets. The E-Machine workbench at present consists of a language and integrated simulation and editing capabilities. It is an important first step to a complete environment. Further discussion of a microprogramming environment would take us into the province of firmware engineering, which is discussed in Chapter 10. Another important step is continued work on compaction and optimization. For a survey of work on compaction, see Chapter 9. Interesting work on optimization was reported by Vegdahl (1985).

Microprogramming languages have greatly increased in sophistication and number since the early 1970s. New, successful languages are described each year. As advances in compiler technology continue and the job of creating a compiler becomes easier, we can expect to see more languages. As the amount of applications microprograms increase, there is an increased need for machine-independent microprogramming languages that will support these applications. Perhaps one day an HLML for a widely distributed bit-slice microprogrammable microprocessor will become commercially available. In any case, microprogramming languages will continue to drive the study of firmware engineering.

REFERENCES

Baba, T., and H. Hagiwara. 1981. "The MPG System: A Machine-Independent Efficient Microprogram Generator." *IEEE Transactions on Computers* C-30 (6):373–94.

Bartlett, J. F. 1981. "MicroTAL—A Machine-Dependent, High-Level Microprogramming Language." *Proceedings 14th Annual Microprogramming Workshop*, 109–14. Silver Spring: IEEE Computer Society Press.

Bell, C. G., and A. Newell.   1971. *Computer Structures: Readings and Examples.* New York: McGraw-Hill.

Damm, W.   1984. "An Axiomatization of Low-Level Parallelism in Microarchitectures." *Proceedings 17th Annual Microprogramming Workshop,* 314–23. Silver Spring: IEEE Computer Society Press.

Dasgupta, S.   1978. "Towards a Microprogramming Language Schema." *Proceedings 11th Annual Microprogramming Workshop,* 144–53. Silver Spring: IEEE Computer Society Press.

———.   1980. "Some Aspects of High Level Microprogramming." *ACM Computing Surveys* 12(3):295–324.

Davidson, S.   1980. "Design and Construction of a Virtual Machine Resource Binding Language." Ph.D. diss. University of Southwestern Louisiana, Computer Science Department.

———.   1986. "Progress in High Level Microprogramming." *IEEE Software* 3 (4):18–26.

Davidson, S., and B. D. Shriver.   1981. "Specifying Target Resources in a Machine Independent High Level Language." *AFIPS Proceedings of the National Computer Conference* 50:81–85.

DeWitt, D. J.   1976. "A Machine-Independent Approach to the Production of Horizontal Microcode." Ph.D. diss. University of Michigan at Ann Arbor.

Duda, M. R., and R. A. Mueller.   1985. "u-C Microprogramming Language (Version 3.1) Reference Manual." *Technical Report CS-85-11.* Fort Collins, CO: Colorado State University.

Eager, M. J. 1983.   "M29—An Advanced Retargetable Microcode Assembler." *Proceedings 16th Annual Microprogramming Workshop,* 92–100. Silver Spring: IEEE Computer Society Press.

Eckhouse, R. H.   1971. "A High-Level Microprogramming Language (MPL)." *Proceedings of AFIPS Spring Joint Computer Conference.*

Goessling, D. F., and J. F. McDonald.   1972. "ISPMET—A Study in Automatic Emulator Generation." *Proceedings 5th Annual Microprogramming Workshop,* 90–95. New York: ACM Press.

Guffin, R. M.   1982. "A Microprogramming Language Directed Architecture." *Proceedings 15th Annual Microprogramming Workshop,* 42–49. Silver Spring: IEEE Computer Society Press.

Gurd, R. P.   1983. "Experience Developing Microcode Using a High Level Language." *Proceedings 16th Annual Microprogramming Workshop,* 179–84. Silver Spring: IEEE Computer Society Press.

Heinanen, J.   1983. "A Programmer Controlled Approach to Data and Control Abstraction." *Proceedings of SIGPLAN '83 Symposium on Programming Language Issues in Software Systems,* 41–52. New York: ACM Press.

Hobson, R. F., P. Hannon, and J. Thornburg. 1981. "High-Level Microprogramming with APL Syntax." *Proceedings 14th Annual Microprogramming Workshop*, 131–39. Silver Spring: IEEE Computer Society Press.

Hopkins, W. C., M. R. Horton, and C. S. Arnold. 1985. "Target-Independent High Level Microprogramming." *Proceedings 18th Annual Microprogramming Workshop*, 137–44. Washington: IEEE Computer Society Press.

Husson, S. S. 1970. *Microprogramming Principles and Practices*. Englewood Cliffs, NJ: Prentice Hall.

Kernighan, B. W., and D. M. Richie. 1978. *The C Programming Language*. Englewood Cliffs, NJ: Prentice Hall.

Klassen, A., and S. Dasgupta. 1981. "S* (QM-1): An Instantiation of the High Level Microprogramming Language Schema S* for the Nanodata QM-1." *Proceedings 14th Annual Microprogramming Workshop*, 124–30. Silver Spring: IEEE Computer Society Press.

Laws, B. A. 1977. "Microbe: A Self Commenting Microassembler." *Proceedings 10th Annual Microprogramming Workshop*, 61–65. Silver Spring: IEEE Computer Society Press.

Lawson, H. W., and L. Blomberg. 1973. "The DataSaab FPCU Microprogramming Language." *Proceedings ACM SIGPLAN-SIGMICRO Interface Meeting*, 86–97. New York: ACM Press.

Linn, J. L., B. D. Shriver, and S. Dasgupta. 1983. "Component Identification for a Portable, Retargetable Firmware Development System." *Proceedings Computer Systems Organization Conference*, 164–70. New Orleans, LA.

Ma P., and T. G. Lewis. 1981. "On the Design of a Microcode Compiler for a Machine-Independent High-Level Language." *IEEE Transactions on Software Engineering* SE-7 (3):261–73.

Marwedel, P. 1981. "A Retargetable Microcode Generation System for a High-Level Microprogramming Language." *Proceedings 14th Annual Microprogramming Workshop*, 115–23. Silver Spring: IEEE Computer Society Press.

Oestreicher, D. R. 1973. "A Microprogramming Language for the MLP-900." *Proceedings ACM SIGPLAN-SIGMICRO Interface Meeting*, 113–6. New York: ACM Press.

Patterson, D. A. 1975. "The Design of a System for the Synthesis of Correct Microprograms." *Proceedings 8th Annual Microprogramming Workshop*, 13–17. Silver Spring: IEEE Computer Society Press.

———. 1976. "STRUM: Structured Microprogramming Development System for Correct Firmware." *IEEE Transactions on Computers* C-25 (10):975–85.

———. 1981. "An Experiment in High Level Language Microprogramming and Verification." *Communications of the ACM* 24 (10):699–709.

Patterson, D. A., K. Lew, and R. Tuck. 1979. "Towards an Efficient, Machine-Independent Language for Microprogramming." *Proceedings 12th Annual Microprogramming Workshop*, 22–35. Silver Spring: IEEE Computer Society Press.

Patterson, D. A., R. Goodell, M. D. Poe, and S. C. Steely, Jr.   1981. "V-Compiler: A Next Generation Tool for Microprogramming." *AFIPS Proceedings of National Computer Conference* 50:103–9.

Ramamoorthy, C. V., M. Tabendeh, and M. Tsuchiya.   1973. "A Higher Level Language for Microprogramming." *Proceedings 6th Annual Workshop on Microprogramming*, 139–44. New York: ACM Press.

Ramamoorthy, C. V., and M. Tscuchiya.   1973. "A High Level Language for Horizontal Microprogramming." *IEEE Transactions on Computers* C-23 (8):791–802.

Rauscher, T. G.   1973. "Towards a Specification of Syntax and Semantics for Languages for Horizontally Microprogrammed Machines." *Proceedings of ACM SIGPLAN-SIGMICRO Interface Meeting*, 98–111. New York: ACM Press.

Sheraga, R. J., and J. L. Gieser.   1981. "Automatic Microcode Generation for Horizontally Microprogrammed Processors." *Proceedings 14th Annual Microprogramming Workshop*, 154–68. Silver Spring: IEEE Computer Society Press.

Sint, M.   1980. "A Survey of High Level Microprogramming Languages." *Proceedings 13th Annual Microprogramming Workshop*, 141–53. Silver Spring: IEEE Computer Society Press.

_____.   1981. "MIDL—A Microinstruction Description Language." *Proceedings 14th Annual Microprogramming Workshop*, 95–106. Silver Spring: IEEE Computer Society Press.

Skordalakis, E.   1983. "Meta-assemblers." *IEEE Micro* 3 (2):6-16.

Sommerville, J. F.   1979. "Towards Machine-Independent Microprogramming." *EUROMICRO Journal* 5:219–24.

Tirrell, A. K.   1973. "A Study of the Application of Compiler Techniques to the Generation of Micro-Code." *Proceedings ACM SIGPLAN-SIGMICRO Interface Meeting*, 67–84. New York: ACM Press.

Tucker, A. B., and M. J. Flynn.   1971. "Dynamic Microprogramming: Processor Organization and Programming." *Communications of the ACM* 14 (4):240–50.

Vegdahl, S. R.   1985. "The Design of an Interactive Compiler for Optimizing Microprograms." *Proceedings 18th Annual Microprogramming Workshop*, 129–36. New York: IEEE Computer Society Press.

Wagnon, G., and D. J. W. Maine.   1983. "An E-Machine Workbench." *Proceedings 16th Annual Microprogramming Workshop*, 101–11. Silver Spring: IEEE Computer Society Press.

Weidner, T. G.   1980. "CHAMIL, A Case Study in Microprogramming Language Design." *SIGPLAN Notices* 15 (1):156–66.

Young, J. L.   1988. "The Software Foundry: Almost Too Good to be True." *Electronics* 61 (2):47–51.

five
VERTICAL MIGRATION

TOM WEIDNER
JOHN STANKOVIC

Relocation of functionality is and always has been an unavoidable phenomenon associated with computer-systems design and development. Several factors combine to ensure nonoptimal functional placement regardless of the amount of effort spent in planning and preparation. Most of these factors reflect the dynamics of the problems faced in the computer industry. We constantly attempt the impossible, resulting in the inevitable compromises, shortcuts in systems methodology, and fluctuations in project direction. We consistently demand more than our technology can deliver. We typically design without detailed foreknowledge of the application to be supported. It is not surprising that we continually discover more appropriate functional partitionings in computer systems.

Migration of functionality denotes a methodological strategy in relocation. Three forms of migration are prominent:

- Outboard migration
- Horizontal migration
- Vertical migration

Outboard and horizontal migration deal with establishing a good division of labor between multiple processing sites responsible for accomplishing a task. Vertical migration is substantially different: it is concerned with reducing overhead in individual systems constructed with multiple levels of interpretation (Heller and Van Dam 1981).

Improved performance is the primary motivation of all three techniques. Isolation of function is rapidly increasing as an ulterior motive. Vertical migration, in particular, provides a means of isolating and thereby protecting proprietary objects by effectively making them more difficult to access and modify. Increasing instances of industrial espionage lend credence to this practice (Tinnen 1983).

Outboard migration is an established technique dating back to first-generation systems. Such systems were characterized by overworked CPUs. Outboard migration involves off-loading specific functions to additional specialized processing elements. These processing elements are usually dedicated devices with restricted architectures that operate in a master/slave environment. I/O channels and arithmetic processors are examples.

The notions of outboard migration are again becoming prominent due to heavy use of the client/server model within the context of distributed systems. The server off-loads an overburdened client by performing specialized activity on its behalf. The client acts as a master. The dedication of these logical devices and their assumed roles are analogous to earlier applications of the technique involving physical devices.

Horizontal migration is a relatively new technique in which division of labor is partitioned among cooperating and equal tasks. It owes its feasibility to improved hardware economics and connectivity. The technique relies on the availability of several general-purpose processing elements. Since each of the processing elements can perform any portion of the task, performance enhancement through concurrent activity is possible. In reality, this remains an untapped potential. It is another instance in which technology precedes an understanding of the problem. In this case, the problem involves the intricacies of parallelism.

Vertical migration approaches the problem of an overburdened processing resource from a different perspective and is applicable in a different environment. This technique assumes the existence of a multilevel interpretive system and restricts itself to a single processing site. The relocation of functionality takes place among the levels of the interpretive system. Higher levels are more general in terms of applicability and more demanding in terms of processing activity. Lower levels are more specific in terms of applicability and less demanding of processing resources. Migration from higher to lower levels reduces the processing burden of the CPU.

The multilayered interpretive model is not atypical of existing systems. The least sophisticated systems contain at least a single software layer that is interpreted by a hardware layer (fig. 5-1). More commonly, the software of a system consists of several layers. The hardware interprets an operating-system kernel.

Figure 5-1. Common two-level interpretive system.

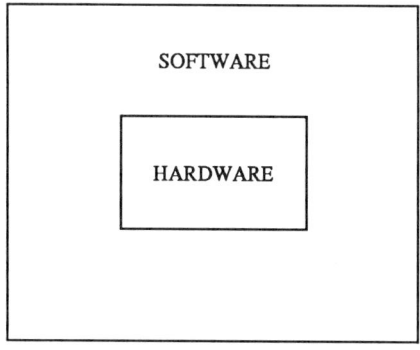

This kernel interprets more sophisticated operating-system functions. The more sophisticated operating-system primitives interpret the application software. It is not uncommon to find database-management and communications-software layers in between the application and operating-system layers.

Additional layering between the hardware and software, called firmware, is now commonplace, due to increased application of microprogramming techniques during the past decade (fig. 5-2). Migration of software from a given level to a lower level in a system is called vertical migration. A special case of vertical migration, migration from any software level into the firmware level, is called classical migration. This chapter describes vertical migration but in many cases focuses on classical migration because of the nature of this book.

The potential of vertical migration as a performance-enhancement technique was recognized over three decades ago. Wilkes drew attention to the technique while giving birth to the concept of microprogramming (1951). However, the overwhelming cost of equipment at the time stifled its development. Since then, the technique has experienced two periods of renaissance. One was spurred by software-engineering disciplines advocating design of layered architectures during the late 1960s, and the other occurred as the result of improved control-store technology during the mid 1970s.

Layered architectures continue to promote application of vertical migration. The availability of large amounts of inexpensive writable control store (WCS) also continues to motivate use. However, current fascination surrounding distributed systems seems to be overshadowing vertical migration in favor of other forms of migration. All three forms seemingly hold their own in relation to other types of performance-enhancement techniques such as compiler optimization, caching, pipelining, paging, and specialization of architecture. Statistical analysis in support of the previous statement remains scarce.

Figure 5-2. Typical multilevel interpretive system.

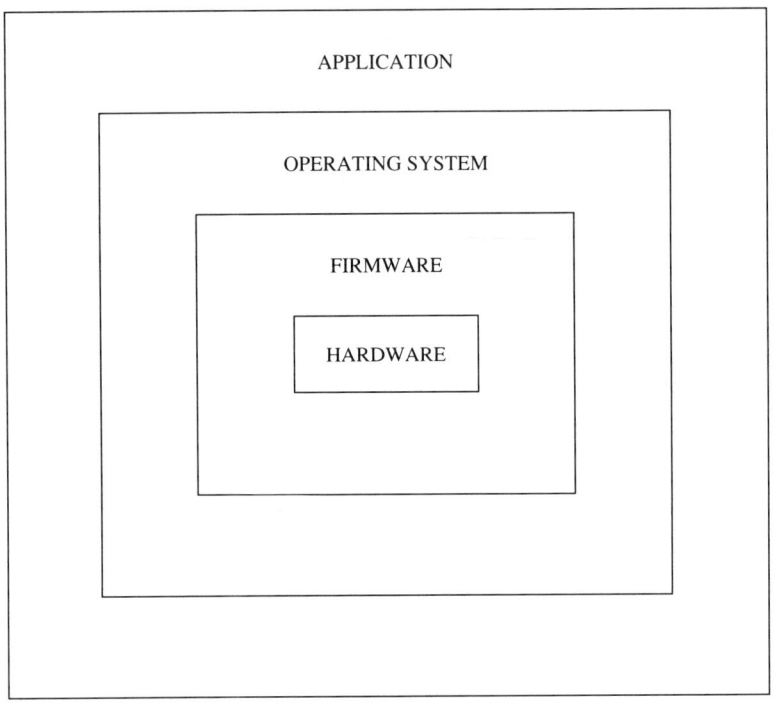

Hesitancy in adopting vertical migration is only partially due to the perceived advantages of distribution. Its most formidable obstacles have always been a genuine lack of theoretical foundation and the harsh realities of firmware engineering. The limited capabilities of firmware engineering are a factor because of the predominance of the use of vertical migration at the interface between software and firmware layers (classical migration). Analytical results to support vertical migration are rare. Tools are often inappropriate or incomplete.

The remainder of this chapter is organized as follows. First, we discuss applications of the vertical migration technique in survey style. This is not an exhaustive presentation; the types of variation of applications are too numerous. Instead, we focus on a few representative cases. Function-oriented and instruction-oriented approaches are contrasted. The relationship of vertical migration to architectural synthesis is outlined. Manual and heuristic methods are described. Evolution of the technique is traced from early ad hoc methods to recent efforts involving tools for capture and analysis of performance characteristics.

The following section provides a more theoretical description of vertical migration and presents an analysis of the constituent elements and interactions of a model. The model is a generalized multilevel interpretive system. The overhead introduced by each component is described in detail. Possible reductions in overhead due to migration from higher to lower layers are identified. The reader is referred elsewhere for more extensive treatment of the model, including quantification of savings based on formulas and theorems (Stankovic 1981a).

Future directions are discussed next. Automatic synthesis, tools for sampling without undue overhead, and legitimacy through analytical and theoretical effort are established goals. Much more work is required in comparing migrational and nonmigrational methods of performance enhancement. Technological advances in storage and VLSI continue to influence classical migrations. Emerging areas of applications are identified. References are provided should the reader care to delve deeper.

APPLICATION OF THE TECHNIQUE

Vertical migration is often perceived in a very narrow context as simply a technique for performance improvement. It is properly viewed as much more. Not only is it motivated by other factors, including security, propriety, protection, and basic engineering strategy, but it also represents an evolving methodology. The methodology is comprised of several fundamentally distinct elements including:

- Partitioning
- Load analysis
- Synthesis
- Verification
- Integration

Refer to figure 5-3. Partitioning identifies those sections of a system that are candidates for migration. This often involves flawed methods such as soliciting expert subjectivity. However, selecting a representative workload remains critical to the success of the entire process. Load analysis refers to the techniques employed to identify areas of activity within the selected partition. Most common are tracing and sampling mechanisms. We contrast these methods later in this section. Synthesis is the creation of equivalent functionality at a lower level of the hierarchy. Verification is the process of ensuring the same result given a new and different method of achieving it. Integration involves the steps necessary to incorporate a new realization of some function into the existing system.

Figure 5-3. Vertical migration as an engineering methodology.

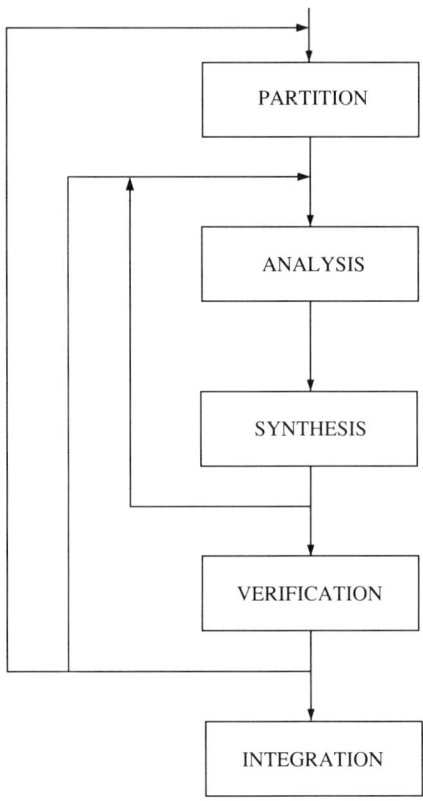

The rest of this section focuses on instances of the methodology applied to the interface between software and firmware (classical migration). We do not wish to give the impression that software-to-software migrations are rare or in some sense uninteresting. On the contrary, performance improvements are readily attainable. Reductions in mapping overhead between software layers can often be measured at more than an order of magnitude (Stockenberg and van Dam 1978). Synthesis is actually easier in this circumstance because the same instruction set is involved. Vertical migration between software layers is constantly being employed, especially by software-system producers, but it frequently appears in the guise of a cleanup activity and is not recognized as such. It is also frequently complicated by unmanageable structuring with existing operating-systems software.

Manual Methods

Several recent computer architectures demonstrate the now-common practice of migrating elements of an operating-systems kernel into microcode (Soltis 1981; Intel 1981). See figures 5-4 and 5-5. Early attempts at this type of migration can be traced to the problem of modifying a system architecture in order to make it more amenable to a specific problem set. A flurry of such activity took place in the early 1970s. It centered around the prospect of user-microprogrammable machines and readily available writable control store (WCS).

The Burroughs 1700 is a good example of such a universal host. It was a vertically oriented microinstruction machine with a wealth (at the time) of WCS available to the microprogrammer. The system architecture (S-machine) provided to the user was defined by the microcode resident in the WCS at any

Figure 5-4. IBM System/38 horizontal microcode layer.

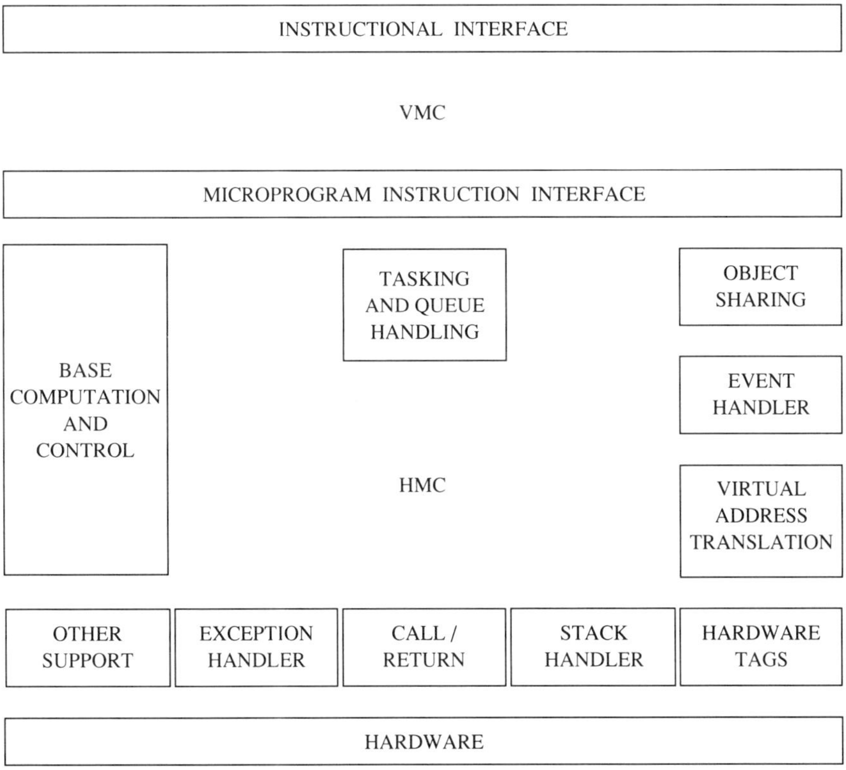

INSTRUCTIONAL INTERFACE

VMC

MICROPROGRAM INSTRUCTION INTERFACE

BASE COMPUTATION AND CONTROL	TASKING AND QUEUE HANDLING		OBJECT SHARING
			EVENT HANDLER
	HMC		VIRTUAL ADDRESS TRANSLATION

OTHER SUPPORT	EXCEPTION HANDLER	CALL / RETURN	STACK HANDLER	HARDWARE TAGS

HARDWARE

Figure 5-5. IBM System/38 vertical microcode layer.

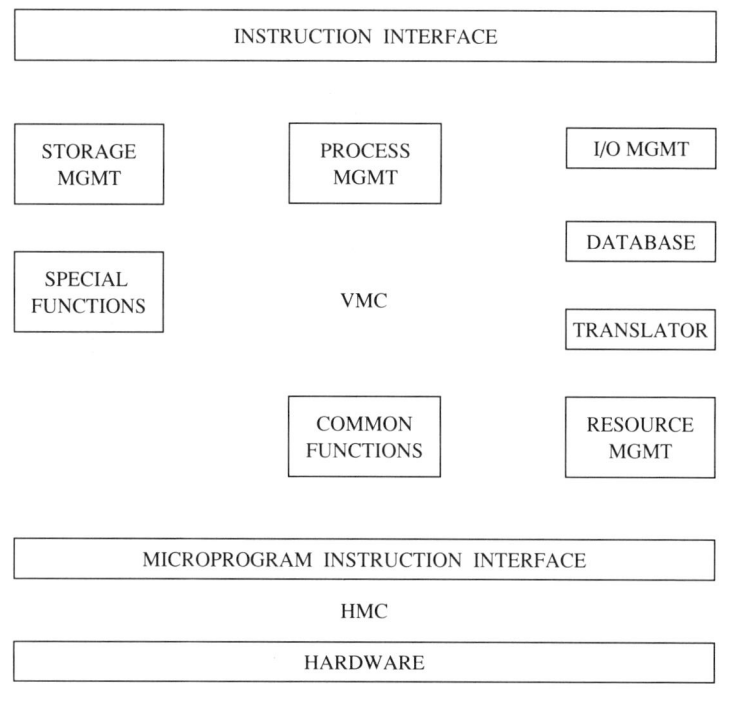

given instant, and the WCS could be overwritten by microcode representing another S-machine dynamically.

Establishing overall performance gains due to migration was a fairly simple exercise for the B1700. Microinstructions could be fetched from either WCS or main memory. In fact, the hardware of the machine hid the boundary from the software. The more expensive members of the family had several kilobytes of WCS; the least expensive member had none. Performance improvements could be ascertained by running the same benchmark on both machines.

Early interpreters were relatively small, leaving plenty of space in WCS for experimentation. The first experiments involved elements of the system traditionally associated with the operating system. Migration of physical I/O handlers improved system performance in that area by approximately a factor of two. Logical I/O routines followed. Methods for selecting appropriate routines were not supported by execution monitoring.

Spoolers and the schedule were next. Performance improvements became less dramatic. The interrelationships of the multiple migrations definitely had an impact, but the method employed did not really attempt to analyze the situation. Analysis would have been further complicated by simultaneous efforts at modularizing and splitting off OS functionality.

At this stage, logical I/O was reorganized. This is important because it demonstrated the inadequacy of ad hoc application after a certain threshold and the need for well-defined interfaces in order to keep a handle on migration methods. The fact that a system is hierarchically layered does not imply that the system is well structured. Without good structure migrations are of little use. The motivation was completeness, not performance. Following the reorganization, real-time-device support and queue handling for data communications found their way into WCS.

During this process, the physical structure of the B1700 changed to incorporate a microinstruction caching mechanism. It evolved into the B1800 family. At the same time the interpreters were growing and becoming considerably more sophisticated. Suddenly, expected performance gains due to migration were not realized. This demonstrated the effect of alternative performance-enhancement techniques (caching) on migration. Analysis of these relationships remains an outstanding problem area. In this circumstance the working-set characteristics of the large interpreters using the caching method nullified performance gains due to migration.

The benefits of even these early manual techniques cannot be dismissed. This experimentation resulted in significant overall applicational performance improvement. It resulted in a reasonable partitioning of operating-system functionality. It drew attention to the necessity of explicit, well-formed interfaces. And it also motivated investigations into issues of multiple migrations and the effects of instruction caching on migration. The next generation of this architecture, the B1900, became the direct beneficiary; other Burroughs architectures, including those currently being designed, have also been influenced.

Too often, vertical migration is seen as a universal panacea. Economic factors such as the cost of writable control store lead the unsuspecting to suggest that everything possible be migrated. Migration has very little to do with control-store space. More relevant issues include the extent of good hierarchical structuring, the widespread sharing of global data items, and even whether a function is typically I/O bound.

Recent trends toward loosely coupled distributed systems have influenced systems designs to avoid global data items and shared memory. The resulting clean interfaces enhance migration methods. Improved hardware-description tools also aid the methodology by making it easier to identify interactions and verify results.

When considering candidates for migration, recognition of Rauscher's Law seems appropriate (Rauscher and Adams 1980). In substance it states: microprogramming an inefficient algorithm does not make it efficient.

Heuristic Methods

As early as 1974 improvements to the slow and expensive manual architecture-tuning process were proposed (Abd-Alla and Karlgaard 1974). Their attempts to automate the manual tuning process represent the initial formulation of a vertical-migration method. This heuristic tuning involved all the previously described phases.

The methodology proposed establishing categories of similar program entities, usually oriented towards particular language environments such as FORTRAN or COBOL. The motivation was creation of a specialized architecture for each partition, each existing as a specialized instruction set interpreted from control store. The prospect of dynamically selecting the appropriate machine was considered in light of WCS implementations.

Each category is then analyzed in terms of its execution behavior. This phase incorporates a monitoring mechanism. We discuss the relative merits of tracing and sampling in subsequent paragraphs; this methodology employed the former. The trace would gather statistics on instruction-execution frequencies, dependencies, and data-referencing patterns. The analysis took place following execution of the algorithm.

Two fundamental approaches, function-oriented and instruction-oriented, exist in establishing the object of migration. In the function-oriented approach, migration objects are functions as defined by programming-language constructs such as procedures and subroutines (Holtkamp and Kastner 1982). In the instruction-oriented approach, migration objects are sequences of instructions that occur or are executed frequently. These blocks of instructions are independent of the logical structure imposed by the programming environment. The approach selected can have an effect on the method of measurement selected.

The Abd-Alla method used the instruction-oriented approach. In fact, the literature on the method focused on an algorithm for synthesis based on iterative replacement of frequently executed loops. Only suggestions were offered concerning the other aspects of the methodology.

El-Ayat and Howard extend this basic proposal, refining the algorithm for analyzing execution profiles and suggesting individual mechanisms for synthesizing loops and nonloops (El-Ayat and Howard 1977). Their method is instruction-oriented, like its predecessor, and also employs tracing techniques in the analysis phase. They report execution improvement from 30% to 45% for complete programs.

The experiments with vertical migration at Brown University are landmarks in several respects (Stockenberg and van Dam 1978; Stankovic 1982a, 1982b). Most importantly, we notice that the theoretical foundations are laid using Parnas's USES relation (Parnas 1972), and that a model identifying the fundamental concepts and constituent elements of the method is created.

Secondly, the designers of the Brown University methodology proposed an elegant and sophisticated marriage between vertical migration and the mechanisms used in its analysis. BUGS (Brown University Graphics Systems) in conjunction with STRUCT (Stockenberg and Van Dam 1975), a system allowing examination of both static and dynamic program behavior, provide what may still be the most advanced system of its kind for these purposes. In any case, a system using interactive graphics in an attempt to automate portions of the methodology was well ahead of its time. Analogous efforts elsewhere are now being applied to horizontal and outboard migrations with graphics-capable workstations acting as sampling devices for the network.

These experiments resulted in several interesting observations. For instance, low-level migrations yielded smaller improvements, but more applications were affected. Migrating a few high-level functions worked best for special-purpose applications. Migrating a number of low-level functions worked best for general-purpose applications. And the combined effect of several migrations was always better than a single migration (Stankovic 1982a).

Analytical Approach

In the late 1970s Rauscher and Agrawala presented a technique for synthesizing architecture that differed considerably from previous methods (Rauscher and Agrawala 1978). Much of the work was done by the compilation process. The compiler was responsible for generation of both the microprograms for the new instruction set and the machine-language representation of the problem.

Selection of candidates for migration and construction of optimal instructional groupings involves considerable mathematical modeling. It also involves changes to the code-generation phases of a compiler. The obvious advantage is the reduced emphasis of familiarity with microprogram organization. These mechanisms can be categorized as instruction-oriented. The authors use firmware tracing mechanisms in establishing behavior. And they also report overall performance improvements in the neighborhood of 30% to 45%.

Luque, Ripoll, and Ruz suggest another rigorous but static analytic methodology (Luque, Ripoll, and Ruz 1980). Their proposal identifies all sequences of instructions that may be microprogrammed. In this sense, it is more complete than the previously described method. The static analysis for identification of sequences applies to loops and segments (nonloops). Information derived from the statistic analysis is used by the subsequent dynamic-analysis phase, which obtains an execution profile of the program. Analytical expressions are developed to evaluate time savings produced by microprogramming the sequences. Two methods are proposed for selecting appropriate sequences. One is based on integer linear programming. The other is based on a linear iterative algorithm, which is less time-consuming but does not guarantee the best solution in every case. The authors report improvements in execution speed up to 50%.

Means of Gathering Statistics

Legitimate vertical-migration methodologies require the ability to monitor the behavior of a system. Without this capability the decision process involving what to migrate becomes entirely subjective. Given the critical nature of this process to the methods previously described, it is not surprising to find considerable activity in the development of optimal monitoring mechanisms.

Software monitors are programs that run concurrently with the programs they observe. They typically distort system operation (i.e., systems running with a monitor usually have different characteristics than without). This interference can degrade system performance and result in at best dubious measurements. However, monitors do provide flexibility in specifying what to record and the limits for doing so. Hardware monitors lack this flexibility. They have predefined capabilities so far as what to record and where to find the information. This usually results in massive amounts of data, most of which is difficult to associate with higher-level functionality. The advantage is low interference and the associated improvement in realistic behavior tracking.

Recent efforts suggest a hybrid approach of firmware monitoring. It provides the advantages of both while at the same time reducing the drawbacks. Firmware monitors are typically realized as microprogrammed instructions that can be used by the software levels. They are flexible enough to allow selection, exclusion, and granularity specification for sample spaces, yet they don't interfere to any considerable extent (Armbruster 1979).

Firmware monitors can be used to observe objects of the following classes (Gratsch and Kastner 1981):

- Mapping actions
- Execution actions
- Hardware-level interface
- Software functions

The first two are most useful in the instruction-oriented approach (see below). The third is the focus of microdiagnostics and is not particularly relevant to this discussion. The last is most useful for the function-oriented approach.

Mapping actions include observation of instruction tapes, instruction addresses, addressing modes, register usage, and operand addresses. Execution actions monitor successful branching, register alteration, and memory updates. Software functions incorporate logical grouping of numbers of instructions based on environmental factors. Techniques for measurement include tracing and sampling.

Tracing is event-driven. At each occurrence of the event, certain data is collected. Information content is high. However, the raw amount of data can be prohibitive. This technique is more appropriate given the larger objects of the function-oriented approaches.

Sampling can be controlled outside the context of events. Raw-data collection is reducible. The 80/20 rule (the phenomenon in which a program spends 80% of its time in 20% of its code) results in acceptable accuracy. This technique is most appropriate given the smaller objects typical of the instruction-oriented approaches.

Industrial Manifestations

Over the past decade, IBM has invested significant effort and resources in establishing a methodology for vertical (classical) migration. It is one of the few reasonably documented efforts of the past decade (Tallman 1974; Olbert 1978). As such, we distinguish it as representative of the state-of-the-art in the industry.

Most of the effort was applied to Extended Control Program Support (ECPS) for the VM/370 software system. This system is a standard feature on several central processing units. Reported reductions of 48% to 55% in control-program execution time and overall elapsed-time reductions of 9% to 27% were characteristic.

The ECPS:VM assist methodology consists of the following steps:

- Benchmark selection
- Load analysis
- High-execution-frequency identification
- High-usage-area analysis
- Area-stability determination
- Performance-improvement projection
- Formal documentation of function
- Implementation/test
- Measurement of actual performance improvement

The first is analogous to that described previously as partitioning. The next four represent a considerable refinement to the global notion described earlier as load analysis. In contrast to many of the methodologies previously described, IBM's migration methodology draws heavily upon firmware monitoring of the sampling variety.

Performance projections through implementation and test again refine the general area of synthesis. The last step is analogous to the previously described verification phase. Although not explicitly identified above, integration involves creation of a new instruction opcode that is inserted preceding the machine-level code it replaces. If a particular CPU supports the assist, the microcode is invoked. If not, the new instruction becomes a no-op and the machine-language code is executed.

Considerable effort is consumed within the methodology in establishing reasons for excluding candidates for migration. The candidate can be tagged as using too much WCS. The area of software may be prone to change (unstable). It may need normal optimizations before it is seriously considered. Or it may be too closely linked to direct hardware support, resulting in too little or no performance improvement if microcoded.

While the IBM ECPS:VM assist methodology has been described in the open literature, few other industrial efforts (of which there have been many) have been so documented, primarily for proprietary reasons.

DESCRIPTION OF THE TECHNIQUE

The classical form of vertical migration is the migration of functions from software to firmware. A generalization of this classical form is the migration of functions from a high-level (abstract) machine to a lower-level (abstract) machine (Stockenberg and Van Dam 1978). The abstract machines can be implemented in hardware or software. Hence, vertical migration includes software-to-software migrations as well as the classical software-to-firmware migrations.

The performance improvements attainable by vertical migration have been well established in practice. Such improvements arise in two ways: (1) the movement of a function to a lower level means the movement to a faster level, and (2) in the process of moving higher-level functions "excess" generality is often omitted. Before describing the vertical-migration technique in depth we first informally discuss why vertical migration improves performance.

It is obvious that a software-to-firmware migration is a movement from a slower to a faster level. But what about the more general software-to-software migrations? In these cases, each level incurs an overhead with higher-level overheads being more costly in execution time than lower levels. This is due to the fact that the higher levels typically make use of the lower levels, incurring the overhead of the lower levels in addition to their own overhead. By reimplementing the higher-level function in the lower level the overheads of the higher level are avoided. When reimplementing there is also the possibility of replacing expensive (in time) interlevel calls with cheaper intralevel calls.

The second reason for performance improvements in vertical migration is more a consequence of practicality than any fundamental law. Functions (especially those implemented at higher levels in the system) are often general enough to handle a variety of inputs. For a given application program, the particular paths needed from a function might be quite restrictive. By making this function less general, it can be optimized. For example, it is often possible to remove tests to determine just what paths of the general function are needed. A slow version of the more general functions would still exist for those presumably infrequent applications needing that generality.

We now present a more formal description of the vertical-migration technique concentrating on the previously noted reasons for performance improvement.

Vertical migration is a systematic method for improving the performance of a dedicated application or class of applications in a multilevel firmware-software hierarchical system (fig. 5-6) by reducing CPU overhead. Each level in figure 5-6 has an associated execution-time overhead. The execution-time overhead of a level is lowest for the hardware and increases for each level as you proceed up the hierarchy from the hardware to the application-program level. As stated above, this is due to the fact that the higher levels typically make use of the lower levels, incurring the overhead of the lower levels in addition to their own overhead. The method for reducing overhead involves reimplementing either entire functions or paths through them that are CPU-intensive on lower levels. An example would be the reimplementation of an OS-level 1 function as an OS-level 0 function, or the reimplementation of an OS-level 2 function in the firmware. Elements contributing to this overhead are described below as part of what is referred to as the VM model.

The VM model is a multilevel interpretive model and is based on both the USES relation (Parnas 1972) and the mapping/execution model (Fuller et al. 1976), also called fetch and recognition cycles (Hartenstein 1973). The utility of the VM model consists of identifying the control structure and overhead of layered systems for purposes of performance improvement.

In the VM model the invocation and execution of a function that exists at a particular level in a multilevel interpreter system consists of two components, mapping actions and execution actions. Mapping actions are actions performed

Figure 5-6. Brown University graphics system: a typical multilevel firmware-software hierarchical system.

APPLICATION PROGRAMS
OS-LEVEL 1 Functions include program storage and loading, file manipulation, and high-level I/O
OS LEVEL 0 Functions include automatic storage management, multiprogramming support and low-level I/O
FIRMWARE Produces IBM 360-like instruction set
HARDWARE Digital Scientific Corp. Meta 4

to map flow of control and data parameters from the caller level to the level of the invoked function and back. Execution actions refer to steps that perform the semantic operations for the invoked function.

The mapping actions may be viewed as overhead in that they implement the actual interlevel call mechanism as well as the processing conventions common to each level. For software-level to firmware-level calls, these mapping actions include instruction fetch and decode, operand-address computation, fetch, and so on. For interlevel software calls the mapping actions will likely include the use of an interrupt mechanism (i.e., supervisor call [SVC] on 360s or EMT on PDP/11s), with the associated common processing of context saving, manipulation, and restoring. At each level the common processing constituting the mapping actions for invoking and returning from the execution actions is defined as mapping prologue and epilogue. The selector is defined as that part of the mapping-action prologue that determines whether the function exists at this level. The reader is encouraged to remember these specific *examples* of mapping actions to better understand the more formal treatment presented below.

Figure 5-7 is a high-level symbolic model of three software levels and a firmware level with the processing at each level partitioned into mapping actions and execution actions. The mapping actions of each level are shown as common prologues and epilogues. The execution actions for each function on the firmware level are labeled T_1 (target instruction 1), T_2, T_3,. . .; for level 0, P_{01} (function at level 0), P_{02},. . .; P_{11} (function at level 1), P_{12}, P_{13},. . .; and finally for the application level A1 (application module 1), etc.

When P_{13}, a function at level 1, is invoked at the application level, it is executed by going through the level 1 prologue, the four execution actions of P_{13} (i.e., the calls to function T_3, T_2, P_{02}, P_{01} of which it is comprised), and the epilogue. For each of the execution actions T_3 and T_2 the firmware prologue (and epilogue) must be executed, and similarly for each of the execution actions P_{02}, P_{01} the level 0 prologue (and epilogue) must be executed. The logical flow of control to these four prologues is shown in figure 5-7; flow of control returns to P_{13} after the respective epilogues have been executed. Note that logically the interlevel flow of control is top down from level i to level $k(k \leq i)$. In reality, the flow of control is bottom up, with the hardware doing the executing and trapping to the firmware level when necessary, the firmware level trapping to OS level 1 when it cannot perform the requested function, and so on. This bottom-up mechanism is entirely transparent to the programmer. Only the selector portion of the prologue is executed when a level cannot perform a particular function, and the selector simply passes control upwards in the hierarchy. For example, in figure 5-7 when P_{13} is invoked, control first passes to the firmware-level selector, then to the level 0 selector, then to the level 1 selector. The level 1 selector recognizes function P_{13} as existing on this level and then completes the remainder of the prologue that contains the common processing for this level.

Figure 5-7. The VM model.

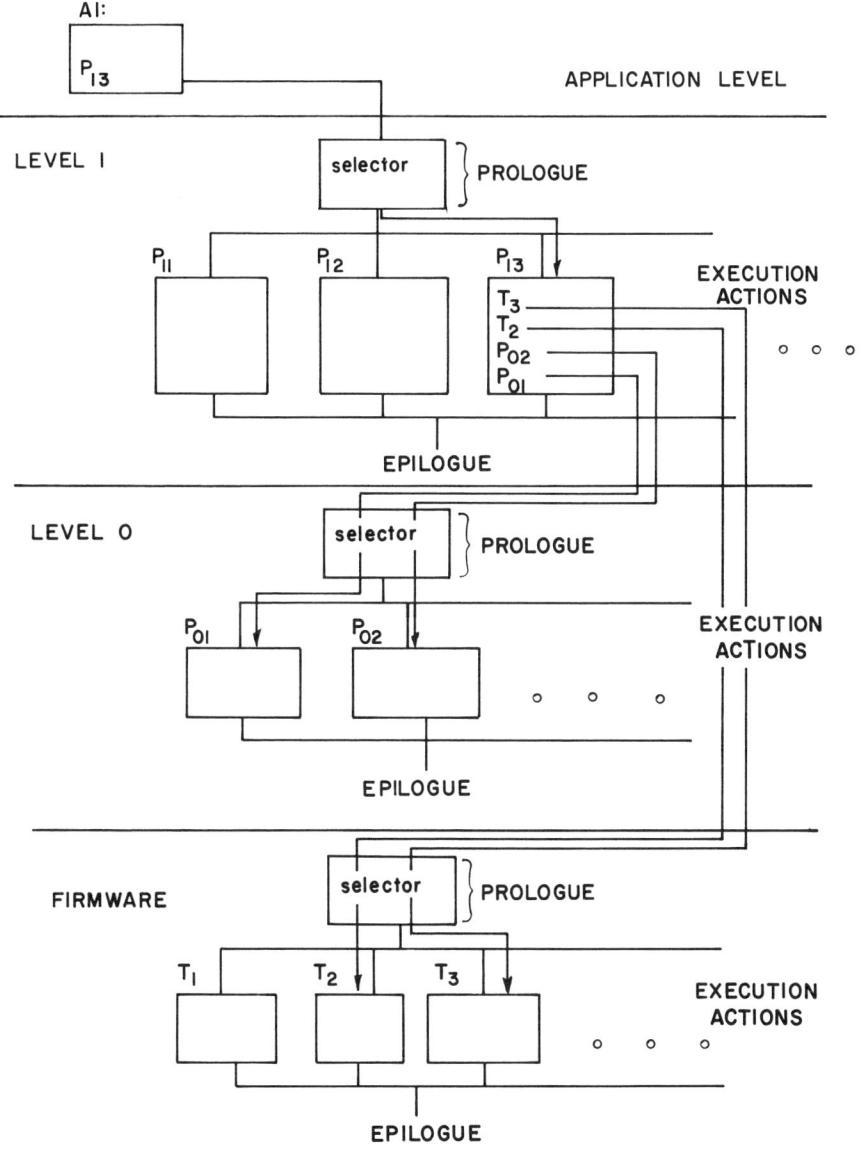

In the vertical-migration methodology, performance is improved by migrating specific functions (i.e., their execution actions) to a lower level. For example, P_{13} is migrated down to level 0 by reimplementing P_{13}, and is labeled P'_{13} in figure 5-8. In order to preserve the hierarchy when implementing P'_{13}, functions above level 0 cannot be employed. The performance improvement of migrating the execution actions to a lower level is realized for two distinct reasons. First, migrating a complete function allows a lower-level mapping action to be substituted for a higher-level mapping function—i.e., in place of the AIs invoking the level 1 prologue/epilogue for P_{13}, it invokes level 0 prologue/epilogue for P'_{13}. Remember the mapping-action execution costs increase with increasing level number as described above. Note that the mapping-action costs are machine-dependent.

The second reason for savings in migrating execution actions arises when interlevel calls that were part of the migrated execution action become simple intralevel calls (i.e., calls to P_{02} and P_{01}). Intralevel calls transfer control within a level without invoking the mapping action of that level (fig. 5-8). The mapping actions for the P_{02} and P_{01} interlevel calls are therefore saved. The extent of the performance improvement is therefore dependent on the relative cost of the various mapping actions and the number of mapping actions that are saved. This cost can be automatically approximated by using run-time statistics of how often each routine is invoked and prior calculations of mapping-action overhead for each level.

As an example, consider a level 0 function migrated to the firmware level. One saving results from the substitution of a firmware mapping action for a level 0 mapping action. The second saving is due to the replacement of the sequence of target instructions that comprised the level 0 function's execution action by the functionally equivalent sequence of microinstructions of the firmware-level execution action. Logically speaking, the interlevel mapping action (including target-instruction fetch) of each target instruction is deleted when we replace the level 0 execution action with the equivalent firmware-level execution action.

Note that all computer systems exhibit the behavior described by the VM model for at least two levels (software and hardware). Most systems have at least several additional levels—firmware and/or one or more operating-system levels. The model then is widely applicable to uniprocessor systems in use today.

Of course, it is also sometimes possible to further improve performance by eliminating execution actions altogether. This occurs when certain execution actions are deemed excess code as far as the particular migration (special-purpose) is concerned. These actions were originally installed to handle more general invocations of the functions, as described earlier.

Three important issues that still must be treated to fully understand vertical migration are (1) interactions of multiple simultaneous migrations, (2) two other

Figure 5-8. An example of migration.

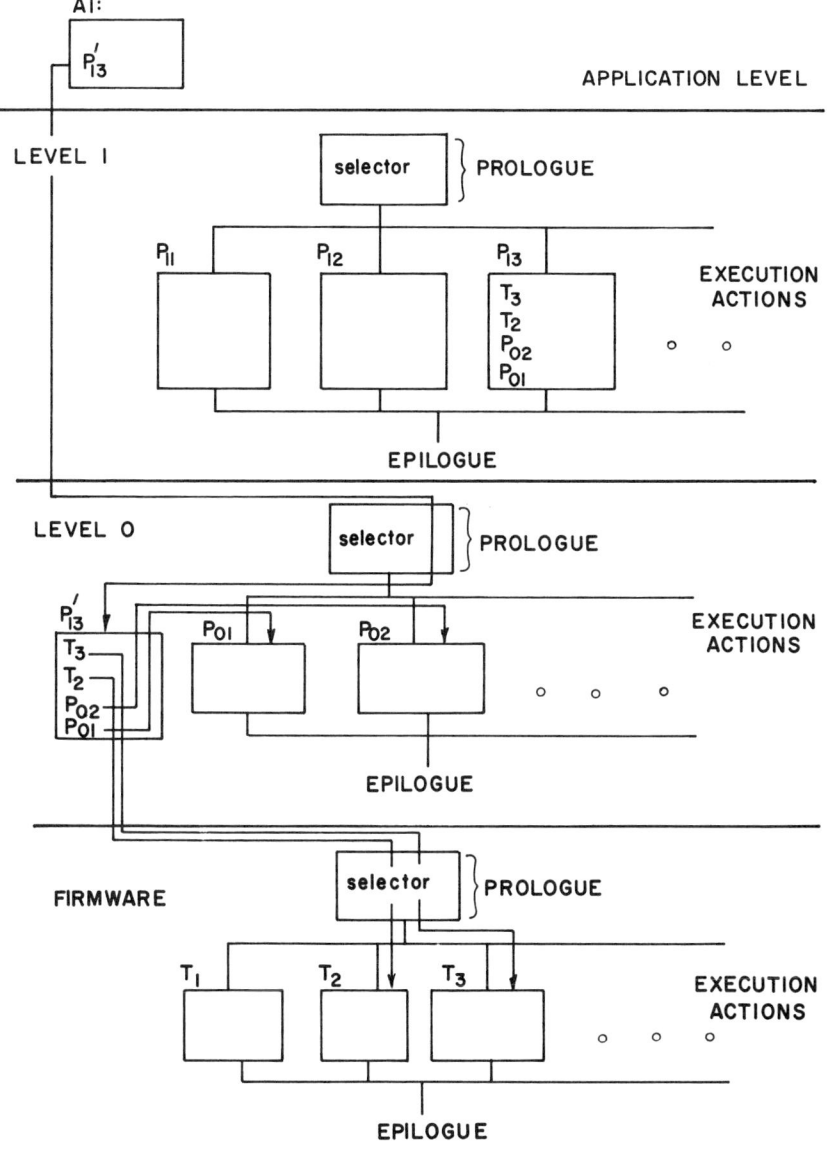

variations of vertical migration called new instructions and replacement, and (3) data migration.

The above VM model is used to describe the interaction of migrations (Stankovic 1981a). The results include the identification of how both positive and negative performance effects of multiple migrations can occur and how the magnitude of these effects can be large. The order of migrations is shown to be irrelevant. It is also shown that a migration may negate the performance improvement of previous migrations, implying that the "total" performance improvement is degraded.

It is also shown that three distinct types of migration are possible for a multilevel interpreter systems. The first type possesses the greatest potential for performance improvement. This results when the invocation of the migrated function takes place at a lower level after the migration than prior to the migration. Strictly speaking, this is vertical migration as described in the above model. The second type of migration occurs when a new (target) instruction is defined to replace a sequence of higher-level primitives. The third type of migration consists of replacement of a function invocation by its equivalent lower-level instructions. It was shown that if one is not careful, replacement could easily lead to a loss in performance rather than an improvement. For each of the above types of migration precise formulas have been derived for execution-time savings on a per-invocation basis. Comparison of these formulas indicates that vertical migration has the largest potential performance improvement (Stankovic 1981a).

The migrations referred to as new instructions and replacement are now described in more depth, and the savings formula for vertical migration is given to provide a clear comparison among these forms of migration. Figure 5-9 depicts the situation of creating a new (target) instruction at level 0 (i.e., P'_{00}). This is a second type of migration, different from vertical migration. Let z be the number of instructions at level m (here $m = 1$) that are condensed into a new instruction. In this example, $z = 3$ (P_{01}, P_{02}, P_{03}). Each of the P_{01}, P_{02}, and P_{03} functions invoke the mapping actions of level 0. The new instruction P'_{00} will only invoke the mapping actions of level 0 once. In general, $(z - 1) M(0)$ is saved where $M(0)$ is the mapping overhead of level 0. New "target" instructions may be defined at any level, but would not typically be called target instructions above the firmware level. For the case in which all the combined instructions exist at the same level, as in our example, we obtain a general savings of

$$(z - 1)(\Sigma \text{Selector}(j - 1) + M(m - 1)), 1 \leq j \leq m - 1$$

Figure 5-10 depicts a more general case within the software levels, but the resultant savings formula does not change. Here P_{02}, P_{12}, and P_{11} are combined into T'. Since P_{02} does not exist on level 1, it must be repeated within the new instruction T' at level 1. This is true of all functions defined at levels lower than $i - 1$, where i is the original level at which combined instructions existed.

Figure 5-9. New target instruction (firmware).

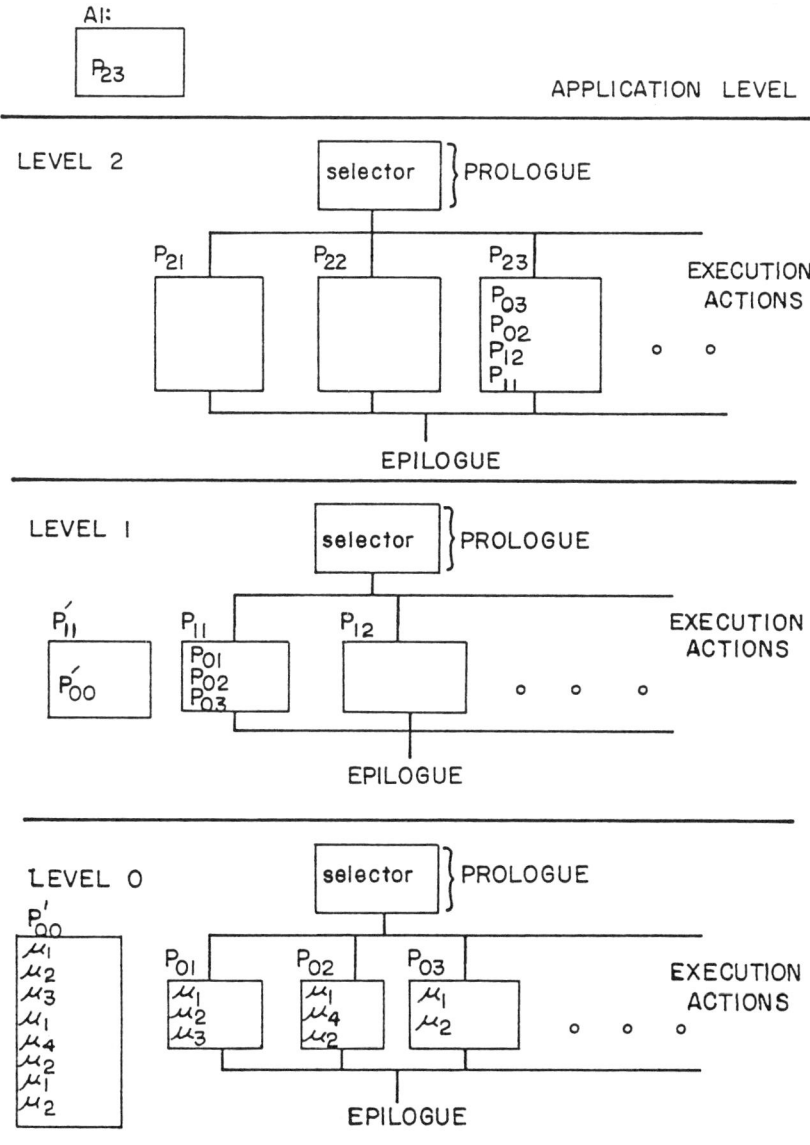

Figure 5-10. New target instruction (software).

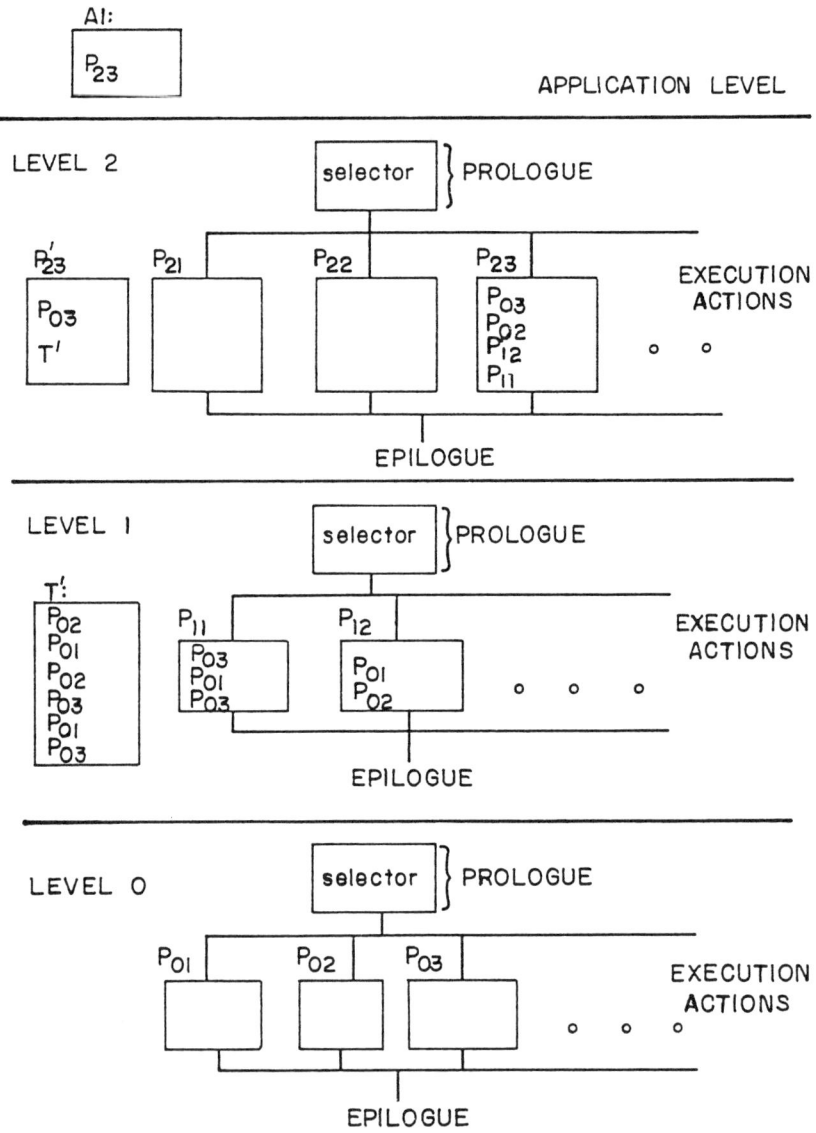

Hence, no change is needed in the previous formula expressing this type of savings.

As an example of replacement we will replace P_{23} in application program A1 by its equivalent instructions P_{03}, P_{22}, and P_{11} (fig. 5-11). We immediately recognize that it is no longer necessary to invoke P_{23}, which saves $M(2) +$ Selector(0) + Selector(1); i.e., in general

$$M(i) + \Sigma \text{Selector}(j), \quad 0 \leq j \leq i - 1$$

where i is the level at which the function exists (in this case P_{23} exists on level 2) and $M(i)$ is the mapping overhead of level i. This is the maximum savings that can accrue and assumes that the replacing instructions (P_{03}, P_{22}, P_{12}, and P_{11}) do not add any additional mapping actions. In our example (fig. 5-11) if P_{22}, executing within the execution action of P_{23}, requires $M(2)$ (dashed line), then after the replacement P_{22} will also require $M(2)$, but now it is merely being invoked from level 3. In this case no additional mapping actions are necessary and the maximum savings are accrued. Alternatively, assume that prior to replacement, P_{22} directly activates its execution actions (solid line) without going through the mapping action of level 2. After replacement, P_{22} must now use the mapping action of level 2 because it is on a lower level. This reduces our expected saving by $(M(2) + \text{Selector}(0) + \text{Selector}(1))$. Hence, this cancels the saving accrued by not having to execute P_{23} and there is no saving at all in this case. We can now state the following.

Theorem: If all instructions in the replaced function exist at a level less than level i, or all those on level i go through the mapping action of level i, then we accrue maximum savings given by

$$M(i) + \Sigma \text{Selector}(j), \quad 0 \leq j \leq i - 1$$

Corollary: If exactly one instruction on level i does not use the mapping action of level i, then a cancellation occurs and there is no savings.

Corollary: If more than one instruction on level i does not use the mapping action of level i, then each of these instructions may need to be invoked from level $i + 1$, in which case there is a negative effect and replacement causes a loss in execution time. The loss is precisely

$$(n - 1)(M(i) + \Sigma \text{Selector}(j)), \quad 0 \leq j \leq i - 1$$

where n is the number of instructions on level i that now need to invoke the mapping action of level i.

The saving S due to the classical form of vertical migration is given by

$$S = M(m) - M(m-1) + \text{Selector}(m-1) + w(M(m-1) + \Sigma \text{Selector}(j)),$$
$$i \leq j \leq m - 2$$

where w is the number of primitives that can avoid the mapping actions of level $m - 1$ due to the migration (refer back to the description of vertical migration

Figure 5-11. Replacement.

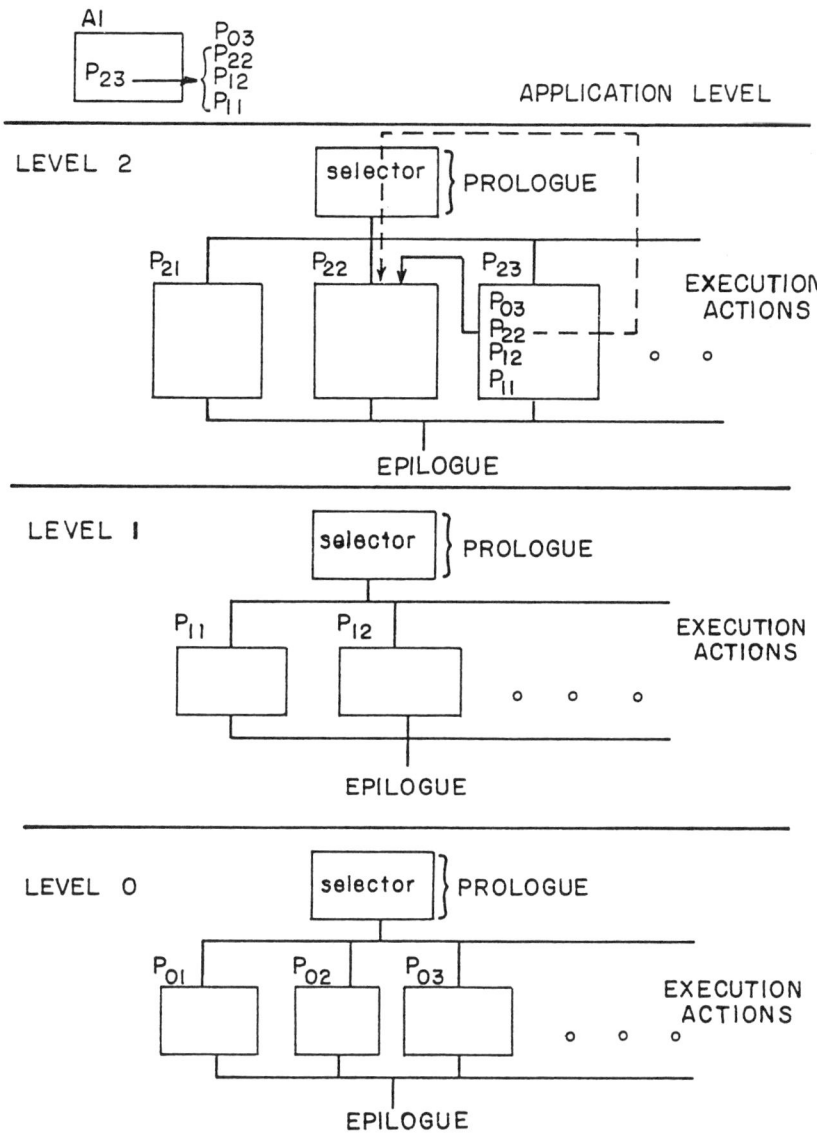

given in figs. 5-7 and 5-8). By examining all these formulas it is clear that this classical form gives greatest potential performance improvement.

We now consider data migration. Data migration refers to moving data in addition to control instructions to a lower level. In a very general sense this can be considered as migrating an abstract data type (data plus the operations on the data) or object. An extension of the VM model, called the VM-object model, has been proposed to deal with both complexity and performance issues (Stankovic 1981b). This model also treats both data and control migration.

Figure 5-12 graphically depicts a typical level in terms of the VM-object model. The model, like the VM model discussed above, is a general multilevel model and can be extended to any number of interpretive levels.

To model the implementation support of objects, the VM-object model requires an object to consist of (1) data, (2) a set of operations on the data, and (3) an object manager. An object manager is the execution time code thought of as overhead for supporting the environment of the object and its operations. At a minimum, the object manager serves as an invocation mechanism for the object and must

1. Locate the procedure implementing the operation
2. Acquire or construct an environment to make available to the procedure those objects required for its correct execution
3. Cause execution of the procedure to begin at the procedure entry point

Other tasks that may be performed by the object manager include:

- Synchronization
- Protection (including capability-based protection schemes)
- Type checking
- Creating and destroying objects
- Controlling which user gets which instance of the data
- Initializing data values on first access to the module
- Concurrency

The mapping action of a level (the same as the VM model) performs tasks common to the entire level and then initiates the object manager. The object manager performs some subset of the actions listed above and is considered the mapping action for the individual object. In some cases (typically at lower levels in the operating system) the object manager can be null. For example, this occurs when the support required for an object is accomplished at compile time.

Consider figure 5-12 as modeling the first software level, level 1. The mapping actions of level 1 may include a selector, register saves, setting up inputs for modules, and checking masks that enable or disable certain functions. The

Figure 5-12. VM-object model, level 1 software.

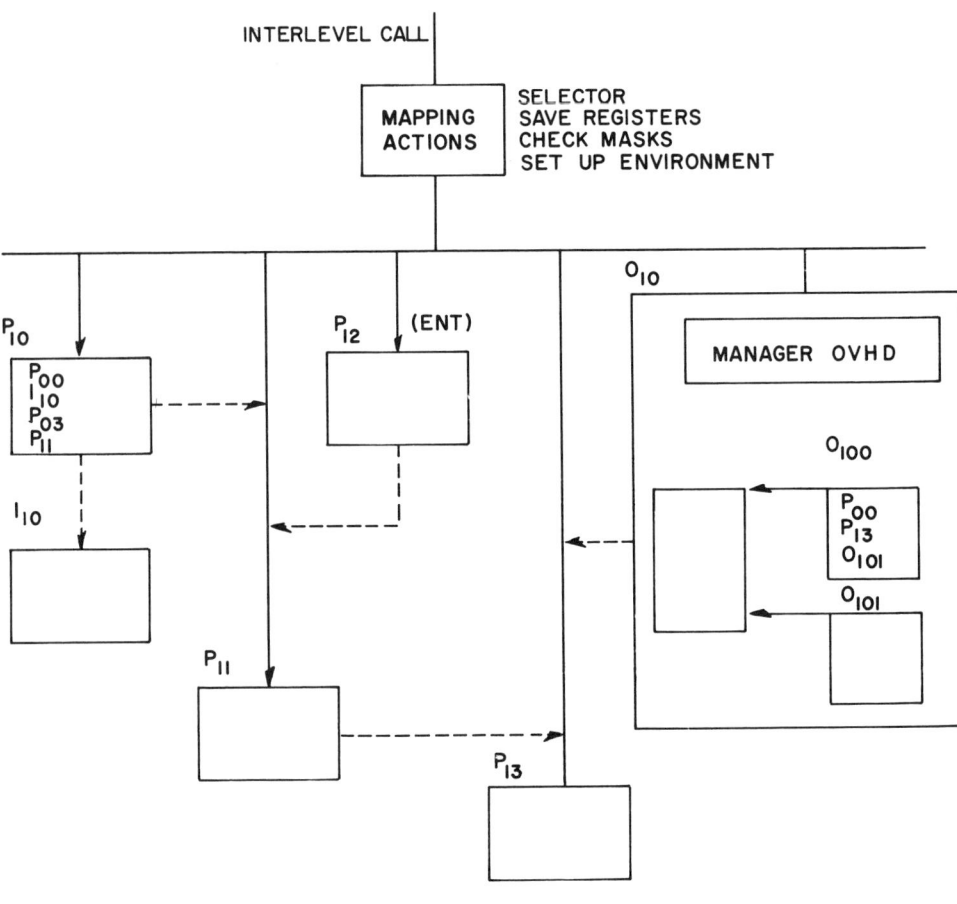

level is invoked by some unique invocation mechanism (e.g., an SVC). The execution actions P_{10}, P_{11}, P_{12}, and P_{13} can be invoked from higher levels, while P_{11} and P_{13} are also invoked by level 1 modules. This induces the level 1 intralevel hierarchy. Typically the intralevel hierarchy for software levels is much greater than for firmware. The execution actions labeled P_{ij} implement abstract action behavior (control).

The object O_{10} implements abstract data behavior; its operations, labeled O_{100} and O_{101}, can be invoked from higher levels. The object manager represents the overhead of using the data abstraction. This overhead is particular to the data abstraction and hence is drawn with the data abstraction in question rather than with the level overhead. The object manager is the mapping action of the object. Consequently, when doing vertical migration on objects both data and operations should migrate together.

Using the VM-object model, it is now clear that there are three ways to improve performance for objects. The first is the standard vertical-migration technique of implementing the function on a faster level. The second is also a standard vertical-migration technique of potentially removing "excess" generality when the migration occurs. This "excess" is removed from the execution actions. The third improvement is for objects, and it occurs both by replacing the overhead of the higher-level object manager by a cheaper lower-level object manager and also by migrating the data.

FUTURE DIRECTIONS

Work will continue on efforts to automate as much of the vertical-migration process as possible. There is a need for automatically determining the feasibility of migrating particular functions based on a cost-benefit ratio and subject to control-store-size constraints. An integral part of this automation is the need to predict the performance improvement of the migration, which is a function of the frequency of its use, its interactions with other migrations, and overheads of the various levels involved. Good estimates of frequency of use often cannot be predicted in advance, and therefore there is a need for a more dynamic and adaptive migration policy. That is, it is necessary to devise a system that can automatically determine the set of functions to migrate and automatically implement the migrations (assuming a writable control store), all as a function of time (dynamically). The above scenario is quite optimistic, and we are a long way from achieving it.

In the meantime, we can expect better and more sophisticated heuristics and tools to help support various parts of the migration process (Armbruster 1979; Luque and Ripoll 1981; Holtkamp and Kastner 1982). In general, current work is attempting to rely less and less on ad hoc techniques and to develop more systematic and complete methods. To do this, vertical-migration researchers are borrowing from the software-engineering field (Stankovic 1982a). Tools such as firmware monitors and microcode generators are already in use. In conjunction with developing useful methods there is a need for a firm theoretical basis for vertical migration. Very little theory has been developed in conjunction with vertical migration to date (Stankovic 1981a).

Analytical models to deal with performance prediction are also required. These models should include ingredients for instruction (control) and data migration, for modeling interactions of migrations, and for handling the dynamic nature of systems (Rauscher and Agrawala 1978; Liu and Mowle 1978;

Luque, Ripoll, and Ruz 1980). The analytical models should be part of a larger package of tools and also use computer graphics for "user-friendly" display of results. Some work is beginning in this area.

A general trend, which should continue into the foreseeable future, is the use of vertical migration for dedicated, special-purpose applications. Applications most suitable to vertical migration include database systems, layered communication protocols, operating systems (Brown 1977, et al.), computer-graphics systems, individual programming languages (e.g., the language accelerator for COBOL), and expert systems. For these dedicated applications the majority of the migrations can be done in a static fashion with dramatic performance improvements. In these dedicated systems there is less need for the more difficult dynamic migrations described above. The dynamic migrations are more suitable for general-purpose systems.

A major influence on vertical migration may come about due to reduced cost of control stores. If control stores reach the point of negligible cost, it may be feasible to put entire systems in microcode. In this case, compilers would have to generate microcode directly, and many complicated issues discussed above are thereby avoided.

Since vertical migration is primarily a performance-improvement technique, it is necessary to understand its influence on and interaction with other performance-improvement techniques. This list includes compiler-code optimization techniques, microcode optimization techniques, caches, increasing memory size, tuning-system parameters, distributed processing (outboard migration), and efforts such as RISC (reduced-instruction-set computer). Little research has been done to compare various performance-enhancement techniques.

In general, microprogramming (not vertical migration) has been used as a method to define architecture, sometimes dynamically. On the other hand, vertical migration is a performance-improvement method largely employing microprogramming. What is the influence of these two methods on each other? To date these methods have been treated separately, although they should be better integrated.

Some claims have been made that in designing innovative multicomputer systems with complex functionality both vertical and horizontal migration are inadequate, as are combinations—at least as they are used today (Giloi and Behr 1983). Significant improvements in these techniques that incorporate more ideas from software engineering (Stankovic 1981b) or entirely new techniques (Giloi and Behr 1983) might be necessary.

In conclusion, relocation of functionality in computer systems will continue to occur in various forms including outboard, horizontal, and vertical migration. This chapter has discussed one of these forms, vertical migration, in detail.

REFERENCES

Abd-Alla, A. M., and Karlgaard, D. C. 1974. "Heuristic Synthesis of Microprogrammed Computer Architecture." *IEEE Transactions on Computers* C-23:802-7.

Abd-Alla, A. M., and Moffett, L. H. 1976. "On-Line Architecture Tuning Using Microcapture." *Proceedings of the Third Annual Symposium on Computer Architecture, ACM Computer Architecture News* 4 (4):165-71.

Agrawala, A. K., and Rauscher, T. G. 1976. *Foundations of Microprogramming: Architecture, Software and Applications.* New York: Academic Press.

Albert, A., Bode, A., and Handler, W. 1981. "A Case Study in Vertical Migration: The Implementation of a Dedicated Associative Instruction Set." *Microprocessing and Microprogramming* 8 (3,4,5).

Anceau, F. 1972. "A Microprogrammed System for Task Management." *1971 NATO International Advanced Summer School Proceedings.* Paris: Hermann.

Armbruster, C. 1979. "A Tool to Sample the Software Instruction Address for Systems/370 Machines." IBM Technical Report TR 01.2225.

Ballieu, G., Lewi, J., and Willems, Y. D. 1981. "A Microprogramming Language at Register Transfer Level." *Microprocessing and Microprogramming* 8 (3,4,5).

Block, H., and Graetsch, W. 1981. "An Experiment in Data Migration." Technical Report 3, University of Dortmund.

Bode, A. 1980. "Vertical Processing: The Emulation of Associative and Parallel Behaviour on Conventional Hardware." Semi, Thompson, and Mezzalira (eds.), *Microprocessor Systems,* EUROMICRO 1980: 215-20. Amsterdam: North-Holland.

Brown, G.E. et al. 1977. "Operating System Enhancement through Firmware." *SIGMICRO Newsletter* 8 (3):119-33.

Chroust, G., and Meuhlbacher, J., eds. 1980. "Firmware Microprogramming and Restructurable Hardware." *Proceedings of the IFIP Conference.* Amsterdam: North-Holland.

Chroust, G., Kreuzer, A., and Stadler, K. 1981. "A Microprogrammed Page Fault Monitor." *Microprocessing and Microprogramming* 8 (3,4,5).

El-Ayat, K., and Howard, J. 1977. "Algorithms for a Self-Tuning Microprogrammed Computer." *Proceedings of the Tenth Annual Workshop on Microprogramming.* 85-91.

Fuller, S. H., Lesser, V. R., Bell, C. G., and Kaman, C. H. 1976. "Microprogramming and its Relationship to Emulation and Technology." *IEEE Transactions on Computers* C-25 (10):1000-1009.

Giloi, W., and Behr, P. 1983. "Hierarchical Function Distribution—A Design Principle for Advanced Multicomputer Architectures." *SIGARCH* 11 (3):318-25.

Gratsch, W., Holtkamp, B., and Kastner, H. 1982. "Literature Review on Vertical Migration." Technical Report 1, University of Dortmund.

Gratsch, W., and Kastner, H. 1981. "Firmware Monitoring—History and Perspective." *Microprocessing and Microprogramming* 8 (3,4,5).

Hartenstein, R. W. 1973. "Increasing Hardware Complexity— A Challenge to Computer Architecture Education." *Proceedings of the First Annual Symposium on Computer Architecture.* New York: IEEE.

Heller, A., and Van Dam, A. 1981. "Vertical and Outboard Migration—A Progress Report." *NCC Conference Proceedings:* 69–74. New York: IEEE.

Hojka, N. 1981. "Increasing Performance by Microcoding." *Microprocessing and Microprogramming* 8 (3,4,5).

Holtkamp, B., and Kastner, H. 1981. "Instruction Set Analysis of Commercial Computer Systems." Technical Report 3, University of Dortmund.

⸺. 1982. "A Firmware Monitor to Support Vertical Migration Decisions in the UNIX Operating System." *SIGMICRO Newsletter* 13(4):153–62.

Husson, S. S. 1970. *Microprogramming—Principles and Practices.* Englewood Cliffs, NJ: Prentice-Hall.

Intel. 1981. *Introduction to the iAPX43 2 Architecture* Document #171821-001. Portland, Oregon: Intel Corporation.

Liu, P. S., and Mowle, F. J. 1978. "Techniques of Program Execution with a Writable Control Memory." *IEEE Transactions on Computers* C-27:816–27.

Luque, E., Ripoll, A., and Ruz, J. J. 1980. "Dynamic Microprogramming in Computer Architecture Redefinition." *EUROMICRO Journal* 6:98–103.

Luque, E., and Ripoll, A. 1980a. "Tuning User Programs in a Microprogrammable Environment." G. Chroust and J. R. Muhlbacher (eds.), *Firmware, Microprogramming and Restructurable Hardware.* Amsterdam: North-Holland.

⸺. 1980b. "Tuning Architecture via Microprogramming." *Information Processing and Microprogramming* 8 (3,4,5).

⸺. 1981. "Microprogramming: A Tool for Vertical Migration." *Microprocessing and Microprogramming* 8 (3,4,5).

Maekawa, M., Sakamura, K., Tanaka, A., and Ishikawa, C. 1981. "Firmware Realization of an Operating System." *Microprocessing and Microprogramming* 8 (3,4,5).

Maier, H., and Burkhardt, W. H. 1978. "Implementation and Performance Comparison for a Microprogrammed Hierarchical Operating System Nucleus." W. K. Giloi and H. K Berg (eds.), *Fachgesprach Mikroprogrammierung.* Berlin: North-Holland.

Olbert, A. G. 1978. "Extended Control Program Support: VM/370." *SIGMICRO Newsletter* 9 (3):8–25.

Parnas, D. L. 1972. "On the Criteria to be Used in Decomposing Systems into Modules." *CACM* (5):1053–58.

Rauscher, T. G. 1975. "Dynamic Problem Oriented Redefinition of Computer Architecture via Microprogramming." Ph.D. diss. Department of Computer Science, University of Maryland.

Rauscher, T. G., and Agrawala, A. K. 1978. "Dynamic Problem Oriented Redefinition of Computer Architecture via Microprogramming." *IEEE Transactions on Computers* C-27:1006-4.

Rauscher, T. G., and Adams, P. 1980. "Microprogramming: A Tutorial and Survey of Recent Developments." *IEEE Transactions on Computers* C-29 (1):2–18.

Richter, A. 1980. "Vertikale Migration—Anwendungen, Methoden und Erfahrungen." *Hardware für Software*. Constance: Verlag Teubner.

Soltis, F. 1981. "Design of a Small Business Data Processing System." *IEEE Computer* 14 (9):77–94.

Stankovic, John A. 1981a. "The Types of Interactions of Vertical Migrations of Functions in a Multilevel Interpretive System." *IEEE Transactions on Computers* C-30 (7):505–13.

———. 1981b. "Improving System Structure and its Effect on Vertical Migration." *Microprocessing and Microprogramming* 8 (3,4,5).

———. 1982a. "Good System Structure Features: Their Complexity and Execution Time Cost." *IEEE Transactions on Software Engineering* SE-8 (4):306–18.

———. 1982b. *Structured Systems and Their Performance Improvement through Vertical Migration*. Ann Arbor, Michigan: UMI Research Press.

Stockenberg, J., and van Dam, A. 1978. "STRUCT Programming Analysis System." *IEEE Transactions on Software Engineering* SE-1 (4):384–89.

Stockenberg, J., and Van Dam, A. 1975. "Vertical Migration for Performance Enhancement in Layered Hardware/Firmware/Software Systems." *IEEE Computer* 11 (5):35–50.

Tallman, P. et al. 1974. "Virtual Machine Assist Feature Architecture Description." IBM Technical Report RT 00.2506.

Tinnen, C. 1983. "How IBM Stung Hitachi." *Fortune* (7 March).

Tsuchiya, M. 1981. "FREM: Firmware Requirements Engineering Methodology." *Microprocessing and Microprogramming* 8 (3,4,5).

Wilkes, M. 1951. "The Best Way to Design an Automatic Calculating Machine." Manchester University Computer Inaugural Conference. Manchester: University of Manchester.

Winner, R., and Carter, E. 1986. "Automated Vertical Migration to Dynamic Microcode: An Overview and Example." *IEEE Software* 3 (4):6–17.

six
DYNAMIC MICROPROGRAMMING

ROBERT I. WINNER

Dynamic microprogramming involves taking advantage of writable control store (WCS) by altering its contents from time to time. It can be thought of as a technique for both total system implementation and performance enhancement of software systems and applications. This being the case, the purpose of this chapter is to acquaint system architects, sophisticated users, and the toolmakers who support users and architects with the possibilities presented by this scheme. In particular, we hope to provide a model that can be used to describe different kinds of dynamism and to illustrate some implementations of subsystems that support dynamic microprogramming.

In the past, dynamic microprogramming has been little utilized, but new technology and low-overhead management techniques suggest a rethinking of the problem. As a system-implementation technique, its efficiency has been questionable, and the cost of WCS has been relatively high. Today, however, except in single-chip-processor implementations, the cost of a custom ROM may be greater than a WCS with a mechanism to bootload it. There is also considerable flexibility obtainable with WCS, even if it is loaded only at startup time and is static while the system is running. (We do not consider this dynamic microprogramming even though it is dynamic in a restricted sense.) For example, microcoded hardware diagnostics can be provided as if they were a separate instruction set. Extensive microcoded system-status verification, such as interprocessor handshaking, can be loaded into WCS at startup and then overwritten with the standard instruction-set emulator. As to the question of efficiency, the main source of inefficiency in dynamic microprogramming comes from swapping the WCS. We shall argue later in the chapter that, given current technology, multiprocessor and local-area-network environments may eliminate the sources of inefficiency that remain in the dynamic management of WCS.

As a means for users to enhance the performance of their systems and applications, dynamic microprogramming has never been popular. There are several reasons for this, but the two major considerations have to do with tool availability and system security. Our view is that the second is a result of the first. The tools for microprogramming, at least those made available to users by system vendors, have been on the whole unsupportive of user requirements. Since the systems have been designed so that microcode is executed with no protections whatsoever and since the tools make no effort to enforce even the most rudimentary security measures, system managers are loath to allow anyone access to the microcode. In fact, WCS microcode routines are at the same level of security as the operating system. Errors in either can cause disasters on a systemwide scale, although admittedly only microprograms can cause physical damage on some systems. We shall show that sufficiently secure and useful management techniques can be implemented.

Our intent, then, is to present a model of the problem for which we contend dynamic microprogramming is a suitable solution. We shall describe how several pieces of that model can be realized to produce a dynamic microprogramming system. We assume that the reader is familiar with the concept of vertical migration as described in Chapter 5 as well as with several ideas from the software arena, notably memory management and linkage editing.

We use several terms adopted from the realm of operating systems. An *object* is a piece of data or code worthy of having a name or of being pointed to by another object. Objects may contain other objects. For example, a procedure is an object; so are arrays and elements of arrays. A *macroobject* is an object within a conventional machine-language-level program. That is, it is an object within the purview of the macromachine. Similarly, a *microobject* is an object in a microprogram. Every process executing in the system has a piece of primary memory. The contents of that piece form the process *macroimage*. The macroimage is composed of macroobjects, some of which are macroroutines. There is also a *microimage* that must be present in the micromachine's control store for the process to execute. The microimage consists of microobjects, all of which typically are microroutines.

In a conventional, statically microprogrammed computer, all processes share the same microimage, the conventional machine-language emulator. A machine-language instruction implicitly refers to microobjects that are the routines that execute the parts of the instruction (e.g., an addressing mode or an arithmetic operation).

DYNAMIC MICROPROGRAMMING AND ITS RELATIONSHIP TO OTHER CONCEPTS

There are several concepts related in various ways to dynamic microprogramming. The problem of *assigning functionality* to layers in a computer system is related because dynamic microprogramming is a potential solution to the problem. *Vertical migration* is related because dynamic microprogramming is often used as the vehicle for migration into the fastest available layer in an existing system. *Language accelerators* are related because they are restricted examples of vertical migration into microcode. We shall show that restrictions typically placed on language accelerators are not necessary in a properly managed dynamic microprogramming system. *Multiprogramming* is related because it places a significant functional and performance load on the dynamic microprogramming system. That is, in a multiprogramming system the dynamic microprogramming system needs to be able to do certain things and needs to do them quickly. *Multiprocessing* and *local area networking* are related in that they provide the opportunity for eliminating the overhead of dynamic microprogramming in a multiprogrammed system. In the rest of this section, we shall discuss these relationships in greater detail.

The Function-Assignment Problem

The function-assignment problem is one for which dynamic microprogramming is a potential solution. It is the problem of where to place various functions in the several layers of the computer system. We can think of function assignment in terms of data types as well as control structures. For example, should the management of system queues be the province and responsibility of the operating system? In this case, should the software realize the queues in terms of the low-level data types provided by the language in which the system is written? Or should the language provide a data-type QUEUE, which is realized by compilation into the low-level data types of the machine language? Or should the machine language include a data-type QUEUE with associated operations realized by microcoded interpretation? Or should the micromachine have embedded in its hardware the data type? All these are possible.

For instance, consider systems written in Concurrent Pascal or Ada. Such systems use facilities that have queuing mechanisms built into the language (monitors and rendezvous, respectively). Systems written to run on the Digital Equipment Corporation VAX machines can make use of machine language instructions related to double-linked queues.

So there is a problem faced by a system architect concerning which functions to place where. Typically, this problem is solved by negotiation among hardware, firmware, and software designers and at some time the solution, that is, the design of an architecture and its implementation, is frozen. The person responsible for designing a later software product, perhaps a new operating system (e.g., a UNIX port) or a new compiler, is faced with a fait accompli.

One of the features of the recent reduced-instruction-set-computer vs. complex-instruction-set-computer (RISC vs. CISC) controversy is related to this conventional way of solving the function-placement problem (Radin 1982; Patterson and Sequin 1981; Patterson and Ditzel 1980; Clark and Strecker 1980). RISC proponents point out that freezing complicated instructions (e.g., queuing) and suboperations (e.g., autoincrement addressing modes) yields a design that is suboptimal for the later development of software such as compilers (Patterson and Piepho 1982; Wulf 1981). Their conclusion, supported by other arguments as well, is that complicated instructions should not be in the design at all. Another valid conclusion, however, is that the design of the conventional-level, macromachine architecture should not be frozen when it is. If dynamic microprogramming could be used to allow the macromachine architecture to be adapted to the software, the problems pointed out by the RISC proponents about poor matches between the needs of the software and the macromachine architecture would no longer exist. This argument has been presented in greater detail elsewhere (Winner 1983; Carter 1983; Hopkins 1983). It is not clear, however, whether there are real gains to be achieved from dynamic matching of architectures to software or how important these gains might be. Since we cannot yet address these questions, this chapter will deal mainly with practical matters related to how dynamic microprogramming can be made to work and how it fits into the more general problem of function placement.

Relationship to Vertical Migration

Chapter 5 of this book deals extensively with the notion of vertical migration. In this section we discuss the relationship between vertical migration and dynamic microprogramming.

First, vertical migration does not necessarily entail the use of microprogramming at all. Vertical migration means the movement of a function from one layer of the system's hierarchical organization to another. Let us, however, restrict the discussion to vertical migration downward to or upward from microcode.

We also assume that dynamic microprogramming implies vertical migration. That is, we assume that dynamic microprogramming is being used to create a better match between software and macromachine architecture rather than for the emulation of more than one conventional architecture. Even though it is conceivable that dynamic microprogramming might be used profitably to emulate more than one conventional machine on one host, we are not really concerned with this application. Since we are using dynamic microprogramming to implement functions that otherwise would have to be done in the software, the performance or security of which is to be improved, this implies that a decision has been made to migrate the functions into microcode. Note that this decision might be made by a human or by the system.

On the other hand, the existence of vertical-migration decisions does not require a *dynamic* microprogramming implementation. Examples include machines with extended architectures for the support of operating-systems functions. This assumes that a previous machine has existed with only the base architecture and with all operating-system functions handled in software. In this case, the time between the decision to migrate and the placement in control store of the programs implementing the migrated functions might be the entire design cycle for a new machine (Olbert 1982). Since the extended functionality is to be static in the new machine, dynamic microprogramming is not required.

In this chapter it will be assumed that a vertical-migration decision-making mechanism exists in the system or in the environment. The policies implemented by the vertical-migration mechanism are not of concern here, so the objects of migration, be they instruction sequences, functions and procedures, abstract data types, or some combination of these, are not of interest. We are, however, interested in certain characteristics of these objects, such as size and the ways they refer to each other and to other objects in the system. We are also interested in ways in which these objects might be collected and archived. Thus, we have severed the problem of how to make vertical-migration decisions from how to make the system environment hospitable to vertical migration. This hospitality is provided by the dynamic microprogramming subsystem.

Relationship with Language Accelerators

Systems have been constructed in which language accelerators are convenient to use if certain constraints hold. Sometimes only one accelerator can be used on a system. This is because dynamic microprogramming is not really being used. The accelerator is loaded into WCS at system startup, and WCS is static thereafter. In virtually all cases, the language compiler knows of the existence of the accelerator and compiles programs to use the accelerator or not. Even if this is not the case and programs may be linked to microroutines at linkage editing time, the routines in microcode (typically, the mathematical functions such as sin, cos, sqrt, and so on) are characterized by the fact that they refer to macroobjects, if at all, only through parameter passing and are bound absolutely to the other microroutines. A set of trigonometric functions, for example, receives values from the macroprograms only via parameter passing and refers to other microcoded functions much in the same way that absolute assembly-language programs refer to each other.

In a properly designed and implemented dynamic microprogramming system, none of these constraints is necessary. As we shall show later, there are ways to manage the WCS so that the right accelerator taken from a collection is present in WCS whenever a macroobject needs it. Also, microobjects can be made to see macroobjects and other microobjects in arbitrarily complicated linkage chains. This being the case, language accelerators are simply a particular form of microobject resulting from a particular kind of vertical-migration mechanism and policy.

Relationship with the Multiprogramming Environment

In this chapter, we assume that the environment in which the dynamic microprogramming subsystem is to be placed is one supporting multiprogramming. That is, several processes share primary memory and the central processor. Since processes share the central processor, they must share WCS in some way.

Several problems arise because of this. How may the WCS be protected from erroneous entry? When should WCS be loaded and with what? For example, should the entire microimage of a process be required, or is a partial load satisfactory? How might the system take advantage of the fact that several processes use the same image? How may the system facilitate the sharing of microimages by processes? Are there implications for the processor scheduler (hereafter, simply the scheduler)? For example, should the scheduling policy take into account the current contents of WCS? If it does, how much is gained and are there dangers to be avoided?

The first few of these questions are of a "how-to-do-it" type. These will be addressed in this chapter. The last few have mostly to do with performance evaluation, about which very little is known. Only a short part of the chapter deals with these issues.

Relationship with Multiprocessing and Local-Area-Network Environments

Multiprocessing may eliminate some overhead associated with time-sharing the WCS in a multiprogramming environment. Suppose that a multiprocessing or local-area-network environment is available in which any process may run on any of several processors. It seems reasonable that processes could be scheduled in such a way as to reduce WCS-sharing overhead by dispatching processes to those processors already containing the correct WCS image. As with the uniprocessor multiprogramming environment, the gains achievable depend on how bad the overhead is. It is probable that the overhead and the gains are dependent on the work load.

Suppose, for example, we define a *class of jobs* as those processes that share a certain microimage. Obviously, if there are two processors and only two images and these images are equally popular, there will be very little WCS-sharing overhead. If one image is significantly more popular than the other and WCS swapping is required to change images, then the scheduling problem is more complex and depends on the arrival characteristics of the two classes of jobs, the cost of a WCS fault, etc. Analytic and experimental work on this situation is just now being done.

Since we cannot yet report conclusive results, we must assume that for typical work loads scheduling can be used to alleviate some (if not all) of the WCS-sharing overhead. This is justifiable by the fact that future multiprocessor systems are clearly going to have many more processors than previously. Since a typical system may have ten or more (e.g., 10,000) processors, we might predict that the number of job classes could be overwhelmed by the number of available processors, each with WCS. This seems to be the understanding, for example, in unpublished studies by Perkin–Elmer Corporation on machines similar to those proposed in a reference cited earlier (Winner 1983). Conversely, lack of a multiprocessor or network environment may be the reason that dynamically microprogrammed machines such as the Burroughs B1800 have not been used very often in multiclass environments. (In the B1800 case, all programs written in a given language form a class, since the WCS images are language-specific.)

Summary

In this section, we have stated why dynamic microprogramming is of interest. Dynamic microprogramming is a possible solution to certain aspects of the function-assignment problem especially with respect to bridging the gap between the microarchitecture and the software actually running on a given system. We assume that a vertical-migration policy and mechanism exist to determine which actually are the objects to be placed in microcode, but we are not concerned in this chapter with the details of either the policy or mechanism. We simply assume that for a given process a set of objects should be in WCS at a given time. We will discuss options on the nature and interrelations of those objects and on the timing of WCS loading as they bear on the problems of managing dynamic microprogramming.

We have discussed briefly the nature of language accelerators and have found that they are simply a kind of WCS image with certain specific characteristics. Their main use in this chapter will be as a contrast with other kinds of microobjects with more difficult-to-manage characteristics.

Finally, we showed how dynamic microprogramming might fit into both multiprogramming and multiprocessing environments. Our claim is that multiprogramming forces certain issues to be faced in the management of WCS, and multiprocessing alleviates some of the costs of WCS sharing introduced by multiprogramming.

MODELING FUNCTION PLACEMENT

In the previous section, we saw that dynamic microprogramming is one solution to the problem of assigning functions in the various layers of the computer system. In this section, we describe a model of function assignment that can be used to identify the subparts of a dynamic microprogramming system. This will allow us to pinpoint where dynamism might be used as well as show the relationship between dynamic microprogramming and other solutions to the problem.

Before proceeding several terms must be reviewed. A *process* can be thought of as what happens when a program is executed. We take, however, the bureaucratic view that a process really is whatever the operating system identifies via its descriptor table as such an execution. In some systems these might be called jobs or tasks. A process has certain attributes, such as its primary (or virtual) memory image and its processor state image. We shall divide a process's memory image into two parts, its *macroimage* and its *microimage*, corresponding, respectively, to the part that resides in primary memory and the part that resides in WCS. (We assume throughout that WCS is separate from primary memory.)

A process's macroimage is made up of *macroobjects*, and its microimage is made up of *microobjects*. For example, the executable code portion of a procedure or subroutine can be a macroobject. A data item can also be a macroobject. Similarly, a routine or data item might be a microobject. Objects can be parts of other objects. For example, a data item might be part of the data segment of a procedure. In some situations, we are interested in only larger objects, while in others we are interested in any object, regardless of size, referred to by another object of a certain kind. For example, if a macroroutine refers by name to a routine that has been migrated into microcode, at some point we must consider the object consisting of the entry point of the microroutine.

All this brings up the issue of naming. All objects have *names*. These names may be ambiguous (more than one object may have a given name), and they may be synonymous (an object may have more than one name). Objects refer to other objects using names. The system must *resolve* these references by mapping names used in references to objects. This sometimes requires the use of other objects and other names requiring several levels of name resolution. When a reference becomes resolved either to another name or to an object, the reference is said to be *bound* to that name or object. In order for a command containing a reference to be executed, the reference must be completely resolved, that is, bound to an object.

A familiar software example concerns the action of conventional linkage editors. A reference to an external procedure (usually a call) generally translates into either a machine-language instruction or data item that must be filled in prior to execution. The linkage editor uses a table of entry points to find out which address should be filled in to the object with the "blank" reference. The entry-point table is itself an object, containing the names and addresses of other objects. Thus, the linkage editor resolves references to objects. The entry-point table is a kind of *context object*, an object containing name bindings. Returning to the example of a macroroutine referring to a microroutine, if the macroroutine wishes actually to call the microroutine during execution, the reference to the microroutine within the jump instruction must have been resolved to the real WCS entry point for the appropriate routine. Note that this resolution might occur early or late and therein lies much of the problem of successful management of dynamism in general and dynamic microprogramming specifically. An excellent treatment of the general issues of naming and binding can be found in "Naming and Binding of Objects" (Saltzer 1979). Having presented the required definitions, we may now detail the model of function assignment.

The Parts of the Model

The goal of this section is to provide a framework for discussion and comparison of solutions to the function-assignment problem. In order to assign functions and actually to place the mechanisms that implement the functions, several actions must be taken. Our model of function assignment will be a characterization of these actions. It should be realized that this model is slanted toward dynamic microprogramming as a solution. In some solutions some actions are combined, while in others the actions must be carefully delineated both for clarity and in order to achieve a good implementation. The order in which these actions are presented here is not the order appropriate for all possible methods of function assignment. Instead, one can think of the described actions as tasks that interact in various ways. We shall present the actions and then illustrate the model's applicability to several relevant classes of solutions to function assignment.

All the actions described in the following combine to achieve one goal: to be able to execute processes on a computer system. These actions are geared to creation, loading, and execution of memory images through a chain of interpretation that ends with the base hardware. In the present discussion, we are concerned with macroimages, microimages, and their interrelationships. Thus, the activities described typically exist both at the macroimage level and at the microimage level. At the two levels, the activities have similar functions but different implementations. In addition, every action has its policies and its mechanisms. The mechanisms implement the policies. For example, the idea that a program may execute only if all its references have been resolved to named objects included in the primary memory image is a policy implemented by the linkage editor, a mechanism. It is helpful to separate policy and mechanism in one's mind.

We assume that details of the underlying hardware are not of interest at this point. Of course, in reality the decisions of functionality of the hardware are at least as important as those of the microcode. In a sense, we are abstracting from the hardware in order to isolate the problem of software/microcode tradeoffs.

The actions are as follows. They are related as shown in figure 6-1.

Figure 6-1. Action within function assignment.

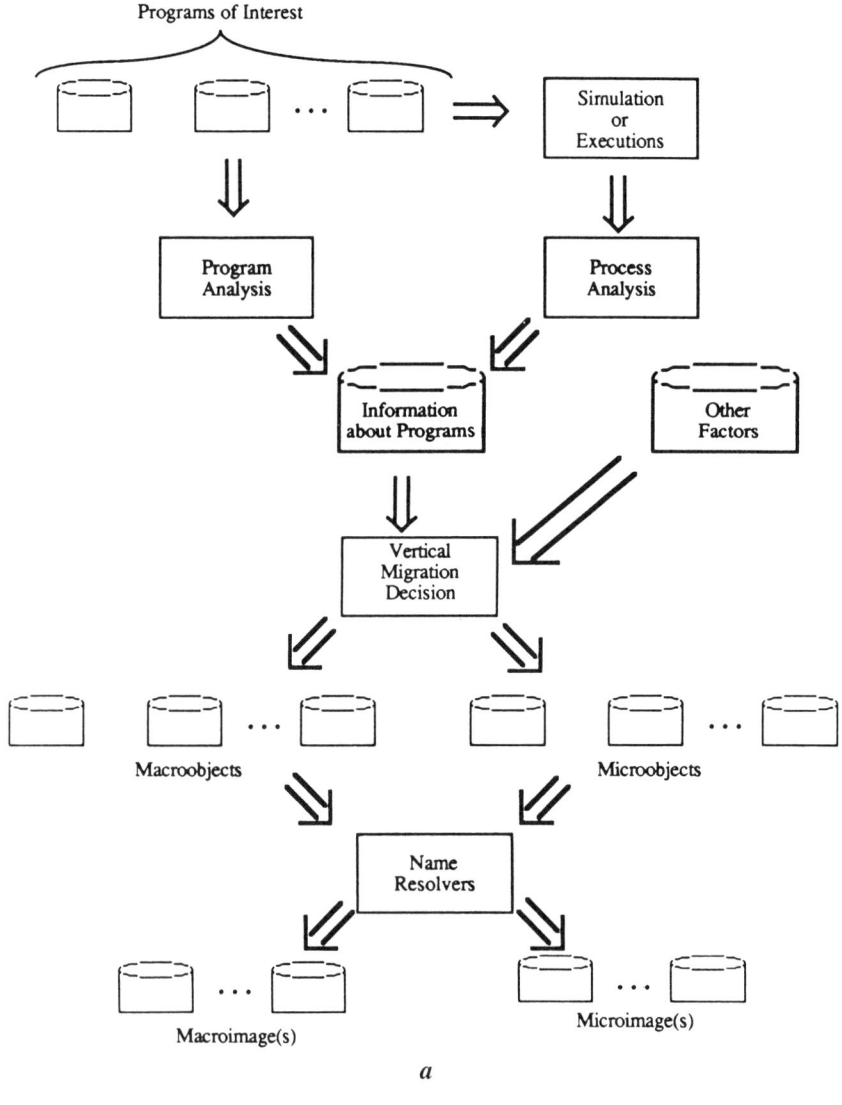

a

Figure 6-1. (continued).

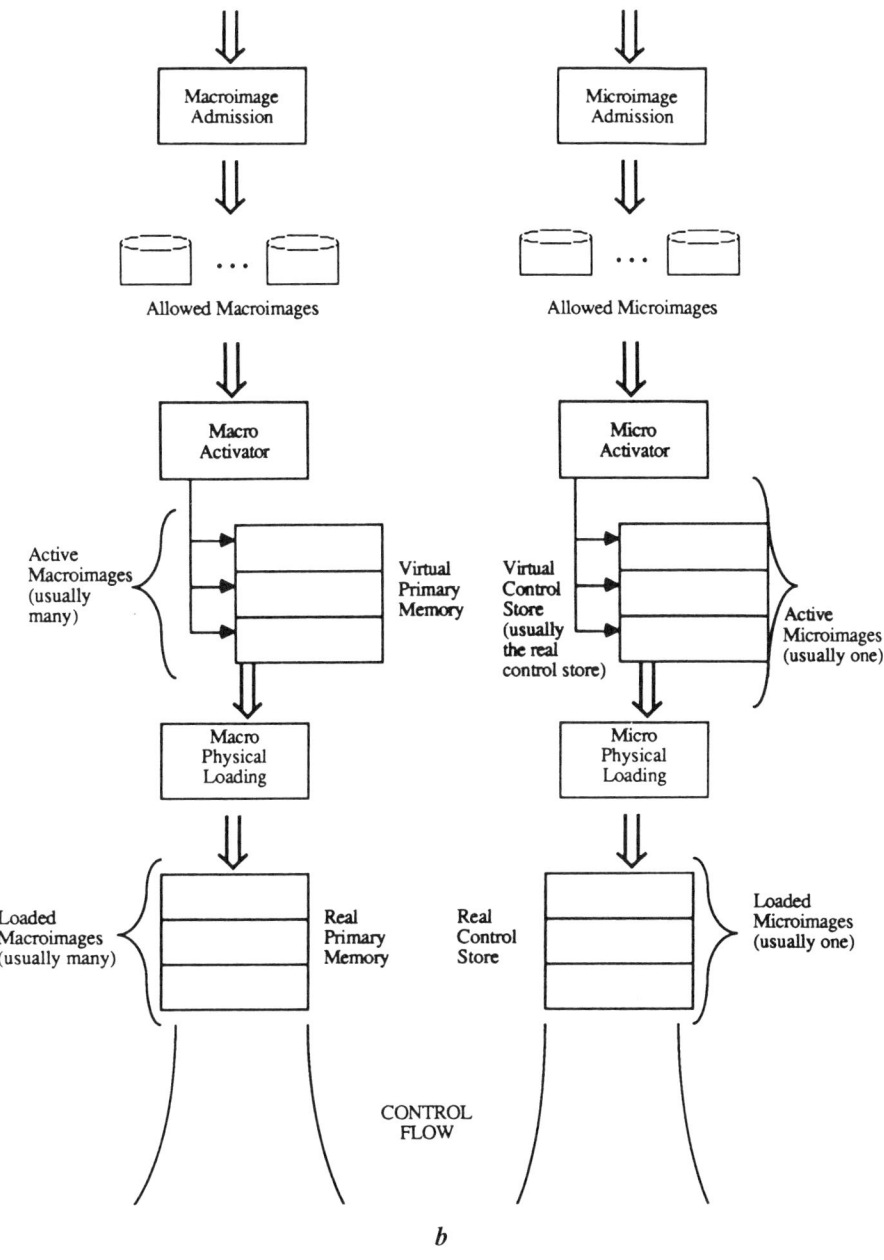

b

Figure 6-1. (continued).

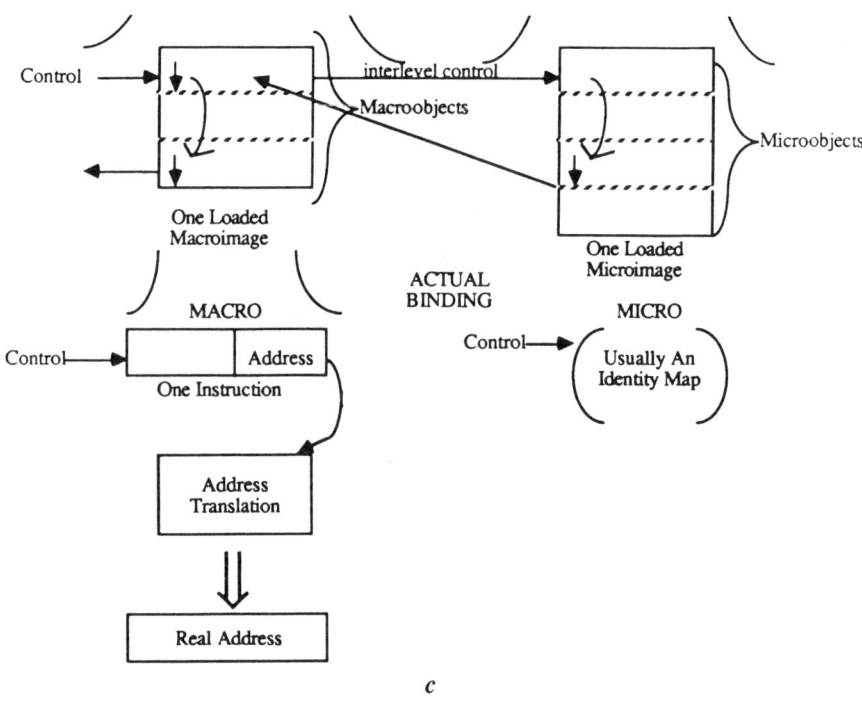

c

- Program and process analysis: This is the process used to gather data concerning the behavior of the programs and processes of interest. We ask the questions: What applications will run on this system? To what functions is their performance sensitive? Methods to accomplish this range from guesswork to very complex performance monitoring, mathematical analysis, and simulation.
- Vertical-migration decision: The data and results from the above analysis as well as other factors depending on the environment drive a decision as to which objects are to be put into control store and which are destined for primary memory.
- Interobject-name resolution: Objects refer to other objects by name. These names must be resolved. The result of this is an augmented set of objects that become bound into images.
- Image admission: The fact that an image is officially allowed to be used must be established. This is an example of a part in which the implementation for microimages is quite different from that for macroimages.

- Image activation: This is the logical loading of an image. If you will, this is the loading of an image into virtual (micro- or macro-) memory.
- Image loading: This is the physical loading of an image into memory. For microimages this means the physical load into control store.
- Transfer of control to an image (or to an object in an image): By this we mean the initiation of execution of an image or object. Control may be transferred many times to objects within an image even though the image might be loaded just once.
- Actual binding: References are finally bound to real locations.

Dynamism in a Solution

Various solutions may be more or less dynamic. In order to understand what that means, we must first understand that dynamism is always with respect to some *locus of control*. For example, dynamism may be with respect to the operating system or to an ordinary process. This gives a reference point for uses of the terms "dynamic" and "static." By and large, for example, if some part of the above model can occur during the execution of a process, then that part is dynamic relative to processes. Thus, in a virtual-memory system actual binding of references to macroobjects is dynamic relative to processes. If an action must happen prior to the execution of a process but can happen during the execution of the operating system, it is static with respect to processes but dynamic with respect to the operating system. For example, process activation might be of this class.

It is also helpful to differentiate between things that must happen during the initialization of a locus of control from those that can occur later during execution. Thus, we shall use the terms "static," "initial," and "dynamic" with respect to some locus of control. For example, say that WCS is altered when a new scope is entered in the execution of a program. This means that microimage activation or microimage loading is dynamic with respect to processes and initial with respect to the subprocesses identified with the parts of a program within a scope (Winner and Carter 1983).

Sometimes an action may be dynamic with respect to some locus of control but restricted to occur only once during that execution. We shall regard this as "initial" whether or not the activity actually occurs during initialization. For example, suppose an operating system allowed the use of only one microimage—say, a language accelerator—but deferred the actual loading of WCS until a process requiring that microimage was scheduled. In this case, since the operating system will load WCS only once, microimage loading is initial relative to the operating system rather than dynamic even though loading occurs sometime in the midst of execution of the operating system rather than during initialization.

Examples

Following are several examples of solutions to function placement as modeled within the scheme presented above. They proceed from the more familiar to the more speculative and tend to move from static to dynamic.

Static Instruction-Set Design of a Typical Architecture

Program and process analysis and vertical-migration decision: Compiler writers, operating-system designers, and architects have an understanding of what they like to see in instruction sets based on experience, the dictates of marketing factors, and so on. They discuss this and negotiate an instruction-set design, visible processor data structures, compiler functionality, and operating-system functionality. An attempt is made to show that compilers and operating system are implementable in the processor as described.

Name resolution: Operation codes, address-mode numbers, and register names and numbers are assigned. Macroaddressing routines and hardware are built. These are, in fact, naming and binding operations. This can be seen by inspection of the objects produced at this point. The microobjects are the interpreters of various parts of the instruction set. The macroobjects are systems and applications programs. The microobjects are bound to each other into a microimage by virtue of the fact that they have been written in absolute assembly language, hand-coded in micromachine code, or in some cases assembled or compiled and link-edited.

Macro-to-micro references consist of uses of opcodes, addressing-mode numbers, and the like. Since they are absolute, no active, separate binding mechanism need be used. Micro-to-macro references are of two kinds. There are references in microcode to fixed locations of macromemory—for example, to interrupt vectors. These are absolute and thus bound when the code is written. The second kind of micro-to-macro references are bound dynamically during execution. These are references provided by the macrocode such as direct primary memory references contained within an instruction. Typically, these are resolved by the combination of microcode and hardware devices.

Image admission: The establishment of a macroimage is usually provided by the linkage editor and operating system. In UNIX, for example, the linkage editor produces output with a code word indicating that the object is of the correct form to be run as a bound program. The operating system may be called upon to mark the resulting file "executable." Thus, a program is officially established as a macroimage. The microimage is officially established by human management decision. That is, someone says, "This is now the official instruction-set emulator."

Image activation: The microimage is the native instruction set emulator; it is logically loaded as soon as the appropriate person decides that this, in fact, is the correct interpreter and announces, "The microcode is frozen." (Since we ignore the debugging phase of development, this logically happens only once.)

Macroimages are activated at user command by the operating system. The OS activates itself.

Image loading: The microimage is set into ROM.

Transfer of control: The power-up mechanism causes execution of the microimage, which thereafter interprets various macroimages. (Hereafter, in order to avoid confusion, the interpreter of ordinary macroprograms by the native emulator, if there is one, will be viewed as if the macroprogram were in control. WCS is passed control by the macroprogram. This view, however, is inappropriate for certain examples such as multilanguage architectures like the Burroughs B1800.)

The reader may have noticed that the existence of language processors has largely been ignored in the previous example. That is because the language-translation mechanism and the associated naming and binding of names to lower-level names are logically transparent within this discussion. That is not to diminish their importance. Clearly, if dynamic microprogramming is to be used in support of a truly flexible vertical-migration system, language processing must be a central function.

WCS Used to Accelerate a Dedicated Application System

Analysis and migration decision: The application system is divided into parts according to decisions made by humans, supported, perhaps, by monitoring tools.

Name resolution: A single microobject with several absolute entry points is created. This occurs in the process of coding the part of the program intended for microcode. References to the absolute entry points are coded into the macroobjects, perhaps, in special gateway routines coded in assembly language.

Admission, activation, and loading: The start-up mechanism for the application (either the initialization procedure of the application or, possibly, the invocation of a system utility) causes the microimage file to be loaded. The fact that the microimage is physically loaded implies that it is logically loaded and assumes, without further checking, that it is a valid microimage.

Control: The image executes whenever called by the macroimage.

This example is initial with respect to the dedicated application system and is similar in the way it is supported by the operating system to the following example.

Using a Language Accelerator

This example assumes that the operating system allows only one language accelerator to be used. The system will ensure that the accelerator is loaded prior to the execution of user processes, but the system itself does not depend on the accelerator at all. The familiar case of a FORTRAN accelerator containing the microcoded versions of the intrinsic mathematical functions is the paradigm.

Analysis and migration decisions: The analysis leading to the decision to place certain language support in microcode usually depends on a designer's understanding of the contents of typical user programs. Benchmark analysis sometimes enters into the decision.

Name resolution: Name resolution is built into the language compiler. For example, if a program is to be compiled so that the object program uses the accelerator, the compiler typically must be told about it. The names of the intrinsic functions or other language support are known to the compiler in the form of absolute WCS entry points. References to these are compiled into the object program. Micro-to-micro references are resolved via absolute coding or, possibly, by a microlinkage editor. There are no micro-to-macro references.

Admission: The accelerator is admitted as an image specially known by the operating system via management decision and special coding in the OS.

Activation and loading: The image is logically and physically loaded during operating-system initialization. If the system is restarted after a failure, the accelerator gets reloaded as well.

Control: The image executes whenever called by the specially compiled macrocode.

Multilanguage Machine

The idea here is to have a different architecture for each programming language. The compilers each compile to a different machine language, and it is up to the operating system to see to it that the appropriate image is resident in WCS when an object program runs. The best-known example of this to date is the Burroughs B1700 and descendants (Organick and Hinds 1978). There is a possibility that other manufacturers will take advantage of multiprocessor capabilities to try this scheme again.

In terms of the model, all actions from analysis through image admission are all static with respect to the operating system. Activation is dynamic with respect to the operating system but static with respect to a user process. That is because the system must activate a microimage prior to starting a user program that expects that architecture. The image expected by the operating system might be handled separately.

Loading, transfer of control, and actual binding depend on the implementation. In the Burroughs B1720, for example, microcode may be executed from WCS or specially allocated main memory at the option of a master control program. In the B1800, WCS is handled like an instruction cache, and all microimages are in main memory. Thus, only the currently used portions of the control program are in WCS. This implies that actual binding in the B1800 is also dynamic, since actual bindings to physical WCS will vary depending on what is in the control cache at a given moment.

Note that binding of macro-to-micro references is built into the compilers for the various languages and is therefore static.

What Follows in Terms of the Model

The previous examples are all familiar but are not very dynamic. The remainder of the chapter, however, will show how certain parts of the model can be made to support greater dynamism at the operating-system and process levels. We are going to concentrate on name resolution, image admission, image activation, and image loading. As stated earlier, we assume that analysis and vertical-migration decisions provide the objects for migration to microcode. What remains is for the system to link those objects to form usable microimages, to manage admission by archiving those images in a secure way, and to manage the loading process for images so that WCS will contain the right image for a using process. Before investigating these aspects of system support for dynamic microprogramming, a short discussion of image sharing is necessary.

MICROIMAGE SHARING

Because of the potential overhead of loading WCS, especially if WCS is large, it is necessary for the system to support and encourage sharing of microimages. There are many aspects of this support permeating the linkage editing, archiving, and logical and physical WCS loading subsystems. In this section, we discuss different kinds of microimage sharing.

Microimage sharing can be taken as independent of whether more than one image can be coresident in WCS, because even if this is allowed, it is beneficial for the images to be shared. In practice, the vertical-migration process is greedy for WCS space and WCS is relatively scarce. Thus, it is unusual for WCS sharing to be implemented via packing of more than one image at a time into WCS. (We except the case in which WCS is partitioned into two parts, one reserved for an operating-system assist that is initial with respect to the operating system. In this case, the dynamic microprogramming is essentially restricted to the other partition.)

There are three levels of microimage sharing.

1. *No sharing*: Every process must have its own microimage even if the processes are running identical macro- and microcode. This might happen if the microimage is not reentrant because variable data (or references) from the macroimage are stored in the microimage. This might happen in environments in which microcode is being developed using an interactive debugging aid (Winner and Reed 1984; Roskos and Winner 1981). The debugging aid can unload the image, alter it, and reload it, resulting in a nonreentrant image. In a production environment, such test images do not exist and the failure to allow sharing, therefore, is unwarranted.

2. *Program-specific sharing*: Processes executing the same program, with the same static data in the macroimage, may share a microimage. Note that the executable macrocode of the program must be regarded as static data. Thus, if a microimage contains a direct reference to an entry point in the macroimage, the microimage probably is restricted to program-specific sharing. This happens, for example, if the microcode calls a macroroutine.
3. *General sharing*: Processes containing various macroimages can share a microimage. This requires that the microimage be able to resolve references to the macroimage at run time.

Two nontrivial approaches can result in generally sharable microimages. The first is typical of language accelerators: every macroimage reference is supplied by the macrocode as part of each calling sequence to the microcode. For example, the value to be imported by the microcoded sine routine is in the macroimage but passed (perhaps by reference) as a parameter during the call by the calling macroroutine. Native machine-language emulators are also of this type.

The second way to achieve general sharing is via the presence of a context object in the macroimage. This is simply a table of name bindings stored so that the microimage knows where to find it. Every microreference to data listed in the context object is indirect via the table. Since the table location is fixed (or reachable via a fixed-location pointer) in the macroimage, different macroimages may use the same microimage.

Let us contrast program-specific and general sharing by example. Consider figure 6-2. Suppose that two processes A and B, running two different macroimages A.M and B.M, share a microimage C. Suppose that C has a microroutine, msub, and that msub is called by A and B. Also suppose msub calls a macroroutine named error. Since A.M and B.M are different, the entry point of error will occur at different locations in the two images even if A.M and B.M are memory-mapped in primary memory. If C contains in msub a jump directly to x.a, then the jump (and C) cannot be used with B. This makes C program-specific in that only macroimages that are copies of A (as far as static data are concerned) can share C.

The problem is: how does msub effect the jump to x.a (error's entry point within A) and x.b (error's entry point within B) with a reentrant transfer of control? The use of a context object, as shown in figure 6-3, solves the problem by making the reference to error indirect or context-dependent. Note that the context object itself must be reachable by the microimage in a fixed way.

It is also important to see that the context objects are tied to the particular microimage. That is because "error" must be represented by the same slot (1) for all current and future macroimages that use the microimage C. These contexts

Figure 6-2. Different macroimages sharing a microimage.

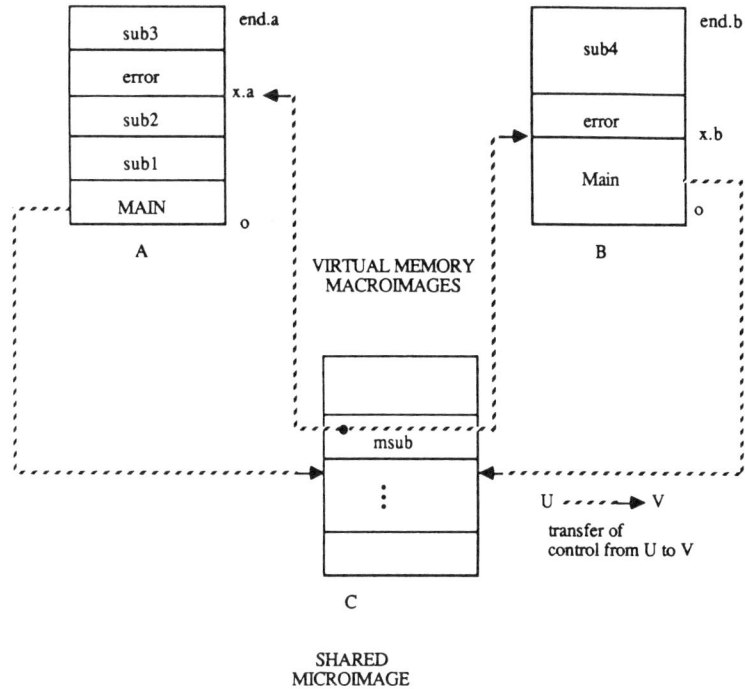

should be called, for instance, "the context of A for C." All and only those of the macroimage's names referred to by the microimage need be in this context.

The reader may have noticed that the different kinds of sharing have been described largely in terms of characteristics of the macro- and microimages. This means that the allowed level of sharing depends to a great extent on the way the language processors code the microimages. In practice, this means that the operating system including the linkage editor and loaders provides a level of support, and it is up to the language processors to take advantage of this. Details will be presented in the section on naming and binding.

Another totally different kind of sharing involves the sharing of unbound object code in the form of template microimages. For example, there may be a set of microobjects that can be linked together to form a microimage but with the restriction that the result is program-specific. The difference between the images as bound with different macroobjects may simply be in the resolved values of micro-to-macro references. This may be particularly common in systems that do not implement context objects as mentioned above. In this case, there still should be a method for creation of program-specific sharable images from

Figure 6-3. General sharing through a context object.

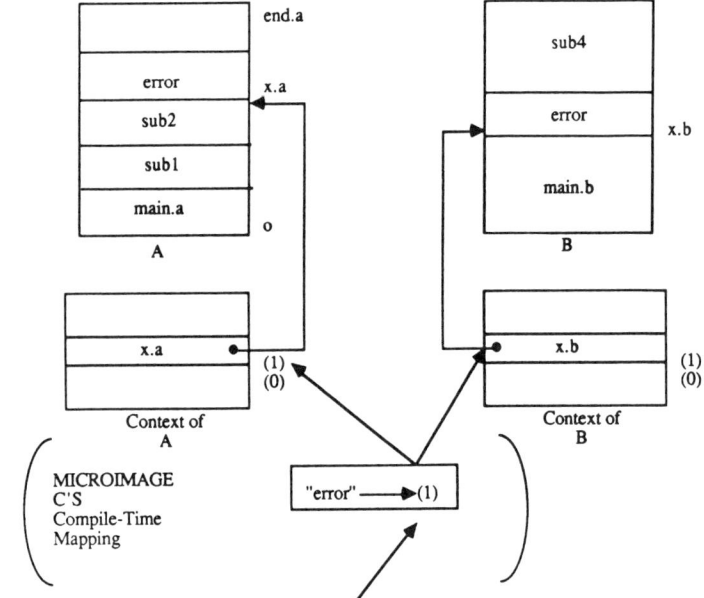

some sort of template image. In the implementation described later, such a template is called a *pseudoimage*. Thus, it is possible to archive a generally applicable package (for example, a matrix data type) as a set of micro- and macroobjects. Even though the microobjects might refer to the macroobjects and the location of the macroobjects cannot be known in advance, a program-specific microimage can be generated at link-edit time from the information given in the pseudoimage stored in an archive.

Thus, microimages may be sharable in a program-specific or general way or not at all. A pseudoimage may be used to generate custom or program-specific microimages from a generally applicable template. From a user and system point of view, however, it is preferable to have generally sharable microimages result from generally applicable microobjects (by using the context-object approach) than to have less sharable images generated using the pseudoimage approach. An advantage of the pseudoimage approach is that it makes it easier to combine two images into one larger image in order to increase sharing. This is because the pseudoimage is unbound, consisting of a set of commands to the micro- and macrolinkage editors.

So far, the discussion has been quite general. We have seen what dynamic microprogramming is for, namely to delay the assignment of functionality to microcode until the nature of the software is known in detail. We have discussed a model of the way functions actually get assigned in terms of the activities necessary to perform the assignment. Lastly, we have defined some ways in which microimages can be shared by macroimages.

In the next sections, we present a more detailed view of the activities of naming and binding, microimage activation, and physical loading. We shall pay special attention to dynamic approaches to these actions. Then we shall look at the question of archiving and admission of microimages. Prior to all that, however, we need a model of the architecture of WCS.

MODEL OF WCS

In the following discussion of parts of the dynamic microprogramming system, a certain model of WCS is assumed. WCS is simply a word-oriented memory with lower and upper boundaries for addresses. The software might define either or both boundary addresses by reserving part of WCS for its own use or for an operating-system assist.

In order to execute code in WCS, there are two available instructions:

1. ENTER CONTROL STORE (ECS), a user-mode instruction with one (possibly short, say, 6- to 10-bit) parameter and one physical entry-point number (2 to 4 bits)
2. SUPERVISOR JUMP INTO CONTROL STORE (SJCS), a supervisor-mode instruction that jumps into WCS at an arbitrary point.

The instruction we are concerned with is ECS. The parameter might be within a register or within the instruction. The physical entry point is probably in the instruction. It is very important that this instruction be user-mode so that entries into control store can be fast, avoiding the necessity of executing a trap. In order to control these entries, however, it is necessary that the number of possible entry points in WCS be limited to a few in low or high WCS.

In the Perkin–Elmer 3220 system there are 16 entry points (Reed 1983; Winner and Reed 1984). This may, in fact, be more than is desirable. If the dynamic microprogramming system is going to control the security of entering control store as described in the section on physical loading of microimages, there need be only two or three entry points. One is for ordinary entries, and one is for reentries after departing WCS so that an interrupt can be handled or for similar purposes such as returns from called macroroutines. The parameter within the ECS can indicate which logical entry point to jump to on ordinary entries. Logical entry points can be managed as a boundary-controlled jump table managed in firmware. In that way, the dynamic microprogramming system may set a maximum number of logical entry points but it only has to manage very few physical entry points for security reasons. This will be detailed later.

There are two other relevant instructions. One loads control store in a block move from primary memory, and the other copies from control store in a block move to primary memory. Both instructions need source and destination addresses and a count and are supervisor-mode. The read writable control store (RWCS) is rarely used but necessary for certain kinds of hard debugging aids. Both RWCS and load writable control store (LWCS) are used within the operating-system kernel in a device driver for WCS. This should look to the user like any other simple driver (Roskos and Winner 1981). It is very important that the hardware connection from primary memory to WCS have a high band width.

DYNAMISM IN MICROIMAGE ACTIVATION

The purpose of the activation subsystem is to associate a macroimage with the appropriate microimage at the correct moment. This means that microimages must be maintained both as files when not in use and as logically but not physically loaded microimages when associated with a live process. Since much of the work of activating a microimage has to do with establishing it as one of the logically loaded images, this section will deal with the management of such images.

Other goals of the microimage-activation subsystem are:

- Simplicity of the user interface
- Recognition of the use of a shared image
- Impossibility of deadlock
- Avoidance of infinite blocking of processes
- Security enforcement of rules concerning the ownership and integrity of microimages
- Avoidance of performance degradation due to interactions with the virtual memory system (e.g., primary/secondary memory swapping)

In addition, image activation must help the image-loading subsystem enforce rules concerning illegal entering of WCS when either no image or the wrong image is loaded. According to the model of WCS described in the previous

DYNAMIC MICROPROGRAMMING

section, this simply requires the separate management of WCS physical entry points.

The image-activation subsystem must take the following steps:

1. Accept information identifying the microimage to be associated with the macroimage
2. Discover if the microimage is sharable and, if so, if it is already in use
3. If necessary, move the microimage to the appropriate backing store for WCS
4. Ensure that the microimage is safe to use in whatever sense the system defines this
5. Ensure that the file from which the microimage came cannot be tampered with while the microimage is logically in use
6. Update the data structures used by the microimage-loading mechanism to reflect the new usage of the microimage

These steps are discussed in the following subsections.

Image Declaration and Naming

Steps one and two imply that a decision must be made as to what identifies an image. We think the most appropriate name for an image is its physical name as stored on secondary memory. In this way, if the operating system supports different file-naming contexts for different users sharing files, the microimage-activation mechanism can recognize the use of a share image even if the users refer to the image by different names.

For example, UNIX has a three-level file-naming mechanism. A user process has a table of open files known by file numbers. Entries in this table point to a file-table entry, which in turn points to a physical file-table entry called an *inode*. Two processes might share a file-table entry, or they might share an inode entry with different file-table entries. If two processes share a file-table entry, they originally knew the file by the same name, but if they share the file at the inode level, they might know the file by completely different names. The original file-naming mechanism uses directory files to map user-level file names to inodes. Taking all this into account, the microimage-activation subsystem should be able to identify microimages by inode number rather than any higher-level name. At the same time, however, the user process should be able to name the microimage by its directory name. Therefore, the activation subsystem must be able to resolve the name to an inode number. The situation is illustrated in figure 6-4.

In the interest of simplicity of interface, then, all that need be done is that the user process identify the file name of the appropriate microimage, and the activation subsystem should be able to do the rest of its tasks. The moments when activation might occur are:

Figure 6-4. Activating a Sharable Microimage.

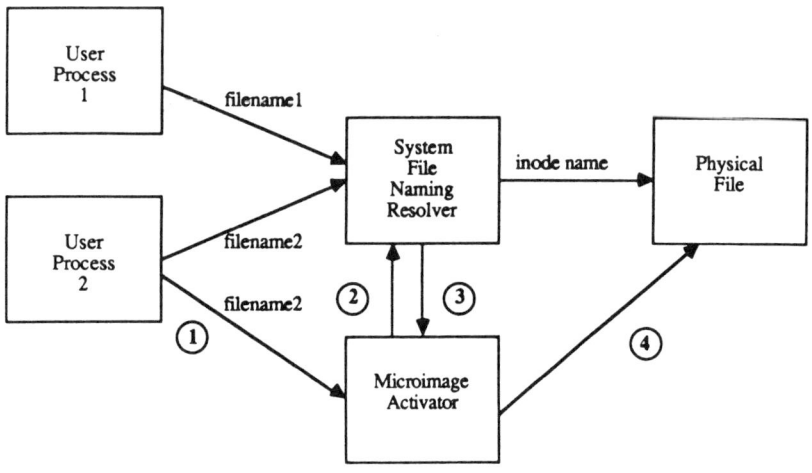

① User process 2 announces name of microimage file to activator.

② Activator queries system file name resolver: What is this file's physical name?

③ Resolver passes physical name to activator.

④ Activator recognizes microimage is already in use (by user process1) and sharable.

- When the process becomes associated with its macroimage
- When the macroimage asks the system to activate the microimage
- When an attempt is made to use the microimage

If image activation is to be more than initial, then at least the second option should be allowed. The advantage of the second option compared to being restricted to the first is that full dynamism with respect to the process can be implemented if desired. The added cost in the case that the macroimage actually uses only one microimage is the overhead of one system call necessary to announce to the system the name of the microimage. If the first option is used, the call that associates the process with the macroimage can also associate with the microimage. The advantage of the third option over the second is that if the process terminates prior to using the microimage, the work of activation is avoided. The cost of the third is that every attempted entry into WCS will have to check to see if the image has been activated. This means that the WCS entry will have to carry the name of the microimage or that the name will have to be announced at a prior time, splitting the task into logical activation and physical activation. Since it is important that jumps into WCS be as fast as possible, it is reasonable to complete the activation prior to the first attempted use. We conclude that the second option should be adopted.

Therefore, there must be a system call with one parameter. The parameter is the logical name of the microimage file, and the result of the call is the activation of that file in association with the calling process. This system call is WCSLOAD (Winner and Reed 1984; Reed 1983).

There is one other situation in which a microimage should be attached to a process. If a process already has an attached microimage and the process spawns a child process with the same macroimage, the child should inherit the parent's microimage as well. In UNIX, this occurs when the parent issues a FORK system call. On the other hand, if a UNIX process calls EXEC, it becomes associated with a new macroimage. In this case, it should lose the association with its previous microimage if there is one. According to the argument above, the EXEC should carry a microimage name only as an option and not as a requirement.

A Backing Store for WCS

Once the image name has been announced by the user process, the image must be activated and managed in a backing store for WCS. Obviously, the appropriate backing store for WCS is primary memory. An implementation of dynamic microprogramming in which images were swapped to secondary memory resulted in unacceptable performance overhead (Gulia 1977). This has been recognized, and later experiments took measures to avoid interactions with secondary-memory swapping (Reed 1983). How this should be done depends on how primary memory is managed. If demand paging is the policy, WCS images can be in pages locked into primary memory if that is allowed. If, however, all user space is subject to swapping to secondary memory, it might be necessary to reserve space in the operating system kernel for a microimage cache. This term is chosen to reflect its purpose in hiding WCS images from secondary memory swapping. It also happens that it can be managed somewhat like an instruction cache in the sense that it has a least-recently-used replacement policy. Thus, the microimages in the cache will neither be swapped to secondary memory nor will they cause primary memory fragmentation.

Such a kernel cache was implemented as an option that could be compiled into the kernel or not (Reed 1983; Winner and Reed 1984). In either case, active images that cannot be fit into the cache must be allowed in order to prevent infinite blocking. (If the operating system does not prevent infinite blocking, the WCS support system should not be the factor that causes the blocking. This is the case with UNIX.) The following situation must be prevented.

Suppose the cache holds three images, all of which are very popular. In other words, the images currently in cache are used by classes of processes with arrival rates high enough to guarantee that all three images are always activated. A process arrives that uses a fourth image but finds the cache full. Even though the scheduler would schedule this process in some fair manner in competition with the others, the process is blocked because of the inability to activate its WCS image.

We feel, therefore, that a cache-overflow mechanism must be implemented. The images held outside the cache are, of course, subject to secondary memory swapping. Therefore, if a propitious moment arises at which it is discovered that room can be found in the cache for a microimage held in user space, the microimage should be migrated into the cache.

Accepting all this, it is necessary to state management policies both for the microimage cache and for microimages held in user space. Again, if swapping is not a problem in a given installation, the cache need not be configured in the kernel.

User-Space Microimage Management

In this case, management of a microimage is very similar to the way in which UNIX managed shared macroimages on machines without paging. The basic idea is to keep a table of microimages associating two counts with each: the number of active using processes and the number of primary-memory-resident using processes. If the number of resident processes drops to zero and the number of active processes is above zero, the image should be swapped to secondary memory along with the last resident process.

In reality, if the image is reentrant, it should be swapped to secondary memory at most once. The secondary memory copy should then be maintained unchanged in case a second swap-out appears to be needed. Since the image is already on the swap device, it need not physically be swapped out but simply overwritten in primary memory. This is also a convenient time to check for space in the cache. Rather than swap an image to secondary memory, it may be possible to move it into the cache if there is one.

Microimage Cache Management

It is important to remember that this is a software cache, not a hardware cache. Therefore, different management techniques are in order. First, we assume that the cache is of fixed size, at least large enough to hold one maximal microimage. Since we are trying to pack variable-length objects, the microimages, into a fixed-length scarce object, the cache, we must be concerned with fragmentation issues.

The classic choice arises here. Should we keep the images contiguous and cause external fragmentation requiring memory compaction, or should we page the cache and incur internal fragmentation and increased table size? The cost of tables being negligible, we should like to avoid the performance cost of compaction. Therefore, paging is the method of choice. The page-size choice results from a tradeoff between the time it takes to perform a physical load of WCS and the expected cost of internal fragmentation. These are system dependencies that are not too hard to work out for any given system.

Thus, the cache consists of a collection of pages. The space in the cache at any moment is divided into three classes:

- In-use list: pages holding microimages currently associated with live processes
- Available list: pages holding microimages not currently in use
- Free list: pages not holding microimages

Pages are allocated to incoming images first from the free list and then from the available list. The latter is managed in order of most recent use. Thus, the pages of the least recently used image are freed first. An alternate method is to search the list for best fit in an attempt to keep as many pages on the available list (as opposed to the free list) as possible. Or one could use a best fit biased toward least recently used. The comparative efficacy of these methods is unknown.

It seems clear, however, that the available list should be maintained rather than just freeing the space held by an image that is being released by a process. The reason is that there is the possibility of another user process arriving prior to any demand for the space. The cost of maintaining the available list is practically zero. Thus, secondary-memory I/O and the rest of the activation cost are almost completely avoided, in some cases free of charge.

Of course, migration of an overflow image from user space into cache should occur if there is sufficient space in the combination of available and free lists. The size of the cache should be a configuration parameter, since it is so dependent on other factors in the configuration, the expected work load, and so on.

Other Matters Occurring during Activation

Naturally, various descriptors must be kept up-to-date when a microimage is activated. The physical-file descriptor should indicate that this is a microimage in use. The process descriptor of the using process should indicate its association with this microimage. There will also have to be a table of descriptors of the active microimages with counts of user processes, resident processes, a header into the sublist of pages allocated to the image, and so on.

The physical file in which the microimage is stored when inactive must be locked. This prevents tampering with the file version of a shared image while the image is in use. Suppose, for example, that process A activates image I. Process B then opens file I and writes on it. Process B then activates image

I, but since I is already active, B gets the old version already activated by A. Locking the physical file while the image is active prevents this. On the other hand, if process A terminates prior to process B's creation and if image I is moved to the available list within the microimage cache and unlocked, when process B opens file I, the version of I in the cache must be voided and the space placed on the free list. Thus, whenever a file is opened for output, it must be checked to see if it is a microimage, and if so, appropriate action must be taken by the dynamic microprogramming system.

This is an example of how system support for dynamic microprogramming permeates the system even in places where one might not expect it.

Another goal stated at the beginning of this section is that the integrity of microimages must be checked at activation time. One method of accomplishing this at little cost is to checksum the image. This, in combination with restricted ownership and write privileges on image files, is not foolproof but works reasonably well. Since microimages are maintained as files, or at best as kernel routines, the microimages are only as secure as the kernel routines that maintain them. It is, therefore, arguable that microimage files should be maintained on read-only or write-once secondary-memory devices.

DYNAMISM IN PHYSICAL LOADING OF MICROIMAGES

Given that a microimage has been activated, that is, that a microimage is associated with a given macroimage and is being maintained in primary memory in its role as a backing store for WCS, the problem now is when and how to load WCS with the microimage. This decision and its implementation should be completely invisible to the macroimage and therefore to the user process.

We have previously assumed that WCS is managed such that only one microimage may be present at one time. Although we shall continue with that assumption, an alternate approach (Guha 1977) will be described at the end of this section.

Given that only one image is to reside in WCS at a time, there are only three possible times when WCS can be physically loaded:

1. When a process is initiated and WCS is reserved for that microimage until all processes using that microimage terminate
2. When a scheduling quantum is reached for a process that has activated a microimage
3. When the first ECS is executed within a scheduling quantum for a process that has activated a microimage

There are problems with the first choice that make it applicable only to certain applications. Since WCS is reserved for a particular image as long as there is a live process that uses it, this becomes an overriding scheduling policy. This policy is applicable when there is only one set of processes using WCS—for example, for a time-critical application for which WCS is permanently reserved—or when a given processor within a multiprocessor is to be dedicated to some class of processes, for example, those that were compiled from a particular source language. In the first case, WCS might as well be loaded during system start-up and kept static. It is not known whether the first option is a wise scheduling policy in the second case or, if it is, under what constraints. If implemented, the danger of deadlock among cooperating processes using different images must be avoided.

In either the second or third options, there is a possibility of a process being chosen to execute by the scheduler at a time when the wrong microimage is in WCS. This is called a WCS *fault*.

The differences between the second and third options are slight. The third adds the possibility of the overhead of a WCS-fault interrupt to the first ECS in a quantum. The second can handle the possible WCS fault during context switching but admits the possibility of handling a WCS fault for a quantum in which no ECS is executed. There are several reasons why a process might not use an image every time it is scheduled. Among them are the following.

- The process may enter a report writing or checkpointing phase, causing it to become I/O-bound.
- The user may have activated a premature image or one that is not used much. This might be a result of bad programming or a generally applied or poor vertical-migration policy. The problem is that this user is not the only one punished. The next user of the displaced microimage might incur an unnecessary WCS fault as well.

We therefore conclude that the third option is the method of choice.

This option of trapping WCS faults at ECS time depends on the WCS model described earlier. The key is that the macroimage can transfer control to WCS only via one of the few WCS physical-entry points. That means that the entry points can be separately managed as follows.

The WCS entry points become part of the context of a process. However, during a process switch the current state of WCS is checked. During a process switch, there is an outgoing process and an incoming process. Each might or might not have an active microimage and each might or might not actually be using or getting ready to use its microimage. The following five cases can occur.

1. The desired image is fully loaded in WCS. In this case, nothing need be done.

2. The desired image (that of the incoming process) is fully loaded except for the entry points. In this case, the correct entry points should be loaded during the context switch.
3. Another image is fully loaded. In this case, only the entry points need to be altered. They are loaded with "trap" values, explained below.
4. Another image is loaded except for the entry points. In this case, the entry points must already have the "trap" values, so there is nothing to do.
5. The process has not activated a microimage. In this case, the "trap" values must be loaded into the entry points if they are not already there. This prevents erroneous entry into WCS.

The "trap" values cause a processor trap to occur. For example, the illegal instruction trap might be used. The kernel routine responsible for handling such traps can see if the ECS was a legal instruction, that is, if the process has an activated microimage and that image is not currently loaded. In case the ECS was illegal, it should be handled as any other illegal instruction. In case it was legal, the system must load WCS with the proper microimage.

Note that this can happen only with the first ECS in a scheduling Quantum. A subsequent ECS within the quantum will not cause interrupts because the entry points will be properly loaded. (Unused entry points should contain "trap" values so that a valid microcode user still cannot make an erroneous entry. It is up to the microlinkage editor to ensure this when it sets up the entry points within the microimage.)

An example should give the reader a feeling for the implications of this kind of management. Suppose there are two processes, A1 and A2, each using microimage A; one process, B1, using microimage B; and one process C1, using no microimage. Let us assume WCS contains A and its entry points during a quantum in which A1 is actually using WCS. Let the following be the schedule chosen by the scheduler with accents indicating quanta in which an ECS is executed.

$$\{A1', A2, A1', B1, A2', B1', A1, A2', C1\}$$

Then the actions taken by the WCS manager would be as shown in Table 6-1. There are two points of interest in this table that may not be obvious to the reader. At the beginning of quantum 4, it is not known whether an ECS will be done or not. An entry-point load is done anyway. This is because the presence of the correct image at the beginning of the quantum implies a sufficient probability of an ECS during that quantum to warrant the short load, avoiding the possibility of a WCS fault trap unnecessarily being

Table 6-1 Sample process schedule with WCS faults.

Quantum	Process	Image in WCS	Entry Points in WCS	WCS Load	Entry Point Load
0 end	A1	A	A		
1 start	A2	A	A		
end		A	A		
2 start	A1'	A	A		
end		A	A		
3 start	B1	A	trap		x
end		A	trap		
4 start	A2'	A	A		x
end		A	A		
5 start	B1'	A	trap		x
end		B	B	x	x
6 start	A1	B	trap		x
end		B	trap		
7 start	A2'	B	trap		
end		A	A	x	x
8 start	C1	A	trap		x
end		A	trap		

taken during the quantum. Also note that the scheduling of a process with no activated microimage is not strictly neutral with respect to performance since it can cause an entry-point load while switching contexts. This can be seen at quantum 8.

Performance of this Management Policy

Only preliminary work has been done to date on the overhead associated with WCS demand loading. There are three main factors to consider in analyzing the overhead.

1. Length of quantum
2. Probability of a fault in a given quantum
3. Cost of a load

The cost of a load is linear in the expected length of a microimage and is dominated by the block transfer rate from primary memory. The appropriate quantum length depends on many factors, but it is not yet known how sensitive overall system performance is to this choice in realistic cases. The probability of a fault in a given quantum and, generalizing, of the fault distribution over a sequence of quanta is dependent on both the work load and the scheduling policy.

We reported a worst-case measure of overhead in a system implemented on a superminicomputer with 2Kw × 32b WCS (Winner and Reed 1984). The quantum of 200ms was chosen for reasons having nothing to do with dynamic microprogramming. Assuming a fault every quantum, all processes to be completely compute-bound, and all microimages to be of maximum size, the performance degradation due to the demand-loading scheme is

$$\text{fault time/quantum length}$$

where fault time is the time required to service one WCS fault. In the example implementation, the maximum degradation was approximately 2.25%. Typical degradation was less than 1%. This compares favorably with the benefits achievable through vertical migration. However, since these figures are linear with (and almost proportional to) the image length, a larger WCS might result in unacceptable performance. In this case, a paged WCS might be called for. The implications of such paging have been discussed (Winner 1983), but very little actual experience has been reported in the open literature.

Another Approach: Simultaneous Activation, Loading, and Binding

Guha reports a system in which activation, loading, and interobject binding are all dynamic and occur at the same time (Guha 1977). The key point here is the load-time binding and relocation. This is similar to virtual-memory segmentation in the style of the MULTICS operating system. The advantage of this approach is that commonly used microobjects tend to stay in WCS. Macroobjects and other microobjects are bound to them as needed. Unfortunately, this system also admits infinite blocking because microobjects are never overwritten if in use by any process. It is also possible for such a system to deadlock because of the piece-by-piece allocation of WCS. These objections, however, can be overcome. It is also possible to envision hardware to support the segmentation and binding.

The question then is: does the saving in WCS swapping override the cost of complicated dynamic binding? Since this is clearly work-load-dependent, the analysis of this question would be quite complex and as far as we know has not been attempted. We do note, however, that few systems have followed the MULTICS lead at the primary-memory level.

NAMING AND BINDING

In typical software systems, naming and binding activities are the task of a linkage editor or a dynamic segmentation system or both.[1] Binding in a dynamic microprogramming system has some unusual aspects that must be considered in the design of the system. In such a system, binding is the process of linking microobjects to form a microimage, linking macroobjects to from a macroimage, and handling interlayer (macro-to-micro and micro-to-macro) linkages to form the bound program. A goal of the interobject name-resolution subsystem should be to support as general a form of image sharing as possible while incurring as little performance overhead as can be arranged. The following deals with effecting macro-to-micro, micro-to-macro, and micro-to-micro references with this goal in mind.

In this section of the chapter, we assume that sharing of macroimages is allowed by the operating system and that the reader is familiar with typical means of accomplishing this. Hence, we are concerned with the sharing of microimages and the various linkages involving microimages.

The first question that arises is when binding should occur. Possibilities are:

- Prior to microimage admission: binding results in the creation of a new microimage added to the collection of microimages
- After admission and prior to microimage activation: binding results in the selection of an existing microimage from the microimage archive
- During activation and prior to microimage loading: binding is done in response to the activation request using an image selected from the microimage archive by the running program
- At the time of image loading: binding is done in the style of a segmented virtual-memory system

The fourth approach is the one described at the end of the section on microimage loading. We believe that in order to make this work, significant hardware support would have to be provided for segmentation at the micromachine level. Even then, we doubt that acceptable performance levels could be achieved.

All other approaches assume that linkage editing is done at some time before the microimage is loaded. In the first approach the linkage editor would select

---

1. In this section, we ignore the possibility that WCS has memory-address-translation hardware. Thus, we assume that WCS is not paged and therefore references to microobjects must be to WCS addresses. The addition of paging or some other form of WCS address-translation mechanism does not alter the analysis here. It does add the extra activity of actual binding. Thus, in the presence of paging, the linkage editor binds references to addresses in a one-dimensional virtual-address space.

the microobjects to be used according to some vertical-migration policy, search the archive of existing images for a microimage that includes all the selected microobjects, and, if one were not found, create a new microimage. Wood considered this approach but rejected it because of the complexity of the knapsack problem it entails and because it unnecessarily confuses the two tasks of microimage creation and linkage editing (Wood 1983). Thus, it was decided to split the two tasks into different sets of tools, with the linkage editor always selecting from existing images if possible and, otherwise, producing an error message. This is a form of the second approach listed above.

The third approach is an interesting one but has never been tried as far as we know. It is similar to the second approach but delays binding until the macroprogram is already running but prior to the physical loading. Thus, it differs form the fourth approach in that in the latter the image is actually created while the loading proceeds. In the third approach, the microimage, as in the second, is selected from those previously created but is bound at run time to the macroimage. At first glance, it might appear that the advantage over the second approach is that two processes sharing the same macroimage could be using different microimages. This, however, can also be accomplished using the second method. The reason is that the technique rests on the ability to have dynamic microimage activation and really has nothing to do with the time at which binding occurs. The problem with the third approach is that it requires dynamic binding at the macroimage level as well because micro-to-macro references might require the presence of different macroobjects for different microobjects. We conclude, therefore, that the second approach is the best of the four. The description that follows is based on Wood's implementation, referenced above.

Resolving Macro-to-Micro References

We assume that two kinds of microobject references might occur in the macroimage—those that refer to code sequences that the compiler of the macroobjects knew about and those that refer to routines that the compiler assumed were macroobjects but that were later chosen for migration to microcode. In both cases, the references in the macroobject must be mapped to entry-point numbers in WCS. Whether these entry-point numbers are physically realized in the design of WCS and the ECS instruction or whether they are entries in a branch table maintained in WCS by system firmware is only of minor importance; we postpone further discussion of the difference. There is an important difference between compiler-known references and linkage-editor-discovered ones. In case the compiler knows the reference is to a microobject, the compiler can generate an ECS instruction in the unbound macroobject. In case it does not know the reference is to a microobject, the compiler might generate various forms of macrosubroutine jumps. The job of the linkage editor in the former case is easy and analogous to its typical job in resolving macro-to-macro references.

In case the nature of a reference is being changed by the linkage editor from macro-to-macro to macro-to-micro, the situation is not so simple. Two approaches are possible. In the first, an ECS instruction is substituted for the subroutine call in the text of the unbound macroobject. Unfortunately, in some implementations of ECS this assumes that the object of the reference is known at linking time. This is because the ECS must contain the entry-point number. In fact, the nature of the source language may be such that it cannot be determined which routine is being called at linking time because the choice of routines is made at run time.

For example, in the programming language C there are arrays of pointers to functions. Consider a call to a function pointed to by an element in this array. In figure 6-5, suppose f0 is in macrocode, f1 is in microcode, and other procedures are at various levels. Two conclusions emerge from this situation. One is that the compiler must compile the call in a way that is neutral with respect to the level of the routine called, and the linkage editor cannot alter that. The second conclusion is that there must be a way to represent the locations

Figure 6-5. The object code of CALL*(X(i)) cannot depend on the level of the routine called.

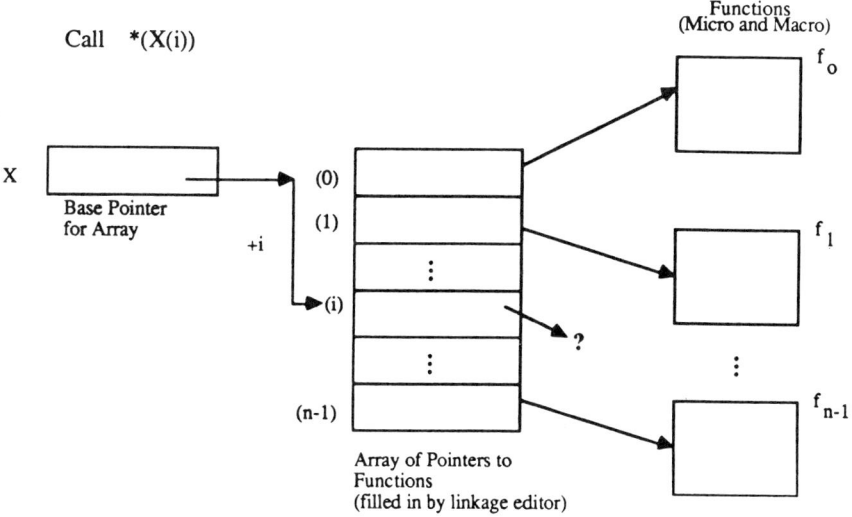

of the functions whether they are in macrocode or microcode. No architectures that we know of have the latter capability directly. In effect, a call is made to an object pointed to by an object pointed to by the base-array pointer.

The solution is to use a *gateway routine*, a macroobject with the name of the original macroroutine but containing the ECS to the microroutine. Almost all users of vertically migrated routines use this approach whether they need to or not. The Vanderbilt system, however, has elaborated the role of the gateway to a greater extent than usual and has made the creation of the gateway invisible to the user. In most systems, the user must write his own gateways; in the Vanderbilt system, the gateways are created and linked by the system.

The relationship between a microroutine and its gateway is illustrated in figure 6-6. The ECS instruction always uses a fixed physical entry point regardless of the routine called. The ECS parameter (i) indicates which routine is called and can be supplied by the linkage editor. Thus, as far as the compiler is concerned, the call is to a macroroutine regardless of the ultimate target. The physical entry point branches via a logical entry-point table to the actual microroutine. If there is a large number of physical entry points, the roles of the logical and physical entry points can be combined. Observations on the

Figure 6-6. Macro-to-micro call using a gateway.

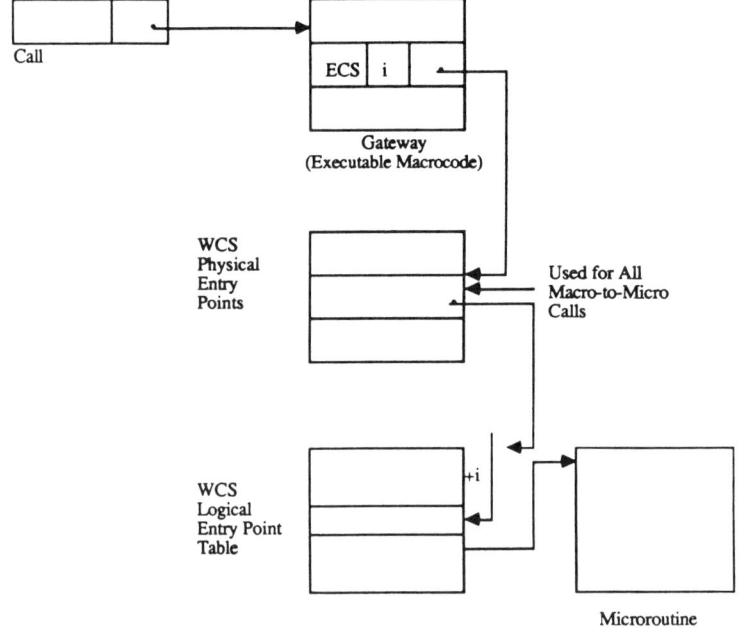

management of the entry points follows in the section on physical loading of microimages.

The exact nature of gateway routines has been described (Carter 1983; Carter and Winner 1983). A gateway has several functions:

- To provide an object for macroreferences to migrated routines
- To provide a mechanism for micro-to-macro calls
- To provide a control point for exits from microcode to allow the handling of interrupts
- To provide a control switch so that calls can be made either to the macro version or the micro version of a given routine

Of these, the first is what we have just been looking at. The second will be explained in the section on micro-to-macro references. According to Wood, the third should not be in the gateway; this will be explained in the section on interrupt handling (Wood 1983). The fourth function of the gateway is necessary if microimage activation or loading is to be dynamic (rather than either initial or static) with respect to the user process.

Suppose, for example, that we accept the suggestion that architectures be initial with respect to some scopes within a program (Winner and Carter 1983). A new microimage might be loaded upon entry to a scope using a particular package because that package is not used elsewhere in the program but is used intensively within this scope. This means that among the set of objects represented in the union of all microimages activated during a given process there are some that will be called while residents in WCS and also while not resident in WCS.

For example, a program might have the structure shown in figure 6-7. Suppose WCS is large enough to hold the sets {A,C} and {B} but not {A,B}. It might be reasonable to have {B} in WCS during the execution of the outer scope (including loop2) and {A,C} in WCS during the execution of the scope labeled L1. During the execution of this program, A is called sometimes when it is in the microimage and sometimes when it is not.

Thus, the gateway that actually performs the call must be sensitive to a switch telling it which version, the macro or micro, is currently in use (figs. 6-8 and 6-9). This is easy to implement efficiently if all microimages are linkage-edited with the macroimage in advance of being used. If the advantage of overlaying the control store in such a situation outweighs the overhead, there is no reason to reject this approach.

Given that the function of the gateway has been determined, there are some interesting implementation aspects to be considered. Suppose there are only a few types of gateway. For example, there might be one type that allows only calls to a microobject and one that is switchable. There should be only one gateway template for each type in the archive. Then it should be the responsibility of

Figure 6-7. Sample program block structure.

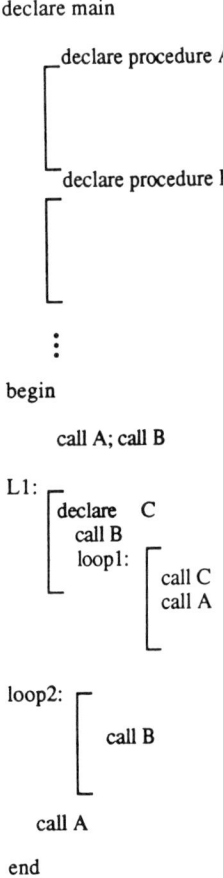

the linkage editor to instantiate a gateway for each microobject callable from the macroimage. This is accomplished via a naming convention.

Consider, for example, a switchable gateway template. It will contain two calls, one for the macro version and one for the micro version of the object for which it will be instantiated. The call that ultimately will be to the macroobject uses the generic name @macro and the call intended for the microobject uses the generic name @micro. The linkage editor will find the macroobject in the usual fashion, and it will find the microobject according to the rules set forth in the microarchiving system. Now it has the original call in the calling macroobject and two objects with the same name that might be called from time

Figure 6-8. Switchable gateways.

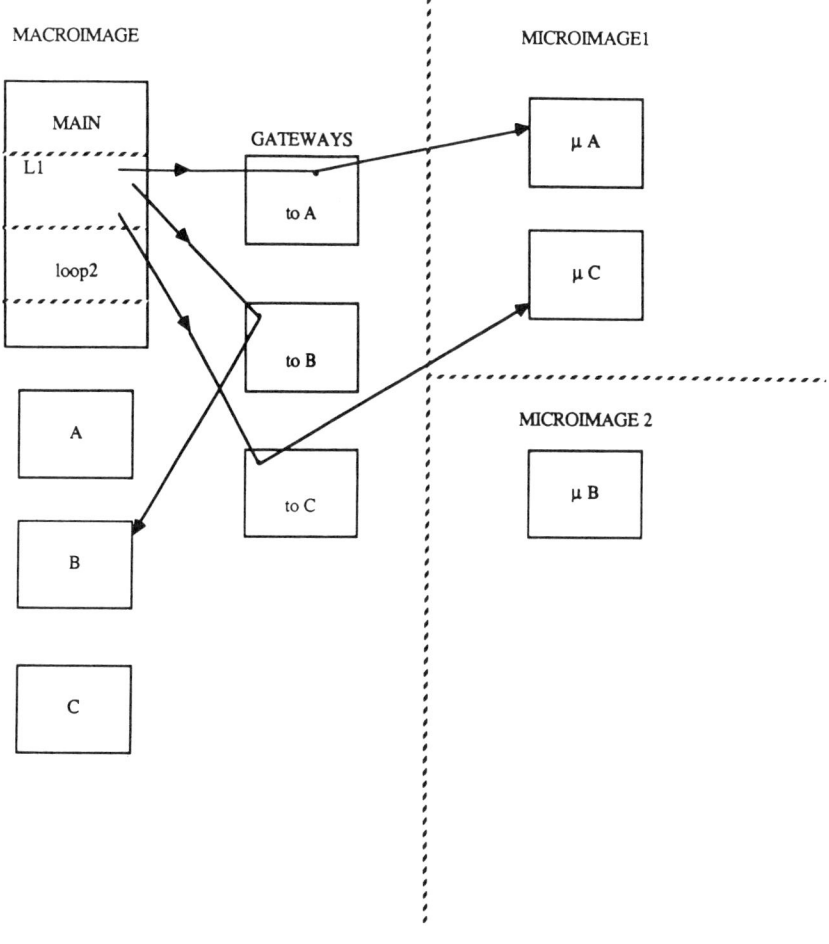

to time during the execution. The linkage editor simply interposes the gateway between the calling macroobject and its two potential targets. It renames the called macroobject and links the gateway macrocall symbol @macro to that new name. It links the gateway microcall to the appropriate WCS entry point. Then it renames the gateway to the original name of the called macroobject and links the calling macroobject to the gateway in the obvious fashion. Note that it does not matter how the original call is actually coded. Whatever the calling sequence, instead of calling the original macroobject directly, the call will be to the gateway, which will then decide which version to call. This makes the

Figure 6-9. Switchable gateways.

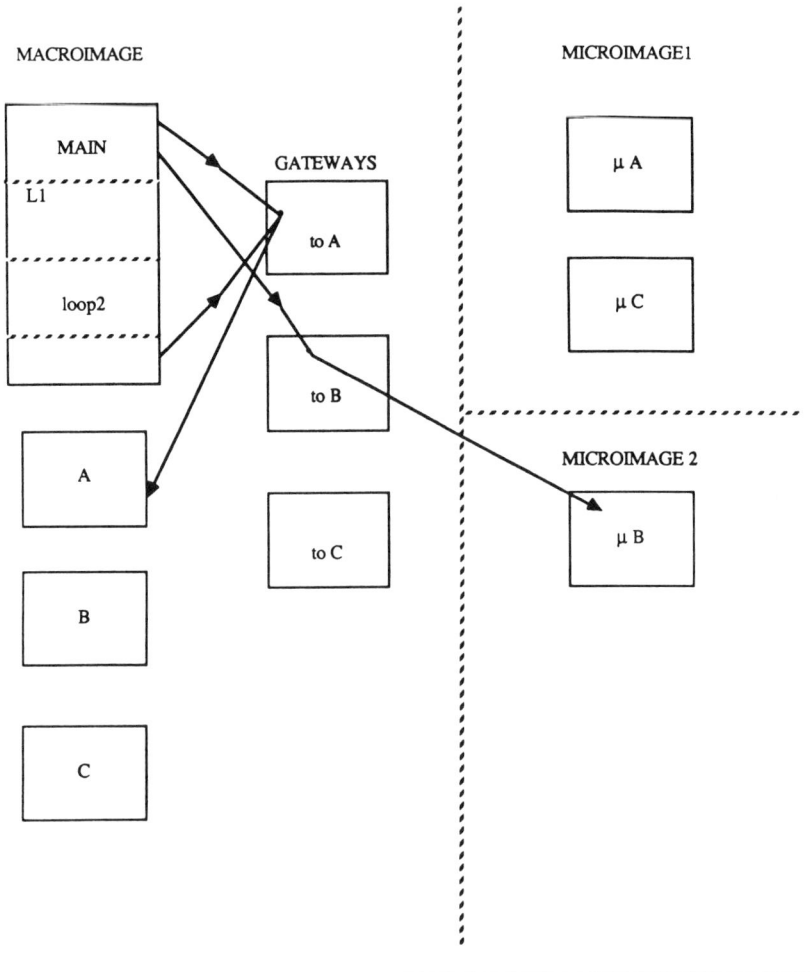

dynamic loading of the WCS invisible to the compiler. All the compiler has to do is generate a call to a special run-time routine upon entry to a new scope where there is to be a scope-specific microimage. This routine activates the microimage and resets the switch describing the WCS-resident routines for the gateways.

It might be thought that if the compiler knows that there will be a change of microimages, then it can generate the correct kind of calls within that scope. But consider the following example (fig. 6-10). Suppose there are two scopes;

Figure 6-10. Compiling the call from B to C.

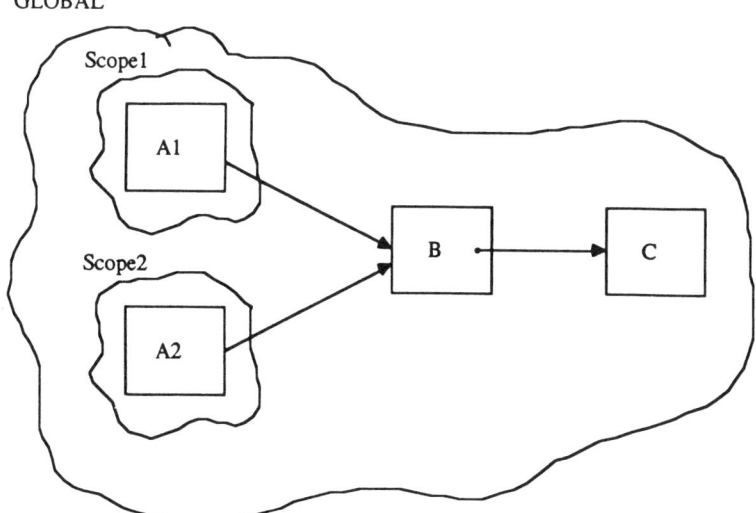

Visible in Scope1 = {A1, B, C}

Visible in Scope2 = {A2, B, C}

C ∈ Microimage (Scope1)

C ∉ Microimage (Scope2)

The call in B to C must be switchable.

---

the routine A1 is in the first and A2 is in the second. Routines B and C are global to both scopes. In the first scope, it is decided by the vertical-migration policy that C be in microcode. In the second scope, C is to remain in macrocode. Suppose both A1 and A2 call B and B calls C. Even though the compiler might know when compiling A1 that C is represented by a microobject and that C might be called indirectly from A1, it cannot know that when compiling B. Thus, it is appropriate for B, unbeknownst to the compiler, to end up calling a switchable gateway.

It is interesting to note that a system like this, actually implemented in prototype in the Vanderbilt project, provides *effective* bindings that are even more dynamic than those proposed above (Guha 1977). This occurs even though the real bindings performed by the linkage editor are all static from linkage-editing time onward. Thus, the advantages of dynamic loading can be realized without the cost of run-time linkage editing. The comparative disadvantage of the Vanderbilt scheme is that the entire microimage is overlaid, whereas Guha's scheme allows part of the image to remain with the new parts being dynamically linked to it.

In sum, we find that gateways are necessary in resolving macro-to-micro references. The gateways need not actually be separate routines (they could be compiled at the entry point of every macroroutine), but the above-described logical properties must be present. One might envision these properties themselves being migrated into the machine architecture. This is being considered in current work. Next, we consider the relatively easy resolution of micro-to-micro references.

Resolving Micro-to-Micro References

There are two kinds of microobjects that might be referred to by another microobject. These are microobjects that are known always to be microobjects at compile time and those that are the objects of vertical migration. The former are linked by a relocating microlinkage editor (Roskos and Winner 1981). There are no aspects of this peculiar to dynamic microprogramming, and so it will not be discussed further at this point.

If an object is a candidate for migration to microcode, we assume that it must be a routine that is called. If a call is generated by a compiler when the compiler does not know the level of the target, a gateway must be used. Whether that gateway is implemented in microcode or macrocode is a performance-evaluation question. In either case, the activity of the linkage editor is largely as described in the previous section. In the Vanderbilt system, the linkage editor could handle a macrocode gateway but would have to be extended to be able to create microcoded gateways from a template. The prototype compiler does not deal with this situation at all. That is, it knows whether a call within a microobject refers to another microobject or to a macroobject. To our knowledge, no system has yet been implemented to cover this situation.

Resolving Micro-to-Macro References

References to macroobjects from microobjects have been disallowed in most systems to date. One class of exceptions to this is described in this section on microimage sharing above. These are generally sharable microimages that assume that all references to macroobjects will be provided when the microobject is called from a macroobject. For example, a microcoded matrix-inversion routine assumes that certain registers will hold the address of the matrix and its size and that there is a stack pointer available for the allocation of workspace in primary memory. The only system we know of that allows microobjects actually to name macroobjects as data objects, routines to call, or what have you is the system we implemented at Vanderbilt, referred to in the previous sections. In that system, it becomes the responsibility of the linkage editor to resolve these references.

There are two ways that macroobjects can be named by a microobject. Both entail naming conventions. In the first method, the microcode can name the parts of a primary-memory address necessary for building the full address in microcode. Assume, for example, that a memory address is 24 bits but the maximum constant that can be put into a microinstruction is 8 bits. (This says little about the actual width of a WCS word but rather is a result of the microinstruction format.) A microprogram, therefore, must build primary-memory addresses byte by byte and must have a method of naming the individual bytes of the address. For example, the microC compiler users $C\_NAME.m$ to indicate the middle byte of the macroobject named NAME (Carter and Winner 1983). The microassembler passes this on as an external reference to be resolved by the linkage editor. The disadvantage of this approach is that the resulting microimage is program-specific; it can still be shared but only by processes executing the same macroimage or copies of the same macroimage.

In the second method, the microcode makes all references to macroobjects indirectly through a context object, a primary-memory-resident table of locations of macroobjects. In the actual implementation at Vanderbilt, this table always resides at location 0 of the microimage and has a maximum length of 256 bytes (64 object locations). Thus, the microcode name of a macroobject is resolved by the linkage editor into a single-byte index into the context object. This has the advantage that all microcode generated by the compiler for the purpose of accessing macroobjects is of constant length. In the alternate method of naming macroobjects in byte-to-byte fashion, the length of the microcode can depend on the length of the macroaddress if the compiler knows this. In fact, the compiler probably does not know the macroaddress, so it must generate for a worst case every time. Depending on the micromachine, the context-object approach can be more compact and faster than the direct-naming approach. In our compiler, using the context object takes three microinstructions, while the direct-naming approach takes seven. The cost is an extra primary-memory reference and a limitation on the number of macroobjects that can be named. This limitation can, of course, be avoided by allowing another step of indirection if the context object overflows.

The main advantage of the context-object approach has nothing to do with microcode size or speed, however. By using a context object, the microimage becomes generally sharable, whereas the direct-naming approach limits the microimage to program-specific sharing. Given the goal of facilitating sharing, which can then be taken advantage of by the scheduler and WCS loading subsystem, the context object is clearly the method of choice.

It is necessary for the linkage editor to build the context object. Thus, the context-object approach results in a somewhat more complicated linkage editor. This complication, however, is manageable in our experience. If, however, there are reasons why the context-object approach cannot be used, there should at least be a method of archiving a microimage template that can be used to ease the generation of program-specific but isomorphic microimages from assembled, unbound microobjects. The Vanderbilt system accomplishes this by allowing *pseudoimages* to be archived along with actual microimages. A pseudoimage consists of header information, a command list instructing the linkage editor as to what to include in the microimage to be created, a list of microentry points, and a list of external macrosymbols. This suffices to allow the linkage editor to create a program-specific sharable microimage. In a sense, the pseudoimage is a generic microimage with macroreferences as parameters.

Interrupt Handling and the Linkage Editor

It is necessary on some systems for microcoded routines to check for the existence of interrupts and to exit so that the operating system may handle any pending ones. Wood points out that there need be only one control point in the macroimage in order to cause a return to the correct place in microcode (Wood 1983). Essentially, what is done is that the microcode, on discovering the existence of a pending interrupt request, sets a reserved user-visible register with the WCS return point, alters the macroprogram counter to point to a fixed location at which can be found an ECS to a reserved microentry point, and exits. The interrupt is then taken by the macromachine and handled by the operating system in the usual fashion. When the process that allowed the interrupt to be taken is rescheduled, its processor-state image will be such that the processor will begin executing at the special ECS. This is accomplished as follows.

When the process is suspended by the interrupt mechanism, both the current macroprogram counter and the user registers are saved by the operating system. Upon rescheduling, these are restored. Thus, the program counter points to the special ECS, and the reserved-user register contains the WCS return point. The ECS enters WCS at a routine that moves the contents of the reserved register into the microprogram counter. This will cause a return to the correct spot in the microroutine.

All of this results from cooperation between the microcode compiler and the linkage editor. The linkage editor will see to it that the special ECS is in the macroimage at the appropriate spot. Part of the run-time package assumed by the compiler is the microcode necessary to effect the exit and return.

Summary of Naming and Binding

We have seen that the problem of naming and binding across the boundary between macromachine and micromachine has some unusual complications. Most of these can be viewed as problems of determining the proper context of reference and making sure that the contextual information is present at the right time.

For example, the switchable gateway can be thought of simply as an element in a context table that indicates which routines are where. Another example can be found in the operation of an ordinary linkage editor (micro-to-micro or macro-to-macro only). The external-reference tables and entry-point tables provide the context for name resolution. Yet another example is the context object used to resolve micro-to-macro references. This allows microimages to be shared by dissimilar macroimages even in the presence of micro-to-macro references.

An important point to remember here is that none of this complexity should be visible to the user. Otherwise, the vertical-migration dynamic microprogramming system will not be used!

ARCHIVING MICROOBJECTS AND MICROIMAGES

We have seen how microobjects are linked together into microimages, how the microimages are linked with macroimages to form bound programs, how the microimages are activated by the macroimages, and how the active microimages are loaded into WCS and executed. It remains to describe how the microobjects and microimages are archived. The goals of the microlibrarian, the subsystem responsible for archiving, are similar to any object-library-maintenance software. The microlibrarian must maintain a set of files containing the objects of interest and maintain directory information as to what objects are located in which files. The latter needs to be organized in such a way as to facilitate linkage editing, since linkage-editor performance depends largely on the speed at which these directories can be searched. This is a standard data-structures problem that need not be described here.

Unusual Aspects of Archiving Microobjects and Microimages

There are some unusual aspects to archiving in a dynamic microprogramming/vertical-migration environment. Two kinds of interrelated entities are of interest—microobjects and microimages. Moreover, information about microobjects and about microobjects within microimages must be kept so that the vertical-migration policy may be obeyed by the linkage editor and so that new images may be created according to this policy.

One method of passing information from the vertical-migration analysis mechanism to the linkage editor and image builder is as follows. Every unbound microobject has a *local profit* associated with it. This is a number that has been determined by the vertical-migration subsystem. It indicates the advantage of executing this routine once in microcode compared with the macrocode version. This local profit might or might not make assumptions about the migration of objects the microobject refers to, depending on the migration policy. An *aggregate local profit* might be computable for any microobject within a collection of microobjects forming a prospective microimage. Since the level (micro- or macro-) of each referenced object is known once a microimage is formed, this aggregate local profit can account for the profit, if any, of referenced objects. A macroimage contains references to many objects, some of which are candidates for migration. For each candidate, there is a global profit associated with the macroimage independent of the local profit. For example, this might simply be the expected number of times this object is to be called during a typical execution. Of course, the exact definition of the local and global profits are within the vertical-migration policy.

The librarian must maintain the local profits and aggregate local profits so that the linkage editor, presented with the global profits, can attempt to choose the most profitable feasible image. Since it chooses only among the existing microimages, it need not worry about the size of the microobjects. It might, however, consider such matters as the size of the microimage (since this bears on loading overhead) and the popularity of the image (since this bears on the expected occurrence of WCS faults). The image-creation software presumably must know the size of each microobject.

Thus, we see that the kinds of information needed in the archive in readily available form are:

1. For each microobject:
   - the set of microimages in which it can be found
   - its entry points and its external references
   - its local profit
   - its size

2. For each microimage:
   - the set of microobjects in it
   - its external macroreferences
   - aggregate local profits for each of its microobjects
   - its popularity
   - its size

The popularity information might be a collection of data from which may be derived use frequency and load frequency. Use frequency is the number of processes using the microimage per unit time, and the load frequency is the number of times the microimage file actually had to be loaded from secondary memory per unit time. Presumably, a very popular image has a high use frequency and a low load frequency. This information can be used not only to choose a microimage for a macroimage but also to tune the system. For example, if both the use and load frequencies are high for several images, the microimage cache is probably too small.

Security of the Archive

In addition to the above, there must be some form of protection placed on the manipulation of images and objects. The security of the microlibrary depends on the security of the file system of the operating system to some extent. In UNIX, we have found that extra precautions are advisable. For example, there can be a fictional administrative user, named MICRO on the system. This user owns all microobjects and microimages. Other users may only read these images. There is a set of language processors, each of which may set its effective user-ID to MICRO so that it may create microobjects. There is also a set of users who have permission to create test microobjects and test images, although this would not be necessary at most installations where there is no active research into vertical migration. Microobjects may not be created by any ordinary users unless they use the approved language processors. Nor may microobjects be altered without breaking the file-system security and the internal consistency checks made by the microimage activation subsystem.

The latter can be as simple or complex as desired. In our system, we checksum the body of every microobject and microimage before using it. In order for a microobject to be linked into a usable microimage, its checksum must check out. In order for a microimage to be archived or activated, its checksum must check out. This decreases both the possibility of tampering with authorized images and the possibility of a system crash due to dropping a bit in reading a microimage from secondary memory.

It is clear that a determined user could break these security measures and place a dangerous microimage in the archive. This entails, however, more work than necessary to break the security of the operating system without the dynamic microprogramming subsystem in place. Thus, a saboteur only makes more work by trying to break this additional level of security.

It is not hard to see that the security of this system is only as good as the quality of the language processors that produce microobjects. For example, after hanging our system several times using microcode produced by our prototype compiler, it became clear that infinite loops in microcode would lock out all interrupt processing. Thus, every backward jump and register jump is compiled with a check for interrupts and exits if necessary as described in the section on linkage editing. In this way, time limits on programs, swapping of WCS, and so on can be enforced. Without this feature, virtual time in the processor stops because even clock interrupts are masked![2]

Conclusions about Archiving

The microlibrarian maintains the interface between the vertical-migration subsystem and both the tools that combine microobjects into microimages and the linkage editor that combines micro- and macroimages into bound programs. It must also provide a link in the security chain that tries to keep the system secure from dangerous microobjects.

The reader may have noticed that very little has been said about the nature of the tools that combine microobjects into microimages. There are two reasons for this. First, very little has actually been accomplished in the automatic selection of objects to pack into images. Second, because little has been accomplished, it is not clear whether such tools can be built in a migration-policy-independent fashion. Tools have been built that do the actual construction of images given some user direction about the objects to be included (Wood 1983). We know of no system, however, that performs the system-monitoring tasks necessary to automate fully the selection of microobjects for images.

Wood suggests that microimages can be viewed as "dynamic sharable libraries." Thus, it should be that two unrelated images that have the following characteristic should be combined automatically by the system into one image. Essentially, the requirement is that the highly profitable fraction of both images should be able to fit into WCS together.

This has implications for the tools that create images and for the linkage editor. To see the connection with linkage editing, consider the following. Suppose image A and image B meet the requirement above and are both quite popular. The routines of image A, however, require the presence of certain routines in the macroobject that are not required by the routines in image B. The linkage editor should be able to arrange matters such that macroimages using image B need not contain the macroroutines required by image A and that the macroimages for A and B cannot erroneously call the routines in the wrong image. This can be accomplished by manipulating the logical-entry-point table in WCS, but it is not clear whether the cost is sufficiently low to counteract the cost of the WCS swapping that the marriage of the two images is trying to prevent.

---

2. A side benefit of this approach was that it was very easy to code micro- and macroimages that measured the interrupt density within the system very accurately.

PLACING THE FUNCTIONS OF THE DYNAMIC MICROPROGRAMMING SYSTEM

Several sections of this chapter mention WCS memory-management hardware, WCS paging, run-time binding of memory references, and load-time linkage editing of WCS. It is worth considering the nature of these suggestions in the light of the general model of the function-assignment problem and its solutions.

If it is decided that dynamic microprogramming should be implemented in a system, then it has been decided that dynamic microprogramming is, at least, a partial solution to the function assignment problem, and the dynamic microprogramming system itself presents a function-assignment problem. In other words, now that we see what the parts of the dynamic microprogramming system are, we must decide at what level in the software/firmware/hardware hierarchy to place these parts. This is the real nature of the decision, for example, of doing linkage editing in software prior to activation time rather than using a dynamic WCS segmentation system. That, also, is the nature of the decision whether to page WCS rather than swap it.

Very little experience exists in actual dynamic microprogramming and virtually no predictive analysis has been done to aid in making these decisions. The era of multiprocessors is only just now beginning, and, as argued in the introductory section of the chapter, this may have overriding importance in such decisions. For example, the decision to page WCS, making it into a true virtual-memory system, may have less to do with preventing WCS faults for microimages that would fit into WCS than with providing the ability to have microimages that are too large for WCS. The reason is that the multiprocessor environment may eliminate WCS faults on microimages that fit at the same time that large images are seen to be desirable.

The details of this decision are dependent on knowledge of the *functional locality* exhibited by typical work loads (Winner 1983). This can be thought of as a kind of WCS working-set problem. As Flynn points out, careful systems analysis will have to be brought to bear on this problem (Flynn 1979). In the meantime, experimental and commercial systems are being developed with virtualized control stores, the design of which are driven purely by the existence of large microimages and the tradeoffs presented by the cost of WCS, the speed of instruction decoding, and so forth.

CONCLUSION

Previous analyses of dynamic microprogramming, leading to decisions not to use such a scheme, have been based on assumptions that now are questionable.

Performance and hardware costs of this potential solution to parts of the function-assignment problem are not what they once were, due largely to changes in the underlying hardware technology and the effects of these changes on the ability to produce reasonably priced microprogrammable multiprocessor systems.

It is now certain that appropriate operating-system and hardware support can be built at reasonable cost. While the solutions sketched in this chapter are largely software-based, there is no implication that firmware and hardware support are inappropriate. That in itself is a vertical-migration question.

It also seems that the mechanisms for support of dynamic microprogramming can be separated from the vertical-migration policies that might be brought to bear on the problem of selection of migration candidates. Except where indicated, all the tools described in this chapter have been implemented at reasonable cost and run at low levels of overhead compared with the benefits achievable.

The next step is the construction of experimental systems to support various approaches to vertical migration and dynamic microprogramming at the same time that analytical work and appropriate models are fashioned to help guide the development of future systems.

REFERENCES

Bird, R. 1981. "A Dynamically Microprogrammable Machine as a Variable Function Resource in a Local Area Network Systems Architecture." *Proceedings of the Sixth ACM European Regional Conference.*

Burke, G. 1982. "Control Schemes for VLSI Microprocessors." *Proceedings of the 15th Annual Workshop on Microprogramming,* 91–96. Palo Alto, CA, October 5–7. New York: IEEE Computer Society Press.

Carter, E. 1983. "Abstract Type Oriented Dynamic Vertical Migration." Ph.D. diss., Vanderbilt University.

Carter, E., and R. Winner. 1983. "A Microcode Compiler Based on the C Programming Language." Technical Report CS-83-08. Nashville, TN: Vanderbilt University.

Clark, D., and W. Strecker. 1980. Comments on "The Case for the Reduced Instruction Set Computer" by Patterson and Ditzel. *Computer Architecture News* 8/6 (October):34–8.

Flynn, M. 1979. "Computer Organization and Architecture." *Operating Systems: An Advanced Course,* R. Bayer (ed.), 17–99. Berlin: Springer-Verlag.

Guffin. T. 1982. "A Microprogramming Language-Directed Microarchitecture." *Proceedings of the 15th Annual Workshop on Microprogramming.* 42–49. Palo Alto, CA, October 5–7. New York: IEEE Computer Society Press.

Guha, R. 1977. "Dynamic Microprogramming in a Time Sharing Environment." *Proceedings of the 10th Annual Workshop on Microprogramming*, 55–61. Niagara Falls, NY, October 5–7. Long Beach, CA: IEEE Computer Society Press.

Hopkins, W. 1983. "HLLDA Defies RISC: Thoughts on RISC's, CISC's, and HLL-DA's." *Proceedings of the 16th Annual Workshop on Microprogramming*, 70–76. Downingtown, PA, October 11–14. Los Angeles: IEEE Computer Society Press.

Olbert, A. 1982. "Crossing the Machine Interface." *Proceedings of the 15th Annual Workshop On Microprogramming*, 163–72. Palo Alto, CA, October 5–7. New York: IEEE Computer Society Press.

Organick, E., and J. Hinds. 1978. *Interpreting Machines: Architecture and Programming of the B1700/B1800 Series*. New York: North Holland.

Patterson, D., and D. Ditzel. 1980. "The Case for the Reduced Instruction Set Computer." *Computer Architecture News* 8/6 (October):25–33.

Patterson, D., and C. Sequin. 1981. "RISC-1: A Reduced Instruction Set VLSI Computer." *Proceedings of the Eighth Annual Symposium on Computer Architecture*, 443–58. Minneapolis, MN, May 12–14. Los Angeles: IEEE Computer Society Press.

Patterson, D., and R. Piepho. 1982. "Assessing RISCs in High-Level Language Support." *IEEE Micro* 2/4 (November):9–14, 16–19.

Rauscher, T., and A. Agrawala. 1978. "Dynamic Problem-Oriented Redefinition of Computer Architecture via Microprogramming." *IEEE Transactions on Computers* C-27/11 (November):1006–14.

Radin, G. 1982. "The 801 minicomputer." *Proceedings of the SIGARCH/SIGPLAN Symposium on Architectural Support for Programming Languages and Operating Systems*, 39–47. Palo Alto, CA, March 1–3. New York: ACM.

Reed, L. 1983. "Virtualization of the Writable Control Store on the Perkin-Elmer 3220 Running Unix." M.S. thesis, Vanderbilt University.

Rosin, R.; G. Frieder; and R. Eckaurs. 1972. "An Environment for Research in Microprogramming and Emulation." *Communications of the ACM* 15/8 (August):748–60.

Roskos, J., and R. Winner. 1981. "Toward User Sharing of the Microprogramming Level under Unix on the Perkin-Elmer 3220." *Proceedings of the 14th Annual Workshop on Microprogramming*, 67–73. Chatham, MA, October 12–15. Los Angeles: IEEE Computer Society Press.

Saltzer, J. 1979. "Naming and Binding of Objects." *Operating Systems: An Advanced Course*, R. Bayer (ed.), 99–209. Berlin: Springer-Verlag.

Winner, R. 1983. "Adaptive Instruction Sets and Instruction Set Locality Phenomena." *Proceedings of the IEEE International Workshop on Computer Systems Organization*, 147–53. New Orleans, LA, March 29–31. Silver Spring, MD: IEEE Computer Society Press.

Winner, R., and E. Carter. 1983. "Toward Type-Oriented Dynamic Vertical Migration." *Proceedings of the 16th Annual Workshop on Microprogramming*, 128–39. Downingtown, PA, October 11–14. Long Beach, CA: IEEE Computer Society Press.

Winner, R., and L. Reed. 1984. "Operating System Support for Sharing Writable Control Store." *Software: Practice and Experience* 14/12 (December):1183–95.

Wood, T. 1983. "A Linker and Librarian for Vertical Migration." M.S. thesis, Vanderbilt University.

Wulf, W. 1981. "Compilers and Computer Architecture." *Computer* 14/7 (July):41–48.

seven
AN EMULATION ENVIRONMENT AND ITS APPLICATION

CHARLES J. NEUHAUSER
MICHAEL J. FLYNN

Algorithms can be represented for execution in many ways. Typically, programmers deal with representation in high-level language or assembly language. On occasion, they may even work directly with the machine-language interface. Usually, however, this is the lowest level at which they work, under the assumption that the execution hardware and associated resources are fixed and beyond user manipulation.

Machine language is only a representation of the original algorithm, and its execution may be carried out by programmable engine whose sole task is to fetch machine language, decode instructions, determine their intent, and perform the required data transformations. This process is termed *interpretation* or *emulation*.

Emulation techniques have been used commercially for many years to provide a flexible implementation base upon which to build specific and well-defined machine-language interfaces, such as the IBM System 360/370 family. In this context, emulation provides ease of implementation, flexibility to support field changes, and the capability of supporting different machine-language interfaces on common hardware.

The flexibility of the emulation approach can be exploited by computer architects and designers to provide a test bed for implementing, measuring, and assessing quantitatively the worth of architectural concepts. In this chapter we will discuss the characteristics of an emulation environment that would be useful for architectural evaluation and how such an environment can be applied to the qualitative assessment of various instruction-set design issues.

As an example of an emulation environment, we will describe in some detail the Stanford Emulation Laboratory. This facility was constructed expressly for the purpose of supporting educational and research activity in the area of emulation. We have used this laboratory to conduct research in the conventional machine architectures and also to investigate the characteristics of unconventional machines, such as those that can directly support execution of high-level languages. Selected examples of results are provided.

EMULATION AND INTERPRETIVE MONITORING

Basic Emulation

Emulation is the process by which the actions of one machine may stand for those of another. We refer here to the *host machine* as the machine that supports the emulation. The *target machine* is the machine being emulated. Figure 7-1 shows the relationship between the host and target machines during execution of a target instruction. In emulation, we are generally concerned only with the *state* of the target machine, which is composed of all internally maintained information that could influence the machine behavior in a way detectable to the user. The state of the target machine might consist of memory, registers, stack, device status, program counter, and condition codes. Our simplifying assumption here is that the target-machine state is valid and stable only between the execution of instructions. State changes made during instruction execution are normally not visible to the user.

Figure 7-1 illustrates the basic issues related to emulation of a target-machine instruction. The host machine must begin with state information that corresponds to that of the target machine before execution of the instruction. This initial host state need not be an exact bit-for-bit representation of the initial target state. We only require that there be some mapping between the two. In fact, it is usually advantageous to represent certain aspects of the target state differently in the host. For example, target-condition codes might be held in a decoded form.

During execution of the target instruction, the host will usually transform the initial state through application of a sequence of host instructions or primitives. At some point, a final host state must be established, which can be mapped to the final target state (i.e., the state after instruction execution). We do not require that the final host state be mapped to the final target state after every instruction, only that user-visible aspects of the state correspond. Thus, for the condition-code example above, we would require that the proper encoding to be

Figure 7-1. Host/target relationship.

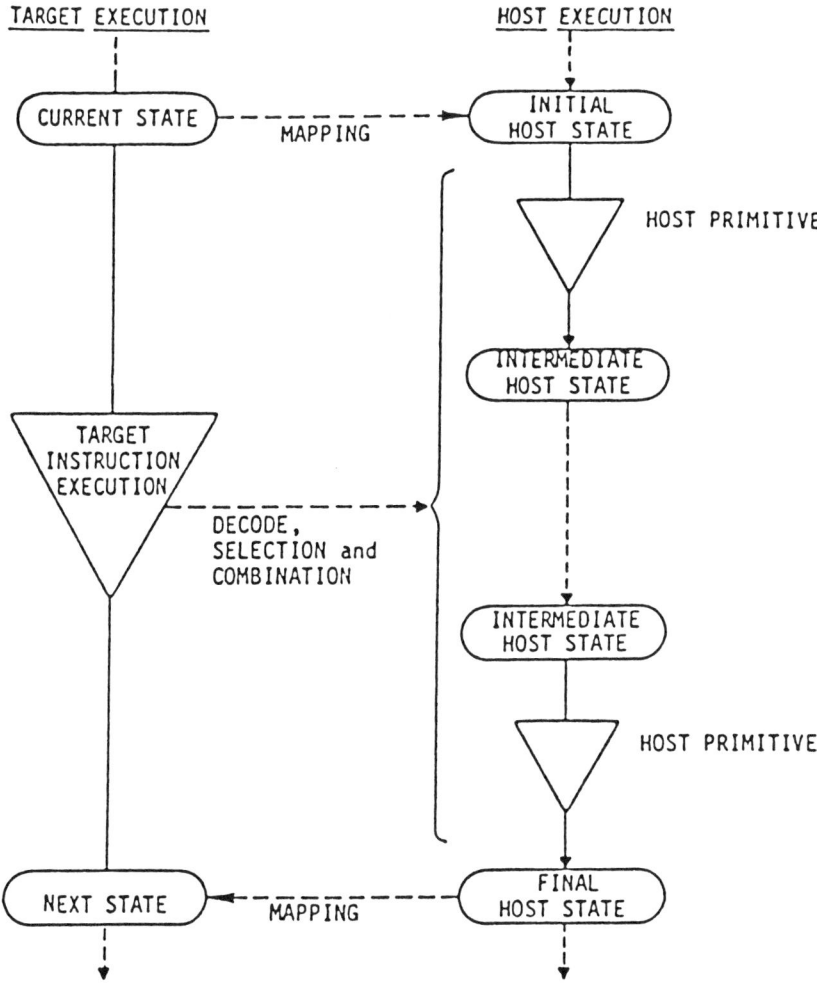

done, if the instruction had stored the condition codes in a memory cell, which would now be accessed in an arbitrary way.

Based on the simple outline of emulation presented above, we can see intuitively that an efficient host machine should have the following characteristics:

- Mechanisms to map between target and host states
- A selection of host primitives with which to build target instructions (We believe that these should be very simple so that arbitrary target-state transitions may be constructed. Complex host

instructions would probably be inefficient for general use, since complex host-state transitions might have to be undone to produce the proper state transition for the target.)
- Support for decoding of the target instruction and methods for selecting the appropriate host primitives to sequence the host-state transition

The use of microprogrammable engines in the emulation of specific target architectures is widespread. Almost all major instruction-set processors, such as System/370 (Pittler, Powers, and Schnable 1982) and DEC VAX™, make use of microprogramming techniques for implementing at least part of the processor range. Usually, these machines are intentionally biased toward emulation of a particular target architecture. Our interest is in host machines that are unbiased and efficiently support a range of target processors. We refer to such machines as *universal host machines*. Examples of such machines would include the Varian 73 (Varian 1973), Nanodata QM-1 (Nanodata 1974), and the MIP-9000 (Standard 1970).

Accuracy of Emulation

One concern in the construction of emulators, especially in the experimental environment, is the degree of accuracy required. For many measurement purposes, perfect emulation of the target machine is not necessary and would be very inefficient. A simple classification of emulators may be made along the following lines (Flynn 1977).

In *Class A emulation* the emulated machine-state transformations would precisely duplicate those of the actual target machine. The most important aspect of this is that program-induced failures would occur in an identical manner in both target and emulated machines. A user would not be able to differentiate operation of the machines, except perhaps on the basis of time.

Class A emulators are the standard goal of industrial practice, where all user programs must behave (or misbehave) in a precise manner. A considerable part of the construction effort in the industrial setting is duplicating the effects of failing programs or those that intentionally induce errors. This is particularly true when the emulator makes use of structures, such as pipelining or prefetching, to gain efficiency but must still fail as though strictly sequential execution had been taking place.

In *Class B emulation* "correct" programs produce the proper state change, but incorrect usage may cause arbitrary behavior. This class of emulation is what we usually try to attain in the emulation laboratory. Emulation at this level allows one to execute benchmarks and make realistic measurements of instruction-stream characteristics. Usually, such emulators are much easier to construct than an equivalent Class A emulation. In particular, manufacturers' architectural specifications are usually an adequate guide for proper implementation of the emulator, where a Class A emulator may require examination of target-machine microcode and circuitry.

In *Class C emulation* the emulator performs properly for a subset of the target environment. Such an emulator might not emulate certain instructions or features. This would not be a problem in experimental situations if the unsupported functions were not used by the benchmarks under test.

In *Class D emulation* some aspects of the target emulation are performed differently. An example might be a different implementation of floating-point formats. The important issue in this type of emulation is that the behavior of the target machine can be predicted from the equivalent behavior of the emulator. Class D emulation can be useful for research if the important target-machine behavior is preserved, such as instruction and reference-stream characteristics.

In *Class E emulation* functions or subroutines from the target machine are performed differently. Under such an emulation, the state of the emulator may be equivalent to that of the target machine at two points in the instruction sequence, but intermediate states may differ. This approach is useful for experimental emulations of complex environments. An example might be an emulator that can provide a highly accurate emulation of user code, but the systems calls (e.g., SVCs in S/370) are emulated to produce the appropriate effect without actually executing the equivalent target-machine instruction sequence. Such an emulator would still be useful in the assessment of user-stream characteristics.

Interpretive Monitoring

In our laboratory, one of the important uses of emulation is in the evaluation of instruction-set performance and effectiveness. Our evaluations are based on measuring certain dynamic characteristics of the instruction stream, such as memory accesses, register accesses, and breaks. This data could be gathered in several ways. The primary approach we use is *interpretive monitoring*, in which a basic emulator is modified to capture events related to the instruction stream under execution.

Figure 7-2 is a schematic illustration of methods for detecting instruction-stream events. Each has associated costs, benefits, and disadvantages.

For limited instruction-stream measurements, the *hardware monitor* has proven useful (Noe 1974). Under this regimen, a specialized event detector is attached electrically to the target machine being measured. The advantage of hardware monitoring is that target execution is not affected by the measurement. The weakness is that event generation may be at such a high rate that detailed data collection is expensive or impossible. The target machine under test must also be physically available. The hardware-monitor approach is used primarily by machine manufacturers and their largest customers to assess very general performance characteristics.

Figure 7-2. Monitoring methods.

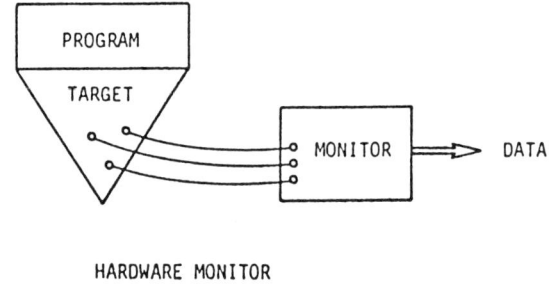

HARDWARE MONITOR

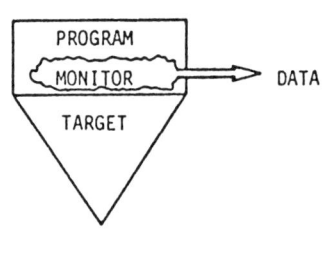

SOFTWARE MONITOR

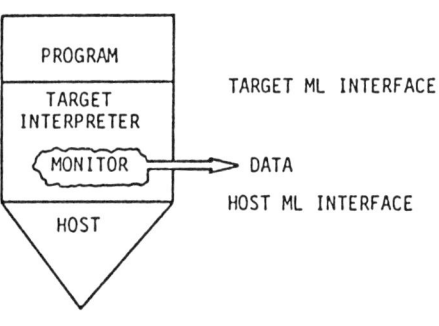

INTERPRETIVE MONITORING

The *software monitor* requires modification of the code under test to include calls to event-capture routines, which update counters for the parameters under test. Although no target-machine modification is required, this approach can have a large impact on the execution speed of code, slowing execution by several orders of magnitude if detailed instruction-level measurements are made. Its primary use has been in the dynamics measurement of high-level-language characteristics (Knuth 1971).

Interpretive monitoring has characteristics and costs that lie between the two techniques outlined above. Implementation requires modification of the target-machine emulator to detect and tabulate events. This impedes emulator execution, perhaps by a factor of two, but allows detailed examination of instruction-stream characteristics. For research purposes, the major advantage of interpretive monitoring is that a specific target machine under measurement does not need to be physically available but instead may be emulated. This allows a range of machines to be measured on a single facility.

Research results presented later were based on data gathered in the Stanford Emulation Laboratory using both software and interpretive monitoring. One expense associated with interpretive monitoring is the construction and validation of target-machine emulators. We have been fortunate in that most of our emulators were developed as a part of the educational mission of our facility and then later augmented to provide interpretive-monitor capability.

High-Level-Language Emulation

An important application of emulation environments is in the experimental construction and measurement of new and possibly unconventional architectures. In our laboratory, we have been concerned with architecture that can directly support the execution of high-level languages with a minimum of translation. This research has been oriented towards understanding the appropriate architectural mechanism to preserve language-level characteristics, such as locality of reference, for explicit use during execution rather than detect them in the instruction stream of the translated code. For example, cache mechanisms in conventional architectures are used to detect locality at the point of execution because this information is diluted when the high-level-language program is translated to machine language. We refer to our architectures for high-level language as *direct-execution languages* (DELs).

Figure 7-3 outlines the different means by which a problem represented in a high-level language can be executed in conventional (say, S/370) or unconventional (DEL) environments. Availability of a universal host machine allows a single facility to execute or measure both conventional and unconventional execution of benchmarks. In a later section we present selected results for high-level-language execution of PASCAL.

Figure 7-3. Interpretation of a problem in an HLL representation.

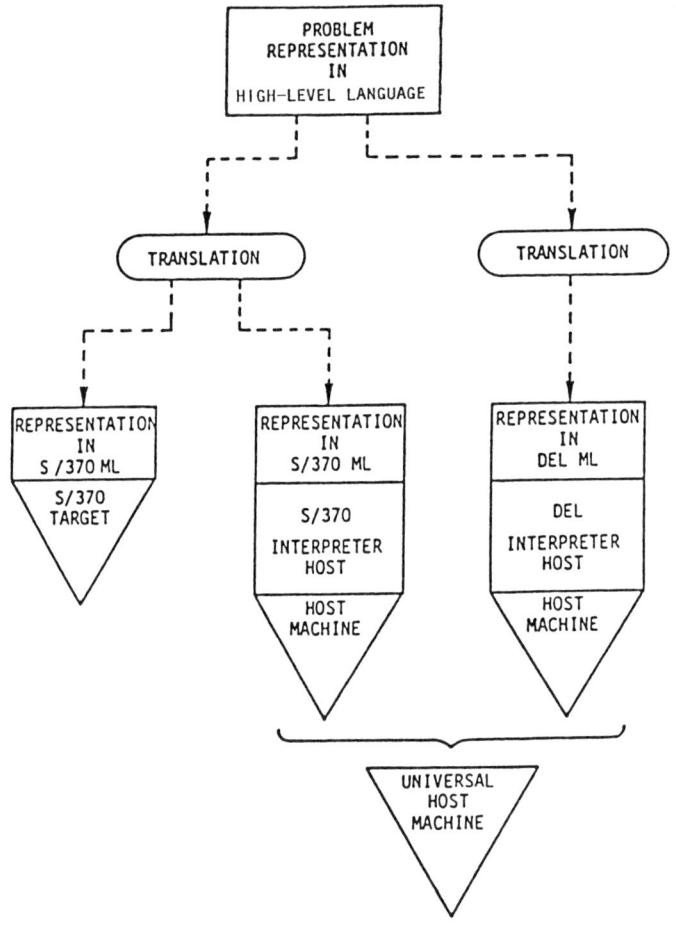

EXAMPLE ENVIRONMENT: THE STANFORD EMULATION LAB

In this section we will examine an example of a reasonably complete emulation environment, the Stanford Emulation Laboratory (Neuhauser 1977 a, b). The primary goal of the laboratory is to provide students and researchers with a friendly, efficient, and flexible environment for exploring conventional and unconventional machine architectures. Some of the objectives that we felt were important are the following.

Full emulation capability: One of the principle functions of the laboratory is to support special study courses in the design of conventional machine emulations to familiarize students with the problems and complexities of completely emulating a machine architecture. This means that the laboratory itself must have efficient mechanisms to support all aspects of emulation, including a sufficiently large micro and macro memory resource, a rich set of primitive instructions, and a method for accessing peripheral equipment.

I/O emulation support: Our laboratory was designed to support realistic programming environments for target processors. This meant that a flexible and efficient I/O emulation environment was a necessity. We have found that accurate emulation of even a small set of a target processor's peripheral environment can be challenging. To support this, we have tried to provide a set of I/O emulation primitives that can be structured into more complex I/O actions by the host microprogram.

Ease of use: The quick and accurate construction of emulators is more important in the educational and research environment than absolute performance. We have attempted to make use of familiar tools such as UNIX in establishing the overall user environment.

Reasonable performance: General-purpose emulation will usually have poorer cost/performance characteristics than that of a specific target-processor implementation. This is a consequence of the fact that the general emulation environment is structured to provide flexibility as a substitute for a priori knowledge of the target machine. Since cost was a very real constraint in our design, we have had to compromise performance to some extent. Our basic performance goal was that emulations of ordinary commercial machines should perform well enough that interactive programs run on them would not be painful to use, at least for a single user.

Basic Structure of the Environment

Figure 7-4 illustrates the functional structure of the emulation laboratory. There are two primary elements: a specialized host processor (the EMMY) and a general-purpose support processor. The two elements are connected with a bus-to-bus interface that allows each processor to access the other's address space.

The EMMY processor is a special-purpose processor whose design was optimized for emulation, as opposed to communication, computation, string processing, and so forth. The host-processor element contains its own memory hierarchy, consisting of a main memory, a microstore and a small register file. The microstore is directly accessible for reads and writes from the host processor and serves as both a control store and a data store. Access to the microstore is about three times slower than a register access.

Since the microstore holds data and control information, we chose a common word size of 32 bits. This size works well for most conventional emula-

Figure 7-4. Functional structure of emulation laboratory.

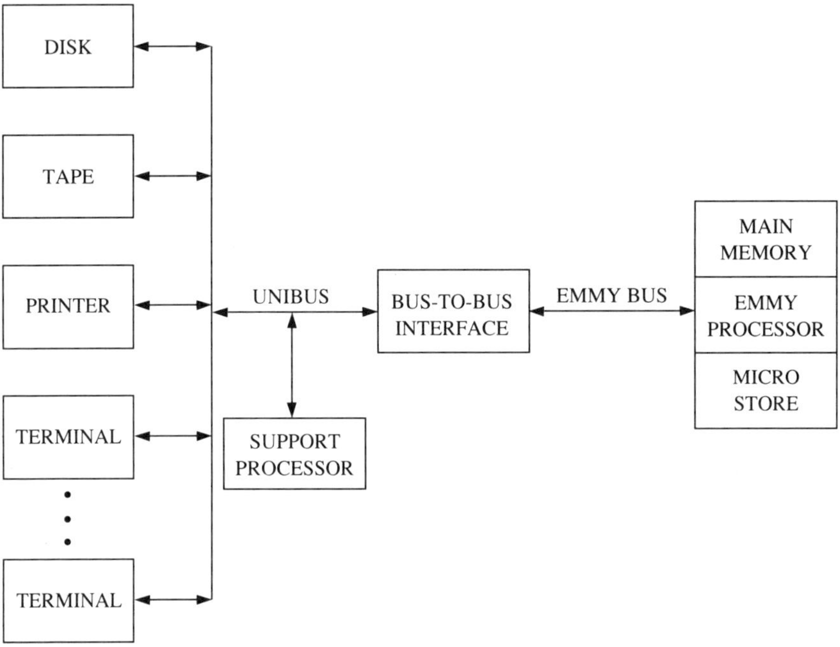

```
┌─────────┐
│  DISK   │◄──────┐
└─────────┘       │
                  │
┌─────────┐       │
│  TAPE   │◄──────┤
└─────────┘       │                                    ┌──────────┐
                  │                                    │   MAIN   │
┌─────────┐       │   UNIBUS   ┌───────────┐ EMMY BUS  │  MEMORY  │
│ PRINTER │◄─────►├───────────►│ BUS-TO-BUS│──────────►├──────────┤
└─────────┘       │            │ INTERFACE │           │   EMMY   │
                  │            └───────────┘           │PROCESSOR │
                  ▲                                    ├──────────┤
                  │                                    │  MICRO   │
┌─────────┐       │                                    │  STORE   │
│TERMINAL │◄─────►│      ┌───────────┐                 └──────────┘
└─────────┘       └─────►│  SUPPORT  │
    •                    │ PROCESSOR │
    •                    └───────────┘
    •
┌─────────┐
│TERMINAL │◄──────
└─────────┘
```

tions, in which data is usually a multiple of the common 8-bit byte. The size does, however, compromise the expressive power of the microinstruction, and we have compensated for this by an instruction-structuring scheme we will outline later. In conventional terms the EMMY microinstruction word would be labeled "vertically encoded," since the basic components are short and highly encoded.

The support processor element of the laboratory is based on a DEC minicomputer (the PDP-11™ series), which runs UNIX. After investing considerable effort in the architecture, design, and construction of the host engine, we decided that the use of a popular, conventional processor would be the most cost-effective method of providing peripherals. Although the EMMY processor bus is fast and reasonably flexible, the cost of designing one-of-a-kind peripheral controllers would have been prohibitive. By using a standard processor system we also obtained the services of UNIX.

Our original plan was to access the support-processor peripheral controllers directly and to perform all peripheral emulation activities in the EMMY processor. This would, however, have led to fairly complex microprogramming of the host, since it would also need to coordinate file accesses with the UNIX system. Instead, we decided to use UNIX as a sort of front-end processor for the peripheral subsystem. In operation UNIX, through a group of processes, packages peripheral accesses into a set of primitive operations (e.g., SEEK, WRITE, READ), which are made available to the host through a simple channellike interface. The host-processor microcode is responsible for maintaining the state of the target-specific peripherals. Details are given later.

The Host Processor

All data and instructions in the EMMY processor are 32 bits wide. This uniformity simplifies the internal processor structure and allows data and instructions to be easily mixed in microstore. Figure 7-5 illustrates the internal functional structure of EMMY, which is basically that of a register-oriented architecture.

Eight 32-bit registers form the central storage resource of the processor. All are available for general-purpose usage, but one (register 0) contains the state of the processor, and its contents have side effects, such as indicating the next microinstruction to be fetched. The architectural intent of the machine is that the register file would be the central object of operation. It is surrounded logically by three independent processing mechanisms, designated as the T, A, and I machines, with functions as follows:

- The *T machine* element controls register-to-register data transformations and usually takes two registers as operands and returns the result to the register file. T-machine operations are primarily ALU-like operations.
- All data movements, initiated by the processor within the memory hierarchy, are controlled by the *A machine*. This includes register transfers between registers, microstore, and main memory. The A machine supports very limited-address arithmetic and assumes that memory addresses are first calculated by the T machine.
- Selection of the next microinstruction and the handling of interrupts is carried out by the *I machine*. Because of the limited instruction-word size, microinstructions are fetched sequentially unless explicitly directed otherwise. The I machine evaluates condition codes and other flags to determine the source of the next microinstruction.

Microinstruction and emulation data reside in the microstore together. There is no partitioning enforced, but instances of a single word being used as both instruction and data are very rare. Sharing of the microstore is primarily an economic consideration in our system and also provides flexibility to trade off program and data space as particular applications require.

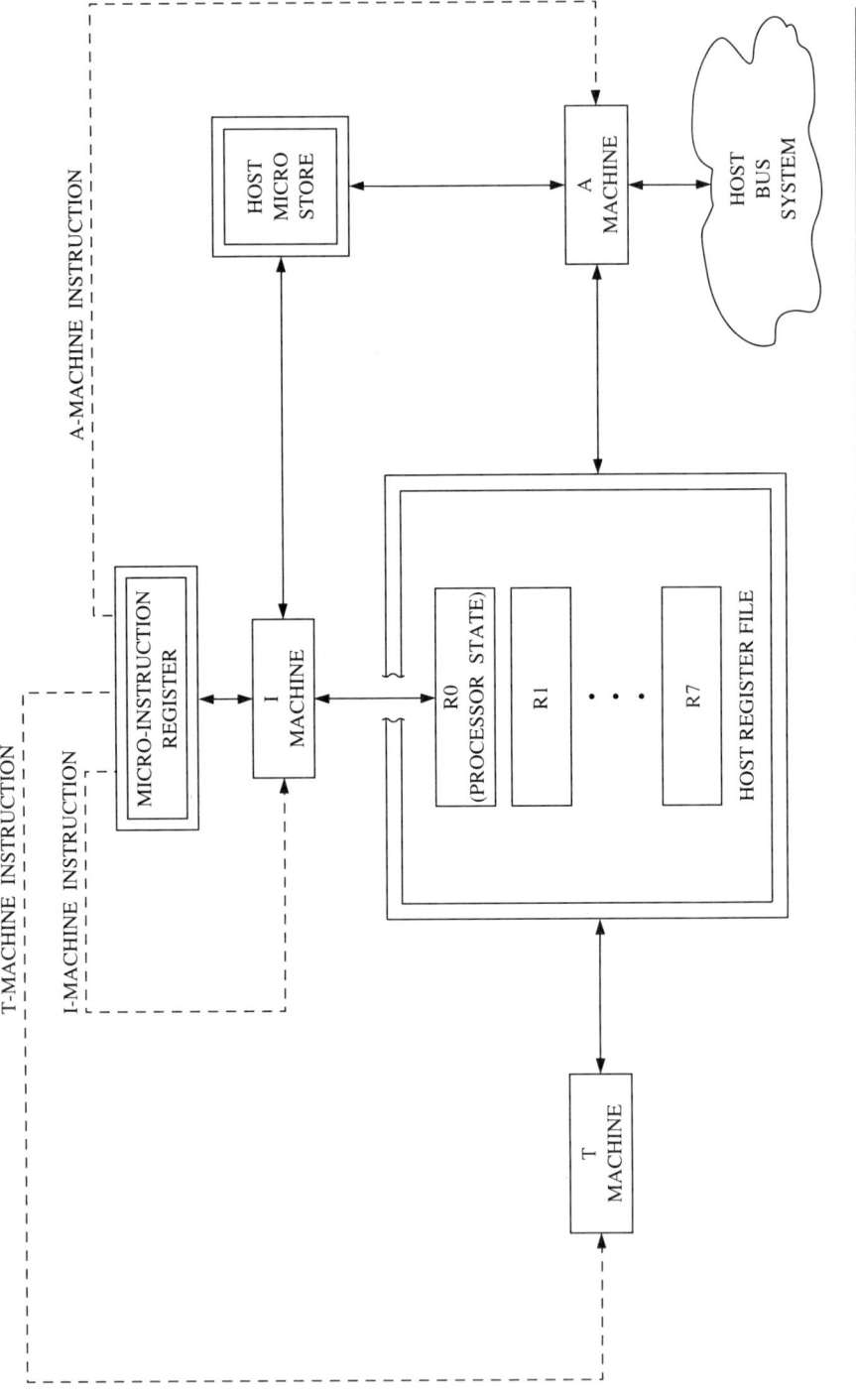

Figure 7-5. Functional structure of EMMY host processor.

Each microinstruction word would ideally be able to specify operations to each of the three host processing elements. The limited width of the 32-bit word, however, constrains the expressive power of the microinstruction, especially when data and address constants must be defined. We have solved the problem in two ways. First, most I-machine operations are implicit, fetching the next microinstruction. Second, we divide the microinstruction word in half and assign one side to T-machine control and the other to A-machine control. When explicit I-machine control is needed, one or both sides of the instruction are preempted. T-machine immediate data is generated by preempting the A-machine side of the instruction. Thus, the five basic instruction types are:

Left Side	Right Side
I. T-machine control	T-immediate data
II. T-machine control	A-machine control
III. T-machine control	I-machine control
IV. I-machine control	A-machine control
V. I-machine control	I-machine control

Details of the instruction set are given in the appendix to this chapter, together with an example of a conventional emulator sequence.

Some of the design principles we used were the following:

Instructions should be simple: Our experience has been that it is better to use multiple simple instructions to structure a target-processor instruction than to modify a complex instruction that is not exactly right. A similar observation has been made with respect to conventional machines (Wulf 1981). In keeping with this notion, we do not provide true multiplication or division instructions but rather offer single-bit computational steps that can be used iteratively to construct the precision required.

Field operations are important: One area where emulation and conventional processing differ is that interpretation of target-processor instructions relies heavily on the extraction and manipulation of fields and bits within a word. This is especially true when the host must emulate a device interface, in which each bit may have an independent function. Field manipulation is also important in matching host computational resources with target-machine requirements when basic computational objects are different. The EMMY instruction repertoire includes a set of powerful selection, insertion, and alignment functions for this purpose. A similar approach has been used in some recent RISC-like architectures (Hao, Markstein, and Radin 1986).

Address generation should be simple: Within EMMY, addresses to microstore and main store are either specified directly or indirectly through a register. There is no address arithmetic, except for limited incrementing or decrementing. Access to objects in microstore is equivalent to the target-machine access to internal-machine state and register. Thus, addressing to support these accesses should be simple. Main-storage addressing in actual target machines is handled by microcode or special hardware units. Cost constraints in our case dictated a microcoded approach.

Host Processor Main Memory

Since every executed target instruction makes at least one access to memory, we felt that the host resource that supported target main-memory operations should be designed to contribute to the efficiency of the emulation. Our approach was to design a host main-memory element that provided considerable flexibility in data addressing and alignment.

Figure 7-6 shows the functional structure of the EMMY host memory design. The memory resources are structured as a linear string of bytes, but accesses to it are mediated by a memory controller, which interprets host processor addresses as either byte, half-word (i.e., 16-bit), or full-word pointers.

Although the host processor always transmits or receives a full (32-bit) word when accessing the memory, the memory controller is able to select and/or align byte subsections of the word when transferring the data. The result is that the memory system can efficiently support 8-, 16-, 24-, and 32-bit target architectures.

Control of the main memory is specified dynamically by the host processor using a command word, which is transmitted to the memory controller on every access. This allows the host to handle different types of accesses in the appropriate way. For example, it is usually better to left-align data and instructions received from memory, but addresses (i.e., indirection) are easier to work with if right-aligned in the host processor.

In figure 7-7 we outline the memory-alignment functions. On READ, one, two, three, or four bytes of data may be read. The results are shifted and filled (zero or sign) as shown. When data is written to memory, a contiguous string of bits (one to four) is selected from the right or left side of the data word and written to the target location. We do not support byte or half-word "swapping" when translating the address, and this complicates the emulation of some processor architectures.

The memory controller also allows dynamic reconfiguration of parity checking. This is sometimes used to emulate simple protection schemes or to provide a form of memory limit detection.

Interfacing to the Support Processor

All real-world I/O for the EMMY host processor is performed by a PDP-11 processor and its associated peripheral set. The EMMY and the PDP-11 bus systems communicate via a bus interface (fig. 7-8), which allows a bus master

Figure 7-6. EMMY main-memory operations.

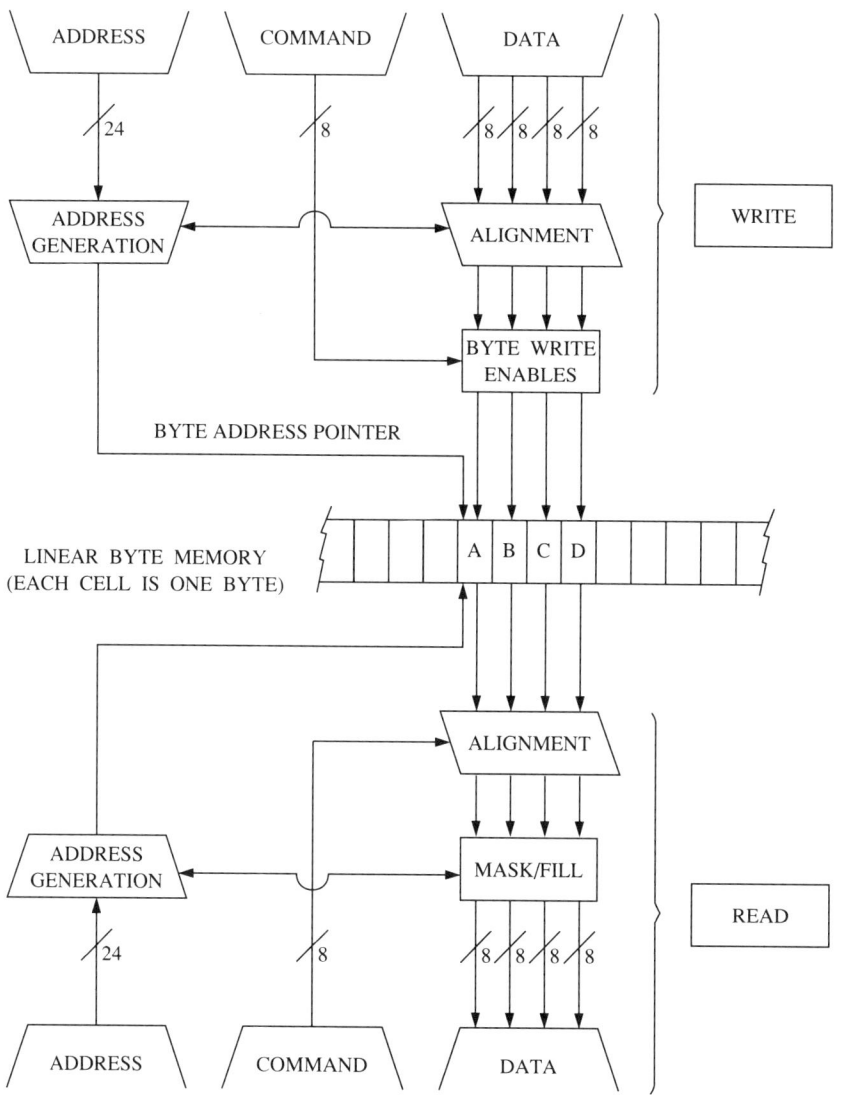

Figure 7-7. Examples of memory alignment.

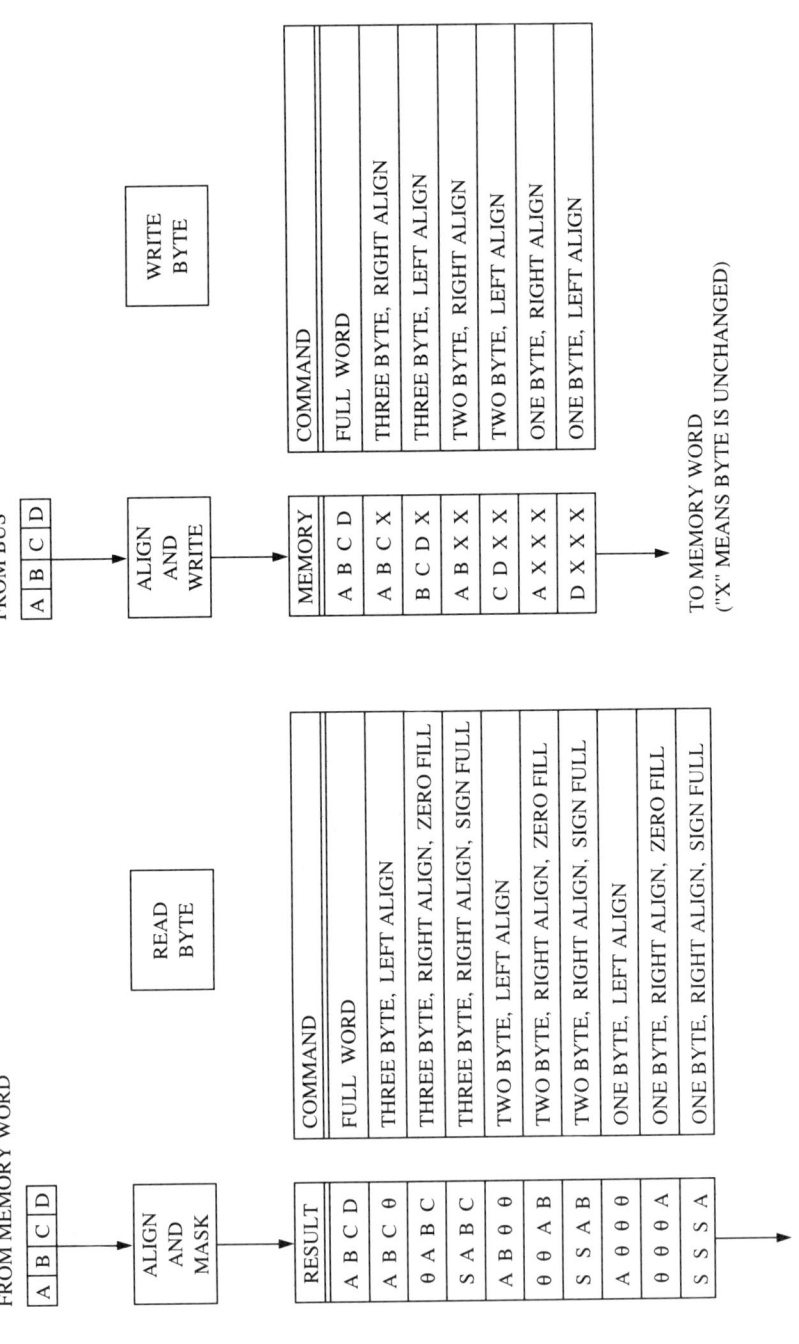

Figure 7-8. Bus-to-bus interface.

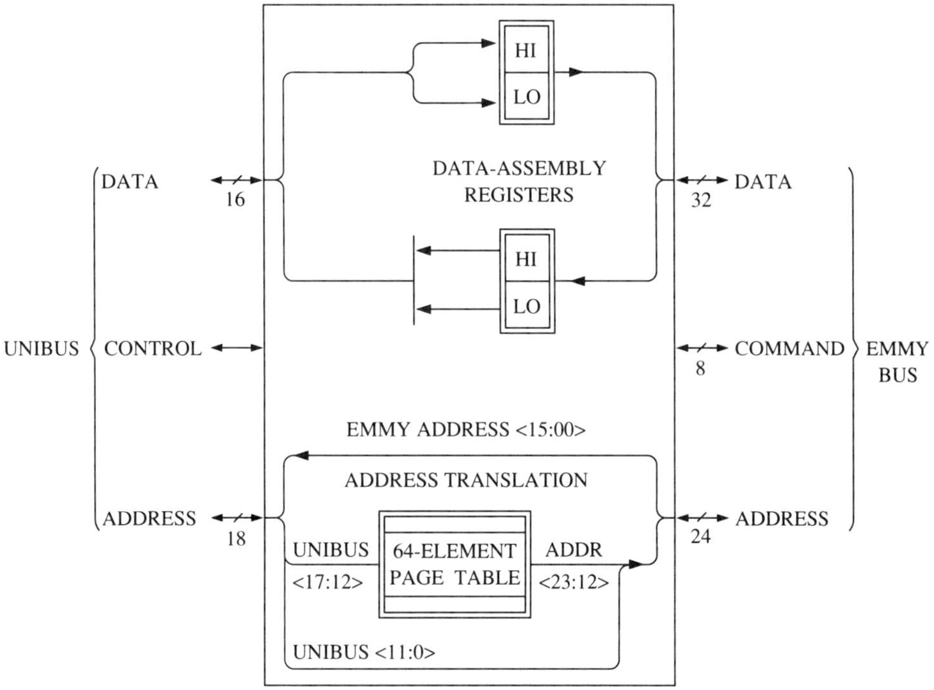

on one system to appear as a bus master in the other system (Shih 1977). Interrupts are handled within each bus system by their respective CPUs, which can use the bus interface to generate an interrupt in the other bus system when required.

The EMMY bus is quite similar to the UNIbus in that it is asynchronous and allows multiple masters. There is one small refinement, which is the addition of a "reject" mechanism, allowing a slave to signal the accessing master that it is unable to complete a request. The master then pulls back and tries the request later. This mechanism prevents the bus systems from entering a "deadly embrace," since the EMMY master can always retract its request.

EMMY bus addresses are 24-bit word addresses, and the 18-bit (byte) addresses of the UNIbus are mapped directly into in area of the EMMY address space. For UNIbus accesses to the EMMY bus, a page-translation mechanism allows 2K-byte blocks of memory to be mapped into arbitrary blocks of the EMMY address space. Usually, only a few blocks are mapped this way, since the PDP-11 processor requires some address space for its programs.

I/O Device Support System

An important aspect of the emulation laboratory is the manner in which device emulation is supported (Huck and Neuhauser 1979). Our experience has been that about half the development effort related to emulator construction is due to device emulation. It is also an area of considerable intellectual difficulty, since device specifications are usually not so rigorous and systematic as those for processors.

We had several objectives in designing our device-emulation approach. Fortunately, the requirements are limited somewhat by our research/educational environment in that we did not need to support complete operation of any device. We require efficient support only of normal, nonfailing operational modes. We have ignored issues related to diagnostic modes, physical failures, and specific physical characteristics, such as time-related actions. This assumption greatly simplifies the support of device emulation.

To provide an adequate level of service, we tried to make the basic transfer rates as fast as possible. A reasonable performance objective is to have the byte data-transfer rate (bytes/second) approximate the instruction-execution rate (instruction per second).

Flexibility in representation was another important goal. We tried to separate the physical aspects of the target device from those of the host. In many cases, for example, it is desirable that the output of an emulated line printer be actually directed to a disk file. Fortunately, the structure of UNIX, which provided the basis for our device emulation, supported this type of mapping in a natural way.

One interesting issue we encountered early on was the necessity for emulating the man-machine interface of a device. If an emulator supports a diskette drive, for example, there must be a way to emulate the insertion, extraction, and changing of the diskette. This is done through a console, which provides overall control of the emulation process.

To simplify the task of supporting emulation, we force all devices to conform to one of three basic device types:

Type	Example
Serial	Terminal, printer, card reader
Linear	Disk, diskette
Variable-record	Magnetic tape

Serial devices are used to support simple, character-oriented devices such as terminals. The data stream is not reusable, at least not without a physical action. Characters are sent and received one at a time, and therefore this mode of operation has considerable overhead.

Linear devices are used to emulate media, such as drums and disks, that have a simple, regular, and fixed internal structure. The device emulated is simply one with a one-dimensional data stream that may be read or written at any point. The point to be assessed is specified by a seek. The I/O support system has no knowledge of the physical structure of the device being emulated. This structure is imposed by the specific device-emulator code on the EMMY processor. In a disk emulation, for example, the device emulator must understand the disk structure (tracks, cylinders, sectors) and from this calculate the appropriate linear data position.

Variable-record devices are used to support tapelike target devices where the information is unstructured and is specified by explicit physical marks on the medium. A variable-record device is emulated from a linear device within UNIX by keeping a separate file that denotes the start and end of records within the linear file. Provisions are made for the I/O support software to understand commands related to record separators (e.g., tape marks) and record terminators (e.g., end-of-file marks).

Figure 7-9 shows the overall structure of device emulation in the laboratory. The target-machine code and device emulator run on the EMMY host. A program called VACCESS (virtual access) runs on UNIX and communicates with the host-based device emulator via a set of mailboxes in the PDP-11 memory. VACCESS provides all the services to support the three generic device types outlined above. The EMMY-based device emulator assumes responsibility for mapping specific host requirements into these device types.

Within VACCESS are several processes. One is P mail, which coordinates the exchange of commands and responses with the device emulator. Another is P control, which carries out the specific device actions. A third process supports debugging by allowing the user to monitor the mailboxes and issue commands and responses directly.

The P control process communicates directly with UNIX files and devices in the standard manner. This means that all the power and flexibility of UNIX can be employed to direct, divert, and manipulate files. A dedicated device is required to control the VACCESS process. This device is usually a terminal and is used to configure the emulator, control physical device operation, and debug emulator transactions. This device can also be time-shared with one of the serial devices being emulated, such as the target-system console.

Figure 7-10 shows the basic interaction between UNIX and the EMMY device emulator. There are two mailboxes connecting the subsystem. One sends commands from the device emulator to UNIX, and the other returns responses to the emulator. Generally, the device emulator initiates all transactions. This is done by waiting for the outgoing mailbox to empty and placing the command in it. UNIX will pick up the command, when it has time to process it, by polling and generating a response. When UNIX sends a response to the emulator,

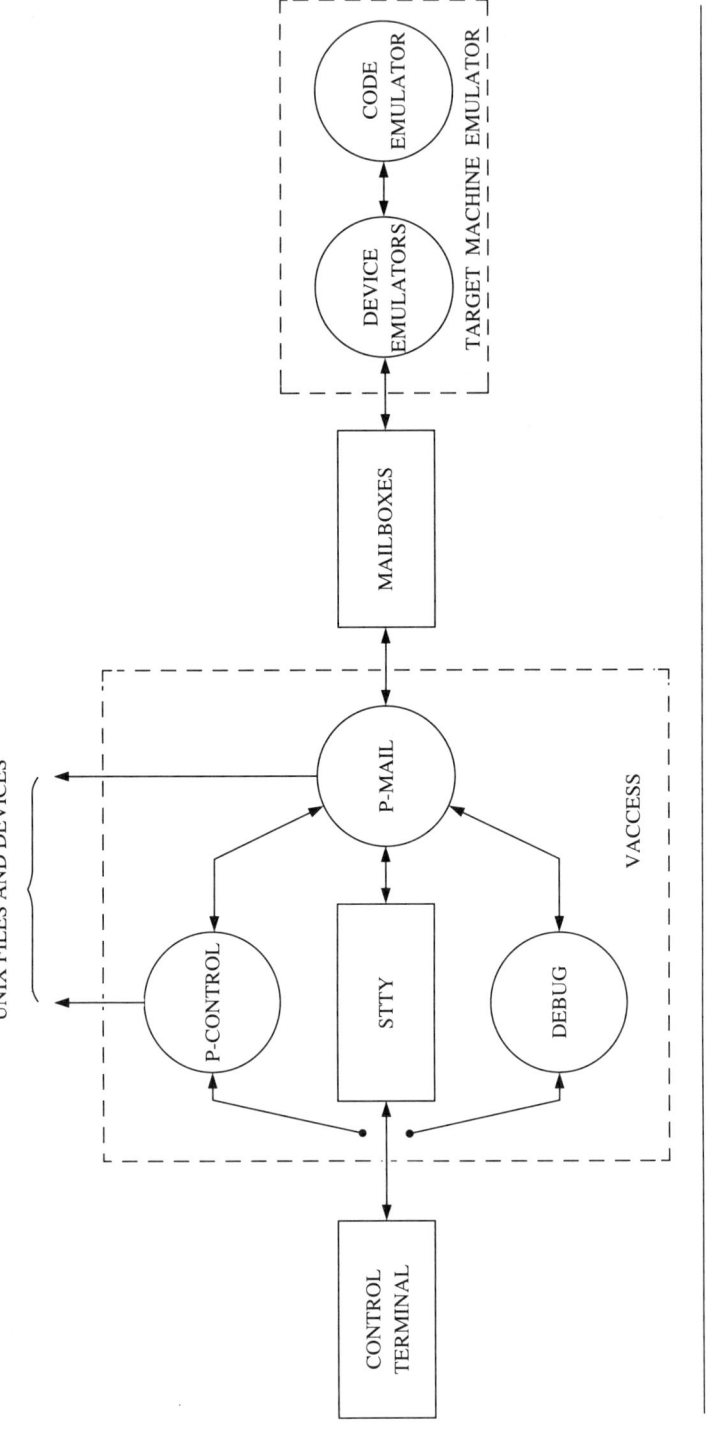

Figure 7-9. Basic emulation structure.

Figure 7-10. UNIX/EMMY Microcode Interaction.

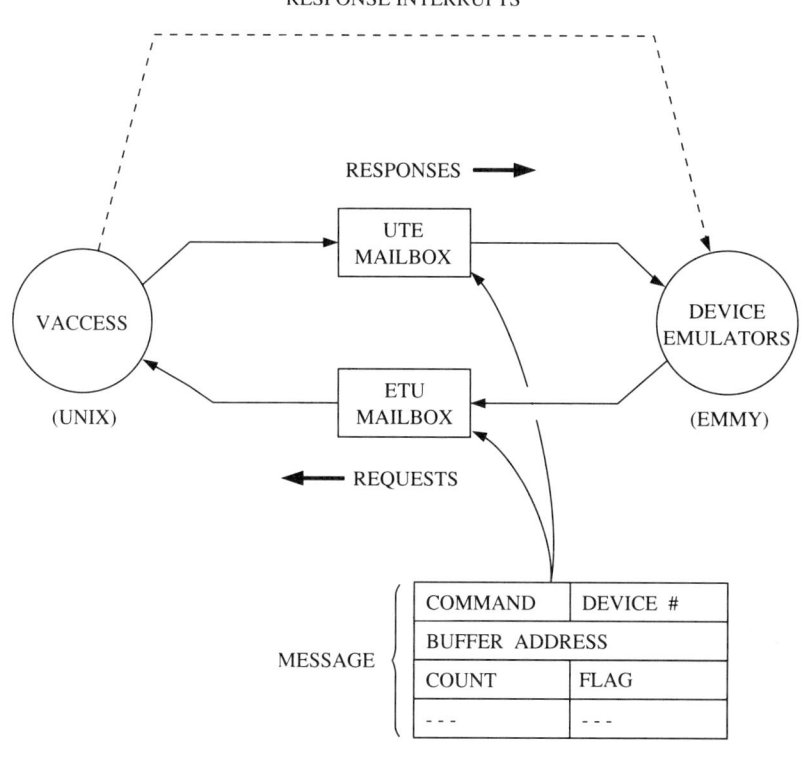

it generates a response interrupt. UNIX will generate an unsolicited response when, for example, a device experiences a "physical" change of state generated by an operator action.

A mailbox entry consists of the following:

> *Command:* defines the action or response
> *Device number:* the ID of an emulated device
> *Buffer address:* the source or destination of data in EMMY storage
> *Count:* the length of the data
> *Flag:* availability indication for the mailbox

A serial device can transfer data directly in the buffer-address field of the message, reducing the overhead for per-character transfers.

Examples of the commands that the emulator may make use of are the following:

Device	Command
Serial	READ_IMMEDIATE
	WRITE_IMMEDIATE
Linear	READ
	WRITE
	SEEK
	REWRITE
Variable	READ
	WRITE
	GO TO TAPE MARK
	WRITE TAPE MARK
	REWIND
General	ABORT
	RESET_ALL_DEVICES
	EXIT

Among the unsolicited responses from the VACCESS facility are: DEVICE RESET DETECTED, BREAK_DETECTED, DEVICE_READY, DEVICE_NOT_READY.

The facilities outlined above have been used to support a range of real and virtual devices in the laboratory. Some examples and performance data will be given later.

Tools for Emulation

Host processor code can be produced using one of two assemblers. The EMMYXL assembler (Hedges 1975) produces one EMMY instruction code per line of input code. It allows exact control of the contents of an EMMY instruction and is the preferred method of producing efficient code.

The EMMY PL assembler (Polstra 1975) is patterned after the PL360 language (Wirth 1968) and is a cross between an assembler and a compiler. Its primary advantage is that one statement may produce more than one EMMY instruction, and thus it is usually a faster method of producing code. EMMY PL provides basic control and data structures, which make the overall structure of an emulator easier to read. Figure 7-11 shows a fragment of a 360/370 emulator coded in each language.

Most tools for debugging emulators have been constructed on an "as needed" basis. All EMMY memory resources (register, control store, and memory) can be accessed directly from UNIX even if the EMMY is halted. The EMMY can be instruction-stepped, but there are no hardware break points or trace facilities. These are usually emulated by programs in UNIX, which will repetitively step

Figure 7-11. Examples of EMMY microcode. These examples are taken from S/360 emulators. They are approximately equivalent, although the emulators use different fetch and decode approaches.

```
              OP10:   .LOAD POSITIVE
                      XR,IR << 4      ; P=M(XR)          .R2 VALUE
                      PC:=PC+2        ; IR=X(PC)         .PREFETCH NEXT INSTRUCTION
                      P:=P            ; (NEG => PCOMP)   .TEST FOR NEGATIVE
                                      ; M(R)=P           .STORE RESULT
                      MAR:=DECODE                        .DECODE NEXT INSTRUCTION

              PCOMP:  .COMPLEMENT NEGATIVE NUMBER
                      XR:=-1          ; S=S-S            .COMPLEMENT NUMBER
 EMMY XL              S:=S-P          ; M(CC)=MAR        .FORM 2'S COMP AND SET CC
                                      ; M(R)=S           .STORE RESULT
                      (NOT OVERFLOW   => MAR=DECODE      .DECODE NEXT INSTRUCTION
                                      ; MAR=ARITHOFL     .HANDLE ARITHMETIC EXCEPTION

              OP12:   .LOAD AND TEST (RR FORM)
                      XR,IR << 4      ; P=M(XR)          .GET R2 VALUE
                      PC:=PC+2        ; IR=X(PC)         .PREFETCH NEXT INSTRUCTION
                      P:=P            ; M(CC)=MAR        .TEST AND SET CC
                      XR:=-1          ; M(R)=P           .UPDATE R1 VALUE
                      MAR:=DECODE                        .DECODE NEXT INSTRUCTION
```

```
              #10:   DO                                ** LPR INSTRUCTION;
                       R2:=X(R1);                     ** PREFETCH NEXT INSTRUCTION;
                       R5:=M(R7);                     ** FETCH OPERAND;
                       IF R5 < 0 THEN R5:=NOT R5+1;   ** COMPLEMENT IF NEGATIVE;
                       SET_CC; AGAIN OPWAIT;          ** SET CC AND CONTINUE DECODE;
                     END;

              #11:   DO                                ** LNR INSTRUCTION;
                       R2:=X(R1);                     ** PREFETCH NEXT INSTRUCTION;
                       R5:=M(R7);                     ** FETCH OPERAND;
 EMMY PL               IF R5>=0 THEN R5:=NOT R5+1;    ** COMPLEMENT IF POSITIVE;
                       SET_CC; AGAIN OPWAIT;          ** SET CC AND CONTINUE DECODE;
                     END;

              #12:   DO                                ** LTR INSTRUCTION (RR FORM);
                       R2:=X(R1);                     ** PREFETCH NEXT INSTRUCTION;
                       R5:=M(R5)-0;                   ** FETCH OPERAND AND TEST;
                       SET_CC; AGAIN OPWAIT;          ** SET CC AND CONTINUE DECODE;
                     END;
```

and test the target addresses. These sorts of simple tools have proven adequate for debugging.

There is a general-purpose program to emulate the control console of a target machine. This allows one to map EMMY memory into formatted and labeled display fields, thus supporting inspection of the target machine state directly.

Performance

Host Processor Performance

The architectural intent of the EMMY design was to support independent execution of T-, A-, and I-machine instruction fragments. Given the simple nature of the instruction set, we expected to execute each fragment in one clock cycle. Unfortunately, the reality of university research financing intruded on the ideals of the implementation. Our implementation approach attempted to obtain moderate performance at low cost. To this end, we implemented the basic structure so that the expensive resources (e.g., ALU, shifter, register/file) were serially reused by the T, A, and I machines. Instead of a parallel shifter, we used a serial-shift mechanism. The full 32-bit data paths were retained.

The basic processor technology was ECL, which allowed us to regain some of the speed lost to serialization. Our prototype (wire-wrapped) clock cycle was 50 nsec, although later work showed that 35 nsec was easily attainable in a proper physical environment.

Empirical measurements have shown that the average host-instruction execution time is 15 clocks, about 750 nsec. One instruction, in this context, includes full operation of the T, A, and I machines in sequence. This average time includes the serial-shift time required by many important EMMY instructions.

A conventional target machine, such as the S/360 or PDP-11, can be emulated at rates of about 50 KIPS. This means that, on the average, about 25 EMMY instructions are required to emulate one conventional target-machine instruction. The Appendix presents some data on Emmy instruction usage.

I/O System Performance

The performance of an emulated I/O device is a function of many different factors, the most important of which is the *block size*. Mailbox requests require a fixed amount of time to initially parse the request type and device assignment. Once a device is identified, the transfer is started. The transfer time between the operating system and the VACCESS program is directly proportional to the block size. So, for small block sizes, the initial overhead dominates the total interaction time, while for larger blocksizes the transfer rate is constant. Because of the buffering scheme used by the UNIX operating system, block sizes above 512 bytes result in near constant transfer rates. There is one notable exception, which involves the use of the *raw* device interface. Raw devices bypass the normal buffer mechanism and use direct-disk transfers to the VACCESS program. For raw devices, the transfer rate is proportional to the block size. This provides much higher throughput when the block size exceeds 1,024 bytes.

UNIX makes no logical distinction between the physical devices connected to it and its file system, but the transfer rates can vary dramatically. Ordinary files are organized into a file system and are maintained by the operating system. Special files are the actual devices available on the system. Raw special files are special files that bypass the UNIX buffering scheme. They are restricted to complete-block transfer (multiple of 512) but are ideal for disk emulation because of the considerable speed advantage.

Figure 7-12 shows the expected transfer rates for the various file types and device structures. Tape devices refer to ordinary files used as variable-record structured devices. The curve labeled "character" refers to the expected transfer rates of ordinary files connected as serial-structured devices. The ordinary, special, and raw-special labeled curves refer to the rates when connected as

Figure 7-12. I/O system performance: *a.* large block sizes; *b.* small block sizes.

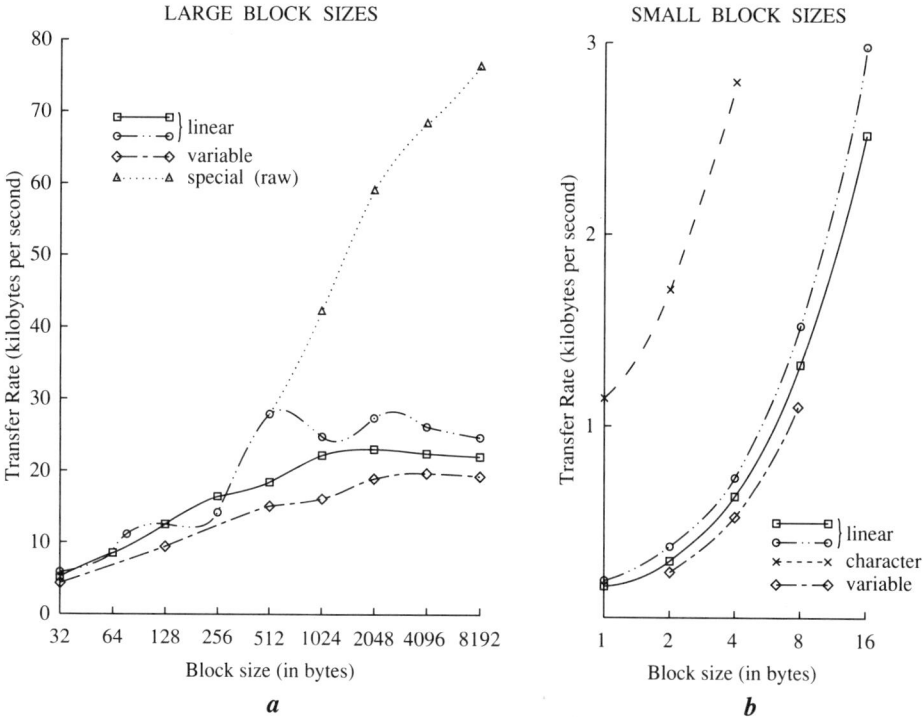

linear devices. The curves were generated using block sizes that are powers of two, but the actual curve between these points may be lower because of the internal blocking used by the UNIX file system. Data for block sizes corresponding to card image and print images (80 and 132 bytes, respectively) fit very closely to the curve.

LABORATORY USAGE EXAMPLES

In this section we will examine several examples of experimental laboratory usage. At Stanford, we have pursued three basic areas of experimentation:

1. Emulation of conventional architectures
2. Interpretation monitoring
3. High-level-language emulation

Our efforts at monitoring have covered both conventional and high-level-language machines.

An Example of Conventional Emulation

We have undertaken the construction of about a dozen conventional-machine emulators in our laboratory. One of the first complete systems was that for a PDP-11, which we will discuss here (Neuhauser 1977a). In most conventional machines, the emulator structure follows that of the PDP-11, but some details will be different. Although the instruction set of the PDP-11 is small, its architectural structures are such that they pose some real problems for efficient emulation.

Structure of the PDP-11 Emulator

Figure 7-13 shows the basic structure of the PDP-11 emulator, which consists of two major mechanisms. One decodes and executes PDP-11 instructions, and the other deals with I/O emulation. The basic mechanism, which handles instruction execution, has the following phases:

1. Fetch target instruction and decode
2. Form operands, which includes
   a. Decoding of operand mode
   b. Formation of operand address
   c. Fetch of operand(s)
3. Execution of the required operation
4. Storage of result
5. Setting condition codes (if required)

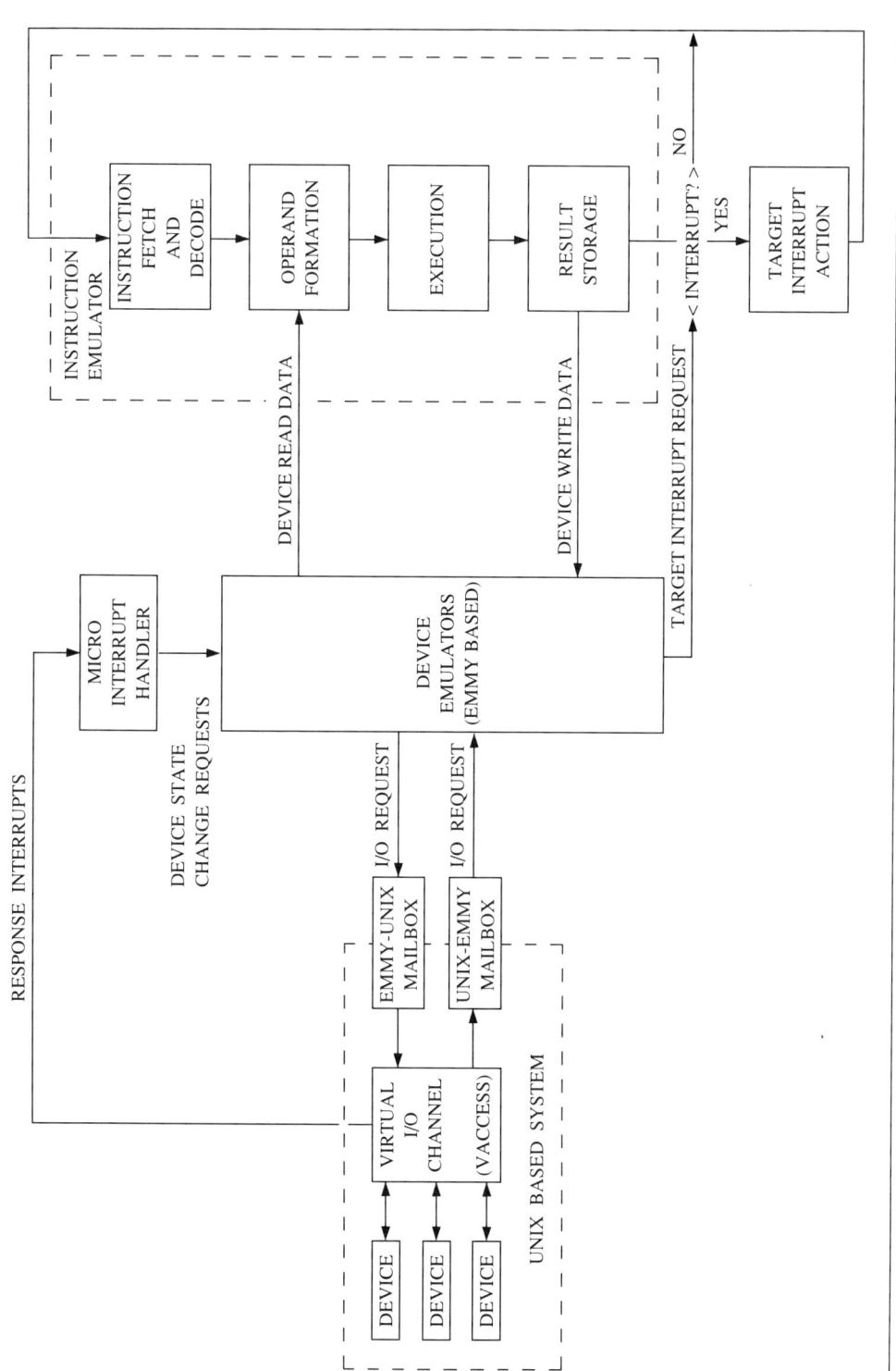

Figure 7-13. Structure of PDP-11 emulator.

The appendix gives an example of the PDP-11 decode, which is probably more complex than that required for most conventional machines.

The mapping of target-processor resources onto host resources in the PDP-11 emulator follows the same general approach as most other emulators. Because the host-processor register set is limited in size, the natural mapping of host registers to target registers is not possible. Instead, we follow this outline:

Host	Usage
Registers	State of current target instruction
	Instruction register
	Source address/operand
	Destination address/operand
	PDP-11 condition code state
Microstore	State target machine
	Register set
	Device emulator state
	Interrupt state
	Decode tables
	Instruction emulator code
	Device emulator code
Main memory	Target main memory

PDP-11 I/O is memory-mapped, meaning that I/O devices are activated as a side effect of accessing a memory location. As a result, every memory access must be checked to see if it refers to an I/O device, and if it does then special action must be taken. If the location accessed is an I/O data register (i.e., where the access will communicate to the I/O device), then the appropriate VACCESS command is formulated, and the I/O action is carried out. When the accessed location is an I/O control register, then the emulator makes a state change to the emulated image of the device, as appropriate. This device image is held in the host processor (the EMMY) and its maintenance is the responsibility of emulator code.

Most of our conventional emulators allow the microcode to be interrupted at any point in the target execution cycle. Interrupts are directed to the indicated device emulator, where the appropriate state change is made. In some cases, this will necessitate an interrupt to the target machine. This interrupt is set aside and will occur only when the target machine begins to fetch a new instruction and is in a state to accept interrupts.

Problems in Conventional Emulation

There are several problems that arise in the construction of a conventional emulated system, some of which include:

1. Target instruction decoding
2. Maintenance of the processor internal state
3. Generation and control of target interrupts
4. Emulation of I/O device actions
5. Validation

Decoding required for PDP-11 instructions is substantially more complex than that for many other processors, such as the S/370. This is because the instruction formats of the PDP-11 are highly encoded and consequently require several decoding steps and some backtracking. In a few cases, all 16 bits of the instruction word must be examined to determine the operation to be performed. Fortunately, the most frequently used instructions are simple, so the average decode time is not excessive. On the whole, however, the PDP-11 decode process consumes more time and space than any other emulator used in the laboratory.

Maintenance of the target processor state in the PDP-11 is a difficult task. This is a result of the "open" structure of the processor state (i.e., PS and PC are maintained in the general register file), which allows any instruction to manipulate the current state in an unstructured way. In many other architectures, the processor state is hidden and may only be accessed by selected instructions. Another aspect of this problem is that condition codes are generated by nearly every PDP-11 instruction execution, and these codes do not correspond directly to the host processor codes either syntactically or semantically. This situation requires that either condition codes be mapped on every target-instruction execution or every access be checked for potential access to the processor state. Both approaches consume host-processor time, but the latter approach was judged to be the most efficient and is used here and in other target-processor emulations. Note that the most frequent condition-code access is by conditional branches, and these instructions can be implemented to access the EMMY-generated codes directly. Fortunately, the processor-state word is in the reserved I/O memory area, and normal operand checks for an I/O access can also trap the PSW accesses without additional overhead. When accesses to the PSW do occur, the internal EMMY formatted codes must be converted to an equivalent PDP-11 format.

Interrupts and the detection of changes in interrupt priority level also present an emulation problem. In hardware realizations of the PDP-11, potential interrupts are maintained in the device controllers and are sent to the processor only when the CPU priority is appropriate. In the emulator, this action must be simulated and requires the use of a list of pending interrupts, which must be scanned whenever the priority level changes. Since program actions can change the conditions under which interrupts may be generated, provisions must be made to remove interrupts from the pending list. Unfortunately, the exact conditions under which a device generates interrupts were not always clear from the PDP-11 documentation, and it was sometimes necessary to consult schematic drawings or perform tests on actual hardware to determine the proper sequence of actions.

Emulation of I/O devices can sometimes require as much effort as the construction of the basic code emulator. This task is usually simplified somewhat by ignoring complex error and maintenance modes, that is, assuming that target programs operate the devices correctly. Because I/O status registers are memory-mapped, every memory access must be checked to determine if it lies in the I/O address spectrum when required to activate the appropriate I/O device emulation microcode.

The emulated processor must be identical functionally to the intended target. Although an existing ISP description of the PDP-11 processor was used (DEC 1971), it was found to be ambiguous and in places erroneous. Initial checkout of the emulator was performed by hand, using the processor description as a guide. Next, the processor diagnostic tests were executed (DEC 1970) until all applicable tests were completed correctly (i.e., not all tests for error actions were performed). Finally, actual user code consisting of the UNIX operating system and associated programs was run.

Interestingly, the diagnostic tests did not detect all errors in the emulation. This was because they were limited in nature and could only check conditions foreseen by the diagnostic programmer, who must ultimately rely on the processor description. In a sense, the only true test for target-processor validity is the ability to transfer programs between the emulated and actual machines and have their execution produce equivalent results.

Emulator Characteristics

Performance of the PDP-11 emulation of the EMMY was measured directly by a program that executed each target instruction 10,000 times and measured the execution time required. Figure 7-14 summarizes the results of this measurement and compares it with representative execution times for the PDP-11/05 (DEC 1975). Basic instruction-execution time in the emulator includes the time spent in instruction fetch, decoding, and execution. In this area, the emulator was about six to seven times slower than the actual PDP-11/05. Most of this degradation is due to the complex decoding process required. Operand formation by the emulator is only about one-half the speed of the hardware target processor, reflecting the simpler nature of this task.

Direct measurements of the emulator execution rate were also made by a frequency counter triggered once every target fetch cycle. These measurements indicated that the target processor executes about 50,000 instructions per second, which corresponds to approximately one-fifth of the hardware execution rate (Snow and Siewiorek 1978). Emulation of the PDP-11 architecture requires about 2K words of control store, allocated as follows:

Function	Words
PDP-11 state and registers	16
Operand decode tables	40
EMMY interrupt vectors	18
Constants and masks	76
Code emulator	1,128
I/O and device emulator	462
Total	1,740

Although most of the microstore words need only be read, about 50 words are required to be read/write. These include PDP-11 state information, EMMY interrupt vectors, and device-status registers. Storage requirements for this emulator are about equivalent to those reported for a PDP-11/20 emulation on the Nanodata QM-1 (Demco and Marsland 1975).

Other emulators constructed on the emulation laboratory base show performance figures similar to the PDP-11/05. Figure 7-15 summarizes the characteristics of the emulators written to date. For most conventional processors (i.e., machine-language-based) performance is in the range of 50K IPS regardless of the apparent external complexity.

Interpretive-Monitoring Examples

One of the most important uses of our emulation facility is in the collection of detailed instruction-stream (I-stream) data. This is done through a process called interpretive monitoring, in which a target-machine emulator is instrumented to capture I-stream events during program execution. Although the event detection and counting process requires some overhead, it is small enough that the overall emulator still runs at a usable and comfortable rate.

The EMMY architecture is well suited to the process of interpretive monitoring, since the microstore is writable and is usually only 50% utilized (i.e., 2K words) by the emulator code. The remaining area is available for counter storage. Storing of the counters in microstore also prevents interference with the use of main memory for representation of the target main-memory resource. A major advantage of the interpretive-monitoring approach is that the event-counting mechanism may be designed to capture data related to a particular architectural artifact. We will give an example where a specific call sequence is identified and tabulated. Because the target machine is interpreted, its internal state is completely available. This allows reasonably complex events to be detected.

Another important advantage of interpretive monitoring is that event detection may be enabled or disabled by a number of means, especially methods related to execution conditions. For example, in some experiments we have

Figure 7-14. PDP-11 emulator performance. All timings are in μsec. Additional time is required by both processors to access byte operands.

Operation	EMMY	PDP-11/05
ADD, BIS ...	24-25	3.7
CMP, BIT ...	21	2.5
MOV ...	25	3.7
CLR, COM ...	20-22	3.4
ASL, ROR ...	20-25	3.4
TST ...	17	2.2

Operation Timing

Mode	Form	EMMY SRC/DST	PDP-11/05 SRC	PDP-11/05 DST
0	R	0.0	0.0	0.0
1	(R)	1.4	0.9	0.9
2	(R)+	2.3	0.9	2.4
3	@(R)+	5.1	2.4	3.4
4	-(R)	2.4	0.9	2.4
5	@-(R)	5.3	2.4	3.4
6	X(R)	6.5	2.4	3.4
7	@X(R)	6.5	3.4	4.7

Operand Timing

Branch Result	EMMY	PDP-11/05
Successful	15	2.5
Unsuccessful	12	1.9

Branch Timing

disabled the counting mechanism during operating-system or user execution, thus allowing us to determine execution characteristics of each area independently. Some experiments have disabled event counting during the computation of mathematical functions to determine the effect of coprocessor operation on instruction-stream characteristics.

In the sections that follow, we will briefly outline the interpretive-monitoring approach used on several emulators, the PDP-11 (Neuhauser 1979), the S/370, and a P-code machine (Alpert 1979). Selected results are presented to give the reader a feel for the types of analysis carried out in the laboratory and how the use of interpretive monitoring has made these analyses possible.

Figure 7-15. Summary of laboratory emulators.

EMULATOR	WORDS	KIPS	SUPPORTS
IBM S/370	2600	50	PL 360 O/S, FORTRAN, and PASCAL object
DEC PDP-11	1700	50	Mini-UNIX
DG NOVA 3	1000	50	RDOS
R/C 4000	1000	45	Simple O/S
MDS (8080)	1000	80	Basic ROM monitor
CDC 6400	1700	45	Test programs
P- CODE	1900	70	PASCAL compiler
DELTRAN	800	80	FORTRAN benchmarks
ADEPT	2500	-	PASCAL benchmarks

The PDP-11 Interpretive Monitor and Examples

Analysis of the PDP-11 architecture by interpretive monitoring was a direct follow-up to the construction and debugging of the emulator. One attractive feature was that the emulator had an I/O device repertoire capable of supporting UNIX, and this would allow examination of a wide variety of code bases, including UNIX utilities, applications, and tools.

Once the emulator was operational, the structure was modified at selected points to gather data as the interpreter unraveled the instruction execution. Figure 7-16 shows the overall flow of instruction emulation and the placement of data-capture points. During emulator execution, the information at each point is encoded (in a very simple way) and set aside. When target-instruction execution is complete, the monitor is entered, and the captured data is decoded and used to activate counters.

Approximately 2,000 counters were maintained by the emulator. These tabulated the following information:

- *Operator type:* There is one counter for each of the PDP-11 opcodes (about 100 in all).
- *Operand mode and register:* Each source and destination mode and its associated registers were recorded. Registers were grouped as PC, stack pointers, and general registers following the UNIX convention for this machine.
- *Branch offset:* The direction and amount of relative branches are recorded when the branch is taken.
- *Branch outcome:* The branch outcome and direction are tabulated for all the types of conditional branches.

For the PDP-11 emulation, the measurement environment was primarily UNIX. We made a small architectural extension to the PDP-11 PSW, which allowed the emulator to control the enabling of the monitor. We also made small changes to the UNIX kernel to flag entrances and exits to the operating system and to indicate when "interpreted" execution of unavailable PDP-11 instruction was undertaken. This later extension was quite useful, since it allowed us to tabulate execution of a floating-point instruction as one instruction, even though our emulator did not support floating point. Instead, these operations were carried out by the PDP-11 target machine but masked from the event-monitor mechanism. For programs with a very low floating-point content (i.e., 1% or 2%), this was an adequate and not inefficient approach.

A major analysis effort in the laboratory related to the PDP-11 architecture involved 28 programs, many consisting of over a million executed instructions. Details are given in figure 7-17. Most data taken included user and operating-system-code execution. At the completion of each run, the counter data was unloaded and analyzed in the support processor. This included correlating the counter data with known characteristics of the PDP-11 architecture.

Figure 7-16. PDP-11 interpretive monitor structure.

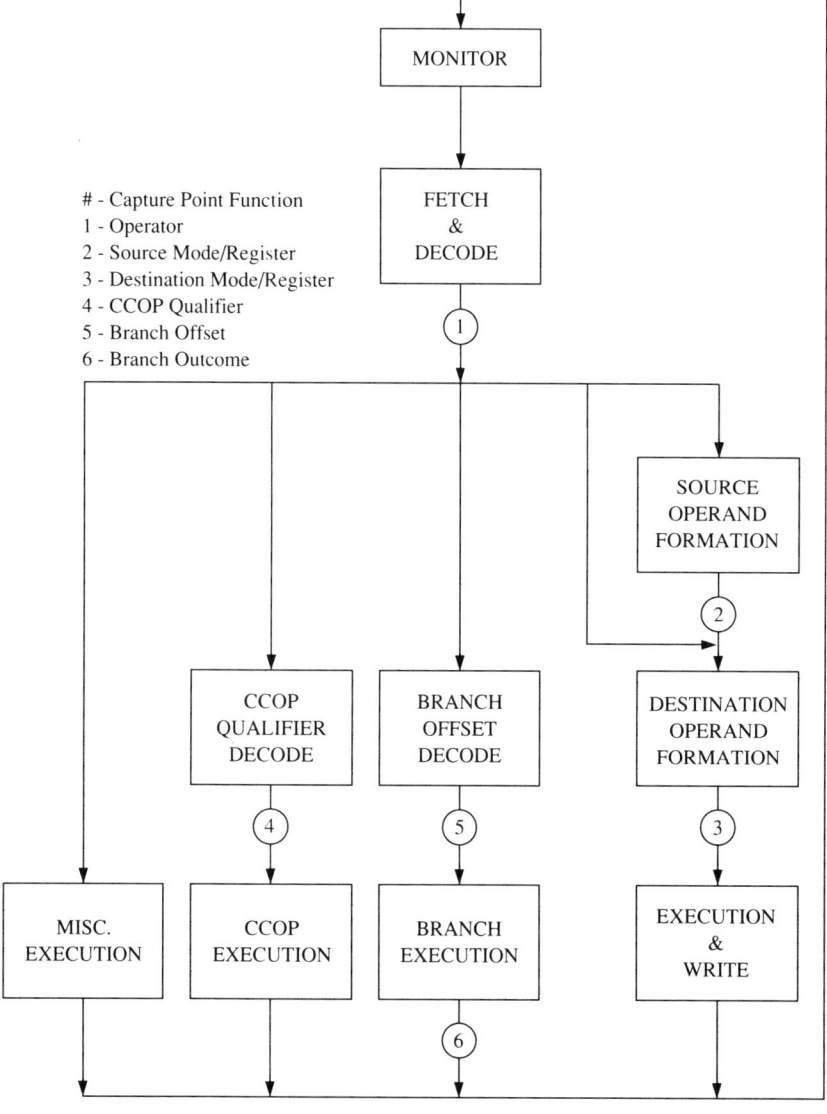

Figure 7-18 gives an example of the results, in which the operand access modes are analyzed to produce data related to the memory and register-access characteristics of each mode.

Branch direction and distance for taken branches is easily measured, since the results of every branch are known by the emulator. Figure 7-19 shows the results averaged over all programs run.

One interesting result of our study is the overhead related to subroutine calling in C programs. Since this is very stylized in UNIX, we were able to detect

Figure 7-17. PDP-11 analyzed program set.

Name	Command	Lang	Length	Description
Translation				
T1	cc -P	c	1,525,427	Macro preprocessor for C compiler
T2	cc -s	c	3,024,003	Compiler from C to assembly code
T3	emxl	c	5,125,722	EMMY microassembler
T4	rc	c	9,373,978	Ratfor FORTRAN preprocessor
T5	as	asm	2,138,721	Assembly of ASM language program
T6	as	asm	2,935,479	Assembly of C produced ASM code
T7	fc	asm	10,331,547	FORTRAN compilation
Information Organizing				
I1	icheck	c	1,592,082	File system consistency check
I2	cref	c	10,135,141	C program cross-reference generation
I3	sort	c	1,077,105	General file sort
I4	diff	c	754,765	File comparison
I5	typo	c	8.767,411	Locate spelling errors
I6	nroff	asm	15,040,112	Text formatting
I7	chess	asm/c	7,280,244	One move in chess
I8	db	asm	4,870,364	Object code decompilation
System-oriented				
S1	ls	c	1,352,584	Show directory contents
S2	ps	c	572,909	Show process status
S3	cp	c	421,742	Copy a file
S4	date	c	123,021	Show time of day
S5	ar	c	1,105,739	Show contents of archive file
S6	strip	asm	408,265	Compress a load module
S7	du	asm	549,873	Show current disk usage
S8	mkdir	asm	142,735	Make a directory node
S9	rmdir	asm	147,567	Remove a directory node
S10	time	asm	224,867	Measure "null" program execution time
Computational				
C1	janzen	fort	351,271	Computation of constants
C2	whetstone	fort	592,633	Synthetic FORTRAN benchmark (reduced)
C3	fft	fort	953,596	Fast Fourier transform benchmark
		Total	90,918,903	

Figure 7-18. PDP-11 operand access characteristics (accesses per instruction).

Access	Register	Memory
Instruction		1.000
Displacement		0.209
Data Read	0.329	0.453
Data Write	0.292	0.220
Address	0.706	0.040
Misc. Read	0.075	0.033
Misc. Write	0.075	0.050
All Reads	1.110	1.755
All Writes	0.366	0.270
Total	1.476	2.005

each instance of a call and establish from the code used a cost (in instructions executed) for calls. Results for the C-coded programs are shown in figure 7-20. On the average, calling accounts for over 20% of the executed instruction stream.

We tested several programs to determine the percentage of the I stream devoted to user and operating-system execution. Even though the results varied widely, as shown in figure 7-21, the operating system always accounted for a very large share of total execution. We were also able to characterize dynamic characteristics of system and user code independently, since we could control monitor enabling as discussed earlier. Generally, our measurements showed that system code was slightly more efficient in that it used shorter instructions and fewer memory and state accesses per instruction and made more use of registers. This is probably a natural result of the more careful coding practices that are applied to system-code development.

The S/370 Interpretive Monitor and Examples

An extensive study of machine architectures and compiler effects was conducted in the laboratory (Huck 1983). In this study, the S/370, VAX, PDP-11, and a P-code machine were compared across a set of common programs. Various levels of compiler optimization were also tried on the S/370 and VAX in an attempt to separate architectural and compiler effects. Interpretive monitors, supported by EMMY, were used to gather data for all machines except VAX. For this architecture, a software-monitoring approach was used, in which a control program single-stepped the program under test on a VAX host.

Instrumentation of the S/370 was simpler than that required for the PDP-11, reflecting the more organized structure of the S/370 emulation. Basically, a

Figure 7-19. Branch distance for taken relative branches.

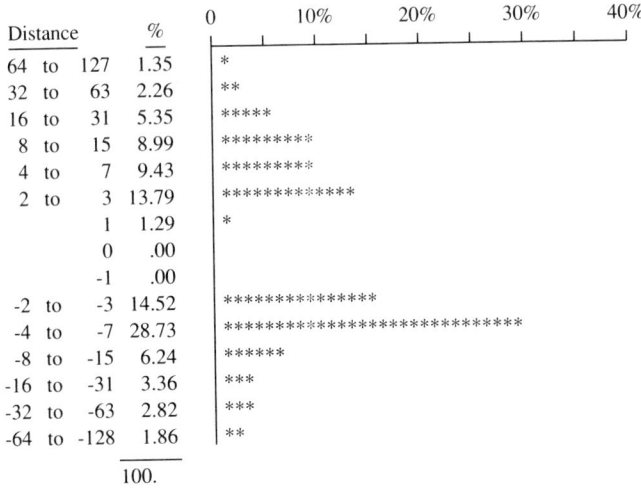

Distance			%
64	to	127	1.35
32	to	63	2.26
16	to	31	5.35
8	to	15	8.99
4	to	7	9.43
2	to	3	13.79
		1	1.29
		0	.00
		-1	.00
-2	to	-3	14.52
-4	to	-7	28.73
-8	to	-15	6.24
-16	to	-31	3.36
-32	to	-63	2.82
-64	to	-128	1.86
			100.

tabulation of the first byte of the instruction is sufficient to determine opcode and operand requirements of an instruction. Branch statistics (direction, outcome, and distance) are also collected. Monitoring was added to the S/370 emulator quite a while after the original emulator design (Wallach 1975), and thus a "bolt on" approach was used in which the monitor was entered at the start of

Figure 7-20. C-program calling-sequence characteristics.

Pgm	% JSR	% JSR's with R5	% Calls	% Calling Overhead	Command
T1	6.03	36.76	2.22	35.52	cc -P
T2	4.32	32.51	1.40	22.40	cc
T3	6.42	20.68	1.33	21.28	emxl
T4	4.66	31.24	1.46	23.36	rc
I1	3.57	36.46	1.30	20.80	icheck
I2	5.20	22.51	1.15	18.40	cref
I3	5.37	19.29	1.04	16.64	sort
I4	4.47	35.93	1.61	25.76	diff
I5	5.67	30.13	1.71	27.36	typo
S1	5.90	20.71	1.22	19.52	ls
S2	7.01	20.02	1.40	22.40	ps
S3	2.91	25.26	1.00	16.00	cp
S4	2.67	26.10	.70	11.20	date
S5	6.67	23.31	1.55	24.80	ar
mean	5.06	27.21	1.36	21.76	

Figure 7-21. System/user instruction usage.

Prog	% User	% System	Description
T2	70.6	29.4	C compilation
T6	51.2	48.8	FORTRAN compilation
I3	49.9	50.1	Cross-reference listing
S1	26.1	73.1	Directory listing

every instruction. At this point, the next instruction to be executed is decoded by the monitor and tabulated. Although the instruction is redecoded by the emulator for execution, the loss of efficiency is not important.

Programs examined in the comparative-analysis study were smaller than those used in the PDP-11 study discussed above. This resulted from the goal of executing common benchmarks on several architectures and the necessity of simplifying the benchmarks so that comparable results could be obtained. For the S/370, the benchmarks were also run under five different compiler-optimization schemes. The four benchmarks were:

> FFT: Calculate a 256-point complex FFT
> SORT: Quick sort of 100 random elements
> MOST: Translation of FORTRAN to MORTRAN
> NORM: Integration of a system of differential equations based on an adaptive technique

Figure 7-22 shows a sample result for the four benchmarks on four different architectures. The data presented is the number of register references per instruction executed. Figure 7-23 compares total memory read and write accesses across the architectures and benchmarks.

To detect compiler effects, the benchmark programs were measured after being compiled at several different optimization levels (G, H0, H1, H2, H3). Results are compared to the instruction stream of an idealized architecture, referred to as the CIF, or canonical interpretive form (Flynn and Hoevel 1979; Flynn 1980). The CIF characteristics are determined directly from the high-level-language representation of the benchmark.

Figure 7-22. Register references per executed instruction.

	FFT	Mort	Norm	Sort	Average
S/370 FORTRAN Hopt1	2.43	2.04	2.41	2.15	2.26
P-code PASCAL	2.26	2.13	2.22	2.16	2.20
VAX FORTRAN	2.51	1.90	2.83	2.03	2.32
PDP-11 C	2.31	1.74	2.31	2.86	2.06

Figure 7-23. Memory object accesses.

		FFT	Mort	Norm	Sort
READS	CI	104,512	4,695,823	1,235,963	1,243,603
	S/370 FORTRAN Hopt1	71,501	2,926,849	638,385	369,326
	P-code PASCAL	194,291	3,054,908	1,493,070	1,062,216
	VAX FORTRAN	202,853	2,975,244	1,458,185	824,856
	PDP-11 C	206,660	3,043,367	1,452,330	771,243

		FFT	Mort	Norm	Sort
WRITES	CI	22,459	567,463	207,573	246,665
	S/370 FORTRAN Hopt1	28,583	586,084	177,709	97,120
	P-code	23,357	556,242	209,878	246,665
	VAX FORTRAN	71,031	666,794	271,272	248,873
	PDP-11 C	30,162	586,474	258,145	247,056

Figure 7-24 shows the improvement in number of instructions executed (relative to CIF) for higher levels of compiler optimization. Memory read and write references are shown in figure 7-25.

High-Level-Language Emulation

For many years, our laboratory has been engaged in the study of architectures to directly support the execution of high-level languages (Hoevel and Flynn 1979; Flynn 1980; Wakefield 1983). The emulation facility has provided an efficient way to construct, operate, and measure various high-level-language execution architectures, which we refer to here as direct-execution languages (DELs). We have developed DEL emulators for FORTRAN and Pascal.

Figure 7-24. Instructions executed per CI operation.

		FFT	Mort	Norm	Sort	Average
CI		1	1	1	1	1
S/370 FORTRAN	G	4.76	3.47	4.50	3.01	3.93
	Hopt0	7.19	3.23	6.03	3.28	4.93
	Hopt1	4.27	2.21	3.79	2.11	3.10
	Hopt2	2.34	1.83	1.40	1.73	1.83
	Hopt3	2.30	1.82	1.26	1.73	1.78
S/370 PASCAL/VS		3.57	2.97	3.04	2.66	3.06

Figure 7-25. Memory access (in thousands).

			FFT	Mort	Norm	Sort
READS		CI	23	567	208	247
	S/370 FORTRAN	G	46	618	365	258
		Hopt0	95	964	730	295
		Hopt1	29	586	178	97
		Hopt2	24	614	157	108
		Hopt3	24	614	156	108
	S/370 PASCAL/VS		27	589	274	247

			FFT	Mort	Norm	Sort
WRITES		CI	105	4,696	1,236	1,244
	S/370 FORTRAN	G	147	6,270	1,773	1,301
		Hopt0	221	5,425	2,195	1,348
		Hopt1	72	2,926	638	369
		Hopt2	53	2,219	403	292
		Hopt3	51	2,208	397	292
	S/370 PASCAL/VS		110	3,760	1,222	987

The theory behind DEL processor architecture is fairly complex, but the basic issues are:

1. Direct correspondence between verbs in the target language and the instructions in the DEL host
2. Structuring of operations to provide all the basic forms necessary, thus minimizing the use of temporary storage
3. Explicit representation of current execution environments so that object accesses can be encoded in an efficient way (The current environment usually corresponds to the subroutine.)

In general, the DEL equivalent for a particular high-level language should improve program size, I-stream and data-stream performance, and execution time relative to conventional architecture. In fact, it should approach the ideal performance characteristics of the executed program, as represented by the CIF, or canonical interpretive form, referred to earlier.

To test the above claims, we have developed a DEL architecture for Pascal called ADEPT (Wakefield 1983). The basic ADEPT instruction format consists of a variable number of variable width fields, where the initial field (the "format" field) defines the organization of the following fields. Emulation is structurally similar to that for conventional architectures consisting of a decode, operand formation, execute, and result-storage stage. Operand formations differ from conventional emulations in that operand "addresses" are really pointers to the descriptors, which are valid for the current environment, referred to as a "contour" (Johnston 1971). The emulator manages the "caching" of the contours so that the descriptors most likely to be referenced are maintained in the host microstore. In the case of EMMY, the writable microstore is a real efficiency benefit, and about half the 4K words are used for descriptor storage. The ADEPT emulator also contains facilities for monitoring the activity of execution and gathering performance data.

Our major experiment with the ADEPT DEL involved a set of five benchmark programs. These were executed on five target machines: the HP-1000, S/370, VAX, P-code engine (Alpert 1979), and ADEPT. Statistics for the HP-1000 and VAX were gathered by step simulators, hosted by the target machines. The other architectures were hosted on EMMY. Specific measures were taken in a number of areas, including:

- Static program size
- Instructions executed
- Instruction bytes fetched
- Data bytes read
- Data bytes written

A summary of the data is presented in figures 7-26, 7-27, and 7-28. Figure 7-28 summarizes the average across architectures and programs, showing the characteristics of other architectures relative to ADEPT.

The quantitative case for DEL structures is quite strong. Further research remains to be done to determine the cost/performance tradeoffs between DELs and conventional architectures.

CONCLUSIONS AND DIRECTIONS
Improving the Emulation Environment

While the basic emulation-laboratory architecture and implementation has proven adequate to the tasks undertaken, there are many areas where improvements could be made, particularly if costs were less of a constraint. The comments that follow apply to the EMMY host and support system in the experimental "one of a kind" environment. If EMMY were required to be successful in a commercial environment, a different set of basic constraints would apply, and thus the avenues for enhancement might be different.

The application of parallelism to several areas of the emulator host architec-

Figure 7-26. Architecture/program characteristics for memory accesses.

	Test Program	ADEPT	HP 1000	IBM 370	P-code	VAX
MEMORY BYTES READ	FFT	171,344	888,915	402,906	691,916	n.a.
	Kalman	50,792	426,058	425,898	459,931	358,628
	Puzzle	3,673,524	11,457,546	16,935,356	18,546,857	10,535,920
	Sort	657,696	2,973,946	3,535,328	4,964,928	n.a.
	Walk	222,972	616,728	1,864,263	741,429	n.a.

	Test Program	ADEPT	HP 1000	IBM 370	P-code	VAX
MEMORY BYTES WRITTEN	FFT	1.00	3.84	2.39	1.51	n.a.
	Kalman	1.00	12.50	20.27	10.34	18.90
	Puzzle	1.00	31.51	31.97	25.30	21.98
	Sort	1.00	4.09	4.33	4.27	n.a.
	Walk	1.00	10.87	41.78	4.54	n.a.

ture would yield the greatest improvement in performance. There are several areas which could be considered:

1. Parallelism within basic microinstruction execution
2. Independent instruction decode
3. Special support for address formation and memory access

Figure 7-27. Architecture/program characteristics relative to ADEPT.

	Test Program	ADEPT	HP 1000	IBM 370	P-code	VAX
INSTRUCTIONS EXECUTED	FFT	1.00	3.87	1.35	3.46	n.a.
	Kalman	1.00	3.70	3.53	3.80	3.84
	Puzzle	1.00	2.52	3.16	3.69	2.29
	Sort	1.00	4.21	3.02	3.97	n.a.
	Walk	1.00	3.44	6.05	2.93	n.a.
	Average	1.00	3.55	3.42	3.57	3.07

	Test Program	ADEPT	HP 1000	IBM 370	P-code	VAX
INSTRUCTION BYTES READ (PER INSTR.)	FFT	1.00	3.67	1.87	5.09	n.a.
	Kalman	1.00	3.15	3.88	4.51	5.54
	Puzzle	1.00	1.89	3.54	4.49	1.83
	Sort	1.00	2.46	3.24	4.53	n.a.
	Walk	1.00	1.68	3.92	1.99	n.a.
	Average	1.00	2.57	3.29	4.12	3.69

Figure 7-28. Measures relative to ADEPT (average across architecture and programs).

Measure	Relative to ADEPT
Instructions executed	3.46
Main memory bytes read for instructions	3.37
Main memory object reads for data	6.74
Main memroy bytes read for data	5.42
Main memory object writes for data	16.00
Main memory bytes written for data	14.73
Instructions executed between branches taken	2.26
Instruction bytes read between branches taken	2.40
Static size of executable code	2.76
Static size of executable code and environmental data	2.11

Although the basic structure of microexecution was intended to operate in a parallel manner, cost constraints required that an instruction be executed in a strictly serial manner. Thus, the T-, A-, and I-machine parallelism discussed previously was replaced with strictly sequential execution. To reduce resource cost even more, we have used multiple clock steps to implement basic micromachine operations, such as long shifts. Most EMMY instructions could be executed within one clock cycle, since they usually make a single state change to the register set. A few A-machine instructions (such as those modifying indirect pointers) would probably still require multiple cycles in any reasonable implementation. A parallel implementation, on a technology base comparable to that used in the original EMMY (10K ECL), would probably yield a processor with five to ten times the current performance.

Parallelism could profitably be applied at a higher level with the addition of specialized units to support independent target-instruction decode, address generation, and memory access. This would, of course, result in a structure similar to that of pipelined mainframe processors. Instruction fetch and decode, for example, occupies about 50% to 60% of the host emulator time in conventional machine emulations we have tested. This is partially a result of the heavy dependence that emulators make of host instructions that shift and rotate data. In the EMMY, this is not efficiently supported, due to cost limitations. Our estimate is that an adequate instruction-decode unit would enhance target-processor performance by almost a factor of two.

An independent unit for address formation and limited memory protection would also enhance performance, although to a lesser extent. We estimate that address-decode assist would lead to about 30% improvement in target performance.

Limited use of residual control techniques might also yield some performance improvements. The current architecture makes no use of residual control, and as a result every target instruction is handled without any a priori knowledge of its characteristics. For example, our current main-memory interface is very flexible, but on every access the microcoder must form and issue the appropriate command to cause translation of the address, alignment of data, and parity checking. A useful extension would be to allow the microcoder to establish the parameters of a limited set of accesses in the memory controller. These would be called out directly by a code embedded in the microinstruction, initiating the access. This simple extension would save a few host cycles on every main-memory access. Residual control techniques might also be applied to the specification of insert/extract rotation and masking parameters, since very few types of insert/extract instructions constitute a large majority of the host execution cycle for a given target architecture.

Other suggestions for improving laboratory capabilities include:

- Specialized hardware for the support of interpretive monitoring, such as counters that could be triggered from microcode (Huck 1983)
- Special support for the implementation of DEL contours (Wakefield 1983)

Experience in the Emulation Laboratory

When we began construction of our emulation facility, we had several potential uses in mind. The first was purely educational, in that the laboratory would provide a convenient base for students to undertake emulation construction of existing machines. The second and third objectives were basically research-oriented. We hoped to apply our emulators to the dynamic measurement of instruction-stream characteristics and to the development of unconventional architectures. Below we review our experiences in these areas.

Conventional Emulation

As an educational tool, we feel that the laboratory has proven itself very useful. For a number of years, our laboratory was the basic instrument used to support an ongoing series of graduate-level seminars and special projects in computer architecture and emulation. A number of projects involved constructing and testing emulators for conventional processor architectures. It is usually possible to build an emulator for the basic instruction set of a processor in about one academic quarter of effort. For simple machines, this might also include some limited I/O. For complex machines, additional time is required to extend their capabilities to I/O, floating point, and special instruction sets.

Students have found the emulation task to be manageable and quite rewarding, since the final result is a target machine that can run real code. The process of construction provides very useful experience in a number of areas, such as interpreting architectural specifications, resolving ambiguities, and validating the design. We believe that these are important lessons and that the experience transfers well to the "real world," industrial environment.

Interpretive Monitoring

In the area of interpretive monitoring, the laboratory has proven useful, but cannot be viewed as an unqualified success. If we discount the effort to construct and validate an emulator, the interpretive-monitor approach is a reasonably efficient approach to data collection. It has the advantage of allowing one to collect data over a very large program base, to examine all aspects of execution (i.e., user and system code), and to do so at relatively low cost. A further advantage is that one need not have the actual target machine available.

The cost in time and effort of emulator construction, however, is not trivial. The three machines we examined in depth through interpretive monitoring (PDP-11, S/370, and P-code) were built initially as student projects and later modified to support monitoring. Adding a monitor to an emulator is about the same level of effort as would be required to add a "single step" monitor to a real implementation of a target processor. If the code base to be studied does not require efficient operation, that is, it is not interactive and is of a reasonable size, then the use of the actual machine is probably more efficient from the user's point of view. Statistics for the VAX architecture were gathered with a software monitor and were quite satisfactory, although they consumed a prodigious number of machine cycles.

Recent architectural studies in the laboratory have been carried out using a different technique, called basic-block analysis (Mitchell 1988). In this approach, a benchmark program is compiled into a specific target language (usually P-code) and divided into *basic blocks*, which are unbroken sequences of instructions. The resultant code is executed interpretively, and execution counts are obtained for each basic block as a unit. This, together with the compiled code, represents general characteristics of the benchmark without reference to its execution on a particular architecture. Characteristics from architectures to be compared are calculated algorithmically from the basic-block information and the specific way an architecture would handle each basic block. Our work so far has indicated that this approach will be an efficient way to compare a range of architectural features. The level of detail of the comparison should approximate that of our previous interpretively based studies.

High-Level-Language Emulation

Experimentation with high-level-language execution, as represented by DELs, has been very rewarding. We have been able to demonstrate that certain architectural structures will lead to significant improvement in important execution parameters, such as code size and memory traffic. Results obtained in the laboratory are limited in some important ways. First, the constructed emulations only support a particular high-level language (one supports Pascal and the other FORTRAN). The characteristics of an efficient multilanguage DEL have yet to be determined.

Second, the hardware cost of an efficient DEL engine relative to a conventional engine has not been characterized. Efficient support of a DEL would require hardware structures that are much different from conventional machines. Although the EMMY host and its environment support DEL emulations reasonably well, they were really designed for conventional machine emulation. More work needs to be done to determine the nature of an efficient DEL host machine.

APPENDIX A: DETAILS OF EMMY INSTRUCTION SET

For completeness, we present here the details of the EMMY host instruction set and an example of its usage. Some data on code frequency is also provided.

Basic Instruction Format

An EMMY "instruction" is a 32-bit word, which provides encoded control information to the T, A, and I machines. Ideally, the instruction word would provide simultaneous control of all three resource machines. Given the limited word width and the need for introducing immediate data quantities, we had to compromise on full generality. Our approach was to partition the instruction into two parts (left and right). These are assigned to functions, as shown in figure 7-29.

Instructions sometimes specify no action for a particular machine. If no I-machine action is specified, then the next microinstruction is taken implicitly from the following word.

Register Resources

The register file is the central EMMY resource. There are eight registers, all of which may be accessed by any instruction. Only register 0 has unusual properties, since it controls the state of the processor. In fact, it controls and presents *all* the user-visible states of the processor. Figure 7-30 outlines the format of register 0. Its basic components are:

Item	Bits	Description
CC	8	Processor-generated condition codes
IC	8	Target-generated indicator codes
STATE	4	Host processor state
MAR	12	Next microinstruction address

Figure 7-29. Basic microinstruction formats.

Format	31 — "LEFT HALF" — 18	17 — "RIGHT HALF" — 00
I	T MACHINE CONTROL	IMMEDIATE DATA
II	T MACHINE CONTROL	A MACHINE CONTROL
III	T MACHINE CONTROL	I MACHINE CONTROL
IV	I MACHINE CONTROL	A MACHINE CONTROL
V	I MACHINE CONTROL	I MACHINE CONTROL

The CC flags contain the usual set of condition codes, which are generated by T-machine operations. Operations in the other machines have no effect on the condition codes.

The IC, or indicator codes, are flags that may be set by the user to indicate the state of the target machine. They differ from bits in the other registers in that they may be tested directly by certain instructions.

The processor-state field relates to the control of interrupts and processor execution rate.

The 12-bit MAR provides access for up to 4K of instruction; there is no provision for banking or extending this range. Since the MAR is directly accessible, the next address may be computed using any host instruction. This is very useful in directing the decoding of target-machine instructions. The usual technique is to extract a field from the target instruction and insert it into the MAR, affecting a multiway "case" branch.

T-machine Microinstructions

T-machine instructions provide the primary support for data manipulation. They usually combine two registers and return the result to one of the source registers. T-machine instructions can only appear in the left half of the EMMY instruction word, although some may obtain immediate data from the right half. Figure 7-31 outlines the basic T-machine instruction forms.

When immediate data is required, the right half of the microinstruction provides it. A simple encoding scheme allows an 18-bit quantity to represent useful masks and data, as shown in figure 7-32. This approach is also simple to implement.

The arithmetic, logical and shift/rotate instructions are fairly standard. Arithmetic is limited to simple add and subtract variations. More complex

AN EMULATION ENVIRONMENT AND ITS APPLICATION 323

Figure 7-30. Processor state register.

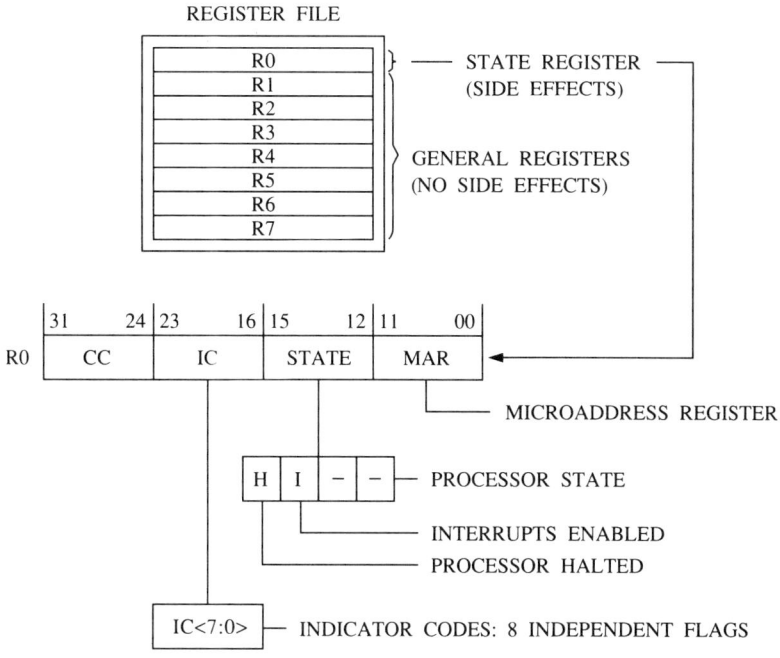
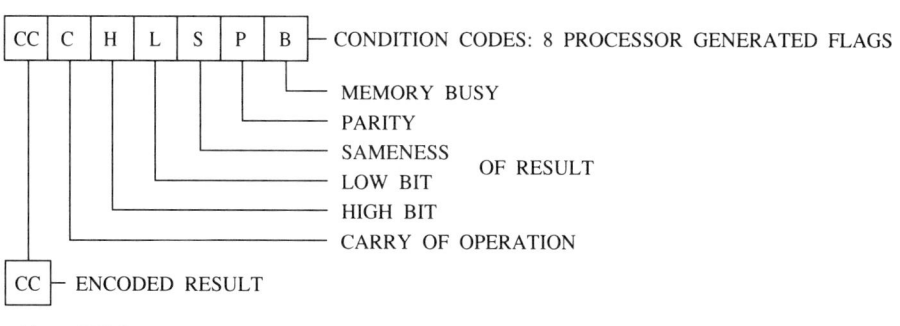

00 — ZERO
01 — LESS THAN
10 — GREATER THAN
11 — OVERFLOW

Figure 7-31. T-machine microinstructions.

31	30	29	28	27	26	25	24	23	22	21	20	19	18	17	16	15	14	13	12	11	10	09	08	07	06	05	04	03	02	01	00
					LEFT HALF																			RIGHT HALF							

	I	OP	BF	AF	OPTIONAL IMMEDIATE DATA

LOGICAL   000
ARITHMETIC   001
SHIFT/ROTATE   010
EXTENDED   011

I - USE IMMEDIATE DATA

OP - OPERATION

BF - OPERAND B REGISTER ADDRESS

AF - OPERAND A REGISTER ADDRESS

EXAMPLES: Reg [AF] ⟸ Reg [AF] OP Reg [BF]

Reg [AF] ⟸ Reg [AF] OP Immediate Data

	POS	BF	AF	MANDATORY IMMEDIATE DATA

100
101

POS - ROTATE AMOUNT

EXAMPLES: Reg [AF] ⟸ (Reg [BF] rotate by POS) ^Immediate Data

Reg [AF] ⟸ ((Reg [BF] rotate by POS) ^Immediate Data) v (Reg [AF]^~Immediate Data))

arithmetic operations are built from the extended-class operations, which perform the following:

- Single-bit multiplication step
- Single-bit conditional divide step
- Addition/subtraction with "excess six" indicator

Repetition on these basic units provides multiply and divide operations for multibit operations.

The insert and extract T-machine microinstructions require a full 32-bit word to specify. These instructions are used for field and bit manipulation. Insert is the more general and works as follows:

1. Rotate contents of source register by amount specified in SHIFT field
2. Insert this quantity into the target register under control of the MASK specified in the immediate-data field
   - If MASK bit is 1, then target register bit takes on rotated source bit value
   - If MASK bit is 0, then target register bit is unchanged

Extract is like insert, except the target register is cleared before insertion; thus, the operation will isolate and align fields from the source register.

A-machine Microinstructions

Figure 7-33 summarizes the A-machine microinstructions, which are primarily concerned with transferring data between memory resources (registers, microstore, and main memory). The three basic instruction forms are:

1. Load register with address
2. Load/store register to microstore
3. Register indirect data movement

The load-address instruction simply loads the lowest 12 bits of a register with 12 bits of immediate data. Its primary purpose is to load the register 0 MAR field with a new microcode address, thus effecting a microcode branch.

Two A-machine instructions allow control-store contents to be moved to and from registers, based on a directly specified 12-bit address.

The indirect-access instruction allows one to move data between registers, microstore, and main memory, based on pointers held in specified registers. These are usually used to communicate with the external memory system. Since all EMMY I/O is memory-mapped, these serve as I/O instructions also. The microprogrammer may also specify optional incrementing or documenting of the pointer registers by small amounts.

Figure 7-32. Expansion of immediate data to full word.

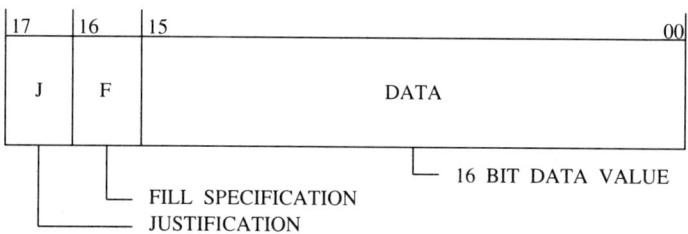

I-machine Microinstructions

I-machine microinstructions may appear on either side of the microinstruction (fig. 7-34). These microinstructions provide a means of introducing conditional executions into the microcode. There are two types of I-machine instructions: conditional and looping.

The conditional I-machine microinstruction may appear in either the left or right half of the microinstruction. Basically, it tests condition or indicator codes under a mask that selects a subset of the codes. The related bits can be combined in simple ways (AND, OR, INVERT) to produce a final result condition. If the condition instruction is in the left half of the microinstruction, it can, depending on the result, suppress the execution of the microinstruction coded in the right half of the instruction. If the conditional microinstruction is coded in the right half, it controls updating of the MAR in register 0, which

Figure 7-33. A-machine microinstructions.

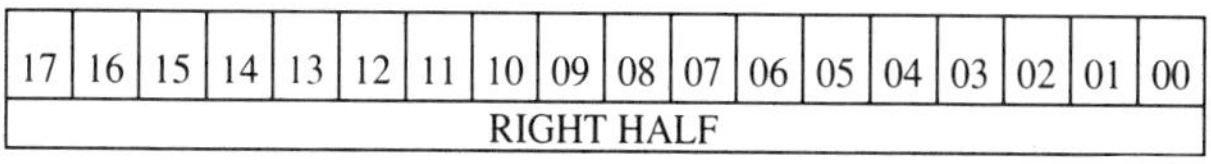

```
|17|16|15|14|13|12|11|10|09|08|07|06|05|04|03|02|01|00|
                        RIGHT HALF
```

LOAD ADDRESS   0 0 1
LOAD REGISTER   0 1 1 | CF | ADDRESS |
STORE REGISTER   1 1 1

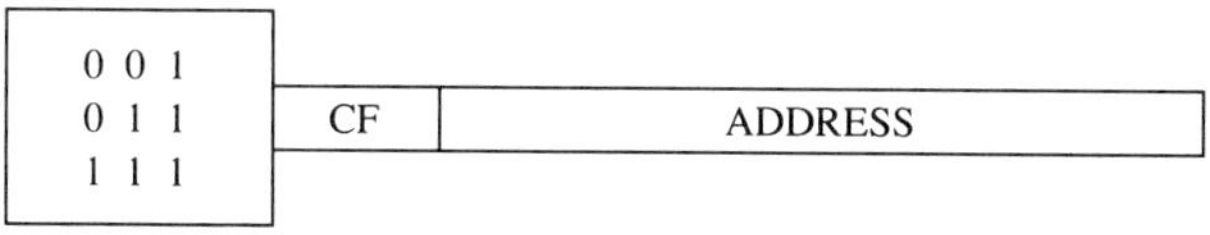

CF – REGISTER FILE OPERAND ADDRESS

ADDRESS – MICROSTORE OPERAND ADDRESS

EXAMPLES: Reg [CF] ⇐ ADDRESS   ; Load Address

Reg [CF] ⇐ MicroStore [Address]   ; Load Register

MicroStore [Address] ⇐ Reg [CF]   ; Store Register

```
                    18   12 11   09 08  07 06   04 03      00
INDIRECT   1 0 1  | CF  |  DF   |  EF  |  OP  |   VAL     |
```

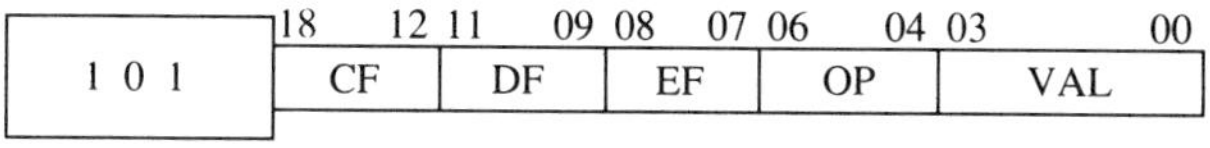

CF – REGISTER FILE OPERAND ADDRESS

DF – REGISTER FILE OPERAND ADDRESS

EF – REGISTER UPDATE SPECIFICATION

OP – OPERAND SOURCE/SINK SPECIFICATION
      – REGISTER FILE
      – MICROSTORE
      – MEMORY SYSTEM

VAL – UPDATE VALUE

EXAMPLES: Reg [CF] ⇐ Reg [DF] ;

Reg [CF] ⇐ MicroStore [DF] ; Reg [DF] ⇐ Reg[DF] + VAL

Memory [CF] ⇐ MicroStore [DF] ; Reg [CF] ⇐ Reg [CF] + VAL

may be incremented by a small value. Two conditionals may be coded in one microinstruction to produce a fairly complex conditional microcode jump.

The loop microinstruction appears only in the right half of a microinstruction. It allows the codes to modify a register by a small constant and, based on the result, to take a short conditional branch. It simplifies coding of short loops, especially those involving repetition of multiply and divide steps.

Interrupts are handled in a very simple manner. They may only occur between microword fetches (*not* between T- and A-machine execution). Register 0 contains the complete state of the host, and when an interrupt occurs, this register is saved in control store at an address specified by the interrupting device. The microinstruction contained in the location following the save location is loaded into register 0, thus effecting a complete change of state.

Instruction Set Usage

Figure 7-35 summarizes the dynamic opcode distribution of the EMMY performing emulation of the ICL 1900 (Rigg 1977). These figures count individual halves of the microinstruction as if they were stand-alone instructions. If a T-machine instruction uses immediate data, it is counted as a single instruction, and the right half (i.e., the immediate data) is not counted as an instruction.

We have made some static and dynamic measurements of instruction format usage with the following results:

Instruction Half		PDP-11	ICL 1900
Left	Right	Static	Dynamic
T control	Immediate data	17%	25%
T or I control	A or I control	34%	47%
Null	A or I control	47%	28%
T control	Null	2%	0%

The high percentage of null usage of the left half of the instruction indicates that our basic instruction-set structure is not so well balanced as it could be. What appears to be needed is a more powerful mechanism to transport data to the register file for use by the T-machine. Perhaps a slightly larger register file would also help, since more useful data would reside there rather than in microstore.

We have examined emulator code on a subjective basis and found that the dynamic usage to which microinstructions are put is roughly the following:

Instruction fetch and decode	60%
Operand formation and fetch	20%
Execution and condition code setting	20%

Figure 7-34. I-machine microinstructions.

```
 31 30 29 28 27 26 25 24 23 22 21 20 19 18
              LEFT HALF
```

T-CONDITIONAL

EXAMPLES:
MASK – SELECT BITS FROM R0 FOR TESTING
OP – TYPE OF TEST
<u>if</u> any bit set in (mask^R0<IC>) <u>then</u> skip right half instruction
<u>if</u> all bits set in (mask^R0<IC>) <u>then</u> execute right half instruction

```
 17 16 15 14 13 12 11 10 09 08 07 06 05 04 03 02 01 00
                     RIGHT HALF
```

A-CONDITIONAL

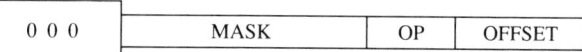

EXAMPLE:
MASK – SELECT BITS FROM R0 FOR TESTING
OP – TYPE OF TEST
OFFSET – VALUE TO ADD TO MAR IF CONDITION MET
<u>if</u> any bit set in (mask^R0<IC>) <u>then</u> goto MAR + VAL

```
 17 16 15 14 13 12 11 10 09 08 07 06 05 04 03 02 01 00
                     RIGHT HALF
```

LOOPING

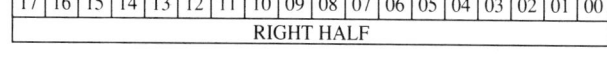

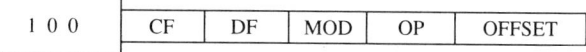

CF – REGISTER OPERAND
DF – REGISTER OPERAND
MOD – REGISTER UPDATE SPECIFICATION
COND – CONDITIONAL TEST SPECIFICATION
OFFSET – VALUE TO ADD TO MAR IF CONDITION IS MET

EXAMPLES:
Reg [CF] ⇐ Reg [CF] -1 ; <u>if</u> Reg [CF] = 0 <u>then</u> <u>goto</u> MAR + 5;
Reg [CF] ⇐ Reg [CF] +1 ; <u>if</u> Reg [CF] > 0 <u>then</u> <u>goto</u> MAR - 5;
Reg [CF] ⇐ Reg [CF] +Reg DF ; <u>if</u> Reg [CF] < 0 <u>then</u> <u>goto</u> $;

Figure 7-35. EMMY microinstruction frequency.

Machine	Instruction	Number	%
T-Machine	Logical	4306	15.4
	Arithmetic	2011	7.2
	Shift/Rotate	0	.0
	Null	4379	15.6
	Extract	1675	6.0
	Insert	600	2.1
	Total	12971	46.3
A-Machine	Load Address	625	2.2
	Load Register	3856	13.7
	Store Register	1700	6.1
	Internal Access	2118	7.5
	External Access	1009	3.6
	Pointer Update	550	2.0
	Total	9858	35.1
I-Machine	T-Conditional	3135	11.2
	A-Conditional	1437	5.1
	Looping	631	2.3
	Total	5203	18.6
Total for all instructions		28032	100.0

APPENDIX B: FRAGMENTS OF A PDP-11 EMULATOR

This appendix contains a partial listing (EMMYXL) of the PDP-11 emulator. We include this for completeness and to give the reader a feel for the capabilities of the EMMY instruction set. The pages included show the main microinstruction paths for execution of operand instructions such as MOV, CMP, and ADD. If the instruction were:

　　　　MOV#20, R3　　　;LOADRegisterR3with20

the path would be:

Label	Action
FETCH	Fetch, update PC, and decode first four bits
SRCWD	Decode source operand
SRCWD2	Form source operand (mode 2)
DSTWD	Decode destination operand
DSTWD0	Form source operand address (mode 0)
EXECWD	Execute as required
WCC1	Set condition codes (case I)
MONITOR	Collect data (details not supplied here)

AN EMULATION ENVIRONMENT AND ITS APPLICATION   331

Most references in the instructions are to registers, which are given the following names:

Name	Register	Function
MPC	R0	EMMY state register
OP	R1	PDP-11 opcode information
IR	R2	PDP-11 instruction register
DCR	R3	Decode register and destination address
A	R4	Scratch
B	R5	Scratch
SRC	R6	Source operand formation
DST	R7	Destination operand formation

M (reg) denotes indirect access of microstore
X (reg) denotes indirect access of main memory

Example of a PDP-11 Emulation in Emmy Microcode

```
                         990  .
                         991  .     THE FIRST TWO INSTRUCTIONS OF THE FETCH SEQUENCE ARE
                         992  .     OVERWRITTEN TO SELECT THE ACTION REQUIRED.
                         993  .     FETCH:      - PDP-11 INSTRUCTION FETCH
                         994  .                 - SOFT INTERRUPT JUMP
                         995  .     CTLPOINT:   - PDP-11 INSTRUCTION FETCH
                         996  .                 - CONTROL EMULATOR JUMP
                         997  .

FF0198  6A01C007    998  FETCH:    SYNC(R0,R0)      ; A = M(PC)       .FETCH AND SIGNAL
FF0199  1B12B800    999  CTLPOINT: A = A OR HMONES                    .SET '1' CONTROL BITS
FF019A  1E13B800   1000            A = A AND HWNZEROS                 .SET '0' CONTROL BITS
FF019B  0C0EA810   1001            DCR = 0          ; IR = X(A)       .INSTRUCTION FETCH
FF019C  2650C007   1002            A = A+2          ; M(PC) = A       .UPDATE PC
FF019D  C033819D   1003            ( BUSY           => MPC = * )      .I/O WAIT
FF019E  4C8E0700   1004            DCR, IR << 4     ; MPC = MPC+DCR   .CASE DECODE OF IR<15:12>
                   1005  .
                   1006  .         DECODE JUMP TABLE FOR IR<15:12>
                   1007  .         OP REGISTER         FORMAT ROUTINE     OP   OPCODE
FF019F  0C0F81AF   1008            DCR = 0             ; MPC = LODECODE   . 0 - LOW DECODE
FF01A0  6D038231   1009                                ; MPC = SRCWRD     . 1 - MOV
FF01A1  6D038231   1010                                ; MPC = SRCWRD     . 2 - CMP
FF01A2  6D038231   1011                                ; MPC = SRCWRD     . 3 - BIT
FF01A3  6D038231   1012                                ; MPC = SRCWRD     . 4 - BIC
FF01A4  6D038231   1013                                ; MPC = SRCWRD     . 5 - BIS
FF01A5  6D038231   1014                                ; MPC = SRCWRD     . 6 - ADD
FF01A6  0C0F8572   1015            DCR = 0             ; MPC = EXTOP      . 7 - 11/40 EXTENDED OPS
FF01A7  0C0F81F0   1016            DCR = 0             ; MPC = HIDECODE   .10 - HIGH DECODE
FF01A8  6D67827B   1017            OP = DCR            ; MPC = SRCBYT     .11 - MOVB
FF01A9  6D67827B   1018            OP = DCR            ; MPC = SRCBYT     .12 - CMPB
FF01AA  6D67827B   1019            OP = DCR            ; MPC = SRCBYT     .13 - BITB
FF01AB  6D67827B   1020            OP = DCR            ; MPC = SRCBYT     .14 - BICB
FF01AC  6D67827B   1021            OP = DCR            ; MPC = SRCBYT     .15 - BISB
FF01AD  24EF8231   1022            DCR = DCR-7         ; MPC = SRCWRD     .16 - SUB
FF01AE  0C0F8588   1023            DCR = 0             ; MPC = FLOAT      .17 - 11/45 FLOATING OPS

                   1169  .
                   1170  .         IR<11:09> IS DECODED TO DETERMINE SOURCE MODE
                   1171  .         IR<08:06> IS DECODED TO DETERMINE REGISTER
                   1172  .
                   1173  .         ON EXIT: DCR CONTAINS THE OPCODE.  THIS REDUNDANCY IS
                   1174  .                  NECESSARY FOR COMMONALITY WITH THE DST ROUTINES
```

```
                          1175
FF0231 6D67B002 1176  SRCWRD:    OP = DCR              ; DCR = SWADR
FF0232 A046FFF0 1177             OP(31:20) = IR(31:20)                  . SAVE MODE-REG INFO
FF0233 4C6EC640 1178             DCR,IR << 3           ; A = M(DCR)
FF0234 0C0E8060 1179             DCR := REGADR
FF0235 4C6EE640 1180             DCR,IR << 3           ; SRC = M(DCR)
FF0236 A0800FFF 1181             MPC(11:00) = A(11:00)
                          1182  .
                          1183  .
FF0237 50180010 1184  SRCWRD0:   SRC << 16
FF0238 6D2F82CC 1185             DCR = OP              ; MPC = DSTWRD
                          1186  .
FF0239 A0D0FFFF 1187  SRCWRD2:   A(15:00) = SRC(15:00)
FF023A 265ABC50 1188             SRC := SRC+2          ; M(DCR) = SRC
FF023B 6D2EE810 1189             DCR = OP              ; SRC = X(A)
FF023C 1B111FFF 1190             A := A OR IOMASK
FF023D C08382CC 1191             ( NOT SAME            => MPC = DSTWRD )
FF023E 6D0385AE 1192                                   ; MPC = SRCWIO
                          1193  .
FF023F 245ABC50 1194  SRCWRD4:   SRC := SRC-2          ; M(DCR) = SRC
FF0240 A0D0FFFF 1195             A(15:00) = SRC(15:00)
FF0241 6D2EE810 1196             DCR = OP              ; SRC = X(A)
FF0242 1B111FFF 1197             A := A OR IOMASK
FF0243 C08382CC 1198             ( NOT SAME            => MPC = DSTWRD )
FF0244 6D0385AE 1199                                   ; MPC = SRCWIO
                          1200  .
FF0245 6D01D007 1201  SRCWRD6:                         ; B = M(PC)
FF0246 A0B0FFFF 1202             A(15:00) = B(15:00)
FF0247 2654D007 1203             B := B+2              ; M(PC) = B
FF0248 6D02D810 1204                                   ; B = X(A)
FF0249 19120800 1205             A := A XOR ALIGN
FF024A 6D02E640 1206                                   ; SRC = M(DCR)  .REFETCH REG
FF024B C033824B 1207             ( BUSY                => MPC = * )
FF024C 22BA8060 1208             SRC := SRC+B
FF024D A0D0FFFF 1209             A(15:00) = SRC(15:00)
FF024E 6D2EE810 1210             DCR = OP              ; SRC = X(A)
FF024F 1B111FFF 1211             A := A OR IOMASK
FF0250 C08382CC 1212             ( NOT SAME            => MPC = DSTWRD )
FF0251 6D0385AE 1213                                   ; MPC = SRCWIO
                          1214  .
FF0252 A0D0FFFF 1215  SRCWRD1:   A(15:00) = SRC(15:00)
FF0253 6D2EE810 1216             DCR = OP              ; SRC = X(A)
FF0254 1B111FFF 1217             A := A OR IOMASK
FF0255 C08382CC 1218             ( NOT SAME            => MPC = DSTWRD )
FF0256 6D0385AE 1219                                   ; MPC = SRCWIO
                          1220  .
FF0257 A0D0FFFF 1221  SRCWRD3:   A(15:00) = SRC(15:00)


                          1352  .
                          1353  .         IR<05:03> IS DECODED AS DESTINATION MODE
                          1354  .         IR<02:00> IS DECODED AS REGISTER IDENTIFICATION
                          1355  .
                          1356  .         ON EXIT DCR CONTAINS ADDRESS OF ACCESS
                          1357  .
FF02CA 300C001D 1358  DSTWRDA:   DCR := DCR - 29                        .OFFSET FOR OPCODES
FF02CB A04EFC00 1359             DCR(31:26) = IR(31:26)                 . SAVE MODE-REG INFO
FF02CC 6D67B004 1360  DSTWRD:    OP = DCR              ; DCR = DWADR
FF02CD 4C6EC640 1361             DCR,IR << 3           ; A = M(DCR)     .MODE DECODE
FF02CE 0C0E8060 1362             DCR := REGADR
FF02CF 4C6EF640 1363             DCR,IR << 3           ; DST = M(DCR)   .REGISTER DECODE
FF02D0 A0800FFF 1364             MPC(11:00) = A(11:00)
                          1365  .
FF02D1 501C0010 1366  DSTWRD0:   DST << 16
FF02D2 6D0383A6 1367                                   ; MPC = EXECWRD
                          1368  .
FF02D3 A0F0FFFF 1369  DSTWRD2:   A(15:00) = DST(15:00)
FF02D4 265EBE50 1370             DST := DST+2          ; M(DCR) = DST
FF02D5 6D8EF810 1371             DCR = A               ; DST = X(A)
FF02D6 1B111FFF 1372             A := A OR IOMASK
FF02D7 C08383A6 1373             ( NOT SAME            => MPC = EXECWRD )
FF02D8 6D0385B2 1374                                   ; MPC = DSTWIO
```

AN EMULATION ENVIRONMENT AND ITS APPLICATION

```
                       1375  .
FF02D9  245EBE50       1376        DSTWRD4:    DST := DST-2        ; M(DCR) = DST
FF02DA  A0F0FFFF       1377                    A(15:00) := DST(15:00)
FF02DB  6D8EF810       1378                    DCR  := A           ; DST := X(A)
FF02DC  1B111FFF       1379                    A    := A OR IOMASK
FF02DD  C08383A6       1380                    ( NOT SAME          => MPC := EXECWRD )
FF02DE  6D0385B2       1381                                        ; MPC := DSTWIO
                       1382  .
FF02DF  6D01D007       1383        DSTWRD6:                        ; B := M(PC)
FF02E0  A0B0FFFF       1384                    A(15:00) := B(15:00)
FF02E1  2654D007       1385                    B    := B+2         ; M(PC) := B
FF02E2  6D02D810       1386                                        ; B := X(A)
FF02E3  6D02F640       1387                                        ; DST := M(DCR)   .REFETCH REG
FF02E4  C03382E4       1388                    ( BUSY              => MPC := * )
FF02E5  19120800       1389                    A    := A XOR ALIGN
FF02E6  22BE8060       1390                    DST  := DST+B
FF02E7  A0F0FFFF       1391                    A(15:00) := DST(15:00)
FF02E8  6D8EF810       1392                    DCR  := A           ; DST := X(A)
FF02E9  1B111FFF       1393                    A    := A OR IOMASK
FF02EA  C08383A6       1394                    ( NOT SAME          => MPC := EXECWRD )
FF02EB  6D0385B2       1395                                        ; MPC := DSTWIO
                       1396  .
FF02EC  A0F0FFFF       1397        DSTWRD1:    A(15:00) := DST(15:00)
FF02ED  6D8EF810       1398                    DCR  := A           ; DST := X(A)
FF02EE  1B111FFF       1399                    A    := A OR IOMASK
FF02EF  C08383A6       1400                    ( NOT SAME          => MPC := EXECWRD )
FF02F0  6D0385B2       1401                                        ; MPC := DSTWIO
                       1402  .
FF02F1  A0F0FFFF       1403        DSTWRD3:    A(15:00) := DST(15:00)
FF02F2  265EBE50       1404                    DST  := DST+2       ; M(DCR) := DST


                       1620  .               ON ENTRY: DCR - DESTINATION ADDRESS AND CONTROL BITS
                       1621  .                         SRC - SOURCE OPERAND
                       1622  .                         DST - DESTINATION OPERAND
                       1623  .
                       1624  .               SIMPLE OPERATIONS ARE PERFORMED DIRECTLY.
                       1625  .               AFTER PROCESSING A ROUTINE IS SELECTED TO SET
                       1626  .               TARGET CONDITION CODES AND STORE THE RESULT.
                       1627  .
FF03A6  8028001F       1628        EXECWRD:    IR(4:0) := OP(4:0) CLEAR            .ISOLATE OPCODE
FF03A7  320408A1       1629                    OP   := OP + DUMMY1                 .SET COUNTER BASE
FF03A8  22428060       1630                    MPC  := MPC + IR                    .CASE JUMP
FF03A9  00000000       1631                    DC   0                              .DUMMY
                       1632  .               *** WARNING: ASSUMES DATA VALIDITY BASED ON ELAPSED TIME ***
                       1633  .
FF03AA  0ADF83E8       1634                    DST  := SRC         ; MPC := WCC1   .MOV
FF03AB  28FB840C       1635                    SRC  - DST          ; MPC := WCC3X  .CMP
FF03AC  0EDF8406       1636                    DST  := DST AND SRC ; MPC := WCC1X  .BIT
FF03AD  0DDF83E8       1637                    DC   X'0DDF8000' ++ WCC1            .BIC
FF03AE  0BDF83E8       1638                    DST  := DST OR SRC  ; MPC := WCC1   .BIS
FF03AF  22DF83F3       1639                    DST  := DST + SRC   ; MPC := WCC2   .ADD
FF03B0  20DF83FC       1640                    DST  := DST - SRC   ; MPC := WCC3   .SUB
FF03B1  6D0384CB       1641                                        ; MPC := JMPIO  .JMP
FF03B2  6D0383E3       1642                                        ; MPC := SWAB   .SWAB
FF03B3  6D0384D1       1643                                        ; MPC := JSRIO  .JSR
FF03B4  0C1F83F3       1644                    DST  := 0           ; MPC := WCC2   .CLR
FF03B5  6D0383D3       1645                                        ; MPC := COM    .COM
FF03B6  6D0383D7       1646                                        ; MPC := INCR   .INC
FF03B7  6D0383D9       1647                                        ; MPC := DECR   .DEC
FF03B8  6DF383E1       1648                                        ; MPC := NEG    .NEG
FF03B9  6D0383DB       1649                                        ; MPC := ADC    .ADC
FF03BA  6D0383E0       1650                                        ; MPC := SBC    .SBC
FF03BB  0AFF840A       1651                    DST  := DST         ; MPC := WCC2X  .TST
FF03BC  6D0383C0       1652                                        ; MPC := ROR    .ROR
FF03BD  6D0383C6       1653                                        ; MPC := ROL    .ROL
FF03BE  6D0383CB       1654                                        ; MPC := ASR    .ASR
FF03BF  6D0383D2       1655                                        ; MPC := ASL    .ASL


                       1728  .               THESE ROUTINES SET CONDITION CODES AND STORE
                       1729  .               THE RESULT AS REQUIRED.
```

```
                         1730  .            ON ENTRY: MPC - CONTAINS CONDITION CODES
                         1731  .                      DCR - RESULT ADDRESS  (BIT<31>=0 => REGISTER)
                         1732  .                      DST - CONTAINS RESULT
                         1733  .
                         1734  .            N X V C   STORE   ROUTINE
                         1735  .            R R R -   YES     WCC1
                         1736  .            R R R R   YES     WCC2
                         1737  .            R R R T   YES     WCC3
                         1738  .            R R R -   NO      WCC1X
                         1739  .            R R R R   NO      WCC2X
                         1740  .            R R R T   NO      WCC3X
                         1741  .
                         1742  .            WHERE: R -- BIT IS PROPERLY SET ON RESULT OF OPERATION
                         1743  .                   - -- BIT IS TO BE UNCHANGED
                         1744  .                   1 -- BIT IS FORCED TO ONE
                         1745  .                   T -- RESULT BIT IS COMPLEMENTED
                         1746  .
FF03E8  6D01C008         1747   WCC1:                          ; A = M(COND)
FF03E9  A0822000         1748            MPC(29) = A(29:29)
FF03EA  6D008008         1749                                  ; M(COND) = MPC
FF03EB  0A6C0842         1750   WCCCPUT: DCR '= DCR            ; ( NOT HIGH => WCC1$ )
FF03EC  6D02BE20         1751                                  ; X(DCR) = DST
FF03ED  6D038160         1752                                  ; MPC = MONITOR
FF03EE  2CEC0A01         1753   WCC1$:   DCR - 7               ; ( LTE => WCC1$$ )
FF03EF  6D0385E1         1754                                  ; MPC = PUTWIO
FF03F0  521C0010         1755   WCC1$$:  DCR >> 16
FF03F1  6D02BE50         1756                                  ; M(DCR) = DST
FF03F2  6D038160         1757                                  ; MPC = MONITOR
                         1758
                         1759
FF03F3  6D008008         1760   WCC2:                          ; M(COND) = MPC
FF03F4  0A6C0842         1761            DCR '= DCR            ; ( NOT HIGH => WCC2$ )
FF03F5  6D02BE20         1762                                  ; X(DCR) = DST
FF03F6  6D038160         1763                                  ; MPC = MONITOR
FF03F7  2CEC0A01         1764   WCC2$:   DCR - 7               ; ( LTE => WCC2$$ )
FF03F8  6D0385E1         1765                                  ; MPC = PUTWIO
FF03F9  521C0010         1766   WCC2$$:  DCR >> 16
FF03FA  6D02BE50         1767                                  ; M(DCR) = DST
FF03FB  6D038160         1768                                  ; MPC = MONITOR
                         1769
                         1770
FF03FC  6D11D067         1771   WCC3:    A = MPC               ; B = M(CBCON)
FF03FD  09B0C008         1772            A '= A XOR B          ; M(COND) = A
FF03FE  0A6C0842         1773            DCR '= DCR            ; ( NOT HIGH => WCC3$ )   .MEMORY?
FF03FF  6D02BE20         1774                                  ; X(DCR) = DST            .YES: STORE IT
FF0400  6D038160         1775                                  ; MPC = MONITOR
FF0401  2CEC0A01         1776   WCC3$:   DCR - 7               ; ( LTE => WCC3$$ )       .REGISTER?
FF0402  6D0385E1         1777                                  ; MPC = PUTWIO            .NO: I/O
FF0403  521C0010         1778   WCC3$$:  DCR >> 16                                       .REGISTER
FF0404  6D02BE50         1779                                  ; M(DCR) = DST
FF0405  6D038160         1780                                  ; MPC = MONITOR
```

REFERENCES

Alpert, D. 1979. "A PASCAL P-code Interpreter for the Stanford EMMY." Computer Systems Laboratory, Technical Note 164. Palo Alto, CA: Stanford University.

Digital Equipment, 1970. "MAINDEC-11 DOAA Diagnostic Test Sequence." Maynard, MA: Digital Equipment Corporation.

――――. 1971. "PDP-11/20 Processor Handbook." Maynard, MA: Digital Equipment Corporation.

――――. 1975. "PDP-11/05 Engineering Drawings." Maynard, MA: Digital Equipment Corporation.

Demco, V., and *Marsland*, T. 1975. "A Complete PDP-11 Emulation." Technical Report TR75-13, Department of Computer Science. Alberta, Canada: University of Alberta.

Flynn, M. J. 1977. "Classes of Emulation." *ACM SIGMicro Newsletter* 8 (4):34–35.

———. 1980. "Directions and Issues in Architecture and Languages." *Computer* 13 (10):5–22.

Flynn, M. J., and *Hoevel*, L. W. 1979. "A Theory of Interpretive Architectures: Ideal Languages Machines." Technical Report 170, Computer Systems Laboratory. Palo Alto, CA: Stanford University.

Hao, H.T.; *Markstein*, P. W.; and *Radin*, G. 1986. "Mechanism for Implementing One Machine Cycle Executable Mask and Rotate Instruction in a Primitive Instruction Set Computing System." U.S. Patent No. 4,569,016.

Hedges, T. S. 1975. "EMMY/360 Cross Assembler." Technical Note 74, Computer Systems Laboratory. Palo Alto, CA: Stanford University.

Hoevel, L. W., and *Flynn*, M. J. 1979. "A Theory of Interpretive Architectures: Some Notes on DEL Design and a FORTRAN Case Study." Technical Report 170, Computer Systems Laboratory. Palo Alto, CA: Stanford University.

Huck, J. C. 1983. "Comparative Analysis of Computer Architectures." Technical Report 83-243, Computer Systems Laboratory. Palo Alto, CA: Stanford University.

Huck, J. C., and *Neuhauser*, C. J. 1979. "I/O Device Emulation in the Stanford Emulation Laboratory." *SIGMICRO Newsletter* 10 (4):101–8.

Johnston, J. B. 1971. "The Contour Model of Block Structured Processes." *Sigplan Notices* 6 (2):55–82.

Knuth, D. 1971. "An Empirical Study of FORTRAN Programs." Technical Report CS-186, Computer Science Department. Palo Alto, CA: Stanford University.

Mitchell, C., and *Flynn*, M. 1988. "A Workbench for Computer Architects." *IEEE Design & Test* 5 (1):19–29.

Nanodata, 1974. "QM-1." Buffalo, NY: Nanodata Corporation.

Neuhauser, C. J. 1975. "EMMY System Peripherals—Principles of Operation." Technical Note 77, Computer Systems Laboratory. Palo Alto, CA: Stanford University.

———. 1977a. "An EMMY Based PDP-11/20 Emulation." Technical Report TN-110, Computer Systems Laboratory. Palo Alto, CA: Stanford University.

———. 1977b. "An EMMY System Processor—Principles of Operation." Technical Note 114, Computer Systems Laboratory. Palo Alto, CA: Stanford University.

———. 1979. "Instruction Stream Monitoring of the PDP-11." Technical Note 156, Computer Systems Laboratory. Palo Alto, CA: Stanford University.

Noe, J. 1974. "Acquiring and Using a Hardware Monitor." *Datamation* (April):89–95.

Pittler, M. S.; *Powers*, D. M.; and *Schnabel*, D. L. 1982. "System Development and Technology Aspects of the IBM 3081 Processor Complex." *IBM Journal of Research and Development* 26 (1):2–12.

Polstra, J., and Proskurski, A. 1970. "EMMYPL: A Description and Implementation." Technical Report 74, Computer Systems Laboratory. Palo Alto, CA: Stanford University.

Rigg, C. 1977. Private communication with author.

Shih, M. 1977. "EMMY/Unibus Interface Design Specification." Technical Note 109, Computer Systems Laboratory. Palo Alto, CA: Stanford University.

Snow, E. and Siewiorek, D. 1978. "Impact of Implementation Design Trade-offs on Performance: The PDP-11, A Case Study." Technical Report CMU-CS-78-104. Pittsburgh: Carnegie-Mellon University.

Standard Computer, 1970. "MLP-900 Multilingual Processor—Principles of Operation." Santa Ana, CA: Standard Computer Corporation.

Varian Data. 1977. "Varian Micro-programming Guide." Palo Alto, CA: Varian Data Machines.

Wakefield, S. 1983. "Studies in Execution Architectures." Technical Report 277, Computer Systems Laboratory. Palo Alto, CA: Stanford University.

Wallach, W. 1975. "System/360 Emulator Performance Estimate." Technical Note 66, Computer Systems Laboratory. Palo Alto, CA: Stanford University.

Wirth, N. 1968. "PL360: A Programming Language for the 360 Computers." *Journal of the ACM* 15 (1):37–74.

Wulf, W. A. 1981. "Compiler and Computer Architecture." *Computer* 14 (7):41–48.

Note: UNIX is a trademark of AT&T Bell Laboratories; VAX is a trademark of Digital Equipment Corporation; PDP-11 is a trademark of Digital Equipment Corporation.

eight
TRADITIONAL MICROPROGRAM DEVELOPMENT TOOLS

WILL TRACZ

Microprogramming is an alternative method of implementing the control logic of a digital device. It requires analyzing the requirements and identifying hardware, firmware, and software tradeoffs. Writing microprograms, one aspect of firmware engineering, usually takes place after the microarchitecture data flow has been designed and the microword defined. Microcode support software plays a crucial role in providing the tools (e.g., assembler, linkage editor, and simulator) necessary for microprogram development. These support tools can also provide a vehicle for the logic designers, system engineers, and microprogrammers to model a system before the hardware is available, thus obtaining valuable analysis of system performance. The data gathered from simulation or from a breadboard version of the system may often suggest a more desirable hardware/firmware tradeoff, in which case the support software must be updated to reflect the new system architecture. This short scenario illustrates the dynamic nature of microprogram development tools and is a unique requirement of their design and functional capability.

This chapter describes the traditional microprogram-development tools or microcode support software used to facilitate the generation of microprograms. It is organized into five sections. The first section covers the evolution of microcode development tools. The next three sections describe the functions and features found in microcode assemblers, linkage editors, and simulators, respectively.

Microcode compiler technology has been described in Chapter 4. The last portion of this document contains an overview of the microprogramming tools currently being used in industry. Tools such as PROM programmers and ROS/control-store simulators/hardware debuggers are not within the scope of this chapter. For more information on these topics, the reader is urged to consult *Digital System Design with LSI Bit-Slice Logic* (Myers 1980), which also contains a chapter on microprogram development tools.

THE EVOLUTION OF MICROPROGRAM DEVELOPMENT TOOLS

One can observe that the methodology for developing microprograms strongly parallels the methodology for developing software but that it has trailed that methodology by at least ten years. Microprogramming tools also parallel software development tools in philosophy, but the comparable functions and features have evolved at a slower pace. Historically, software system and application programming has had a 15-year head start on microprogramming. Microprogram development did not become a significant activity until the mid 1960s when read-only memories (ROMs) became an economically viable manufacturing technology. Even then, only a relatively small amount of microcode was being developed for each computer system.

In the case of the IBM System/360 computer family, less than 280K bytes of microcode were written for the entire model line, including the 1400 and 7090 emulation microcode on some of the eight microprogrammed models (Padegs 1981). This can be contrasted with the tens of thousands of lines of emulation, microdiagnostic, and operating-system-assist microcode that are being developed for each mainframe processor today. A typical IBM 308x system is shipped with over 380K bytes of microcode.

First-Generation Microprogramming Tools

In the early days of microprogramming (mid to late 1960s), support software was still an art, not a science. The small amount of microcode being written did not justify the generation of sophisticated tools. Simple tools were developed to meet the user's needs. Straightforward substitution of bit patterns for mnemonics (bit-stuffing) was the most prevalent approach. Direct specification of instruction contents in binary through the use of special coding forms was not unheard of when small amounts of microcode were required. Assembler input was mostly fixed-format, because of the batch/card-oriented systems they were developed on.

Two other factors influenced the type of microcode development tools that were available. Sometimes, a short development schedule precluded the generation of anything but the least complex set of tools or mandated the modification of existing ones. In such instances, the user might also not have been fully aware of the advantages of having better tools because of the lack of exposure to programming or software methodology in general. Writing microprograms was (and probably still is) considered a hardware-oriented activity. The early representations of microprograms such as IBM CASS closely resembled circuit-logic drawings (Husson 1970). This was due in part to the logic designers who were recruited to be microprogrammers and in part to their familiarity with wiring diagrams. A secondary factor was the field engineer's desire for consistent documentation of hard-wired and programmed logic.

Second-Generation Microprogramming Tools

The development of inexpensive read-only memories and bit-slice microprocessor devices in the early to mid 1970s, coupled with expanding user needs, led to the development of larger microprograms with further emphasis on microprogram development tools. A second generation of microcode support tools was created to provide the operational microprogrammer, diagnostic microprogrammer, and customer with a better environment in which to develop, in turn, more sophisticated and complex microprograms. These tools are characterized by:

- Increased readability of mnemonics
- Macro capability in the microcode assemblers
- Register-transfer-level syntax in microprogramming languages
- Microcode linkage editors or binders (These were developed to facilitate the increased size of microprograms, which had themselves been modularized.)
- Microcode simulators for simultaneous microcode and hardware debug (This further supported concurrent, modularized microcode development activities by many microprogrammers.)
- Early investigation of microcode compilers (Schlaeppi 1973; Eckhouse 1979).

Third-Generation Microprogramming Tools

Microprogramming tools are rapidly approaching the sophistication of low-level software development tools. While high-level-language microprogramming has not achieved any sweeping commercial success, it has been used at Burroughs (Wagnon and Maine 1983) and Tandem (Bartlett 1981) and explored by IBM (Ris 1984) and DEC (Poe 1981; Goodell 1981). In addition, it has been shown to be feasible in several academic environments (Sint 1980; Davidson 1983).

The number of microprogrammers has increased as well as the diversification of their backgrounds. Today, microprogrammers are either former programmers or they have more extensive software experience than ever before, either from formal schooling, recreational computing (a home computer), or job-related activities. Consequently, microprogrammers have begun to demand the same level of support software that programmers have accepted as standard in a software development environment. External driving factors, such as vertical migration (placing more software into firmware), have influenced the perspective of how microcode is viewed. The military standard for weapon-system software development, MIL-STD-1679, also influenced microprogram development. This Department of Defense standard states that firmware (microcode) shall be treated as software in the development and documentation processes. These and other factors have resulted in the current, third generation of microcode support software tools. Some characteristics are:

- A well-integrated package of development tools: The microcode tool suite contains an assembler (or compiler), linkage editor, simulator, library manager/release mechanism, and editor (Wagnon and Maine 1983)
- A microcode simulator/debug package that maintains the same user interface as the hardware tester: Burroughs (Wagnon and Maine 1983), DEC (Sherwood 1984), Bell (Chadwick 1983)
- Microcode tool-generator packages: Data General (Beauchamp and Firth 1982), IBM (Dubbs 1979; Tracz 1985), and NEC (Takahashi et al. 1982); these tools are specification-driven and allow for rapid implementation and easy modification

THE MICROCODE ASSEMBLER/TRANSLATOR

The purpose of a microcode assembler/translator is to take a machine/human-readable form of a microprogram and translate it into a binary object file (fig. 8-1). The exact format of the input may take on various levels of sophistication. For example, let us assume we wish to specify the generation of a microword that adds the value in a staging register called A to the contents of the user general-purpose register 15, placing the results back in the staging register A and at the same time branching to the overflow handling microcode if an overflow is detected. One approach to specifying these actions would be traditional assembler-language format of opcode followed by a list of operands:

MW ADD, LS, A, X'F', A, , , , OVF, X'200'

In this case, default operands are implied by the missing operands illustrated by the series of commas separating **A** and **OVF**. Notice, also, that all addresses are in hexadecimal.

A second approach is the *"bit-stuffer,"* where each field in the microword has a corresponding mnemonic that is assigned a value explicitly by the microprogrammer on a per-field basis. The same microinstruction expressed in this form would be written as:

```
ALU = L + R;
L = A;
R = LS;
LS = X'F';
DEST = A;
COND = OVR;
BRADDR = X'200';;
```

In this instance the positions of the microorders are not fixed, as was the case in the previous example.

The final example illustrates a pseudo-high-level language, with register-transfer level and pseudostructured control syntax:

```
A = A + LS(X'F');
IF OVF GOTO OVERFLOW_PROCESSING;;
```

A single microword definition can be specified on one input record or spread over many in a fixed or free input format. As long as no more than one microword is generated from one input record, the microcode assembler/translator is, by definition, not a microcode compiler. Although one may argue that an assembler with macro expansion capability results in the generation of multiple microwords from a single macro call, the translation process is still not classified as compilation. No local or global optimization or compaction is performed, but some static analysis, in the form of conflicts in field usage, generally occurs.

The differences between a microcode assembler and a macrocode assembler are as follows:

- *The amount of code that is processed:* A microcode assembler has only a fraction of the amount of use a macrocode assembler has. Therefore, a microcode assembler can be and generally is less efficient in the time it takes to translate microprograms.
- *Wider words:* A microinstruction is typically wider than a machine instruction. This is attributable to the inherent parallelism designed into most microinstructions.
- *Built-in sequencing:* Most high-performance, horizontal microwords are designed with next address information as part of each instruction. Furthermore, as is the case with DEC, IBM, and NEC mainframe microarchitectures, the microsequencing mechanism can be N-way and discontiguous. (Discontiguous

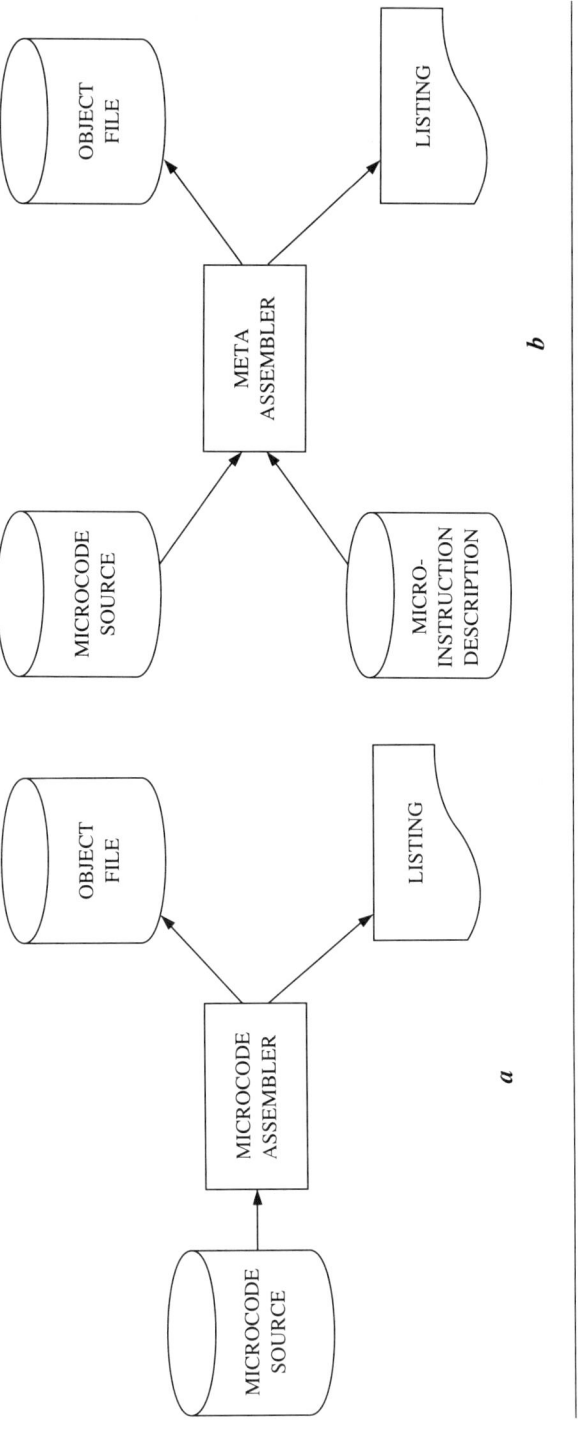

Figure 8-1. Microcode assembler block diagram: *a.* standalone; *b.* meta-assembler; *c.* compiler-compiler.

Figure 8-1. (continued)

branches are multiway branches that have possible target addresses that are not sequential. For example,

GOTO X'200' + 0,0,ZD,0;

is a 16-way branch that has been constrained to be only a 2-way branch. If the Zero Detect (ZD) branch condition is set, then the branch address (or branch leg) will be X'202'. If the branch condition is not set, the branch address will be X'200'. In this case the next two possible addresses are not contiguous.)
- *Validity tests:* A microcode assembler test for many more error conditions attributable to hardware constraints, or abnormalities

The Evolution of Microcode Assemblers/Translators

Initially, the microcode assembler was the only microprogramming tool available to the microprogrammer. There were no linkage editors or software simulators. The microcode assembler consisted of a simple substitution mechanism, a bit pattern for a mnemonic, with possibly some primitive error-checking capability. The output of the microcode assembler was an object file capable of being loaded into control store (or burned into ROM) for debug, along with a listing file and possibly a load map and cross-reference listing of labels. Input to the microcode assembler was a list, sometimes free format, of mnemonics or field operand pairs.

A second popular input format was fixed-field position as used in the RCA-Spectra system (Husson 1970). In this approach, every field in the microword was assigned a field in the input record. If a mnemonic was present in that field, then the respective bit value would be assigned to that field in the microword through a simple table-look-up mechanism. This technique is still used today for extremely horizontal microwords in heavily pipelined microarchitectures (IBM 3838), where the fixed-field format shows the movement of data through the different stages of the pipe. (Each stage of the pipeline is controlled by a different and adjacent field in the microword.) A similar fixed sequence of mnemonics, separated by commas, was used in the MV-8000 microcode (Firth 1980).

Register-transfer-level syntax (Tracz 1981; Beauchamp 1982; Guffin 1982) can be provided as the microprogramming language format for microword definition, thus increasing readability and writability of the microcode. This "syntactic sugar" is relatively simple to implement using the translator-writing-system (YACC and LEX) approach described in the section entitled "Second-Generation Microcode Support Software."

A third format of microprogram input is flow charts. A graphic representation of the microprogram is entered in a high-resolution graphics display (Husson 1970; Takahashi et al. 1982); and the intermediate form is processed by the microcode assembler, with the output listing taking the form of a flow chart. The advantage of using this approach is that it succinctly documents the flow of control of the microcode, which can become very complex given the multiway branching structure in high-performance processors (Fisher 1981). This method of microcode representation has been the mainstay of the IBM high-performance and avionics processors (fig. 8-2) and has recently been adapted by NEC. Motorola (Nash and Spak 1979; Tredennick 1980) has used a stylized version of flow charts for their nanocode on the MC6800 microprocessor.

Finally, a microprogram can be written in a high-level machine-dependent or -independent microprogramming language; in either case the microcode assembler/translator accepts the output of the microcode compiler. This is covered in Chapter 4.

Microcode Assembler/Translator Requirements

A microcode assembler/translator should satisfy the basic requirements of its users. It must assist rather than hinder the microprogrammer in writing microprograms. In order to meet these needs and enhance productivity, the following attributes are characteristic of a good microcode assembler/translator:

- *Rapidly implementable*: This feature is defined as the amount of time it takes to design, implement, document, and debug the microcode assembler program. Schedule constraints often require rapid definition of a microprogramming language and development of a program for translating it into microwords.
- *Efficient*: The throughput of the microcode assembler is a quick measure of its usefulness. Effective throughput can be improved by providing a facility to support separate translation of microprogram modules, thus minimizing the time it would take to make a change to a single microword. Separate assembly may be construed as a tradeoff in implementation speed versus execution speed, since this facility in turn necessitates the existence of a microcode linkage editor or binder (as described in the next section), which incurs more development time and money.
- *Easily modifiable*: The microprogramming effort is often started before the microarchitecture is completely specified or defined. The microcode assembler should be flexible enough to provide easy modification of field and mnemonic definitions.
- *Robust*: The microcode assembler should provide the following features or exhibit the following characteristics:
  - *User-friendly syntax*: (at the RTL level, if possible): The microprogram input format should make specifying and documenting microcode easy. A high-level, intuitive mapping between

Figure 8-2. Microcode flow-chart representation.

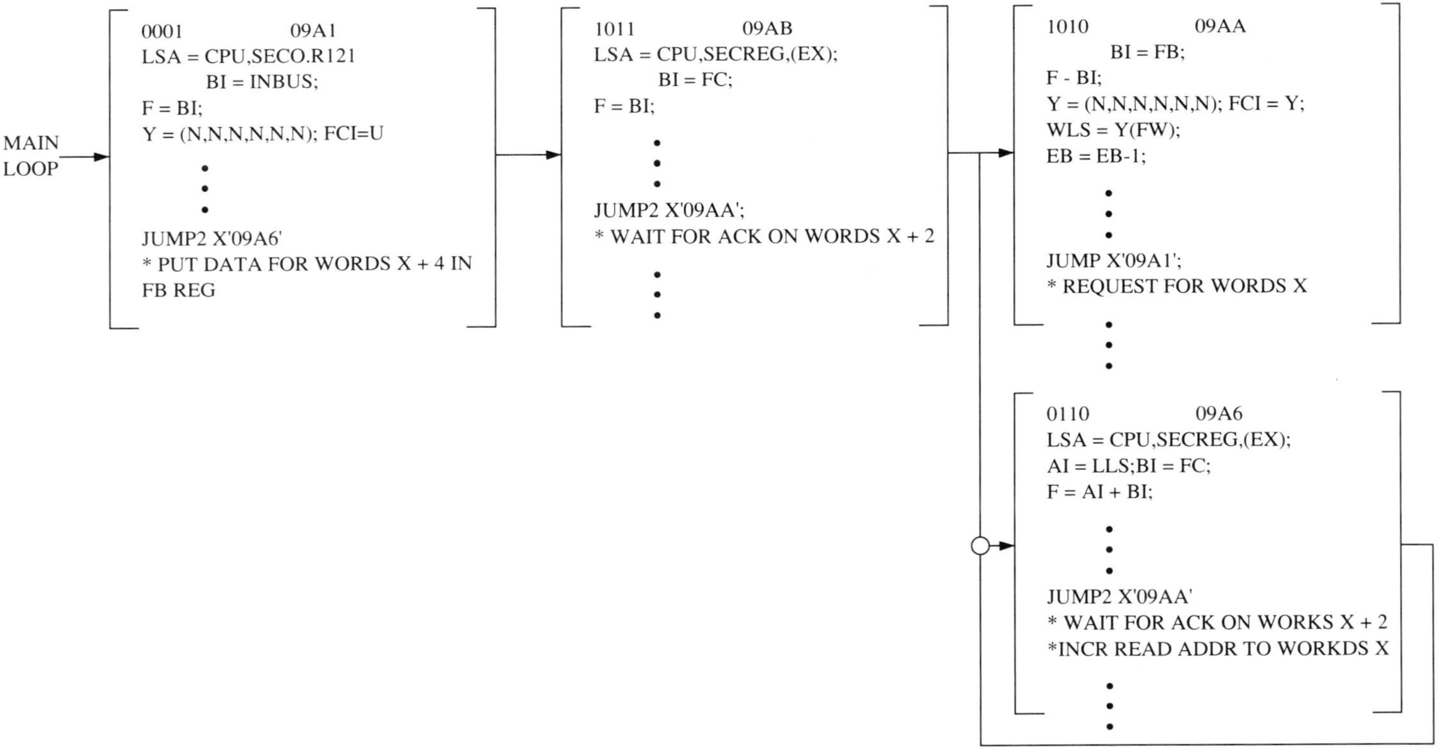

MAIN LOOP

```
        0001        09A1
     LSA = CPU,SECO,R121
         BI = INBUS;
         F = BI;
         Y = (N,N,N,N,N,N); FCI=U
         ...
         JUMP2 X'09A6'
         * PUT DATA FOR WORDS X + 4 IN
           FB REG
```

```
        1011        09AB
     LSA = CPU,SECREG,(EX);
         BI = FC;
         F = BI;
         ...
         JUMP2 X'09AA';
         * WAIT FOR ACK ON WORDS X + 2
```

```
        1010        09AA
         BI = FB;
         F - BI;
         Y = (N,N,N,N,N,N); FCI = Y;
         WLS = Y(FW);
         EB = EB-1;
         ...
         JUMP X'09A1';
         * REQUEST FOR WORDS X
```

```
        0110        09A6
     LSA = CPU,SECREG,(EX);
         AI = LLS;BI = FC;
         F = AI + BI;
         ...
         JUMP2 X'09AA'
         * WAIT FOR ACK ON WORKS X + 2
         *INCR READ ADDR TO WORKDS X
```

the semantics of the operation and the syntax used to express it should exist. Furthermore, the syntax should be compact to minimize the entry and update effort.
- *Free format:* Microorders can be entered in any sequence, in any position on the input record.
- *Meaningful mnemonics:* Cryptic and terse mnemonics should be avoided.
- *Macro expansion capability:* The amount of source microcode written and debugged can be reduced through macros.
- *Listing format control:* This increases readability through page ejects and user-inserted blank lines.
- *Cross-referencing of labels:* This will improve debug and maintenance efforts.
- *Convenient commenting mechanism:* This facilitates readability and encourages documentation.
- *Expression evaluation:* This is useful for absolute or relocatable expressions in macros.
- *Structured control syntax:* This aids in modularization, although it may be limited by the microarchitecture. As a minimum a CALL and RETURN mechanism should exist, with some sort of conditional, or CASE, statement also desirable.
- *Support for assembly of separate microprogram segments:* This minimizes the cost of small changes to the microcode.
- *Relocatability and external-address referencing:* The user should be able to write microcode without regard to which location in control store it will occupy. Furthermore, the microprogrammer should be able to reference symbolic microword locations external to the microprogram unit being translated. (This necessitates a microcode linkage editor or loader program.)
- *Conditional assembly:* This is normally part of the macro facility.
- *Address assignment:* As previously stated, certain horizontal microwords have n-way noncontiguous branching capability. In this circumstance, the assembler should assist in address allocation.
- *Additional functionality:* It is often desirable to perform static analysis of microprograms at assembly time. Checks for timing conflicts as well as illegal or conflicting combinations of microword fields may be performed. (This supports the well-worn maxim: the sooner errors are found, the cheaper they are to fix.)

These features in general add to the overall readability and writability of a microprogram, thus increasing the ease of development and debugging.

Microcode-Assembler Implementation Issues

In the early days, microcode assemblers were basically "roll your own" (i.e., ad hoc) two-pass programs (programs that read the microprogram source two times). The first pass of the assembler built a symbol table. During the second pass, the microcode bit image was generated. Sometimes an additional pass was necessary to perform address assignment, or macro expansion. Each microcode support-software system was developed from scratch, derived from the one that existed previously, or a result of modifying a generalized baseline system. A popular method of implementing microcode assemblers was to use a set of macros (Tanenbaum 1976), one for each microorder. A similar implementation strategy was used for implementations written in the programming language APL, where each microorder is an APL function. In either case, a list of keyword constants is retained for assigning a value to a microword field. Each of the fields to be assigned represents a separate macro or function call. A microword definition is thus a series of macro or function calls that combines all the microword fields into a large assignment (literally, stuffs the bits in), then reinitializes the default field values. This was illustrated in the bit-stuffer example above.

With the introduction of the microprocessor came the concept of a meta-assembler with logical extensions into bit-slice microarchitectures (Habib and Yang 1981; Berglass 1980). A meta-assembler is a specifications-driven approach to tool development (see fig. 8-1b). The microword fields, mnemonics, and a mapping between each must be specified in the form of tables. The advantages to this approach are rapid development time and ease of modification. The disadvantages include loss of flexibility because of a somewhat rigid format, loss of certain error-detection capability, and slow processing due to the overhead of reading in the tables each time the assembler is run (Powers and Hernandez 1978; Skordalakis 1983). Two recent commercially available microcode development systems that include meta-assemblers are M-29 (Eager 1983) and STEP-29 (Wilburn and Mick 1984). The STEP system has recently introduced an extensive facility that detects conflicting field assignments and values (Wilburn 1985).

Support software has gradually become more sophisticated, as software developers assumed the role of generating microcode tools rather than leaving them to microprogrammers. As compiler writing technology evolved, compiler generator techniques and translator writing-system technology (see fig. 8-1c) have been applied to microcode assembler generation (Dubbs 1972; Tracz 1981; Patterson, Lew, and Tuck 1979).

A separate but related tool-development strategy is based on the use of computer-hardware description languages (CHDLs). This approach has been demonstrated to automatically generate microcode development tools from hardware descriptions, thus minimizing or eliminating the explicit development of a microcode assembler or translator and the related suite of tools (Sheraga and Gieser 1981; Takahashi et al. 1982; Tracz 1985).

MICROCODE LINKAGE EDITORS

A microcode linkage editor (also referred to as a linking loader, linker, or binder) takes on many variations other than the traditional ones provided by machine-language linkage-editor programs. This section describes the types of functions that can be found in microcode linkage editors and which subsets of these functions and extensions are applicable to various microcode development systems. Microcode linkage editors serve a wide variety of microprogrammer's needs. The amount of function contained in a microcode linkage editor is dependent on the size of the microarchitecture and the amount of microcode to be written. Microcode linkage editors are more than just "utility programs" that reformat data; they can be used to debug and analyze microcode as well.

The Link-Edit Process

A linkage-editor program is classically defined as a program for combining separately assembled program segments into one large program load module. In conjunction with this process, certain other functions may be performed on the program segments. These are generally specified in a control file and include the following:

- *Object-code relocation:* A program segment can be assigned to reside at different locations in memory. This requires all branch-address and local-data-address references to be adjusted to reflect the effects of relocation.
- *External-symbol address resolution:* The addresses of labels external to a program segment may not be known until the program segment in which the external reference is defined is assigned a location by the linkage editor. At this time all references to such symbols can be resolved using the assigned address.
- *Load-module generation:* The last step in the link-edit process is the generation of the load module, the format of which is dependent on the target-system requirements. In the case of a cross-linkage editor (i.e., the target system is different from the linkage-editor host system), the load module is typically produced on a transportable medium such as magnetic or punched tape or diskette.

- *Diagnostic/error checking:* The linkage editor generates reports on duplicate usage of storage, improper boundary alignment, unresolved external references, and numerous other errors.
- *Absolute listing:* When assembler output listings are used for documentation, it is desirable to have them reflect the effects of relocation and external-address resolution. Absolute-listing generation consists of reading separate assembly listings and modifying them to show the updated instructions and address assignments.
- *Load-map generation:* The load-map-generation capability allows the user to obtain a map of the contents of the memory locations within the load module.
- *Patch capability:* To avoid the costs of recompiling or reassembling, the patch capability is available at link-edit time. This allows the user to specify explicitly the contents of a word in memory, overriding the previously defined contents.
- *Overlay generation:* A linkage editor can automatically generate program-segment overlays. This allows large programs to be partitioned to run in smaller regions of memory by only having portions of them in memory at one time, with the other program segments residing in auxiliary storage.
- *External-symbol-dictionary generation:* This capability provides the user with a listing of external symbols and assigned addresses. Optionally, a cross-reference may be generated showing the locations that reference each external symbol.
- *Initialization of unused locations:* Under some circumstances (e.g., program debugging) it may be desirable to initialize the contents of unused locations to a particular value (e.g., machine stop). This facility can be provided for at link-edit time.

Figure 8-3 shows a generalized top-level data flow of the link-edit process. There are two distinct inputs to the linkage editor: the control file and the object/text files (output from the assembler/compiler). Control-file processing determines the type of function to be performed by the linkage editor and which program segments are to be linked together. Processing the object file is generally a multipass process, depending on the type of function being performed. The first pass sets up the external-symbol dictionary, the second does address resolution. Three types of information must be contained in the object file. They are:

1. Machine-code representation of the instruction and data
2. Relocation information
3. External-symbol information

Figure 8-3. Generalized link-edit process.

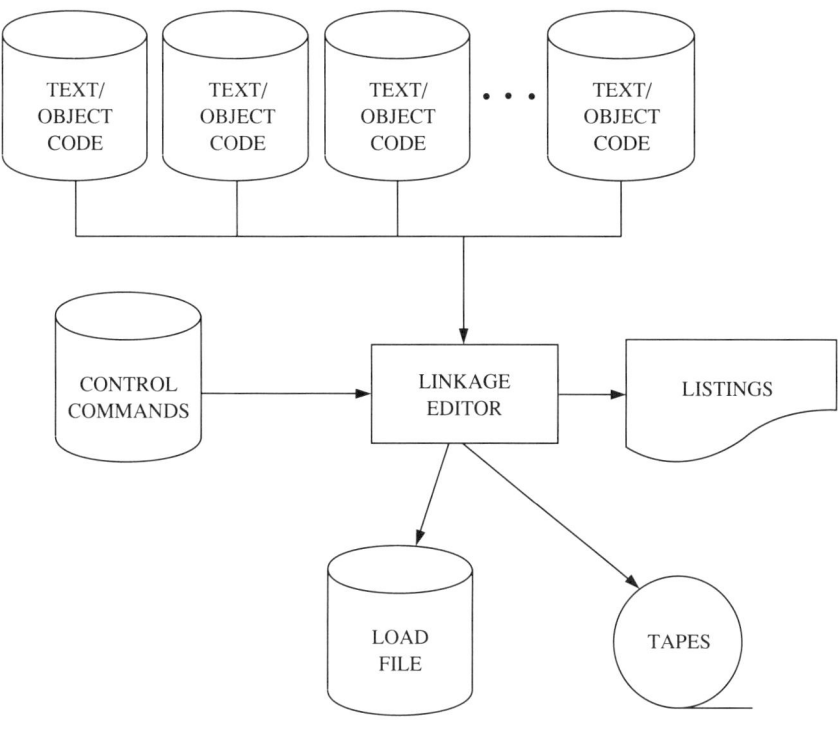

Output of the linkage editor is in the form of listings, data files, and/or load modules/tapes. Special output may also be generated for other programs such as a simulator.

Microcode Linkage-Editor Requirements

Microcode linkage editors cover a broad spectrum of performance and function in order to serve the needs of the microprogrammer of microprogrammable architectures (Myers 1980). These architectures can vary in their degrees of complexity and performance, thus directly influencing the amount of function necessary to be incorporated into a microcode linkage editor.

A microcode linkage editor's functional capability consists of a subset of the function found in traditional linkage editors plus additional processing capability especially tailored for microcode development. The type of functions that are unique to microcode linkage editors include the following:

- *Fan-in/fan-out reports:* The fan-in/fan-out report gives the microprogrammer detailed flow analysis of the microcode. This function can also be described as a cross-reference by location or a branch-tree/connectivity-table analysis report, which lists all the microwords that branch into a location, all the locations that a microword branches to, and all undefined branch targets. It is especially useful in microarchitectures in which multiway branches (ranging from contiguous and noncontiguous 2-way through 16-way branches) are prevalent, as with horizontal microcode (Fisher 1980). The fan-in/fan-out report is also helpful in finding errors such as microwords that are unaccessible or unspecified paths (or legs) down a branch tree.
- *Control-store map:* The control-store map-generation process gives the microprogrammer a listing of all locations in control store and identifies unused locations as potential patch areas.
- *Control-store simulator tapes:* An alternate method for representing the control store, especially in a development system, is to use an ROS simulator such as STEP 27 (Wilburn and Mick 1984). The contents of control store (ROS) can then be loaded across a data link from the microcode development system or with an ROS simulator tape. The ROS simulator tape is used for system debugging before PROMs are actually burned, giving the flexibility needed in a development environment.
- *PROM burn tape:* The generation of a PROM burn tape coupled with the EC (engineering-change) report results in the generation of only the PROM burn tapes that contain microwords that differ from those in control store at the previous link-edit time, thus saving time and money in burning the PROMS and offering a trace of changes made to the system.
- *Control-store static analysis by field and value:* The last feature unique to microcode linkage editors is the control-store static analysis function. This feature allows the microprogrammer to investigate where certain microword field values are used in a microword in control store, thus allowing determination of the effects of changes in microarchitectures or microword definition.

One area not covered, though of special interest to microprogrammers, concerns the area of pipelined microprogrammable architectures. Here, scheduling analysis and verification can be performed by the linkage editor in an effort to optimize the microcode. The whole concept of optimization can also be addressed at link-edit time, although traditionally it has been done at compile time (Fisher 1981).

Microcode Linkage-Editor Implementation Issues

This section discusses the cost/function tradeoffs that should be considered in designing a linkage editor for a microcode development system. Microarchitectures vary in size of control store and amount of microcode. An architecture that contains 256 locations of 16-bit microwords has no need for overlay capability or relocatable microcode. Similarly, a microarchitecture with a simple sequence control (in which the default address of the next microword is the next sequential address unless a branch microword is executed) has less use for fan in and fan out than a microarchitecture with multiway multicondition sequence control. Therefore, not all the functions mentioned need be incorporated into a microcode development system.

From the standpoint of implementation cost and schedule, a relatively basic microcode assembler and linkage editor may be sufficient tools for microcode development. Furthermore, some of the linkage-editor functions may be embedded into the assembler itself, thus eliminating the need for a linkage editor at all. Figure 8-4 shows an approximate ordering of microcode linkage-editor functions by cost. Cost is represented in the number of lines of high-level-language code required to implement the particular facility or function (note: the costs are shown as summations of previous costs). Microprogram size is represented by the total number of microcode bits to be written in the lifetime of the microarchitecture.

The curve is a linear approximation drawn from experience based on over a dozen avionics processors' microcode development systems (Tracz 1985). It can be interpreted as follows: for very small microcoding projects (.5K, 24-bit microwords) no microcode linkage editor is necessary. The functions of a linkage editor can be built into the translator or microcode assembler. Single microprograms become unmanageable in the 64K-bit region (2K × 32 bits). At this time the microprogram should be broken into separate modules.

The need for intermodule communication and relocation can be avoided if the microprogrammer specifies fixed addresses at assembly time (does his own memory management) and external addresses in the form of equates or constants. This is an unnecessary practice but eliminates the need for relocation. The next step in adding function is to introduce external symbols and entry statements to the source code, with the linkage editor taking care of external-address resolution. As a result of this change, the microcode assembly listing (if used) no longer reflects the true contents of each microword and a control-store map becomes increasingly important. The absolute listing feature can also be incorporated to supplement the documentation of the microprogram. An absolute listing is the assembler output listing modified to reflect the microword contents after relocation and external-address resolution.

When relocation is introduced into the microcode linkage editor, the microcode development system will have reached a level of sophistication that

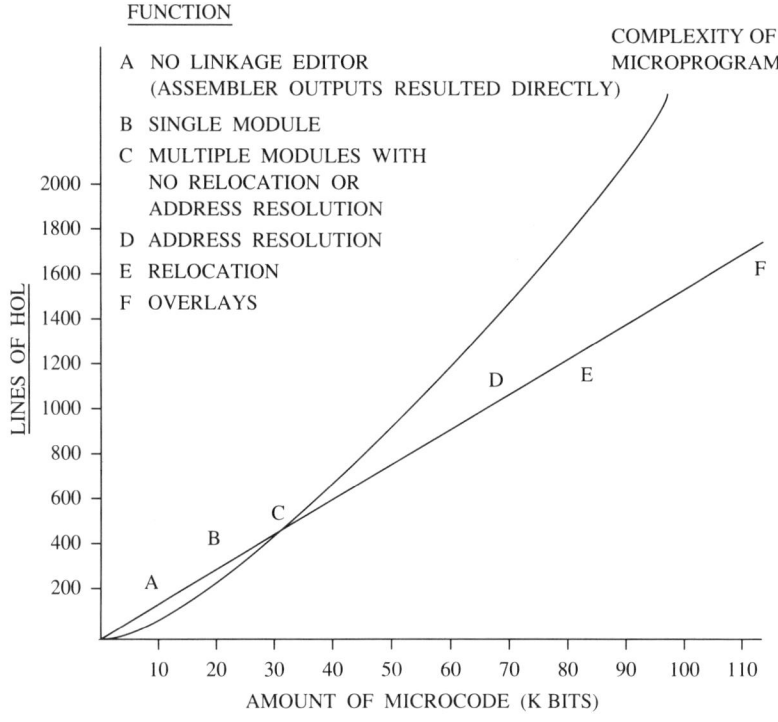

Figure 8-4. Link-edit function and microprogram size.

most assembler-language programmers consider a standard operating environment.

Superimposed on the graph in figure 8-4 is a line representing the complexity of the microprogram as it grows in size (Zincke 1981). Complexity is defined as the amount of function to be implemented in microcode and the degree it maps onto the microarchitecture at the assembler-language level. The intersection of the two lines shows the breakeven point where the benefits of improved link-edit functions are needed to manage the increasing complexity of microcode.

It should be noted that this analysis of cost and performance is based on the assumption of using a register-transfer-level microcode assembler and does not reflect the effects of using a high-level microprogramming language. The requirements of a linkage editor resulting from the use of a high-level microprogramming language are not as dependent on the amount of microcode to be written. That is, the amount of effort necessary to develop a compiler should result in increased microprogram productivity and performance that outweighs the development cost.

MICROCODE SIMULATORS

Software simulators for microcode modeling and debugging have existed since the early days of the IBM S/360. They have evolved from cumbersome batch jobs to powerful interactive programs. The advantages of generating and utilizing a microcode simulator cited by Myers and Hocker (1981) are as follows:

- *Parallel microprogram/hardware development:* As soon as the microword template is defined (or even earlier), the microprogrammers and logic designers can begin their jobs, along with the microcode toolsmiths. When the assembler and simulator are operational, the microprogrammer can begin debugging. The primary advantage to having debugged microcode before it goes on the hardware is that one source of error is eliminated when the hardware/software/firmware system does not properly function.
- *Easier debugging:* Software simulators generally provide a better debug environment for microcode testing than those found on the prototype or production hardware, although hardware test tools are becoming more sophisticated (Wagnon and Maine 1983; Wilburn and Mick 1984).
- *Special error checks:* The simulator can test for and trap certain subtle errors in the microprogram such as illegal combinations of microorders or sequences of microwords that might prove too difficult to detect, observe, and isolate on the hardware.
- *Parallel debugging:* Many microprogrammers can use the simulator simultaneously, thus eliminating the need for duplicate hardware and testers or multishift work.
- *Performance analysis:* System bottlenecks can be detected early with the simulation results.
- *Teaching tool:* The simulator is a good way to introduce a new microprogrammer to the microarchitecture of a machine or to introduce the concept of microprogramming (Mathur 1977; Prosser and Winkel 1983).
- *Reduced microcode-development cost:* Assuming that the actual cost of the simulator is reasonable, the payback in savings from less test hardware, reduced schedule time, and improved quality should more than compensate for the initial investment.

Simulator Requirements

In order to be a useful tool, a microcode simulator should demonstrate the following characteristics:

- *Visibility:* The microprogrammer should be able to display the value of each register, latch, or any state data in the processor.
- *State modifiability:* The microprogrammer should be able to change the value of any register, latch, or state data in the processor.
- *Controllability:* The user should be able to control the execution sequence of the microprogram by having:
  - *Single-step capability:* The ability to execute one microword at a time
  - *Multiple-step capability:* The ability to specify the execution of a fixed number of microinstructions or macroinstructions at a time
  - *Break-point capability:* The ability to execute microwords until a certain instruction address or data value in a register is reached
- *User-friendly:* The simulator's user interface should be designed so that:
  - The simulator is interactive as well as capable of being run in batch mode.
  - The user interface is easy to learn and use. When possible, it should be the same as the system-console diagnostic interface.
  - In batch mode, condition commands and looping is available for the construction of sophisticated tests.
  - There is automatic disassembly of microwords and assembly of patches
  - Symbolic debugging is supported. The symbol table is available from the assembly or compilation and link-edit phases for referencing microword locations or data values.
  - A reasonable response time is maintained for simulating a single instruction and user-command processing.
- *Checkpoint capability:* The microprogrammer should be able to save the current state of the machine at any time during the simulation and restore it to that state if desired at a later date. In a similar manner, the user should be able to reinitialize the processor to a known state.
- *Trace capability:* The microprogrammer should be able to specify which state information should be output at each step of the simulation or under what circumstances trace information should be output.
- *Functional completeness:* The simulator should faithfully reproduce the functions incorporated in the hardware.

- *Maintainability:* When hardware changes occur, the simulator and its command interface should be modifiable in a reasonable amount of time.

These and other features are available in most microcode simulators found in commercial use today (Guyer 1981; Schleimer and Meyers 1979; Tracz 1979; Firth 1980; Staas 1984), as well as in those developed in universities (Mezzalama, Prinetto, and Visintin 1981).

Microcode-Simulator Implementation Issues

Different strategies are available upon which to base the development of microcode simulators. The primary implementation tradeoff decision focuses at the level at which the simulator program chooses to simulate the microarchitecture. There are three levels at which simulation is possible:

1. *Functional or register-transfer level:* This is generally the easiest to implement because it views the microarchitecture at the highest level. It can be developed as a black box, independent of the actual hardware implementation, and runs the fastest of all three levels of simulators.
2. *Gate level:* This implements the circuit logic. This type of simulator is usually a byproduct of the design-automation tools, and is used for logic-design debug and fault analysis. It is sometimes used for microcode debug, but in general the user interface is more cumbersome and the throughput an order of magnitude slower than the functional simulator.
3. *Transistor level:* At this level, the physical properties of the circuit components are simulated. This is especially necessary for timing analysis in VLSI circuits. Simulation at this level is not practical for microcode debug because of the large overhead involved.

A second issue is whether the simulation does lazy evaluation or implicit full simulation. Lazy evaluation saves processing time and increases simulator performance because only the functions explicitly specified by the microinstruction are executed. In the case of implicit full simulation, all circuitry is executed, even though it doesn't participate in the generation of an explicitly specified result.

Another implementation technique is to create program modules for each major functional unit or logic device used in the microarchitecture design (multiplexors, ALU slices, sequencers, shifters, and so on). These subroutines can then be used as basic building blocks in future simulator development efforts.

The User Interface

It is advantageous to modularize the simulator design so that the user interface is separate from the data-flow simulator (fig. 8-5). The user interface can be thought of as the front end of the simulator. It can be reused across architectures with little modification, provided that it was designed to have a common interface and is table-driven.

Having the same user interface available on all levels of simulation as well as on the system diagnostic console or hardware tester results in a large return on investment (Wagnon and Maine 1983). Under these circumstances it is possible to run a test case on the simulator and the hardware simultaneously, side by side, on two adjacent terminals using the same set of commands. Discrepancies may be found by comparing the results, which are displayed in the same format on the adjacent terminals.

The same translator writing-system techniques used to implement microcode assemblers can be used to implement the user interface of any simulator (Tracz 1979). (The command syntax can be specified in Backus normal form (BNF) and the parsing tables generated automatically; see the section on aerospace processors below.)

CURRENT MICROCODE DEVELOPMENT FACILITIES

Microprogramming tools currently being used in industry are still somewhat primitive compared with the tools being used for software development. No machine-independent high-level microprogramming language is used for emulation microcode, but machine-dependent high-level microprogramming languages have been used by Burroughs and NEC. Some work is being done using variations of C as a machine-independent high-level microprogramming language for application microcode. The remaining portion of this chapter contains a description of the microprogramming tools being used to develop microcode by the following computer manufacturers:

- Burroughs
- Data General
- Digital Equipment Corporation
- IBM
- Nippon Electric Corporation

Burroughs Microprogram Development Tools

The microprogramming support for the high-performance processors developed by Burroughs Corporation is probably more advanced than any other major computer manufacturer (Wagnon and Maine 1983). The tools evolved from

Figure 8-5. Simulator block diagram.

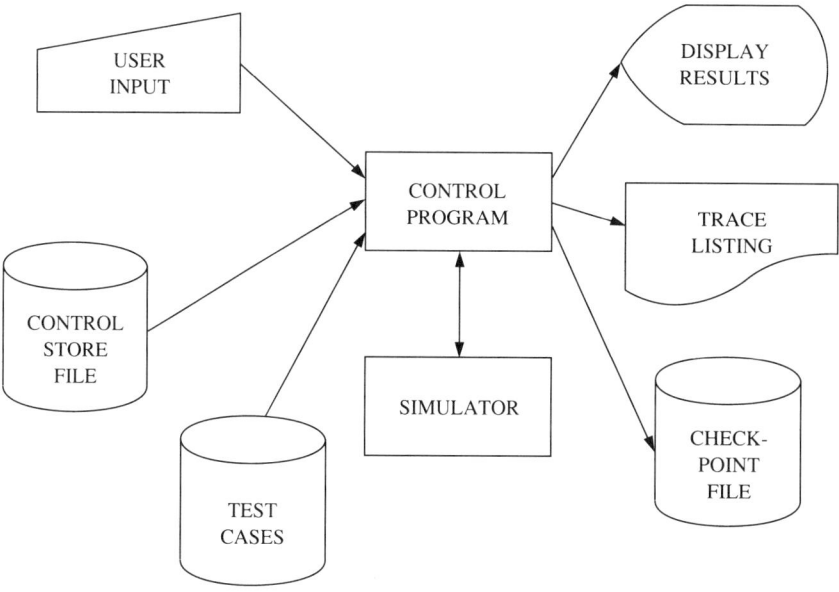

the adaptation of the support software used for operating-system development and maintenance. The suite of tools in the E-machine workbench (fig. 8-6) include:

- *Integrated library system:* This program keeps track of patches and changes to all microcode modules in a single data base. It provides the control capability for several microprogrammers developing different versions of the same microcode simultaneously.
- *High-level partially machine-independent microprogramming language* (OHNE): This language has no branch instruction and is tailored to the stack architecture the emulation is targeted for. Early versions of the compiler had a machine language back end to provide simulation capability before the microcode simulator was available.
- *Integrated editor:* The editor is integrated with the compiler and library system. If the compilation process generates any error messages, they are saved in an error file. The next time the source file is edited, the editor positions the source file to the line at which the error was detected. Additional errors may be subsequently scrolled. Any changes in the file are noted in the

Figure 8-6. The Burroughs E-machine microcode tool suite.

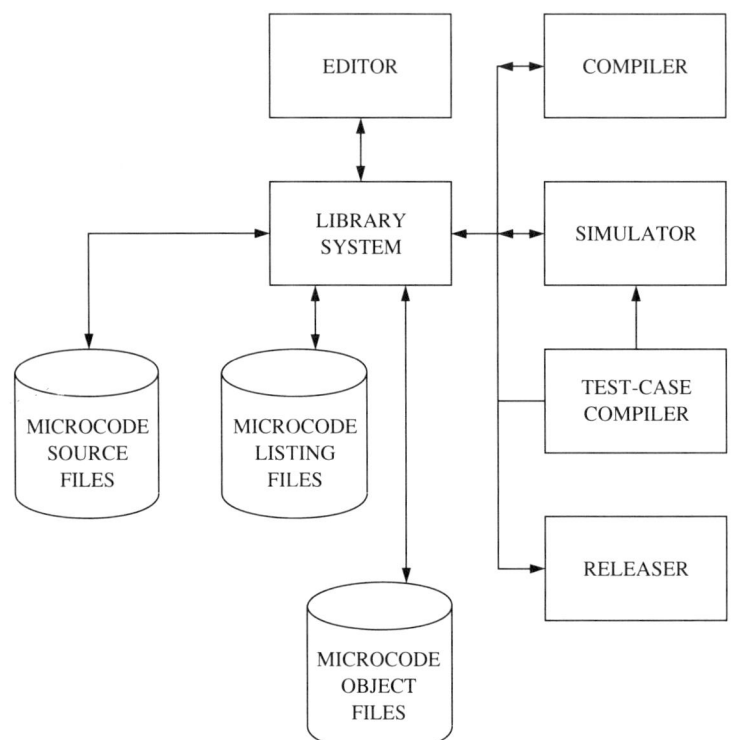

patch file by the library manager for controlling future release control.
- *Releaser:* This program is a function of the library system and handles all backups, version-number assignment, and configuration management.
- *Simulator:* The E-machine simulator provides a powerful debug environment for verifying the microcode for the E-machine. Furthermore, the user interface is the same as the console diagnostic interface, so microcode or macrocode can be run simultaneously by the hardware and the simulator using the same commands and test cases with the results available, side by side, for comparison in the same format. The simulator has many additional tests for conflict detection. It is used for early checkout of the microcode, performance evaluation, as well as freeing the prototype for hardware debug.

- *Test-case compiler:* An automated test facility provides easy regression analysis, as well as new test-case generation.

Using the E-machine workbench, the microprogrammers were able to write and simulate over 54,000 lines of microcode in less than one year.

Data General Microprogram Development Tools

Data General's microprogramming tools evolved from the MV/8000 project. They consisted of a microcode preprocessor, microcode assembler, and simulator (fig. 8-7a). The microcode preprocessor was created to overcome the inflexibility of the assembler. The assembler required a free-formatted, fixed sequence of mnemonics to appear on a single input record for each microword (Firth 1980). This, however, made the microcode difficult to edit, so a preprocessor was put in place that converted free-formatted microcode into formatted microcode. The advantages to this approach were that:

- It provided a uniform method of initializing unused fields.
- It minimized the amount of microcode to be reformatted.
- It provided an automatic reformatting of source code if the microword changed format.

The microcode assembler was table-driven, with the fields-template-mnemonic definition tables parsed by the assembler during the first pass of an assembly. Each microword could be followed by a template name, which selected the particular format of the microword and its default values to be assembled.

The output of the microcode assembler was a fixed-field listing, with the specified mnemonic or the default value appearing under the respective field of the microword. As an additional and unique documentation aid, a disassembler was used to generate register-transfer-level type comments regarding the actions being performed by each microword (Laws 1977).

For the MV/8000, a functional simulator was extensively used to debug the microcode and microdiagnostics. It provided an interactive simulation capability with

- Trace capability of the full machine state
- Micro- and macroinstruction breakpoint capability
- Display and modification capability on any value in the machine

For the MV/4000 and MV/10000, a new set of tools (fig. 8-7b), the UDSYS system, was created (Beauchamp and Firth 1982; Data General 1982). The microcode assembler was modified to be definition/table-driven. The tables are generated by a program known as MAKEPS, which contains a permanent symbol file that drives the microcode assembler. The UDSYS system provides:

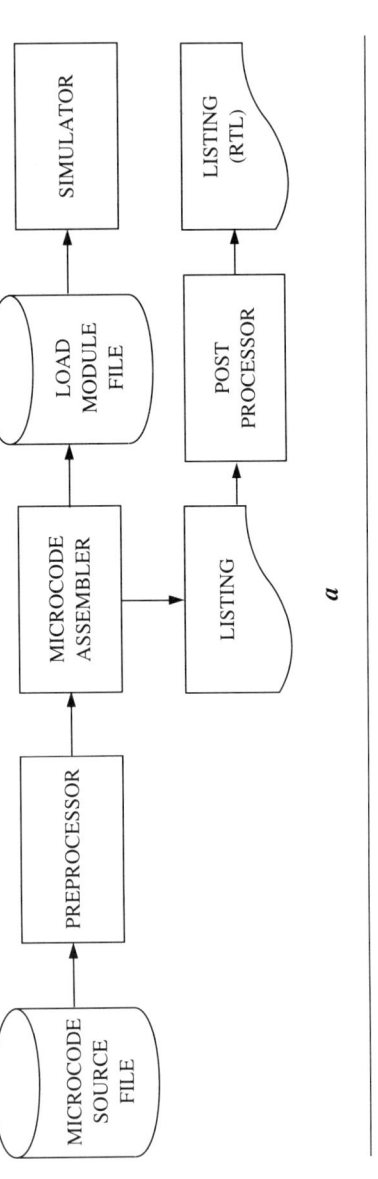

Figure 8-7. Data General microcode tool suite: *a*. MV/8000; *b*. MV/4000 and MV/10000.

Figure 8-7. (continued)

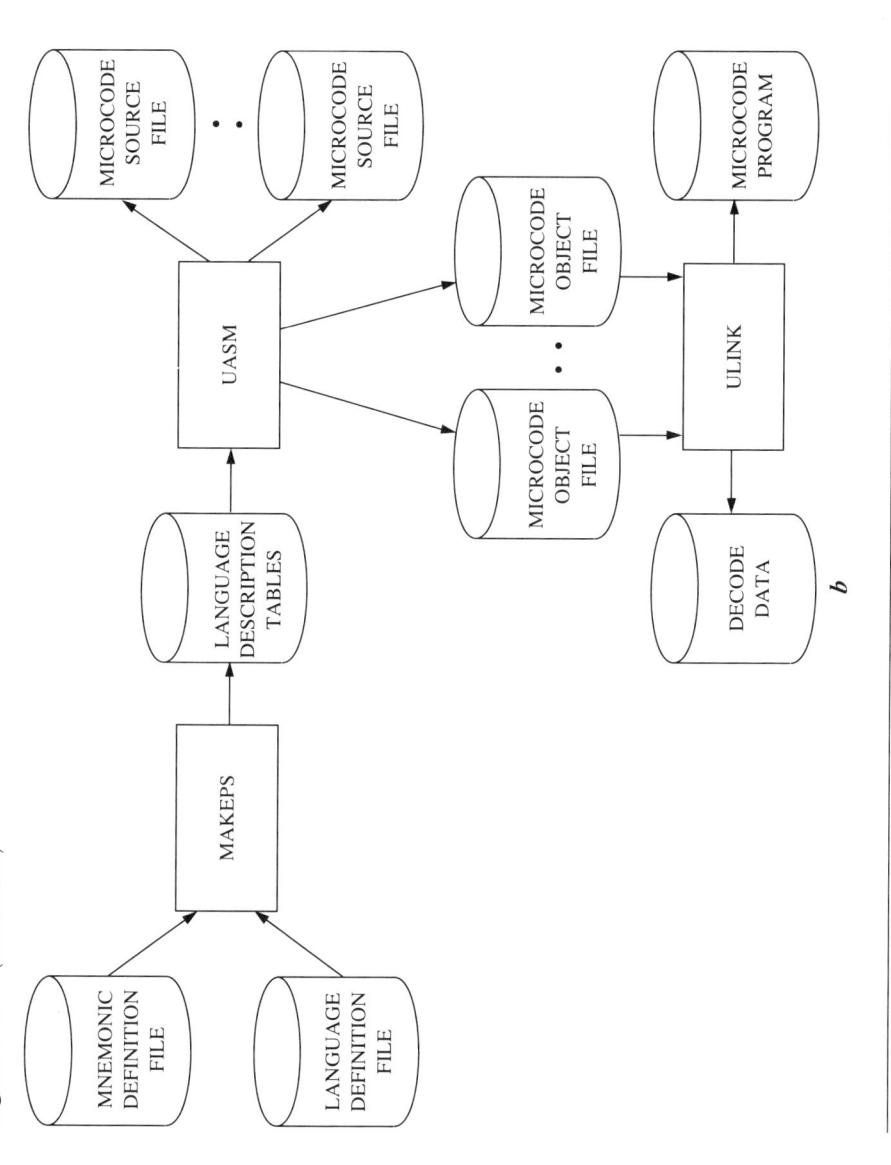

b

- A general purpose, table-driven system
- Modular assembly and linking
- Well-formatted mnemonic disassemblies in the listings
- The ability to provide timing conformance verification
- The ability to encode any mixture of vertical and horizontal microword formats (including micro-/nanocode)
- The ability to provide the user with meaningful error messages

The ULINK (Data General 1982) microcode linker is used to bind separately assembled microcode modules. A separate simulator is available for the MV/4000 and MV/8000, each with the same user interface.

DEC Microprogram Development Tools

Digital Equipment Corporation's MICRO2 microcode development system (fig. 8-8) provides support for the VAX and VLSI VAX series of processors (Digital Equipment 1981). It consists of an assembler and loader but no linkage editor. MICRO2 is definition-driven and provides:

- Free-format fields
- Macro expansion capability
- Validity checking of microorders
- Formatted output with cross-reference listing
- Register-transfer-appearing syntax (partly attributable to a powerful naming convention that allows spaces)

The MICRO2 microcode assembler has recently been enhanced to perform automatic address assignment as determined by stylized comments (Gries and Woodward 1984). This greatly simplifies the microprogrammer's task of allocating control-store addresses that conform to certain branch-boundary constraints imposed by the n-way branching mechanism found in most high-performance microsequencers.

The DEC microcode tool suite, as used to develop the VLSI VAX, included an integrated set of system simulators and testers, each utilizing the same set of commands to provide a consistent user interface. At the highest level was the functional simulator (FUNSIM), written in DECSIM. Below that, a logic simulator (LOGSIM) and transistor-level simulator (TRSIM) were also used. Finally, an engineering tester (ET) was developed to control the tester hardware and prototype computer, which maintained the same command structure as all three software simulators.

The V-System (Sites 1981; Poe, Goodell, and Steely 1981) was a research-oriented microcode development system at DEC based on the STRUM system (Patterson 1976; Patterson, Lew, and Tuck 1979). Its objective was to demonstrate the feasibility of an easily retargetable microcode compiler as well as to

Figure 8-8. DEC microcode tool suite.

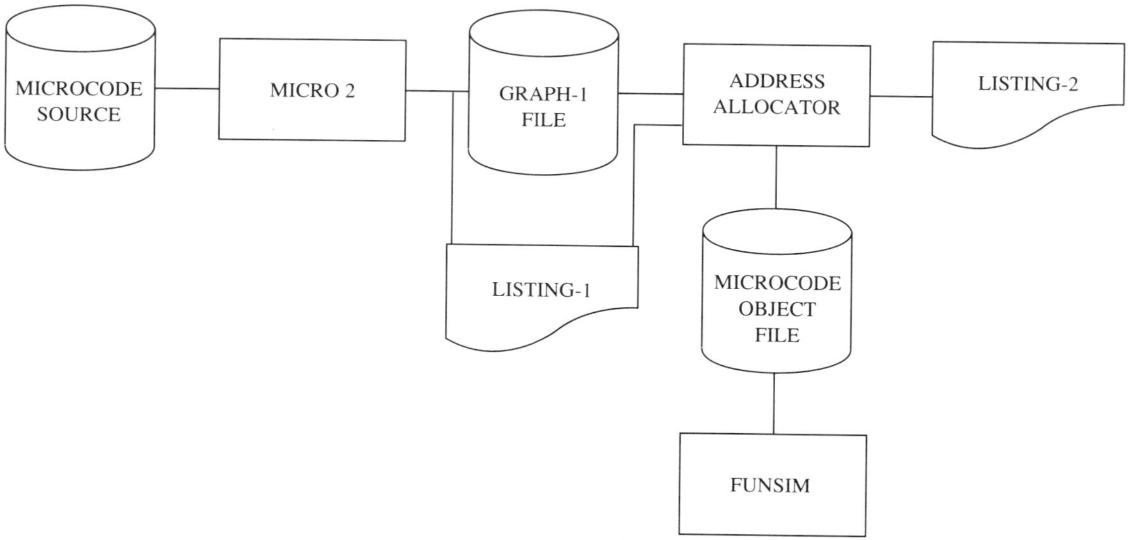

impose a top-down microcode development methodology in which the specifications for the microcode were refined and verified at each level of abstraction through the use of assertions and theorem proving.

IBM Microprogram Development Tools

Microprogramming within the IBM Corporation is organized by product. ISA (instruction-set architecture) emulation microcodes are written in Poughkeepsie, New York (38xx Series), Endicott, New York (43xx Series), Rochester, Minnesota (System 38), Owego, New York, and Manassas, Virginia (aerospace/military processors). Operating-system assists are developed in Poughkeepsie, Endicott (Olbert 1982), and Rochester. Device-control microcode for printers, disk drives, tapes, and mass-storage devices are manufactured at the San Jose, California (Wang 1982), and Tucson, Arizona (Skibbe 1982) locations. This section discusses the microprogram development tools used to develop ISA microcode.

Commercial Processors

Microprogramming support tools within IBM originated with the CAS system in Poughkeepsie (Carter 1984). This tool set consisted of a microcode assembler, an address-assignment program, and the CAS logic drawing (CLD) program. It has been the main baseline for microcode support software for mainframe efforts. The CAS system was even used for the control logic on early disk drives (2341) until a more vertical microword was selected. CLDs, until recently adopted by NEC, were a unique form of microprogram documentation (fig. 8-2). They are a cross between a program flow chart and a circuit logic diagram. They are highly suitable for specifying the control flow of microprogram logic for highly horizontal (80-125 bits wide) microinstructions with a high degree of parallel branching (2-, 4-, 8-, 16-, 32-, and 256-way). The 43xx Series 32-bit microword is the only IBM mainframe architecture not to use CLDs for microprogram documentation.

Two microcode support packages have evolved from the CAS base line. The first, used on the IBM 3033, consists of a microcode assembler and the graphic microcode editor (GME). GME allows the microprogrammer to edit the microword contents and net lines of each CLD page by using an IBM 3277 dual-screen graphics attachment and joystick. The microprogrammer also has the option of assembling each microword upon entering it in the assembler.

The second microcode development system originated in Santa Teresa, California for the 370 model 158 (Dubbs 1974). It has also been used on the 3031 and current 3081 processors as well as for the System 38. Based on a register-transfer-level syntax for microprogram specification, it features a microcode assembler, address-assigning program, linkage editor, block-drawing generator (another term for CLD), and simulator. The translator/assembler is based on the

LaLonde grammar analyzer and translator writing system. The microcode support-software developer specifies the syntax of the microprogramming language in BNF, and the parsing tables and code-generation skeleton are automatically produced.

Aerospace Processors

This section describes the evolution of microprogramming methodology and microcode support software that has taken place in the Federal Systems Division, Owego Laboratory. Microprogramming, like programming, has experienced a significant technical refinement, partially due to the need to develop timely, cost-effective, quality products. The improvement in microprogramming tools has also been motivated by the increase in microprogramming efforts in Owego for systems such as B52G/H, NATO/AWACs, and B-1B, and in Manassas for various signal-processing applications.

Military microcode support software has evolved in three distinct stages or generations. Figure 8-9 shows this evolution of microprogram support software. Each generation will be described in the following sections.

First-Generation Microcode Support Software The first generation of microcode tools consisted of an assortment of ad hoc programs based on existing microcode support tools used in Poughkeepsie on the IBM/360 development effort control automation system (CAS) or one-of-a-kind cross-assemblers built from Assembler H macros or APL functions. There were no linkage editors, since the microprograms were small, and no simulators, since the microprogrammer used the hardware for testing microprograms.

Second-Generation Microcode Support Software The second generation of microcode support software appeared as a result of experiences on the Space Shuttle on-board computer effort. The Space Shuttle microcode was written by a small group of individuals who also developed a simulator to facilitate parallel checkout while the hardware was being developed. It was at this time that a reevaluation of the Assembler H and APL cross-assembler approach revealed limitations on error detection and recovery that could possibly have jeopardized the quality of the microprogram. A new approach was taken for microcode translator development, adapting compiler writing expertise and experience with LaLonde's LALR grammar analyzer (a translator writing system). Figure 8-10 shows the components used in this approach. A microcode assembler is developed by first analyzing the format and fields in the microword and then deriving a language or grammar with respect to the operations and operators associated with each field. This grammar is written in Backus normal form (BNF) and used as input to the grammar analyzer, which generates the parsing tables and code-build or synthesis skeleton routines. The parsing tables are then combined with an existing "front end," or generalized lexicographical analysis and parsing

Figure 8-9. Evolution of microprogramming development at IBM-FSD.

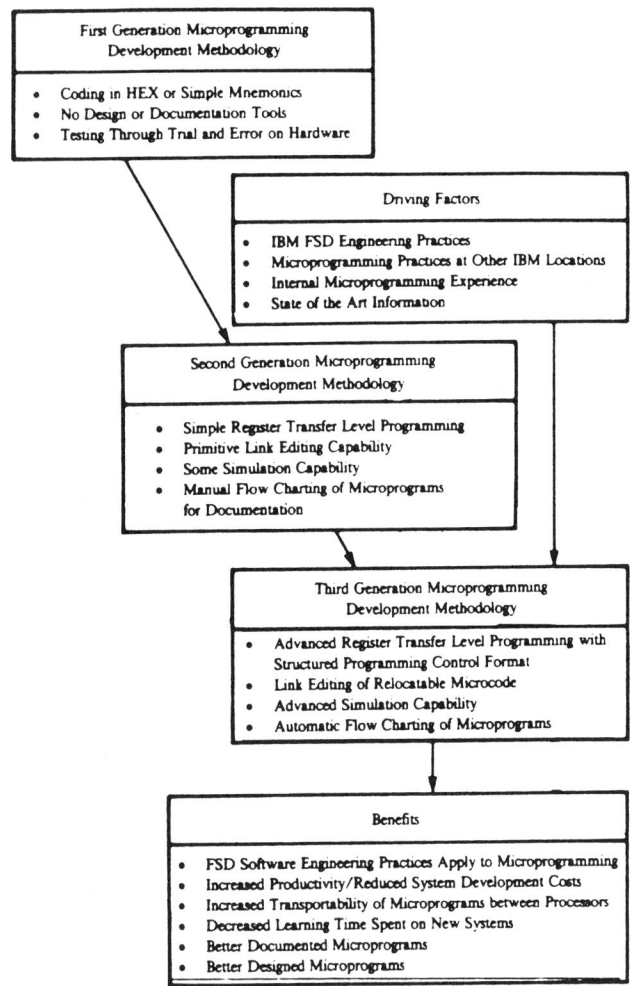

program, and the synthesis skeleton, or "back end," filled in with microcode bit field values. This approach has resulted in considerable savings in development costs and time. The previous approaches took an average of four person-months of effort, while the grammar analyzer approach takes only two. The user benefited by increased flexibility, facility, and savings in processing time and cost halving over previous methods.

Other tools introduced as part of the second generation of microcode support software were a linkage editor and a microcode simulator. The linkage editor

Figure 8-10. Microcode assembler implementation structure.

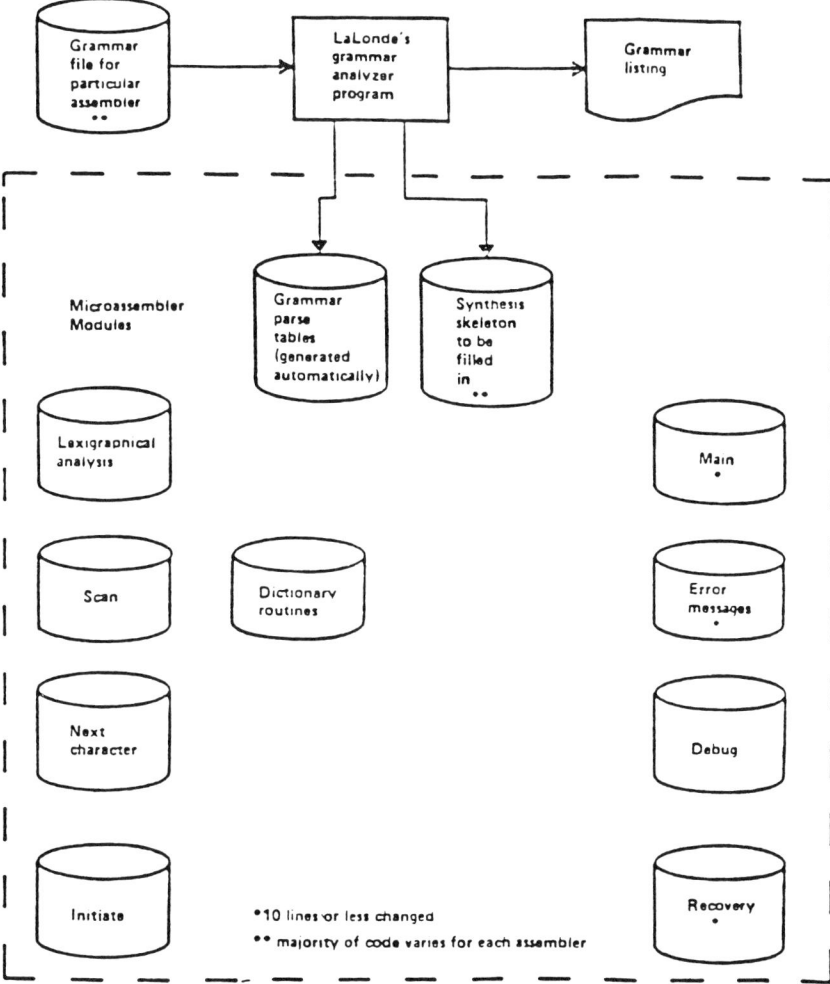

combined separately assembled microprogram segments and did external address resolution but did not have relocation capability. The simulator made use of the 3270 terminal to allow full-screen display of the simulated contents of the microarchitecture with interactive modification and displaying of simulation results (see fig. 8-11). The linkage editor resulted in cost savings to the user, who could now efficiently modularize microprograms. When a change was made, only the modules affected needed to be modified and reassembled, rather than a costly reassembly of all the source microcode. The simulator provided an early

Figure 8-11. Microcode simulator, full-screen format.

```
RETIRED:      I COUNT: 0000      TIME: 00000000      SIMTEST       — ISA SIMULATION —
-->
                    ROS_IC     000      FA 0 00000000 0    AI 0 00000000 0    EA    00  IUIC   0000
  - CURRENT -       ICOUNT     0001     FB 0 00000000 0    BI 0 00000000 0    EB    00  PC     0000
                    TIME       00010000 FC 0 00000000 0    FS 0 00000000 0    EC    00  MC     0000
                    RD SDR 00000000     00000000 00000000  FW                 STATA 00  STATB  00
              +0 +1            +2 +3    +4 +5    +6 +7     +8 +9    +A +B     +C +D     +E +F
        LS  0 00000000    00000000      00000000 00000000  00000000 00000000  00000000  00000000
              00000000    00000000      00000000 00000000  00000000 00000000  00000000  00000000
        SEC 1 00000000    00000000      00000000 00000000  00000000 00000000  00000000  00000000
              00000000    00000000      00000000 00000000  00000000 00000000  00000000  00000000
        RDS  000  0800C0077  086 C0000  000000C9
                                                          • ─────────── ADSTOP ─────────── •
                                                          - AD 0  •••          AD 3  •••   -   05/29/80
              • ─────────── •  OP    00    R1  00   ISEC 0 - AD 1  •••         AD 4  •••   -   11:29:45
              - OPDECODE -    OPX   00    R2  00   CSEC 0 - AD 2  •••          AD 5  •••   -
              • ─────────── •  DISP8 00                   • ─────────────────────────────── •

                    ROS_IC     000      FA 0 00000000 0    AI 0 00000000 0    EA    00  IJIC   0000
  - PREVIOUS -      ICOUNT     0000     FB 0 00000000 0    BI 0 00000000 0    EB -  00  PC     0000
                    TIME       00000000 FC 0 00000000 0    FS 0 00000000 0    EC -  00  MC     0000
                    ROSDR 00000000      00000000 00000000                     STATA 00  STATB  00
```

checkout tool and increased the quality of the microcode by detecting illegal microcode sequences and operations as well as by providing shorter development schedules by allowing overlapped microprogram verification by multiple users.

Third-Generation Microcode Support Software The third generation of microcode support software tools is a result of the experience gathered from developing support software for over a dozen processors during the previous two years and the desire to provide a development environment to support FSD software standards. Analysis showed that a good base line of tools was in place. However, short (one-to-two-month) development schedules and requirements that tended to "mature" over that period required a modified approach that departed from conventional development.

The ideal solution to cope with the dynamic requirements and short schedule constraints is an automatic tool-generation capability (fig. 8-12). This process would accept as input a description of the microarchitecture written in a computer-hardware description language (CHDL) and generate as output an assembler, linkage editor, and simulator tailored for that architecture. One advantage of this approach is the obvious savings in time and money to develop the support software. Another advantage is an improved function description of the architecture from which the microprogrammer can develop the microcode and which serves as a document for hardware design review. There are three disadvantages. First, the development of the "automatic tool-generating process" requires substantial investment. Second, the tools often suffer from inflexibility and inefficiency, since they use a generalized base line. Finally, the quality of

Figure 8-12. The ideal automatic tool-generation system.

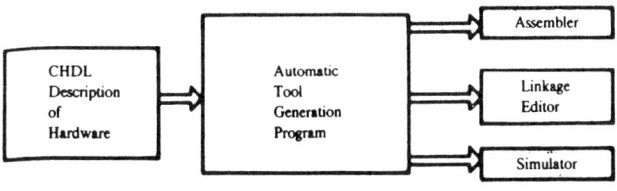

the tools can only be as good as the quality of the input to the program. In other words, translating the architecture into the CHDL is a precise and potentially time-consuming activity.

Automatic Microcode Support Software Generation The Microprogrammers' workbench (Brubaker 1986) is a result of the effort to automate the generation of microcode tools in Owego. This approach simplifies the ideal solution previously described. The microcode assemblers and linkage editors are partially derived through the automation process shown in figure 8-13. All tools (assembler, linkage editor, CLD generator, and simulator) have been designed

Figure 8-13. Current assembler-generation approach.

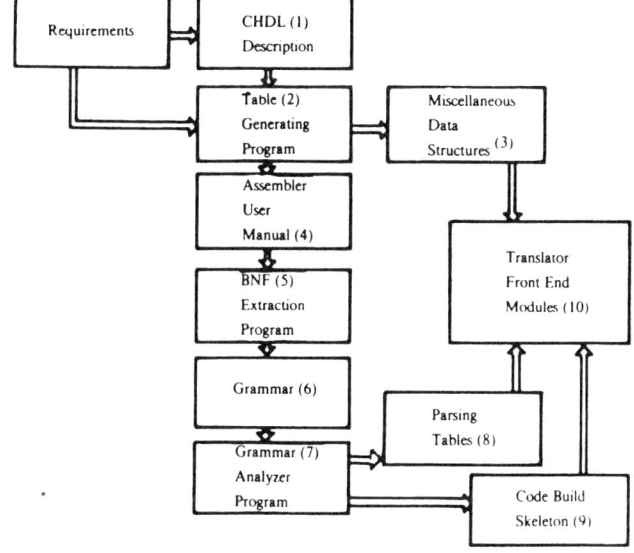

and implemented with retargetability in mind. Preprocessor variables and data abstraction have been used to facilitate changes in various system parameters.

When microcode tools are developed, the requirements must first be translated into a CHDL description (see fig. 8-13, item 1) of the microarchitecture (microword size, data flow, and control flow). A user manual is also developed incorporating the programming syntax rules and mnemonics for microprogramming the computer. BNF is used to describe the microprogramming language. Before any more work is done, a requirements review is conducted with the engineers. Their concurrence that the user manual properly reflects the desired software products is sought. The user manual is then updated, if necessary, to achieve compliance. All subsequent changes result in updates to these two documents (CHDL description and user manual). The documents also serve as a requirements-control vehicle, which may be updated in the future if changes are made to the product.

Once requirements have been defined, the automatic tool-generation process begins. A table-generation program (item 2) processes the CHDL description, which results in the generation of bit-assignment tables (item 3) and various data structures that become part of the user manual (item 4) and are used directly in all later programs. The next phase is the extraction of the formal grammar (item 5) from the user manual. Once the grammar (item 6) is extracted, development proceeds in the same manner discussed in the previous section, with the grammar processed by the grammar analyzer (item 7). The grammar analyzer produces the parsing tables (item 8) and synthesis skeletons (item 9) for the microcode assembler. These are combined with the existing front-end translator-processing modules (item 10) to implement the microcode assembler program.

Simulator development proceeds in a similar manner. The CHDL is used as a high-level design document with the data structures derived from it used directly in the simulator source. The simulator user manual contains a description of the interactive commands available to the user. It is subjected to the same automation process, with the outputs combined with an existing simulator-control-program front end. The actual processor simulation is developed manually from the CHDL description or taken from a library of chip-simulation routines derived from previous simulators. The full-screen interface is based on using the display management system to define the screen layout and to display the simulated results and allow direct manipulation of the simulated hardware resources. The use of this partial automation process has resulted in further reductions in microcode assembler and simulator development costs by 50% and 20%, respectively.

Other Enhancements The third-generation microcode support-software tools have increased in functional capability beyond the scope of automatic tool generation. The microcode-assembler base line now features a macroprocessor, user-defined opcodes and mnemonics, and automatic boundary alignment for branch addresses. The microcode linkage editor provides valuable static analysis to branching and field usage as well as relocation and external address resolution.

Two other tools, the CLD generator and the CLD line-editor program (CLEP), have advanced in capability, while aiding in the documentation of microprograms by providing control-logic diagrams. The CLD generator performs automatic line routing of microwords specified on a CLD page (see fig. 8-2). CLEP, like GME, provides the user with a convenient interactive editor to enter CLD information and easily update microprogram source and documentation/design.

NEC Microprogram Development Tools

The Nippon Electric Company's Microcode Design-Support System (MDS) provides machine-dependent, retargetable, high-level microprogramming-language support for horizontal, vertical and split (micro/nano) microcode implementation and simulation (Takahashi et al. 1982, 1985). The tools available include (fig. 8-14):

- *Source-file management program:* This is the microcode data base manager.
- *Library processor:* Since all the microcode tools are definition-driven, this program converts the microinstruction format, mnemonics, and branching mechanism into the tables necessary to drive the rest of the tools.
- *Preprocessor:* This is a macroprocessor or compiler of sorts. It converts the tailorable machine-dependent high-level language into the standard assembler format.
- *Address-assignment program:* This assigns microwords to addresses in control store according to the branch boundary required.
- *Assembler:* This is a table-driven, free-format macroassembler with a wide assortment of options (cross-reference listings, fan-in and fan-out list, microword field validity checking, and so on).
- *Linker:* This combines separately assembled modules.
- *Analyzer:* This performs a symbolic execution of microcode.
- *Simulator:* The simulator, called mixed-level simulator (MIXS), takes a microarchitecture description written in FDL (functional description language) and generates a simulator on which the microcode may be executed (Yamada 1980).
- *Postprocessor:* This consists of an assortment of utility routines for creating control-store load tapes or PROM burn tapes.

The microprogramming environment consists of desktop PCs, which each microprogrammer uses for initial entry and update of microprogram segments

Figure 8-14. The NEC suite of microprogramming tools.

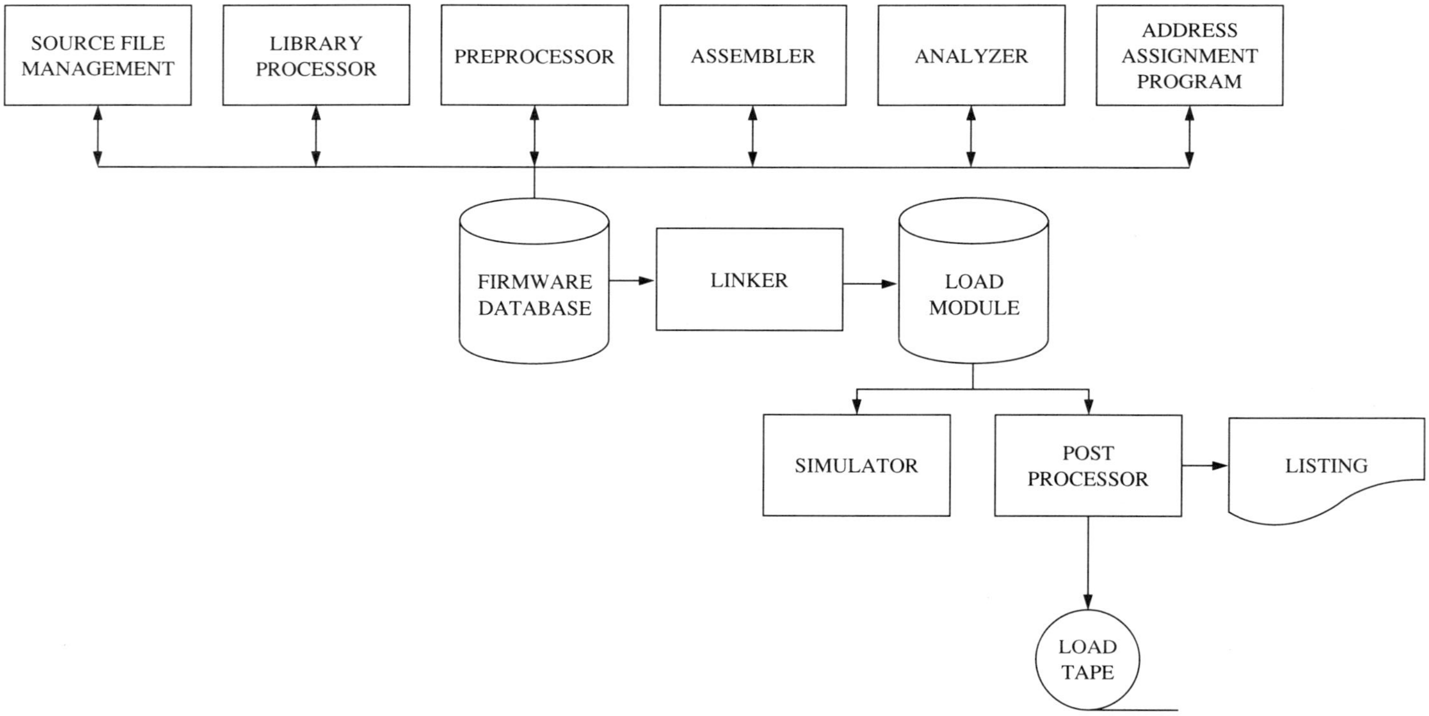

off-line. These files are then downloaded for a batch run to a mainframe for assembly and link-edit. Simulations are done interactively or in batch mode. The microcode flow charts are produced on the mainframe and are vertical, not horizontal, in format (control flows top to bottom, not left to right as in the IBM format).

In other applications of microcode-tool technology, NEC has successfully implemented a microprogram-converter program (Takahashi 1984) that translates a microprogram written in the machine-dependent microprogramming language of one processor into the machine-dependent microprogramming language of another. NEC has also applied expert system technology to create a self-configuring microcode development system (Shimizu and Sakamura 1983).

CONCLUSION

The primary factors for determining the types of functions to be incorporated into a microcode support software system are cost, schedule, and technical worth. The cost of developing all microprogramming support software tools should be in proportion to the amount of microcode to be written and the complexity of the architecture. A flexible base line of easily modifiable support software tools is one approach to decreasing the cost of development and shortening the development process. A specification-driven tool suite is another approach. The benefits of increased microprogrammer productivity and improved quality of microprograms result directly from the increased functional capabilities in the support tools. The evolution of support-software technology will continue as new tools and more powerful workstations are made possible through advances in related technologies.

In summary, for any tools to be successful, they must be:

- *Integrated:* The tools should exhibit a user interface that is self-consistent as well as consistent with other tools the microprogrammer may use.
- *Robust:* The tools must provide basic and enhanced functional capability. The microprogrammer must perceive a significant return on investment of time spent in learning how to use them.
- *Of the utmost quality:* Finally, above all, the tools must work and work well. The user should have confidence in their ability to do the job, otherwise, they will be misused or not used at all.

REFERENCES

Bartlett, J. F. 1981. "MicroTAL—A Machine Dependent, High-Level Microprogramming Language." *Proceedings of the 14th Annual Workshop on Microprogramming,* 109–14. New York: ACM.

Beauchamp, R. W., and Firth, N. R. 1982. "UDSYS: A Microcode Development System." *Proceedings of the 15th Annual Workshop on Microprogramming*, 35–41. New York: ACM.

Berglass, G. R. 1980. "A Meta-Assembler for Highly Parallel Microprogrammable Systems." *Proceedings of the 13th Annual Workshop on Microprogramming*, 181–89. New York: ACM.

Brubaker, W. J. 1986. "Owego's Microprogrammers Workbench Software Products to be Released Soon." *FSD Technology News* 3 (2).

Carter, W. J. 1984. Private communication.

Chadwick, D. 1983. "Firmware Engineering Tools and Methodology." Panel discussion at 16th Annual Workshop on Microprogramming. Downingtown, PA.

Charlton, C. C., Jackson, D., and Leng, P. H. 1984. "The Generation of Simulator Based Systems for Microcode Development." *Proceedings of the 17th Annual Workshop on Microprogramming*. 114–21. New York: ACM.

Data General. 1982. *UASM Microassembler Manual* (093-400030) Westboro, MA.

Data General. 1982. *ULINK Microcode Linker Manual* (093-400029) Westboro, MA.

Data General. 1982. *SIMx Microcode Simulator* (093-400031) Westboro, MA.

Davidson, S. 1983. "High Level Microprogramming—Current Usage, Future Prospects." *Proceedings of the 16th Annual Workshop on Microprogramming*, 193–200. New York: ACM.

Digital Equipment. 1981. *The VAX 11/780 Microprogramming Tools User's Guide.* AAH306A-TE: Digital Equipment Corporation.

Dubbs, E. W.; Parsons, R. L.; and Petersen, J. E. 1972. "A Microprogram Design System Translator, an Introduction Proceedings of Compcon-72," 95–98. Northridge, CA: IEEE Computer Society Press.

Eager, Michael J. 1983. "M29—An Advanced Retargetable Microcode Assembler." *Proceedings of the 16th Annual Workshop on Microprogramming*, 92–100. New York: ACM.

Eckhouse, R. H. 1979. "A High Level Microprogramming Language (MPL)." *AFIPS Conference Proceedings*, 38:169–77. Arlington, VA: AFIPS Press.

Firth, N. R. 1980. "The Role of Software Tools in the Development of the ECLIPSE MV/8000 Microcode." *Proceedings of the 13th Annual Workshop on Microprogramming*, 54–58. New York: ACM.

Fisher, J. A. 1981. "Two to the N-Way Jump Microinstruction Hardware and an Effective Instruction Binding." *Proceedings of the 13th Annual Workshop on Microprogramming*, 64–78. New York: ACM.

————. 1981. "Microcode compaction: Looking forward and looking backward." *AFIPS Proceedings* 50: 95–102. Arlington, VA: AFIPS Press.

Geyer, S., and Lake, A. 1981. "Development Tools for User Microprogramming." *Proceedings of the 14th Annual Workshop on Microprogramming*, 74–77. New York: ACM.

Gieser, J. L., and Sheraga, R. J. 1982. "Microarchitecture Description Techniques." *Proceedings of the 15th Annual Workshop on Microprogramming*, 23–33. New York: ACM.

Goodell, R. 1979. "An ISPS Microassembler," *Proceedings of the 4th International Symposium on Computer Hardware Description Language*, 62–68. New York: ACM.

———. 1981. "Using Semantic Productions to Compile Microcode in the V-Compiler." *Proceedings of the Euromicro Symposium*, 341–49. Amsterdam: North-Holland.

Greenberg, K. F. 1981. "The Micro8 Microcode Assembler." *Proceedings of the 14th Annual Workshop on Microprogramming*, 78–82. New York: ACM.

Gries, R., and Woodward, J. A. 1984. "Software Tools Used in the Development of the VLSI VAX Microcomputer." *Proceedings of the 17th Annual Workshop on Microprogramming*, 55–58. New York: ACM.

Guffin, R. M. 1982. "A Microprogramming Language Directed Microarchitecture." *Proceedings of the 15th Annual Workshop on Microprogramming*, 42–49. New York: ACM.

Habib, S., and Yang, X-L. 1981. "The Use of a Meta-Assembler to Design an M code Interpreter on AMD2900 Chips." *Proceedings of the 14th Annual Workshop on Microprogramming*, 38–50. New York: ACM.

Husson, S. S. 1970. *Microprogramming: Principles and Practices*. Englewood Cliffs, NJ: Prentice-Hall.

Kott, R. K., and Ambroziak, K. 1981. "The Cross-Assembler Universality Versus Standardization of Microcomputer Assembly Languages." *Euromicro Symposium*, 209–17. Amsterdam: North-Holland.

Laws, B. A. 1977. "Microbe: A self-commenting microassembler." *Proceedings of the 10th Annual Workshop on Microprogramming*: 61–65. New York: ACM.

Mathur, F. P. 1977. "MICROSIM: A Microinstruction Simulator for Teaching Microprogramming and Emulation." *Proceedings of the 10th Annual Workshop on Microprogramming*, 109–18. New York: ACM.

Meith, W. H., and Richter, L. 1981. "MMDS—A Microprogram Development Tool." *Euromicro Symposium*, 261–68. Amsterdam: North-Holland.

Meyers, W. 1981. "Design of a Microcode Linkage Editor." *Proceedings of the 14th Annual Workshop on Microprogramming*. New York: ACM.

Mezzalama, M., and Prinetto, P. 1979. "Design and Implementation of a Flexible and Interactive Microprogram Simulator." *Proceedings of the 12th Annual Workshop on Microprogramming*, 42–48. New York: ACM.

Mezzalama, M.; Prinetto, P.; and Visintin, I. 1981. "A Hierarchical Integrated System For Microcode Development." *Euromicro Symposium*, 251–60. Amsterdam: North-Holland.

Myers, G. J. 1980. *Digital System Design with LSI Bit-Slice Logic*. New York: John Wiley & Sons.

Myers, G. J., and Hocker, D. G. 1981. "The Use of Software Simulators in the Testing and Debugging of Microprogram Logic." *IEEE Transactions on Computers* C-30 (7):519–24.

Nash, J., and Spak, M. 1979. "Hardware and Software Tools for the Development of a Micro-Programmed Microprocessor." *Proceedings of the 12th Annual Workshop on Microprogramming*, 73–83. New York: ACM.

Olbert, A. G. 1982. "Crossing the Machine Interface." *Proceedings of the 15th Annual Workshop on Microprogramming*, 163–72. New York: ACM.

Padegs, A. 1981. "System/360 and Beyond." *IBM Journal of Research and Development* 25 (5):377–90.

Patterson, D. A. 1976. "STRUM: Structured Microprogramming System for Correct Firmware." *IEEE Transactions on Computers* C-25 (10):974–85.

Patterson, D. A.; Lew, K.; and Tuck, R. 1979. "Towards an Efficient, Machine Independent Language for Microprogramming." *Proceedings of the 12th Annual Workshop on Microprogramming*, 22–35. New York: ACM.

Poe, M. D.; Goodell, R.; and Steely, S. 1981. "Issues of the Design of a Low Level Microprogramming for Global Microcode Compaction." *Proceedings of the 14th Annual Workshop on Microprogramming*, 88–94. New York: ACM.

Powers, V. M., and Hernandez, J. H. 1978. "Microprogram Assemblers for Bit-Slice Microprocessors." *Computer* 18 (7):108–20.

Prosser, F., and Winkel, D. 1983. "The Logic Engine Development System Support for Microprogrammed Bit-Slice Development." *Proceedings of the 16th Annual Workshop on Microprogramming*, 84–91. New York: ACM.

Ris, F. 1984. "Experience with Access Functions in an Experimental Compiler." *IBM Journal of Research and Development* 28 (1):40–51.

Schlaeppi, H. 1974. "A Microcode Compiler." Presentation at IBM FSD, Owego, NY.

Schleimer, S., and Meyers, W. J. 1979. "Experience with a High Level Micromachine Simulator." *Proceedings of the 12th Annual Workshop on Microprogramming*, 49–54. New York: ACM.

Sheraga, R. J., and Gieser, J. L. 1981. "Automatic Microcode Generation for Horizontally Microprogrammed Processors." *Proceedings of the 14th Annual Workshop on Microprogramming*, 154–68. New York: ACM.

Sherwood, W. 1984. "A Prototype Engineering Tester for Microcode and Hardware Debugging." *Proceedings of the 17th Annual Workshop on Microprogramming*, 64–69. New York: ACM.

Shimizu, T., and Sakamura, K. 1983. "MIXER: An Expert System for Microprogramming." *Proceedings of the 16th Annual Workshop on Microprogramming*, 168–75. New York: ACM.

Sint, M. 1980. "A Survey of High Level Microprogramming Languages." *Proceedings of the 13th Annual Workshop on Microprogramming*, 141–53. New York: ACM.

Sites, D. 1981. "Microprogramming Tools at DEC." Panel discussion at the 14th Annual Workshop on Microprogramming, Palo Alto, CA.

Skibbe, R. E. 1982. "PACE: A Microprogram Evaluation System." *Proceedings of the 15th Annual Workshop on Microprogramming*, 181–96. New York: ACM.

Skordahkis, E. 1983. "Meta-Assemblies." *IEEE Micro* 3 (2):6–16.

Staas, G. "TDL: A Hardware/Microcode Test Language Interpreter." 1984. *Proceedings of the 17th Annual Workshop on Microprogramming*, 122–28. New York: ACM.

Takahashi, K., Takahashi, E., Bitoh, T., Aoyama, T., and Yamada, A. 1982. "MDS: An Improved Total System for Firmware Development." *Proceedings of the 15th Annual Workshop on Microprogramming*. 50–59. New York: ACM.

Takahashi, K., Takahashi, E., Bitoh, T., Sugimoto, T., et al. 1985. "A New Universal Microprogram Converter." *Proceedings of the 17th Annual Workshop on Microprogramming*: 264–66. New York: ACM.

Tanenbaum, A. S. 1976. "A General Purpose Macro Processor as a Poor Man's Compiler-Compiler." *IEEE Transactions on Software Engineering* 2: 121–23.

Tracz, W. J. 1979. "IBM Advanced System/4 PI Computer and Microcode Simulators." *Proceedings Summer Computer Simulation Conference, AFIPS*: 788–90. Arlington, VA: AFIPS Press.

———. 1981. "Modular Computer System Microcode Support Software." *SIGMICRO Newsletter:* 12(2): 6–18.

———. 1985. "Advances in Microcode Support Software." *Proceedings of the 18th Annual Workshop on Microprogramming:* 57–60. New York: ACM.

Tredennick, N. 1980. "How to do Flowcharts for a Controller." *IBM Technical Report* RC 8426 (#36569). Yorktown Heights, NY.

Wagnon, C., and Maine, D. J. L. 1983. "An E-Machine Workbench." *Proceedings of the 16th Annual Workshop on Microprogramming:* 101–11. New York: ACM.

Wang, D. T. 1982. "Defensive Microprogramming." *Proceedings of the 15th Annual Workshop on Microprogramming:* 84–90. New York: ACM.

Wilburn, D. L., and Mick, J. 1982. "Step-27 Development Station." *SIGMICRO Newsletter* 15 (2):22–36.

Wilburn, D. L., and Schleimer, S. 1985. "STEP Development Tools: METASTEP Language System." *Proceedings of the 18th Annual Workshop on Microprogramming*, 157–65. New York: ACM.

Yamada, A. et al. 1980. "Mixed Level Simulator for Large Digital System Logic Verification." *Proceedings of the 17th Design Automation Conference*, 626–33. Piscataway, NJ: IEEE.

Zinke, G. D. 1981. "Why is Microprogramming So Difficult? Some Thoughts about a Generally Accepted Problem." *Microprocessors and Microprogramming.* 7(6).

nine
HORIZONTAL MICROCODE COMPACTION

JOSEPH L. LINN

Horizontal microcode compaction has been a widely studied area since the mid 1970s. The work in this area has been fueled by a perceived need to automate, at least partially, the production of high-quality microcode for host architectures supporting a large amount of parallelism in its microinstruction set. Before proceeding further, it is important to understand exactly the problem that is being addressed, since there is a potential terminology conflict.

The term "horizontal microcode compaction" must be parsed as meaning the compaction of horizontal microcode. The term "compaction" is used here to mean the production of a microprogram that executes as many fundamental operations as possible in each unit of time. Thus, the objective of compaction is to produce a microprogram that runs as quickly as possible; that the amount of control-store space utilized might also be reduced is incidental to the process.

A number of authors and practitioners in the microprogramming arena have used the term "compaction" in a different sense—that is, to reduce the amount of control store utilized by a microprogram. Used in this way, the terms "horizontal compaction" and "vertical compaction" denote procedures that reduce the microinstruction width and the number of control-store words, respectively. Unfortunately, horizontal code compaction applied to straight-line microcode sequences has the effect of reducing the number of words required to store the microprogram, i.e., the concept of "vertical control-store compaction" of this paragraph. Except to point out this potential terminology conflict, we will not deal further with control-store reduction techniques.

In order to understand the environment in which compaction takes place, consider the microcode development diagram of figure 9-1. In the leftmost development path, the microprogrammer essentially considers all the details of the machine and of the specified program together as the microprogram is coded. This is considerably more difficult than "normal programming," in which many of the machine details are intentionally masked. Further, it is even more difficult than conventional machine/assembly-language programming because the details of the machine can be quite complex. For example, a typical horizontal microinstruction is able to execute several fundamental operations in

Figure 9-1. Possible scenarios for horizontal microcode development.

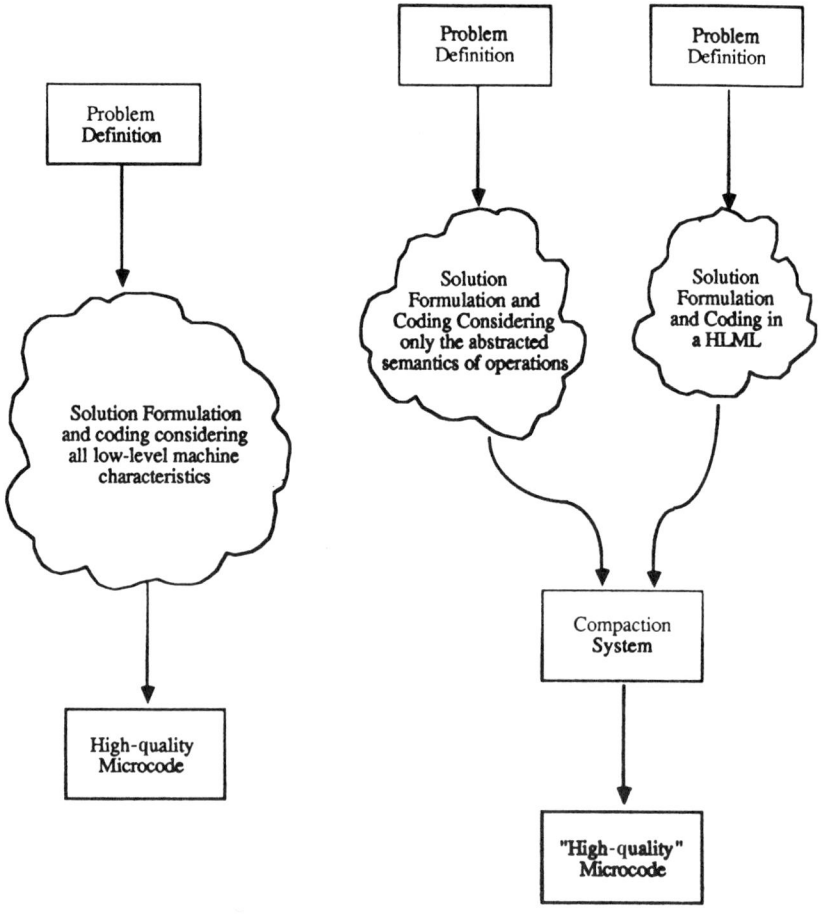

parallel. However, any particular pair of operations might not be executable in parallel because the bits used in the microinstruction to encode the various operations may conflict, e.g., one operation requires a multiplexor to be set in one way while the other requires a different multiplexor input to be passed. Moreover, this is only one class of detail that the microprogrammer must manage; clearly, this task is very challenging (and some microprogrammers actually enjoy it!).

The left fork of the right development path shows one way that a compactor can be used. Here, the microprogrammer thinks and writes the microprogram in terms of fundamental machine operations; then the compaction system determines an appropriate microprogram that is semantically equivalent to its input program and is "conformant" with the underlying horizontal architecture. In this way, the compaction system makes the task of producing horizontal microcode more manageable; the questions that arise are, "Is the code produced by the compactor as good as code produced by a human microprogrammer?" and "How much does it cost to run the compactor itself?" The latter question is addressed later in this chapter. As for the efficacy of the code, the question turns largely on the size of the program involved, on the match between the program specification and the underlying architecture, and on the "quality" of the generated code.

First, there is every reason to believe that a human microprogrammer will not be able to keep track of enough of the architectural details to do as well as an automatic compactor for sufficiently large microprograms. Second, there are situations where either a human microprogrammer or automatic compactor will have no difficulty in arriving at the best solution. These occur when the host architecture has exactly the hardware desired for the task at hand. As an example, a number of horizontally programmed machines have all the appropriate resources to do a multiply step (of Booth's algorithm) in one microinstruction. Clearly, either the microprogrammer or the compactor will probably choose a sequence of 16 (say) multiply steps scheduled in 16 consecutive instructions to solve the problem of multiplying two 32-bit words, particularly if the compactor's input consists of the 16 multiply step operations. The point is that both these situations occur reasonably frequently, and in both one can expect that an automatic compactor will do quite well.

However, the automatic compactor shown is limited in that its input program is completely bound with respect to its host resources. As will be seen, the compaction algorithms assume that part of the specification of a fundamental operation is a listing of the host registers read and written by the operation. Thus, the compactor is limited as to what code sequences are considered feasible. The human microprogrammer can take into account such resources conflicts as the code is generated and, importantly, change the register allocation and code generation on the fly to obtain a more satisfactory microprogram. Such an approach to the generation and compaction of microcode is a ripe topic for future research but is beyond what is possible currently. Thus, in this chapter we consider compaction as a postprocessing step that takes as its input a program expressed in the fundamental operations of a host architecture and handles the resource conflict and sequencing problems to ensure that the resulting microprogram is valid for the given architecture.

As a final thought, consider the right path of the Y in figure 9-1; here, the figure shows that a high-level microprogramming-language (HLML) compiler generates code that is subsequently treated by the compaction system. The hope here, and another topic ripe for research, is that the code generated by the high-level microprogramming-language compiler will be sufficiently efficient that reliance on the other two styles of development will decrease dramatically. For this to be achieved, the compaction algorithms presented here, though perhaps integrated into a compiler in a different way, will be important.

MODELS FOR COMPACTION

In this section, models are presented that are used to represent the salient characteristics of the program to be compacted and of the architecture upon which the compacted code is to execute. The models used for microcode compaction are rather complicated because microarchitectures are frequently very idiomatic; failure of a compaction system to deal with highly irregular architectures results in poor code quality, lack of applicability of the compaction system, or both. Essentially, the program model contains information that is used to ensure the correct sequencing of the fundamental operations due to data dependencies. The machine model contains information by which the compaction system can determine whether any candidate-compacted program can actually be represented correctly by the instruction set of the architecture. As the presentation unfolds, it will hopefully be clear that there is some duality between the models—that is, that some of the information needed to perform compaction directly can be represented either in the program model or in the machine model. Thus, the machine and program models for any particular microarchitecture are not unique.

Several items should be considered before presenting the models. First, the program model contains significant machine-specific information. This is in keeping with the view that the program being compacted is itself machine-specific, i.e., the program is composed entirely of fundamental machine operations (at some level of abstraction) for the architecture at hand. Part of the information needed for correct sequencing concerns the propagation delay encountered on various paths in the data path of the machine. It is conceivable (and desirable) that this information could be added in a prepass and not supplied directly by the programmer. Nevertheless, we will assume that the information required is available at the beginning of compaction. Second, one might claim that the models presented here are baroque and contain considerable information not really necessary in practical cases. Hopefully, the reader will be able to determine when a particular case at hand is simpler than the general case and will then be able to make appropriate simplifications.

The Machine Model

As with most so-called general methods, the techniques presented here generalize over a reasonably large class of machines but do not apply to every conceivable architecture. Intuitively, there are two conditions that must be met for an architecture to be considered as a member of the applicable class. First, it must be straightforward to determine whether a set of operations can coreside in the same instruction word. Indeed, since the issuing of an operation in a particular instruction cycle can make demands for machine resources in later cycles, the determination must extend to whether a set of operations can coreside in a specified sequence of instruction words. Second, it must be straightforward to determine the latency of each datum output by any operation to be read by a subsequent operation. In the same vein, it must be straightforward to determine when a register written by some operation overwrites a value written by a previous operation, thereby making the previous value unavailable to be read subsequently.

Notice here the use of the word "straightforward" rather than either "possible" or "simple." This is an important distinction because the complexity of the horizontal-code-compaction problem requires that a balance be struck between the efficacy of the compacted code and the complexity of the machine modeled versus the amount of time that is spent in the compaction process. Thus, "compactors" have come to adopt a particular compaction process, based on list scheduling, that has a reasonable time complexity and have broadened the machine and program models to encompass essentially whatever machines can be dealt with under this structure. Note that considerable work has been done using enumerative (exhaustive) techniques whereby the compacted program can be guaranteed to be optimal. Pointers to such work may be found at the end of the chapter.

A simple example will serve to show the class of microarchitectures that are under consideration, i.e., polyphase microarchitectures with relatively simple timing for reading and writing of machine registers. Essentially, the main requirement is that any particular register in the microarchitecture has a unique clock phase when that register is written. As an example, consider the hardware fragment of figure 9-2 and the program fragment:

> memory_address_register := program_counter;
> program_counter := program_counter + 1;

Such a situation is very common in microprograms that define emulations for machine instruction sets—that is, very common among microprograms.

The program fragment can be executed in two microinstructions by performing load_MAR on the first microinstruction and inc_PC on the second. Here,

Figure 9-2. A hardware fragment for loading the next instruction from memory and updating the program counter.

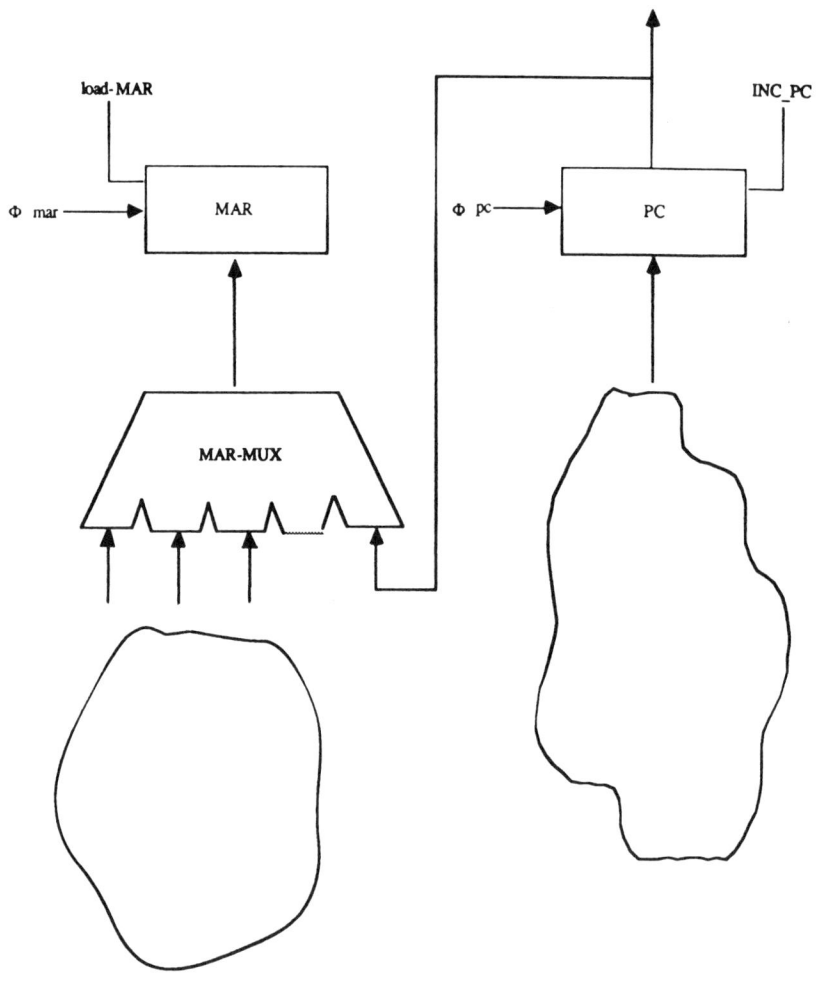

we assume that the MAR is latched on phase Φ_{MAR} and the PC is latched on phase Φ_{PC}. Further, assume that the microinstruction format is such that the fields required to encode the two operations are disjoint. Then, for most architectures of interest, both these operations may be issued in the same microinstruction. For any polyphase case where Φ_{MAR} occurs before Φ_{PC}, the proper semantics are obtained so long as Φ_{MAR} trails Φ_{PC} by no more than the best-case delay of the multiplexor, MAR-MUX. In a typical monophase microarchitecture,

Φ_{MAR} and Φ_{PC} will be the same. Thus, same-cycle issue for these primitives is correct whenever

$$t_{store\_PC} \geq t_{store\_MAR} - \text{logic\_delay\_from\_PC\_to\_MAR} \qquad (***)$$

Of particular interest is the fact that the inc_PC operation can actually be issued by the microinstruction preceding the one issuing the load_MAR operation as long as (***) is maintained. Clearly, it is highly desirable that the compactor find all necessary information for determining microinstruction coresidency in the machine and instruction models and apply this information dynamically during scheduling.

In order to specify these timing dependencies, the model for microarchitectures specifies (a) the registers (data stores) supported by the microarchitecture, (b) the phases utilized by the microarchitecture, and (c) the phase in which each register is stored. A partial order $<_\Phi$ must also be supplied that gives the relative ordering of the phases within the microinstruction cycle. A partial order is required since many microarchitectures allow some phases to be missing, or "stretched," on any particular cycle. Actually, $<_\Phi$ is normally a linear order. For example, the VAX-11/780 has four phases T0, T1, T2, and T3 with $T0<_\Phi T1<_\Phi T2<_\Phi T3$. (When no confusion can result, we will use $<$ instead of $<_\Phi$). As it happens, we will require that each operation of the input program be represented by a template that indicates for each register read by that operation what the last cycle is when the data must be present. Then, correct execution of the two operations from within the same microinstruction may be inferred whenever

$$\text{last\_read\_cycle}(ma := pc)[PC] < \text{store\_cycle}[PC]$$

instead of the more complicated (***) above. In summary, then, the machine model for microarchitectures under consideration must specify (1) the set of registers that can store data, (2) the set of clock phases of the microinstruction cycle where data is stored, (3) for each register, the unique phase when data is actually stored into that register, and (4) the partial order $<$ describing the order of the phases in time. Specifically, $<$ is a partial order so that for any operations I1 and I2 and with I2 data antidependent on I1, the execution of I2 in the same microinstruction as I1 will be semantically correct whenever

last_read_phase(I1)[R] < STORE_PHASE[R],

for each R read by I1 and written by I2

Data antidependence here means that some previous operation has written a value in register 4 to be read by I1 and that I2 overwrites register r. Clearly, the read by I1 must precede the write by I2.

The second facet of the machine model that must be considered is the description of the various fields of the microinstruction. As it happens, the only item that is really a part of our machine description (as opposed to the program description) is the microinstruction's length. The settings of the various fields of the control word (microinstruction register) are contained in the specification of the input operations themselves. A specification of an operation containing all the appropriate model information is called an *instruction template*, or just a template. Now, in general, the appropriate settings for the bits of the control word for any particular instruction could be specified by any Boolean function over these bits. Such a scheme is, however, clumsy in both description and implementation. In attempting to simplify this situation, we might attempt to specify in the templates just the values certain fields must contain in order that the instruction will execute properly.

Unfortunately, this method is not sufficiently general to handle all cases of interest. Consider the situation of figure 9-3 where several registers may be gated onto a bus, depending on the values of several fields. Here, if we desire that register R-D be gated onto the bus, we must ensure not only that field1 contains the value 6 but also that field2 contains neither 5 nor 11, and field3 does not contain 7. Situations such as this one are not uncommon when a designer has used some control-store-width minimization procedure. One technique for handling such a situation would be to require that instruction templates include not only the valid field settings but also the "invalidating" ones. In order to see that a more general scheme is needed, a more elaborate but nevertheless realistic case will be examined.

Consider the data-path fragment depicted in figure 9-4; the fragment consists of a three-ported register file, two ALUs, and two result registers. Two points are of particular interest. First, the ALUs are not general-purpose in that neither are they interchangeable nor does either perform all the desired operations. Second, the register-file ports are not interchangeable, either, in that the data from the second port is used as an input to both ALUs. If we require that that the input program specify exactly which register ports and exactly which ALU are to be used for each input operation, we may not expect a compaction system to obtain much concurrency from the code. If, however, we allow the compaction system to make some simple bindings, then we may expect much better code to be obtained. The type of bindings that the compactor is allowed to make include choosing exactly which path through the data path will be used to compute a given set of output registers from the given input registers. Thus, in this case, an input operation might be something like $X := R11 + R5$. Now, there are at least four different ways to produce this result using the hardware fragment shown in figure 9-5. Exactly which of these should be chosen depends on what other input operations are available to be executed in parallel. For example, if the operation $Y := R3$ **xor** $R5$ is available, then the first of the four forms should be chosen so that parallel execution is possible. Conversely, if $Y := R3 - R11$ is available, then the third form would be the correct choice.

The key question is how this information may be represented. One way of viewing the situation is that the input operations that are to be examined to

Figure 9-3. Tristate multiplexing onto a bus from separate encoded fields.

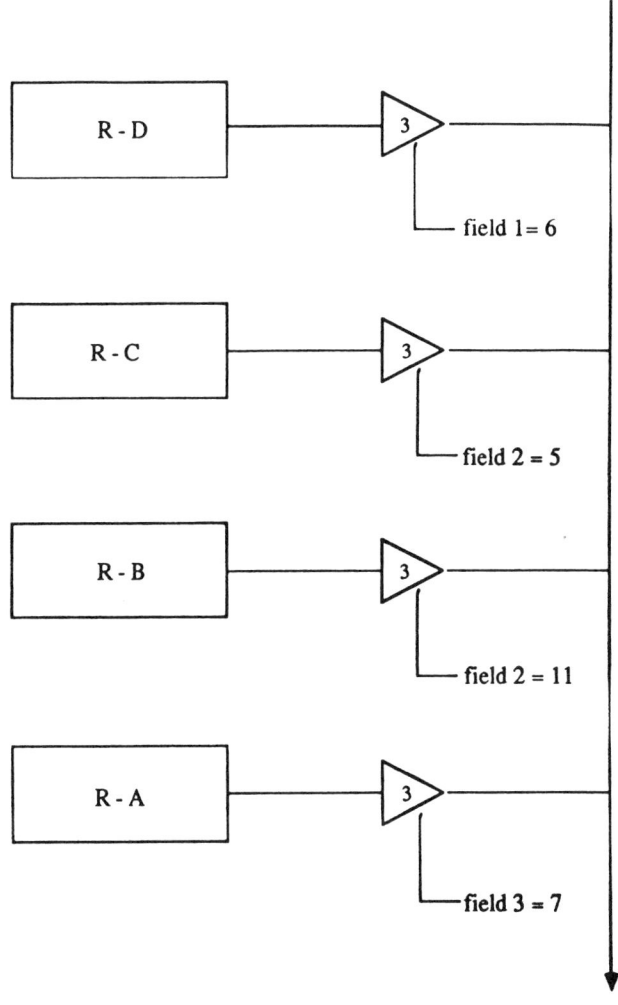

determine possible concurrency are the input symbols of a language. In such a case, a finite-state machine (FSM) may be utilized to make the determination in the following way: if the machine has seen an initial string of operations $o_1 o_2 \ldots o_n$ and has entered state k and if there is a transition from state k to some state k' for input o', then the set of operations $\{o_1, o_2, \ldots, o_n, o'\}$ may be executed in parallel. If no such transition exists, then o' may not be executed in parallel with $\{o_1, o_2, \ldots, o_n\}$. First, note that an FSM used in this way

Figure 9-4. A data path with multiple ALUs.

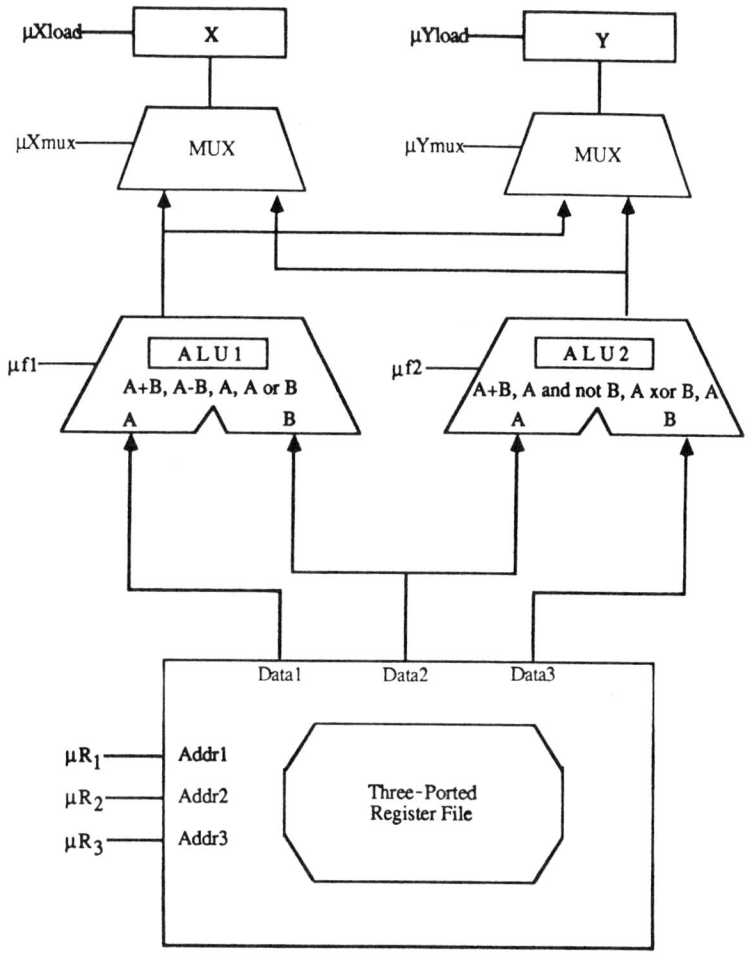

Figure 9-5. Possible field settings to produce X := R11 + R5

	µR$_1$	µR$_2$	µR$_3$	µf$_1$	µf$_2$	µxmux
1.	R11	R5	∅	+	∅	ALU1
2.	R5	R11	∅	+	∅	ALU1
3.	∅	R11	R5	∅	+	ALU2
4.	∅	R5	RU	∅	+	ALU2

may be conservative; that is, it must never indicate potential parallelism where none is possible, but it may indicate "nonparallelness" when, in fact, parallel execution is possible. Of course, the efficacy of the compacted code may suffer if "nonparallelness" is indicated too often when parallel execution is possible. Second, we are not interested here in how the FSM is actually implemented; many ways are possible and some require exponentially more space than others. The appropriate approach is left as an implementation issue.

Consider, then, the FSM fragment of figure 9-6, keeping in mind that only a portion of the machine is depicted. Focusing on the wavy lines, one may note that the machines accepts $\{X := R1 + R2; Y := R3 - R1\}$ and $\{X := R1 + R2; Y := R3 - R2\}$ but not $\{X := R1 + R2; Y := R1 - R3\}$ or $\{X := R1 + R2; Y := R2 - R3\}$. Clearly, this is because the shared register must be the right operand of the subtraction operator. Focusing on the dashed lines, $\{X := R1 - R2; Y := R2\}$ is allowed but not $\{X := R1 - R2; Y := R1\}$ or $\{X := R1 - R2; Y := R3\}$. Again, this simply reflects the capabilities of the hardware.

The last concept to be understood with respect to the encoding capabilities of these FSMs is that we must make explicit the idea that the final state of the FSM determines the eventual setting of some of the bits within the control word. If the FSM state requires that particular control word bits be set in a particular way and various previously scheduled operations require other settings, then all the work done in determining parallelism by the FSM will have been wasted. Thus, when these FSMs are being employed, the bits that are used by the FSM must be reserved in the control word. The term *pseudofield* is used to denote such an FSM, the bits of the control word that it reserves, and the mapping of final states into control-word bit settings. The input symbols of the FSMs are not limited to the instructions themselves; rather, an instruction template will (as will be seen below) specify an input symbol to be "executed" by a transition in the FSM. These input symbols are called "events."

As another example, consider the situation in figure 9-7. Here, there are four possible events:

1. Register R-A gated onto bus 1
2. Register R-B gated onto bus 2.
3. Register R-C gated onto bus 3.
4. Register R-D gated onto bus 3.

Figure 9-8a shows a possible state-encoding and transition function for a pseudofield that will handle the situation. Note that the state-set size is exponential in the number of events. This is, of course, the worst case as predicted by the theory. Figure 9-8b gives a reduced transition function that could be obtained by using existing algorithms for minimizing finite-state machines, and figure 9-8c gives the mapping from pseudofield states to bit settings in the control word. Remember that these fields must be somehow reserved for use by the pseudofield; that is, at the end of determining which operations are to be

Figure 9-6. An FSM fragment to determine coresidency of a pair of ALU operations.

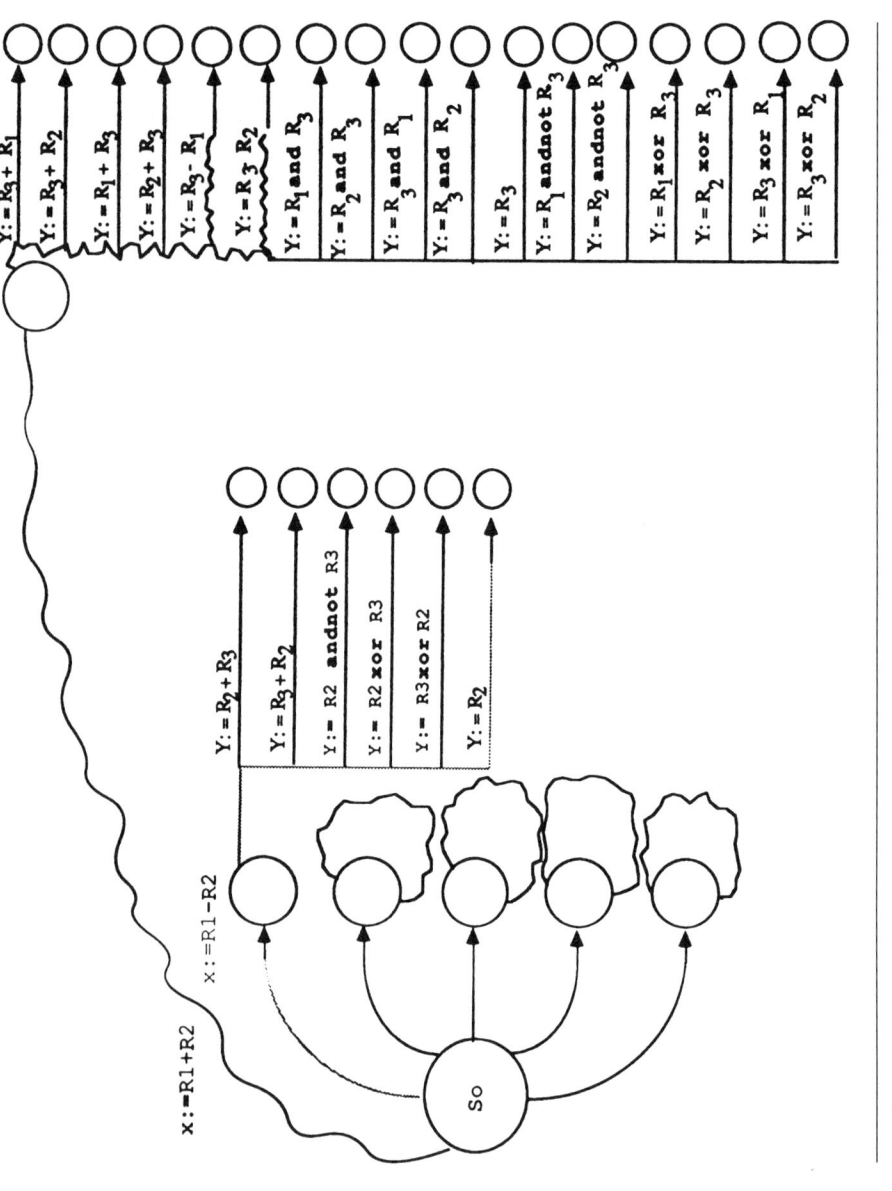

Figure 9-7. A case solvable by pseudofields.

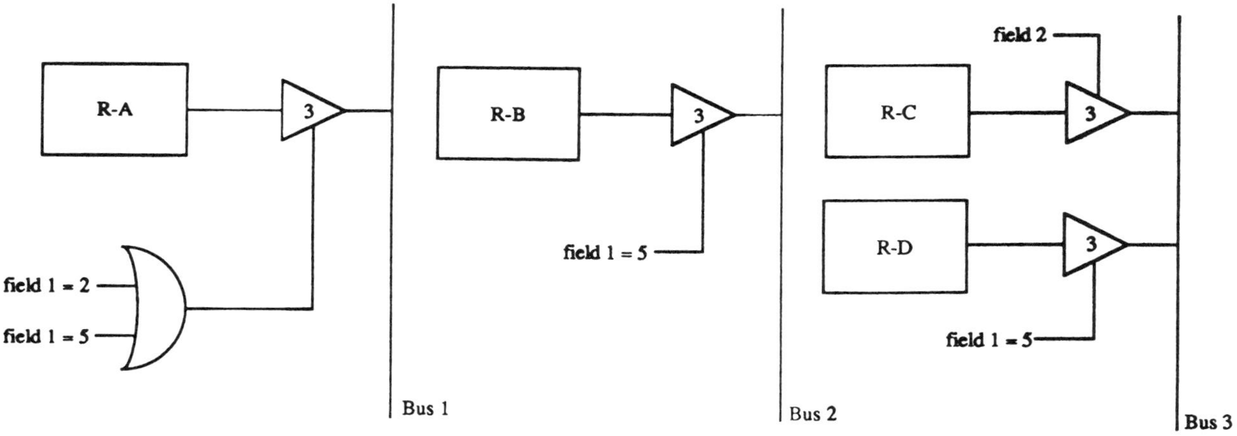

Figure 9-8. *a.* The transition function; *b.* a reduced function; *c.* the associated field description.

	A	B	C	D
∅	A	B	C	D
A	A	AB	AC	AD
B	AB	B	invalid	BD
C	AC	invalid	C	invalid
D	AD	BD	invalid	D
AB	AB	AB	invalid	ABD
AC	AC	invalid	AC	invalid
AD	AD	ABD	invalid	AD
BC	--	--	--	--
BD	ABD	BD	invalid	BD
CD	--	--	--	--
ABC	--	--	--	--
ABD	ABD	ABD	invalid	ABD
BCD	--	--	--	--
ABCD	--	--	--	--

a

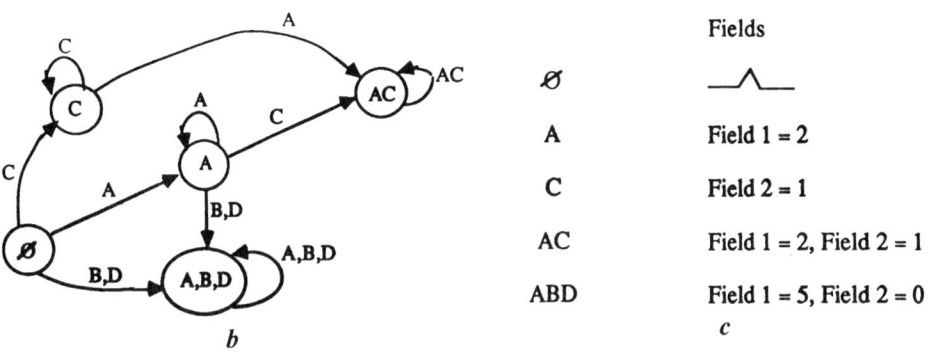

b

Fields	⎯⋀⎯
∅	
A	Field 1 = 2
C	Field 2 = 1
AC	Field 1 = 2, Field 2 = 1
ABD	Field 1 = 5, Field 2 = 0

c

issued in a particular cycle, the compactor must not find that some other instructions have used the pseudofield's control-word bits. How this is accomplished is discussed in the next section.

In summary, then, a microarchitecture may be modeled for the purposes of compaction as a function of six entities:

1. Its control-word length
2. Its pseudofields
3. Its registers
4. Its phases
5. The phase when each register is stored
6. Its phase-ordering relation

In order to complete our understanding of the machine/instruction model, we now turn to the definition of instruction templates.

The Instruction Template Model

A program, for the purposes of compaction, is represented by special types of graphs whose atomic entities are the "instructions" of the program. Actually, these atomic entities, called "instruction templates," convey more information than might be initially imagined. Some of this information has been alluded to or at least hinted at by the discussion of the machine model. Informally then, an instruction template contains the following information:

- The registers to be read by the instruction, called "read registers"
- The registers to be written by the instruction, called "write registers"
- The microinstruction cycle and phase when each read register is read, relative to the cycle when the instruction is initiated; this cycle is called the "start cycle"
- The microinstruction cycle relative to the start cycle when each write register is written
- The fields and pseudofields required by the instruction on each cycle while it is in execution

There are several significant concepts that are implicit in this model. First, a template potentially executes over several microinstruction cycles, and in particular a template may consume fields and pseudofields over several microinstruction cycles. This concept may be utilized in a number of interesting ways. For example, in the fragment shown in figure 9-9 consider the execution of an instruction such as LATCH := LATCH + 255 where 255 is a constant in the CONSTANT_ROM. Suppose further that the access time of the ROM is slightly greater than the microinstruction cycle time. In such a case, one would have to set up 255 on the output of the ROM on the previous cycle and hold it through the cycle containing the addition.

A second important consideration is that the read registers and write registers are not assumed to be "monolithically utilized" throughout the execution of a template. In particular, there may be a latency or delay between the cycle after which an instruction no longer consumes resources and the cycle in which a data value written by the instruction is available to the next instruction. Continuing with the fragment in figure 9-9, we can see from the previous discussion that the instruction template for LATCH := LATCH + 255 has the LATCH register as its only read register and its only write register. In this case, the read register is read with a delay of one cycle after the cycle in which the operation is issued.

Figure 9-9. A micro architecture with operations executing over more than one instruction cycle.

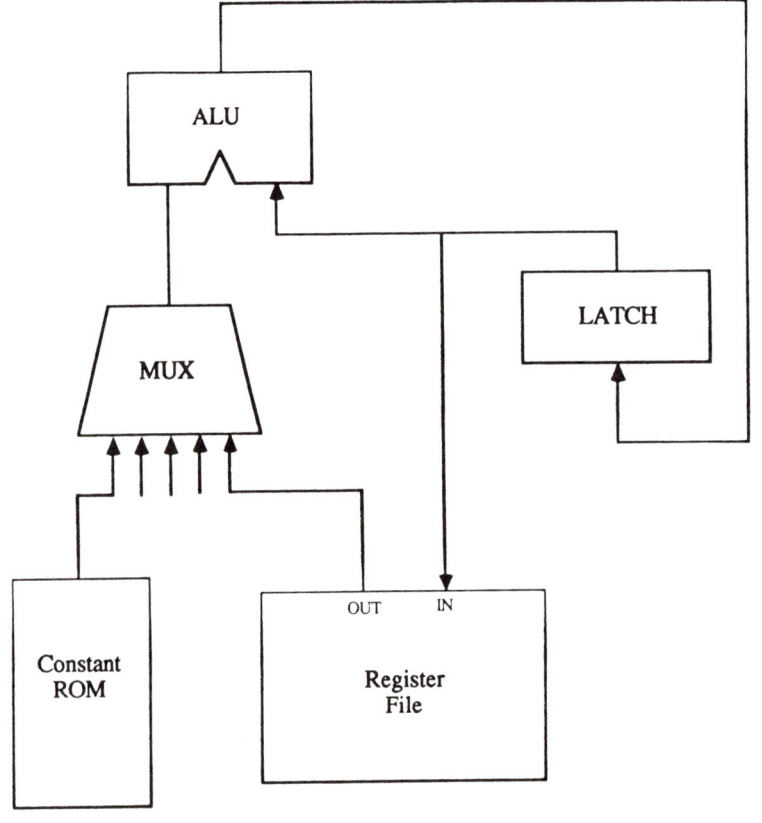

Another important concept is the concept of *versions,* that is, different realizations of the same instruction. Versions of operations serve the same sort of purpose as pseudofields, that is, to delay the binding of the exact bit patterns that will cause the semantics of the operation to be realized. Only the read registers and write registers are constant among versions of an instruction. The register timing and field utilizations may change from version to version. Lastly, note that the semantics of the operation are of no consequence to the compactor; accordingly, no model of the "value of an operation" is included.

Consider the hardware fragment of figure 9-10. Here, we assume that both ALUs have $f(x, y) = 0$ in their repertoires and that we desire to set register S2 to zero. Clearly, there are two reasonable ways to do this: either ALU1 or ALU2 should be used. The one that should be chosen depends on the context in which the instruction is to be issued. For example, if an F := F + S1 is to be executed in parallel, then clearly ALU2 should be used to form the zero. In other situations, ALU1 should be used. What one does with versions, then, is to enumerate the various ways that an instruction can be executed. The compactor may try each of the various versions until it either finds one that is compatible with the other instructions scheduled to start in a particular cycle or until it determines that no version is compatible. In the latter case, issuing of this operation is deferred to a later cycle.

In summary, an instruction template specifies the read registers and write registers of a particular instruction as well as the different versions of the instruction. Each version must detail the read delay for each read register and the write delay for each write register. Further, each version must specify the fields used in the control word, the values that those fields must assume, the pseudofields used, and the events to be executed on the respective pseudofields.

In the next two sections, we will take up the topic of how to use all this information contained in the model to approach the problem of the compaction of linear sequences of instruction templates. Then we will take up the problem of compaction beyond the basic blocks of a program.

LOCAL HORIZONTAL-CODE COMPACTION

In this section, we consider the topics of representing a program so that a compaction algorithm may proceed efficiently and of actually performing the compaction step. Keep in mind that the compaction process has two major inputs: (1) the machine description and (2) the program to be compacted. Programs to be compacted may be classified into three categories. The most restrictive form of program is one in which there are no branches into or out of the program. These have been referred to as straight-line microprograms (SLMs); in traditional compiler optimization, a sequence that may only be entered at the beginning and where only the last instruction may be a branch

Figure 9-10. A fragment that utilizes two versions for $f(x,y) = 0$.

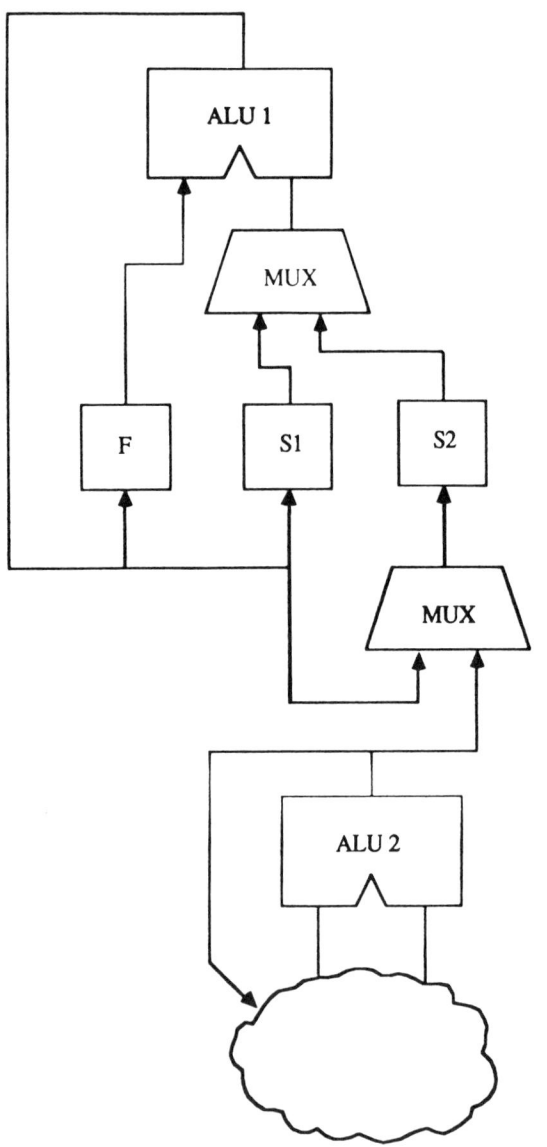

has been termed a "basic block." The latter term is used here. The next most restrictive form of program is one in which branches are allowed but in which there are no loops. The third category of program has unrestricted branching among the basic blocks. Initially, we are only concerned with the most restrictive style of program, that is, branchless programs. This type of compaction is called *local compaction*, since it deals only with instructions local to a particular basic block. The local-compaction problem may be stated simply (and slightly inaccurately) as follows:

> Given a machine description and a linear sequence of instruction templates, find the minimum sequence of microinstructions that would effect the same semantics as the input sequence.

Several problems very similar to this one have already been shown to be NP-complete, that is, it is unlikely that a program that runs in polynomial time will be likely to find the optimal solution in all cases. Thus, we must be satisfied in finding an algorithm that produces small but not necessarily minimum sequences in polynomial time.

A second important point is that the compaction program should not expect that the input sequence is a legal program. This occurs because instructions are permitted to write values into registers long after the instruction has finished consuming instruction words. Consider figure 9-11a; depicted is a hardware fragment with two registers R1 and pipeout register and with a 10-stage pipeline unit. The intended semantics is that the initiation of the pipelined unit causes its input to be processed, with the answer appearing in pipeout register 10 cycles later without further intervention of program control. The pipeout register is then stable until 10 cycles after the next initiation. The sequence of instruction templates depicted in figure 9-11b cannot execute without the introduction of the NO-OP microinstructions (fig. 9-11c) because of the delay inherent in producing the answer. Since whoever created the input has no way of predicting a priori which versions of the templates will eventually be chosen, information as to how many NO-OPs are required cannot be supplied as part of the input.

A subtle inaccuracy in the above problem formulation is that we should not be overly restrictive about the "intended semantics" of the input sequence. In particular, we should not care which values end up in registers whose values are not meaningful after the execution of the instruction sequence. In other words, we expect that the sequence is part of a larger program and that not all the registers written are necessarily used elsewhere in the program. The concept that applies here is called *liveness*. A register is live at some point in the program if there is some later instruction in the program that will read that register before any intervening instruction overwrites its current contents. The set of registers that are live at the bottom of the basic block has a tremendous effect on the possible "equivalent" rearrangements of the instruction sequence. Therefore, we must include the concept of live registers in our compaction scheme.

Figure 9-11. *a.* Hardware fragment; *b.* instruction templates; *c.* microinstructions.

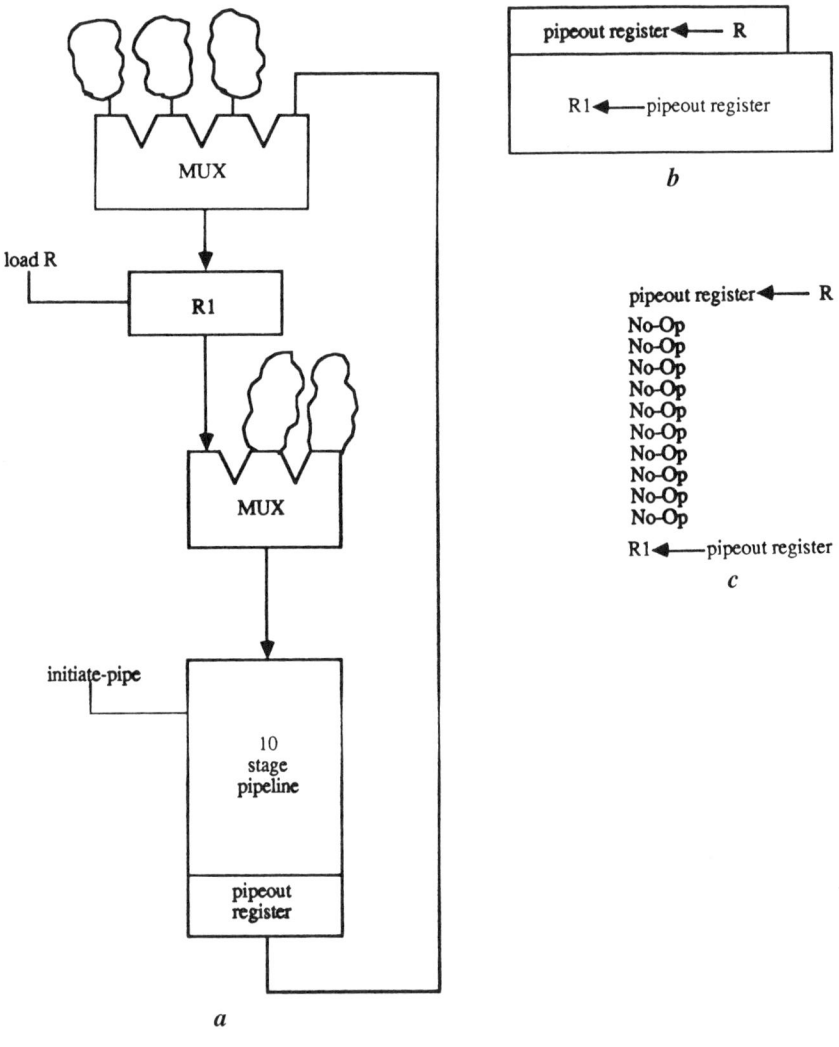

Initial Data-Precedence Graph

Having decided that it is too expensive to enumerate all the possible (or even feasible) arrangements of the code, another technique must be discovered by which a reasonable number of good rearrangements can be explored. The technique to be used is to essentially schedule the instructions of a program in a manner similar to deterministic scheduling in operating systems (Coffman and Denning 1973). Thus, the instructions are considered in a suitable order and the compactor attempts to discover a set of start times for the instructions so that (1) the program can actually be represented on the machine with the start times determined, and (2) the semantics of the original program are preserved.

The first problem, machine representability, is solved by taking cognizance of the machine description during scheduling; the details of this are presented in the next section where we present the scheduling algorithm. The latter problem, perserving semantics, is solved by constructing and maintaining relationships among the instructions that dictate the order in which the instructions must execute. These relationships can be encoded into a directed acyclic graph called the *data-precedence graph* (DPG). The nodes of the DPG are the instruction templates of the program to be compacted. The arcs of the graph are labeled with machine registers, and an arc from instruction template i to instruction template j indicates that the instruction issue time, or start time, of instruction template i must be determined before the start time of instruction template j can be determined.

There are three types of arcs, each indicating a different reason why one instruction must "data precede" (or at least not follow) a second instruction. The first type of arc is a data-dependency arc. If a data-dependency arc exists from template i to template j and the label on the arc is r, then template i writes a value into register r and template j reads that value from register r. The second type of arc is a data-antidependency arc. If a data-antidependency arc exists from template i to template j and the label on the arc is r, then template j writes a register r that template i reads. Thus, template j must be prevented from writing register r between the time that the value to be read by template i is stored and the time when template i reads that value. The third type of arc is an output-dependency arc. If an output-dependency arc exists from template i to template j and the label on the arc is r, both templates write register r and template j must write register r after template i.

By calculating an initial DPG and by maintaining all of the appropriate relations in the DPG as compaction ensues, we can always have at hand all the restrictions that must hold among the various templates. Note that as compaction progresses, more antidependency and output-dependency and output-dependency arcs are added to the DPG. There are, however, five types of static arcs in the DPG and together these form the initial DPG. First, all the data-dependency and output-dependency arcs are in the initial DPG. These may be obtained by the following simple rule: (1) if instruction template I1 precedes instruction template I2 in the input sequence, then for each register r so that I2 reads register r, I1 writes register r, and no template that is between I1 and I2 in the input sequence writes register r, there is a data dependency from I1 to I2 on register r; and (2) if register r is live at the end of the sequence and template I is the last template in the sequence to write register r, then there is an output dependency from template J to template I on register r for each other template J that writes register r. These arcs enforce the register liveness requirements.

The next type of static arcs formed during initialization are data-antidependency arcs used to essentially reserve registers that are needed in a computation. Consider the program fragment in figure 9-12a. Here, we are assuming a machine with two- and three-address instructions and hardware resources available to execute these instructions two at a time. The data dependencies are shown in figure 9-12b. Careful examination of the program and the data dependencies reveals that instruction L2 must be scheduled before L4 or the computation cannot be completed. Further, this implies that L3 is data-antidependent on L4 since it must read the information that L2 writes. Thus, the antidependency arc depicted in figure 9-12c is required. What is now needed is a general rule that will allow these arcs to be placed correctly.

The first rule to be discussed is called (for historical reasons) "the old rule." The old rule is very similar to the rule for data-dependency arcs. Simply, if template I precedes template J in the input sequence and there is a register r so that I reads r and J writes r, then a data-antidependency arc is formed from I to J labeled r. This rule would account for the antidependency arc in figure 9-12c. However, if we consider the program and graph of figure 9-12d and figure 9-12e, then the old rule requires antidependency arcs in figure 9-12f from L3 to L5 and from L4 to L6. Now, the best code that satisfies the constraints of this graph is the original code. But the true optimal code is shown in figure 9-12g. Note that the optimal code is essentially half the size of the original. Thus, the situation that is obtained with the old rule is that correct code is generated but that too many antidependency arcs are placed to obtain the optimal code.

It turns out that devising a rule that both gives correct code and allows full deadlock-free operation of the scheduler is not a simple proposition. Nevertheless, "the new rule" has been devised, which gives greater schedul-

Figure 9-12. Example of antidependencies.

L1: mov #2,r2
L2: mov #3,r3
L3: add r2,r3,r5
L4: mov #3,r3
L5: add r3, r5
;: r5 is live

a

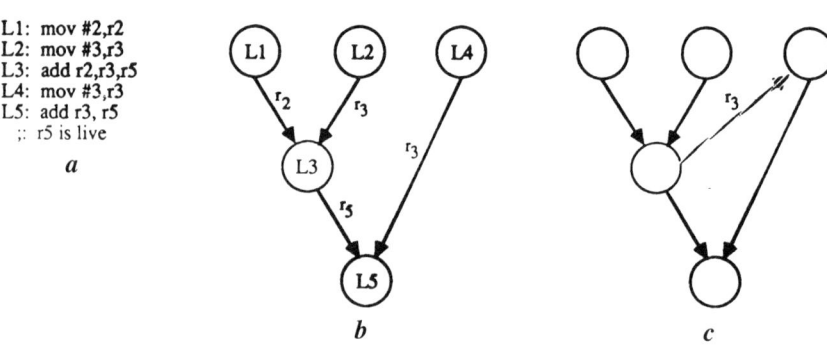

b *c*

Figure 9-12. *(continued).*

L1: mov #1,r2
L2: add #1,r2,r3
L3: add #1,r3,r4
L4: add #1,r4,r10
L5: mov #1,r3
L6: add #1,r3,r4
L7: add #1,r4,r5
L8: add #1,r5,r6
L9: add #1,r6,r7
;: r7,r10 live

d

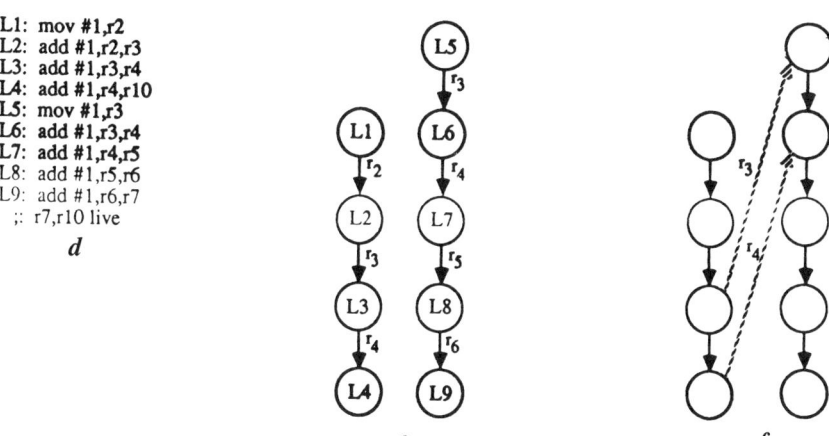

e   *f*

at t_1: L5//L1   ; // is "in parallel with"
     t : L6
     t_2: L7//L2
     t : L8//L3
     t_3: L9//L4

4

0

g

---

ing freedom than the old rule (but not full freedom) but which costs more in execution time. In order to apply the new rule, several items must be discovered for each node in the graph. Specifically, one must discover for each node and for each register the data-dependency ancestors of that node, if any, where that register is read. Note that here a node is considered to be among its own ancestors. In addition, one must discover for each node and for each register all data-dependency ancestors that write the given register. Again, a node is considered to be among its ancestors for this calculation. Last, one must discover all nodes that are data-dependency ancestors of a given node.

Having this information at hand, we may now explore the problem in more detail and present a solution. Consider again figure 9-12a and b. The actual reason why L3 must execute before L4 is that if L4 is executed, then we cannot produce the correct result for L3 since L3 reads r3 from L2 and the execution of L2 would destroy the result written by L4. Thus, the compactor must be careful about the "evaluation order" of multioperand operations. Specifically, if some node T has parents T_i and T_j, a safe situation results if the registers needed in the computation of T_i are used before those registers are written in the computation of T_j (assuming T_i precedes T_j in the source).

Thus, the antidependency arcs may be added by the following method. Consider each node T in the DPG in reverse topological order and for each pair of parents of T, T_i and T_j, with T_i preceding T_j in the source order, create an antidependency arc from T_i' to T_j' labeled r for any $<T_i'T_j', r>$ where T_i' is an ancestor of T_i reading r and T_j' is an ancestor of T_j writing r.

Let us consider a few examples to see how this rule operates. First, reconsider figure 9-12b. Since L5 has two parents, we must consider the pair L3, L4. The question is whether or not there is a reader among L3 and its ancestors that reads r3; since the answer is yes, we construct data-antidependency arcs from the readers of r3 among L3 and its ancestors (in this case just L3 itself) to the writers of r3 among L4 and its ancestors. Thus, the arc shown in figure 9-12c is the result. If we reconsider the graph of figure 9-12e, we find that no nodes have more than one parent; therefore, no arcs are formed.

Now let us consider some less obvious cases. Figure 9-13a and b shows the same program and graph as figure 9-12d and e except that r5 and r7 are live and L4 writes r5 instead of r10. The difference in the graph is the output-dependency arc as shown. A moment of reflection reveals that this constraint actually requires that most of the "left path" be scheduled before the "right path"; how is this reflected by the new rule? Consider L7. It has parents L4

Figure 9-13. More complicated examples of static antidependencies

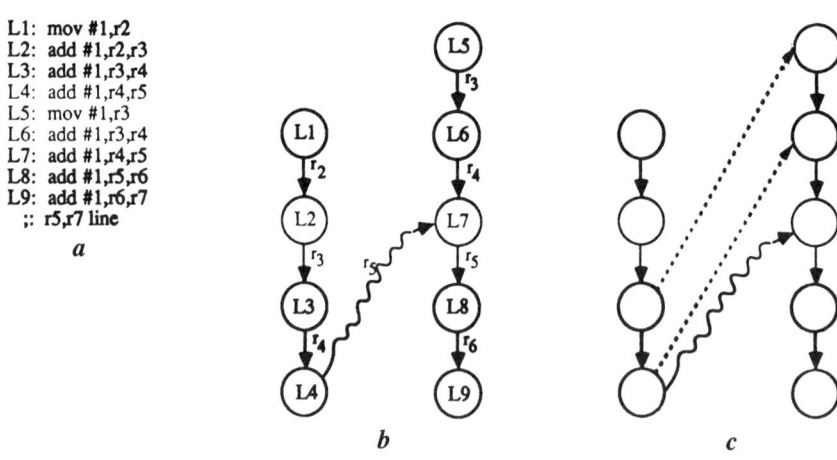

Figure 9-13. (continued).

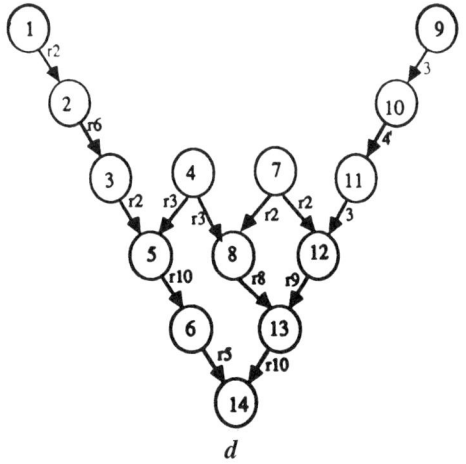

d

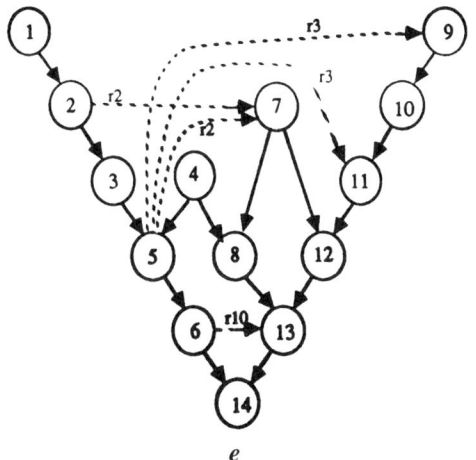

e

and L6; since there is a reader of r4 among L4 and its ancestors, we place antidependency arcs from register reader in L4's family to register writers in L6's family. The result is the two arcs shown in figure 9-13c.

As a last example (and a complicated one at that), consider the DPG of figure 9-13d. The updated graph shown in figure 9-13e is the result of considering node 14 with parents 6 and 13. A few comments are in order. First, note that the arcs <2,7,r2> and <5,11,r3> are in some sense redundant since <5,7,r2> and <5,9,r3> are in fact more constraining. Second, notice that although node 4 is an ancestor of node 13 that writes r3, no in-arcs are formed for node 4 since it is also an ancestor of node 6. Lastly, the graph implies that there is no legal ordering with node 9 preceding node 5. This is not correct. Thus, the new rule is less restrictive than the old rule but still does not provide the scheduler with the flexibility to consider all legal schedules.

Note that the new rule by itself does not correctly handle static antidependencies that are caused by reading a register that is live at the top of a block. Thus, an antidependency arc must be placed from each template I that reads a value live at the top of the block to each writer distinct from I that writes the register. These arcs must be placed before the new rule is applied.

The fourth and fifth types of static arcs are needed in order to allow the scheduler not to have to check for two special cases. The fourth kind is shown in figure 9-14a. Here, a certain node A writes register r1 to its descendants; one descendant, node B, also writes register r1. Clearly, node B must execute after each of its siblings; rather than having the scheduler check for this case as part of the firing of node A, it is somewhat quicker to add statically the antidependency arcs shown. The last kind of static arc added during initialization is to handle the situation shown in figure 9-14b. An enumeration of the possibilities reveals that node B must execute before node A. As will be seen in the next section, this will cause the output-dependency arc shown from E to A to be added dynamically as part of the firing of B. However, the scheduler does not look ahead to see node D, and this causes a special case. To resolve this, the output-dependency arc shown is preadded during the initialization. In fact, another copy of the arc will be added dynamically.

In summary, there are six steps in the formation of the static data-precedence graph:

1. Form the data-dependency graph.
2. Add output-dependency arcs to preserve the last store of each register live at the bottom of the block.
3. Add antidependency arcs to preserve values live at the top of the block.
4. Add data-antidependency arcs to ensure register availability as shown in figure 9-12.
5. Add antidependency arcs for the case of siblings of instructions that read and write the same register.
6. Add output-dependency arcs for the case of figure 9-14b. Actually, the scheduler described in the next section would deadlock if faced with figure 9-14b without the antidependency arc.

The use of these relationships is detailed next.

Figure 9-14. Special case of static dependencies.

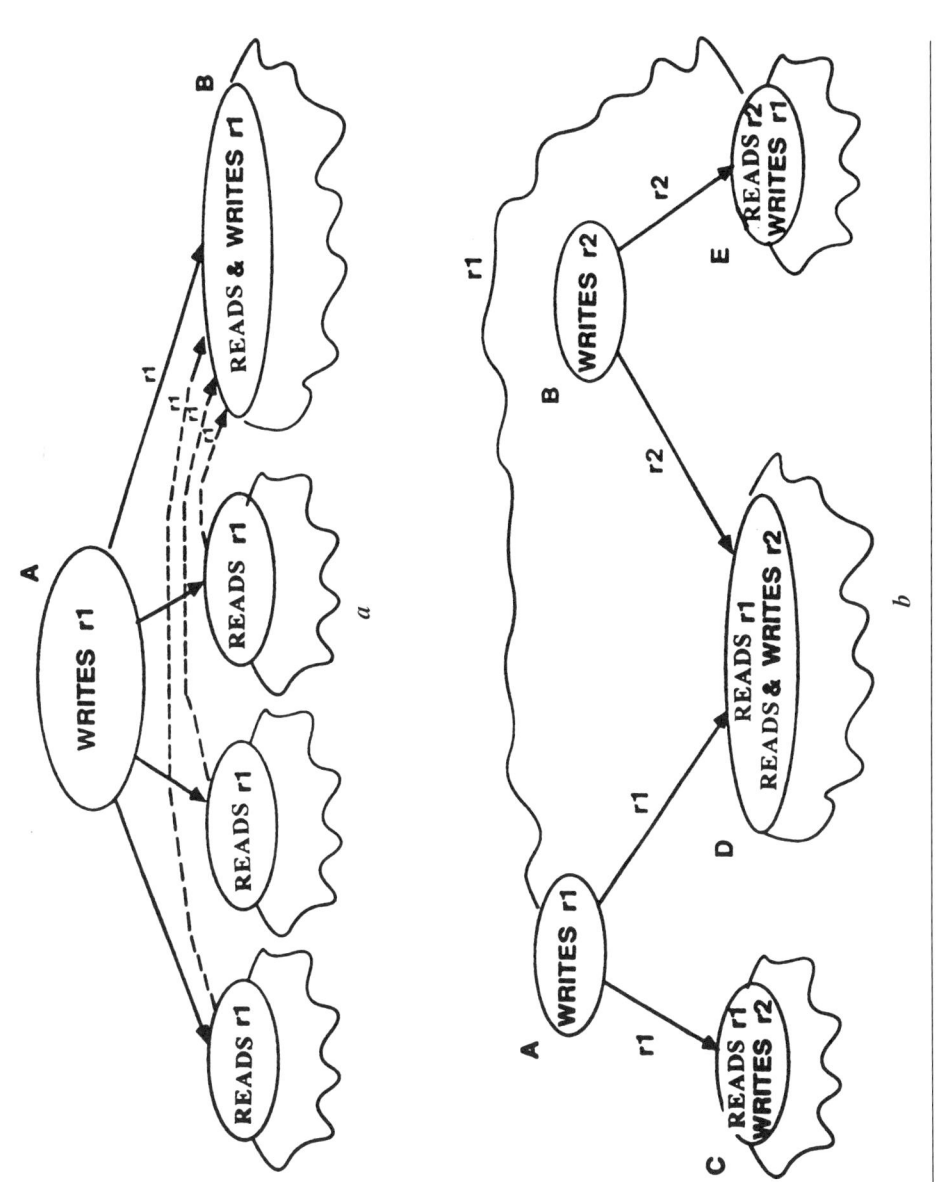

The Scheduling Step

As was mentioned previously, the scheduling algorithm is similar to the type of deterministic schedulers found in the study of operating systems. The scheduler essentially begins at "time zero" and proceeds forward one microinstruction cycle at a time, scheduling as many templates into each microinstruction as it can by considering the templates one at a time for insertion into the current working microinstruction. Given the preceding concepts, the scheduling step is relatively straightforward except for three items:

- How does the DPG change as compaction progresses?
- How are field and pseudofield values maintained?
- How is the earliest start time for each instruction template determined?

Scheduler Data Structures and Procedure

At any particular time during the compaction process, the DPG will indicate the relations that must hold among the templates; further, some of the templates will have been packed into microinstructions. Clearly, we will need to keep track of the required field and pseudofield settings in the working microinstruction so that we can tell if another template is "field-compatible" with the working microinstruction. Less obvious, but nevertheless crucial, is the fact that we must keep track of the field and pseudofield setting in future microinstruction cycles as well. Additionally, unless we intend to search for available, unscheduled templates on each iteration, we must keep a list of such templates. Because of write delays, however, not all such templates will necessarily be available on the same cycle. Obtaining the templates available on the current cycle is greatly facilitated by having a separate list for each cycle.

Thus, we begin by selecting an appropriate t_{max} so that fewer than t_{max} microinstructions are required. We maintain two vectors of this size. One of these, FIELDS, contains both the current setting for each bit of the control word and the current state of each pseudofield. A control-word bit may be in one of several states. It may be undefined, defined to be zero, defined to be one, or (less obviously) declared to be under the control of a particular pseudofield. In the scheduling algorithm that follows, we will need to understand the concept of field compatibility and also how to update the control-word settings to conform with a newly scheduled template. With respect to control-word fields, an instruction template may specify that a particular bit is to be set to zero or set to one. Depending on the current setting, such a specification may or may not be "field-compatible" with the current setting. If the specification is not field-compatible, then the template may not be scheduled into the slot under consideration. If field compatibility is achieved, the current setting is updated to align with the specification. Table 9-1 gives the appropriate conditions for field compatibility and the correct updating function.

Table 9-1 Field compatibility and updating.

Current Setting	Desired Setting	
	Set to Zero	Set to One
Undefined	OK / DEFINED ZERO	OK / DEFINED ONE
Defined zero	OK / DEFINED ZERO	BAD
Defined one	BAD	OK / DEFINED ONE
Controlled by PS	BAD	BAD

If an event E on pseudofield PS is specified, field compatibility is achieved if both these conditions are satisfied:

1. All bits controlled by the pseudofield either are undefined or are already controlled by this pseudofield.
2. There is a next state defined for event E on the current state of pseudofield PS.

In case of field compatibility, the update is performed by setting the current state to the appropriate next state and by setting all the controlled bits to be controlled_by_pseudofield_PS.

The next of the major data structures is the vector, DATAV, of data-available template lists. At any particular point in the scheduling process, either a template is not on any data available list or it is available at time i. If a template is not on any list, either it has already been scheduled or it has parent templates that have not yet been scheduled. If a template is on DATAV[i], then it is available for scheduling at time i; it may ensue that it is not scheduled at time i for a variety of reasons that are discussed below. Using multiple DATAV lists is the simplest technique for dealing with write delays. For example, if a template that writes register R1 is scheduled at time t and it has a write delay of 10 cycles on register R1, then its R1 descendants become available no sooner than $t + 10$., The scheduling algorithm sweeps forward in time beginning with $t = 1$ and scheduling all compatible instructions at $t = 1$. Then, it moves on to $t = 2, t = 3, \ldots$ until all instructions have been scheduled. Originally, all instructions in the block are initially placed into DATAV[1]; any template that is not available—that is, one with unscheduled ancestors in the DPG—is eliminated from the list by a simple check until its ancestors have been scheduled.

With this understood, it is simple to state the scheduling algorithm:

```
procedure compaction_scheduler;
    Setup; t := 0;
    while all instructions not scheduled do
        t := t + 1;
        while DATAV[t] not empty do
            foreach template T in DATAV[t] do
                if T is not available then delete T from DATAV[t] endif;
                if any version V of T is both
                        field compatible with the current state beginning at
                        time t and continuing for as many cycles as V needs
                        to consume fields
                    and
                        V is timing compatible along each DPG in-arc for T
                then remember which V is a good one
                else delete T from DATAV[t]; add T to DATAV[t+1]
                endif;
            endforeach;
            if DATAV[t] is not empty then
                select the "best" instruction I;
                mark I as having been scheduled;
                update FIELDS[t] according to the remembered version V;
                foreach descendant D of I do
                    mark D as a current descendant;
                    If each parent of D has now been scheduled then place
                        D on the appropriate DATAV list endif;
                endforeach;
                update DPG with dynamic antidependency and output-
                dependency arcs;
                foreach descendant D of I
                    unmark D as a current descendant
                endforeach;
            endif;
        endwhile;
    endwhile;
endprocedure;
```

Two items can be made clear immediately. First, one might wonder why it is necessary to test an entry on a DATAV for having all parents scheduled. This is because a previously available template can become unavailable as arcs are added to the DPG dynamically. It would be possible to remember the DATAV, if any, into which each template is currently entered. This would actually be slightly faster than the procedure presented here. (Note that in such a case only the initially available templates should be placed in DATAV[1] in the setup.) Another item that can be immediately dealt with is the marking of the "current descendants" followed by the unmarking. This is needed because the routines that update the DPG (detailed below) need to know which templates are descendants of the template that is currently being scheduled.

A further item to consider is the selection of the "best" candidate by the scheduler. One of the advantages of this type of scheduler is the ease with which it can be parameterized by an appropriate prioritizing heuristic. The presentation makes no mention of whether a static or a dynamic priority function is intended since different techniques are appropriate in different situations. Several authors report good success may be obtained by ranking templates according to their respective number of descendants in the DPG. Conversely, one might know that scheduling a template before the third, say, cycle of the block will cause an interlock or "stall" to be initiated. In such a case, one might want to derate the ranking of that particular template for the first three cycles. The situation here is similar to one frequently encountered when discussing hashing functions—most implementors have one that they like based on their experience. Only the static ranking mentioned above has received much favorable press.

We may now proceed to discuss (1) computation of the appropriate DATAV for a newly available instruction, and (2) the procedures for updating the DPG.

Timing Issues

In this section, we address the problem of discovering the cycle when a particular template becomes available based on the previously determined start cycles of its parents. In the following, let us assume that template I is the template that has become available. Then, to determine its earliest start time, we must example each of the in-arcs for this template since each one represents a timing constraint. From each arc, we may determine the earliest "slot" into which template I may be scheduled according to that constraint. The earliest time, then, is the latest of these earliest times, or

earliest_slot = max{ x | x is the earliest slot according to $<J, I, r>$,

an in-arc of I}

Now, for any arc $<J,I,r>$—that is, an arc from J to I labeled r—the exact form of the constraint expression depends on whether the arc is a data-dependency arc, a data-antidependency arc, or an output-dependency arc. Let us now address how each type of arc dictates a particular slot selection. Let us assume in what follows that instruction J has been scheduled at time tJ and that it writes register r on the cth cycle after tJ according to the version of J that was scheduled. Then, the earliest_slot indicated by a given arc $A = <J,I,r>$ is given by

$$\text{earliest\_slot}(A) = \begin{cases} tJ + c + 1 & \text{If A is an output-dependency arc.} \\ tJ + c - d & \text{if A is a data-dependency arc and } d \text{ is the latest delay for any version of I.} \\ tJ + d - e + f & \text{if A is a data-antidependency arc, d is the delay for for the scheduled version V of J to read } r, e \text{ is the earliest cycle for a version of I to write } r, \text{ and f is given below.} \end{cases}$$

$$f = \begin{cases} 1 & \text{if STORE\_PHASE}[r] > \text{last\_read\_phase}(V)[r]. \\ 0 & \text{otherwise} \end{cases}$$

Taking each case in turn, the first is certainly straightforward. If I must write after J and J writes on cycle $tJ + c$, then I cannot write before $tJ + c + 1$. The second case occurs where I is reading data written by J. Clearly, the earliest slot is obtained when we assume that the value is read as late in the microinstruction execution as possible. Now, it may turn out that no version of I that gives this best-case behavior may be scheduled at the time specified. In such a case, the test for timing compatibility will ensure that some other version that is field-compatible but not timing-compatible will not be scheduled. In the last case, we want to ensure that I does not write r before J reads r. The formula given here is simply a restatement of what was presented earlier. Note that we are optimistic in our treatment of data dependencies and pessimistic in our treatment of data antidependencies. It is possible to adjust the formula above for antidependencies and the definition of timing compatibility below to treat both arc types optimistically; this variation is not treated here.

Although the meaning of timing compatibility by now is intuitively clear, the definition is presented for completeness. A data-precedence arc $A = <J,I,r>$ is satisfied (i.e., timing-compatible) at time t for some version V of I if J has been scheduled on or before time t and

$$t > tJ + c - d + f$$

where
   tJ is the start time for template J
   c is the write delay for r for the scheduled version of J
   d is the read delay for r for V

Figure 9-15. A single example showing DPG updates.

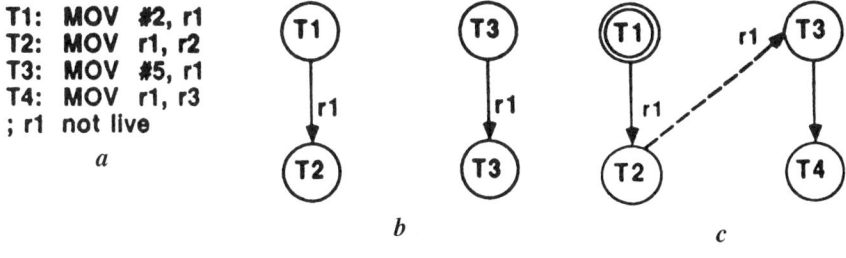

```
T1:  MOV  #2, r1
T2:  MOV  r1, r2
T3:  MOV  #5, r1
T4:  MOV  r1, r3
; r1 not live
        a
```

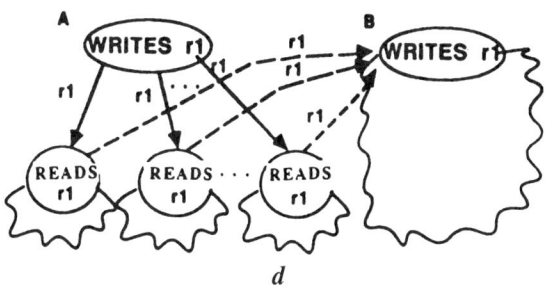

$$f = \begin{cases} 1 & \text{if STORE\_PHASE}[r] <= \text{last\_read\_phase}(V)[r]. \\ 0 & \text{otherwise} \end{cases}$$

Again, this essentially restates the material in the section on microarchitecture modeling.

Updating the DPG

The last item to be addressed on the topic of local compaction is the procedure for updating the DPG; this procedure must be invoked after each node is scheduled. The essential idea here is that scheduling a particular template can cause changes in the relationships among the templates. Consider, for example, figure 9-15a and b, a possible program and its DPG, respectively. Looking at the DPG, we see that both T1 and T3 are available initially since R1 is not live at the end of the block. If we suppose that T1 is selected, then the DPG must be updated as shown in figure 9-15c since T3 is now data-antidependent on T2—that is, T2 must precede T3 so that T3 does not overwrite the data to be read by T2. The general case is seen pictorially in figure 9-15d. Here, we have nodes A and B both data-available. Now, if node A is scheduled, the issue for node B must be delayed until after all of A's children (by data dependency on register r1) have executed. Thus, we must create a data-antidependency arc from each such child to node B; the label of each arc will be r1. In fact, it is not necessary that node B be available for this problem to occur since B could become available on a later cycle and do the overwriting later. In general then, an antidependency arc labeled r1 must be created for each appropriate child of A to each node that has not yet been scheduled, writes r1, and is not a child of A. Execution efficiency can be greatly increased by implementing this blocking in a semaphore arrangement; in fact, a linear factor can be saved on the execution time in this way.

The second situation in which new arcs must be created is shown in figure 9-16a and b. The essential problem here is that if T1 is scheduled first, then T4 cannot be immediately scheduled because no possible further scheduling can lead to a correct solution. To see this, study figure 9-16c and d, which

Figure 9-16. A more complicated updating of the DPG.

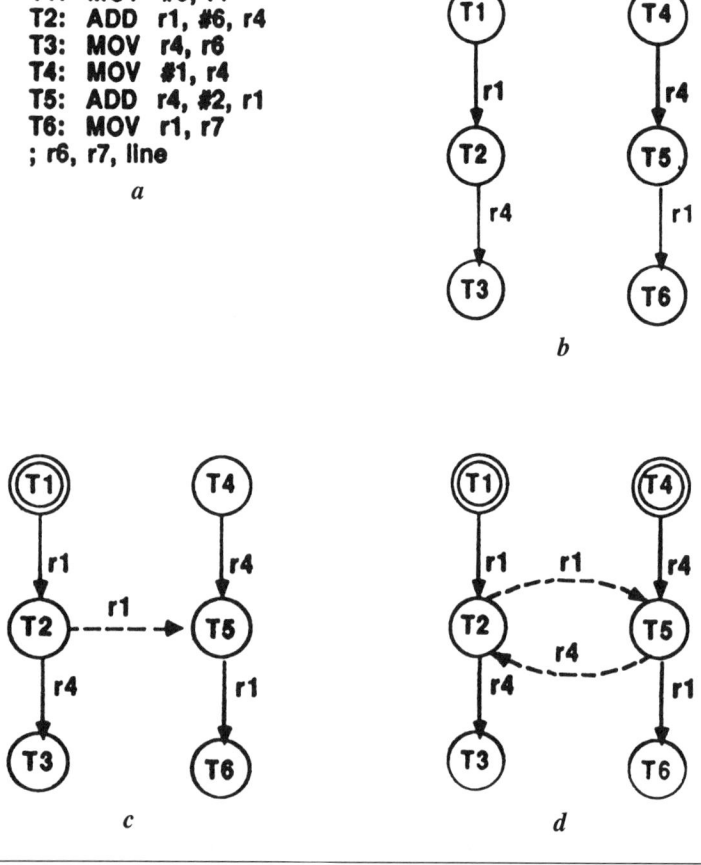

Figure 9-16 *(continued)*.

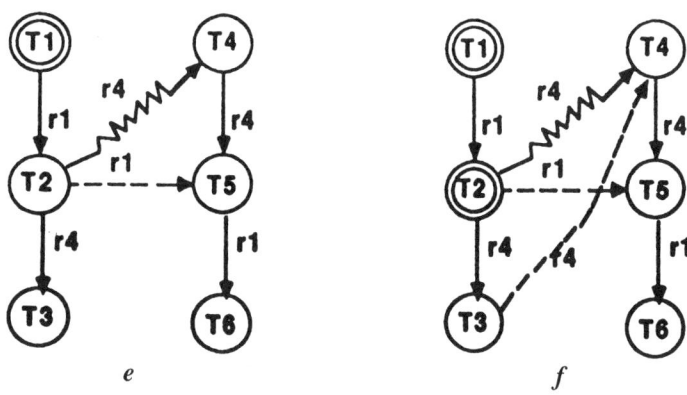

give the correct DPG after T1 has been scheduled and then after T4 has been scheduled, respectively. Clearly, T2 and T5 are on a cycle; thus, no further templates may be scheduled. The method used to circumvent this problem is to create an output-dependency arc from the r1 children of T1 to T4. Again, T4 doesn't have to be available when T1 is scheduled to cause the problem. Here, figure 9-16e shows the updated DPG after T1 is scheduled, and figure 9-16f shows the situation after T2 is subsequently scheduled. A picture of the general case is shown in figure 9-17. At least in this case, the register setup for B is very specific, that is, it must write the same register as a child C of the

Figure 9-17. The general case for adding antidependency arcs.

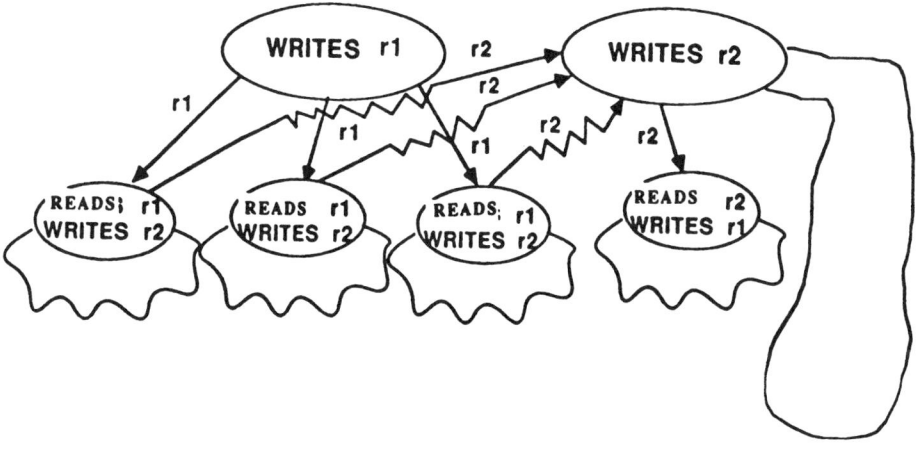

Figure 9-18. A demonstration of the interblock dependency problem.

```
start 1:  mov #1,r1              start 1:  mov #1,r1
          mov #2,r2                        mov #2,r2
          jmp L                            jmp L

start 2:  mov #2,r2              start 2:  mov #2,r2
          mov #1,r1                        move #1,r1
          jmp L                            jmp L'

     L:   mov r1,r3                   L':  nop
          mov #6,r5                   L:   mov r1, r3
          nop                              mov #6, r5
          add r2,r3                        nop
          nop                              add r2,r3
          nop                              nop
          add r3,r5                        nop
                                           add r3,r5
```

current node being scheduled and it must have a child that writes one of the registers that the child reads from the current node being scheduled. Since it is easy (and somewhat justifiable) to predict that such Bs will not occur often, no more efficient technique for doing the blocking (as in semaphor-band blocking above) has been sought.

Actually, the above discussion is not quite precise enough. Specifically, suppose that a node B' reads r2 and writes r2 and B reads r2 from B', where B is the node from figure 9-17. Then it is necessary to block B' as well as B. A precise statement of the appropriate nodes to block is: assume A is the current node, A writes r' to C, and C writes r. Then, C must block I_0 and there exist $I_0 I_1, \ldots I_k$ such that I_{j+1} is data-dependent on I_j, $0 <= j < k$, and I_k writes r'.

COMPACTION OF LOOP-FREE PROGRAMS

For some programs, compaction at the basic-block level followed by a step of pasting the compacted blocks together will result in a program with sufficient performance that further optimization is not necessary. However, there are other programs for which the level of optimization that may be obtained by this technique is insufficient. Moreover, when long write and branch delays are involved, the job of pasting the blocks together can be very difficult. These two reasons—that is, the need for faster execution and for a uniform way to handle interblock write and branch delays—have led to the development of so-called global compaction techniques.

The problem of interblock write delays has nothing to do with "compaction" per se; even very simple, vertical instruction sets exhibit write-delay problems if, say, a pipelined ALU is used that requires multiple instruction cycles to complete. Consider the program shown in figure 9-18a; here, a PDP-11ish instruction set is employed and an ALU instruction (either MOVE or ADD) is assumed to require three cycles (i.e., that two instructions must be executed between the issuing of an instruction and the use of its result). As can be seen, there are three basic blocks in the program. Each of the blocks is correct as far as write delays are concerned. But, the sequence of instructions executed beginning at start2 will not execute correctly because the value of r1 is not available at the beginning of the block labeled L. Unless one is willing to "recompact" the block labeled start2, then a NO-OP instruction must be inserted, as in figure 9-18b. While the compaction system that offers completely satisfactory solutions to this problem is beyond the state of the art, the compactor should at least offer some assistance in this domain since the most compact of programs that executes incorrectly is of little use.

Global Compaction Concepts

Since global compaction deals with arbitrary loop-free programs, we will have to augment some of our previous notions. The only change in the machine/instruction model that is needed is to introduce a model for branch instructions. The primary difference between a branch template and a normal instruction template is that the versions of branch instructions must specify a branch delay value. This is because some microarchitectures implement a *delayed branch*, that is, a branch that takes effect some possibly nonzero number of cycles after the branch instruction is issued. Branch delays of zero and one are quite common; branch delays for heavily pipelined microarchitectures could be much larger. Also, note that all versions of a branch instruction should not be required to have the same branch delay.

The major way that global compaction achieves a faster running program than local compaction is to find ways of moving templates among the various blocks of the program. It is noteworthy that the microarchitecture at hand must have either considerable extent in its horizontal characteristic or reasonably long write and/or branch delays for reasonable utility to be obtained by global methods. With this caveat, let us turn to the problem of moving templates across block boundaries to increase the available templates for compaction.

A template is said to be "free at the top of a block" if it does not read a value produced by another template in that block. Similarly, a template is "free at the bottom of a block" if it does not produce a value read by some other template in the block. The combination of a template and a block constitute what is called a *definition* (or def) of each of the write registers for that template. Further, a definition is said to *reach* a particular point in a program if the register is live at that point and there is some execution sequence from the definition to the program point in question so that no intervening template writes the register defined. Similarly, each template that reads a register is said to be a *use* of each of the definitions of the register that reach the template. A great deal of compiler optimization is involved with solving questions such as, "What are all the uses of this definition?" and "What are all the definitions that reach this use?" Algorithms for answering these questions are not presented here; rather, the reader is pointed in the right direction(s) in the bibliographic references.

Now, consider the portion of a flow graph depicted in figure 9-19. Here, TB, MB, and BB stand for top block, middle block, and bottom block, respectively. The question is this: "Under what conditions may a template be moved from one block to another without changing the semantics of the program?" As it happens, movement of templates between adjacent blocks is governed by four rules.

1f. If a nonempty subset $S = \{TB_{i1}, \ldots, TB_{ik}\}$ each contains a template T and T is free at the bottom of each block in S and for each write register w in T either w is not live at the top of MB or the only definitions of w that reach the top of MB originate in the blocks of S, then (whew!) template T may be moved by deleting it from each block in S and adding it to the top of MB.

1b. A template T that is free at the top of MB may be moved by deleting it from MB and adding it to the bottom of all TBs.

Figure 9-19. Legal moves between blocks.

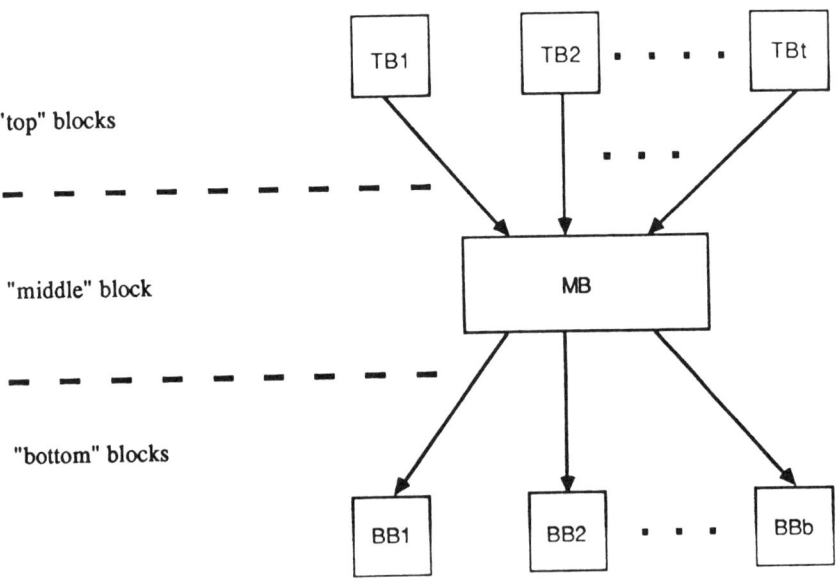

2f. A template T that is free at the bottom of MB may be moved by deleting it from MB and adding it to the top of each BB where any write register of T is live.

2b. If a nonempty subset $S = \{BB_{i1}, \ldots, BB_{ik}\}$ each contains a template T and T is free at the top of each block in S and for each write register w in T w is not live at the top of any block in $\{BBs\} - S$, then template T may be moved by deleting it from each block in S and adding it to the bottom of MB.

The rules have been numbered according to whether or not a fork or a join is involved and according to whether the templates move forward (along the arcs) or backward. In reality, we would like to move templates so that they execute as soon as possible; this corresponds to moving backward along the arcs. How these rules are utilized in global compaction is the subject of the next section.

Global-Compaction Procedure

In this section, the algorithm for global compaction is presented. In order to motivate what follows, first let us consider the problem from a high-level point of view. Recall that the program will be given to us as a loop-free flow graph. In addition, we will require that entrances to the flow graph not have any in-arcs and exits from the flow graph not have any out-arcs. In order to accomplish this, we will add special entry and exit blocks to a given flow graph to ensure this condition. These blocks will be assumed to be precompacted. Here, then, is a high-level view of the procedure.

```
procedure global_compaction(inout P:program);
  begin
    reduce_graph_and_compute_flow_information(P);
    while not (all blocks of P are compacted) do
      select_compaction_tree(T,P);
      get_new_prog_with_root_of_T_compacted(T,P);
      reduce_graph_and_compute_flow_information(P);
    endwhile;
  endprocedure;
```

In this presentation, a graph-reduction procedure is shown explicitly. This procedure, reduce_graph_and_compute_flow_information, effects several important transformations on the program. First, empty blocks are deleted and strings of blocks coalesced when possible. Second, updated live register and use/def information is computed; in the same step, useless microinstructions can be eliminated. Although the procedure as shown recomputes this information for the entire graph on each iteration, execution time may be saved by recomputing this information only for those blocks changed or created in the current iteration and their predecessors. The implementation of such a scheme is not detailed here.

Cursory inspection of the procedure reveals that each iteration consists of three steps: (1) selecting a subtree of the whole program graph, (2) compacting the root block of the tree compacted, and (3) setting up for the next iteration with a "reduced" graph and new flow information. Our presentation concentrates on the root compaction step. However, even though a thorough discussion of the subtree selection will be deferred to a later section, we must at least understand what a legal subtree would look like. Specifically, the subtree must not contain any blocks that have already been compacted. Any subtree that has this property is legal, although we shall see later some of the selection criteria that have been used.

The DPG for Global Compaction

Since we are using a tree flow graph with each block of the flow graph being a template sequence, we will clearly have to change our procedure for generating the initial DPG. Interestingly, only a few concepts will have to be modified; indeed, only the first two steps—the placement of the initial data-dependency arcs and the placement of the initial output-dependency arcs—are changed.

The change in the case of data dependency is a simple generalization of our previous concept. The rule is this—template J is data-dependent on template I using register r in a subtree T of a program P exactly when there is some register r so that template I is a definition of r that reaches J in T. Note specifically that a definition that reaches template J via a path not in T does not generate a data-dependency arc. A second minor change is that conditional branch instructions are treated as reading all the registers live at the top of all successor blocks.

Consider the program shown in figure 9-20a and its flow graph, shown in figure 9-20b. Here, the corner embellishment of a block implies that it is already compacted. A legal subtree to choose from the program is the one depicted in figure 9-20c; the resulting data-dependency arcs are shown in figure 9-20d. Please take special note that there are no arcs $<T3,T10,r5>$ or $<T5,T9,r2>$. These arcs are not present because the reaching definitions that they represent are not present in the subtree even though they are present in the program.

The placement of initial output-dependency arcs based on live variables generalizes to trees in a similar way. Thus, if template I writes register r and this definition reaches the bottom of the block B that contains template I, then all templates that write register r and reside in blocks higher in the tree than B must have output-dependency out-arcs linking to I and labeled with register r. These arcs are, of course, in addition to the ones that are in the same block with I; these are placed exactly as for local compaction. As a final difference, arcs are placed from the branch template of the root block, if any, to each of the other branch templates so that the order of the branches in the program is not altered. These output-dependency arcs are also shown in figure 9-20d.

Figure 9-20. A demonstration of the initial setup for global compaction.

```
T0:   mov #9,r9
T1:   mov #1,r1
T2:   mov #2,r2
T3:   mov #5,r5
T4:   go to if r8 then T5 else T7

T5:   mov #4,r2
T6:   go to T9

T7:   mov #8,r5
T8:   go to T9

T9:   add r1,r2,r3
T10:  add r3,r5
```
a

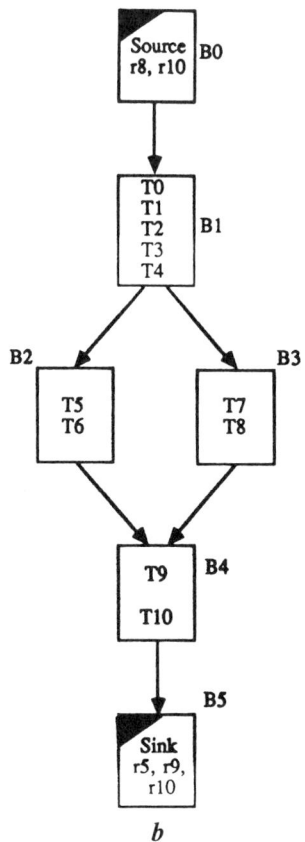

b

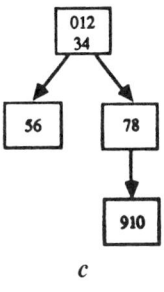

c

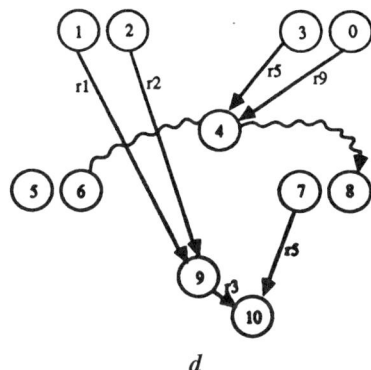

d

As a final comment, the compaction-time penalty for utilizing the new rule over the old one is increased considerably for global compaction. However, tradeoffs can be established in the use of the rules. For example, one might decide to use the new rule only when considering nodes located in the root block, since this is the block that is going to be compacted. Antidependencies outside the root block could be handled by the old rule. Or, one might decide to use the new rule only on certain registers with very high use frequencies, and the rest of the registers would be handled by the old rule. However it is accomplished, the eventual DPG must have the property that nodes do not become available if the scheduling of such nodes would lead the scheduler into deadlock.

The Root-Compaction Step

Thus, we turn our attention to the root-compaction procedure. There are two features of the tree compactor's instruction placement that differ from that of local compaction: the need for bookkeeping operations to preserve the semantics of the program, and the need to deal with delayed branching, interblock latency, and interblock field utilization.

There are two types of "bookkeeping" operations. The first type is possible whenever a template is moved to the root block of the compaction subtree from another block. Referring again to figure 9-20, this situation would occur if T9 is moved into the root after T1 and T2 are scheduled. This is an extended use of rule (1b) above for moving templates among blocks. However, in order to complete the use of the rule, we must consider the rest of the flow graph. In particular, we must also place a copy of T9 in the same block as T5. Rule (1b) requires that the template be moved into all parent blocks of the "moved-out-of" block. In reality, fewer copies of the template can be "pushed up" by considering reaching definitions; such extensions are not detailed further here.

The other type of bookkeeping operation is essentially a form of rule (2f). It comes into play when not all templates in the root have been scheduled when the block has been terminated by scheduling the branch. Let us assume here that two ALU templates or one branch template may be scheduled in a cycle. Referring again to figure 9-20, the root block of the tree might be scheduled as shown in figure 9-21a. Note, however, that T0 was not scheduled in this block. Thus, rule (2f) must be applied in order to preserve the semantics of the program. The resulting program showing this effect and also the effect of pushing up T9 is shown in figure 9-21b. Possible compactions of the new B2 and B3 show that in this case no performance penalty was obtained by the pushing down operation.

The actual implementation of "pushing up" and "pushing down" operations is actually somewhat more complicated than might be surmised from this example. Suppose that block B2 had instead consisted of the templates shown in figure 9-22a and the resulting program had been as in figure 9-22b. Further,

Figure 9-21. The global-compaction problem.

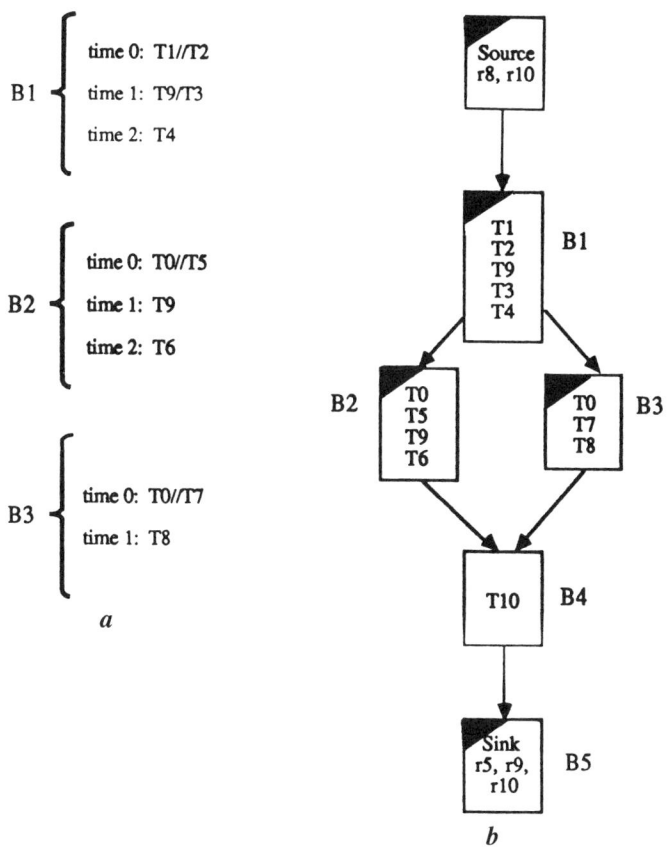

assume a new entry into B3 sourcing r9 as depicted. In such a case, the pushing-up procedure could not have moved T9 into block B2'; rather, a new block would have been created, as in figure 9-22c. Also, T0 could not have been pushed down directly into B3; again, a new block must be formed to hold the copy. As a last note, if B3 had contained a definition of register r9 and no uses, then the copy pushed down into r9 would have been useless and could have been eliminated.

The other difference from local compaction, dealing with delayed branches, is a very thorny problem. On the one hand, if the write delays and field utilization could be perfectly meshed across block boundaries, then we could expect a significant speedup. On the other hand, no straightforward formulation of the problem that is not exponential in its time complexity has been advanced.

Figure 9-22. The plan of global compaction.

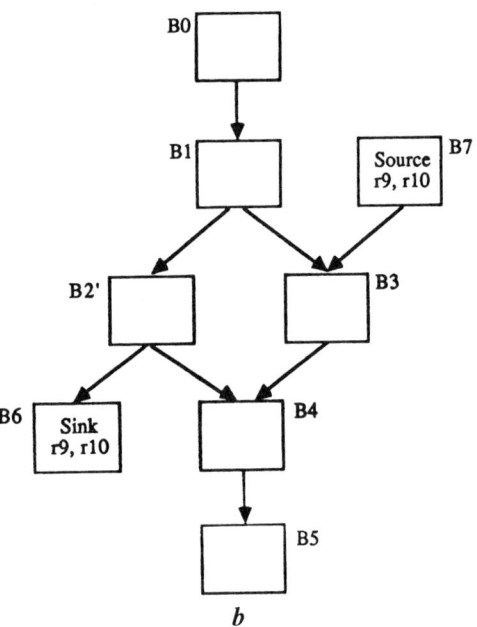

```
B2'.1:  mov #4,r2
B2'.2:  mov #7,r3
B2'.3:  if r3 > r10 go to T9 else exit
```
a

b

It's essentially a chicken-and-egg problem. If the write delays from all the predecessors of a given block are known, then the scheduler can take those delays into account when scheduling. Or, if all of the successor blocks have already been compacted, the scheduler can try to advance the writes of registers to be read early in successor blocks. Continuing (vainly) on this latter course, the problem that obtains is that different successor blocks will have been compacted so that the same register will have different "first-read-delays" in the different blocks. Thus, it is impossible to always have the delays mesh cleanly. Several researchers are reportedly working to solve this type of problem; the most likely attack is to try to maximize efficiency for the most probable execution path.

As it turns out, the interblock field-utilization problem is even harder to solve; this leads us to the other hand, where we find that a correct program, albeit

Figure 9-22. *(continued).*

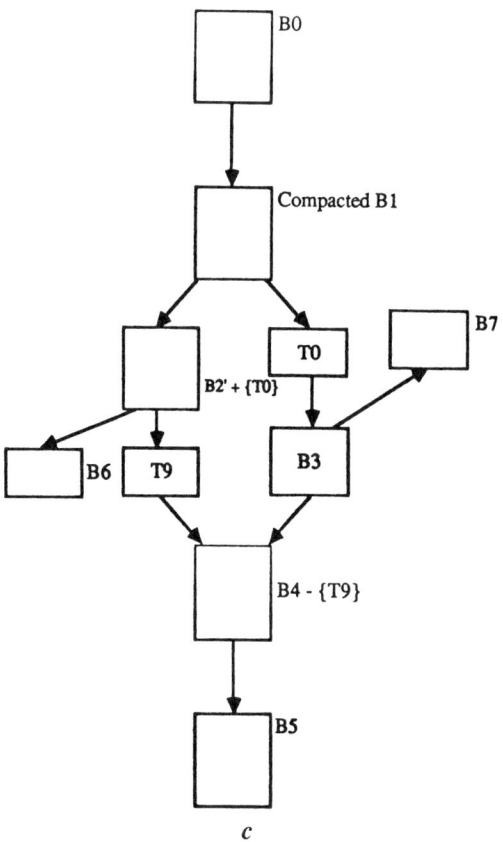

c

somewhat slower, may be obtained if write delays and field utilizations are not permitted to propagate beyond the block being scheduled. This can be handled within the current framework fairly simply, as follows. First, the branch is not considered for scheduling until the sum of the current cycle plus the branch delay is a cycle beyond where any already scheduled template writes a register or consumes any fields. Once the branch has been scheduled, no template is considered schedulable that writes registers or consumes fields in the cycle following the branch delay or beyond. Note that this still allows templates to be scheduled into the branch-delay cycles if these write-delay and field-utilization constraints are not violated. Also, we must ensure that only one branch is scheduled per block.

Having discussed fully these preliminaries, the algorithm for compaction of the root may now be presented.

```
procedure global_compaction_scheduler;
    Setup; t := 0; t_limit := MAXINT;
    max_use := 0; max_write := 0;
    while (all instructions not scheduled) and (t < t_limit) do
        t := t+1;
        while DATAV[t] not empty do
            foreach template T in DATAV[t] do
                if T is not available then delete T from DATAV[t] endif;
                if for any version V of T, all of the following are true:
                    • V is field compatible with the current state
                      beginning at time t and continuing for as many
                      cycles as V needs to consume fields;
                    • V does not write any registers as late as
                      t_limit;
                    • V does not consume any fields as late as
                      t_limit;
                    • V is timing compatible along each DPG
                      in-arc for T;
                    • if T is a branch template then
                      t_limit = MAXINT; and
                    • if T is a branch template with branch delay of
                      b associated with V then t+bd>max_write and
                      t+bd> =max_use
                then remember which V is a good one
                else delete T from DATAV[t]; add T to DATAV[t+1]
                endif;
            endforeach;
            if DATAV[t] is not empty then
            select the "best" template T;
            mark T as having been scheduled;
            adjust FIELDS[t], max_use and max_write to account for
            fields required by the remembered version V endif;
            if T is a branch template then t_limit := first cycle after
            the branch delay associated with this version V endif;
            if T is not located in the root block then "push up" T, as
            appropriate endif;
            foreach descendant D of T do
                mark D as a current descendant;
                if each parent of D has now been scheduled then place
                D on the appropriate DATAV list endif;
            endforeach;
```

>   update DPG with dynamic antidependency and output-
>   dependency links;
>   **foreach** descendant D of T
>   unmark D as a current descendant
>   **endforeach**;
>   **endif**;
>   **endwhile**;
>   **endwhile**;
>   **foreach** template T that was originally in the root block but that is
>   not now marked as scheduled do
>   push down T along out-arcs of the root block
>   **endforeach**;
>   **endprocedure**;

This procedure may seem very formidable; fortunately, close inspection reveals that it is essentially the same as the local compaction scheduler but that it has been augmented to take into account the concepts discussed in this section. In essence, then, it serves mostly as a summary. It is now the time to revisit the problem of selecting a subtree for compaction.

Selecting a Subtree for Compaction

As with most concepts of global compaction, even the procedure for picking a subgraph used as the basis for compacting the root is a multifaceted problem. There are essentially four possibilities we would like to consider; choosing (1) a tree consisting of a single node, (2) a maximal path through the program, (3) a maximal tree in the program, and (4) a maximal directed acyclic subgraph. The first choice amounts to local compaction except that the option of pushing down does open up some global possibilities. The last option is under research consideration but is yet in a very immature stage. Let us consider, then, just the choice between (2) and (3).

It seems intuitively clear that (3) is a much better choice than (2), since the scheduler has more templates available with which to make scheduling decisions. However, consider figure 9-23a. Using the "two-ALUs-or-a-branch" assumption and assuming a branch delay of two, we would obtain the compacted block of figure 9-23b. This might, in fact, be a reasonable result. However, if we assume that the program is 100 times more likely to branch to Y1 than to X1, then the two branch-delay slots have essentially been wasted. In this case, we would have been much better off by ignoring the X block completely and just using the T-Y path.

In general, then, the idea of *path compaction* (generally called *trace scheduling* in the literature) is that we choose at each opportunity the maximal path through the program that has the highest likelihood of being executed. This will cause us to focus our attention to a great extent on the part of the program where optimization will do the most good. Clearly, we would have to keep track of the various branching probabilities associated with each arc; indeed, it has been suggested that it might not even be that easy to obtain these probabilities for a particular program. However, this does not seem to be a major practical problem.

Now, one might naively assume that one could adjust the scheduling priority heuristic to take the branching probabilities into account. While this is possible (and perhaps desirable), it does not solve the basic problem. Consider the program of figure 9-23c, making the same assumptions. Figure 9-23d shows the compaction that will result. The problem here is that the scheduler greedily latches onto X1 for scheduling in the first instruction cycle. This, in turn, creates an antidependency from X2 to Y1 and from X3 to Y1. The compaction desired is the one shown in figure 9-23e. However, the only way to obtain this compaction is to ensure that the scheduler never sees X1 become available.

Thus, there is a quandary here. Choose a tree and get more available templates, or choose a "trace" and get the "right" available templates. The recommendation here is that one begin with a high-probability maximal tree and then prune off subtrees with very low execution probabilities; in this way, one obtains some of the better properties of each technique.

FUTURE WORK

Essentially, horizontal code compaction may be viewed as the extension of traditional compiler optimization techniques into the domain of horizontal instruction sets. As such, it owes a great deal of its background to traditional code optimization (Aho and Ullman 1977). In addition, the style of the presentation here owes much to the philosophy employed there—that is, that the algorithms presented represent points on a spectrum ranging from very complicated and very effective algorithms to rather trivial and less effective algorithms. Surprisingly, the presentation here is somewhat biased toward the latter for purposes of exposition, with the view that this information is basic to still more complicated algorithms as yet unexplored that will be used in production microcode compilers. A fundamental reference for deterministic scheduling is *Operating Systems Theory* (Coffman and Denning 1973).

A fundamental reference and survey of local-compaction techniques is given by Landskov et al. (1980). This reference also gives a reasonably exhaustive bibliography on enumerative techniques and early heuristics used to attack the local compaction problem. The concept of the microinstruction template is first elaborated in Tokoro, Tamura, and Takizuka (1981). Vegdahl (1982) is an early reference that calls into question the use of the old antidependency rule; Hennessy and Gross (1983) describe essentially a dynamic version of the new rule.

The fundamental paper in global compaction is Fisher (1981). Linn (1983), while naively enthusiastic about an incorrect formulation of general dag-based (as opposed to tree-based) loop-free compaction, provides some reasonable insights into the difficulties encountered in allowing the order of the branch instruction to interchange. Lah and Atkins (1983) give a version of global compaction based on trace scheduling that has less code-space expansion due to pushing up; it is essentially a different technique for choosing the initial compaction tree.

Several important papers have emerged dealing with programs with loops. While Fisher (1981) contains some background on programs with loops, two

Figure 9-23. Example of path compaction.

```
T0:  mov #1,r1                          time 0: T0//T1
T1:  mov #2,r2                          time 1: T2
T2:  go if r8 > r10 then X1 else Y1     time 2: X1
                                        time 3: X2

Y1:  add r1,r2,r3                            b
Y2:  add r3,r8
Y3:  exit


     ;r3, r8 dead here
X1:  move #6,r3
X2:  add r3, #1,r4
X3:  add r4, #1,r5
X4:  add r5, #1,r6
         :
         a
```

```
T0:  mov #1,r1                    time 0: T0//X1      time 0: T0
T1:  go if r8 > r10 then X1 else Y1   time 1: T1      time 1: T1
                                  time 2: X2          time 2: Y1
Y1:  add #1,r1,r2                 time 3: X3          time 3: Y2
Y2:  add r2,r2,r3                      d                   e
Y3:  exit


X1:  mov #6,r2
X2:  add #1,r2,r3
X3:  add r2,r3,r4
X4:  add #1,r4,r5
         c
```

papers that go significantly beyond the basics are Su, Ding, and Jin (1984) and Isoda, Kobayashi, and Ishida (1983). The latter is especially important since it also contains a completely orthogonal approach to expanding from local to global compaction that should be given some consideration when space is at a premium.

However, the greatest payoffs are to be expected when local and global scheduling become integrated with register allocation and instruction selection. For example, the register allocator could make compaction considerably more efficacious by not having the work registers of one block also be live for some sibling block; for the current compaction technology, this type of register interaction essentially defeats global compaction. Great payoffs may also accrue when general solutions to the interblock write-delay and field-utilization problems are found. Replacing restrictive rules (such as the new rule) by less restrictive rules will also lead to better compactions; similarly, greater use of the template-moving rules will lead to greater freedom in scheduling. Again, more general yet still efficient solutions to the problems are under investigation now.

REFERENCES

Aho, A. V., and J. D. Ullman. 1977. *Principles of Compiler Design.* Reading, MA: Addison-Wesley.

Coffman, E. J., and P. J. Denning. 1973. *Operating Systems Theory.* Englewood Cliffs, NJ: Prentice-Hall.

Fisher, J. A. 1981. "Trace Scheduling: A Technique for Global Microcode Compaction." *IEEE Transactions on Computers* C-30 (July):478–90.

Hennessy, J., and T. Gross. 1983. "Postpass Code Optimization of Pipeline Constraints." *ACM Transactions on Programming Languages and Systems* 5/3 (July):422–48.

Isoda, S.; Y. Kobayashi; and I. Ishida. 1983. "Global Compaction of Horizontal Microprograms Based on the Generalized Data Dependency Graph." *IEEE Transactions on Computers* C-32 (October):922–32.

Lah, J., and D. E. Atkins. 1983. "Tree Compaction of Microprograms." *Proceedings of the Sixteenth Annual Workshop on Microprogramming,* 23–33. Downingtown, PA, October 11–14. Los Angeles: IEEE Computer Society Press.

Landskov, D.; S. Davidson; B. D. Shriver; and P. W. Mallet. 1980. "Local Microcode Compaction Techniques." *ACM Computering Surveys* 12 (3):261–94.

Linn, J. L. 1983. "SRDAG Compaction—A Generalization of Trace Scheduling to Increase the Use of Global Context Information." *Proceedings of the Sixteenth Annual Workshop on Microprogramming,* 11–22. Downingtown, PA, October 11–14. Los Angeles: IEEE Computer Society Press.

Su, B.; S. Ding; and L. Jin. 1984. "An Improvement of Trace Scheduling for Global Microcode Compaction." *Proceedings of the Seventeenth Annual Workshop on Microprogramming*, 78–85. New Orleans, LA, October 30–November 2. Silver Spring, MD: IEEE Computer Society Press.

Tokoro, M.; E. Tamura; and T. Takizuka. 1981. "Optimization of Microprograms." *IEEE Transactions on Computers* C-30 (July):491–504.

Vegdahl, S. R. 1982. "Phase coupling and constant generation in an optimizing microcode compiler." *Proceedings of the Fifteenth Annual Workshop on Microprogramming*, 125–33. Palo Alto, CA, October 5–7. New York: IEEE Computer Society Press.

ten
PRINCIPLES OF FIRMWARE VERIFICATION

SUBRATA DASGUPTA

In the 35 or so years since its inception, the use of microprogramming for both implementation of control units and emulation has become commonplace. With the emergence and development of VLSI technology the general expectation is that microprogramming will continue to play a significant role in the implementation of complex single-chip processors, largely because of the regularity of microprogrammed control-unit structures (Parker and Wilner 1981; Stritter and Tredennick 1978; Mead and Conway 1980). Furthermore, in order to enhance system performance, functionality, reliability, and security, many heavily used functions that have heretofore been implemented in software are being migrated down into firmware, leading to much larger and more complex microprograms than were usually encountered in the past (Stankovic 1981; Bawden et al. 1979).

Because of these facts much attention has been paid in the last decade to the development of tools and techniques for the construction of reliable yet efficient firmware. The firmware development process has become an object of study in its own right, resulting in the emergence of a subdiscipline of *firmware engineering* (Davidson and Shriver 1981a; Giloi 1980; Dasgupta and Shriver 1985), which we may loosely define as being concerned with the identification of scientific principles underlying microprogramming and the application of these principles to the firmware development process. Some of the more important issues in this domain include the design and implementation of high-level microprogramming languages and their compilers (Baba and Hagiwara 1981; Dasgupta 1980; Davidson and Shriver 1980b; Davidson 1983; Linn, Shriver, and Dasgupta 1983; Ma and Lewis 1980; Patterson 1976) and mechanized strategies for optimizing and compacting microcode (Davidson et al. 1981; Fisher 1981; Landskov et al. 1980; Tokoro et al. 1981; Nagle, Cloutier, and Parker 1982; Vegdahl 1982; Wood 1980; Linn 1983).

One of the major objectives of firmware engineering is to develop theoretical and practical foundations for the *formal verification* of microprograms. The importance of this issue can hardly be overstated, for it will be clearly seen that since firmware constitutes one of the lower levels in the hierarchic, multilevel structure of computer systems, any error in the microcode would have serious and costly repercussions on the reliability of each of the higher software levels executing on the machine.

As in the case of software, firmware correctness can be approached from the viewpoint of either formal (mathematical) verification or empirical testing. The advantages of each of these approaches are well documented, both in the software (Wegner 1979; Yeh 1977) and the firmware (Berg 1980) domains; hence the relative merits of these alternative approaches will not be further discussed here. Clearly, both approaches are necessary and can play complementary roles in the development of firmware.

The focus of this chapter is on the formal verification of firmware. We will begin by establishing the theoretical framework on which most of the work on firmware verification is based. For obvious historical and practical reasons, much of this theory originated in the work on program correctness. However, we shall show in this chapter that the application of program-correctness techniques to firmware is not simply a matter of the uncritical transfer of technology from one domain to another. Rather, it involves the judicious selection of the appropriate concepts in program verification and their adaptation, modification, and extension to suit the very distinctive pragmatics that characterize the microprogramming environment. This whole process is by no means a trivial task.

Following is a detailed historical review of state-of-the-art firmware verification, which constitutes the main body of this chapter. In this section we will trace the different strands of ideas and techniques, their relationships, and their relative strengths and weaknesses. We hope that this review will give some indication of the progress made in firmware verification over the ten-odd years since the first paper on the topic appeared.

Finally, in the last section, we conclude by discussing some ongoing projects and speculate on future research directions.

FOUNDATIONS

Formal verification or proof of correctness of an information processing system rests essentially on an independent *specification* S of the intended behavior of the system and a *formal description* D of the system itself. The process of verification, then, involves a demonstration that the system as described by D does indeed behave in the manner prescribed by S. This requires, in turn, the availability of a precisely defined *semantics* σ for the description language by means of which the verifier—human or machine—proves that D satisfies S. Thus, verification requires as its starting point, a 3 Tuple

$$< S, D, \sigma >$$

and the distinctions between different approaches rests partly on the differences in the nature of their respective elements and partly on the method of proof itself.[1]

As we shall see below, there are a number of approaches to system verification, and one can only make sense of the whole picture by imposing some kind of structure on these different methods. It has become customary in recent years to classify different verification approaches according to the nature of the semantic definitions of the description languages and, furthermore, to classify language semantics as being *operational*, *denotational*, or *axiomatic* (or propositional) (Donahue 1976; Berg et al. 1982). Accordingly, one can talk of verification approaches as broadly belonging to one of these classes.

Operational Semantics

Intuitively, the notion of operational semantics originated in the way that language designers traditionally conceive and specify the meanings of their languages, viz., in terms of how constructs in such languages would be executed by an abstract machine.

Wegner (1972a, b) has made the distinction between compiler-oriented and interpreter-oriented operational semantics. A *compiler-oriented* language definition associates with each production

$$X ::= Y$$

in the grammar (where X is a nonterminal symbol and Y a symbol string) a *compile-time* semantic function $f_X(Y)$ that specifies the generation of target-

---

[1]. In this section we shall use the generic term "information processing system" or simply "system" to denote software, firmware, or hardware entities unless a specific reference is made to one of these particular classes of entities.

language code together with some updating of compile-time state variables. At the same time, Y is replaced in the input string representing the program by the symbol X. Thus, in compiler-oriented definitions, "meaning" is specified in terms of a set of *translations* performed on the syntactic entities of the language. This form of semantics was exemplified by Knuth (1968).

An *interpreter-oriented* language definition associates with each construct X ::= Y a state transformation from the "current" state of an abstract machine to a new state. In Wegner's model, states may be viewed as an ordered pair $<P, \sigma>$ where P is the (invariant) program component, while σ denotes the *state vector* component that may change during the execution of P. Included in σ is an *instruction-pointer* component, ip, which is updated to point to the new instruction. Thus, in an interpreter-oriented definition the occurrence of a given syntactic entity gives rise to the execution of a sequence of operations of an abstract machine. The most well-known example of this form of semantics is in the use of the Vienna definition language (VDL) for specifying the semantics of PL/1 (Wegner 1972b; Lucas and Walk 1969). However, the development of interpreter-oriented operational semantics originated in the seminal work by McCarthy (1963a, b) and Landin (1964).

Later in this chapter we shall illustrate the use of interpreter-oriented operational semantics in firmware verification when we discuss the IBM microcode certification system.

Denotational Semantics

A fundamental characteristic of the operational semantic model is that the actions performed by the abstract machine in interpreting programs result in the appearance of a *state sequence*.

However, it may be evident to the reader that operational semantics is in some sense not abstract enough: it may lead to a definition that is overspecified. For example, we may feel that the only states that matter are the initial and the final states and that how we arrive at a final state is irrelevant to the meaning of a syntactic entity. In a sense, an operational definition of a language is specified in terms of its implementation on a *particular* machine, albeit an abstract one.

In the *denotational* approach, the underlying interpretive mechanism is abstracted away and a model is used that views programs as functions from states to states and assigns purely mathematical meanings (i.e., in terms of mathematical objects such as sets and functions) to syntactic entities in such a way that the meaning or *value* of more complex entities may be determined in terms of the meanings or values of its components.

We illustrate this idea with a simple example taken from deBakker (1980). A *state* is defined as simply a function from integer variables to integers. Thus, if σ is a state, and a, b are integer variables, it may be that $\sigma(a) = 3$, and $\sigma(b) = 4$. Let V be the function that maps integer expressions E to their *val-*

ues, which are, in turn, functions from state to integers. Examples of definitions involving V are

$$V(a)(\sigma) = \sigma(a) = 3$$
$$V(E1 + E2)(\sigma) = V(E1)(\sigma) + V(E2)(\sigma)$$
$$V(E1 * E2)(\sigma) = V(E1)(\sigma) * V(E2)(\sigma)$$

Thus, if σ is such that $\sigma(a) = 3$, $\sigma(b) = 4$, we may obtain

$$V(a)(\sigma) = \sigma(a) = 3$$
$$V(a + b)(\sigma) = V(a)(\sigma) + V(b)(\sigma) = 7$$

Now, let M be the function that maps *statements* to their values, which are functions from states to states. Thus $\sigma' = M(s)(\sigma)$ denotes that the effect of statement S is to transform the initial state σ to the final state σ'. σ and σ' will determine the values of the variables before and after executing S, respectively. A typical example in the definition of M is, for the assignment statement $X := E$:

$$M(X := E)(\sigma) = V(E)(\sigma)/X$$

where $V(E)(\sigma)/X$ denotes a state σ' that is identical to σ except that its value at X is set to $V(E)(\sigma)$—i.e., to the value of E in σ. Applying this definition to the statement $X := a + b$, we obtain:

$$M(X := a + b)(\sigma) = \sigma\{7/X\}$$

That is, the effect of executing this statement in state σ is another state that differs from σ only in that the value of the variable X is 7.

While the historical antecedents of denotational semantics goes back to McCarthy (1963a, b), its main development is due to Scott and Strachey (Scott 1970; Scott and Strachey 1971). An excellent introduction to the topic is found in Gordon (1979), while more extensive treatments are given in Stoy (1977), deBakker (1980), and in the treatise by Milne and Strachey (1976).

Axiomatic Semantics

In the axiomatic approach the meanings of syntactic entities are given in terms of *assertions* or *formulas* in some deductive system (Floyd 1967; Hoare 1969; Dijkstra 1976; Gries 1981). In particular, a Hoare-type deductive system consists of formulas of the type {P} S {Q} where P,Q are predicates and S is some legal program statement. The formula {P} S {Q} is to be read as: if the state of the set of program variables is such that the assertion P is true before the execution of S, then the execution of S leads to a state such that the assertion Q is true when (and if) S terminates. P and Q are often called the *precondition* and *postcondition*, respectively, of the statement S.

438 SUBRATA DASGUPTA

In essence, Hoare logic consists of axioms and inference rules that describe the effects of the execution of composite statements in the language. Such inference (or proof) rules are usually expressed in the notation

$$\frac{H1, H2, \ldots, Hn}{H}$$

which states that if the premises H1,H2, . . . ,Hn are valid, then the conclusion H is also valid.

The semantics of objects in any given language L, then, are expressed in terms of *axioms* and *proof rules*. Given a program S in L, with prespecified precondition P and postcondition Q, one can construct a proof of S's correctness by applying these axioms and proof rules in a deductive fashion. Conversely, given precondition P and postcondition Q, one can, in a stepwise and systematic fashion, construct valid sequences of statements S for which {P} S {Q} can be shown to be true.

As an example of axiomatic semantics, we show first, the standard axiom of assignment:

$$\{P[X/E]\}\ x := E\{P\}$$

where the notation P[X/E] denotes the assertion P with all free occurrences of X in P replaced by E. This rule simply states that if P is the postcondition of an assignment statement, then its precondition will be P[X/E].

The semantics of two composite statements in typical Algol-like languages are given below in the form of proof rules:

$$\frac{\{P1\}\ S1\ \{P2\}, \{P2\}\ S2\ \{P3\}}{\{P1\}\ S1; S2\ \{P3\}}$$

$$\frac{\{P\&B\}\ S1\ \{Q\}, \{P\&\neg B\}\ S2\ \{Q\}}{\{P\}\ \text{IF B THEN S1 ELSE S2}\ \{Q\}}$$

The first equation specifies the rule for sequential composition and states that if the premises {P1} S1 {P2} , and {P2} S2 {P3} are valid—i.e., can be shown to be true—then the formula {P1} S1;S2 {P3} will be true.

The second equation defines the rule for the IF statement. According to this, if the assertion P holds on entry to an IF statement, and if we can prove that {P&B} S1 {Q} and {P&¬B} S2 {Q} are true, then the consequence

$$\{P\}\ \text{IF B THEN S2 ELSE S2}\ \{Q\}$$

will be true—that is, regardless of whether or not the Boolean condition B is true or not, the postcondition Q will always be true.

As a trivial illustration of how axiomatic semantics may be applied to verification, consider the following Pascal statement

$$\text{IF } a \geq 0 \text{ THEN } b := a \text{ ELSE } b := -a$$

the execution of which sets b to the absolute value $|a|$ of an integer a. The appropriate pre- and postconditions are TRUE and $b = |a|$, respectively, where TRUE is the predicate that is true for all machine states. Inserting these assertions leads to the formula

$$\{\text{TRUE}\} \text{ IF } a \geq 0 \text{ THEN } b := a \text{ ELSE } b := -a \{b = |a|\}$$

To prove this applying the rule for the IF statement requires us to show that the following antecedent formulas hold (here we have simply ignored the predicate TRUE):

$$\{a \geq 0\} \, b := a \, \{b = |a|\}$$

$$\{a < 0\} \, b := -a \, \{b = |a|\}$$

Applying the axiom of assignment backward in the first equation, since the postcondition P is $b = |a|$, $P[b/a]$ is $a = |a|$, which implies $a \geq 0$, the precondition. Thus, this formula is true. Similar application of the assignment rule in the second equation produces the assertion $-a = |a|$, which implies $a < 0$, the precondition here, hence the truth of this formula. We can then conclude, by the proof rule for the IF statement, that the TRUE formula holds.

Discussion

Some authors, notably Donahue (1976) and Ashcroft and Wadge (1982), have pointed out that these different modes of defining the semantics of a language are not simply alternative or conflicting modes of definition but are complementary in the sense that they define language semantics at different levels of abstractions, and consequently, each approach may serve distinct but complementary roles.

We observe, for example, that the operational approach defines semantics that are strongly suggestive as to how the language may be implemented by prescribing sequences of state transformations that result from the interpretation of a syntactic object. The denotational approach abstracts from state-transformation sequences but retains the concept of states and defines meanings in terms of functions. The axiomatic model abstracts still further in that states are only implicitly present in such a definition, which relies on relating syntactic objects to logical formulas or propositions expressed in some logical calculus. Futhermore, axiomatic semantics is, by design, more conducive to the activities of program design and verification than other forms of semantics.

In his treatise on program correctness, deBakker (1980) illustrates how denotational semantics can be used to define the semantics of programming and assertion languages and to provide a rigorous basis for establishing the *reliability* of proof systems of the axiomatic kind. By "reliability" we mean that the axiomatic proof system is *sound* (i.e., only true formulas $\{P\} S \{Q\}$ can be proved by the system) and *complete* (i.e., all true formulas can be proved by the system).

In the present chapter we shall discuss firmware verification within the operational and axiomatic frameworks. For a discussion of a denotational approach to the problem the reader is referred to Gordon (1981).

DEVELOPMENTS IN FIRMWARE VERIFICATION

As noted at the beginning of the chapter, the purpose of this section is to trace, in some detail, the development of firmware-verification ideas. Our aim is as much to show the evolution and growth of a particular techological discipline as it is to identify important results in firmware verification.

The first published works on microprogram correctness were by Ramamoorthy and Shankar (1973, 1974), Maurer (1974), and the initial theory developed by Carter and his coworkers (Birman 1974; Leeman, Carter, and Birman (1974), which eventually led to their microcode certification system.

Ramamoorthy and Shankar (1974) were primarily concerned with the problem of proving the equivalence of two *loop-free* microprograms M1 and M2. We may suppose that M1 and M2 are executed on the same host machine or on distinct hosts H1 and H2. The former situation may arise, for example, in the course of a development process using stepwise refinement in which M1 is an "earlier," more "abstract" version of M2. "The situation crops up in the transformation of an emulator M1 running on H1 (denoted as M1(H1)) into an equivalent emulator M2 running on H2 (denoted as M2(H2))." Thus, the issue at hand was to demonstrate the equivalence of M1(H1) and M2(H2).

Unfortunately, there are some very serious problems with the theory formulated by Ramamoorthy and Shankar for solving this problem. Apart from the fact that it is restricted to loop-free microprograms, the theory assumes a very simple model of host micromachines that ignores several important properties of microarchitectures such as side effects and timing. Even more seriously, the formalism underlying and leading to their definition of equivalence is mathematically so imprecise as to render the whole approach of very little value.

The Microcode Certification System

Starting from about 1974, Carter and his coworkers at IBM published a series of papers in which the evolution of a system called the microcode certification system (MCS) is described (Birman 1974; Leeman, Carter, and Birman 1974; Leeman 1975; Joyner, Carter, and Leeman 1976; Carter, Joyner, and Brand 1978). Their approach is a textbook example of the application of operational semantics to verification.

As is well known, a computer C can be viewed at several distinct levels of abstraction (Siewiorek, Bell, and Newell 1982; Dasgupta 1984). In particular, consider two abstract representations of C, H and μH. H is a specification of C's *exoarchitecture* (Dasgupta 1982, 1984) — that is, the structure and behavior of C as seen by the compiler writer or operating-system designer. The machine μH is at a lower abstraction level and consists of a specification of a (host) microarchitecture together with a microprogram being interpreted by the host machine. The problem, then, is to prove that μH and H are in some sense equivalent — that is, μH correctly implements H — using Milner's concept of algebraic simulation of one program, P, by another, $\hat{P}$ (Milner 1971).

Informally stated, a simulation of P by $\hat{P}$ means that whatever can be computed by P can also be computed by $\hat{P}$. Basically, the approach taken by Carter et al. involves the following steps:

1. Define the abstract machine H.
2. Define the abstract machine μH.
3. Establish the desired simulation relation R.
4. Prove that μH simulates H with respect to R.

The language used to define H and μH was originally the Vienna Definition Language (VDL) extended with operators from APL. Subsequently, a very similar language called LSS (language for symbolic simulation) was developed and used.

To prove that μH is a correct implementation of H, it must be shown, using the notion of a simulation relation between H and μH, that any instruction of H is correctly simulated by a sequence of microinstructions in μH. The heart of this approach, then, is the concept of a simulation relation, which we now explain.

Notation

For a given set $S = \{a, b, c, \ldots\}$, the notation $\{a, b, c, \ldots\}^k$ denotes the set of k-bit strings (vectors) over the alphabet S.

Given two sets, D, $\hat{D}$, R is a relation if $R \subseteq D \times \hat{D}$. We denote an element of R by $(d, \hat{d}) \in R$, while the inverse of R, $R^{-1} = \{(\hat{d}, d) \mid (d, \hat{d}) \in R\}$. The relation R is a partial function if for each $d \in D$ there is at most one $\hat{d} \in \hat{D}$ such that $(d, \hat{d}) \in R$. In this case we use the usual notations for functions, viz., $R : D \rightarrow \hat{D}, R(d) = \hat{d}$, or $Rd = \hat{d}$. If R is a function and there exists $d \in D, \hat{d} \in \hat{D}$ such that $R(d) = \hat{d}$, we say that R is defined at d and denote this as $<Rd>$.

Let $F : D \rightarrow D$ be a function from D to D, and let $d \in D$. $F^i d$ is defined by

$$F^0 d = d$$
$$F^i d = F(F^{i-1} d) \text{ if } <F^{i-1} d>$$
$$= \text{undefined otherwise}$$

Definition 1

An *abstract program* $P = (D, D_0, F)$ where D is a set called the *domain* of P, $D_0 \subseteq D$ is a set of initial values, and $F : D \rightarrow D$ is a partial function. A *computation* is a sequence $(d_0, d_1, d_2, \ldots)$ in which $d_0 \in D_0$ and $d_{i+1} = Fd_i, i = 1, 2, \ldots$

Consider, for example, the program P in figure 10-1. Here, x is an integer and y a 32-bit vector. Denoting the set of integers by N, the domain $D = M \times E$ where

$$E = \{(x, y) \mid x \in N, \ y \in \{0, 1\}^{32}\}$$

$$M = \{1, 2, 3\}$$

and

$$D_0 = \{(1, e) \mid e \in E\}$$

Definition 2

Let $P = (D, D_0, F), \hat{P} = (\hat{D}, \hat{D}_0, \hat{F})$ be two programs. A relation $R \subseteq D \times \hat{D}$ is a *strong simulation* (or simply *simulation*) of P by $\hat{P}$ if

(C1) $\forall (d, \hat{d}) \in R$, $<Fd>$ if $<\hat{F}\hat{d}>$ and if both are defined ($<Fd>$, $<\hat{F}\hat{d}>$) $\in R$. This is also called the condition of weak simulation.

(C2) $\forall d_0 \in D_0, \exists \hat{d}_0 \in \hat{D}_0, (d, \hat{d}_0) \in R$. That is, R is total on D_0.

(C3) $\forall \hat{d}_0 \in \hat{D}_0, \exists d_0 \in D_0, (d_0, \hat{d}_0) \in R$. That is, R^{-1} is total on $\hat{D}_0$.

(C4) $\forall d \in D, \forall \hat{d} \in \hat{D}, (d, \hat{d}) \in R$ implies $\forall d_1 \in D$ if $(d_1, \hat{d}) \in R$ then $d_1 = d$. That is, R is single-valued.

Informally, if R is a strong simulation of P by $\hat{P}$, then the latter can compute anything that can be computed by the former. This is formalized in the following.

Theorem 1

Let $P = (D, D_0, F)$ and $\hat{P} = (\hat{D}, \hat{D}_0, \hat{F})$ be two programs, and $R \subseteq D \times \hat{D}$ be such that R is a strong simulation of P by $\hat{P}$. Then $\forall d_0 \in D_0, \forall \hat{d}_0 \in \hat{D}_0, (d_0, \hat{d}_0) \in R$ implies $<F^i d_0>$ if and only if $<\hat{F}^i \hat{d}_0>$, $i = 1, 2, \ldots$, and if both are defined, then $F^i d_0 = R^{-1}[\hat{F}^i \hat{d}_0]$.

For a proof of this theorem, the reader is referred to Birman (1974). Informally, the theorem asserts that if $(d_0, \hat{d}_0) \in R$ and we repeatedly apply F and $\hat{F}$, respectively, to the states of P and $\hat{P}$, then all pairs of resulting states are in R. Furthermore, we can determine the state in P from the state in $\hat{P}$ because of the single-valued nature of R^{-1}. Thus for any computation in P which takes $d_0 \in D$ to $d \in D$, we can use R to obtain the same result as follows: let $\hat{d}_0$ be such that $(d_0, \hat{d}_0) \in R$. We know that such a $\hat{d}_0$ exists by condition C2 of Definition 2. We then use $\hat{P}$ to obtain $\hat{d} \in \hat{D}$ such that $(d, \hat{d}) \in R$. We finally compute $d = R^{-1}(\hat{d})$.

Birman (1974) illustrates the application of these results with two programs P (fig. 10-1) and $\hat{P}$ (fig. 10-2). P and $\hat{P}$ are formally characterized as follows:

For P:

$$E = \{(x, y) \mid x \in N, y \in \{0, 1\}^{32}\}$$
$$M = \{1, 2, 3\}$$
$$D = M \times E$$
$$D_0 = \{(1, e) \mid e \in E\}$$

For $\hat{P}$:

$$\hat{E} = \{\hat{x}, \hat{y}, \hat{z}, A) \mid \hat{x}, \hat{z} \in N, \hat{y} \in \{0, 1\}^{32}, A \in N^4\}$$

where N^4 denotes vectors of integers of length 4.

$$\hat{M} = \{1, 2, 3\}$$
$$\hat{D} = \{(\hat{m}, \hat{e}) \mid \hat{m} \in \{1, 3\}, \hat{e} \in \hat{E}\} \cup \{(2, \hat{e}) \mid \hat{e} \in E, \hat{z} = 1\}$$
$$\hat{D}_0 = \{(1, \hat{e}) \mid \hat{e} \in E\}$$

Suppose we construct the following simulation relation R:

$$R = R11 \cup R22 \cup R33$$

where

$$R11 = \{(d, \hat{d}) \mid m = \hat{m} = 1, x = \hat{x}, y = \hat{y}\}$$
$$R22 = \{(d, \hat{d}) \mid m = \hat{m} = 2, x = \hat{x}, y = \hat{y}, A = (0, 1, 2, 3), \hat{z} = 1\}$$
$$R33 = \{(d, \hat{d}) \mid m = \hat{m} = 3, x = \hat{x}, Y = \hat{y}\}$$

Then, in order to show that $\hat{P}$ simulates P, we have to show that conditions C1-C4 of definition 2 are satisfied by R.

Proof

Condition C1 is proved by cases.

Case 1.1. Let $(d, \hat{d}) \in R11$, i.e., $m = \hat{m} = 1$. The symbolic execution of Fd,F$\hat{d}$ corresponds to the following straight-line programs:

```
P : {m=1}                    P̂ : {m=1}
   begin                        begin
      x ← a ;                      x̂ ← a ;
      y ← h                        ŷ ← h ;
   end                             ẑ ← 1 ;
   {m=2, x=a, y=h}                 A ← (0123)
                               end
                               {m=2, x̂=a, ŷ=h, ẑ=1,
                                A = (0123)}
```

Figure 10-1. The microcode certification system: abstract program P.

```
P :   begin
         x ← a;
         y ← h;
      L1 :  if x ≠ 0 then
               begin
                  x ← x-1
                  y ← LS(y)
                  goto L1
               end
      end
```

Figure 10-2. The microcode certification system: abstract program P'.

```
P' :
   begin
      x' ← a;
      y' ← h;
      z' ← 1;
      A ← 0123
      L2 :  if A[z'] = 0
               then begin
                     if x' ≠ 0
                        then begin
                              z' ← z' + 1;
                              goto L2
                           end
                  end
               else begin
                     if A[z'] = 1
                        then begin
                              x' ← x' - 1;
                              z' ← z' + 1;
                              goto L2
                           end
                        else begin
                              if A[z'] = 2
                                 then begin
                                       y' ← LS(y');
                                       z' ← z' + 1;
                                       goto L2
                                    end
                                 else begin
                                       z' ← 1;
                                       goto L2
                                    end
                           end
                  end
   end
```

Clearly, $(Fd, \hat{F}\hat{d}) \in R22$ since the following relations hold:
$$m = \hat{m} = 2, x = \hat{x}, y = \hat{y}, \hat{z} = 1, A = (0123)$$

Case 1.2. Let $(d, \hat{d}) \in R22$ such that $x = 0$. Then

P : {m=2, x=a, y=h}
    begin end
    {m=3, x=a, y=h}

$\hat{P}$: {$\hat{m}$=2, $\hat{x}$=a, $\hat{y}$=h}
    begin end
    {$\hat{m}$=3, $\hat{x}$=a, $\hat{y}$=h}

Clearly $(Fd, \hat{F}\hat{d}) \in R33$ since $x = \hat{x}, y = \hat{y}, m = \hat{m} = 3$.

Case 1.3. Let $(d, \hat{d}) \in R22$ such that $x \neq 0$. Then

P : {m=2, x=a, y=h}
    begin
        x ← x − 1
        y ← leftshift(y)
    end
        {m=2, x=a−1, y=leftshift(h)}

$\hat{P}$: {$\hat{m}$=2, $\hat{x}$=a, $\hat{y}$=h, A=(0123), $\hat{z}$=1}
    begin
        z ← $\hat{z}$ + 1
        x ← $\hat{x}$ − 1
        z ← $\hat{z}$ + 1
        y ← leftshift($\hat{y}$)
        z ← $\hat{z}$ + 1
        z ← 1
    end
        {$\hat{m}$=2, x=a−1, y=leftshift(h), A=(0123), $\hat{z}$= 1}

Since $m = \hat{m} = 2, x = \hat{x}, y = \hat{y}, A = (0123), \hat{z} = 1, (Fd, \hat{F}\hat{d}) \in R22$.

Conditions C2, C3, and C4 can easily be proved and we leave these as an exercise to the reader.

In the foregoing discussion we have outlined the basic theory developed by Carter et al. In order to apply this theory to the verification of microprograms, it is necessary to transform the abstract machines H and μH into the form of abstract programs. Given the operational nature of the machine specifications (say, in VDL/APL) it is not too difficult to have an intuitive understanding of this transformation. For an abstract machine H, its abstract program form will be (D, D_0, FH) in which the domain D will be composed of a set of state variables together with the control that determines the machine's interpretation mechanism. D_0 will consist of the initial state presumed to hold when H begins execution along with the control, set to begin interpretation. The function FH must be defined so that it accepts a state in D and returns the next state in D. The precise nature of D, D_0, and FH will, of course, depend on the machine being specified.

Initially, MCS was applied to a simple, hypothetical 32-bit, stack-based, vertically microprogrammed computer called the S machine (Birman 1974; Leeman 1975). The system was subsequently applied to a "real" computer, the hybrid technology computer (HTC), a version of the NASA standard spaceborne computer 2. Among the features of this machine are: support for the IBM System/360 standard instruction set, an elaborate I/O system, and a 64-bit-wide (horizontal) read-only control store. Several errors in the micro code were detected during symbolic simulation. The reader is referred to Carter, Joyner, and Brand (1978) for an interesting discussion of the nature of these errors.

One other aspect of this work must be noted. The objective set for the MCS was to prove the correctness of, or detect errors in, microcode that had already been written. The system is not helpful to the *design* of correct firmware or, more generally, to the problem of correctly implementing a given architectural specification.

The Beginnings of Axiomatic Verification

The use of the axiomatic method in firmware verification appears to have been first suggested in a little-known paper by Maurer (1974). Most of this paper is devoted to the problem of verifying machine-language programs, in particular programs that may possibly modify themselves. Maurer suggested that this problem is also relevant in the case of microprograms residing in writable control store and having the capability of altering their own microinstructions.

The specific problem addressed by Maurer is the following: how can we extend the basic Floyd–Hoare approach to verification so as to take into account the possibility that instructions may modify themselves?

Recall (from "Foundations") that the general proof formula has the form

$$\{P\} \ S \ \{Q\}$$

where S is a statement (or statement sequence) and P,Q are pre- and postconditions, respectively. Recall, also, that these assertions are formulas over the domain of S's data object set. The implicit assumption underlying formulas of this type is that S is indeed what gets executed when the precondition P holds, in which case, when S terminates, Q will be true. However, for the class of programs we are considering here, it may be the case that S has been modified by some other instruction, in which case a proof of correctness according to this formula does not guarantee that Q will in fact be true when S is executed.

To take this possibility into account, Maurer extended the formula to the form

$$\{ICA \& P\} \; S \; \{ICA \& Q\}$$

where ICA is an *instruction constancy assertion*, defined as follows:
If W is any address and K is a value, then the assertion

$$W = K$$

states that the word at address W has the value K. The assertion ICA states that $Wi = Ki$ for each instruction code Ki of an instruction in the given program and each address Wi at which that code is assumed to be stored. In other words, the ICA states that every instruction word in the program contains the code it had at the start of the program.

Clearly, if it is shown that the second formula is true, then on executing S the postcondition Q will be assured. This requires, of course, that the invariance of ICA across the execution of S must also be shown.

Maurer's paper is of some interest since it illustrates a type of correctness issue that may arise in microprogramming at the assembly-language level but not in high-level-language programs. The possibility of self-modifiable microprograms may exist in any user-microprogrammable computer that contains microinstructions capable of writing into control store—such instructions exist, for example, in the Nanodata QM-1 (Nanodata 1979) and the Burroughs B1700 (Organick and Hinds 1978).

Unfortunately, Maurer does not explore firmware verification to any further depth except to point out the important issues of side effects and timing that distinguishes firmware from software verification. He noted, for example, that the standard axiom of assignment

$$\{P[X/E]\} \; X := E\{P\}$$

would have to be modified to take into account side effects—an issue that was only probed and explored in greater detail much later by Wagner and Dasgupta (1983) and Dasgupta and Wagner (1984); see also the section "S*(QM-1)" below. In this sense, the significance of this largely neglected paper lies in the fact that several important questions in firmware verification were raised.

STRUM

It is an unfortunate fact that Maurer's paper (1974) had virtually no influence on subsequent work. The first major and systematic investigation of the axiomatic verification of microprograms was carried out by Patterson and reported in his doctoral thesis (1977). His general approach is schematized in figure 10-3.

STRUM is a high-level, Pascal-like microprogramming language oriented toward the Burroughs D machine (Katzan 1977). In verifying a STRUM program, assertions are inserted at key positions in the program and then passed to

Figure 10-3. The STRUM verification system.

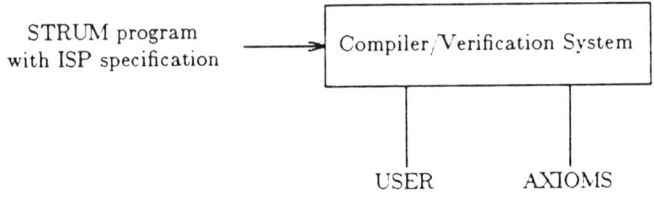

the compiler/verification system, which uses the axioms and proof rules for the language to prove that the microprogram does indeed satisfy the assertions.

It is useful, at this stage, to recall that the verification situation involves a 3 Tuple

$$< S, D, \sigma >$$

where S is the independent specification of the intended behavior of the system, D is a formal description of the system, and σ is the semantics and proof theory for the description language.

In Patterson's approach, D is, of course, specified in STRUM, while the specification S is stated in a modified version of the architecture description language ISP (Barbacci 1979). More precisely, a specification of the target machine that the microprogram is intended to emulate is used as a basis for constructing assertions in this specification (or assertion) language that are then inserted into appropriate positions in the STRUM program.

In designing STRUM, Patterson's main objective was to construct a language and a programming system that would permit well-structured verifiable microprograms to be written for the Burroughs D machine without having to sacrifice object-code efficiency. Thus, a great deal of attention was paid to the structuring facilities in the language, and as a result it has four distinct repetition statements, four alternative selection statements, a macro statement and the procedure statement. A STRUM program can be organized into blocks, thus enabling the "scope" of variables to be explicitly stated.

For purposes of verification, the programmer is required to associate an assertion with each loop and one assertion each at the input and output of every procedure. Loop assertions start with the word ASSERT, and input and output assertions are identified by the key words ASSUME and CONCLUDE.

The proof theory for verifying STRUM programs is based on an axiomatic definition of the language much in the style of the Hoare–Wirth definition of Pascal (1973). One must remember, however, that STRUM is oriented towards a particular host machine. Thus, while many of the axioms and proof rules are identical to those for corresponding constructs in Pascal, others reflect the peculiarities of the D machine. For any firmware-verification system oriented partially or wholly, implicitly or explicitly toward a particular machine this characteristic will always be present, and it is therefore worthwhile to examine some relevant parts of STRUM's formal definition from this viewpoint. Later we shall see a further example of a machine-specific proof theory.

Example 1

STRUM includes two IF statements that on the surface look like IF statements in any other Algol-like programming language:

$$\text{if B then S}$$
$$\text{if B then S1 else S2}$$

However, there are restrictions on the nature of the Boolean expression B. One class of admissible Boolean expressions is the class of *test* expressions and typically these may take the form[2]

$$\text{lst (AE) def if AE} <15> = 1 \text{ then true else false}$$
$$\text{mst (AE) def if AE} <0> = 1 \text{ then true else false}$$
$$\text{ones (AE) def if AE} = \text{FFFF}_{16} \text{ then true else false}$$
$$\text{carry (AE) def carry}_{16} \text{ (AE)}$$

where AE denotes an arithmetic expression. Note that a test expression includes the arithmetic expression upon which the predicate is being tested. An example of an IF statement would be:

$$\text{if carry (X + Y) then temp} := \text{temp} + 1$$

The proof rules for the two IF statements are:

$$\frac{\{P \& B\} S \{Q\} \, P \& \neg B \supset Q}{\{P\} \text{ if B then S } \{Q\}}$$

$$\frac{\{P \& B\} S_1 \{Q\}, \{P \& \neg B\} S_2 \{Q\}}{\{P\} \text{ if B then } S_1 \text{ else } S_2 \{Q\}}$$

As a final point, it should be noted that the four test predicates mentioned above are instances of *machine-specific* Boolean expressions; in the Burroughs D machine they correspond to four "dynamic conditions" that are established dynamically from the adder output by an arithmetic/logic-unit (ALU) operation. These conditions are maintained until the next ALU operation.

---

[2]. Other forms of the Boolean expression include simple Boolean variables, relational expressions, and a predicate that denotes the stack-overflow indicator.

Example 2
The WHILE and REPEAT statement have the forms:

> while B assert A do S od
> assert A repeat S until B Baeper

where B is a Boolean expression and A is a nonexecutable assertion expression that should be true for every iteration of the loop—i.e., A is a loop invariant. The proof rules stated for these constructs are (Patterson 1977):

$$\frac{P \supset A, \{A \& B\} S \{A\}}{\{P\} \text{ while B assert A do S od } \{P \& B\}}$$

$$\frac{P \supset A, \{A\} S \{B \& Q\}, \{A\} S \{\neg B \& A\}}{\{P\} \text{ assert A repeat S until B taeper } \{B \& Q\}}$$

Clearly, the first is incorrect. Even after we alter the postcondition in the consequence to P & ¬B, the resulting proof rule is still wrong since, assuming the antecedents are true, the consequence does not necessarily follow, as A may not imply P. The correct proof rule for the WHILE statement is:

$$\frac{P \supset A, \{A \& B\} S \{A\}}{\{P\} \text{ while B assert A do S od } \{A \& \neg B\}}$$

In the second equation, the forms of the antecedents are confusing. A more appropriate (though equivalent) form that emphasizes the invariant nature of A is

$$\frac{P \supset A, \{A\} S \{Q\}, Q \& \neg B \supset A}{\{P\} \text{ assert A repeat S until B taeper } \{Q \& B\}}$$

Example 3
As a final example, we consider the proof rules for the parallel statement in STRUM. The general form for this statement is

> assign[, assign][, assign], stmt

where ASSIGN is an assignment statement, STMT is any of the executable statements except an assignment, and [. . .] denotes an optional component. Certain restrictions—largely dictated by the nature of the underlying host machine—apply to the nature and form of the assignments that may appear in a parallel statement. Informally stated, the assignment statements are interpreted as executing in parallel, *followed* by the execution of STMT. According to the informal definition, the assignment statements must be "independent" of one another—however, this notion is not developed formally, which weakens the proof rule considerably.

The proof rule itself is unusual, compared to other kinds of rules for parallel statements. Its general form is somewhat complex, so we present below a simplified version for the following special case of the parallel statement:

$$S : b1 := a1, b2 := a2, v := e, s$$

where $b1$, $b2$ are Boolean variables, $a1$, $a2$ are Boolean constants, v is an integer variable and e an integer valued expression. Then the proof rule is, according to Patterson (1977):

$$\frac{\{P\}\,s\,\{Q\}}{\{P\,[b1/a1][b2/a2][v/e]\}\,S\,\{Q\}}$$

where $P[b1/a1][b2/a2][v/e]$ denotes the assertion P with all free occurrences of $b1$ replaced by $a1$, $b2$ replaced by $a2$, and v replaced by e, respectively.

The STRUM system was used to emulate the architecture of the HP-2115 on the Burroughs D machine. The emulator was verified and then translated and optimized to produce object microcode. The verification procedure uncovered 10 errors in the STRUM program, 11 errors in the specifications, and 10 errors in the assertions.

The significance of Patterson's work lies in demonstrating convincingly the feasibility of verifying high-level-language microprograms reflecting the characteristics of a real machine and in translating such programs into efficient object microcode. (For a discussion of the compilation and efficiency aspects, see Patterson [1981].) It also provides some data on the complexity, size, and computational requirements demanded of the verification procedure. There were, of course, several issues that were not addressed in this investigation partly because they were considered irrelevant in the present context—those having to do with some of the "unpleasant" features characteristic of microarchitectures. We shall return to these issues later when we discuss the S*(QM-1) project.

The MIDDLE Approach

Patterson's approach reflects a standard paradigm underlying software design in the last three decades and much of the recent work in firmware engineering: because of the inherent complexity of microprograms at the actual microarchitectural level it is generally agreed that both the firmware development process as well as verification can be greatly eased by appropriately abstracting from the microarchitectural level—that is, by using an appropriate high-level microprogramming language. Of course, the success of this approach rests on the practicality of compiling high-level source code into object microcode and on the assumption that the compiler would function correctly. The STRUM project demonstrates, at least for the D machine, that a compiler could indeed be constructed that would emit efficient microcode (Patterson 1981), and more recent studies have yielded further evidence of the practicality of such compilers (Ma and Lewis 1980, Sheraga and Gieser 1983). On the other hand, as far as it is known to this author, no microcode compiler has yet been proven to be correct.

A somewhat different approach to the firmware-verification problem was taken by Budowski and Dembinski (1978). The problem they consider is the following: let us suppose that we have a document describing a microprogrammed processor at the "implementation" (i.e., microarchitectural) level. This description is of a type that may be produced by the hardware designer or manufacturer. The desired objective is to prove that the microprogram as represented by the object microcode specified in the documentation is correct with respect to a higher specification of the target architecture.

As a means for facilitating this proof, Budkowski and Dembinski have designed a language called MIDDLE (1978a, b), the main characteristic of which is that it allows the microprogram to be specified at different levels of abstraction, starting from the implementation through the register-transfer to the algorithmic level.[3] Thus, this same language can be used to describe both the implementation level as originally specified in the design documentation as well as the target level. Once this is done, some suitable verification tech-

---

3. Unfortunately, how exactly the "implementation" and "register-transfer" levels differ, or what are the precise characteristics of the "algorithmic" level as far as MIDDLE is concerned, are issues that have not been pursued by the authors in any of their papers.

Figure 10-4. Verification strategy in the MIDDLE approach.

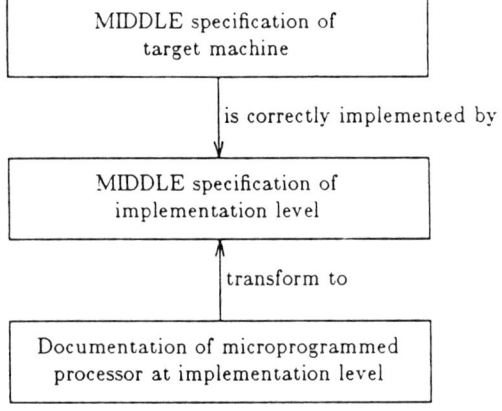

nique, for example, algebraic simulation (see "The Beginnings of Axiomatic Verification" above) can be applied to prove that the lower level is a correct implementation of the target-level description (fig. 10-4).

As figure 10-4 indicates, there are two steps in this scheme: the first transforms the document description of the microprogrammed processor into a MIDDLE specification; the second is the proof of correctness. The main point of interest in the MIDDLE approach is the first step. For this purpose it is assumed that the documentation of the implementation-level processor gives a specification of the functional units and their interconnections and a description of the control unit itself (including the microcode). The task of transforming this specification to a MIDDLE description may then be viewed as a decompilation process.

The approach is of interest in the case of verifying implemented microprograms since it takes as the starting point of verification the implementation itself; however, we are not convinced that the model of the microarchitecture used by Budkowski and Dembinski is adequate for capturing the typical characteristics of machines of any realistic level of complexity nor that MIDDLE is able to describe these realities. The evidence has simply not been provided. For further details on the language and the general approach, the interested reader is referred to Dembinski and Budkowsi (1978a, b).

The State Delta Approach

In this approach (Crocker et al. 1980; Levy 1984; Marcus et al. 1984) both host and target machines were specified in the architecture description language ISPS (Barbacci 1979). The heart of the proof system is a formalism called *state deltas*, due originally to Crocker (1977), which is essentially an extension to the first-order predicate calculus and provides a means for reasoning about situations that change with time. The state-delta formalism uses the following concepts.

Definition 3

A *modification list* denotes that part of the "present" state vector that may be altered by some microcode sequence.

Definition 4

An *environment list* denotes that part of the present state vector that is identical to some particular prior state.

A state delta can now be formulated as follows:

1. If the values listed in the environment list remains unchanged from now until some future time
2. If the precondition holds at that time

Then

3. At the end of some succeeding time interval during which at most only the values in the modification list will have changed
4. The post condition will hold

The syntax of a state delta is

(SD (pre : P)
    (mod : M)
    (env : E)
    (post : Q))

It may be noticed that state deltas have some similarity to formulas in temporal logic (Manna and Pnueli 1981). As a specific example, the following state delta

(SD (pre : $R > 0$)
    (mod : R)
    (env : E)
    (post : $R' = .R-1$)

means that if the value of R is greater than 0, than at some later time the new value of R will be one less. Here, .R refers to the contents of R at the time of the precondition and R' refers to R's contents at the time of the postcondition.

Clearly, a state delta can be used to formulate an input-output specification for a program or a program segment. Note also that in contrast to the meaning of the formula

$$\{P\}\, S\, \{Q\}$$

in the standard Hoare logic, a state delta specifies both safety (partial correctness) as well as termination. That is, it says that a system *will* reach a state such that the postcondition holds.

Suppose we are given an ordered collection of state deltas and an initial state. The first state delta whose precondition is true in the current state may be "applied," thus transforming the state into that specified by the postcondition and the modification list. The process is now repeated in the new state and so on. This execution of state deltas is a form of *symbolic simulation*. Clearly, it is possible to view an arbitrary program as a set of state deltas or to translate a program written in some other language into state deltas.

The process of microcode verification in the state-delta approach thus proceeds by modeling both the host machine (together with its microcode) and the target machine as ordered sets of state deltas and then using symbolic simulation to prove the equivalence of the two machines. Initially, both host and target machines are described in ISPS (Barbacci 1979). These descriptions are then translated into state-delta representations.

PRINCIPLES OF FIRMWARE VERIFICATION

As a specific example, taken from Marcus et al. (1984), consider the following simple ISPS program for shifting an 8-bit register S left by the contents of another 8-bit register B:

```
SHIFTMACHINE :=
    (
    **Registers **
        S <7:0>, B <7:0>
    **Processes **
        SHIFT :=
        BEGIN
            S < - S SLO B
        END
    **Execution Cycle **
        CYCLE :=
        BEGIN
            SHIFT ( )
        END
```

Given below is the state delta describing the assertion that if the above program is executed and S has enough high-order zeros, then the value of S will be multiplied by 2 to the power of the value of B.

SD   pre : $(|.S < 7:8 - |.B| > | = 0)$
         env : NIL
         mod : ALL
         post : $|S'| = |.S| * 2 \uparrow |.B|$

The state-delta approach was originally implemented as the ISI microcode-verification project at the University of Southern California Information Science Institute (Crocker et al. 1980). The current version—called SDVS (Marcus et al. 1984; Levy 1984) and developed at the Aerospace Corporation—is an interactive program that checks proofs of microcode correctness, specified by the user using a formal *proof language*. In a certain sense the proof language may be viewed as a programming language: if the "program" is accepted by SDVS, the proof is correct.

The system can determine whether a proof step that the user wishes SDVS to apply is in fact applicable. The user may request SDVS to execute from state to state to initiate case analysis at a branch point and so on by specifying proof commands such as the following:

- APPLY <sd>: Apply <sd>. <sd> can be a named or a typed out state delta. If <sd> is NIL then apply the highest applicable state delta

- CASES <cond><thenproof><elseproof>: Start two cases assuming <cond> and ~<cond> and use the proof command in <thenproof> and <elseproof> if they are provided
- LET <symbol><exp>: Instantiate <symbol> to the current value of <exp>
- PROVE <sd><proof>: Start a proof of <sd> and use the proof commands in <proof> if they are provided

The state-delta formalism as reported here has been developed for sequential programs and is therefore unable to deal with concurrency and timing—issues of the kind commonly encountered in microprogramming. Thus, the scope of the state-delta approach is largely restricted to vertically microprogrammed computers. In a recent paper Overman and Crocker (1982) describe an extended form of the formalism called concurrent state deltas (CSDs) in which time appears in an explicit form. CSDs have the general syntax:

(CSD (pre : Q
       read : R
       mod : M
       procs : P
       post : S
       time : T))

which states that if the process (or system of processes) P for which the CSD is defined is in a state satisfying the precondition Q, then it will get to a state satisfying the postcondition S after a time T and during that time only the variables in the read list R may be read and only the variables in the modification list mod may be modified. The application of CSDs to the verification of horizontal microprograms remains to be demonstrated.

S*(QM-1)

A more recent application of the axiomatic approach to firmware verification is due to Wagner and Dasgupta (Wagner and Dasgupta 1983; Dasgupta and Wagner 1984), who have developed a proof system for a machine-specific microprogramming language called S*(QM-1). This work extends but also differs from Patterson's work on STRUM in a number of significant ways:

1. There are sharp differences in the languages. More specifically, S*(QM-1) is an *instantiation* of the machine-independent microprogramming language schema S*(Dasgupta 1978, 1980) with respect to the Nanodata QM-1 (Nanodata 1979). S* contains a fairly comprehensive set of primitive and structured data types and a number of constructs for expressing low-level parallelism appropriate for monophase, polyphase, and multi-

cycle timing schemes. In addition, the instantiated language S*(QM-1) reflects specific characteristics of the QM-1 host machine.
2. The feature known as *residual control* (Flynn and Rosin 1971) present in the QM-1 posed rather unique problems in the axiomatization of S*(QM-1). Since residual control is present in several other machines (Kornerup and Shriver 1975; Kraley et al. 1980) the solution offered by Wagner and Dasgupta to this problem may be useful in a wider context than for the QM-1 alone. Similarly, the presence and use of *transient variables* posed an additional problem that also had to be resolved in order to formulate a realistic basis for proving correctness of S*(QM-1) programs.
3. The highly horizontal nature of the QM-1 as well as the presence of nearly a dozen buses around which the QM-1 dataflow is organized raised issues concerning *low-level parallelism* and, in particular, *side-effects* that had to be reflected in the proof theory. From a consideration of the various earlier researches reviewed in this article, it should be clear that the S*(QM-1) study was addressing a number of issues that had been more or less ignored in the past, issues that although in this case are specific to the QM-1 are observed in one form or another in many host-machine architectures.
4. At a more general level, Wagner and Dasgupta were interested in constructing a deductive system for *developing* correct microprograms. While it seems clear that automating the verification process (to some extent at least) may be necessary from a practical point of view, the focus of this project, unlike that in the case of STRUM, MCS, or the SDVS system, was to provide a basis for *reasoning formally* about architecture design and the microprogrammed implementation of such designs in the context of a real host-machine architecture.

Basically, the schema S* consists of the following features (Dasgupta 1980):

1. The primitive data types BIT and SEQUENCE and a set of structured data types including ARRAY, TUPLE (which is identical to the Pascal RECORD), and STACK.
2. A set of *simple* statements that may be used to represent microoperations, i.e., the most primitive indivisible units of action available to the microprogrammer. The principal simple statements include:
    - A generic *assignment* the syntax and semantics of which are not specified in S*. Their valid forms and meanings are assumed to be machine-dependent and are determined during instantiation.

- The simple *selection* statement

  if C1 → S1 || C2 → S2 || . . . || Cn → Sn fi

  where Ci denotes testable conditions and Si simple statements (other than selections). Here again, the construct merely provides a template for valid selections—the legal testable conditions and simple statements are machine-dependent and are determined during instantiation.
- The procedure CALL statement and the GOTO statement.
3. A set of structured statements that allow for the composition of larger program entities. These include the CASE, WHILE, .. DO, and REPEAT..UNTIL statements and, of course, sequential composition. In addition there are two constructs

  cocycle. . . coend
  stcycle. . . stend

  that allow for the specification of parallelism between simple statements.
4. The *synonym* declaration, which allows the programmer to arbitrarily rename previously declared data objects or parts thereof.

As noted before, the syntax and semantics of the constructs in S* are only partially defined. An instantiation of S* with respect to a particular host machine M specifically tailors the constructs in S* to M. The fully defined language S*(M) thus derived would contain the machine-dependent information necessary for the efficient utilization of the microarchitecture. Such an instantiation was carried out for the Nanodata QM-1, resulting in the language we call S*(QM-1) (Klassen and Dasgupta 1981).

A Synopsis of the QM-1 Architecture

The presence of residual control and side effects in the QM-1 posed special problems in the axiomatization of S*(QM-1). It is not possible for the reader to understand the nature and logic of the proof rules without some understanding of the host machine itself. Thus we present here a very brief description of the QM-1 architecture.

The Nanodata QM-1 is a user-microprogrammable general emulation engine with two rather distinctive features: the *two-level control store* and the extensive use of *residual control*.

The higher of the control-store levels is referred to simply as the *control store*. The *microinstructions* at this level may interpret conventional *machine instructions* residing in *main store*. The microinstructions are 18-bit vertical words and have no capacity for specifying concurrent operations. They are in turn interpreted by highly horizontal *nanoinstructions* from the lower-level control store, known as *nanostore*. At this level, a high degree of parallelism is possible between *nanooperations*. S∗(QM-1) is an instantiation of S∗ with respect to the QM-1 nanolevel architecture. A compiler would generate nanoprograms from a given S∗(QM-1) source program.

The idea of *residual control* (Flynn and Rosin 1971) rests on the observation that in emulating a target architecture a part of the control information, once "set up," will remain relatively invariant for significant periods of time. Thus, instead of holding this information in the microword (or, in the case of the QM-1, in the nanoword), it can be placed in special registers and held there for any desired period of time until it needs to be altered. By reducing the amount of information that needs to be held in a micro- or nanoword the width of the latter can be significantly reduced. The states of these special residual-control registers can, of course, be altered under micro- or nanoprogram control. In the QM-1 the control function rests partly in the nanoword (providing what Kornerup and Shriver (1975) termed "immediate control") and partly in a set of residual-control registers called *F registers*.

The nanostore consists of 360-bit-wide nanowords each divided into five 72-bit subwords (fig. 10-5). The first of these, called the *K vector*, contains fields that serve to specify certain conditions and operations (e.g., ALU functions). The remaining subwords, the *T vectors*, are identical in format and contain a number of fields that encode for the various nanooperations. When a T vector is activated, its fields are decoded and used to initiate specific hardware functions. At any given time only one of the T vectors is active, while the K vector is active throughout the execution of all four T vectors in the associated nanoword. Thus, from a logical viewpoint the combination of the K vector and the active T vector constitutes a single nanoinstruction.

Most of the residual control resides in the 32 6-bit F registers. These can be set to values from certain fields in the K vector ("K fields") or from resources whose contents are only known at run time. For example, an F register may be loaded with values obtained from a microinstruction residing in the control store.

The QM-1 also contains a *local store* consisting of 32 18-bit registers linked to other resources in the machine by a number of buses.

Precisely which local-store register is connected to a particular bus is under the (residual) control of a specific F register. For example, one of the F registers, FAOD determines which local-store register is connected to the ALU output

Figure 10-5. Format of nanoinstructions in the QM-1.

K-vector	T-vector1	T-vector2	T-vector3	T-vector4

bus AOD, while the value in the F register FAIL determines the local-store source to the left ALU input bus AIL (fig. 10-6).

Finally, it should also be noted that since the K vector can remain unchanged in value across the scope of a nanoword, a certain amount of residual control also resides in the K vector.

Axiomatization of S*(QM-1)

If the F registers were made invisible at the S*(QM-1) level of abstraction, the programmer would be prevented from exploiting the parallelism available in the QM-1 by explicit control of these registers. The need to declare residual-control locations has had a major impact on the axiomatization and instantiation of S*(QM-1). The part of the data declaration containing this information is prefixed by the key word STRUCT, and it specifies the relationships between residual-control registers and the source or sink locations that they select for data transfers. In effect, part of the QM-1 data-path *structure* is specified in the language.

This is done by means of two constructs—the ARRAY-*with-pointer* and the UNION-*with-selector*.

Example 4

In the QM-1 a source of input data for the control store is one of 64 "logical" local-store registers, and this can be determined by the setting of the 6-bit residual-control register fcid. This relationship may be denoted by the declarations:

> type ls_ register = seq [17..0] bit;
>
> cs_ source : array [0..63] of ls_ register with fcid;

Given this declaration the only legal reference to cs_source (say, in an assignment statement) would be cs_source[fcid].

Figure 10-6. A part of the Qm-1 data path.

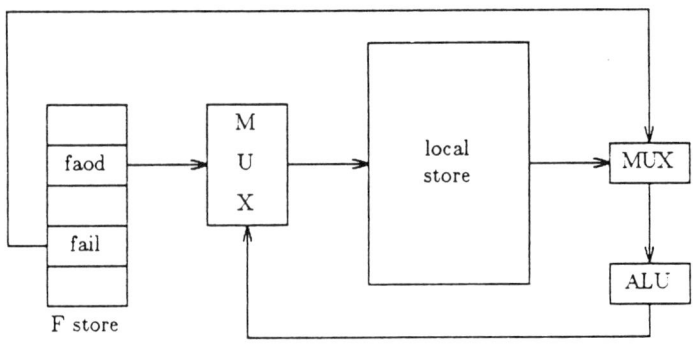

Example 5
This same control-store input source can also be declared as:

  cs_source : selector fcid
   union
    local_store : array [0..31] of ls_register
    all_ones : array [0..31] of ones
   endun

Given this declaration, one legal reference to cs_source could be cs_source.fcid.local_store [12]. This reference would, as a side effect, set fcid to 12. In fact, the object nanocode corresponding to this reference would first set fcid to 12 and then use this value in fcid to access local store.

In order to illustrate some of the axioms and proof rules for S*(QM-1), we shall use the following notation:

1. Let P be an assertion. Then $P[x/y]$ denotes P with all free occurrences of x being replaced by y.
2. Let $P[x1/y1][x2/y2]...[xn/yn]$ denote the simultaneous substitution of the entities $y1, y2, ..., yn$ for free occurrences of $x1, x2, ..., xn$, respectively, in P. Note that occurrences of some xi in $y1, y2, ...yn$ are not replaced. Furthermore, the substitution is invalid if the variables $x1, x2, ..., xn$ are not distinct.

Consider now, the *simple assignment statement*

$$x := y$$

where x, y are locations. This statement satisfies the axiom

  { $P[x/y][SEL/v]$ }
  $x := y$
  { P }

where SEL denotes all selector locations side-effected by reference (if any) to UNION-with-selector and V denotes the set of values assigned to the selectors. That is, P [SEL/V] denotes P [sel1/v1] [sel2/v2] . . . [sel$n$/vn].

Example 6
Let cs_source be declared as above and let P be the assertion

  {cs[addr] = cs_source.fcid.local_store[15] & fcid = 15}

Then, by the axiom above we have the following formula:

  {P[cs[addr]/cs_source.fcid.local_store[15]] [fcid/15]}
  cs[addr] := cs_source.fcid.local_store [15]
  {P}

On substitution this reduces to

{TRUE}
cs[addr] := cs_source.fcid.local_store[15]
{P}

The second class of assignments are of the form $x := E$ where E is an expression. In the execution of an S*(QM-1) program, *the evaluation of an expression E can lead to side effects.*

This arises because the operations appearing in E are encoded by values of fields in the K vector, which are visible (and therefore manipulable) objects in S*(QM-1). An expression E containing an operator bound to some functional unit will, during execution, side-effect the relevant K vector fields by modifying or selecting the function to be performed. In addition, the output buses of several of the functional units involved in evaluating expressions will be set to the values of the associated expressions.

Example 7
Consider the expression

local_store [fail] 1 << s (5)

This will perform a single left logical shift of 5 positions on local_store [FAIL] and side-effect the K vector fields kshc (which encodes the SHIFT function) and ksha (which encodes the SHIFT amount). Also, the shifter output bus will be set to the value of the expression.

The axiom for assignments involving expressions is:

{P[SEL/V1] [CNTR/V2] [MOD/V3] [MASK/V4] [OUT/E1] [X/E]}
X := E
{P}

where CNTR denotes K vector fields that are side-effected as a result of the operations and V2, the values encoding these operations. MOD denotes any set of K-vector modifier fields side-effected by the operators, and V3 specifies the corresponding modifier values appearing in E. MASK denotes the K field side-effected in the evaluation of the expression if it is a Boolean and V4 specifies its corresponding MASK value (see discussion on test expressions and control constructs below). Finally, OUT denotes any variables corresponding to output buses of devices used in evaluating E that are side-effected, and E1 represents their corresponding values.

Example 8
Let P denote the assertion

{local_store [15] − local_store [13] 1 << S (5)
         & kshc = ko & ksha = 5 & faod = 15 & fail = 13}

where ko is a binary (or equivalent integer) valued constant; then by the axiom for assignments involving expressions we have the formula

{P[faod/15] [fail/13] [kshc/ko] [shft_out_bus/local_store[13]
1 << S(5)] [local_store[15]/local_store[13] 1 << S(5)]}
local_store[15] := local_store[13] 1 << S(5)
{P}

For convenience, the side-effect clause [SEL/V1][CNTR/V2][MOD/V3] [MASK/V4][OUT/E1] will be denoted simply as [EXPR].

Unlike other variables, testable locations in the QM-1 are unstable. However, these are not declared in the data-declaration part of the program but are part of the language itself in the form of *test expressions*. Each legal test expression is bound to a particular machine condition.

Example 9

The machine condition OVERFLOW resulting from an ALU operation is defined by the S*(QM-1) test expression

LOCAL OVERFLOW of (local_store[fail] + local_store[fair])

where LOCAL signifies that this is one of the so-called local (i.e., temporary) conditions generated from ALU and shift operations. Other such local conditions are CARRY, SIGN, RESULT, SHB, SLB. Other types of conditions that may appear in a test expression are GLOBAL conditions, which are similar to the LOCAL ones, except that they are saved in a special F register; and SPECIAL conditions such as MS_BUSY and MS_DATA. The latter, for example, evaluates to true if a main-store read or write is in progress.

In evaluating a test expression additional side effects may occur because of the 6-bit K vector fields ks, kt and kx, which are used as masks for testing, respectively, the local, global, and special conditions. The mask for local condition, for instance, is constructed by placing 1's in the bits corresponding to the conditions tested and 0's elsewhere. The mask and the test condition are ANDed together with a 1 returned if the result is true, 0 otherwise.

Let MASK_SEL denote one of the keywords LOCAL, GLOBAL, SPECIAL and let MASK denote the variables (ks, kx, kt) side-effected by the evaluation of the test expression B. Then the proof rule for the *repeat* statement is as follows:

$$\frac{\{P\} S \{Q [MASK/V] [EXPR]\}, Q \& \neg B => P}{\{P\} \text{ repeat } S \text{ until mask\_sel of } (E) \{Q \& B\}}$$

Proof rules of a similar nature have been defined for the IF and WHILE statements.

Finally, we consider the parallel statement in S*(QM-1). In the schema S*, one of the ways for representing parallelism is by using the COCYCLE statement (Dasgupta 1980). Let

$$S1 \; \Theta \; S2 ::= S1 \; \Box \; S2 \mid S1 \; ; \; S2$$

where $S1 \; \Box \; S2$ denotes the *parallel composition* of statements $S1, S2$ while $S1;S2$ denotes the usual sequential composition. Then, the *cocycle* statement is of the form:

$$\text{cocycle } S1 \; \Theta \; S2 \text{ coend}$$

where $S1, S2$ are simple statements or statements composed of simple statements. The cocycle statement indicates that the composite event $S1\Theta \; S2$ begins and ends in the same microcycle. Note that if Θ is " ; " then the microcycle is, by implication, polyphase.

Two additional features of the general cocycle statement should be noted. First, apart from the fact that the statement's execution begins and ends in a single microcycle (a property that is termed COCYCLIC), the composite statement $S1 \; \Theta \; S2$ must also map into a single microinstruction. This property is termed COMPILABLE.

Secondly, in the case of the parallel version

$$\text{cocycle } S1 \; \Box \; S2 \text{ coend}$$

it is necessary that S1 and S2 do not *interfere* with one another. Informally, this reflects the situation that during the times when they are both in execution, there are no conflicts in their resource usage. We shall simply call this property DISJOINT. COMPILABLE, COCYCLIC, and DISJOINT are all machine-specific properties and are determined during an instantiation of S*.

In S*(QM-1) only the parallel version of the COCYCLIC is instantiated. Furthermore, the only statements that may appear within the COCYCLE are simple assignments. The COCYCLIC and COMPILABLE properties are interpreted in terms of the T step (that is, the duration of execution of a T vector) and the T vector, respectively. The DISJOINT property is characterized using the Owicki–Gries (1976) notion *of interference-free*, defined as follows:

Definition 5

Given a proof $\{P\} \; S \; \{Q\}$ and a statement T with precondition pre(T), we say that T does not interfere with $\{P\} \; S \; \{Q\}$ if:

$$\{Q \; \& \; \text{pre}(T)\} \; T \; \{Q\}$$

and

$$\{P \; \& \; \text{pre}(T)\} \; T \; \{P\}$$

In other words, the execution of T does not affect either the pre- or the postcondition of S.

Definition 6

{P1} S1 {Q1}, . . .,{Pn} Sn {Qn} are interference-free if for all pairs of statements Si, Sj (i = j) Si does not interfere with Sj.

Thus, the proof rule for the S*(QM-1) COCYCLE statement is:

$$\frac{\text{Forall } (1 < i < n) \{Pi\} \text{ Si } \{Qi\}, \text{ COCYCLIC, COMPILABLE, DISJOINT}}{\{P1 \& \ldots \& Pn\} \text{ cocycle } S1 \;\square\; S2 \;\square\ldots\square\; Sn \text{ coend} \{Q1 \& \ldots \& Qn\}}$$

Note that the composite statement is COMPILABLE if and only if the fields that initiate the actions specified by the statement can be encoded into a single T-vector and its corresponding K-vector.

For examples illustrating how these axioms and proof rules can be applied in the derivation of correctness proofs of S*(QM-1) programs, the reader is referred to Dasgupta and Wagner (1984) and Wagner (1983). Additional issues such as the treatment of data types, control statements for invoking procedures, and the method of handling transient variables are also discussed in these references.

In assessing this work, we note the following points. First, it is evident that the proof rules are somewhat cumbersome. Certainly, one of the reasons for this is the inherent complexity of the QM-1 architecture—a fact that tells us that if we really wish to design and implement demonstrably reliable firmware, we are well advised to design architectures that support this goal.

A second cause for the complexity of the proof rules was the fact that such concepts as "operators," "expressions," and "assignments" were taken from the programming-language domain and adapted for use at the microprogramming level. In reality, the interpretation of these entities in the latter domain are very different from their interpretation in the software context. For example, the simple assignment statement in S*(QM-1) is not an assignment at all but denotes an *atomic procedure* that modifies one or more output variables. Similarly, the evaluation of an expression in S*(QM-1) does not return a value; it also causes an atomic procedure to be invoked that modifies one or several state variables. This insight into the actual nature of apparently "primitive" microoperations was, in this author's opinion, an important result of this study.

On the other hand, this project also has a specific objective: to determine whether one could abstract from the properties of real architecture a collection of proof rules appropriate for firmware verification. Prior to this work nothing was really known as to how such problems as residual control, different kinds of side effects, and transient locations could be handled. A second important result emanating from this study was the fact that a relatively small and uniform set of proof rules was identified that captured the behavior of the whole machine.

Finally, a problem that became very evident when constructing proofs of correctness was the very low level of description and verification that may be needed in the case of horizontal microprograms to ensure that the programmer can utilize machine resources both efficiently and correctly: there is a substantial gap between the abstract "function" of a microcoded routine and its concrete machine-specific form. One way of possibly bridging this gap is to use a family of closely related languages, as suggested in Dasgupta and Olafsson (1982), and Dasgupta (1984).

Semantics-Based Automatic Microcode Synthesis

The various projects described above were all concerned with the design of correct firmware or the verification of existing firmware. A somewhat more ambitious system on *automatic microcode synthesis* is currently being developed (Mueller and Johnson 1981; Mueller and Varghese 1982, 1983) at Colorado State University.

The work being done by Mueller and his colleagues involves the application of techniques from artificial intelligence to the synthesis of microcode. Stated briefly, their approach is to input descriptions of the target and host-machine architecture to a knowledge-based system that will synthesize and optimize microcode. The synthesizing system is thus retargetable, since the host-machine description can be changed.

The theory underlying the Mueller–Varghese approach is based on Dijkstra's (1976) *weakest-precondition* operator. An assertion P is a weakest precondition with respect to statement S and postcondition Q whenever the following requirements are satisfied:

- $\{P\} \, S \, \{Q\}$ is true
- For each R, if $\{R\} \, S \, \{Q\}$ is true, then $R \supset P$ is also true

In other words, the WP operator finds a necessary and sufficient precondition for the machine state such that the execution of S produces the desired postcondition Q. Notationally, we say that $P = WP(S,Q)$.

Mueller and Varghese (1982) define the axiomatic semantics of four different classes of actions in terms of WPs. These actions are the null operation, the simple assignment, sequential composition, and parallel (synchronous) composition. For example, the axiom of assignment is

$$WP(X := E, Q) = Q[X/E]$$

The synthesis system has three components—a high-level language (HLL) description of the microprogram, a specification of the host machine, and a set of semantic rules to guide the synthesis process.

The high-level microprogram is first transformed into an intermediate representation using conventional parsing techniques. This intermediate form is then partitioned into a flow graph of basic blocks (i.e., straight-line segments) together with an allocation of host-machine resources to the variables and operators. Each basic block, B, is then symbolically executed to produce a symbolic representation of the block's function. This representation is essentially in the form of a pair <P,Q> of input/output assertions.

Given a host machine description H, the goal of the synthesis system is to generate, for each block B and its input and output assertion pair <P,Q>, a microinstruction sequence SH that may execute on H such that

$$P \supset WP(SH, Q)$$

In that case, starting with the input assertion P, SH is guaranteed to produce the postcondition Q.

The synthesis procedure is guided heuristically by a variety of rules, some of which determine the applicability of host machine microoperations in a particular situation (validity rules) while others (transformational rules) determine the effect of the microoperations when they are applied.

At this writing the system is in a state of development, hence we must defer its assessment until more substantial results have been reported. It is worth noting however, that the basic machine model underlying the Mueller–Varghese system incorporates most of the intricacies of real microarchitectures, viz., side effects, transient variables, parallelism, and mono-/polyphase timing schemes (Mueller 1984).

The Aachen AADL/S* Project

Among a number of ongoing projects, the most notable is the automated, retargetable verification and development system being constructed by Damm and his colleagues at the Technische Hochschule Aachen, West Germany (Damm et al. 1984; Damm 1984a, b, c; Damm et al. 1986).

The main components of the Aachen system are the following:

1. An *axiomatic architecture description language* (AADL) capable of specifying the functional characteristics of both target and host architectures
2. A family of *high-level microprogramming languages*, S*(M), derived from S* on the basis of the AADL specifications of the underlying host M [In the Aachen system, each S*(M) is obtained by instantiating the schema S* with respect to the processor M described in AADL by filling in the definitions of legal assignments and tests according to the AADL descriptions of the microoperations present in M. Figure 10-7 illustrates this process, which thus *formalizes* the notion of instantiation as originally proposed by Dasgupta (1978).
3. A uniform procedure to derive an axiomatization of S*(M) out of M
4. A procedure to derive the precondition/postcondition specification of a target machine N and a mapping of N's storage elements

Figure 10-7. Instantiations of S* in the Aachen AADL/S* system (based on Damm 1984a).

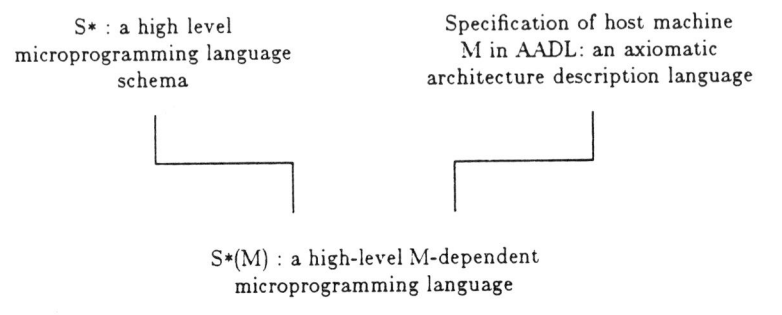

to those of M such that N is correctly realized on M if and only if the S*(M) microprogram designed to implement N is correct with respect to the latter specification

It may be noted that S* may be instantiated with respect to a given host M at a number of different abstraction levels; that is, noted in (2) above, there may be a whole family of S*(M)s depending on the abstraction level at which the AADL specification is provided. This capability contributes to at least two major goals of the Aachen system: support for the incremental development of firmware by stepwise refinement, and the ability on the part of the user to decide the level of detail down to which he or she will conduct the development process before allowing the compiler to generate the low-level microcode.

The overall structure of an AADL description is shown in figure 10-8. The clock specification part describes the (possibly polyphase) clocking scheme controlling the host. This specification describes the various phases of the clock, their durations, and their relative positions in the overall clock cycle. All timing characteristics of microoperations are defined with respect to the clock specification.

The block-diagram part specifies those structural aspects of the architecture that are visible in conventional block diagrams, viz., the storage elements and

Figure 10-8. Organization of an architecture description in AADL.

>Architecture Description:
>   Clock part
>   Block Diagram part
>   Instruction Format part
>   Microoperations part

Figure 10-9. Organization of a microoperation description in AADL.

>   Function
>   Name
>   Pattern
>   Sinks and Sources
>   Condition
>   Semantics
>   Auxiliary Sinks and Sources
>   Side Effects
>   Timing Validity
>   Unit Names
>   Microinstruction Fields

Figure 10-10. Description of an ADD microoperation in AADL.

```
microoperations register_section
   function binary_add_with_carry:
        pattern accu := idlatch+accu+carry
        sink accu
        source idlatch, accu, carry
        condition decimal = 0
        auxiliary sink prstat.N, prstat.A, prstat.V, carry
        auxiliary source decimal
        side effects
            main carry : pre idlatch[7] = 1 & accu[7] = 1
                         post carry = 1
                  overflow : pre accu[7] = idlatch[7]
                             post accu[7] = idlatch[7] → prstat.V = 1
                  zeroflag : pre true
                             post allzero(accu) → prstat.Z = 1
                  negative : pre true
                             post accu[7] = 1 → prstat.N = 1
        end sideeffects
        semantics  +1: bits(8) × bits(8) → bits(8)
                   +2: bits(8) × bits(1) → bits(8)
              allzero: bits(8) → bool
        timing validity low..high
        units ALU, internal_databus
        microinstruction fields F1 = 10011
   end function
end microoperation
```

the functional units together with their data and control paths. The instruction formats specify the structure of the host microinstructions or target instructions (depending on which machine is being described).

The last and most interesting component provides a detailed functional specification of the machine's microoperations. The general form of such a specification is shown in figure 10-9, while figure 10-10 shows the specification for a particular microoperation. These specifications contain all the information required for verification as well as microcode generation and compaction.

Some aspects of figures 10-9 and 10-10 need explaining. The *pattern* serves two roles: first, it provides an appropriate *notation* for referring to the microoperation within an S*(M) program, e.g.

$$\text{accu} := \text{idlatch} + \text{accu} + \text{carry}$$

Second, it highlights or suggests the principal features of its semantics.

The *condition* field prescribes control information that must be true at the time the microoperation begins execution; this condition also remains true during the period the operation is in execution. The *auxiliary source* and *sink* fields list additional data objects whose values are required during or which are set as a result of, the microoperation's execution.

The semantics of the microoperation are specified by its *semantics* and *side-effects* fields. Obviously, it is a matter of opinion as to what are regarded as "main" effects and what are viewed as "side" effects. The semantics clauses will also resolve the overloading of the operators appearing in the pattern by axiomatizing their meaning. The person writing the AADL description will be able to refer to a library of axioms describing the operators commonly available in processors. This library will be part of the knowledge base and will be used in the Aachen system both by a theorem prover and by a simulator when "executing" the microoperation (Damm 1984b). The semantic entry is only partially specified in the example of figure 10-10.

Space does not permit us to describe with any degree of completeness the nature of the proof theory developed by Damm and his colleagues; the reader is referred to Damm (1984a) for a definitive report on the proof system, while more concise accounts are given in Damm (1984b, c) and Damm et al. (1986). However, it should be evident to the reader that by using AADL and the form of AADL specification as illustrated above, many of the issues that remained unsatisfactory in the S*(QM-1) work are resolved here. As Damm (1984a) points out, the Aachen system greatly extends the general approach presented previously (Wagner and Dasgupta 1983; Dasgupta and Wagner 1984) in that:

1. It establishes a precise characterization of such machine-dependent properties as "compilable," "conflict free," and "co-cyclic." These predicates were only informally or partially defined in S*(QM-1).

2. It constructs a more accurate model of very fine-grained, low-level parallelism that reflects the timing characteristics of microoperations to be executed concurrently.
3. By describing microoperations (in AADL) in terms of more primitive entities, it lays visible in a clear and understanding fashion the complexity of their actual behavior; furthermore, the proof rules for the statements in S*(M) are *derived formally* from the formal AADL specification of the machine M. This was not the case in S*(QM-1), since the underlying host machine was never described formally.

We will try to illustrate these points by describing some fragments of the proof theory. Consider firstly, the axiomatization of function microoperations (e.g., the binary_add_with_carry function of fig. 10-10). We know that the so-called "primitive" microoperation, when executed, may in general cause several events to take place—for example, incrementing of an address register, setting status bits, placing data on a bus—in addition to the "main" event. In the section "S*(QM-1)" we noted that it is therefore more accurate to view a microoperation as a complex but uninterruptible *atomic procedure*. This notion forms the basis for the way microoperations are axiomatized in the Aachen system. Basically, a microoperation f is composed of a sequence of indivisible states S1, S2, . . ., S4, guarded by S0, where:

S0: check enabling action
S1: side effects associated with a read access to memory
S2: transformation associated with the function and setting of status information
S3: side effects associated with writing to memory
S4: update of time information

This microoperation f is activated in an S*(M) microprogram through an instance

$$A : a1, a2, \ldots, an := e1, e2, \ldots, en$$

of its pattern. The axiomatic definition of this assignment rests on the fact that its execution actually corresponds to

$$\text{if } S0 \text{ then } S1; \ldots ; S4$$

where Si is a side-effect-free assignment that satisfies the "standard" assignment axiom. Thus, working backwards from a postcondition p, the axiom of assignment for A will essentially have

$$\{S0 \ \& \ p \ [S4][S3][S2][S1]\} \ A \ \{P\}$$

where [Si] is the substitution associated with the axiomatization stage i.

As a second fragmentary example from the proof theory consider the development of a proof rule for low-level parallel statements such as may appear within the cocycle statement in S*. In particular, let the parallel statement be of the form

$$\text{par} : \text{do } S1 \ldots Sn \text{ od}$$

where Si is a microoperation or composition of microoperations. Basically, we require the proof rule for the parallel statement to be of the form

$$\frac{\{p1\}\, S1\, \{q1\},\ldots,\{Pn\}\, Sn\, \{qn\}}{\{p\}\, \text{do } S1 \cdots Sn \text{ od }\{q\}}$$

where p1 &...& pn imply p and q1 &...& qn imply q, and provided that certain additional conditions are met whenever Si, Sj (i $\neq$ j) conflict in their use of microarchitectural resources.

Several key notions must be formalized in order for an appropriate proof rule to be established.

Cooperation

First, the proof rule must take into account the timing dependencies of all the microoperations in PAR and check for conflicts only between those microoperations that are "really" concurrent. Consider, for example, the parallel statement

```
par 1 =
    do A1; A2 od
       B1
    do C1; C2, C3 od
    od
```

which has the timing diagram shown in figure 10-11. The proof rule must be able to express the fact that the properties assumed to be true prior to the execution of C3 are established by those microoperations that establish the state of the machine at the time that C3 begins execution (i.e., A1, B1, and C2). Damm refers to this as the *cooperation test*, and its intent is to show that the pre-/postconditions pA/qA characterizing the state change induced by a single microoperation A in PAR cooperate to establish the truth of the global formula {p} PAR {q}.

This cooperation test can be integrated in the proof rule in the form of a *verification condition* for those time points at which cooperation occurs. For the above example, the relevant verification condition would be

$$\text{VC(time = 12)} : qA1 \,\&\, qB1 \,\&\, .qC2 \rightarrow pC3$$

Without going into the formalism further and relying on the reader's intuitive

Figure 10-11. Timing diagram for the parallel statement PAR1.

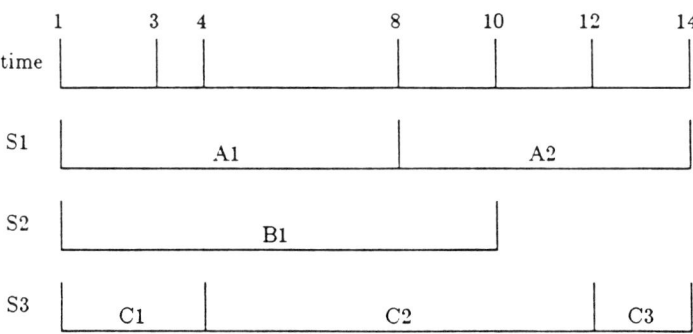

understanding, we simply denote the verification condition for establishing cooperation at time t as VC(t).

It may be the case that even when the proofs of microoperations in PAR cooperate they may still *interfere*. Consider, for example, the case when

$$A1 : a := 4$$
$$B1 : b := 5$$

Clearly, the proofs

$$\{true\} \, A1 \, \{true\}$$
$$\{a = 3\} \, B1 \, \{b = a + 2\}$$

cooperate at time t=1 (figure 10-11) in the sense the preconditions PA1 and PB1 imply the global precondition p : a=3. However, the formula

$$\{a = 3\} \, do \, A1 \, || \, B1 \, od \, \{b = a + 2\}$$

certainly does not hold. Thus, we must ensure that a postcondition does not depend on the sink location of some concurrent microoperations.

Let A d || B be true if and only if A, B occur in parallel in the timing diagram of PAR such that B is started d time units after the start of A, and B starts before A terminates (figure 10-12a).

Let A ||d B be true if and only if A, B occur in parallel in the timing diagram of PAR such that B terminates d time units after the termination of A and B starts before A terminates (fig. 10-12b).

When either of the above predicates hold, A and B are said to constitute a *critical microoperation pair*. We then have:

The proofs {pA} A {qA} are *interference-free* if an only if for all critical microoperation pairs A ||d B

Figure 10-12. Timing diagram: *a*. A d || B; *b*. A ||d B relationships.

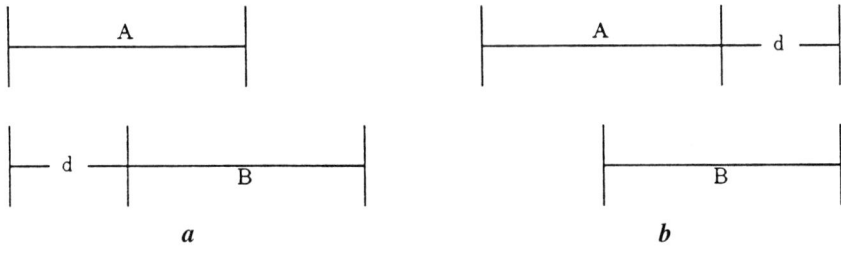

1. If d = 0 then

   outputlocations(A) ∩ free(qB) = ∅
   outputlocations(B) ∩ free(qA) = ∅

2. If d > 0 then

   outputlocations(A) ∩ free(qB) = ∅

where ∅ is the empty set, outputlocations (x) denotes the set of all locations that may be changed by x, and free (q) denotes all the free variables occurring in the assertion q.

Static Disjointness

We must also ensure freedom from resource conflicts between all pairs of critical microoperations. For this purpose it may be required to utilize information available in the AADL definitions of a microoperation that certain input locations or functional units are only required by the microoperation for a certain time period and are freed thereafter. Some other microoperation activated concurrently but after the resource has been freed can then use it.

For a microoperation A, let units (A) denote the functional units used by A. Let needed (A,u) denote the duration for which A requires u. (This information can be extracted from the AADL description of A.) Let inputlocations (A) denote the source locations for microoperation A.

The parallel statement PAR is *statically disjoint* if and only if whenever A ||d B for some microoperations A, B of PAR, some distance d ≥ 0, then

1. {u ∈ inputlocations(A) | needed(A,u) > d} ∩ outputlocations(B) = ∅
2. outputlocations(A) ∩ inputlocations(B) = ∅
3. outputlocations(A) ∩ outputlocations(B) = ∅
4. {a ∈ units(A) | needed(A,u) > d} ∩ units(B) = ∅
5. microinstruction fields(A) ∩ microinstruction fields(B) = ∅

Armed with the above notions of cooperation, interference freedom, and static disjointness, we can formulate a proof rule for PAR that takes into account the timing dependencies among its microoperations:

$$\frac{\{VC(t) \mid t \in ACT\}, \{\{pA\} \, A \, \{qA\} \mid A \text{ is in par}\}, VC(t_{end})}{\{p\} \, do \, S1 \, || \ldots || \, Sn \, od \, \{q\}}$$

provided the proofs {pA} A {qA} are interference-free and PAR is statically disjoint; where ACT = {t | there are some microoperations that are activated at time t} and t_{end} = time when the last microoperation of PAR terminates.

It is important to appreciate the fine level of detail to which the analysis of microparallelism has been taken. However, Damm et al. have in fact gone even further in deriving conditions under which *dynamic data conflicts* may be detected. An example of the latter is when, given a declaration in S* of an array X

$$var \, X : array \, [..] \, of \, seq \, [..] \, bit$$

whose elements are of type SEQ, two microoperations attempt to write to X simultaneously (i.e., X[I], X[J] occur as sinks). Then a conflict will only take place if I = J. Damm has formulated a proof rule taking into account the possibility of such *dynamic disjointness*, which can be used to prove that no conflicts will arise during execution of PAR even though *statically* a conflict is possible. For further details the reader is referred to Damm (1984a, c).

In assessing the current state of the Aachen system, we believe that the system, once completed, will be the most advanced of its kind. It has also established a standard of rigor and exactness in firmware and architecture verification that far exceeds those of its predecessors.

CONCLUSIONS

In this chapter we have attempted to review the status of firmware verification. In tracing the developments from the first paper by Ramamoorthy and Shankar to the current Aachen system, we have tried to convey a sense of the *progress* that has been made. We also hope that the work described here demonstrates quite clearly the feasibility of designing and implementing reliable firmware for "real" machines.

Finally, we observe that these same verification issues that were initially encountered in the software context are also actively being studied not only in the firmware domain but also in the hardware arena (Uehara and Barbacci 1983). While the details may differ, the same kinds of issues are being addressed at all levels of "systems" design. The time seems appropriate for a unified theory of *system* verification that is applicable to any level of system abstraction.

ACKNOWLEDGEMENTS

I am indebted to Werner Damm, Robert Mueller, Scott Davidson, and John Stankovic for their careful readings of versions of this chapter and their many comments and suggestions. This work was supported in part by Grant DCR 84-08750 from the National Science Foundation.

REFERENCES

Apt, K. R. 1981. "Ten Years of Hoare's Logic: A Survey—Part 1." *ACM Transactions on Programming Languages and Systems* 3 (4):431–83.

Ashcroft, E. A., and Wadge, W. W. 1982. "Rx for Semantics." *ACM Transactions on Programming Languages and Systems* 4 (2):283–94.

Baba, T., and Hagiwara, N. 1981. "The MPG System: A Machine-Independent Efficient Microprogram Generator." *IEEE Transactions Computers* C-30 (6):373–95.

Barbacci, M. R. 1981. "Instruction Set Processor Specifications (ISPS): The Notation and its Applications." *IEEE Transactions Computers* C-30 (1):26–40.

Bawden, A., Greenblatt, R.; Holloway, J.; Knight, T.; Moon, D.; and Weinreb, D. 1979. "The LISP Machine." *Artificial Intelligence: An MIT Perspective*, vol. 2. Edited by P.H. Winston and R.H. Brown. Cambridge, MA: MIT Press.

Berg, H. K. 1980. "Correctness of Firmware: An Overview." In Giloi (1980), 173–224.

Berg, H. K., and Franta, W. R. 1980. "Firmware Engineering: Critical Remarks and a Proposed Strategy." In Chroust and Mulbacher (1980), 41–63.

Berg, H. K.; Boebert, W. E.; Franta, W. R.; and Moher, T. G. 1982. *Formal Methods of Program Verification and Specification*. Englewood Cliffs, NJ: Prentice-Hall.

Birman, A. 1974. "On Proving Correctness of Microprograms." *IBM T. J. Research and Development* 9 (5):250–66.

Budkowski, S., and Dembinski, P. 1978. "Firmware versus Software Verification." *Proceedings 11th Annual Workshop on Microprogramming*, 119–27. New York: ACM/IEEE.

Carter, W. C.; Joyner, W. H.; and Brand, D. 1978. "Microprogram Verification Considered Necessary." *Proc. National Computer Conference*, 657–64. Arlington, VA: AFIPS Press.

Chroust, G., and Mulbacher, J. (ed). 1980. *Firmware, Micro-programming and Restructurable Hardware*. Amsterdam: North-Holland.

Crocker, S. D. 1977. "State Deltas: A Formalism for Representing Segments of Computation," Ph.D. diss., Department of Computer Science, UCLA.

Crocker, S. D.; Marcus, L.; and van Microp, D. 1980. "The ISI Microcode Verification System." In Chroust and Mulbacher (1980), 89–102.

Damm, W. 1984a. "A Microprogramming Logic." Tech. Rept. No. 94, Lehrstuhl für Informatik II, Technische Hochschule Aachen, Aachen, West Germany.

———. 1984b. "Automated Generation of Simulation Tools: A Case Study in the Design of a Retargetable Firmware Development System." *Proceedings EUROMICRO 84.* Edited by B. Myrhang. Amsterdam: North-Holland.

———. 1984c. "An Axiomatization of Low Level Parallelism in Microarchitectures." *Proceedings 17th Annual Workshop on Microprogramming.* New York: IEEE Comp. Soc. Press.

Damm, W.; Langmaack, H.; Penner, V.; Richter, M.; and Witt, J. 1984. "Ein System zur Inkrementellen Entwicklung und Verifikation von Microprogrammen und Rechnerarchiteckturen." Lehrstuhl fur Informatik II, Technische Hochschule Aachen, Aachen, West Germany.

Damm, W.; Doehman, G.; Merkel, K.; and Sichelschmidt, M. 1986. "The AADL/S* Approach to Firmware Design Verification." *IEEE Software* 3 (4):27–37.

Dasgupta, S. 1978. "Towards a Microprogramming Language Schema." *Proceedings 11th Annual Workshop on Microprogramming,* 144–53. New York: ACM/IEEE.

———. 1980. "Some Aspects of High Level Microprogramming." *ACM Computing Surveys* 12 (3):295–324.

———. 1982. "Computer Design and Description Languages." *Advances in Computers,* 91–154. Edited by M.C. Yovits. New York: Academic Press.

———. 1983a. "On the Verification of Computer Architectures Using an Architecture Description Language." *Proceedings 10th Annual Symposium on Computer Architecture,* 32–38. *New York: IEEE Comp. Soc. Press.*

———. 1983b. "The Formal Design and Verification of Microprograms." Preliminary Report, Center for Advanced Computer Studies, Univ. of Southwestern Louisiana, Lafayette.

———. 1984a. *The Design and Description of Computer Architectures.* New York: John Wiley & Sons.

———. 1984b. "A Model of Clocked Micro-architectures for Firmware Engineering and Design Automation Applications." *Proceedings 17th Annual Workshop on Microprogramming,* 158–67. New York: IEEE Comp. Soc. Press.

Dasgupta, S., and Olafsson, M. 1982. "Towards a Family of Languages for the Design and Implementation of Machine Architectures." *Proceedings 9th Annual Symposium on Computer Architecture,* 158–67. New York: IEEE Comp. Soc. Press.

Dasgupta, S., and Shriver, B. D. 1985. "Developments in Firmware Engineering." *Advances in Computers,* vol. 24. Edited by M.C. Yovits. New York: Academic Press. 102–76.

Dasgupta, S., and Wagner, A. 1984. "The Use of Hoare Logic in the Verification of Horizontal Microprograms." *Int. J. Computer and Information Sciences,* 13 (6):461–490.

Davidson, S. 1983. "High Level Microprogramming: Current Usage, Future Prospects." *Proceedings 16th Annual Workshop on Microprogramming*, 193–200. New York: IEEE Comp. Soc. Press.

Davidson, S., and Shriver, B. D. 1980a. "Firmware Engineering: An Extensive Update." In Chroust and Mulbacher (1980), 1–30.

Davidson, S., and Shriver, B. D. 1980b. "MARBLE: A High Level Machine Independent Language for Microprogramming." In Chroust and Mulbacher (1980), 253–63.

Davidson, S.; Landskov, D.; Shriver, B. D.; Mallett, P. W. 1981. "Some Experiments in Local Microcode Compaction for Horizontal Machines." *IEEE Transactions on Computers* C-30 (7):460–77.

deBakker, J. 1980. *Mathematical Theory of Program Correctness.* London: Prentice-Hall International.

Dembinski, P., and Budkowski, S. 1978a. "Verification, Design, and Description Oriented Microprogramming Language." *Large Scale Integration*, Euromicro Symposium: 230–40. Edited by H. W. Lawson, H. Berndt, and G. Hermanson. Amsterdam: North-Holland.

Dembinski, P., and Budkowski, S. 1978b. "An Introduction to the Verification Oriented Microprogramming Language MIDDLE." *Proceedings 11th Annual Workshop on Microprogramming*, 139–43. New York: ACM/IEEE.

Dijkstra, E. W. 1976. *A Discipline of Programming.* Englewood Cliffs, NJ: Prentice-Hall.

Donahue, J. E. 1976. *Complementary Definitions of Programming Language Semantics.* New York: Springer-Verlag.

Fisher, J. A. 1981. "Trace Scheduling: A Technique for Global Microcode Compaction." *IEEE Transactions on Computers* 30 (7):478–90.

Floyd, R. W. 1967. "Assigning Meanings to Programs," *Mathematical Aspects of Computer Science*, vol. XIX:19–32. Providence, RI: American Mathematical Society.

Flynn, M. J., and Rosin, R. F. 1971. "Microprogramming: An Introduction and Viewpoint." *IEEE Transactions on Computers* C-20 (7):727–31.

Giloi, W. K. (ed). 1980. *Firmware Engineering.* New York: Springer-Verlag.

Gordon, M. J. C. 1979. *The Denotational Description of Programming Languages.* New York: Springer-Verlag.

―――. 1981. "A Model of Register Transfer Systems with Applications to Microcode and VLSI Correctness." Tech. Rept. CSR-82-81, Dept. of Comp. Science, Univ. of Edinburgh, Edinburgh.

Gries, D. G. 1981. *The Science of Programming.* New York: Springer-Verlag.

Hoare, C. A. R. 1969. "An Axiomatic Basis for Computer Programming." *Communications of the ACM* 12 (10):576–83.

Hoare, C. A. R., and Wirth, N. 1973. "An Axiomatic Definition of the Programming Language Pascal." *Acta Informatica* 2:335–55.

Joyner, W. H.; Carter, W. C.; and Leeman G. B. 1976. "Automated Proofs of Microprogram Correctness." *Proceedings 9th Annual Workshop on Microprogramming*, 51–55. New York: ACM/IEEE.

Katzan, H. 1977. *Microprogramming Primer*. New York: McGraw-Hill.

Klassen, A., and Dasgupta, S. 1981. "S*(QM-1): An Instantiation of the High Level Microprogramming Language Schema S* for the Nanodata QM-1." *Proceedings 14th Annual Workshop on Microprogramming*, 124–30. New York: IEEE Comp. Soc. Press.

Knuth, D. E. 1968. "The Semantics of Context Free Languages." *Math. Systems Theory* 2 (1):127–145.

Kornerup, P., and Shriver, B. D. 1975. "An Overview of the MATHILDA System," *SIGMICRO Newsletter* 5 (4):25–53.

Kraley, M.; Rettberg, R.; Herman, P.; Bressler, R.; and Lake, A. 1980. "Design of a User Microprogrammable Building Block." *Proceedings 13th Annual Workshop on Microprogramming*, 106–14. New York: IEEE Comp. Soc. Press.

Landin, P. J. 1964. "The Mechanical Evaluation of Expressions." *Computer Journal* 6 (4):308–20.

Landskov, D.; Davidson, S.; Shriver, B. D.; and Mallett, P. W. 1980. "Local Microcode Compaction Techniques." *ACM Computing Surveys* 12 (3):261–94.

Leeman, G. B.; Carter, W. C.; and Birman, A. 1974. "Some Techniques for Microprogram Validation." *Information Processing 74, Proceedings IFIP Congress*, 76–80. Amsterdam: North-Holland.

Leeman, G. B. 1975. "Some Problems in Certifying Microprograms." *IEEE Trans. Comput.*, C-24 (5):545–53.

Levy, B. 1984. "Microcode Verification Using SDVS: The Method and a Case Study." *Proceedings 17th Annual Workshop on Microprogramming*, 234–45. New York: IEEE Comp. Soc. Press.

Linn, J. L. 1983. "SRDAG Compaction—A Generalization of Trace Scheduling." *Proceedings 16th Annual Workshop on Microprogramming*, 11–22. New York: IEEE Comp. Soc. Press.

Linn, J. L.; Shriver, B. D.; Dasgupta, S. 1983. "Component Identification for a Portable Retargetable Firmware Development System." *Proceedings IEEE International Workshop on Computer System Organization*, 164–70. IEEE Comp. Soc. Press.

Lucas, P., and Walk, K. 1969. "On the Formal Description of Pl/1." *Annual Rev. of Automatic Prog.* 6 (3):105–82. London: Pergamon Press.

Ma, P-W., and Lewis, T. G. 1980. "Design of a Machine Independent Optimizing System for Emulator Development." *ACM Trans. Prog. Lang. & Syst.* 2 (2):239–62.

Manna, Z., and Pneuli, A. 1981. "Temporal Verification of Concurrent Programs: The Temporal Framework for Concurrent Programs." In *The Correctness Problem in Computer Science*. Edited by R. Boyer and J. Moore. New York: Academic Press.

Marcus, L.; Crocker, S. D.; and Landauer, J. R. 1984. "SDVS: A System for Verifying Microcode Correctness." *Proceedings 17th Annual Workshop on Microprogramming*, 246–55. New York: IEEE Comp. Soc. Press.

Maurer, W. D. 1974. "Some Correctness Principles for Machine Language Programs and Microprograms." *Proceedings 7th Annual Workshop on Microprogramming*, 225–34. New York: ACM/IEEE.

McCarthy, J. 1963a. "A Basis for a Mathematical Science of Computation." In *Formal Programming Languages*. Edited by P. Braffort and D. Hirschberg. Amsterdam: North-Holland.

———. 1963b. "Towards a Mathematical Science of Computation." *Proceedings IFIP Congress*, 21–28. Amsterdam: North-Holland.

Mead, C. A., and Conway, L. 1980. *Introduction to VLSI Systems*. Palo Alto, CA: Addison-Wesley.

Milne, R. E., and Strachey, C. 1976. *A Theory of Programming Language Semantics*, vols. 1 and 2. London: Chapman and Hall.

Milner, R. 1971. "An Algebraic Definition of Simulation between Programs." *Proceedings 2nd Int. Joint Conference on Artificial Intelligence*, 481–89. London.

Moskowski, B. 1983. "A Temporal Logic for Multi-level Reasoning about Hardware." *Computer Hardware Description Languages and their Applications* (6th Symposium). Edited by T. Uehara and M. Barbacci. Amsterdam: North-Holland.

Mueller, R. A. 1984. *Automated Microcode Synthesis*. Ann Arbor, MI: UMI Research Press.

Mueller, R. A., and Johnson, G. R. 1981. "Contrasting Translation, Verification, and Synthesis in Software and Firmware Engineering." *Proceedings 14th Annual Workshop on Microprogramming*, 17–22. New York: IEEE Comp. Soc. Press.

Mueller, R. A., and Varghese, J. 1982. "Formal Semantics for the Automatic Derivation of Microcode." *Proceedings 19th Design Automation Conference*, 15–22. Las Vegas, NV.

Mueller, R. A., and Varghese, J. 1983. "Flowgraph Machine Models in Microcode Synthesis." *Proceedings 16th Annual Workshop on Microprogramming*, 159–67. New York: IEEE Comp. Soc. Press.

Nagle, A.; Cloutier, R.; and Parker, A. C. 1982. "Synthesis of Hardware for the Control of Digital Systems." *IEEE Transactions on Computer Aided Design*, CAD-1(4):201–12.

Nanodata Corporation. 1979. *The QM-1 Hardware User's Manual*, revised edition. New York: Nanodata Corporation.

Organick, E. I., and Hinds, J. A. 1978. *Interpreting Machines: Architecture and Programming of the Burroughs B1700/B1800 Series*. Amsterdam: North-Holland.

Overman, W. T., and Crocker, S. D. 1982. "Verification of Concurrent Systems: Function and Timing." *Protocol Specification, Testing, and Verification*. Edited by C. Sunshine. Amsterdam: North-Holland.

Owicki, S., and Gries, D. G. 1976. "An Axiomatic Proof Technique for Parallel Programs." *Acta Informatica* 6:319–40.

Parker, A. C., and Wilner, W. T. 1981. "Microprogramming: The Challenges of VLSI." *Proceedings National Computer Conference*. Arlington, VA: AFIPS Press.

Patterson, D. A. 1976. "STRUM: A Structured Microprogram Development System for Correct Firmware." *IEEE Transactions Computers* C-25 (10):974–85.

———. 1977. "Verification of Microprograms." Ph.D. diss., Dept. of Comp. Sc., UCLA.

———. 1981. "An Experiment in High Level Language Microprogramming and Verification." *Communications ACM* 24 (10):699–709.

Ramamoorthy, C. V., and Shankar, K. S. 1973. "Correctness and Equivalence of Straight Line Microprograms." *Proceedings 6th Annual Workshop on Microprogramming*. New York: ACM.

———. 1974."Automatic Testing for the Correctness and Equivalence of Loopfree Microprograms." *IEEE Transactions Computers* C-23 (8):768–82.

Rustin, R. (ed.) 1972. *Formal Semantics of Programming Languages*. Englewood Cliffs, NJ: Prentice-Hall.

Scott, D. 1970. "Outline of a Mathematical Theory of Computation." Tech. Monograph PRG-2, Univ. Comp. Lab., Prog. Res. Group, Oxford University, Oxford.

Scott, D., and Strachey, C. 1971. "Towards a Mathematical Semantics for Computer Languages." Tech. Monograph PRG-6, Univ. Comp. Lab., Prog. Res. Group, Oxford University, Oxford.

Sheraga, R. J., and Gieser, J. L. 1983. "Experiments in Automatic Microcode Generation." *IEEE Transactions Computers* C-32 (6):557–68.

Shimizu, T., and Sakamura, K. 1983. "MIXER: An Expert System for Microprogramming." *Proceedings 16th Annual Workshop on Microprogramming*, 168–75. New York: IEEE Comp. Soc. Press.

Siewiorek, D. P.; Bell, C. G.; and Newell, A. 1982. *Computer Structures: Principles and Examples*. New York: McGraw-Hill.

Stankovic, J. 1981. "The Types and Interactions of Vertical Migrations of Functions in a Multilevel Interpretive System." *IEEE Transactions Computers* C-30 (7):505-13.

Stoy, J. E. 1977. *Denotational Semantics: The Scott-Strachey Approach to Programming Languages Theory*. Cambridge, MA: MIT Press.

Stritter, S., and Tredennick, N. 1978. "Microprogrammed Implementation of a Single Chip Microprocessor." *Proceedings 11th Annual Workshop on Microprogramming*, 8–16. New York: ACM/IEEE.

Tokoro, M.; Tamura, E.; and Takizuka, T. 1981. "Optimization of Microprograms." *IEEE Transactions Computers* C-30 (7):491–504.

Uehara, T., and Barbacci, M. R. (ed.) 1983. *Computer Hardware Description Languages and their Applications* (6th Symposium). Amsterdam: North-Holland.

Vegdahl, S. 1982. "Local Code Generation and Compaction in Optimizing Microcode Compilers," Ph.D. diss., Comp. Science Dept., Carnegie-Mellon University, Pittsburgh.

Wagner, A. 1983. "Verification of S*(QM-1) Microprograms," M. Sc. thesis, Dept. of Comp. Science, Univ. of Alberta, Edmonton, Alberta.

Wagner, A., and Dasgupta, S. 1983. "Axiomatic Proof Rules for a Machine-Specific Microprogramming Language." *Proceedings 16th Annual Workshop on Microprogramming*, 151–58. New York: IEEE Comp. Soc. Press.

Wegner, P. 1972a. "Programming Language Semantics." In Rustin (1972), 149–248.

———. 1972b. "The Vienna Definition Language." *ACM Computing Surveys* 4 (1):5–63.

Wegner, P. (ed.) 1979. *Research Directions in Software Technology*. Cambridge, MA: MIT Press.

Wood, W. G. 1980. "Computer-Aided Design of Microprograms." Ph.D. diss., Univ. of Edinburgh, Edinburgh.

Yeh, R. (ed.) 1977. *Current Trends in Programming Methodology, Vol. II: Program Validation*. Englewood Cliffs, NJ: Prentice-Hall.

index

Page numbers in *italics* refer to figures.

Aachen AADL/S* verification project, 467–75
  AADL language, 467–70
    ADD microoperation description, 469
    architecture description, 468
    microoperation description, 469
  cooperation test, 472–74
  S*(m) language instantiation, 467, 468
  static disjointness, 474–75
Accumulator register (AC), 36, 37
Ada (language), 174, 225
ADDRESS field, 43
ADEPT, 315–16, *317, 318*
Aerospace processors, IBM, 367–73
ALGOL (language), 117, 131, 163
A machine (EMMY), 285, 286
AMD 2900 series, 11, 13
ANIMIL (language), 158
Architecture

FCPU (*see* Asynchronous microprogramming)
  future trends in, 132–36
  heuristic, 88, 200–201
  manual, 88, 197–99
  of microprogrammed control, 49
  VLSI (*see* VLSI architecture)
  von Neumann, 33–40
Archives, of microobjects and microimages, 267–70
Arithmetic and logic unit (ALU), 34, 35, 42
  data path with multiple, 390
  FCPU architecture, 97, 98, 99, 109–11
  language and, 137–38, 140–41
  microinstruction format, *119*
Assemblers/translators, 340–49, 371–72
  block diagram, *342–43*
  evolution of, 12–13, 344–45
  implementation, 348–49
  macrocode vs. microcode, 341, 344
  requirements of, 345–47

483

Association for Computing Machinery (ACM), 2
ASUM execution timing, 128, 130
Asynchronous microprogramming, 95–144
　applications, 125–30
　　D23 instruction implementation, 125–27
　　vector operations, 128–30
　arithmetic unit, 97, 98, 109–11
　control unit, 97, 98, 111–15
　design alternatives
　　high-level facilities, 102–4
　　minimally/highly coded microinstructions, 104–5
　　processor data path width, 106–7
　　synchronous or asynchronous processing, 105
　　writable control storage, 105–6
　design, development, testing, production and maintenance, 131–32
　FCPU global architecture, 97–100
　FCPU physical structure, 116–17
　field access unit, 97, 98, 107–9
　future architecture implications, 132–36
　introduction, 96–97
　language, 117–25
　microinstruction processing strategy, 100–102
　statements syntax, 137–42
　variable logic sets, 115–16
Automatic microcode synthesis, semantics-based, 466–67
Axiomatic semantics, 437–39
Axiomatic verification systems, 446–47. See also S* (QM-1) (language)

Bipolar technology, 57
Bit packing, 42
Bit-slice architectures, 12
Bit-steering encoding, 64, 65
"Bit-stuffer" assembler, 341
Branching operations, 15, 43
　control-unit branch microinstructions, 114–15

delayed, 417
instructions for Standard Logic CASH-8, 60
language vectors, 123
minimizing delays in, 81–84, 85
BUGS (Brown University Graphics System), 201, 205
Burroughs 1700 series, 47, 59, 197, 238, 447
Burroughs Corporation, microcode development at, 358–61
Burroughs Interpreter, 6, 58

C (language), 169, 173, 358
　emulator calling-sequence characteristics, 312
Capacitor read-only store (CROS), 45
Card-capacitor read-only memory (CCROM), 56
Card-capacitor read-only store (CCROS), 45
Card-resistor read-only memory (CRROM), 56
CASS system, 366
CASUM execution timing, 128, 130
CHAMIL (language), 174
CLCI (current location counter indicator), 114
COBOL (language), 47, 117, 131
COCYCLIC statements, 464
Commercial machine culture, 85
Compaction. See Horizontal microcode compaction
Compiler(s), 16
　high-level microprogramming language, 148–49, 168, 186–87
　microcode assemblers and, 343, 348
Compiler-oriented language, 435
Complex-instruction-set (CISC), vs. RISC computers, 226
Computer-hardware description languages (CHDL), 348–49, 370–71
Computer Systems Laboratory, Stanford University, 17
Concurrent Pascal, 225
Concurrent state deltas (CSDs), 456
COND field, 43

CONDITIONAL BRANCH microinstruction, 114
Conditional operations, 40–41
Context object, 231
  sharing microimages through, 240, 242
Control and control units
  FCPU architecture, 97, 98, 100, 111–15
    control mechanisms, 113–15
    language, 139–40, 141–42
    registers and functions, *112*
  organization, 47–67
    control store memory types, 55–57
    control store structure, 58–59
    microinstruction execution, 64–67
    microinstruction organization, 62–64
    microinstruction sequencing, 59–61
    microprogrammed control units, 47–55
  in Von Neumann machines, 33–40
    operation, 35–40
    organization, 34, 35
Control storage write-limit (CWL), 114, 121
Control store(s), 41, 48. *See also* Writable control store(s) (WCS)
  development history, 2, 9, 15, 19
  memory, 55–57
  packed, unpacked methods, 42
  structure, 58–59
Control-store address register (CSAR), 48
COUNTING REGISTER, 113
Critical-path partitioning algorithm, 80
CVI (current VLS indicator) field, 114, 115

Data General Corporation, microcode development at, 361–64
Data path, width of, 106–7
Data precedence graphs (DPG),
  global compaction, 420–22
  local compaction, 400–407
DataSaab D23 Computer System, 95, 97. *See also* Asynchronous microprogramming

microprogramming applications, 125–30
ML language for, 157
DEC (Digital Equipment Corporation), microcode development at, 364–66
DEC V Compiler, 174
DEC VAX and VLSI VAX system, 62, 225, 364
Denotational semantics, 436–37
The Design and Description of Computer Architectures, 58
Diagnostics, 3
Digital System Design with LSI Bit-Slice Logic, 338
Directly executed language (DEL), 21, 47, 86–87, 281, 314
DO CASE statement, 123
DO statement, 123
Dynamic disjointness, 475
Dynamic microprogramming, 47, 87, 223–74
  archiving microobjects and microimages, 267–70
  development history, 21–23
  dynamism in microimage activation, 244–50
  dynamism in physical loading of microimages, 250–54
  microimage sharing, 239–43
  modeling function placement, 230–39
  naming and binding activities, 255–67
  placing functions of, 271
  relationship to other concepts, 225–29
  writable control store model, 243–44

Education, microprogramming, 5
Efficiency. *See* Optimization
E-Machine workbench, 180, 186, 187, 359, 360
EMMY host processor, 17, 283, 285–88
  A-machine microinstructions, 325, 327
  assembler emulation tools, 296–98
  basic instruction format, 321, 22
  bus, 291
  I-machine microinstructions, 326–28, 329

EMMY host processor (*continued*)
  instruction set usage, 328, 330
  interfacing to the support processor, 288–91
  I/O device support system, 292–96, 298–300
  main memory, 288, 289
  microcode examples, 297
  microinstruction frequency, 330
  performance, 298–300
  register resources, 321–22, 323
  T-machine microinstructions, 322–25
EMMYPL assembler, 296
EMMYXL assembler, 296
EMPL (language), 12
Emulation, 275–336
  accuracy/classification of, 278–79
  basics of, 276–78
  development history, 4, 5, 6, 11, 14, 17
  interpretive monitoring and, 279–81, 305–14
  language choice and, 185–86
  microprogramming for, 41–46, 85–86
  PDP-11 Emulator, 300–302, 330–34
  Stanford Emulation Lab example, 282–300
    conclusions and directions on, 316–21
    EMMY instruction set, 321–30
    laboratory usage examples, 300–316
Environment list, state delta systems, 453–54
Erasable programmable read-only memory (EPROM), 57
Euromicro Workshops, 2
Explicit sequencing, 61
Extended Control Program Support (ECPS), 203

Fetch/decode/execute method, 37, 38
FFT machine, 16
Field access unit (FU), FCPU architecture, 97, 98, 107–9
  language, 138, 141
Finite-state machine (FSM), 389–95

Firmware
  defined, 193
  monitors on, 202–3
Firmware engineering
  development history, 4, 14, 17–20
  verification (*See* Verification, firmware)
Flexible Central Processing Unit (FCPU). *See* Asynchronous microprogramming
Flow chart microprogram input, 344–45, 346
Flynn, Michael, 6
Format-shifting, microinstruction, 64
FORTRAN (language), 47, 117, 314
Foundations of Microprogramming, 11
Functionality, and microprogramming
  assignment problem, 225–26
  modeling placement of, 230–39
    diagram of, 232–34
    dynamism in a solution, 235
    examples, 236–39
    parts of the model, 231–35
  placing functions, 271
Future trends
  architecture, 132–36
  microcode compaction, 428–30
  vertical migration, 217–18

Gateway routines, 258–59
  switchable, 259–60, 261, 262
GMPL (language), 154, 155–56, 159
GPM (language), 158–59

Hardware monitor, 279, 280
Hardwired implementations, 47–48
Hewlett-Packard 21-MX, 9
High-level languages, 8–12
  emulation, 281, 282, 314–16, 320–21
  vs. high-level microprogramming languages, 145–46
High-level microprogramming language(s), 3–4, 145–50, 167–85
  compilers for, 148–49
  development history, 3–4, 8–12, 18–19

INDEX 487

High-level microprogramming
    language(s) (*continued*)
  emulation, 314–16, 320–21
  vs. high-level languages, 145–46
  machine-dependent, 167–72
  machine-indendent, 172–77
  mixed (HLMXL), 177–85
  vs. system implementation languages, 146–48
History of microprogramming, 1–32, 40–47
  dynamic microprogramming, verification, and specification (mid 1980s), 21–23
  firmware engineering, vertical migration and optimization (early 1980s), 17–20
  high-level language machines and languages (mid 1970s), 8–12
  language enhancement, diagnostics and emulation (1967 to early 1970s), 3–8
  microprogrammable processors and microprogramming tools (late 1970s), 12–17, 338–40
  Wilkes's concept of, 40, *41*
HLL (language), 173, 174, 175–76
Horizontal microcode compaction, 76–81, 381–431
  development diagram for horizontal microcode, 382
  future work in, 428–30
  local compaction, 76, 79–80, 397–416
    data-precedence graph, 400–407
    scheduling step, 408–16
  loop-free program compaction, 416–28
    global compaction, 76, 417–19
    global compaction procedure, 419–27
    selecting subtrees for compaction, 427–28
  models for compaction, 384–97
    instruction-template model, 395–97
    machine model, 385–95
Horizontal migration, 15, 104–5
  vs. vertical, 191–92

Host machine, 42, 85, 276
  host/target relationship, 277
  universal, 278
HP 21-MX hardware, 62
Hybrid technology computer (HTC), 446
Hypothetical-microprogrammed-machine (HMM), 50
  machine-instruction fetch microprogram, 52
  memory-block move, 52, *54*
  polyphase execution, 50, 52, 53
  set repertoire, *51*

IBM 1401, 42
IBM 7000 series, 4, 42
IBM Corporation
  microcode development tools at, 366–73
    aerospace processors, 367–73
    commercial processors, 366–67
  vertical migration methods at, 203–4
IBM System/38
  horizontal microcode layer, *197*
  vertical microcode layer, *198*
IBM System/360 series, 42, 45, 56
IBM VM/370 system, 203
IEEE Transactions on Computers, 2, 23
IFETCH routine, 43
ILI (interrupt level indicator), 113
I machine (EMMY), 285, 286
Image. *See* Macroimage(s); Microimage(s)
Image machine, 42, 86
  sample instruction microprograms, 43, 45
Implicit-addressing sequencing, 59, 60, 61
Index-register sequencing, 59
Inode, 245
Input/output unit, 34, 35, 37
Instantiating into a language, 178, 467, 468
Institute of Electrical and Electronic Engineers Technical Committee on Microprogramming, 2, 3
Instruction(s). *See also* Microinstruction (MI)
  format, 36

Instruction(s). (*continued*)
  versions of, 397, 398
Instruction constancy assertion, 446–47
Instruction pointer, 436
Instruction register (IR), 36, 37. *See also* Microinstruction register (MIR)
Instruction set, 21. *See also* Reduced instruction set
  static design of, in typical architecture, 236–37
Instruction template, 388
  compaction model based on, 395–97
Integrated injector logic (I^2L), 57
Intel 3000, 12, 13
Interdata Model, 85
Interpretation, vs. emulation, 85
Interpreter, 6, 8–9
Interpreter-oriented language, 436
Interpretive hierarchy, 133
Interpretive monitoring, and emulation, 279–81, 305–14, 320
Interpretively driven operations (IDOs), 4
Interrupt handling and the linkage editor, 266
ISA (instruction-set architecture) microcode, 366
ISPMET (language), 165–66

LALR grammar analyzer, 367, 369
Language(s), microprogramming, 16, 17, 117–25, 145–90
  axiomatic semantics, 437–39
  basic language elements, 120
  branch vectors, 123
  built-in names, 137–40
  choosing, 185–87
  computer-hardware description languages (CHDL), 348–49, 370–71
  control storage layout, 121, *122*
  declarations, 121–23
  denotational semantics, 436–37
  directly-executed (*see* Directly-executed language (DEL))
  early microprogramming tools, 150–53
  high-level, 145–50, 167–85 (*see also* High-level microprogramming language(s))
  loop control, 123–24
  lower-level, 153–60
  low-level machine-independent, 160–67
  microinstruction grouping, 123
  microinstruction organization and, 118–20
  microinstruction structure, 124–25
  microprogram structure and, 121, *122*
  multilanguage machines, and function placement, 238
  operational semantics, 435–36
  subroutines and, 124
  syntax, 140–42
Language accelerators
  function placement model using, 237–38
  relationship to dynamic programming, 225, 227–28
Language enhancement, 3–8, 10
Linkage editor, 230–31, 349–54
  in IBM aerospace processors, 368–70
  implementation issues, 353–54
  interrupt handling and, 266
  link-edit process, 349–50, *351*
  naming/binding microobjects to form microimages with, 255–67
  requirements of, 351–52
LK (locking key) field, 114
Load writable control store (LWCS), 244
Local-area networks, relationship to dynamic microprogramming, 225, 228–29
Local profit, 268
Locus of control, 235
Loop-free programs, compacting, 416–28
Low-level microprogramming languages, 153–60
  machine-independent, 160–67
LSS (language), 441
LUKKO (language), 183–84

INDEX 489

Machine-instruction fetch interpreter, 51, 52
Machine model of compaction, 385–95
Macroimage(s), 224, 230
    to microobject references, 256–64
Macroobject, 224, 230
    references from microobjects to, 264–66
MAKEPS program, 361
Mapping actions, 202, 205–8
MARBLE (language), 182–83, *184*
Memory, control store, 55–57
    pages, 58
Memory address register (MAR), 36–37, 43
Memory-block-move microprogram, 52, 54
Memory data register (MDR), 36–37, 43
Meta-assembler, 342, 348
Metal-oxide semiconductor (MOS) technology, 57
MICRO-3 workshop, 3–4
MICRO-4 workshop, 4–6
MICRO-5 workshop, 6
MICRO-6 workshop, 7
MICRO-7 workshop, 8, 9
MICRO-9 workshop, 12
MICRO-10 workshop, 13
MICRO-11 workshop, 15, 16
MICRO-12 workshop, 16
MICRO-13 workshop, 18–19
MICRO-14 workshop, 19, 174
MICRO-15 workshop, 20
MICRO-16 workshop, 21
MICRO-17 workshop, 22
MICRO-18 workshop, 23
Microcode
    bit optimization problem, 70
    code motion optimization technique, 83
    compaction problem, 76–81 (*see also* Horizontal microcode compaction)
    current development facilities, 358–75
    horizontal/vertical layers, *197, 198*
    relationship with processor, *103*
Microcode C (language), *173,* 174, *177*
Microcode certification system (MCS), 440–46
    definitions, 442
    notation, 441
    theorems, 442–46
Microcode Design-Support System (MDS), 373, 374, 375
Microdata 3200, 58
Microimage(s), 224, 230
    activation of, 244–50
        backing store for WCS, 247–49
        declaration and naming, 245–47
        other matters occurring during, 249–50
    archiving microobjects and, 267–70
    caches of, 247, 248–49
    dynamism in physical loading of, 250–54
    naming and binding, 255–67
    paging, 248–49, 255 n.1
    pseudoimage, 242–43
    sharing, 239–43
        macroimages sharing different microimages, 240, *241*
        through a context object, 242–43, *244*
    templates, 241
    user-space management of, 248
Microinstruction (MI), 1, 42, 48
    asynchronous processing strategy, 100–102
        control unit branch, 114–15
        control unit processing/control unit branch, 111–12
        language, 118–20, 124–25
        stream-preparation and control, *101*
        vs. synchronous, 105
    diagonal, 62
    execution, 64–67
    formats, *43*
    horizontal, 61, 63–64
    hypothetical set repertoire, *51*
    minimally or highly encoded design, 104–5
    organization, 62–64, 118–20
    sequencing, 59–61
    vertical, 62, 63, 69, 70

Microinstruction buffer register (MIBR), 48
Microinstruction index register (MIX), 123
Microinstruction location counter (MLC), 101
MICROINSTRUCTION RECOVERY, 115
Microinstruction register (MIR), 40, 42–43, 48, 101
Microobject, 224, 225
  archiving, 267–70
  naming and binding to form microimages, 255–67
Microoperation (MO), 42, 48
  basic blocks, 76, 78
    critical path for, 79–80, *81*
    data-dependency graph for, 78, 79
  compatibility class (CC), 71, 72
  eliminating redundant, 75, 77
  immediate vs. residual control, 64
  maximal compatibles, 73, 74
  monophase vs. polyphase timing, 66, 67
  parallel (PP), 71, 72, 73
  schedule, *44*
  serial vs. parallel, 66, 68
Microprocessors, microprogrammable. *See also* Microprogramming
  design alternatives, 102–7
  development history, 11–12, 12–17
Microprogram(s)
  defined, 42
  language structure and, 120–25
Microprogrammable machine culture, 85
Microprogramming, 33–93
  alternative roles of, 84–88
  asynchronous (*see* Asynchronous microprogramming)
  control in Von Neumann machines, 33–40
    operation, 35–40
  control unit organization and, 34–35, 47–67
  dynamic (*see* Dynamic microprogramming) efficiency in, 67–84 (*see also* Optimization)

evolution/history of, 40–47 (*see also* History of microprogramming)
  tools (*see* Tools, microprogramming)
Microprogramming Principles and Practices, 11
Microprogramming Repository, 24
Microprogram-status register (MPS), 100, *113*
Microstore, 58
MicroTAL (language), 146, 168, *169*, 170
MIDDLE verification system, 451–53
Migration, 4, 14, 18
  horizontal (*see* Horizontal migration)
  outboard, 191–92
  vertical (*see* Vertical migration)
Military microcode support software, 367–71
MIMOLA (language), 174
Minor cycles, 43
MISIM (FCPU simulator), 131
MITRAN (language translator), 131
ML (language), 157–58
Modification list, state delta systems, 453
MODULA (language), 19
MPGL (language), 165, *166*
MPL (language), 174–75
MSU (main storage unit address)
  logical addressing/field selection, *107*
  logical READ/WRITE transmission, *109*
  physical address generation and step control, *108*
Multiprocessing, relationship to microprogramming, 225, 228–29
Multiprogramming environment, relationship to dynamic microprogramming, 225, 228
MV/1000 project, 361, 363
MV/4000 project, 361, 363
MV/8000 project, 361, 362

Name, of an object, 230
Nanodata Corporation, 5, 47. *See also* QM-1 hardware
Nanostore, 58, 458, *459*

NEC (Nippon Electric Company), microcode development at, 373–75
No-operation (NOP) statements, 123

Object, 224. *See also* Macroobject; Microobject
OHNE (language), 149, 180–81, *182*, 359
Operating systems, 4, 10, 13, 227
Operation codes (opcodes), 2, 36
  meanings, 37
Operational semantics, 435–36
Optimization, 67–84. *See also* Compaction; Parallelization
  bit minimization of directly encoded control words, 70–75
  control-word format determination, 69–70
  development history, 3, 17–20
  microcode compaction, 76–81 (*see also* Horizontal microcode compaction)
  minimizing branch delays, 81–84, 85

Parallelization, 18
  natural, in the VLSI environment, 134–35
  natural vs. man-made, 133
Pascal (language), 170, 182, 225, 314, 315
Path compaction, 427–28, *429*
PDP-11 processor emulation, 288, 330–34
  characteristics of, 304–5
  fragments of, 330–34
    EMMY microcode example, 331–34
  interpretive monitor and examples, 308–11
  performance, 306
  problems in conventional emulation with, 302–4
  structure of, 300, *301*, 302
PL/1 (language), 117, 174
Polish-string opcodes, 10–11
Polyphase execution, 50, 52, 53
  compaction and, 385–87
Process
  defined, 230

memory image (*see* Macroimage(s); Microimage(s))
Processors. *See* Microprocessors, microprogrammable
Program counter (PC), 36, 37
Programmable read-only memory (PROM), 57
PROLOG machines, 22
Proof language, 455
Pseudofield, 391, 393
Pseudoimage, 242–43

QM-1 hardware, 5, 47, 53, 58, 63, 96, 447. *See also* S* (QM-1) (language)
  architecture synopsis, 458–60

Random-access memory (RAM), 56–57
Read-only memories (ROMs), 55, 56
Read writable control store (RWCS), 244
Reduced instruction sets (RISC), 20, 47, 82
  vs. complex-instruction-set, 226
Register(s), 36–37. *See also* Microinstruction register (MIR); TFR (to-and-from register)
Resource-binding, 178
Retargetability, 23
RETURN statement, 124
Root-compaction, 422–27

S* (QM-1) (language), 22, 179, *180*, 456–66
  axiomatization of, 460–66
  QM-1 architecture and, 458–60
S/370 interpretive monitor, 311–14
Scheduling algorithm, compaction, 408–16
  data structures and procedure, 408–11
  field compatibility, 408
  timing issues, 411–13
  updating data precedence graphs, 413–16
SDVS system, 455

Security in microprogrammed systems, 224
microimage archives, 269–70
Setup registers, 64
SIMPL (language), 163, *164*
Simulation and simulators, 355–58
block diagram, 359
development history, 4, 13
vs. emulation, 42
IBM aerospace processor, 368–69, 370
implementation issues, 357–58
requirements of, 355–57
symbolic, 454
Single-level (direct) encoding, 64, 65
Software
development tools, 338–40
migration of software-to-, 204
vertical migration (*see* Vertical migration)
Software monitor, *280*, 281
Special Interest Group in Microprogramming (SIGMICRO), 2, 3, 6, 7
Special Interest Group in Programming Languages (SIGPLAN), 6, 7
Specification, development history, 21–23
Standard Computer MLP-900, 96, 118
Standard Logic CASH-8
branching instructions, *60*, 61
organization, 62, 63
Stanford Emulation Lab environment, 282–300
basic environment structure, 283–85
emulation tools, 296–98
host processor (EMMY), 285–88
host processor instruction set, 321–30
host processor main memory, 288, *289*, *290*
improving the emulation environment, 316–19
interfacing to the support processor, 288–91
I/O device support system, 292–96
laboratory usage examples, 300–316
conventional emulation, 300–305, 319–20
high-level language emulation, 314–16, 320–21
interpretive-monitoring examples, 305–14, 320
PDP-11 emulator, 300–302, 330–34
performance, 298–300
review of experiences in, 319–21
START PROCESSOR microinstruction, 114
START TARGET microinstruction, 114
State delta verification system, 453–56
Static disjointness, 474–75
Storage unit, 34, 35, 36
STRUCT system, 201
STRUM (language), 170–71, *172*
verification system, 447–51
Subtree compaction, 427–28
SUILVEN (language), 174, 175, *176*
Symbolic simulation, 454
Synthesis, 19
System-implementation language (SIL), vs. high-level microprogramming languages, 146–48

TAL (language), 169
Target machine, 276. *See also* Image machine
host/target relationship, 277
TFR (to-and-from register), 97, 99
Tirrell's language, 162, *163*
T machine (EMMY), 285, 286
Tools, microprogramming, 337–79. *See also* Compiler(s); Emulation; Language(s), microprogramming
current development facilities, 358–75
Burroughs, 358–61
Data General, 361–64
DEC, 364–66
IBM, 366–73
NEC, 373–75
development history, 12–17, 19, 338–40
early (microassemblers), 150–53
microcode assembler/translator, 340–49 (*see also* Assemblers/translators)
microcode linkage editors, 349–54 (*see also* Linkage editor)
simulators, 4, 13, 42, 455–58
Trace scheduling. *See* Path compaction

Transformer read-only store (TROS), 45
Transient vs. permanent storage elements, 51
Transistor-transistor logic (TTL), 57
Translation systems, 19
Transparency, 86
Two-level (indirect) encoding, 64, 65

UDSYS system, 361, 364
ULINK system, 364
Unconventional (DEL) environments, 281
University of Southern California Information Science Institute, 455
UNIX systems, 245, 247
   microcode interaction with EMMY, 293, 295
User interface, simulator, 358, 359

Vanderbilt project, 263–64
Variable logic sets (VLS), 100, 114, 115–16
Varian 73 hardware, 62
Verification, firmware, 433–82
   Aachen AADL/S* project, 467–75
   automatic microcode synthesis, 466–67
   axiomatic verification, 446–47
   development history, 19, 21–23
   foundations, 435–40
      axiomatic semantics, 437–39
      denotational semantics, 436–37
      operational semantics, 435–36
   microcode certification system (MCS), 440–46
   MIDDLE system, 451–53
   S* (QM-1) system, 456–66 (see also S* (QM-1) (language))
   state delta system, 453–56
   STRUM system, 447–51
Vertical migration, 15, 88, 104–5, 191–221
   development history, 17–20
   future directions in, 217–18
   vs. horizontal and outboard migration, 191–92
   multilayer interpretive model of, 192, *193*, *194*, 195
   relationship to dynamic microprogramming, 225, 226–27
   technique application, 195–204
      analytical approach to, 201
      heuristic methods, 200–201
      industrial manifestations, 203–4
      manual methods, 197–99
      means of gathering statistics, 202–3
   technique description, 204–17
Vienna definition language (VDL), 436, 441
VLSI architecture, 20
   natural parallelism and, 134–35
VM model, vertical migration, 205–17
   migration example, 208, *209*
   new target instruction (firmware), 210, *211*
   new target instruction (software), 210, *212*
   object model, 215, *216*
   replacement, 213, *214*
   software/firmware levels, 206, *207*
VMPL (language), 174
Von Neumann, John, 34
Von Neumann architecture, 33–40

WAIT microinstruction, 115
WCSLOAD, 247
Wilkes, M. V., 1–2, 13–14
   his concept of microprogramming, 40, *41*
Writable control store(s) (WCS), 19, 46–47, 55, 57, 193
   as a design alternative, 105–6
Writable control store(s) (WCS), dynamic microprogramming use of, 223–24, 229
   backing store for, 247–49
   fault, 251–52
   model of, 243–44
   used to accelerate dedicated application systems, 237

YALLL (language), 17, 160, *161*, 162, 164–65